We work with leading authors to develop the strongest educational materials in Industrial Relations, bringing cutting-edge thinking and best learning practice to a global market.

Under a range of well-known imprints, including Financial Times Prentice Hall, we craft high quality print and electronic publications which help readers to understand and apply their content, whether studying or at work.

To find out more about the complete range of our publishing please visit us on the World Wide Web at: www.pearsoneduc.com

Industrial Relations
Theory and practice

Fourth Edition

Michael Salamon

 **FT** Prentice Hall
FINANCIAL TIMES

An imprint of **Pearson Education**
Harlow, England • London • New York • Boston • San Francisco • Toronto • Sydney • Singapore • Hong Kong
Tokyo • Seoul • Taipei • New Delhi • Cape Town • Madrid • Mexico City • Amsterdam • Munich • Paris • Milan

Pearson Education Limited
Edinburgh Gate
Harlow
Essex CM20 2JE
England

and Associated Companies throughout the world

Visit us on the World Wide Web at
www.pearsoneduc.com

———————————

First published in 1987
Fourth edition published in 2000

© Michael Salamon, 2000

ISBN 0 273 64646 X

British Library Cataloguing in Publication data
A CIP catalogue record for this book can be obtained from the British Library.

10 9 8 7 6 5 4 3
07 06 05 04 03

Typeset by Mathematical Composition Setters Ltd, Salisbury, Wiltshire.
Printed in Great Britain by Ashford Colour Press Ltd., Gosport

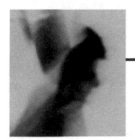

contents

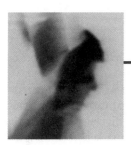

preface

Objectives

This book is intended for students studying industrial or employee relations on undergraduate, postgraduate or post-experience courses. It draws on an extensive range of sources and materials:

- to provide a framework of concepts and knowledge for understanding and analysing approaches to the subject, the roles of the major participants, the issues confronting them and the strategies and processes used; and
- to present that knowledge in a way which facilitates the student's learning.

Approach

Industrial relations is more than simply an area of organisational management. Its development reflects changes in the nature of work within society (in both economic and social terms) and differences of view about the regulation of employment. Liberalisation, internationalisation and globalisation of business, coupled with the challenge from newly industrialised countries, have resulted in significant shifts in the economic context and a realignment of the world economy. The 'older' industrialised countries have been confronted with the need to consider both how to improve their labour competitiveness and how to deal with the consequences of greater labour competition.

During the 1980s and most of the 1990s, management efforts at the organisational level to develop a strategic approach to the management of human resources (emphasising individualism, commitment, performance and flexibility) were, in the UK, supported by government policies directed towards labour market deregulation, reduced social welfare costs and reduced union power. The labour market experienced not only persistent and high levels of unemployment (compared with the 1960s and 1970s) but also significant changes in employment structures, relationships and patterns of work. Organisational changes were inevitably interrelated with wider economic and social issues in what some regard as a post-industrialisation process. For example, attention became more focused on the consequences of unconstrained labour competition (social dumping) and the need for the maintenance of minimum labour standards not only within countries but also across countries (both *within* the European Union and *between* the EU and other trading areas).

We need, therefore, to consider industrial relations not just within a narrow and exclusive UK context but to see it within international variations in styles, institutions and conduct of industrial relations. It is this diversity of industrial relations models and responses to changing economic, market, technological and social environments which, perhaps, provides the *raison d'être* for industrial relations as a subject separate from HRM or Personnel.

■ Structure

The subject matter of industrial relations may be presented in many different ways. However, whatever approach is adopted, it soon becomes apparent that the multidisciplinary nature of the subject combined with its complex inter-relationships mean that it is difficult to comprehend fully one aspect of the subject without reference to other aspects. This book segments the subject matter into four areas:

■ Part I (Perspectives) introduces the student to a range of concepts and approaches which are central to a study and understanding of industrial relations.

■ Part II (Participants) examines the functions, organisation and issues confronting the three main participants within industrial relations – trade unions, management and the government.

■ Part III (Processes) examines the range of processes used by the participants in determining and conducting their relationship.

■ Part IV (Practices) examines the outcome of the participants relationship in two broad areas – the substantive area of pay and working arrangements and the procedural areas of grievances, discipline and redundancy.

■ Presentation

The book seeks to aid the student's learning in a number of ways:

■ Each chapter opens with *learning objectives*, topic *definition* and some suggested *key issues* which the student should keep in mind while reading the chapter.

■ The use of *diagrams* to help explain concepts, institutions, relationships, influences, etc.

■ Most chapters include:

Case studies, drawn from various industries (both manufacturing and service) and different countries, which illustrate the way organisations have handled particular aspects of industrial relations; and

Country profiles, both European and non-European, which illustrate differences in national approaches and systems of industrial relations.

■ Each chapter concludes with *summary propositions* which both highlight significant points and provide areas for discussion, some *student activity* which encourages the student to explore the 'real world' of industrial relations and a short list of *further reading* on that topic.

■ Acknowledgements

I would like not only to express my appreciation to all those people with whom I have worked in industrial relations over the past 35 years (as a trade unionist, manager and lecturer), but also to acknowledge that the contents of this book owe as much, if not more, to the thoughts and efforts of many other writers and researchers over the years, as it does to my own.

All extracts from HMSO publications are reproduced courtesy of the Controller of Her Majesty's Stationery Office.

Michael Salamon
June 2000

abbreviations

ABS	Association of Broadcasting Staffs (merged with NATTKE in 1984 to form BETA)
ACAS	Advisory, Conciliation and Arbitration Service
ACTAT	Association of Cinematograph Television and Allied Technicians (merged with BETA in 1991 to form BECTU)
ACTSS	Association of Clerical, Technical and Supervisory Staffs (white collar section of T&GWU)
ACTU	Australian Council of Trade Unions
AEEU	Amalgamated Engineering and Electrical Union
AEU	Amalgamated Engineering Union (merged with EETPU in 1992 to form AEEU)
AFL-CIO	American Federation of Labour-Congress of Industrial Organizations
ANC	African National Congress
APEX	Association of Professional, Executive, Clerical and Computer Staff (merged with GMB in 1989)
ASBSB&SW	Amalgamated Society of Boilermakers, Shipwrights, Blacksmiths and Structural Workers (merged with GMWU in 1982 to form GMB)
ASEAN	Association of South East Asian Nations
ASLEF	Associated Society of Locomotive Engineers and Fireman
ASTMS	Association of Scientific, Technical and Managerial Staffs (merged with TASS in 1987 to form MSF)
AUEW	Amalgamated Union of Engineering Workers (now AEEU)
BECTU	Broadcasting, Entertainment and Cinematograph Technicians' Union
BETA	Broadcasting and Entertainments Trade Union (merged with ACTAT in 1991 to form BECTU)
BIFU	Banking, Insurance and Finance Union (merged with UniFI in 1998 to form UNIFI)
BMA	British Medical Association
BR	British Rail
BSC	British Steel Corporation
BT	British Telecomm
CAC	Central Arbitration Committee
CATU	Ceramic and Allied Trades Union
CBI	Confederation of British Industry
CEEP	European Centre of Public Enterprise

CIR	Commission on Industrial Relations
COHSE	Confederation of Health Service Employees (merged with NALGO and NUPE in 1993 to form UNISON)
COSATU	Confederation of South African Trades Unions
CPSA	Civil and Public Services Association (merged with PSTCU in 1998 to form PCSU)
CPAUIA	Commissioner for Protection against Unlawful Industrial Action
CRTUM	Commissioner for the Rights of Trade Union Members
CSU	Civil Service Union (merged with SCPS in 1988 to form NUCPS)
CWU	Communication Workers Union
EAT	Employment Appeals Tribunal
EC	European Community
EETPU	Electrical, Electronic, Telecommunications and Plumbing Union (merged with AEU in 1992 to form AEEU)
ETU	Electrical Trades Union (became EEPTU)
ETUC	European Trade Union Confederation
EU	European Union
EWC	European Works Council
FBU	Fire Brigades Union
FTO	Full-Time Officer
GATT	General Agreement on Tariffs and Trade
GCHQ	Government Communications Headquarters
GMB or GMBATU	General, Municipal, Boilermakers' and Allied Trade Union
GMWU	General and Municipal Workers Union (merged with ASBSB&SW in 1982 to form GMB)
GNCTU	Grand National Consolidated Trade Union
GPMU	Graphical, Paper and Media Union
HRM	Human resource management
ICFTU	International Confederation of Free Trade Unions
IDS	Incomes Data Services
ILO	International Labour Organisation
IM	Institute of Management
IoD	Institute of Directors
IPD	Institute of Personnel and Development
IPM	Institute of Personnel Management (now IPD)
IPMS	Institution of Professional Managers and Specialists (formerly Institution of Professional Civil Servants)
IRSF	Inland Revenue Staff Federation (merged with NUCPS in 1996 to form PSTCU)
ISTC	Iron and Steel Trades Confederation
ITB	Industrial Training Board
JIC	Joint Industrial Council
JNCC	Joint Negotiating and Consultation Committee

JRC	Joint Representation Committee
JSSC	Joint Shop Stewards Committee
LPC	Low Pay Commission
LRC	Labour Representation Committee
MATSA	Managerial, Administrative, Technical and Supervisory Association (white collar section of GMB)
MNE	Multinational enterprise
MSC	Manpower Services Commission
MSF	Manufacturing, Science and Finance Union
NAFTA	North Atlantic Free Trade Area
NALGO	National and Local Government Officers' Association (merged with COHSE and NUPE in 1993 to form UNISON)
NAS/UWT	National Association of Schoolmasters and Union of Women Teachers
NATFHE	National Association of Teachers in Further and Higher Education
NATTKE	National Association of Theatrical, Television and Kine Employees (merged with ABS in 1984 to form BETA)
NBPI	National Board for Prices and Incomes
NCB	National Coal Board
NCU	National Communications Union (merged with UCW in 1995 to form CWU)
NEC	National Executive Committee
NEDO	National Economic Development Council
NGA	National Graphical Association (merged with SOGAT in 1990 to form GPMU)
NHS	National Health Service
NJC	National Joint Council or Committee
NJIC	National Joint Industrial Council
NJNC	National Joint Negotiating Committee
NMW	National minimum wage
NUAAW	National Union of Agricultural and Allied Workers (merged with T&GWU in 1981)
NUCPS	National Union of Civil and Public Servants (merged with IRSF in 1996 to form PSTCU)
NUM	National Union of Mineworkers
NUPE	National Union of Public Employees (merged with COHSE and NALGO in 1993 to form UNISON)
NUR	National Union of Railwaymen (merged with NUS in 1990 to form RMT)
NUS	National Union of Seamen (merged with NUR in 1990 to form RMT)
NUT	National Union of Teachers

OECD	Organisation for Economic Co-operation and Development
PBR	Payment by results
PCSU	Public and Commercial Services Union
POEU	Post Office Engineering Union (merged with part of CPSA in 1985 to form NCU)
PRP	Performance–related pay
PSTCU	Public Services Tax and Commerce Union (merged with CPSA in 1998 to form PCSU)
RCM	Royal College of Midwives
RCN	Royal College of Nursing
RMT	National Union of Rail, Maritime and Transport Workers
SAYE	Save as you earn
SOGAT	Society of Graphical and Allied Trades (merged with NGA in 1987 to form GPMU)
STB	Single-table bargaining
STUC	Scottish Trades Union Congress
SUA	Single-union agreement
T&GWU, TGWU or T&G	Transport and General Workers' Union
TQM	Total quality management
TSSA	Transport Salaried Staffs Association
TUC	Trades Union Congress
TULR(C)A	Trade Union and Labour Relations (Consolidation) Act (1992)
TURERA	Trade Union Reform and Employment Rights Act (1993)
UCATT	Union of Construction, Allied Trades and Technicians
UCW	Union of Communication Workers (merged with NCU in 1995 to form CWU)
UMA	Union membership agreement
UNICE	Union of Industrial and Employers' Confederations of Europe
Unison	(formed in 1993 by merger of COHSE, NALGO & NUPE)
USDAW	Union of Shop, Distributive and Allied Workers
WIRS	Workplace Industrial Relations Survey
WTO	World Trade Organisation

part one

Perspectives

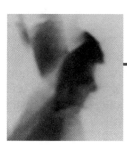

chapter one

Approaches to industrial relations

Learning objectives

In the social sciences, conceptual or analytical frameworks (approaches) help us differentiate, integrate and understand people's behaviour. By the end of this chapter, you should be able to:

■ understand the different views of the employment relationship and the interaction in an 'industrial relations system';

■ appreciate the character of the labour process and labour market within capitalism and the interrelationship between micro (organisational) and macro (society) employment issues;

■ explain the integral nature of the concepts of 'conflict', 'co-operation' and 'regulation' to an understanding of industrial relations;

■ identify the importance and difficulties of comparing industrial relations in different countries.

Definition

Industrial relations encompasses a set of phenomena, both inside and outside the workplace, concerned with determining and regulating the employment relationship.

Key issues

While you are reading this chapter, you should keep the following points in mind:

■ Each approach is partial, derived from a particular perspective or standpoint in time, and focuses on certain concerns and/or aspects of the subject. They are not mutually exclusive; but rather, if taken together, can help us to make better sense of the diverse, complex and dynamic nature of the employment relationship.

■ All approaches involve a mixture of:

  ▮ *assumption and conviction* (implicit socio-political or ethical values and beliefs)
  ▮ *description, explanation and prediction* (discussion or analysis of what is and projection of how it might develop)
  ▮ *prescription* (suggestion of what ought to be done, or how it ought to be done, to achieve a desired objective).

The difficulty, often, is to disentangle these different elements!

■ The way we perceive industrial relations determines, to a large extent, not only how we approach and analyse specific issues and situations but also how we expect others to behave, how we respond to their actual behaviour and the means we adopt to influence or modify their behaviour. Each participant has a different perception of 'reality' which will influence his or her behaviour and actions.

1.1 Introduction

Few would disagree with Blyton and Turnbull that 'work dominates the lives of most men and women' and 'the management of employees, both individually and collectively, remains a central feature of organisational life'[1]. However, it is difficult to define the term 'industrial relations' in a precise and universally accepted way. Any definition must, of necessity, assume and emphasise a particular view of the nature and purpose of industrial relations. The two most frequently used terms of 'industrial relations' and 'employee relations' are, in most practical senses, interchangeable, yet they have very different

Figure 1.1
Approaches to industrial relations

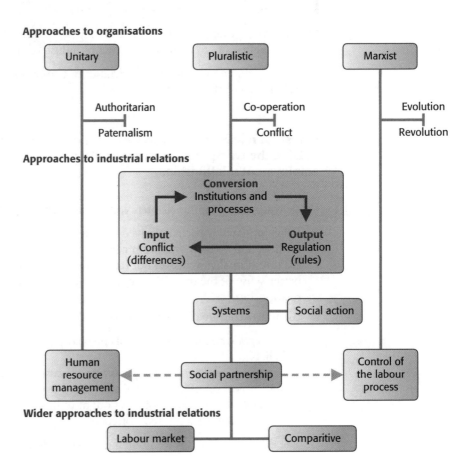

connotations. *Industrial relations* is perceived as being concerned with male, full-time, unionised, manual workers in large manufacturing units involving restrictive practices, strikes and collective bargaining. *Employee relations* is perceived to reflect the development of more diverse employment patterns (non-manual, female, part-time, etc.), the growth of employment in the 'high-tech', service and commercial sectors and reduced level of unionisation coupled with management strategies aimed at individualising the employment relationship.

However, Edwards argues that "industrial relations" has become established, and there is no reason to abandon it once its remit is properly understood'[2]: its focus is the regulation (control, adaptation and adjustment) of the employment relationship which is shaped by legal, political, economic, social and historical contexts. Similarly, Ackers argues that industrial relations 'should concern itself with the employment relationship in every facet ... cover the full panoply of relations between employers or managers and the people they pay to work for them', even though it 'focuses on collective social relations at work'[3]. Even Blyton and Turnbull, who prefer the term 'employee relations', argue that the focal point 'remains the *collective* aspects of relations between workforce and management' and the dual problems of *social welfare* and *social order* so that 'our concern is not simply the efficiency of organisations, the control of labour and the resolution of conflict, but also the interests of workers, the conditions of their labour, and the remuneration of their effort'[4].

In examining different approaches it is useful to differentiate between those concerned with the general nature of employment organisations and those which specifically deal with industrial relations (see Figure 1.1).

1.2   The nature of employment organisations

It is clear from Box 1.1 that the unitary, pluralistic and Marxist approaches make quite different assumptions about the nature of organisations, work and society and, consequently, view conflict and the role of trade unions differently. However, it is important to bear in mind that each approach also encompasses variations: the unitary ranging from authoritarian to paternalistic; the pluralistic including co-operation as well as conflict; the Marxist adopting an evolutionary or revolutionary approach to social change.

Unitary perspective

The unitary perspective assumes the organisation is, or should be, an integrated group of people with a single authority/loyalty structure and a set of common values, interests and objectives shared by all members of the organisation. Management's prerogative (i.e. its right to manage and make decisions) is regarded as legitimate, rational and accepted and any opposition to it (whether formal or informal, internal or external) is seen as irrational. The underlying assumption, therefore, is that the organisational system is in basic harmony and conflict is unnecessary and exceptional: it is not a 'them and us' situation.

Box 1.1	Unitary, pluralistic and marxist approaches

	Unitary	**Pluralistic**	**Marxist**
Assumptions	Capitalist society	Post-capitalist society	Capitalist society
	Integrated group of people	Coalescence of sectional groups	Division between labour and capital
	Common values, interests and objectives	Different values, interests and objectives	Imbalance and inequalities in society (power, economic wealth, etc.)
Nature of conflict	Single authority and loyalty structure (management's)	Competitive authority and loyalty structures (formal and informal)	Inherent in economic and social systems
	Irrational and frictional	Inevitable, rational and structural	Disorder precursor to change
Resolution of conflict	Coercion	Compromise and agreement	Change society
Role of trade unions	Intrusion from outside	Legitimate	Employee response to capitalism
	Historical anachronism	Internal and integral to work organisation	Expression and mobilisation of class consciousness
	Only accepted in economic relations (if forced)	Accepted role in both economic and managerial relations	Develop political awareness and activity

Fox argued it **represents a management ideology** and, as such, can 'create difficulty for [the manager], not simply in acknowledging the legitimacy of challenges to it, but even in fully grasping that such challenges may at least be grounded in legitimacy for those who mount them'[5]. Similarly, factionalism within the organisation may even be regarded as 'a pathological social condition' and collective bargaining as 'an anti-social mechanism'[6] since they are founded on the premise of the existence of conflicting interests. Conflict, when it does arise, is believed to be primarily frictional rather than structural in nature and caused by such factors as: clashes of personalities within the organisation; poor communication by management of its plans and decisions; a lack of understanding on the part of the employees that management's decisions and actions are made for the good of all within the organisation; or by agitators.

Coercion (including the use of law) is regarded as a legitimate use of managerial power. Management does not perceive a need, given the legitimacy of its prerogative, to obtain the consent of employees to decisions or changes.

Certainly, the legislative changes in the UK during the 1980s sought to constrain trade union actions which were regarded as 'disruptive' and 'disorderly'. At the same time, management may concentrate on a human relations approach (improving interpersonal relations and communications within the organisation) or make appeals to the loyalty of the employees (the 'let's pull together, we're all in the same boat' syndrome).

Many **managers perceive trade unions as an intrusion into the organisation from outside which competes for the loyalty of employees**. They are an historical anachronism and, with enlightened human resource management, are no longer necessary to protect the employees' interests – these will be taken fully into account, alongside other factors, in management decision making. Even if management are forced to accept the existence of trade unions in the determination of terms and conditions of employment (market relations), they are certainly reluctant to concede any role for trade unions in the exercise of authority and decision making within the organisation (managerial relations). Trade unions are likely to be seen as little more than a political power vehicle used by a militant minority in order to subvert the existing and legitimate political, social and economic structure of society. The existence of trade unions and collective bargaining, therefore, is suffered rather than welcomed and is to be resisted wherever possible.

Although Fox believed that this view of organisations had 'been abandoned by most social scientists as incongruent with reality and useless for purpose of analysis'[7], it should not be discarded too lightly. It provides the subconscious foundation (the 'right to manage') for managers seeking to maintain a clear distinction between those issues on which they are prepared to negotiate and those issues on which they are prepared only to consult. It certainly appears to have provided the basis for much of the recent 'human resource management' developments and, in particular, the projection of 'common interests, culture and values' ideology within the organisation[8].

Pluralistic perspective

This perspective views society as being 'post-capitalist' – a relatively widespread distribution of authority and power within the society, a separation of ownership from management, and a separation, acceptance and institutionalisation of political and industrial conflict. It assumes the organisation is composed of individuals who coalesce into a variety of distinct sectional groups, each with its own interests, objectives and leadership (either formal or informal). The **organisation is multi-structured and competitive in terms of groupings, leadership, authority and loyalty**, and this, Fox argued, gives rise to 'a complex of tensions and competing claims which have to be "managed" in the interests of maintaining a viable collaborative structure'[9]. The organisation is, therefore, in a permanent state of dynamic tension resulting from the inherent conflict of interest between the various sectional groups and requires to be managed through a variety of roles, institutions and processes.

Conflict, that is, 'the total range of behaviour and attitudes that express opposition and divergent orientation'[10], is perceived as both rational and inevitable. It results from industrial and organisational factors (structurally determined) and the differing roles of the managerial and employee groups. The managerial group is responsible for the efficiency, productivity and profitability of the organisation and for co-ordinating the activities of others to achieve these objectives (this is the basis on which the success of both individual managers and management in general is judged). However, the main concerns of the employee group are more likely to be perceived in personal terms (better pay and working conditions, greater job security, etc.). Conflictual behaviour may be caused by both specific situations and general 'management principles'. The closure of some part of an organisation's operations or introduction of new technology is intended to meet management's objectives of increased efficiency and profitability but may well clash with the employees' objective of job security. Similarly, management will seek to maintain the maximum degree of power and authority to control the organisation's activities while employees may seek to establish safeguards against arbitrary management actions and decisions.

Fox argued that the mutual dependence of the sectional groups exists only in so far as they 'have a common interest in the survival of the whole of which they are parts' and this is, at best, only a 'remote long-term consideration'[11]. However, the pluralistic perspective also assumes that there is a basic consensus that 'the normative divergencies between the parties are not so fundamental or so wide as to be unbridgeable' and that each group is prepared to limit 'its claims and aspirations to a level which the other party finds sufficiently tolerable to enable collaboration to continue'[12]. The resolution of conflict is characterised by the **need to establish accepted procedures and institutions which achieve collaboration through comprehensive, codified systems of negotiated regulation**. There has to be an acceptance of the need for shared decision making; the legitimacy of management's role is not automatic but must be sought and maintained by management itself ('management by consent' rather than 'management by right').

The pluralistic perspective accepts the legitimacy of employees combining in formal organisations to express their interests, influence management decisions and achieve their objectives – trade unions provide a countervailing power to management. Fox argued that such legitimacy is founded not just on industrial power or management acceptance but 'on social values which recognise the right of interest groups to combine and have an effective voice in their own destiny'[13]. It accepts, also, that employees, through their horizontal linkage with employees in other organisations, will owe loyalty to authority structures other than their own management and may pursue not only narrow organisational interests but also wider fraternalistic interests. Trade unions and their representatives are as much an internal part of the organisation and its managerial processes as they are an external body to the organisation. They do not, of themselves, cause the conflict within organisations but 'simply provide a highly organised and continuous form of expression for sectional interests which would exist anyway'[14].

Marxist perspective

Some critics argue that the 'post-capitalist' notion of society which underlies the pluralistic perspective is wrong. The Marxist perspective concentrates on the nature of the capitalist society surrounding the organisation where, Hyman argues, 'the production system is privately owned ...; profit ... is the key influence on company policy ...; and control over production is enforced downwards by the owners' managerial agents'[15]. The Marxist general theory of society argues the following:

- Class (group) conflict is the source of societal change – without such conflict the society would stagnate.

- Class conflict arises primarily from the disparity in the distribution of, and access to, economic power within the society – the principal disparity being between those who own capital and those who supply their labour.

- The nature of the society's social and political institutions is derived from this economic disparity and reinforces the position of the dominant establishment group, for example through differential access to education, the media, employment in government and other establishment bodies, etc.

- Social and political conflict in whatever form is merely an expression of the underlying economic conflict within the society.

Conflict is seen as a reflection of not just organisational demands and tensions but also, and perhaps more importantly, the economic and social divisions within society between those who own or manage the means of production and those who have only their labour to sell. Therefore, it is continuous, unavoidable and synonymous with political and social conflict. The pluralistic perspective is criticised for maintaining an illusion of a balance of power between labour and management which hides the reality of imbalance in social power resulting from two factors:

- Employers do not need to exercise their full industrial power by closing plants and withdrawing their capital; the implicit threat that they have such power is sufficient to balance any direct collective power exercised by employees and trade unions.

- The social and political institutions within the society support the intrinsic position of management; employees, through the influence of education and the mass media, become socialised into accepting the existing system and role of management.

The Marxist perspective sees the processes and institutions of joint regulation as an enhancement rather than reduction in management's position; at best, they provide only a **limited and temporary accommodation of the inherent and fundamental divisions within capitalist-based work and social structures**. Indeed, Marchington has suggested that the attention of management, trade unions and employees may be directed towards the maintenance of the system of regulation to such an extent that 'procedural principles may be elevated above substantive outcomes'[16] – stability through compromise is preferable to a polarisation of conflicting interests and objectives which could destroy the system. Thus, trade unions and collective bargaining become an established, accepted and supportive part of the capitalist system rather than a real challenge to it. Industrial relations becomes, at best, concerned only with marginal issues and power (relative distribution of pay between employees and the exercise of management's operational authority) rather than fundamental issues (the distribution of wealth and control within the society). The legal contractual relationship between the employer and employee is perceived as asymmetrical and not one freely entered into between equals. Hyman believes that in the eyes of the law "equality" of the employment relationship is one which gives the employer the right to issue orders, while imposing on the worker the duty to obey'[17]. Hence, from the Marxist perspective, the reality is that the law is supportive of management's interests and position rather than being an independent referee between competing interests.

The growth of trade unionism is seen as an inevitable employee response to capitalism; trade unions not only enhance collective industrial power by reducing competition between individual employees but also provide a **focus for the expression and protection of the interests of the working classes**. The fraternalism developed within trade unions can then be converted into class-consciousness within the social and political systems. From the Marxist perspective, trade unionism and industrial relations may be viewed as political activities associated with the development of the working classes; they are part of the overall political process for achieving fundamental changes in the nature of the economic and social systems. Therefore, unless this is recognised by the union's members, and acted upon accordingly through the policies and decisions of their organisation, they will not be fulfilling the primary purpose of trade unionism.

1.3   The nature of industrial relations

Industrial relations should be viewed not just in simple organisational job regulation terms but in broader social, political and economic terms – it is *'integrated with* and not *separated from* the political and economic spheres'[18]. For Blyton and Turnbull, the distinctive characteristics of the employment relationship lie in it being more than a simple economic exchange in the marketplace – it is also an asymmetrical power and authority relationship; it is continuous and open-ended; and the interdependent nature of the relationship can engender both conflict and co-operation.

The approaches to industrial relations can be divided broadly into two groups. First, there are the 'input–output', 'systems' and 'social partnership' approaches (broadly derived from the pluralistic concept) which recognise the need within the organisation to manage the different and possibly divergent interests of management and employees. Second, there are the 'human resource management' and 'control of labour process' approaches (derived from the unitary and Marxist perspectives respectively) which, it may be argued, represent opposite forms of analysis of the same phenomenon – control of the human activity of paid work.

Input–output model

This model regards industrial relations primarily as **a process of converting conflict into regulation**. However, while Barbash saw the conflict being generated by the inherent tensions *within* organisations ('technology, scale, organisation, efficiency and uncertainty – the essential features of industrialism' which 'necessarily generate tensions ... of command and subordination, competitiveness, exploitation, physical deprivation at work and economic insecurity'[19]), Fox perceived it to stem from the surrounding capitalist society ('industrial conflict may be rooted in a clash of values as well as a conflict of interests'[20]). Thus, the latent conflict of interest which provides the core of industrial relations can arise from either the micro level of the organisation (the economic exchange and the managerial systems of authority and control) or the macro level (the fundamental divisions and differing values in society). The **transformation of latent conflict into manifest conflict** may be expressed in a number of ways:

- In a hidden, unorganised and individual way through low employee morale, high labour turnover, absenteeism, etc.;

- In an overt, constitutional form (on an individual and/or collective basis) through established procedures and institutions (e.g. the grievance procedure, consultation and collective bargaining machinery);

- Through industrial pressure (industrial action) – for most people this is commonly, but wrongly, what is meant by conflict in industrial relations.

Clearly, the expression of conflict in either of the latter forms requires both a will to change the situation and often, on the part of the employees, a collective consciousness.

The **expression of conflict is regarded as legitimate and functional**, including the use of industrial action, in identifying the differences of interest as a prelude to resolving them so as to maintain stability and equilibrium within the social structure. However, for Barbash there is 'a point beyond which conflict becomes "aberrant", "abnormal", "dysfunctional" or "pathological"'[21] because it may destabilise, if not destroy, the social structure. He suggests conflict is dysfunctional when it involves violence, a major social disorganisation of the community, civil disobedience or the extinction of either management or union. However, Hyman regards the function of conflict as being 'a total transformation of the whole structure of control ... within the organisation of work and in social and economic life more generally'[22]. From this perspective the seeking of order and stability in industrial relations is a constraint on the function of conflict.

It is the apparent need to reconcile conflicts of interest through some form of processes and institutions which led Flanders to define industrial relations as 'a study of the institutions of job regulation'[23]. It concentrates on the nature and variety of interactions which may appropriately be utilised to transform the conflict of interest into rules regulating the organisation. The processes may vary through a spectrum from unilateral decision making (by management, employees or government); through joint management/union processes (consultation, collective bargaining and employee involvement or participation); to tripartite processes involving management, unions and government. The **importance of collective bargaining** lies in the fact that, through trade unions, the employees' collective power is used to counterbalance the power of the employer. Flanders[24] described the process of negotiation as the diplomatic use of coercive power; collective bargaining as a pressure group activity; and collective agreements as compromise settlements of power conflicts. The importance of the ability of employees to exercise some countervailing power if they are to be successful in conducting an exchange based on 'bargaining' led Lumley to suggest that 'in the absence of any organised countervailing force outside an organisation's managerial hierarchy to provide a check on unilateral management decision making over employment relationships, the study of the process of rule making and interpretation is one of administrative procedures and management decision making processes'[25]. It is perhaps more useful, as Bain and Clegg suggest, to include within the study of industrial relations 'all aspects of job regulation – the making and administering of the rules which regulate employment relationships – regardless of whether they are seen as being formal or informal, structured or unstructured'[26].

The **regulatory output** of industrial relations is generally seen to be 'rules'; any organised social structure needs to establish formalised 'norms' of behaviour amongst its members[27]. There are a number of bases on which the rules may be differentiated:

- The **authorship** of rules – unilateral (management or employees), joint or imposed by government.
- **Substantive and procedural rules:** *substantive rules* define the rights and obligations of employer and employee in the contractual wage/work bargain; *procedural rules* define the conduct of the relationship (e.g. grievance, discipline, union recognition, consultation, collective bargaining, etc.).
- Whether the rules are determined **within the organisation or externally**. *External rules*, such as law and national agreements, apply to more than one organisation and place a limitation on the freedom of action and decision making of those at the organisation level. *Internal rules* are specific to the organisation and can be more easily abandoned, modified or replaced as the situation changes.
- Differing **degrees of formality** in the determination and recording of the rules ranging from informal and unwritten 'custom and practice' to codification in formal written documents (policies, procedures, agreements).

The input–output model focuses on the generation, expression and resolution of conflict but does not provide an adequate framework for understanding either the integrative nature of the parts which comprise 'industrial relations' or its relationship to the wider contexts within which it operates. To do this, it is useful to examine the systems approach.

Industrial relations system

Dunlop's original systems view (see Box 1.2) not only identified actors (people in roles) working within contexts to develop a body of rules but also saw them being integrated (a system) through a broadly accepted common ideology. Although his work has, over the years, been subject to a variety of interpretations, uses and criticisms, few writers have suggested its abandonment.

Box 1.2	Dunlop's system approach

Dunlop (1958) applied the systems concept to industrial relations to produce a broad-based integrative model. He sought 'to provide tools of analysis to interpret and gain understanding of the widest possible range of industrial relations facts and practices' and 'to explain why particular rules are established in particular industrial relations systems and how and why they change in response to changes affecting the system' (pp. vi and ix).

The model sees industrial relations as a subsystem of society distinct from, but overlapping, the economic and political subsystems. It has four interrelated elements:

- **Actors:** Management, non-managerial employees and their representatives and specialised government agencies concerned with industrial relations.

- **Contexts:** Influences and constraints on the decisions and actions of the actors which emanate from other parts of society, in particular, the technological character of the organisation; the market or budgetary constraints affecting the organisation; and the locus and distribution of power within society.

- **Ideology:** Beliefs within the system which not only define the role of each actor or group of actors but also define the view that they have of the role of the other actors in the system. If the views of the roles, one with another, are compatible then the system is stable; if the views are incompatible then the system is unstable.

- **Rules:** The regulatory framework, developed by a range of processes and presented in a variety of forms, which expresses the terms and nature of the employment relationship.

Source: J. T. Dunlop, *Industrial Relations Systems*, Henry Holt Ltd, 1958 (quote reprinted by permission of CBS College Publishing).

In the 1970s Wood *et al.*[28] argued that the central feature of the industrial relations *system* was the rule-making process (rather than the much broader totality of interaction between employee, management and government) and that it was important to distinguish between the 'industrial relations system' which produced the rules and the 'production system' which was governed by the rules (see Figure 1.2). This provides a framework for distinguishing between the following:

- Rules which are an output from the industrial relations system to 'govern' behaviour within the production system (substantive rules and, possibly, procedural rules for regulating the interpretation and application of the substantive rules); and

- Rules which are established for the internal regulation of the conduct of the industrial relations system (procedural).

This differentiation also has a significant impact on the perceived purpose of the industrial relations system. Dunlop argued that the objective of the system could be seen primarily in terms of the stability and ultimate survival of the industrial relations system itself – hence his concern for the common ideology among the actors which integrates the system. Wood *et al.* believed that it would be more useful and appropriate to regard 'the goal of the I.R.S. as satisfying the functional need for order within the production system'[29]. This appears to emphasise the social control need of management above the social welfare needs of employees and certainly accords with the empirical evidence of the management

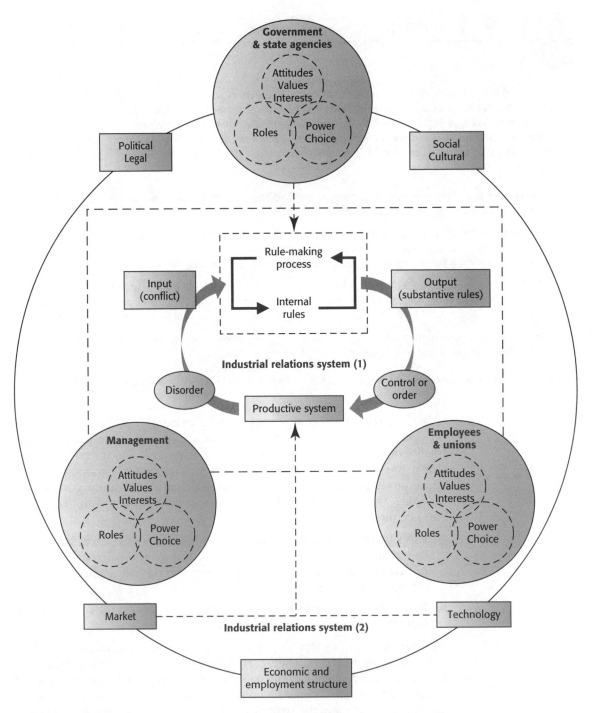

Figure 1.2 The system of industrial relations

attitude towards industrial relations – that industrial relations should be supportive of business objectives rather than an end in itself.

The **role of a common ideology integrating the system** has been criticised because it implies that the industrial relations system is, or should be, naturally stable and orderly. Hyman argues that by concentrating attention on 'how any conflict is contained and controlled rather than on the processes through which disagreements and disputes are generated' an image is projected that 'the various institutions and procedures are compatible and well integrated; and that conflict is therefore largely self-correcting'[30]. The functional view of industrial relations (to produce order) skates over the fact that what constitutes order is a matter of belief and perception of individuals and that the existence of order is a matter of degree rather than an absolute. Certainly, Schienstock believes that the system's apparent 'concentration on the stability issue should ... not be represented as though it presupposes an imminent tendency towards stability in the industrial relations system'[31]. Similarly, Eldridge argued that 'the sources of conflict and co-operation, order and instability must have an equally valid claim to problem status'[32], while Blyton and Turnbull point out that the model must recognise 'conflict as a possible outcome of relations rather than simply a temporary aberration en route to agreed rules'[33]. The systems approach has to accept the existence of a variety of ideologies, which may or may not be congruent, rather than one and they are as likely to produce conflict within the rule-making process as they are to produce consensus.

Another major criticism made of Dunlop's system has been that it **appears to emphasise roles rather than people** and 'ignores such behavioural variables as human motivations, perceptions, and attitudes'[34]. Industrial relations appears to be structurally determined and underestimates the effects and importance of personal leadership in determining the outcomes of industrial relations situations. Similarly, Banks[35] argued that the management hierarchy, as set out by Dunlop, ignores the influential role of the owners of the business which should be accommodated by including them as an actor on the management side and their property ownership interest as a context impinging on the operation of the industrial relations system. Wood *et al.* recognised that behavioural factors should be included within the industrial relations system but argued that such factors are exercised through 'roles' on a structured rather than unstructured basis.

It has also been argued that the systems view does not adequately reflect the **real nature of the wider society**. Wood argued that Dunlop's view of the industrial relations system prefers 'to take the analysis of it [society] as given, presumably leaving it to the other disciplines of the social sciences'[36]. Similarly, Winchester noted that the system view fails because it 'focuses in its analysis on an empirical conception of power at the workplace or organisational level (not the less visible impact of social power) and develops a restricted definition of workers' interests and trade union purpose that concentrates attention largely on the institutions and procedures in collective bargaining (not broader mechanisms for the distribution of power and rewards in society)'[37]. He pointed out that much of the debate and controversy in industrial relations has stemmed 'from policy makers' (especially governments') definitions of social problems or in response to potential or actual policy developments'[38]. Certainly, Shalev argued that 'the social, economic and political environment can be more fruitfully seen as interacting with, and therefore as analytically inseparable from labour relations'[39]. At the same time, Wood *et al.* recognised that Dunlop's 'defocalisation' of power to an external influence on the industrial relations system (derived largely from public policy towards trade unions and collective bargaining) is too narrow. Power, in terms of ability to influence through the possibility of inflicting a 'loss' on the opposition, may be focused on the rule-making process from any of the contextual influences as well as the attitudes of the participants.

This suggests that the system approach should allow for the **study of industrial relations at two levels** – at the narrow level of the rule making process (Industrial relations system (1)) and at a wider level to incorporate the boundary between rule making and the contexts (Industrial relations system (2)).

Social action

Bain and Clegg pointed out that this approach to industrial relations 'emphasises the actors' definition of reality'[40], while Jackson noted that it 'stresses the way in which man influences the social structures and "makes society"'[41]. It is the **individual's perception and definition of reality** which determines his or her behaviour, actions and relationships. In this respect it is important to recognise that people's orientation to work is as much the result of their extra-organisational experiences as their experience within the workplace.

However, over-concentration on the individual's ability to choose and determine his or her own situation has the danger that the individual is not always aware that choice is being restricted by wider structural factors. The essential nature of the relationship between these two elements is that **structural factors may limit the choice of action**, but the action chosen will itself produce a change, however small, in that social structure or relationship. The extent to which it will produce any change is, in part, dependent on the choices made by others. The importance of this view of industrial relations is that it weakens the fatalism of structural determinism and 'stresses that the individual retains at least some freedom of action and ability to influence events'[42] in the direction that he or she believes to be 'right' and 'desirable'.

The 'social action' approach underpins the importance that has been attached to **strategic decision making** in explaining the dynamics of industrial relations. As Poole points out, 'the notion of strategy encapsulates the idea of an overall design within social action, and *rationality* and calculus in the pattern of decisions'[43]. Strategy refers to a focused series of interrelated decisions or actions which represent a significant shift in values, focus, role or relationship. The rationality may be based on instrumental considerations (material interests or gains) or value considerations (ethical, political or other ideals). Through the interrelationship between their *strategic* choices and responses to the strategic choices of others, the actors (management, unions and government) determine the nature of the institutional arrangements of industrial relations.

Control of the labour process

Thompson has defined the labour process as 'the means by which raw materials are transformed by human labour, acting on the objects with tools and machinery; first into products for use and, under capitalism, into commodities to be exchanged on the market'[44]. The concept is just as relevant to the service and public sectors as it is to manufacturing – all transform 'raw materials' into 'commodities to be exchanged'. Significantly, since the early 1980s, the government has imposed capitalist mechanisms and systems on the management of the public sector (privatisation, cash limits, competitive tendering, performance-related pay, etc.) which then directly impact on its methods of operation.

The **core of the labour process approach** rests on the fact that 'the social relations which workers enter into to produce useful things becomes a capitalist labour process when the capacity to work is utilised as a means of producing value' and 'therefore on the unique characteristics of labour as a commodity'[45]. Four elements stem from this core:

■ The labour/capital relationship is essentially one of exploitation wherein surplus value from work activities accrues to capital.

■ The 'logic of accumulation' requires capital continually to develop the production process and cheapen the costs of production.

■ Continual development of the production processes requires the establishment and maintenance of both general and specific 'structures of control'.

■ The resultant 'structured antagonism' relationship includes systematic attempts by capital to obtain co-operation and consent and 'a continuum of possible and overlapping worker responses, from resistance, to accommodation on temporary common objectives, to compliance with the greater power of capital, and consent to production practices'[46].

Braverman[47] argued that the fundamental industrial relationship during the twentieth century has been one of **management exploitation and degradation of labour** by deskilling work through the use of scientific management techniques (Taylorism) to support the achievement of capital's objective. The application of work-study techniques facilitated the breakdown of work into its component tasks which could then be allocated to separate individuals (specialisation). Management thereby cheapened the individual's input value to the production process (the task required less training, skill and/or responsibility and therefore arguably less reward), tied the individual more directly to the technical system (in particular the assembly line) and made the individual or group capable of being subjected to production output controls (bonus payments, quota levels, etc.). Braverman argued that this process was as applicable to non-manual clerical and administrative work as it was to manual production work and consequently many non-manual employees should be regarded, and might come to regard themselves, as part of the 'working class' because they were subject to the same type of work controls and working conditions as manual workers.

However Nichols[48] points out that this general analysis has been criticised and developed in two main ways. First, it does not appear to take sufficient account of **employee resistance** to the introduction of scientific management; yet there is clear evidence (the existence of so-called restrictive practices) that employees have, in different situations and to varying degrees, resisted or modified scientific management approaches and exerted some influence or control over their work situation. Second, it does not take account of **other mechanisms of management control over labour**. Nichols argues that 'the exploitation of labour, though a necessary condition of existence for a capitalist mode of production, always takes place in a particular historical situation, which *inter alia* has its own specific political and ideological components'[49]. While scientific management and deskilling may, in the past, have provided the main plank for management control of labour, management's approach to controlling the labour process has not remained static. Nichols identifies two aspects which have concerned more recent approaches to control of the labour process:

■ The concept of **segmented labour markets** divides 'core' or 'central' employees (whose role, skill and expertise are required for the long-term viability and profitability of the organisation) from 'peripheral' or 'marginal' employees (where there is less commonality between the employee's role/function and the organisation's long-term needs). Such a division in management thinking and organisational strategy can lead to a real or perceived segmentation of interests between these groups and consequently a less effective resistance to management control ('divide and rule').

■ Management has at its disposal a variety of mechanisms, apart from scientific management techniques, to 'control' labour. Friedman[50], for example, differentiates between 'direct control' exercised through the application of scientific management from **'responsible autonomy'** forms of management control over labour. This latter approach involves expanding or enhancing the employee's job or work situation so that it *appears* to allow the employee some degree of 'self control' but only in areas and in a direction which support the achievement of management objectives and increase organisational effectiveness and efficiency. In practice employees are required to adopt and pursue management objectives and ideals as an integral part of their job and working situation. Edwards[51] identifies two forms of managerial control which supplement scientific management's technical or production control of the individual: (1) simple, direct, **personal control** arising from the superior's responsibility for the work and activities of subordinates; and (2) **'bureaucratic' control** stemming from the policies, procedures and rules within the workplace.

Bach and Sisson suggest that within this approach 'managers are agents of capital seeking to maximise profits by intensifying work and systematically reducing labour costs' and 'employers constantly have to devise ways of exerting managerial control'[52]. However, Kelly argues, it is important to understand **the process of employee mobilisation**: how 'workers acquire a collective definition of their interests in response to employer-generated injustice', how 'groups perceive and acquire power resources and deploy them in the construction of different types of conflictual and collaborative relationships' and, in particular, 'how individuals are transformed into collective actors willing and able to create and sustain collective organization and engage in collective action against their employers'[53].

See Chapter 4 –
Trade union
development and
function

Human resource management

The term 'human resource management' (HRM) has become increasingly used in Britain since the early 1980s. However, like 'industrial relations', there is no one universal definition of 'human resource management'. The term has been applied to a diverse range of management strategies and, indeed, sometimes used simply as a more modern, and therefore more acceptable, term for personnel or industrial relations management. Indeed, Keenoy has described it as 'a fluid, multi-faceted and intrinsically ambiguous phenomenon'[54].

Armstrong[55] points out that the roots of human resource management can be found in the 1950s/1960s human relations concepts and approaches of writers such as McGregor, Maslow and Hertzberg combined with the organisational development movement of the l960s/1970s. Its importance for understanding industrial relations lies in its association with **a strategic, integrated and managerial approach to the management of people**. As Guest and Hoque[56] and Storey[57] point out, interest in HRM stemmed from a perceived need to meet competitive challenges in both national and international markets and, consequently, at its heart is the belief that HRM strategy should be driven by business and market considerations with the objective of securing a committed and capable workforce. Certainly Torrington and Hall believe that it is 'totally identified with management interests, being a general management activity, and is relatively distant from the workforce as a whole'[58]. For Guest, the distinctiveness of the HRM model lies in combining established elements of organisational psychology (both what he terms the 'softer' elements of leadership, culture and commitment and 'harder' elements of selection methods, job redesign, goal setting and performance monitoring) with strategic management to provide 'a coherent and distinctive set of propositions about an approach to management – human resource management – which seeks ... to promote positive organisational outcomes'[59]. Storey believes 'it implies something different from the proceduralised approach to handling labour ... it eschews the joint regulative approach ... places emphasis on utilising labour to its full capacity or potential ... HRM is therefore about (and the term is used neutrally here) *exploiting* the labour resource more fully'[60]. This is echoed by Legge who suggests that 'our new enterprise culture demands a different language, one that asserts management's right to manipulate, *and* ability to generate and develop resources'[61].

However, for some writers human resource management should perhaps be retitled **human resource manipulation**. Fowler, for example, questions whether supporters of HRM are 'genuinely concerned with creating a new, equal partnership between employer and employed, or are they really offering a covert form of employee manipulation dressed up as mutuality'[62]. Certainly, the range of personnel practices frequently associated with human resource management (such as psychological testing, appraisal, performance-related pay, individual contracts, quality circles, team briefings, etc.) are regarded by some as HRM policies designed to influence workers' attitudes and 'the use of psychological pressure and group discipline' is seen as 'management by stress'[63]. Storey suggests that there is 'a view of HRM which puts the emphasis on the "resource management" element, with overtones of the dispassionate acquisition, deployment and disposal of resources and an abandonment of the "caring" and empathetic elements in some traditional personnel practice'[64]. Such an approach would seem almost to ignore or dismiss the centrality of people (human beings) in the study of this aspect of organisations. It may be argued that the development of human resource management strategies and approaches provides the evidence of modern management exploitation of labour required by the 'control of the labour process' approach.

Certainly, Guest believes that the values underlying HRM are 'unitarist to the extent that they assume no underlying and inevitable differences of interest between management and workers ... individualistic in that they emphasize the individual-organization linkage in preference to operating through group and representative systems ... [and] leave little scope for collective arrangements and assume little need for collective bargaining'[65]. Quite clearly, therefore, it **questions the collective regulation basis of traditional industrial relations**. Indeed, it may be argued that an essential part of a human resource management approach is that negotiations with trade unions, as the representative of employees, and other such industrial relations activities are to be avoided, removed or, at least, minimised. Storey argues that perhaps the central question is 'can industrial relations be transformed from an adversarial, rule-based institution into a co-operative, commitment-inducing process?'[66] In other words, does human resource management have to equate to a non-union individualistic model of 'industrial relations' or can there be a form of 'dualism' within the organisation where human resource management coexists with industrial relations?

See Chapter 7 –
Management

Social partnership

During the late 1990s attention in the UK shifted towards the concept of 'social partnership' – a term which, as Ackers and Payne point out, 'combines seductive rhetoric with ambiguous and shifting meanings'[67]. Like other new terms such as 'business ethics' and 'stakeholder society', it is capable of a variety of meanings. Sometimes it seems to be applied indiscriminately to any new union recognition agreement, other times it appears to be equated simply to 'good' HRM employment practices. Nevertheless, for Tailby and Winchester it represents a 'qualitatively different form of indirect participation or employee representation'[68] involving employers, trade unions *and* employees, while for Marks *et al.* its distinctiveness lies in its 'emphasis on how the re-constitution of a degree of shared interests in the employment relationship can underpin innovation in the labour process'[69].

It is important to recognise that **'social partnership' has been interpreted in two quite different ways**. In much of Europe (particularly Germany), it has been embedded in the social fabric for 50 years 'as a direct result of social and political forces shaped by the "rupture" of the Second World War'[70]. For example, German postwar reconstruction included state and legal support for the parallel development of, on the one hand, strong centralised sectoral bargaining between single-industry-based trade unions and employers' federations and, on the other hand, the involvement of *employee* representatives in decision making at the workplace (primarily through works councils and co-determination). This allowed for the development of a more co-operative operational relationship between management and employees *within* the organisation, with more conflictual issues, such as wage bargaining, being conducted outside. This took place within a framework of government economic and social policies generally being arrived at by a corporatist approach of consultation with the social partners. However, as Tailby and Winchester point out, the focus in the UK in the 1990s has been almost exclusively on "partnership *at work*" – rather than the broader conception of "*social* partnership" – ... [and] has been interpreted mainly as an attempt to create a more consensual and collaborative relationship between employers, employees and their representatives, and a joint commitment to achieve common goals and mutual benefits'[71]. Certainly, Ackers and Payne believe that the new Labour government's support for 'partnership' is not as all-embracing as it might be, but rather is 'confined to the firm, and bound by unitarist images of identical interests within a united team ... there is little sense that individual interests and rights need collective forms of institutional expression ... [and] an equalisation of power relations'[72].

This interest in the UK in 'social partnership' has been **stimulated by three main developments**:

■ **The election of a Labour government**. 'New' Labour, both before and after the 1997 election, has been keen to project a new image and relationship with both business and trade unions. The 'partnership' or 'stakeholder' concepts are an integral element of its strategy to distinguish 'new' Labour from the perceived union-orientated 'old' Labour. At the same time, it is more committed to the implementation of the EU social dimension which draws heavily on the 'social partnership' model. As with Thatcherism in the 1980s, this creates a perceived political and cultural ideology within which management, unions and employees have to work.

■ **Trade union accommodation to management needs**. Some trade unions argue that it has been necessary to move away from their resistance and reactive 'new realism' of the 1980s and offer management a more proactive and positive relationship in the 1990s. By not only accepting but also encouraging a 'social partnership' approach, it is claimed, they will be better able to represent their members' interests and play their proper part in both the workplace and society.

■ **Shift in emphasis of management strategies**. Previous HRM strategies directed towards *individual* employee involvement, commitment and flexibility may not have been sufficient, on their own, to achieve the desired organisational culture change. Management may view the development of a *collective* 'partnership' as an opportunity to help create a new normative pattern of order, cohesion and stability within the organisation centred around long-term trust between 'stakeholders'.

Perhaps not surprisingly, Ackers and Payne argue that the concept of 'social partnership' can be viewed as either 'yet another unitarist ploy to further compromise the independence of unions from management' or as a 'revamped version of the post-war pluralism' (albeit one which 'makes substantial concessions to the unitarist distaste for conflict and disorder') and therefore needs to be considered within the broader concept of 'participation'[73]. Certainly, in so far

See Chapter 7 –
Management

See Case study 1.1

as the 'social partnership' concept is limited to 'partnership *at work*', it can be viewed as simply the **latest in a continuum of contextually determined management strategies** to change, reform or control the employment relationship to its own advantage. This view may be strengthened by associated management actions intended to by-pass or weaken unionism – using employee representatives and employee councils as an alternative to union recognition; using 'sweetheart deals' or 'beauty contests' to select a preferred union rather than allowing the employees to decide which union they wish to represent them. As Kelly points out, 'it is difficult, if not impossible, [for trade unions] to achieve a partnership with a party who would prefer that you didn't exist'[74].

However, if 'social partnership' is to be developed in its broader sense then, Ferner and Hyman argue, this implies 'first a societal recognition of the different interests of workers and employers; second, an acceptance – indeed encouragement – of the collective representation of these interests; and third, an aspiration that their organized accommodation may provide an effective basis for the regulation of work and the labour market'[75]. Ackers and Payne suggest that 'social partnership' can provide trade unions with a 'foot in the door' which allows them to 'intervene in the lives of ordinary workers today' but is also 'a moveable feast susceptible to redefinitions in a more radical direction'[76] – presumably when circumstances are more favourable for trade unions.

Elements of all of these approaches can be seen in the recent example of call centres. It shows both continuity and change in the nature of the employment relationship. There is a clear continuity, in terms of managing, controlling and regulating people at work, between the factory manufacturing system of the 1890s and the information-processing technology of the 1990s. The case study also highlights the interrelationship between industrial relations and, in particular, changes in technology and the labour market. At the same time, it draws attention to the increasing importance of the international dimension in understanding employment issues.

Case study 1.1 ■ Comeuppance calling
They might be the new assembly lines now but call centres are merely a way-station in an accelerating industrial revolution.

'This week's walk-out by thousands of BT call centre workers – the first ever nationwide strike in the fastest-growing sector of Britain's much-vaunted flexible labour market – will have come as a rude awakening to those who imagined such confrontations to be an anachronism in these engine-rooms of the post-industrial economy.

Faced with an unexpectedly effective campaign of disruption and alarmed that its "customer service" workers' new-found industrial confidence might prove catching, BT managers are now deep in talks with the Communication Workers' Union about how to address its members' grievances.

But their discontent – which is focused on a "19th

Case study 1.1 ■ Comeuppance calling *(continued)*

century management style", impossible targets, stress and understaffing, rather than pay – goes to the heart of the way these white-collar factories operate.

Damned as the "sweatshops of the 21st century", call centres are in reality the logical extension of the Fordist production methods of the early 1900s to the frontline of the emerging 24-hour service economy. They represent the apogee of the "time and motion" theories of industrial management pioneered by Frederick Taylor 100 years ago.

As Sue Fernie, research fellow at the London School of Economics Centre for Economic Performance, puts it: "The possibilities for monitoring behaviour and measuring output in call centres is amazing to behold – the tyranny of the assembly line is but a Sunday school picnic compared with the control that management can exercise in computer telephony."

In the archetypal call centre of the late 90s, thousands of mainly women workers sit in serried ranks in giant hangars, answering telephone inquiries to a predetermined script in relentless succession and under perpetual supervision, each call and its duration recorded, each visit to the lavatory carefully rationed.

Companies such as BT are prickly about what they regard as one-sided stereotypes. But given that a key rallying point in the current dispute has been the threat of disciplinary action if workers fail to complete every call within 285 seconds, it is scarcely a surprise to discover that one popular software package used by a call centre management is marketed as "Total Control Made Easy".

... it has been the combination of the impact of integrated computer and telephone technology, the falling cost of long-distance calls and availability of low-cost labour in areas blighted by industrial decline – Leeds, Liverpool, Sunderland, Glasgow and now Belfast are the industry's "hot spots" – that has fuelled the call centre boom of the past decade.

Banking and financial services led the way, but now call centres are increasingly becoming the crucial contact point between producer and consumer in every imaginable service industry, from travel informa-

tion to tax advice, holidays to health services, and are now spreading to the public sector.

... The consensus is that there are now about 250 000 call centre "agents", as head-set operators are known, working in Britain, accounting for nearly half of the European market. BT, Sky and First Direct – the first bank to operate entirely without branches – are the biggest players in the field and the largest call centres, in Scotland, employ upwards of 4000 people.

... Contrary to industry mythology, most call centre workers are full-time staff and around half are covered by union-negotiated agreements, though some employers are aggressively anti-union. Salary rates range from £8–£17 000, the finance union Unifi says, with the majority in the £10–£13 000 range – roughly half national average pay and heavily dependent on performance bonuses.

But staff turnover is notoriously high and sickness rates are said to be double the average for the finance industry. The stress and tedium means 18 months is the average length of time in each call centre job and in some cases annual turnover can be as high as 80%. With a tightening labour market, employers have been forced to jack up pay and improve conditions to attract new recruits. Some are now even providing on-site jacuzzis.

But, despite its meteoric growth and the added impetus of the internet, most observers believe the call centre will turn out to be only another way-station in an accelerating industrial revolution. With further call-switching to lower labour-cost centres abroad, the expansion of e-commerce and rapid advances in speech recognition technology, call centres are eventually likely to start closing as quickly as they opened.

The OTR Group, a communications consultancy, recently forecast that automation would eliminate 40% of all call centre staff within the next five years. But BT believes that will prove exaggerated. "People will still want human contact," a spokeswoman says.'

Source: Seamus Milne, *Guardian*, 26 November 1999.

1.4   Wider approaches to industrial relations

Recent developments in the study of industrial relations have focused on two approaches (labour markets and comparative) both of which involve considering a wider 'political economy' framework which takes greater account of both the changing economic context and the role of the government.

Labour market

The 'labour market' may be viewed as **the way work is distributed within a society** and involves two overlapping elements: pay (its level and distribution) and work patterns (the level, structure and distribution of employment) (see Figure 1.3). There is little doubt about the **current importance of labour market issues** not just to industrial relations but also to the nature and structure of society. As Fevre[77] points out, labour market conditions in the industrialised countries of western Europe and North America have changed substantially over the past 20 years in a number of ways:

- A significant increase in the economic activity rates among women.
- An increasing level and permanency of unemployment resulting from recession, redistribution of jobs between countries and technological change.

Figure 1.3 The labour market

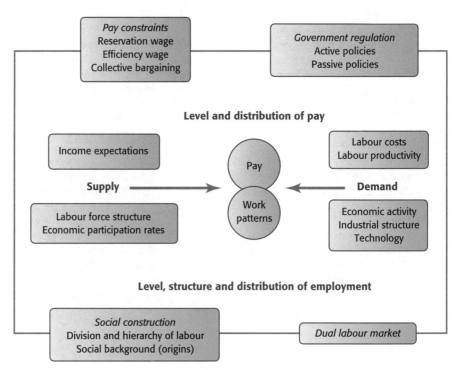

- A shift in the labour force structure from manufacturing to service industries, from manual to non-manual jobs and from unskilled to skilled work.
- Work is increasingly being viewed, by both employees and employers, less in terms of long-term employment and career structures.
- A diversity of government strategies, with some (Japan, Germany and Sweden) taking an active interventionist role in the labour market to help maintain economic development, while others (UK and USA) have sought to deregulate the labour market.

Claydon argues that 'a basic division exists between those approaches which see the labour market as an arena of competition between individuals and those which see it as shaped and controlled by collective institutions, pressures and customs'[78]. Past interest in the operation of the labour market has been the almost exclusive province of labour economists whose 'analytical framework ... is provided by the microeconomic concepts of supply and demand'[79]. The **economic approach to the labour market** concentrates on the role of wages (as a pricing mechanism) in regulating the supply and demand for labour and the effect wages have on inflation and employment within the economy. There is a series of differentiated but interrelated labour markets based on skill, occupation, geographical location, etc. and, within each, the economic model makes three assumptions:

- The individual's income expectation is derived from his or her *utility function* (work is perceived as a 'disutility' and wages are compensation for forsaking leisure – hence, the idea that overtime should be paid at an enhanced hourly rate). The amount of labour supply (i.e. the number of people willing to work and the amount of time each is prepared to work) is determined by the level of wages offered in the labour market.
- The organisation's approach to wages is determined by profit maximisation and labour's *marginal productivity value*. The output of each extra unit of labour will decrease for a constant level of capital and therefore the wage paid will be equal to the value of the 'marginal productivity' of the last unit of labour.
- The competitive forces of supply and demand for labour (in both quantitative and qualitative terms) are constantly operating through the pricing mechanism (wages) seeking to achieve an *equilibrium point* where everyone willing to work at that wage is employed (i.e. there is no 'unemployment').

However, it has long been recognised that there is not a simple free interplay of supply, demand and price in the labour market based on competitive individual maximisation assumptions. Rather, the choices of individuals and organisations within the various labour markets and the associated outcomes of those choices are interrelated and interdependent and, moreover, these choices are constrained to the extent that the **'labour market' is institutionalised** through formal *rules and regulations* and informal *custom and practice*. Certainly, there are a number of ways in which the 'free market' operation of wages may be constrained:

- *Reservation wage:* Unemployment benefit provides, in effect, a 'reservation or replacement wage' (i.e. an income point below which it is unlikely that anyone will be prepared to work). This wage level floor may be further enhanced through the existence of a national minimum wage.

■ *Efficiency wage:* Management may wish to pay at the upper end of the 'market' rate in order to secure labour commitment and greater effort, rather than mere compliance, by 'creaming off' the best labour. There is little evidence to suggest that management seeks to use the wage price mechanism as a regulator. As Claydon notes, 'employers initially go for quantity adjustments to changes in demand rather than wage adjustments'[80]. Indeed, production needs (derived from technology and working methods) may be a more significant determinant of the numbers to be employed than the wage level at any given time.

■ *Collective bargaining:* The existence of trade unions reduces management's ability to treat labour as individual, replaceable units of a commodity and introduces the need to *negotiate* wages. The process of negotiation involves reference to a variety of factors, other than just supply and demand, in determining wage rates, not least, comparability with others (both inside and outside the organisation).

Furthermore, the labour market does not only operate as a series of interactions between organisations and an *external* labour market (hiring and firing). Many organisations have an *internal* labour market characterised by limited entry points, formalised job-evaluated salary structures, internal progression, investment in 'human capital' through training, etc. As Fevre points out, the **concept of the dual labour market** involves 'one [market] in which the laws of supply and demand could operate freely and another in which workers were insulated from competition'[81] – for example, the 'flexible firm' model and its differentiation between core and peripheral employees. The *'organisation-specific'* nature of labour may be further enhanced as a result of increasingly specific technology and systems within organisations coupled with strategic HRM initiatives aimed at developing a distinctive corporate culture. To some, the public sector has been perceived as being labour market 'shelters' or 'gilt-edged' internal labour markets[82] through its apparent concern to be a 'good employer' and lack of competitive pressure.

Alternatively, the labour market may be viewed as primarily a **social construction**. The sociological approach to labour markets is, Fevre suggests, 'more interested in how labour markets put some people in "good" jobs, others in "bad" jobs, and some people on welfare benefits'[83]. It seeks to explain how the labour market allocates jobs and work between groups of people. He argues that the fundamental nature of the labour market rests on two principles: social division and social hierarchy. *Social division* or *labour specialisation* has arisen as societies have evolved to manage more complex tasks. Different people do different things and 'each new type of labour which comes into being and each further subdivision of existing labour adds to the development of the social division of labour'[84]. Over time, labour specialisation has given rise to a *social hierarchy* based on a qualitative perception of different work having different value (a social grading). The labour market has become a crucial element in defining the nature of society and, as such, has 'social' as well as 'economic' dimensions. Fevre argues that 'the development of labour markets therefore depends on the social acceptance and social construction of hierarchies'[85]. In the UK, this has been manifest in many ways:

- The division of work between 'unskilled', 'semi-skilled' and 'skilled' or between 'manual' and 'non-manual'.
- The concept of 'professions' (doctors and lawyers) and the desire of other groups to be accorded the same standing (for example, personnel specialists).
- The lower recognition accorded to 'engineers' in the UK compared to Germany.
- The extent to which the UK 'class' system and its differential access to education (in particular, private schools) appears to underpin many of the above labour divisions.

The sociological approach suggests that labour market patterns (destinations) may be primarily a reflection of social backgrounds (origins). Factors such as race, gender and class are perhaps more significant determinants of access to particular labour markets (and, therefore, the wage level associated with that type of labour) than anything to do with the intrinsic nature of the job or the extent of supply and demand.

At the simplest level, governments have the capacity, through legislation, to determine the boundary of the labour supply by defining when people may join the labour market (school-leaving age), when they are expected to leave (retirement age) and by regulating the terms on which certain groups are employed (e.g. women, young people, migrant labour). However, it appears that **government interest in the labour market** stems primarily from its desire to support economic development and its concern for the social and political consequences of unemployment and only secondarily from any ethical concern to define the nature of the employment relationship. Recent UK changes in the retirement age and the abolition of legislation restricting the work of women were presented as measures to increase labour 'flexibility'; concern in the industrialised countries about the use of prison labour in China or child bonded labour in Pakistan appears to have been highlighted because of its 'cheapness' and its competitive threat rather than because of its inherent ethical unacceptability.

In considering the government's role, it is useful to distinguish between *passive* **labour market policies** (i.e. payments to support people during their period of unemployment) and *active* **labour market policies** (i.e. measures such as training or job support programmes which are intended to influence the level and structure of the supply and demand for labour). Schmid *et al.*[86] suggest that there are two fundamental issues: first, should the cost of these policies be borne by society (from general taxation) or those within the labour market (through direct contributions from employers and employees); and, second, should these policies be managed as separate and distinct strategies or integrated together? As they point out, 'expenditures for passive and active labor market policy compete, especially during a recession when contributions fall and expenditures for passive labor market policy rise almost automatically because of increasing unemployment' and therefore it is 'reasonable to expect that passive labor market policy will crowd out active measures'[87] – perhaps at the very time that they are most needed! Certainly, concern has been expressed, in many industrialised countries, at the difficulty of maintaining the increasing costs of social welfare benefits (not least unemployment pay) at a time of a reducing employment base.

See Chapter 8 –
Government

There has been a clear **diversity of government approach** to labour market issues. On the one hand, some countries (e.g. Sweden, Germany, Singapore) have adopted an interventionist and corporatist approach in the belief that 'the state alone can engage in long-term planning for a country's economy and, in partnership with the representatives of workers and employers, can develop policies to achieve these long-term aims'[88]. On the other hand, there are countries (primarily the UK) which have sought to adopt policies and strategies 'to deregulate labour markets so that they resemble the labour markets of neoclassical theory'[89]. Within the economic model, a 'free' or 'flexible' labour market is one where pay is determined only by the organisation's 'ability to pay' (based on profitability or labour productivity), there is a continual smooth transition flow of labour (individuals move from declining firms, occupations and geographical areas to employment growth areas) and there is a downward movement in average real wages in recession (wages respond to the reduction in demand for labour).

All these labour market developments and issues represent more than simply a changed context within which industrial relations is conducted but are, as Rubery and Wilkinson point out, 'closely linked to the actions and policies of employers'[90]. It is the decisions made within organisations which shape work and, in turn, shape the nature of society. Organisational 'downsizing' (the current antiseptic replacement term for 'redundancy') or 'flexibility' cannot be isolated from the growth or persistence of unemployment or increase in part-time work at the macro-level and the potential social issues that arise from such developments. Decisions within the industrial relations system both reflect and contribute to these wider aspects of the employment situation.

Comparative approach

It is useful to draw a **distinction between 'international or trans-national' and 'comparative' approaches to industrial relations**; although there is an overlap between the two. An 'international or trans-national' approach is concerned with those features of industrial relations which operate *across* national boundaries (multinational corporations, international union organisations and trans-national political institutions such as the European Union and International Labour Organisation) and their capacity to establish trans-national labour standards and challenge national sovereignty. A 'comparative' approach is concerned with examining the industrial relations system *between* countries (analysing the differences in the interrelationship between actors, processes, outcomes and environments).

There are, perhaps, two main **reasons for examining the industrial relations systems in other countries**. First, through comparing (*similarities*) and contrasting (*differences*), it is possible to place the UK within a wider context by gaining a better understanding of not just *how* countries differ but, perhaps more importantly, *why*. Such comparisons often **provide the basis for policy decisions** for modification or reform of parts of the industrial relations system. At different points in the past, for example, it has been suggested that the UK could 'learn' from the perceived success of incomes policies in Sweden and The Netherlands, co-determination in Germany, the legal framework in the USA and, more recently, the management practices and industrial relations systems of Japan and other newly industrialising countries of south-east Asia. Now it is the UK which appears to suggest that other countries could (should) learn from its approach to increasing labour flexibility. Generally, it has been the relative economic success of a country, at a particular time, which has provided the impetus to examine that country's industrial relations system in search of some distinctly different aspect of their system which is perceived to account for their economic success.

However, such a simplistic approach ignores the fact that the economic success of a country depends on a complex set of economic, political and social interrelationships both within the country and beyond rather than just one part of its industrial relations system. Furthermore, even if the industrial relations system (or a part of it) is a major contributor to a country's economic success, it is important to recognise, as Bean notes, that 'when some particular aspect of another country's industrial relations are removed from their social, political and cultural surroundings they may lose their validity and rationale'[91]. It is not possible simply to 'export–import' industrial relations between countries; the ill-fated UK Industrial Relations Act (1971) is a clear example. There is, as Bridgford and Stirling note, 'a need to draw a balance between what is culturally specific and what is generally applicable'[92].

The second reason for having regard to the experience of other countries lies in the **changing world political systems and economy** – these environments are no longer a simple national matter. The political environment for UK industrial relations now clearly exists at two levels – the UK and the European Union; and, as seen during the 1980s and 1990s, there can be conflict between them. The UK's economic environment stretches much wider than even the 'single market' of the European Union. The past 30 years have seen the development of significant newly industrialised countries in south-east Asia (Japan, Korea, Taiwan, Singapore, Malaysia, etc.) to join those of western Europe and North America. Currently the process of industrialisation and the development of market economies is spreading to China, Vietnam and the former Communist eastern European countries (with many of the latter now queuing up to join the EU).

The resultant global 'market' economy, increased international competition and role of multinational corporations have significant consequences for any country's industrial relations system. The overlap between economic trade and social policies (industrial relations) has been clearly demonstrated by the desire of the 'western industrialised countries' to insert 'social clauses' (minimum labour standards) in trade agreements between the EU and ASEAN countries and in the GATT/WTO dialogues. As Bamber and Lansbury point out, 'the realisation that employment standards are important in determining fair international trade between states has further heightened the need for the comparative study of labour relations and its role in export competitiveness'[93]. From the industrialised countries' standpoint, such clauses are seen as necessary to limit 'unfair' trade competition derived from lower labour standards and avoid the consequences of 'social dumping' (the shift of employment from Europe and North America to south-east Asia). From the standpoint of the newly industrialised countries, this is seen as a form of protectionism which will restrict trade competition and their economic development. It is also seen as an attempt to impose a 'western' model of industrial relations and an intrusion into their right to determine their own approach.

However, it is necessary to be aware of the **difficulties of undertaking international comparisons**:

1. **Terminology and functions**: All comparative industrial relations writers point to the difficulty of comparing 'like-to-like'. As Bean notes, problems arise 'in ensuring a measure of concept equivalence across societies, since what are nominally identical practices or institutions may perform varying functions, or have a very different significance'[94]. For example:

   - 'Labour courts' may be only a conciliation body (Ireland) or make statutory binding decisions (Germany)[95]; equally, they may vary in the extent to which they deal with individual and/or collective labour issues; they may be called 'courts' or 'tribunals'.
   - Bamber and Lansbury[96] point out that the terms 'collective agreement' (UK), 'labour contract' (USA) and 'industrial award' (Australia) all refer to the codification of substantive terms and conditions of employment but the differing terms indicate the system differences within which they are determined and their differing status.
   - Bridgford and Stirling note that the term 'workplace representative' 'cannot cover the different roles of the French "*délégués du personnel*", the Danish "*tillidsrepraesentant*" or the British "shop steward"[97]. They may be elected by and represent all employees or only union members; they may or may not have a collective bargaining role.
   - Schregle points out that 'it may have been a mistake (now past remedy) to translate the German word *Betriebsrat* by the English expression "works council"[98] because the UK 'works council' is a voluntary joint consultative body comprising representatives of both management and employees, while the German *Betriebsrat* is composed of only employee representatives and has statutory rights to be informed, consulted and agree to certain organisational changes.
   - Blanpain[99] notes that the French term 'participation' refers to *financial* participation through profit-sharing, whereas in English-speaking countries it is generally used to cover the much wider concept of participation in management decision making.

2. **Practice versus national institutions**: Therefore, when examining the industrial relations experience of other countries, it is necessary to look not just at the formal *macro* system of institutions, processes and legal framework but rather at how particular functions within industrial relations (such as, determining terms and conditions of employment, handling disputes between trade unions and employers, the exercise of managerial decision making, etc.) are actually conducted – who is involved; what type of process, institutions or mechanism are used; what rights and power does each party have within those processes; etc.

2. **Variability within nations as well as between nations**: There are often significant differences between industries, even within the same national system, in the way they conduct their industrial relations (not least, for example, between private and public sectors). Equally, there may be factors (for example technology and market conditions) which are common to an industry across different national cultures. The predominance of a particular industry within a national system may, therefore, distort the perception of the nature of its macro national system and, as a consequence, 'what is really an "industry" effect could be misinterpreted as being a "national" effect'[100]. Certainly, the validity of the Donovan Commission[101] analysis of UK industrial relations in the 1960s has been questioned because of its apparent concentration on the engineering industry.

Perhaps the most important consideration, in trying to understand industrial relations in other countries, is the **analytical framework** to be adopted. As Bean notes, the industrial relations research tradition among western industrialised countries has tended to cluster around two frameworks – the 'pluralist-institutionalist' and 'class-oriented' approaches[102]. However, the expansion of industrialisation, and consequent wider range of countries coming within the scope of the study of industrial relations (particularly south-east Asia), has raised questions about the appropriateness of these frameworks to analysing and understanding their industrial relations.

As Box 1.3 indicates, industrial relations in the newly industrialised and 'developing' countries needs to be viewed within a **political economy framework** and from a **corporatist rather than pluralistic ideology**. It is clear, in the newly industrialised countries of south-east Asia (such as Korea, Malaysia,

| Box 1.3 | A political economic approach to industrial relations in the industrialisation process |

'The ideology of nationalism helps to bring about political independence in developing countries. However, political independence without economic development appears rather meaningless. Hence, the élites of many of the developing countries have seen a need to consolidate political independence by accelerating the process of industrialization to "catch-up" with the more developed countries. Since the private sector is weak and small in these developing countries, it is the state which should embark on the programme of industrialization. However, there are insurmountable difficulties involved in mobilizing and generating domestic savings in these countries. The alternative for the governmental élites in this situation is to look for foreign capital, mainly in the form of foreign direct investment.

  Foreign investors are assumed to be profit makers by design, and other things only by default. If so, host countries should create an appropriate "investment climate" so that foreign investors can be lured to their countries. The labour situation is one of the major factors that figure in the investors' assessment of the investment climate. Mindful of this, the governments of some developing countries have adopted labour policies that limit the role of workers' organizations under the assumption that low wages and industrial peace are inducements to foreign investors.'

Source: B. Sharma, *Aspects of Industrial Relations in ASEAN*, Institute of Southeast Asian Studies, Occasional Paper no. 78, 1985, pp. 16/7.

Singapore and Taiwan), that *nationalism* (emphasising the 'political' relationship between the State and the various elements of the society) is more significant in determining the nature of their industrial relations system than *class* (emphasising the owner/labour relationship between employer(s) and employee(s)). As Bean points out, 'the governments of these countries play a more active and interventionist role in industrial relations ... policies are guided by the requirements of national, growth-orientated development plans and the state itself is much more central to the development process' and that these governments have 'increasingly sought [varying degrees of] control over the trade union movement and its activities – not least, to protect the interests of foreign capital'[103].

At the same time, the role of trade unions and their relationship with government has tended to become one best seen as 'corporatist'. First, in the initial stages of economic development in these countries, trade unions were often in a weak 'economic bargaining' position because of the absence of a significant group of skilled workers (which, in western industrialised countries, provided the core for the early development of trade unions) but an almost unlimited supply of unskilled labour and, therefore, were reliant on political/legal support to maintain their existence. Second, in many of these countries there was, in their pre-independence period, a very close link between the labour movement and 'national liberation' politics (*political unionism*) which has continued post-independence. A similar situation has been seen more recently in South Africa in the drive to remove *apartheid*[104]. Third, governments have sought to restrict the 'sectional interest and consumption' role of trade unions (improving terms and conditions of employment for their members through free collective bargaining) in preference for a 'managerial' role which supports the government by 'guiding' and 'explaining' national economic development needs to their members. The net effect has been the subordination of trade unions to the political system.

At the same time, the **economic structure and labour market** of many *developing* countries show a marked difference to that of western industrialised countries (or even the newly industrialised countries of south-east Asia) and are characterised by 'dualism'. First, often only a small proportion of the working population are in formal 'wage-earning' employment and a large proportion of these are employed in the public sector. Second, the private sector (manufacturing and service) contains both a large number of small, traditional, indigenous organisations alongside a smaller group of larger, modern, multinational 'imports'. Consequently, it is common to find both 'western' and 'eastern' styles of industrial relations being imported within the variety of multinational organisations alongside a strong state-controlled and limited system of industrial relations in the public sector.

An important feature of the comparative approach to industrial relations has been the debate about **convergency and/or divergency between industrial relations systems**. In the early 1970s, Kerr *et al.*[105] argued that there is a 'logic of industrialisation' which produces a *tendency* towards uniformity or **convergence** between industrial relations systems. The universal nature of the technological and market environments will, through the intervening similarity of management production and labour responses supported by government action to maintain and develop their economies, tend to produce similar industrial structures and labour market systems and strategies across different countries. Bridgford and Stirling, while believing 'it is fruitless to join battle with one side or other of a false dichotomy'[106], do identify a number of features common in western European countries; not least, industrial restructuring and changes in employment patterns in response to increased international market competition and the growing influence of the supranational European Union. However, as they point out, the EU countries can conveniently be grouped together because they are 'liberal capitalist democracies with independent trade union movements and free collective bargaining arrangements'[107] (a similar underlying ideology). However, it is important to recognise that while countries may face a similar changed economic environment, nevertheless, as Ferner and Hyman note, there will be a differential impact because they 'vary in their productive base, in their sectoral distribution of output and employment, in their orientation to the international economy, in the extent of foreign and state ownership of industry, and so on'[108]. In addition, they argue that the social structures of industrial relations have a degree of *institutional persistence* in so far as 'they have a life and reality of their own, independent of political (or economic) fluctuations or caprices' and can 'mediate intensifying external pressures with greater or lesser degrees of success' depending on 'the strength and rigidity of the social regulation of employment relations'[109].

The likely extent of any wider convergence, now or in the future, is very much open to question. It is more probable that industrial relations will be characterised by **diversity**:

1. **Countries industrialise at different points in time**. As Bean points out, 'the main characteristics of national industrial relations ... seem to be established at a fairly early stage in the industrial development of a country' and 'in the absence of major dislocations such as war or revolution [they] show a good deal of tenacity, retaining many of their early characteristics and institutions despite subsequent evolution'[110]. Thus, there would appear to be a degree of inbuilt inertia to change. Furthermore, countries which have industrialised in the postwar period have done so within very different economic, political and sociological environments to the industrialisation of western Europe and North America in the nineteenth and early twentieth centuries. It is perhaps inevitable, therefore, that their approach to industrial relations should be different; not least, Dore[111] suggests, because as 'latecomers' they have had the opportunity to 'learn' from the experience of these earlier industrialised countries (and perhaps benefit from the body of industrial relations and human resource management knowledge which has been developed over the postwar period).

2. **Culture and values**. Most importantly, diversity in industrial relations arises from the existence of distinctive value systems and cultural features. Culture can be defined as 'the historically developed and learned pattern of beliefs, values and customs of a people'[112], which 'include views on human nature, the relationship of man to nature, time orientation, orientation towards

activity and types of relation between people'[113], and as such influences the attitudes, behaviours and decisions of all three groups of actors. It is the decisions (choices) of these 'social' actors which determine not just the outcomes of industrial relations but also the nature of the institutional arrangements and relationships that make up the 'system'. Diversity of culture exists even within the relatively homogeneous western Europe: for example, the strong religious and/or political affiliations associated with trade unionism in France, Italy, Belgium and The Netherlands or the development of the 'social partnership' concept within postwar Germany to differentiate it from the previous Nazi era. The expansion of industrialisation has extended the range of cultural diversity. Much has been written about Japanese management styles, both within Japan and the effect and implications of their export/import into western industrialised countries. Similarly, the drive for industrialisation in other countries cannot be divorced from the parallel perceived need to create and/or maintain a distinct national identity. Certainly, Poole believes that 'as more countries become industrialized and as already complex modes of accommodation of interests amongst the parties are shaped by a progressively diverse range of socio-cultural forms, a rich heterogeneous and variegated pattern of industrial relations institutions will unfold'[114].

3. **Heterogeneity *within* national systems**. The existence of significant differences between industries within the same country makes it difficult to characterise any 'national' industrial relations system. Furthermore, there is clear evidence within western Europe of management strategies, in some cases supported by government, directed towards decentralisation and greater flexibility in the operation of the industrial relations system. A reduction in uniformity *within* countries makes the convergence *between* countries more problematical.

Perhaps the most that can be said about the 'convergence/divergence' issue is that similar times and stages in industrialisation combined with broad cultural similarities may tend to produce **regional based convergence of industrial relations systems**. It is possible to identify three major industrial relations models: western European, North American and south-east Asian. There are also countries and regions which are, at present, going through a process of significant economic and social transition. It is not certain that the economic, political and social developments within eastern Europe will result in a simple replication of a western European model of industrial relations and China's move towards a more market economy, but still with a Communist political and social framework, is likely to produce an industrial relations system different to other Asian countries. Similarly, South Africa is different from the rest of Africa (industrialised and with a variant of the western European model of industrial relations which can only be fully understood within the very particular recent economic, social and political context of *apartheid*), while Australia and New Zealand, despite their close historical European cultural links, developed their own arbitration based approach to industrial relations in the early twentieth century but are now looking more closely at their Pacific orientation.

■ Author's note

It is important in any book on industrial relations that the reader is aware of the author's perspective of the subject:

■ Organisations are composed of sectional groups which have different, and frequently divergent, interests and whose members' expectations, perceptions and attitudes are the product of a combination of both social and organisational factors and differences. Within this framework management is simply one of the sectional groups – but one which, within the capitalist context, is the embodiment of 'the organisation' and has privileged access to power through its control of information and resources within the organisation and its linkage to the 'establishment' within society.

■ Industrial relations is concerned with the determination, conduct and regulation of the employment relationship (economic and managerial relations) at both the micro-organisational and macro-society levels and the interrelationship between them – organisational decisions shape work patterns and the nature, role and position of work within society and vice versa. This is inextricably interlinked with wider political and economic issues concerned with economic development and relationships within society and the role and strategy of government.

■ Within industrial relations both management and employees have an equal and legitimate right to seek to protect what they perceive as their interests and to secure their objectives – including the right to exert pressure through industrial power if it is felt by them to be necessary. The relative power relationship between the participants is never 'right' or 'in balance' but constantly varying, dependent on organisational and societal factors. There is never a universally 'right' solution to an industrial relations problem or situation. The only 'right' solution is that which is acceptable to the parties involved.

■ Without collective organisation and representation, employees are unable to influence and regulate the employment relationship effectively. By acting in concert they are better able to establish and maintain institutions, processes and rules to regulate the employment relationship through negotiation and, thereby, secure a genuine partnership with management. *All* parties have to be prepared to accept compromises in resolving problems or issues between them (i.e. not fully to achieve their aspirations and objectives).

■ Summary propositions

■ Industrial relations is a complex and dynamic 'social activity', operating through a diverse structure of relationships and outcomes (both individual and collective) inside and outside the organisation, which is directed towards regulating the employment relationship.

■ By being aware of the underlying values and perspective of each approach – particularly differences in how they perceive issues, problems and solutions – we can make better sense of the changing nature of the employment relationship.

■ Industrial relations should not be regarded as simply an organisational process. Rather it needs to be examined and understood in a broader and changing economic, political and social context. Current developments in the employment relationship cannot be divorced from the globalisation of business and trade.

Activity	Write down briefly what the term 'industrial relations' means to *YOU*, what images it conjures up for you, and what you expect to be the focus and broad content of the subject.
	You can then compare your view with those of Edwards and Ackers (in the introduction to this chapter) and/or those in the Author's note (at the end of this chapter). You might also like to keep what you have written and refer back to it when you have finished your course to see if your views have changed and, if so, in what ways.

■ Further reading

■ A. Fox, 'Industrial relations: a social critique of pluralist ideology', in J. Child (ed.), *Man and Organisation*, Allen & Unwin, 1973. This provides a very useful discussion of unitary, pluralistic and radical frames of reference.

■ R. Hyman, *Industrial Relations: A Marxist introduction*, Macmillan, 1975. A leading, and very readable, book which approaches and explains industrial relations, and particularly the role and problems of trade unions, from a clearly Marxist perspective.

■ P. Thompson, *The Nature of Work: An introduction to debates on the labour process* (2nd edn), Macmillan, 1989. This provides a concise and comprehensive introduction to a range of debates on the labour process.

■ J. Storey (ed.), *Human Resource Management – a critical text*, Routledge, 1995. Chapters 1, 2 and 5 provide a useful discussion of both the overall concept of HRM and its relationship to industrial relations.

■ R. Fevre, *The Sociology of Labour Markets*, Prentice Hall, 1992. This book considers both the economic and sociological perspectives of the labour market.

■ G. J. Bamber and R. D. Lansbury (eds), *International & Comparative Employment Relations*, Sage, 1998. Chapter 1 considers various approaches and issues in examining industrial relations across different national contexts.

■ G. Hollinshead, P. Nicholls and S. Tailby (eds), *Employee Relations*, FT Pitman, 1999 (Chapter 2) and S. Bach and K. Sisson (eds), *Personnel Management* (3rd edn), Blackwell, 2000 (Chapter 1). Both chapters examine the development of various approaches and their influence on the perception of industrial relations.

References

1. P. Blyton and P. Turnbull, *The Dynamics of Employee Relations* (2nd edn), Macmillan, 1998, p. 3.
2. P. Edwards, 'The employment relationship', in P. Edwards (ed.), *Industrial Relations: theory and practice in Britain*, Blackwell, 1995, p. 4.
3. P. Ackers, 'Back to basics? Industrial relations and the enterprise culture', *Employee Relations*, vol. 16, no. 8, 1994, pp. 38 and 39.
4. Blyton and Turnbull, *op. cit.*, pp. 9 and 13.
5. A. Fox, 'Industrial relations: a social critique of pluralist ideology', in J. Child (ed.), *Man and Organization*, Allen & Unwin, 1973, p. 189.
6. D. Farnham and J. Pimlott, *Understanding Industrial Relations* (5th edn), Cassell, 1995, p. 45.
7. A. Fox, 'Industrial Sociology and Industrial Relations', *Royal Commission Research Paper No. 3*, HMSO, 1966, p. 4.
8. C. Provis, 'Unitarism, pluralism, interests and values', *British Journal of Industrial Relations*, vol. 34, no. 4, 1996, pp. 474–6.
9. Fox (1973), *op. cit.*, p. 193.
10. A. Kornhauser, R. Dubin and A. M. Ross (eds), *Industrial Conflict*, McGraw-Hill, 1954, p. 13.
11. Fox (1966), *op cit.*, p. 4.
12. Fox (1973), *op. cit.*, pp. 195–6.
13. Fox (1966), *op. cit.*, p. 7.
14. *Ibid.*, p. 8.
15. R. Hyman, *Industrial Relations: A Marxist Introduction*, Macmillan, 1975, p. 19.
16. M. Marchington, *Managing Industrial Relations*, McGraw-Hill, 1982, p. 48.
17. Hyman, *op. cit.*, p. 24.
18. Blyton and Turnbull, *op. cit.*, p. 25.
19. J. Barbash, 'Collective bargaining and the theory of conflict', *British Journal of Industrial Relations*, vol. 18, 1980, p. 87.
20. A. Fox, *A Sociology of Work in Industry*, Collier Macmillan, 1971, p. 28. Reprinted with permission of the publisher.
21. Barbash, *op. cit.*, p. 88.
22. Hyman, *op. cit.*, p. 203.
23. A. Flanders, *Industrial Relations – What's Wrong with the System?* Faber, 1965, p. 4.
24. A. Flanders, 'Collective bargaining: a theoretical analysis', *British Journal of Industrial Relations*, vol. 6, 1968, pp. 1–26.
25. R. Lumley, 'A modified rules approach to workplace industrial relations', *Industrial Relations Journal*, vol. 10, no. 3, 1979, p. 49.
26. G. S. Bain and H. Clegg, 'Strategy for industrial relations research in Great Britain', *British Journal of Industrial Relations*, vol. 12, 1974, p. 95.
27. J. F. B. Goodman, E. G. A. Armstrong, A. Wagner, J. E. Davis and J. J. Wood, 'Rules in industrial relations theory: a discussion', *Industrial Relations Journal*, vol. 6, no. 1, 1975, pp. 14–30.
28. S. J. Wood, A. Wagner, E. G. A. Armstrong, J. F. B. Goodman and J. E. Davis, 'The "industrial relations system" concept as a basis for theory in industrial relations', *British Journal of Industrial Relations*, vol. 13, 1975, p. 295.
29. *Ibid.*, p. 296.
30. Hyman, *op. cit.*, p. 11.
31. G. Schienstock, 'Towards a theory of industrial relations', *British Journal of Industrial Relations*, vol. 19, 1981, p. 172.
32. J. E. T. Eldridge, *Industrial Disputes*, Routledge & Kegan Paul, 1968, p. 22.
33. Blyton and Turnbull, *op. cit.*, p. 20.
34. M. Jackson, *An Introduction to Industrial Relations*, Routledge, 1991, p. 5.
35. J. A. Banks, *Trade Unionism*, Collier Macmillan, 1974.
36. S. Wood, 'Ideology in industrial relations theory', *Industrial Relations Journal*, vol. 9, no. 4, 1978/79, p. 45.
37. D. Winchester, 'Industrial relations research in Britain', *British Journal of Industrial Relations*, vol. 20, 1983, p. 104.
38. *Ibid.*, p. 105.
39. M. Shalev, 'Industrial relations theory and the comparative study of industrial relations and industrial conflict', *British Journal of Industrial Relations*, vol. 18, 1980, p. 26.
40. Bain and Clegg, *op. cit.*, p. 95.
41. Jackson, *op. cit.*, p. 7.
42. *Ibid.*, p. 9.
43. M. Poole, *Industrial Relations: origins and patterns of national diversity*, Routledge & Kegan Paul, 1986, p. 13.
44. P. Thompson, *The Nature of Work: An introduction to debates on the labour process* (2nd edn), Macmillan, 1989, p. xv.
45. *Ibid.*, p. 242.
46. P. Thompson and E. Bannon (1985), quoted in P. Thompson, *The Nature of Work: An introduction to debates on the labour process* (2nd edn), Macmillan, 1989, p. 245.
47. H. A. Braverman, *Labour and Monopoly*

Capital: The degradation of work in the twentieth century, Monthly Review Press, 1974.

48. T. Nichols, *The British Worker Question*, Routledge & Kegan Paul, 1986.
49. *Ibid.*, p. 31.
50. A. Friedman, *Industry and Labour: Class struggle at work and monopoly capitalism*, Macmillan, 1977.
51. R. Edwards, *Contested Terrain: The transformation of the workplace in the twentieth century*, Heinemann, 1979.
52. S. Bach and K. Sisson, 'Personnel management in perspective', in S. Bach and K. Sisson (eds), *Personnel Management* (3rd edn), Blackwell, 2000, p. 6.
53. J. Kelly, *Rethinking Industrial Relations: Mobilization, collectivism and long waves*, Routledge, 1998, pp. 1, 24 and 38.
54. T. Keenoy, 'HRM as a hologram: a polemic', *Journal of Management Studies*, vol. 36, no. 1, 1999, pp. 1–2.
55. M. Armstrong, 'Human resource management: a case of the emperor's new clothes?' *Personnel Management*, August 1987.
56. D. Guest and K. Hoque, 'Human resource management and the new industrial relations', in I. Beardwell (ed.), *Contemporary Industrial Relations: A critical analysis*, Oxford University Press, 1997, pp. 11–36.
57. J. Storey, 'Human resource management: still marching on, or marching out?', in J. Storey (ed.), *Human Resource Management: A critical text*, Routledge, 1995, pp. 3–32.
58. D. Torrington and L. Hall, *Human Resource Management* (4th edn), Prentice Hall, 1998, p. 12.
59. D. Guest, 'Personnel and HRM: can you tell the difference?' *Personnel Management*, January 1989, p. 49.
60. J. Storey (ed.), *New Perspectives on Human Resource Management*, Routledge, 1989, p. 9.
61. K. Legge, 'Human resource management: a critical analysis' in J. Storey (ed.), *New Perspectives on Human Resource Management*, Routledge, 1989, p. 40.
62. A. Fowler, 'When chief executives discover HRM', *Personnel Management*, January 1987.
63. 'HRM – human resource manipulation', *Labour Research*, August 1989, p. 8.
64. J. Storey, 'Developments in the management of human resources: an interim report', *Warwick Papers in Industrial Relations*, no. 17, November 1987, p. 7.
65. D. Guest, 'Human resource management: its implications for industrial relations and trade unions', in J. Storey (ed.), *New Perspectives on*

Human Resource Management, Routledge, 1989, p. 43.
66. Storey (1987), *op. cit.*, p. 9.
67. P. Ackers and J. Payne, 'British trade unions and social partnership: rhetoric, reality and strategy', *The International Journal of Human Resource Management*, vol. 9, no. 3, 1998, p. 530.
68. S. Tailby and D. Winchester, 'Management and trade unions: towards social partnership?', in Bach and Sisson (eds), *op. cit.*, p. 365.
69. A. Marks, P. Findlay, J. Hine, A. McKinlay and P. Thompson, 'The politics of partnership? Innovation in employment relations in the Scottish spirits industry', *British Journal of Industrial Relations*, vol. 36, no. 2, 1998, p. 209.
70. M. Upchurch, 'Social partnership in grand form: the example of "Rhenish capitalism" ', *Work and Employment*, Issue 8, Spring/Summer 1999, pp. 12–14.
71. Tailby and Winchester, *op. cit.*, p. 374.
72. Ackers and Payne, *op. cit.*, p. 539.
73. *Ibid.*, p. 533.
74. J. Kelly, 'Union militancy and social partnership', in P. Ackers, C. Smith and P. Smith (eds), *The New Workplace and Trade Unionism*, Routledge, 1996, p. 88.
75. A. Ferner and R. Hyman, *Changing Industrial Relations in Europe*, Blackwell, 1998, pp. xv–xvi.
76. Ackers and Payne, *op. cit.*, p. 546.
77. R. Fevre, *The Sociology of Labour Markets*, Prentice Hall, 1992, pp. 2–9.
78. T. Claydon, 'Human resource management and the labour market', in I. Beardwell and L. Holden (eds), *Human Resource Management: A contemporary perspective*, Pitman, 1994, p. 75.
79. R. F. Elliott, *Labor Economics: a comparative text*, McGraw Hill, 1991, p. 4.
80. Claydon, *op. cit.*, p. 80.
81. Fevre, *op. cit.*, p. 34.
82. *Ibid.*, pp. 125–7.
83. *Ibid.*, p. 19.
84. *Ibid.*, p. 49.
85. *Ibid.*, p. 52.
86. G. Schmid, B. Reissert and G. Bruche, *Unemployment Insurance and Active Labor Market Policy*, Wayne State University Press, 1992.
87. *Ibid.*, pp. 22/3.
88. Fevre, *op. cit.*, p. 130.
89. J. Rubery and F. Wilkinson, *Employer Strategy and the Labour Market*, Oxford University Press, 1994, p. 5.
90. *Ibid.*, p. 1.

91. R. Bean, *Comparative Industrial Relations: An introduction to cross-national perspectives* (2nd edn), Routledge, 1994, p. 6.

92. J. Bridgford and J. Stirling, *Employee Relations in Europe*, Blackwell, 1994, p. 3.

93. G. J. Bamber and R. D. Lansbury, 'An introduction to international and comparative employment relations', in G. J. Bamber and R. D. Lansbury (eds), *International and Comparative Employment Relations* (3rd edn), Sage, 1998, pp. 2–3.

94. Bean, *op. cit.*, p. 16.

95. *Ibid.*

96. Bamber and Lansbury, *op. cit.*, p. 5.

97. Bridgford and Stirling, *op. cit.*, p. 5.

98. J. Schregle, 'Workers' participation in the Federal Republic of Germany in an international perspective', *International Labour Review*, vol. 126, no. 3, 1987, p. 320.

99. R. Blanpain, 'The influence of labour on management decision-making: a comparative legal survey', *Industrial Law Journal*, 1974, pp. 5–29.

100. Bean, *op. cit.*, p. 14.

101. *Report of Royal Commission on Trade Unions and Employers Associations*, HMSO, 1968.

102. Bean, *op. cit.*, p. 2.

103. *Ibid.*, p. 218.

104. S. Bendix, *Industrial Relations in South Africa* (3rd edn), Juta & Co (Cape Town), 1996, pp. 243–5.

105. C. Kerr, J. Dunlop, F. Harlison and C. Myers, *Industrialism and Industrial Man: The problems of labour and management in economic growth*, Penguin, 1973. (See also C. Kerr, *The Future of Industrialised Societies: Convergence or continuing diversity?* Harvard University Press, 1983.)

106. Bridgford and Stirling, *op. cit.*, p. 3.

107. *Ibid.*, p. 4.

108. A. Ferner and R. Hyman, *Industrial Relations in the New Europe*, Blackwell, 1992, p. xxxi.

109. *Ibid.*, p. xxxiii.

110. Bean, *op. cit.*, pp. 10/11.

111. R. Dore, *British Factory, Japanese Factory: The origin of national diversity in industrial relations*, Allen & Unwin, 1973.

112. Bean, *op. cit.*, p. 243.

113. Poole, *op. cit.*, p. 18.

114. *Ibid.*, p. 11.

chapter two

The context of industrial relations

<table>
<tr><td>Learning
objectives</td><td>Any social phenomenon, such as industrial relations, cannot and should not be viewed in isolation from its wider context. By the end of this chapter, you should be able to:</td></tr>
</table>

- understand the nature and significance of changes in UK industrial and employment structures and rate of unemployment;

- appreciate the changing character of UK society, the basis of political differentiation and the resulting differences in government policies and strategies;

- set current UK industrial relations within a historical context of the twentieth century (particularly since the 1960s);

- be aware of how our perception of industrial relations is influenced by its portrayal in the mass media.

Definition **Context refers to the background or circumstances surrounding a particular event or situation which may influence or constrain its development.**

Key issues While you are reading this chapter, you should keep the following points in mind:

- The economic, social and political changes being experienced in the UK are not unique and are part of a much wider world economic change. Therefore, it is important that we understand, and learn from, the experiences of other countries.

- The economic context now has a firm international focus, even though the social and political contexts are still primarily national in focus. While there is competition between governments to attract global capital to create wealth and employment in their country, we need to be aware that national governments (or other national bodies such as trade unions) are in a weak position to regulate effectively the activities of global capitalism.

- Although the direction and rate of economic and technological development clearly impacts on the number and types of workers required (*quantitative issues*), we should not underestimate its impact on the very nature of the relationship between the individual, work, organisation and society (*qualitative issues*).

2.1   Introduction

An industrial society is a highly complex and dynamic arrangement of differentiated groups, activities and institutional relationships intertwined with a variety of attitudes, beliefs and expectations. Industrial relations is only one segment of this structure and activity and is influenced by, and in turn influences, other segments of activity (see Figure 2.1). The economic, social and political segments are of particular importance. Actions or changes in these areas may directly stimulate or constrain specific industrial relations activities as well as indirectly influence the attitudes of the participants. It is important to recognise that these environments exert an influence at all levels of industrial relations and therefore, as Fox stated, 'organisational issues, conflicts and values are inextricably bound up with those of society at large'[1].

The roles, relationships, institutions, processes and activities which comprise the phenomenon of industrial relations exist both in a wide variety of industries and services and at a number of levels ranging from the sub-organisational

Figure 2.1 The context of industrial relations

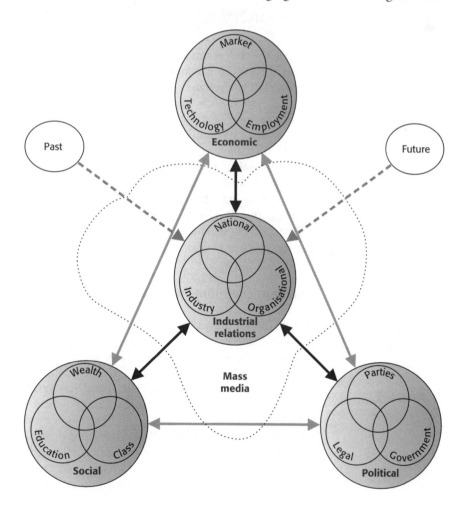

(workgroup, section or department) and organisational (site or company) levels through the industry level to the national level. This inevitably creates a pattern of internal influences both horizontally (between different organisations and industries) and vertically (between different levels). Consequently, the industrial relations system, in terms of the attitudes and activities existing within it at any point in time, provides its own context or climate for the individual industrial relations situations.

At the same time it is important to recognise that the 'mass media' provide an additional, and very significant, context for industrial relations by virtue of their role in shaping attitudes, opinions and expectations. Any individual, whether as a manager, trade unionist or part of the 'general public', has only a partial direct experience of the full range of activities present in a society. Most knowledge and appreciation of economic, social, political and industrial relations affairs is, therefore, gained indirectly from the facts and opinions disseminated through newspapers and television.

2.2 Economic, social and political environments

Each of the environments (economic, social and political) which surround industrial relations is composed of a number of interrelated elements and each environment interrelates with the other environments and with the industrial relations system. For example, the growth of female employment, and its importance for industrial relations, is closely bound up with (a) changing social patterns and expectations in respect of education, work and family arrangements, (b) changes in industrial structure, technology and the level of economic activity, as well as (c) the introduction of legislation directed towards reducing sex discrimination in employment.

It is not the intention of this section to provide a comprehensive analysis of the interactive development of British society but rather to highlight a number of the more important changes which have taken place in these environments over the postwar period.

Economic environment

In 1982 Taylor argued not only that the UK was 'suffering its worst economic slump since the years between the two world wars', but also that 'the first industrial proletariat in the world is fast disappearing with hardly a whimper'[2]. The 1960s were, perhaps, the postwar high point for UK manufacturing industries, but the **process of 'deindustrialisation'** has resulted in manufacturing, in general, declining in its level of output, employment, share of the world market and contribution to the economy. Although other industrialised countries show a similar decline, Nolan and Walsh[3] highlight that the process has been particularly pronounced in the UK: in the period 1960–90, the UK's share of world trade in manufactures declined by a half (from 16.5 per cent to 8.6 per cent), while Japan's share doubled (from 6.9 per cent to 15.9 per cent). This decline has been ascribed to higher labour costs and lower productivity resulting either from management's lack of investment in new plant and new ideas and preference for short-term profit maximisation or from employee and union demands for higher wages and resistance to changes in working arrangements. It can also be seen as the inevitable result of developing economies elsewhere in the world.

Certainly, the world economy has become characterised by **increasing liberalisation, internationalisation and globalisation of trade** through the development of 'free-trade' areas (most importantly, in the case of the UK, the Single European Market but also other groupings such as NAFTA and ASEAN) as well as the more general worldwide liberalisation of trade through GATT and WTO. UK manufacturing faced strong competition, in both home and world markets, not only from other traditionally industrialised countries (such as the USA, Japan, Sweden, Germany, etc.) whose lower inflation, higher productivity or better exchange rate gave them an advantage over UK businesses, but also from an increasing number of newer industrialised countries (perhaps most importantly the south-east Asian 'tiger' economies such as Singapore, Taiwan and Korea) and the 'new' capitalist countries (like China and the former eastern European countries) whose economic growth, although perhaps initially based on low wages, has become increasingly based on high investment in both technology and human resources within a strong framework of governmental support.

While the declining role of manufacturing in the UK economy has, to a certain extent, been offset by an **expansion of the service sector**, Blyton and Turnbull point out that 'the "value added" of manufacturing exports is three times that of services, such that a 1 per cent fall in manufacturing exports requires a 3 per cent rise in services to compensate'[4]. However, major parts of the service sector, like financial services (particularly banks) and the previously 'public' sector utilities, have themselves experienced an increasingly competitive market during the 1990s – perhaps just as severe as manufacturing at the beginning of the 1980s. They too have responded by organisational rationalisation and restructuring accompanied by 'downsizing'. An important element of 'globalisation' has been the **widening range and importance of multinational organisations**. Throughout the 1990s both the manufacturing and service sectors in the UK have witnessed not only transnational take-overs and mergers but also the development of a range of partnership arrangements and joint ventures among organisations operating across different countries and regions of the world. Bach and Sisson[5] note that even in the early 1990s some 60 per cent of organisations employing more than 1,000 people in the UK were part of a multinational organisation (of which over one-third were foreign owned). The multinational organisation is no longer the domain primarily of US, UK or even European companies but now encompasses companies originating in Japan, *See Case study 2.1*   Korea, Taiwan, Australia, etc. The problems experienced by car manufacturers in the UK clearly highlight not only the economic changes experienced by the manufacturing sector but also the increasing power and importance of large multinational corporations.

The process of industrial and employment restructuring has been compounded by the increasing rate of the introduction of **new technology** based on computers and the microchip. The new technology has changed substantially

Case study 2.1 ■ Car manufacture

In the 1960s, the UK motor industry was often held up as a prime example of poor productivity and conflictual industrial relations[1]. In the 1990s, the car industry demonstrates the trends in globalisation of trade, collaboration and organisation as well as retrenchment strategies in the face of worldwide overcapacity.

BMW–Rover

Rover has had a chequered career. In 1975, its predecessor (British Leyland) was nationalised as part of the Labour government's policy to support 'lame ducks'. Over the next decade both Labour and Conservative governments invested £2.25 billion in attempts to modernise BL and, with the support of Mrs Thatcher, it was closely identified with a 'macho-management' style of imposing changes in working practices. In the late 1980s, the bus and truck division was privatised and the remaining car manufacturing (renamed Rover group) was acquired by British Aerospace. In 1992 Rover sought to reform its industrial relations and working practices through a 'New Deal' agreement focusing on 'Japanese-style' working practices – job security in return for team working, functional flexibility, continuous improvement, etc. Rover was sold to BMW in 1994, however, despite a £2.5 billion investment from BMW over the next few years, Rover continued to be less productive and competitive than other European operations. At the end of 1998, BMW announced a further investment of £1.5 billion linked to job reductions following employee acceptance of 'continental-style' working practices – particularly relating to time-flexibility and the creation of unpaid 'overtime'[2]. At the time, BMW indicated that Longbridge was in competition with Hungary for this investment. The government offered £150 million support aid (subject to European Commission approval) but, with continuing losses in early 2000, BMW 'paid' a UK group (Phoenix) to take Rover (and Longbridge) off its hands. The new owners pledged to continue volume car production and provide employment for most of the workers.

Renault–Nissan

Renault 'rescued' Nissan in 1999 by taking a 37 per cent stake for a cost of £3.3 billion to create the fourth largest car manufacturer in the world. It seconded one of its own senior executives to prepare and implement a rescue package which would reduce costs by £5.8 billion and halve the company's debts to £4 billion by 2002. To achieve this involved closing five plants and losing 21,000 jobs in Japan in order to reduce Nissan's 47 per cent overcapacity. Most of the job losses were to be achieved by natural wastage and with financial support for employees to relocate to other Nissan plants. Nevertheless, the plan was perceived within Japan as 'ruthless western methods'[3] which challenged the traditional Japanese employment relationship of lifetime employment combined with seniority-based pay and promotion structures.

Ford–Daewoo

In early 2000 Ford Europe announced plans to restructure its operation including ceasing car production at Dagenham (UK) – but maintaining engine and body building. The company argued their decision was due to poor productivity and industrial relations at the plant (there had been a number of disputes and strikes in recent years) and that the strength of sterling was only a secondary consideration. However, the T&GWU believed that the UK plant was 'being treated unreasonably and unfairly' compared to other European plants because 'low costs and the speed with which workers could be sacked in Britain made the country "a soft touch" for European employers'[4]. Significantly, it was reported at the same time that Ford was considering a bid for Daewoo – the ailing Korean car manufacturer – and was to buy the Land Rover part of Rover from BMW.

'Britain has more vehicle manufacturers than any other country, with plants capable of producing far more cars than they are ever going to sell. Many plants are owned by corporations whose heartlands and major shareholders are in countries with no loyalty to the UK.'[5]

1. H. A. Turner, G. Clack and G. Roberts, *Labour Relations in the Motor Industry*, Allen & Unwin, 1967.
2. D. Gow, 'Job fears over £1.5bn new deal for Rover', *Guardian*, 16 November 1998.
3. J. Watts, 'Beauty and beast of the new Japan', *Guardian*, 15 February 2000.
4. N. Bannister, 'Unions pledge to save Dagenham', *Guardian*, 19 February 2000.
5. P. Brown, 'Too many plants with too much capacity owned by too-distant shareholders', *Guardian*, 6 February 1999.

both manual and non-manual work: in the manual area it has created the possibility of robotic factories serviced by a small number of technicians, while in the non-manual area the development of information-handling technology allows individuals more easily to adopt new work patterns (including working from home). However, as Nolan and Walsh[6] point out, although there has been an increase in the share of UK manufacturing based on high technology since 1980, nevertheless some 50 per cent of UK manufacturing can still be classified as low technology. The creation of new employment opportunities among the 'high technology' industries has been generally too low and of the wrong type to compensate easily or quickly for the rate of job losses in the other industries introducing the new technology. Most new employment growth has been in the 'personal service' industries and lower-grade jobs such as shop assistants, carers, security guards, call-centre staff, etc.

An important feature of the UK economic environment has been the **shift in governmental policy towards the management of the economy**. Postwar economic growth was closely associated with what is often referred to as **Keynsian economic management**. The social objectives of full employment and maintenance of the welfare state were regarded as both of central importance and a governmental responsibility to be achieved, if necessary, by direct action on the demand side of the economy – recession and unemployment were counteracted by deficit government budgeting and increased public expenditure. During the 1960s and 1970s this was frequently accompanied by formal incomes policies in an attempt to contain inflation resulting from either internal or external pressures and governmental support for struggling firms or industries whether in the public or private sector ('lame duck' policy). However, Kessler and Bayliss argue, 'the policies which kept the demand for labour at the full employment level came increasingly to be seen as standing in the way of the long-term adjustment of the British economy to its international position'[7].

After the election of the Conservative government in 1979 the direction of economic policy shifted to a **monetarist approach** which regarded the control of inflation and the achievement of a competitive international position to be of central importance. The government's policy was directed towards reducing public sector expenditure by 'privatisation', 'cash limits', low pay increases, etc. in order to reduce public sector borrowing and taxes and thereby reduce interest rates and divert national resources into investment in the private sector. The public and private sectors were seen in 'competitive' rather than 'complementary' terms and high unemployment was regarded as a necessary, but hopefully temporary, prelude to improved productivity and competitiveness which would result in sustained economic growth. At the same time, the government sought to **reduce labour market regulation** by legal constraints on trade unions and the use of industrial action, by the restriction and then abolition of Wages Councils and by continually resisting any extension of European Union employment protection rights (to the extent of 'opting out' of the Social Chapter to the Maastricht Treaty). The intention was to support and encourage management strategies aimed at securing more competitive, performance-oriented and flexible organisations.

The election of a Labour government in 1997 has introduced a **new 'third way'** – somewhere between Thatcherism's free-market individualism and the

Country profile 2.1   From boom to gloom in Detroit City

'Detroit is famous for two things – cars and stars. It was motor city that gave its name to Tamala Motown four decades ago, when the hits were coming out of Berry Gordy's studio almost as fast as the Buicks and Chryslers were coming off the production lines at the factories of the big three auto companies.

Times change. The big three are still in business, but much shrunken in size and in Chrysler's case only because it has been taken over by Daimler. Car towns such as Flint have become synonymous with the rust-belt decline, 45,000 manufacturing jobs have been lost in the past 20 years.

America's unemployment rate of 4.3% suggests that many of those who have lost their old jobs in industry have found new ones in the service sector. In Detroit, the City wants to create jobs by opening three casinos on the banks of the Detroit River as part of its attempts to revitalise one of the poorest and toughest towns in the US.

It is an appropriate metaphor for the whole of the American labour market. Secure, well paid jobs have been replaced by insecure, badly paid jobs without any of the fringe benefits – such as healthcare. Despite rising real wages in the past two years, labour has largely been left out of the American miracle.

People at the top have done well, and there has been a boom in low paid, low skill, low productivity jobs. In between there is a hole where the middle-class used to be.

There has been much talk about the explosion in America's hi-tech sector, but the real jobs growth has not been in information technology but in home helps, cleaners and security guards as a new servant class has been created for the rich ...

Robert Kuttner, editor of *American Prospect*, says that the old labour market, with its traditions and unspoken bargain between management and workers has been shattered. Workers are just another commodity. "Globalisation and information technology have eroded the power of the two great stewards of the mixed economy – organised labour and the state – and increased the power of business to evade tacit contract with employees."

It was one of Detroit's most famous sons, Henry Ford, who saw the flaw in this process. Ford was an autocrat as well as a plutocrat, but he had a rather different view of business than today's executives. As the Henry Ford Museum in Dearborn Michigan, lovingly explains, Ford decided that he wanted to turn his workers into customers. As a result, he doubled daily pay – from $2.50 to $5. "There is an unwritten bargain with labour," the museum records. "As long as he pays and they work, it holds."

The bargain between management and labour ended in the 80s. Ronald Reagan's breaking of the strike by air traffic controllers was as significant in the US as the miners' strike of 1984–85 was in Britain. Pat Morissey of General Motors, said: "The 80s changed everything. Where there was previously no competition, there was now competition everywhere. Companies were forced to improve product quality and become much more efficient."

After the sustained expansion of the US economy in the 90s, workers are less and less willing to buy this line. Union membership, after falling for decades, appears to have bottomed out. Unions have found that parts of the service sector are not subject to the pressures of globalisation affecting manufacturing, with a major recent success the unionisation of 80,000 home helps in California.

Moreover, a new generation of union leaders has started to adopt a more vigorous approach to industrial relations, in part because of pressure from the shop floor. Discontent has swept through the GM Saturn plant in Tennessee after it became clear that the much-vaunted partnership deal between the company and organised labour had led to union officials becoming a new tier of management.

With unemployment low, unions are starting to flex their muscles. "When times are bad, we're told workers need to tighten their belts," said Elaine Bernard, executive director of Harvard University's trade union programme.

"When times are good, workers need to give concessions to employers to maintain competitiveness. So when do workers get rewarded?"

Source: Larry Elliott, *Guardian*, 30 June 1999.

See also Boxes 4.3 and 5.2, and Case study 10.2.

previous Keynsian welfare approach. Thus, the new government initially continued tight controls on public expenditure and gave control of determining interest rates to the Bank of England (rather than retaining it as an area of political decision making), but has also increased expenditure on police, education and health. In the employment field, its 'new deal' has maintained tight control on payment of welfare benefits (passive policy) while providing supportive action to prepare people to get jobs (skill development, etc.) and encourage employers to take on staff (active policy). It is still seeking to encourage flexibility in the labour market and work patterns but has also been prepared to introduce a National Minimum Wage and statutory rights for the individual to be represented at work, to reintroduce a statutory procedure to support unions seeking recognition at the workplace and to 'sign up' to the EU social dimension.

Employment structure

See Country profile 2.1

An examination of postwar changes in the UK's employment figures shows a number of significant developments (see Figure 2.2 and Table 2.1). However, the UK is not unique and most other industrialised countries have experienced similar changes (see Table 2.2). For example, the USA has experienced not only similar changes in its economic environment and employment structure, but also similar government and management strategies in the 1980s. It also shows that economic expansion and 'full' employment can provide employees with the strength to seek improvements in the employment relationship.

Figure 2.2
Employment structure changes 1951–99

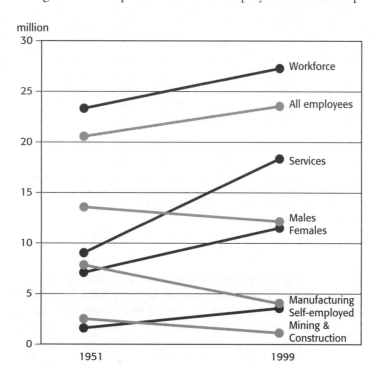

Table 2.1
Employment trends
1981–99 (millions)

	Male		Female		Total
	Full-time	**Part-time**	**Full-time**	**Part-time**	
Manufacturing					
1981	4.2	0.1	1.4	0.4	6.1
1991	3.2	0.1	1.1	0.3	4.6
1999	2.8	0.1	0.9	0.2	3.9
Change 1981–99	*−34.7%*	*−5.8%*	*−33.6%*	*−50.6%*	*−35.2%*
Services					
1981	5.5	0.6	3.8	3.3	13.1
1991	5.7	0.9	4.5	4.2	15.3
1999	6.6	1.4	5.3	4.8	18.0
Change 1981–99	*+20.0%*	*+129.5%*	*+41.3%*	*+45.5%*	*+37.5%*

Sources: 1981 and 1991 Census of Employment results, Employment Gazette; Table B.15, *Labour Market Trends*, January 2000

Table 2.2 International employment (1997)

	Labour force			Sector employment			Part-time employment[2]	
	Change in total labour force 1987–97	Female participation rate	Industry	Change 1987–97	Service	Government employment[1]	All	Female
	(%)	(%)	(%)	(%)	(%)	(%)	(% of total) employment)	(% of part-time) employment)
Australia	19.1	64.7	22.1	−15.7	72.7	14.8	25.6	52.8
France	6.6	59.8	25.6	−16.9	69.9	25.1	15.5	65.1
Germany[3]	*n.a.*	61.8	36.5	−9.7	60.2	15.3	15.0	78.0
Ireland	16.7	50.4	28.4	−1.8	61.7	12.6[4]	16.7	58.8
Japan	11.6	63.7	33.1	−2.1	61.6	5.9	23.2	50.4
Korea	28.0	54.8	31.3	−4.0	57.7	n.a.	5.1	45.3
Netherlands	18.3	62.2	22.2	−17.2	74.1	13.5	29.1	65.2
Sweden	−3.6	74.5	26.0	−12.5	71.3	30.7	15.7	65.1
United Kingdom	2.6	66.8	26.9	−18.2	71.3	14.1[4]	23.1	70.6
United States	12.9	71.3	23.9	−11.8	73.4	13.2	13.6	52.0

[1] Employed in government services; except for Australia, France, Ireland and Netherlands which refer to general government.
[2] Defined as 30 hours worked or less per week, except Australia, Japan and Korea which is based on 35 hours worked or less per week.
[3] Labour force not comparable because of reunification.
[4] 1996 figures.
Source: OECD, Labour Force Statistics: 1977–1997, 1999.

The **size of the total workforce** in the UK has increased by some 4 million people (16 per cent), primarily due to an increase in female economic participation rates (more women working) – only Sweden had a decrease in its total labour force during the 1990s. However, while UK female employment increased by 4.5 million (62 per cent) between 1951 and 1999, male employment declined by 1.5 million (11 per cent). This decline in male employment was due, initially, to an increase in those remaining in school beyond the statutory leaving age and/or entering tertiary education, but more lately appears to have been due to increased early retirement and a shift into self-employment. Certainly, it has been predicted that women will account for nearly 90 per cent of the expected increase in the UK labour force by the year 2006[8].

The UK, like most other industrialised countries, has experienced a continuing **shift in employment from manufacturing to service industries**. UK manufacturing employment has declined by over a half, from 8.5 million employees in 1951 (42 per cent of all employees) to 3.9 million in 1999 (only 17 per cent of all employees), while employment in the service industries has doubled, from 9 million to 18 million employees (77 per cent of all employees). In many countries, service industry employment accounts for over 60 per cent of total employment. Significantly, the decline in UK manufacturing employment was fairly evenly spread across both male and female employment and full- and part-time employment. During the late 1960s and 1970s the decline in manufacturing employment was largely compensated for by an increase in public sector employment[9]. However, the public sector itself became subject to constraints and reduced employment levels after 1979. It was not until the mid-1980s that the private service sector began to grow at a rate of 2 per cent per annum. Significantly, some of this employment growth, for example in the financial services sector, is now under threat from a variety of national and international mergers. The other significant segment of employment growth has been in the 'personal service' industries such as retail and distribution, hotels and catering and leisure, travel and entertainment.

Many of the jobs created have not been full-time permanent ones. There has been a significant increase in the extent of **part-time working** in the UK – from 4 per cent in 1951[10] to 28 per cent in 1999. This represents 6.2 million employees working part-time; of whom 95 per cent are employed in service industries and 78 per cent are female. The development of part-time work has not simply been in response to the needs of those (males or females) who wish, for whatever reason, to combine work with their domestic life but has, along with casual work, temporary contracts, etc., been an integral part of some management's strategies to develop numerical flexibility within the organisation. Certainly, Blyton and Turnbull argue that these strategies have been primarily defensive and short-term and directed more towards reducing labour costs, rather than 'a long-term offensive flexibility strategy by creating a more adaptable workforce, capable of responding to longer-term changes in job requirements'[11]. In addition, **self-employment** expanded by more than 50 per cent during the 1980s[12] and now accounts for about 3.5 million people.

Nolan and Walsh believe that 'Britain emerged from the 1980s as a relatively low-skill, low-productivity economy forced to compete in international markets on the basis of low labour costs'[13]. Although average earnings generally increased throughout the 1980s and 1990s, there has also been a trend for employment to shift away from the middle-wage industries into either high- or low-wage industries (or into unemployment). Certainly, the OECD has commented that achieving labour market flexibility in the UK has been accompanied by **increasing inequality in wage distribution**[14]. Blyton and Turnbull[15] highlight the fact that in the early 1990s 10 million employees in the UK (47 per cent of the working population and 60 per cent of whom were female) earned below the Council of Europe's 'decency threshold' (68 per cent of average full-time earnings). The introduction of the national minimum wage in 1999 has had some, albeit limited, impact on this inequality in wage distribution in so far as an estimated 2 million employees (75 per cent of whom are female) have benefited – but they still remain below the EU 'decency threshold'.

The UK has also endured a **sustained period of high unemployment** (see Figure 2.3). Throughout the 1950s and most of the 1960s, the UK experienced stable and 'full' or 'overfull' employment. The rate of unemployment fluctuated between 1 and 2 per cent and most unemployment was of short duration because a buoyant economy provided a steady demand for labour. Indeed, there were periods of labour shortage (more job vacancies than the number unemployed), particularly among skilled workers, which provided an impetus for both wage competition between employers as they sought to attract the required labour and the development of productivity bargaining as organisations sought to expand their production by making the most effective use of a scarce resource (labour). However, unemployment increased during the late 1970s (primarily because of an increase in the size of the working population), rose very sharply between 1979 and 1981 (due to the severe recession in manufacturing) and remained above 10 per cent for much of the 1980s (reaching a peak of over 3 million in 1985 and 1986). Although it declined to 6 per cent by 1990, the early 1990s saw another recession and a fairly sharp rise in unemployment levels before beginning to decline again – but still remaining well above the levels of the 1950s, 1960s and early 1970s.

Significantly, according to Deaton, the working population reduced by half a million between 1979 and 1981 'as people withdraw from the labour force because of the lack of job opportunities' and 'suggests that there is considerable hidden unemployment in addition to the registered unemployment recorded in the statistics' [16]. The official UK figure has traditionally been based on the number of people who claim unemployment benefits and therefore, as Lawlor and White note, is 'vulnerable to changes in coverage whenever there are changes to the administrative procedures'[17]. Indeed, during the 1980s there

Figure 2.3 UK rate of unemployment 1950–99

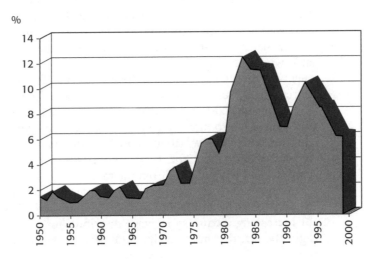

were some 28 changes which, in the main, removed people from the 'claimant count'. While the ILO basis of calculating unemployment – the number of people who are 'seeking work' whether in receipt of benefit or not – generally produces a higher figure, even this will not include "discouraged workers" (those who would like to work but are not actively seeking a job because they do not think any suitable positions are available) and "involuntary part-time workers" (those who are working fewer hours than they would like, or who can find only a part-time job when they want a full-time one)'[18].

However, neither the aggregate number nor the rate of unemployment, on their own, adequately reflect the full extent and nature of the unemployment problem:

▪ Nearly one-quarter of the 2 million unemployed in 1999 could be classified as **long-term unemployed** (more than 12 months); indeed, 15 per cent had been unemployed for more than 24 months. The UK experience is similar to many other countries – although Japan, Korea and the USA have had lower levels of both unemployment and long-term unemployed (see Table 2.3). The long-term unemployed includes those who lack the qualifications, skill, experience or personal attributes which are sought by potential employers; those for whom there is no work in their area; and those whose personal confidence and attractiveness to employers has been undermined by their experience of long unemployment.

▪ Unemployment among **young people** has been of particular concern – 27 per cent of the total and 13 per cent of long-term unemployed in 1999 were under 25 years of age (see Table 2.3 for international comparison).

Table 2.3
International unemployment

	Rate (1999) (%)	Long-term unemployed (over one year) (% of total unemployed – 1997)	Youth unemployed (under 25) (% of youth labour force – 1997)
Australia	7.5	30.7	15.8
France	11.2	41.2	28.7
Germany	9.1	50.1	10.0
Ireland	6.8	57.0	16.1
Japan	4.8	21.8	6.6
Korea	2.6[2]	2.1	8.0
Netherlands	3.3	49.1	9.6
Sweden	7.0	33.4	22.5
United Kingdom	6.1	38.6	13.3
United States	4.3	8.7	11.3

[1] Stadardised rate (based on ILO guidelines) for second quarter.
[2] Rate for 1997 based on national definition.
Sources: OECD, *Labour Force Statistics: 1977–1997*, 1999 and *PAC/COM/NEWS(99)99*.

■ Unemployment is also relatively high among **older people** – 14 per cent of the total and 24 per cent of long-term unemployed in 1999 were over 50 years of age.

■ Unemployment among **ethnic minority groups** has been significantly higher than among white workers – Black and Pakistani workers, for example, have unemployment rates of 14 per cent and 20 per cent respectively[19].

Both Britton[20] and Sen[21] contrast US and European models of unemployment and wage inequality: the USA with lower unemployment but higher wage inequality, Europe with higher unemployment but lower wage inequality. Significantly, perhaps, unemployment in the USA fell in 1999 to its lowest since 1970 (4.2 per cent) – leading to talk about 'running out of new workers'[22] – while Germany's unemployment rate rose to 11.5 per cent (a postwar high)[23]. It has been claimed that the improvement in the UK's unemployment rate, like the low level in the USA, is due primarily to limiting or reducing labour market regulation. Now that unemployment in the UK is predicted to fall to about three-quarters of a million, this raises the issue of redefining **the meaning of 'full employment'**. Britton argues that full employment has to be defined in qualitative and flexible terms (see Box 2.1). Furthermore, although he believes there is scope for increased employment in many service industries (health, education, environment, etc.), nevertheless such expansion, at least in Europe, is constrained by it being within the public sector and, therefore, will involve socio-political decisions about increasing taxation or the introduction of charges.

Box 2.1	The nature of full employment

'Full employment could prove to be a nightmare. It could amount to a return to the conditions of the nineteenth century. It could mean that workers become so impoverished that they are obliged to accept work which is exhausting, soul-destroying or unsafe. It could mean the direction of labour and the loss of personal freedom.

If, therefore, full employment is adopted as an objective it must be accompanied by conditions rendering it acceptable. Those conditions include the distribution of income, the preservation of decent employment conditions and the right to choose whether to work or not. ...

Full employment does not mean that everyone is in fact employed. As the industrialized countries get richer, it becomes possible for more people to retire early or to reduce their involvement in the labour market in other ways. Amongst those who remain in paid work, more people may choose to be self-employed or to have an "atypical" work contract. These are not developments which would be resisted. In a society where men and women enter the labour market on equal terms there is a particular need for a variety of contractual arrangements. ...

Full employment does not mean that no one is ever unemployed. More frequent job changes entail periods of job search. This is acceptable provided that the periods are short and that living standards can be maintained. What is unacceptable is long duration unemployment for any individual, and periods when jobs are simply not available or regions where no jobs are created. ...'.

Source: A. Britton, 'Full employment in the industrialized countries', *International Labour Review*, vol. 136, no. 3, 1997, p. 313.

Social environment

UK society has been generally described, using economic and political terminology, as an **industrialised capitalist democracy** based on the principles of individual freedom of thought, expression and association. Within this society the economic activity of work is supported by social values (often referred to as the 'Protestant work ethic') wherein, as Tawney argued, 'the conscientious discharge of the duties of business is among the loftiest of religious and moral virtues'[24]. Certainly, it is the principle of one individual working for another and accepting superior authority which has given rise to the complex arrangement of economic and social divisions within a modern society. Experiences of this wider society exert a significant influence on an individual's attitude to work and the organisation that employs him or her (see Box 2.2).

However, society has changed over the postwar period. The initial period after the Second World War is perhaps best characterised by the idea of reconstruction – not just of the buildings and economy but also of the social order. The **creation of the welfare state** embodied the beliefs that the strong within society should support the weak and that the state should accept responsibility both for the provision of education, health and other social services and for ensuring that equality of access should prevail, rather than access being dependent on the ability of the individual to pay. In the economic environment, the state took responsibility for maintaining full employment and, through nationalisation, the management of certain key industries which it was felt should operate in the interests of the economy and society as a whole rather than the interests of profit for the shareholder. Society became more 'socialist' in its outlook and based on a mixed economy.

The effects of these changes, particularly in areas such as education, were not fully felt until the 1960s. The 1960s saw the **demise of the deferential society** and a challenge to previously accepted values, attitudes and institutions. Although to some the existence of the welfare state, coupled with the state's acceptance of responsibility for the maintenance of full employment, stifles individual initiative by creating a belief that 'society owes the individual a living', to

---

Box 2.2	The individual, organisation and society link

'... people's attitudes and behaviour towards their managerially-defined work roles, rights and obligations, and towards the roles, rights and obligations of others, are not formed only within the organization. They are formed also by the experiences, values, observations and aspirations which men acquire and construct for themselves in the wider society outside, and by the view they have thereby come to take of that society. Influential here are such factors as family, class, school, friends, locality, and the mass media of newspapers, radio and television. Thus the perspective they bring to bear upon the organization and their place in it, and therefore the way they respond to its rules, rewards and values, is shaped by what they make of this wider frame of reference as well as by the organization itself.'

Source: A. Fox, *Man Mismanagement* (2nd edn), Hutchinson, 1984, p. 16.

others it represents the achievement of independence and an expansion of opportunities for the individual. Certainly, the provision of social benefits in respect of unemployment, sickness, family circumstances, etc. reduces the individual's dependence on the work situation for determining his or her standard of living and the existence of full employment reduces his or her reliance on any particular employer. In this way the individual becomes less constrained to accept low pay, poor working conditions or harsh management. At the same time an expansion of educational opportunities not only increases the individual's awareness of the surrounding world and willingness to question, but also opens up occupational and social possibilities which previously had been denied. Consequently, the developments in education in the 1960s, coupled with economic prosperity, employment stability and the creation of a consumer market through advertising, created a population and workforce which had increased expectations in respect of both material rewards and participation in the decisions at work and outside which affected their lives.

However, despite presenting an appearance of a more egalitarian society, in terms of the distribution of both material rewards and decision making, the UK remains **essentially a class-based society**. The possibility of upward social mobility generated by increased educational opportunities and the overlapping material lifestyles between 'manual' workers and the 'professional' or 'middle' classes created by economic prosperity has not removed the fundamental divisions within society. An individual's position within the economic hierarchy is still an important factor in determining perceived status relative to others within society. In order to gain wider support for the capitalist ethos, the Thatcher government encouraged individual share-ownership in its public-sector privatisation during the 1980s. While there may well now be more individual shareholders than trade union members, most only have a very small holding. Real wealth and power, both economic and political, still remain unequally divided and largely in the hands of a small number of individuals, organisations and financial institutions. In reality, it is a society of inequalities.

High unemployment during the 1980s and 1990s has undermined a number of traditional assumptions associated with the 'Protestant work ethic': for example, 'providing an employee does a "fair day's work", he or she has nothing to worry about'; 'there are three generations of the same family working here'; 'get a trade or skill and you'll always have work'; 'the pay may be low to start with, but there's a good pension at the end'; and 'I'm looking on this as a long-term career'. The reality is that few, if any, jobs have permanent job security and a person's 'working life' is becoming more characterised by the following:

■ Higher probability of a series of jobs interspersed with unemployment (a return to the pre-war situation);

■ Higher probability that some, at least, of these jobs may be either temporary contracts and/or part-time.

There is little doubt that sustained high unemployment has had social as well as economic consequences in the UK. Sen[25] points out that in addition to any economic effects from loss of income and production, unemployment is also associated with loss of motivation and skill, social exclusion, increasing ill health and mortality and loss of social values, responsibility and human relations. Even within those who are employed, the terms 'work-rich' and 'work-poor' are used to describe the situation 'where 40 per cent of those aged 50–65 are not working and one in five children live in workless households; while the better-off work-rich are so time-poor they now employ an army of low-paid workers – from cleaners and nannies to pizza-delivery bikers – to service them'[26]. Another dichotomy can be seen between, on the one hand, the long hours worked at the office or at home by many professionals and managers or the overtime and two jobs found among low-paid manual families and, on the other hand, the desire of the 'new' technocrats for balance and interdependence between work and personal lives[27]. Furthermore, the number of pensioners in the UK is likely to increase by nearly $1\frac{1}{2}$ million over the next 20 years, while the number of children under 16 (potential new entrants to the workforce) is likely to drop by 1 million[28]. This ageing population not only implies a change in the nature of the society (the growth of 'grey' power and the need to meet their needs and interests) but also creates a potential economic problem in funding the benefits and care system needed by an ageing population.

While the Industrial Revolution acted as a catalyst for a major social change by drawing people into factories to work machines and thereby created an urban industrialised society based on the sale of labour, the 'technological revolution' may have created an equally severe social change by removing many people from permanent, secure and adequately paid work. This has **heightened the divisions within society:** between those who have work (sub-divided between those who have relatively secure, well-paid jobs and those with temporary and/or part-time, low-paid work) and those who do not; between economic deprivation in many inner-city and traditional manufacturing areas and relative prosperity in the high-technology business parks, the suburbs and south-east of England; between those who purchase private medicine and education and those who have to rely on the public services. There is evidence to suggest not only polarisation of attitudes and values within society but also frustration among the 'have nots' at their apparent inability to influence governmental policies and achieve change through the normal political processes.

Political environment

It has been suggested that the political environment 'is in many ways the most complex and the most difficult to handle, both because of its impact on the other environments and because of its roles within and without the system'[29] of industrial relations. Certainly, it encompasses both **the means by which society organises itself in order to express and achieve the goals and aspirations of the people** and **the nature of these goals and aspirations themselves**. It comprises not only the formal system of political parties, Parliament and government at the national level but also local authority government, quangos (quasi-autonomous non-governmental organisations with financial support from and senior appointments made by government) and a range of informal pressure groups which seek to influence the decisions of the formal system. However, it is the political parties and government, and their underlying ideologies, which are, perhaps, the most important and active elements within the

See Chapter 8 –
The government

political environment, for it is they who ultimately determine the direction, policies and actions of the governmental process.

Political differentiation, and consequently differential government policies and actions, is determined by differences in view regarding the nature of the society which it is intended to create or at least encourage[30]. In the UK, the type of desired society has tended to be differentiated on the basis of the extent to which it should be **individualist or corporatist** oriented on such issues as the respective roles of the state and the individual in the creation and distribution of economic wealth, the role of the state in the management and control of the economy, the approach and priority afforded to social welfare, and the nature and authority of 'political' decision making and regulation at all levels of the society. The polarisation of political ideologies is clearly reflected in what are perceived to be the **political issues;** indeed, it may be argued that a political issue cannot arise unless there are differences of view about such matters as:

- The government's responsibility for creating and/or resolving the high unemployment level.
- The balance between public and private sectors (privatisation).
- The nature and extent of the power that trade unions may be allowed to exercise within industry and society.
- The 'rule of law', maintenance of 'law and order' and the role of the police in 'social' actions such as strikes and picketing.
- The extent to which government policy and decision making should be conducted within a framework of public debate and involvement.

During the nineteenth century a **liberalist or *laissez-faire* ideology** dominated the emergence of the new social order based on capitalism. The emphasis on an economic regulation of society was closely associated with the concept of individualism. Economic and social matters were perceived as being determined by contracts made between individuals who were equals and responsible for their own destiny. In the economic sphere it was believed that individuals should act alone and not distort the operation of supply and demand forces within the labour market by seeking to combine with others to increase economic power. This approach found expression in the legal doctrines of 'restraint of trade' and 'conspiracy' which, in industrial relations, constrained the development of trade unions until they were granted immunity in the Trade Union Act (1871) and Trade Disputes Act (1906).

However, these enactments were a reflection of a shift in dominant political ideology from the 'liberal individualists of 1830' to the 'democratic socialists of 1905'[31]. The growth of collectivism among the 'working classes' and its resultant pressure for industrial, economic and social reform led to not only the growth of trade unionism but also a realisation of the need for political representation in the form of a distinct political party – the Labour Party. The objective was to ensure that government could not and should not ignore the social problems arising from industrial capitalism but rather should accept responsibility for greater intervention to protect and improve people's quality of life.

This **corporatist or interventionist ideology** is founded on the principle of integration rather than separation of the political, economic and social aspects of life and the involvement of 'capital' and 'labour' in the process of government. This provided the basis for the apparent 'consensus politics' of the postwar period (up until 1979) whereby both Conservative and Labour governments were committed not only to the maintenance of full employment and the welfare state but also to the involvement of trade union and employer representatives in tripartite discussions on a wide range of economic and social issues, including incomes policy. Indeed, it was a Conservative government which both established the National Economic Development Office (NEDO) in 1961 as the main forum for these discussions and confirmed the TUC's predominance by refusing to grant representation to non-affiliated unions. However, this apparent consensus over objectives did not preclude differences of emphasis in government policies or differences in strategy for the achievement of these objectives.

The election of Mrs Thatcher in 1979 brought a return to the more fundamentalist doctrine of the Conservative Party – one involving a *laissez-faire* individualism reminiscent of the early nineteenth century and marked by 'free enterprise, open markets, deregulation, individualism, privatisation'[32] as well as monetarist rather than Keynesian demand management economic policies. No longer were trade unions seen as 'joint managers' *with* government of the industrial and economic system but rather a barrier to the achievement of government objectives and therefore needing to be curtailed through legislation (one Act every two years progressively regulating and reducing union rights and power).

It seemed in the early 1980s that the creation of the Social Democratic Party (by disaffected Labour Party members) and its subsequent alliance and then merger with the Liberal Party (to form the Liberal Democrats) would, given the apparent polarisation between Thatcherism in the Conservative Party and Militant Tendency in the Labour Party, take over the so-called middle ground of politics. However, 'new' Labour's shift to a 'social democratic' ideology, with reformed policies and relationship to the trade union movement, played an important part in securing its landslide election victory in 1997. The approach of the 'new' Labour government has been 'to develop a network of social partnerships in a stakeholder economy, without reverting to tri-partite corporatism'[33]. Rather than directly confront, challenge or restrict the new international capitalism (or champion employee collectivism), the 'new' Labour government is seeking to encourage, incorporate or manage capitalism in such a way that also promotes greater social responsibility. Certainly, the political environment remains favourably disposed towards the needs and interests of business, entrepreneurism and shareholders. However, the 'stakeholder partnership' attitude and ethos which the government is trying to create, and which underpinned the economic success of Germany and Japan, may well involve the development of institutional arrangements which can hinder organisational flexibility and competitiveness.

See Country profile 2.2

An important development in the political environment, so far as UK industrial relations is concerned, has been the **European Union**. There is little doubt that Due *et al*. were right when they stated that 'the interesting feature of EC co-operation is the emergence of quite new actors in industrial relations, such as the EC Commission and the European Parliament – actors whose roles are essentially supra-national'[34]. However, between 1979 and 1997 there was a fundamental conflict of political ideology between the UK Conservative government and its EU partners. The 'social democratic' ideology of most European countries (based on a corporatist social partnership between government, capital and labour) is reflected in the aims of the Social Chapter of the Maastricht Treaty and was at variance with the '*laissez-faire* individualism' ideology of the UK - government. The UK government consistently sought to 'optout' of or water down EU Directives aimed at establishing and regulating employee rights and, frequently, only introduced UK legislation after pressure from European Court decisions. However, since the 1997 election of 'new' Labour, the UK government has presented a more positive and constructive stance towards the EU, albeit also arguing for reforms and developments in line with its own thinking on the process of government and constitutional reform within the UK and its desire to support business and promote labour market flexibility.

Country profile 2.2   Japan, Germany ready to abandon 'stakeholder' capitalism for profits?

Despite being championed by America and Britain, stakeholder capitalism – firms with greater social responsibility – in both Germany and Japan is facing a crop of troubles of its own.

'What goes under the name of capitalism varies a lot from country to country. A big difference is in attitudes to public companies; in particular, in views about their duties and responsibilities beyond their obvious objective of producing goods or services.

In America and Britain, a public company has one over-riding goal: to maximise returns to shareholders.

In Japan and much of continental Europe, in contrast, firms often accept broader obligations that balance the interests of shareholders against those of other "stakeholders", notably employees, but including also suppliers, customers and the wider "community".

It has become fashionable to set shareholder and stakeholder capitalism against one another in a sort of capitalist beauty contest. In America and Britain, many voices now assert that stakeholder capitalism is the more attractive ...

Model economy

Several things differentiate stakeholder from shareholder capitalism. One is near-lifetime employment, at least for a significant number of "core" workers.

In Germany, the leading example of continental Europe's brand of stakeholder capitalism, this is a matter of convention. For large redundancies, compa-

nies must adopt "social plans" to cushion the blow, as well as consulting employee councils.

Sometimes companies are forced to choose whom they sack on the basis of age and family situation rather than competence.

Employees also participate directly in German company management. They are represented on "supervisory" boards of all big public firms.

In Japan, lifetime employment is more formal even than in Germany. Following a rigorous selection process, salarymen have traditionally been guaranteed jobs for life.

The rest of the workforce (more than half of it, including most women) is less fortunate, likely to be on short-term contracts and at risk of being laid off whenever the economy slows.

Customers and suppliers of Japanese firms are also often bound together into broad groups of firms (the *keiretsu*) in a web of cross-shareholdings that gives each firm some pull over all other firms in the group.

At the heart of every *keiretsu*, there is also a bank, which owns shares in each firm in the group. Such banks may be a firm's leading lenders too.

Advocates believe these characteristics of German and Japanese systems confer on stakeholder capitalism big advantages over shareholder capitalism.

Guaranteeing jobs for life gives employees a stronger incentive to acquire skills that are valuable within their firm but may have only limited value outside it. Workers with less job security have more of

Country profile 2.2   Japan, Germany ready to abandon 'stakeholder' capitalism for profits? *(continued)*

an incentive to acquire only the skills that increase their chances of employment elsewhere.

Cross-shareholdings like those in Japan that bind customers and suppliers are also said to encourage investment. Such shareholdings are, moreover, regarded as evidence of a long-term commitment between the parties, which enables each to make investments that will pay off only after several years, confident they will not find that their customer or supplier has gone elsewhere ...

The overall impression ... is that the stakeholder economies, most notably Japan, certainly outperformed the shareholder ones in the first few decades after the war, but the gap has narrowed significantly in the past 20 years or so.

This prompts several questions. Is the stakeholder magic wearing off? Certainly the outperformance of Japan and Germany ended long before the recent recession.

Is stakeholding effective only in periods of rapid growth, such as Japan and Germany enjoyed after the war – and does it crack when put under macro-economic pressure? Did the superior performance of these economies actually stem from factors that had nothing to do with stakeholding, such as a huge injection of fresh capital and new factories after the war, and a better educated workforce?

None of these questions is easily answered. But there is one more significant piece of evidence which suggests the stakeholding model may no longer be as alluring as its fans claim: it is under serious attack at home.

In Germany, the commitment to stakeholder capitalism has been taking a beating in recent years for two related reasons: Germany's high costs of production, caused mainly by high labour costs and a strong Deutschemark, and the pressure to internationalise both production and the raising of capital. German companies have slashed their workforces to cope with recession.

In Japan the stakeholder model has come under pressure. Some *keiretsu* may have begun to unravel; under financial pressure, some partners have started to sell their cross-shareholdings. And the lifetime employment of core workers is increasingly under threat.

Firms have started to export jobs abroad in response to the strong yen and to fears of protectionist measures against goods made in Japan.

Advocates of shareholder capitalism have also risen up in Japan. Some Japanese companies are switching their focus to return on equity to bolster financial discipline. This will become more common as pressures grow on the pension system, which has accepted low returns on shares in Japanese firms. The greying of the Japanese population is likely to create a huge demand for cash from the pension system, which will only be forthcoming if firms pay higher dividends.

Japanese companies are still bending over backwards to protect lifetime employment. The first people to bear the brunt of hard times are always women and part-timers, and potential recruits. The graduate unemployment rate, which has risen from 6 per cent in 1992 to 14 per cent last year [1995], is one of the highest in the OECD. But many firms are beginning to get together on lifetime employees.

Many firms are moving staff to parts of the business, or to affiliates, where they have less job security. It is now possible to find male managers serving coffee in such firms as Honda, in place of the usual office ladies.

System of "up or out"

Above all, Japanese firms are redefining "lifetime employment", pointing out that it applied only to a proportion of workers and whittling down that proportion as much as they can.

Japanese banks have introduced a system of "up or out": those who do not make the grade by the age of 40 are sent to run local banks. Desperate firms are introducing 'voluntary' early retirement.

Official Japanese unemployment is rising, if slowly. Small and medium-sized business shed nearly two million jobs in 1989–94, with many businesses going under. There is a growing belief that the shake-out of jobs has barely begun.

The changes in German and Japanese economic performance should give pause for thought to advocates of stakeholder capitalism. It would be deliciously, if sadly ironic, were Britain and America to shift towards a model just as it was about to be abandoned by its inventors.'

Source: The Economist, 10 February 1996.

See also Country profiles 6.1 and 7.1

2.3 Development of industrial relations

Present-day UK industrial relations are the result of an unplanned evolution over the past 150 years. Although it is possible to identify different stages in this development, it is important to realise that each stage did not supersede and replace the previous stage but rather supplemented and modified it. Furthermore, the rate and strength of these developments have varied from industry to industry and, therefore, the present industrial relations system in each industry is a unique mixture of these developments.

Early development

During the latter part of the nineteenth century trade unionism and collective bargaining were largely confined to the skilled trades and piecework industries. In the former the workers had the industrial strength, through mutual insurance and their control over entry into the trade, to seek employer acceptance of the 'union's rules', while in the latter both workers and employers had an interest in controlling wage competition. Although many trade unions were already organised on a national basis, this early collective bargaining was conducted almost exclusively on either an organisational or a district basis. Wherever trade unions had sufficient organisation and strength, they sought the establishment of a 'common rule' to ensure that different employers within a local labour market applied the same terms of employment. The workers' common interest centred primarily on their immediate geographical locality.

Flanders[35] argued that the main impetus for the development of collective bargaining at the national or industry level came during the First World War. In some industries nationalisation presented the trade unions with the opportunity to negotiate with a single employer, while in others labour shortages and the consequent enhancement of trade union power led employers to seek national agreements as a protection against being 'played-off' one against another. At the same time, inflation coupled with the introduction of a system of compulsory arbitration resulted in a large measure of uniformity in both the wage claims presented on behalf of different groups and the wage increases granted. Perhaps most importantly for the long-term development of national-level bargaining, the Whitley Committee (1916) recommended the establishment of Joint Industrial Councils (JICs) with formal written constitutions and functioning at national, district and work levels. As a result, some 73 JICs and 33 Interim Reconstruction Committees (which were intended to become JICs) were set up between 1918 and 1921.

During the 1920s and early 1930s the economic depression and more repressive attitude of employers and government was reflected in a substantial decline in trade union membership, wage cuts and a high incidence of industrial action (including the General Strike of 1926). At the same time, over half of the JICs were disbanded, particularly in industries that were susceptible to foreign competition. Significantly, and largely as a result of government policy, they survived in industries such as gas, electricity and water, and in national and local government. Improving economic conditions prior to the Second World War, and the need for employee and trade union co-operation in the war effort, provided an impetus for increased unionisation and a resurgence of industrial relations activity.

Since the Second World War, industrial relations in the UK has developed through a number of overlapping phases: pressure on the industry-level system; voluntary reform; government intervention; confrontation; and, possibly, a new realism.

Pressure on the industry-level system

Hawkins has suggested that in the immediate postwar period it was assumed that 'the great industrial conflicts of the past had been resolved by the gradual development of a framework of voluntary institutions'; that the role of trade union leaders 'was to direct industrial conflict into the established framework of industry-wide procedures where peaceful solutions could be found with the minimum disorder', and that 'the more integrated the unions became in the system, the more committed they would be to its success and the more responsibly they would behave'[36]. However, this assumption of an orderly system of industrial relations based on industry-level agreements soon came under pressure.

On the employees' side, full employment, the welfare state and changes in society, coupled with increased union membership at the workplace, resulted in rising aspirations in respect of both material rewards and greater involvement in managerial decision making. At the same time, management's attention was focused increasingly on changing working practices and improving productivity within the organisation, initially to meet rising demand and subsequently to improve its cost competitiveness. However, industry-level bargaining and agreements in the main provided only basic terms of employment (wage rates, hours, holidays, etc.) and had little role in respect of regulating the work relationship and the exercise of authority and decision making within the organisation. Inevitably, the attention of both sides was directed towards collective bargaining at the organisation level.

The consequence of this **shift in the locus of regulation** was increased fragmentation and tension within many segments of the industrial relations system. The development of organisational bargaining, and its associated increase in the power of workgroups and shop steward involvement in negotiations with management, increased the gap between the 'grass roots' union organisation and workplace issues, on the one hand, and the 'official' union organisation and wider policy issues, on the other (as evidenced by an increase in 'unofficial' industrial action). On the management side, a similar tension arose as many organisations sought to act independently by conducting their own negotiations rather than acting collectively with other organisations through their employers' association at the industry level. Thus, in 1967, Flanders described organisational-level collective bargaining as 'largely informal, largely fragmented and largely autonomous'[37].

A central part of the Donovan Commission (1968)[38] analysis of industrial relations was the **conflict between organisational- and industry-level collective bargaining** and their respective underlying assumptions. On the one hand, the formal system of industry-level bargaining made these assumptions:

- It was possible to negotiate and resolve most, if not all, industrial relations issues in a single written agreement which could then be applied throughout an industry.

- The central organs of the trade unions and employers' associations had the capacity to ensure that the terms of any agreement were observed by their members.

- The function of the industrial relations system at the organisation level was primarily one of interpreting and applying the industry agreement and providing a basis for joint consultation between management and employees.

The informal system of organisational bargaining, on the other hand, assumed the following:

- Many industrial relations issues were specific to the organisation and could be regulated by informal arrangements or 'custom and practice' at the workplace.

- Both management and union members at the workplace had a relatively high degree of autonomy to reach decisions independently of their central organisations.

- The distinction between the processes of joint consultation and collective bargaining, and therefore between which issues were appropriate for which process, was blurred.

However, in their view, the conflict between the two systems could not be resolved 'by forcing the informal system to comply with the assumptions of the formal system'[39] but only by management and trade unions accepting the reality and importance of the organisation level and developing it on a more formal and orderly basis.

Voluntary reform

The Donovan Commission's recommendation was, in part, a reflection of a process of reform which had already started among some companies in the early 1960s. However, its recommendation did provide a stimulus for a more widespread and conscious strategy on the part of most managements to formalise and co-ordinate their bargaining arrangements within the organisation. In Hawkins' view the recommendation 'strongly reflected the view that the key to a better system of industrial relations lay in the reform and extension of collective bargaining by management *initiative* and trade union *agreement*' (my italics)[40]. The onus and primary responsibility for reform was placed on management.

See Chapter 7 – Management

Perhaps the most important reform element, and certainly the one most open to management initiative, was the **systematic development of formal**

substantive and procedural agreements at the organisation level. The review of substantive agreements often involved a reform of payment structures and systems (including the removal of piecework or bonus systems, a reduction in the number of grades/jobs, and a linking of such reforms (and pay increases) to changes in working arrangements) as a means for management to regain a measure of control over wages. At the same time, the introduction or reform of procedural agreements provided a clearer identification of not only the procedures and institutions through which industrial relations issues were to be processed but also the various roles and responsibilities for handling such issues. One result of this process was the need for employers' associations to re-examine and, if necessary, adjust their role – to become an advisor/co-ordinator of such activities rather than a regulator – and, consequently, the national agreement became a minimum to be built upon and expanded at the organisation level.

See Chapter 5 –
Trade union
organisation and
structure

At the same time, **trade unions were involved in their own process of reform**. In one direction, the structure of British trade unionism had been 'simplified' during the postwar period through the process of mergers – the reduction in the number of trade unions had, in many cases, simplified collective bargaining arrangements and, in some, made the introduction of new working arrangements easier by reducing the boundary between workgroups. In another direction, the internal organisation and government of trade unions was amended to bridge the gap with their membership: this included the establishment of plant-based branches better able to deal with the workplace issues, more formal and regular meetings between shop stewards and with full-time officials and greater use of postal balloting for elections. In addition, trade unions sought to increase their expertise through the employment of more specialists and the training of shop stewards.

However, the process of voluntary reform did not preclude greater government involvement in industrial relations or, more importantly, attempts to impose greater legal control.

Government intervention

Although both trade unions and management often expound the notion of 'voluntarism' and their freedom to determine the nature and content of their relationship, there is no doubt that the extent of voluntarism has been reduced by government intervention. Under the 'corporatist' ideology of the 1960s and 1970s, trade unions and management were, through NEDO, drawn into **discussions regarding the management of the economy** as part of the government's strategy to achieve their active support for its policies. This presented a major dilemma for trade unions since much of government policy was directed towards controlling inflation and achieving price stability; often through a formal incomes policy involving a temporary restriction on the level of pay increases. Trade unions had the choice of protecting their members' interests either indirectly by co-operating with government economic policies or directly through the collective bargaining process with management. In so far as the trade unions did support government policies of restraint, it not only reduced

See Chapter 8 – The government

the basis of 'voluntarism' in industrial relations but also widened the gap between the unions and their membership at a time when the memberships' autonomy had already been increased by the development of organisational-level bargaining.

The 1970s also saw **increased legal intervention** into industrial relations. Despite the Donovan Commission's emphasis on the benefits of voluntary reform, it was clear that even a Labour government was 'displeased by the absence of any positive recommendations in favour of using the law to deter unofficial strikers in sensitive areas of the economy'[41]. Six months after the publication of the Donovan Commission report, the government published a White Paper setting out proposals which would 'help to control the destructive expression of industrial conflict'[42]. It proposed to give the Secretary of State the power to order a 'cooling-off' period in unconstitutional strikes (i.e. those where the disputes procedure had not been exhausted and which were, in most cases, also unofficial strikes) and to order a ballot where an official strike involved a serious threat to the economy or public interest. Pressure from the trade unions led to the withdrawal of the Paper and replacement by a TUC undertaking to use its authority and influence to secure industrial peace.

Hawkins suggests that the Labour government's withdrawal of its legislative proposals 'simply reinforced the determination of the Conservative Party to enact their own proposals for reforming industrial relations'[43]. This they did in the **Industrial Relations Act (1971)**. The government's attempt to establish greater legal control over trade unions, in particular unofficial industrial action, outweighed the inclusion of some positive rights (notably, unfair dismissal and union recognition) and the legislation failed – but not without a number of court cases[44] which resulted in the brief imprisonment of seven dockers, fines being imposed against trade unions, their funds being sequestrated to pay the fines and 'a growing anxiety about the extent to which [the Act's] provisions could be operated in practice'[45].

On its return to power in 1974, the Labour government adopted a different approach which, McIlroy notes, had at its centre 'an accord between government and unions which was projected as the basis for a new social contract'[46]. The unions, on their part, agreed to consider the needs of the economy in their wage bargaining while the government agreed, in addition to pursuing socially desirable policies, to support trade unions through legislation. Thus, the repeal of the Industrial Relations Act by the Labour government's Trade Union and Labour Relations Acts (1974 and 1976) did not herald a withdrawal of legal intervention but merely a change in direction. The **Employment Protection Act (1975)** not only established a number of employee rights but also provided positive support for trade unionism and collective bargaining by establishing rights in such areas as disclosure of information, consultation in a redundancy and time off for trade union duties. This positive support for trade unionism was reflected also in the terms of reference of the Bullock Committee on Industrial Democracy (1977) which required it to accept 'the need for a radical extension of industrial democracy in the control of companies by means of representation on boards of directors' and 'the essential role of trade union organisations in this process'[47].

Confrontation

However, the 'winter of discontent' (1978/79) arising from, Taylor argues, a 'desire for "more money now" after three years of voluntary pay restraint'[48] and the subsequent election of the Thatcher Conservative government in 1979 once again changed the direction of legislative intervention. The strategy was to impose, in stages, **increasingly greater legal control and restrictions on the activities and affairs of trade unions**:

■ To remove the statutory recognition procedure and the closed shop (Union Membership Agreement) – undermining the union's ability to organise.

■ To withdraw immunity completely from secondary industrial action – removing any support from other trade unionists in a dispute.

■ To require unions to ballot on industrial action under independent scrutiny; make them responsible for unlawful actions authorised by the union's officers, committees or shop stewards unless they repudiate such actions; give individual members the right not to be disciplined by their union for not undertaking industrial action (even if lawful and supported by a majority vote in favour); and make it easier for the employer to dismiss strikers (particularly in an unofficial strike) – all potentially weakening the union's 'strike weapon'.

■ To require unions to elect their NEC, General Secretary and President by direct secret ballot with independent scrutineers, and give individual members legal rights to inspect the union's accounts and challenge unlawful actions – thereby imposing regulation on the union's internal organisation.

■ To abolish Wages Councils as part of the government's strategy to 'price people back into jobs' – the only statutory support to bargaining in a number of poorly organised and low-paid industries.

During the 1980s the government also 'confronted' the established role of unions by downgrading the importance of and then abolishing tripartite bodies on which the TUC was represented (the MSC and NEDO). Furthermore, it no longer regarded the TUC as having exclusive rights to nominate the 'employee' representatives to bodies such as Employment Tribunals and ACAS. At the same time, as an employer, it was prepared to withdraw bargaining rights from teachers and replace it with a review body and confront trade unions in its own disputes: for example, POEU privatisation dispute (1983), GCHQ withdrawal of right to belong to a union (1984), NUM/NCB pit closure dispute (1984/5) and ambulance pay dispute (1988).

However, confrontation was not the sole province of the government. At times it appeared that **confrontational 'macho management'** and the enforcement of the new legal rights might be the standard for industrial relations as some managements in the private sector endured long disputes to 'force through' the major work changes they regarded as necessary to maintain their competitiveness and used the courts to weaken the union's opposition – for example, News International at Wapping (1986) and P&O (1989).

New realism: anomie or partnership?

Alongside the confrontation and increased legislative control, the period since the late 1980s has seen significant **developments in management's approach to industrial relations**. However, there has not been a single cohesive strategy which has been applied uniformly across all organisations but, as during the previous periods of development, different strands have taken place in varying degrees at different speeds in different organisations for different reasons. A number of major strands can be identified:

- **Management proactivity:** Management has introduced HRM approaches and initiatives intended to support and be integrated with the achievement of business objectives (be it improved competitiveness, quality or customer care). This has been closely linked to the strengthening of managerial authority and prerogative within the organisation.

- **Process relationships:** The balance has shifted from an emphasis on the management–union relationship (collectivism) to an emphasis on the management–employee(s) relationship (individualism). This can be seen in shifts from negotiation and agreement to communication and consultation; from 'disclosure' of information to unions for bargaining to 'dissemination' of information to employees; and from union 'participation' to employee 'involvement'. The objective has been to secure the individual's identification with and commitment to the organisation and its goals.

- **Structure of bargaining:** There has been a continuation of the shift from the national 'multi-employer' level to the 'single-employer' organisational level (to better relate pay with work and to take advantage of local labour market conditions). At the same time, some organisations have sought to rationalise structures by limiting recognition to a 'single table' or 'single union' basis to support the development of more flexible working arrangements.

- **Pay and working arrangements**: The new emphasis among most organisations has been on 'flexibility' and greater individualisation of the contractual relationship. This has resulted in an extension of part-time and temporary working (leading to a potential differentiation between core and periphery employees in the organisation) as well as changes in working arrangements to secure greater functional (task) and time flexibility. At the same time, more emphasis has been placed on organisational or individual performance in determining pay and less on a uniform rate for the job.

Throughout the 1980s and early 1990s UK trade unions were largely 'on the defensive' because of the unsupportive economic, political and organisational environments. Consequently, few employers felt it necessary to attack trade unionism directly through wholesale derecognition. Rather, they maintained a relationship with trade unions but only by incorporating it into the new-style organisational relationships on their (management's) terms and, in some cases at least, it was offered as the only alternative to non-unionism. Brown and Sisson believed, in the early 1980s, that this 'new realism' did not reflect a genuine joint acceptance of a new relationship framework but was 'likely to be as ephemeral in the face of economic recovery as were the attitudes of the 1930s when wartime restored job security'[49]. Rose[50], again writing before the election of the 'new' Labour government, argued (see Box 2.3) that the developments in industrial relations could best be understood within the context of both an increasing dominance *and* a fragmentation of capitalism. This would result in increasing disorganisation of the social control mechanisms – both at the governmental level and at the level of the organisation (in particular the fragmentation of the industrial relations system and reduction in generalisation of norms within societies, industries or even organisations).

However, despite a decline in membership of $5\frac{1}{2}$ million between 1979 and 1998 (almost 50 per cent), trade unions have not, as some expected, been 'wiped out' and still account for some 35 per cent of the workforce. They have responded to the adverse conditions in three main ways:

- Targeting their recruitment efforts in the employment growth areas (women, part-timers, service sector, etc.);

- Developing individual member services ('plastic card' unionism) and supporting the individual member in his or her dealings with management;

- Offering management a more proactive and positive relationship based on the concept of 'social partnership' which not only recognises shared interests in the employment relationship (co-operation) but also accepts management's desire to maintain and strengthen its relationship with employees

---

Box 2.3   Disorganisation, disintegration and anomie – a future paradigm

- *Changing nature of capitalism:* The globalisation and internationalisation of markets and liberalisation of trade, coupled with the increasing number and size of multinational corporations (or international co-operation between organisations), results in less corporate interest in and concern for national interests and reduces individual government's ability to control or influence the operation of capitalism. National governments in both the developed and developing worlds, rather than co-operating to control capitalism, compete to offer the 'best' conditions for capitalism in order to secure *their* share of the limited capitalist investment, production, wealth and employment.

- *Changing nature of employment in society:* The decline of manufacturing (particularly in western industrialised countries), reduction in the size of organisations and the displacement of labour to unemployment, under-employed part-time or casual labour and the service sectors has eroded and dispersed 'working class solidarity'. Political representation of labour has, at the same time, weakened as the political parties shift their focus from 'representing labour' to 'being electable'.

- *Changing nature of industrial relations:* Management strategies, supported by government policies of de-regulation and weakening trade unions, have resulted in the disintegration or fragmentation of social regulation (the industrial relations system) through decentralisation (disorganisation) of industrial relations structures, differentiation of management strategies *between* organisations, the individualisation of strategies *within* organisations and the introduction of competition between different labour segments.

Source: E. Rose, 'The "disorganised paradigm": British industrial relations in the 1990s', *Employee Relations*, vol. 16, no. 1, 1994, pp. 27–40.

on an individual basis (a parallel relationship of employees and union with management).

The trade unions' position has been strengthened to a certain extent by the actions of the 'new' Labour government. Although the new government made it clear that it did not intend to repeal the Conservative legislation of the 1980s, it has nevertheless enacted two major pieces of legislation:

- National Minimum Wage Act (1998) which, as its title indicates, establishes a universal minimum pay rate to fill the vacuum created by the abolition of the previous selective Wages Councils.

- Employment Relations Act (1999) which has strengthened union representation in a number of ways:

  - Reintroduced a statutory procedure for union recognition;
  - Abolished the requirement for unions to provide employers with a list of members being balloted or called on to undertake industrial action;
  - Constrained the employer's ability to dismiss lawful strikers;
  - Given employees the right to be accompanied by a union representative or fellow worker during grievance or disciplinary hearings;
  - Protected employees against dismissal because they refuse to accept an individual contract on different terms from those applicable under a collective agreement.

In addition, the new government redressed two long-standing sores remaining from the height of 1980s Thatcherism. First, it restored union rights at GCHQ and compensated those who had been sacked for refusing to give up their union membership and, second, it restored pension rights to those miners who were sacked during the NUM 1984–5 strike but not reinstated after the strike. Perhaps more importantly, in terms of trying to create a new social consensus around a restructured employment relationship, the government set up a Partnership Fund to provide financial support for training and any other measure to assist the development of 'partnership at the workplace'.

2.4 The mass media

Industrial relations provided a major focus for the UK media throughout the 1960s, 1970s and most of the 1980s. Beharrell and Philo argue that the mass media of newspapers and television 'play a crucial role in the battle of ideas, over what is held by people to be important, necessary or possible within society'[51] and consequently 'never simply gives "the news" but always offers us a way of understanding the world'[52]. In their view the mass media's projection of industrial relations has often in the past been 'a world populated by inflationary wage claims, strikes and disruptions, and the perpetual battle between the responsible majority and the small minority who always want to spoil everything for the rest'[53]. It is, therefore, perhaps not surprising that trade union leaders and active trade union members have been suspicious of the mass media and, as Seaton notes, fear 'that the long-term political and social role of the unions is being eroded and distorted by the effects of increasingly hostile reporting' [54].

Extensive research by the Glasgow Media Group in the 1970s[55] showed that the media's reporting of industrial relations was both **selective and subjective**.

What constitutes 'news' which should be presented to the public?

In one sense, Beharrell and Philo pointed out, the answer is tautological – news is news because it is in a newspaper or on television. However, the fact that something is presented as 'news' inevitably creates a mass media impetus as journalists seek to enhance the item by inviting people in authority roles, whether government, trade unions or management, to comment on the validity and importance of the original item. This process is seen clearly in what is often referred to as 'negotiation through the mass media' as journalists seek information and comments from both sides and outsiders at each development, or supposed development, in a dispute. On the other hand, it may be argued that the mass media can only report what they are given and therefore 'news' is, at least in part, determined by what the participants want to have reported. In this respect, the trade unions' public and press relations have, in the past, been much less positive and successful than those of either government or management – particularly the management of large corporations. Management is usually better able to project, through the mass media's reporting of industrial, economic and financial matters, its values of a basic consensus between employees and itself and the need for organisational productivity, competitiveness and profitability. Nevertheless, in recent years UK trade unions have sought to focus their publicity more on their campaigns for social justice – particularly in respect of women and part-time workers.

Imbalanced reporting

Although the mass media seek to project an image of balanced reporting, in reality their reporting is imbalanced by virtue of the 'slant' or 'wording' of the item. This can be seen in two important ways:

- Most 'front page' items relating to industrial relations, and therefore of greatest impact on the public, have tended to report disputes, conflicts and failures to agree rather than the successful situations. Indeed, quite often the resolution of a dispute has gone unannounced or reported only as a small item of news, while the conflict generated during the dispute has received wide coverage. The successful industrial relations situations, when they are reported, are usually found as serious items on the business pages or in current affairs programmes and even then have been presented as examples which other organisations ought to be copying.

- There has also been a tendency, in the words used by the reporter or interviewer, to personalise and politicise a situation by the use of phrases such as 'left and right wing', 'militant', 'bid for power', etc. Some may argue that this is simply good journalese, but its influence is great. It was the media which applied phrases such as the 'winter of discontent', 'flying pickets' and 'secondary picketing' to industrial relations, some of which have 'since passed into political mythology and in fact have come to form the basis for legislation'[56].

Incomplete reporting of the facts

Perhaps most importantly, the mass media do not present a complete reporting of the facts and issues because of either a shortage of space/time or the complexities of the situation. No industrial relations situation is ever simple and yet they are generally projected as such – often related to pay. The reporting of 'facts' is often enmeshed in the expression of opinion and frequently journalists will 'read between the lines' of a statement or situation and offer their own interpretation rather than the views and thinking of the participants. Even a statement of 'no comment' will be interpreted in some way by the reporter or interviewer. Finally, it is not just the reporting of 'industrial relations' situations which influences people's perceptions of industrial relations but also its almost throwaway inclusion in other items. For example, Beharrell and Philo refer to the inclusion of the phrase 'strikes permitting' in a television news item in the 1970s dealing with the launch of a new British Leyland car[57].

Whether the selectivity and subjectivity of the mass media are parts of a conspiracy against trade unions or simply the result of the process of gathering and disseminating news is a matter of personal judgement.

■ Summary propositions

- ■ The UK has experienced a number of significant, and continuing, developments in its economic context – deindustrialisation, the growth of new technology and, in particular, the increasing competitiveness and globalisation of capitalism (trade, organisations and work).

- ■ More people in the UK are working now than ever before (due to a higher female economic participation rate), but many of the new jobs are part-time and low-paid in the personal service industries and, at the same time, UK unemployment has remained high – which raises concerns about what constitutes 'full employment'.

- ■ The technological revolution, changing employment structures and management demands for greater flexibility have led to a number of social concerns: the potential division between the 'work-rich' and 'work-poor', the need for a better balance between work and personal life and the effects of the increasing size of the 'retired' population (relative to the size and nature of the working population).

- ■ The postwar political environment has shifted from a *regulation* of capital and labour through incorporation into government decision making, through a *free enterprise* deregulated market individualism, to a form of *supportive constraint* of international capitalism within the principles of stakeholder partnership and social responsibility.

Activity

1. *Changes in employment and unemployment.*
This chapter provides some statistics on UK employment structures and unemployment. You can find up-to-date figures in *Labour Market Trends*. While you are updating the aggregate figures, you might like also to examine the differences between industries and regions (particularly between male/female and full-time/part-time employment) and the differences in duration of unemployment linked to age and sex. You can also find detailed information in *Labour Market Trends* on other aspects of employment, such as self-employment, hours of work, earnings, etc.

2. *The mass media's reporting of industrial relations.*
It would be useful if, while you are studying industrial relations, you check national newspapers (and television) and note down what items relating to industrial relations are reported. This will help to give you not only up-to-date information on what is happening in the field, but also a better understanding of how it is reported:

(a)   What topics or aspects are covered – contextual matters (such as employment, technological change, etc.), disputes and strikes, the introduction of new working arrangements in organisations, etc.?

(b)   Are they short news reports or in-depth articles?

(c)   What is the overall impression given by the report or article?

(d)   Are there any good examples of the use of emotive language?

(e)   Are fact and opinion clearly differentiated?

▮ Further reading

▮ P. Blyton and P. Turnbull, *The Dynamics of Employee Relations* (2nd edn), Macmillan, 1998. Chapter 3 examines a number of changes at organisation, industry and society levels which have impacted on the nature of work in the UK.

▮ S. Kessler and F. Bayliss, *Contemporary British Industrial Relations* (3rd edn), Macmillan, 1998. The first two chapters explore the development of UK industrial relations during the postwar period up to 1979, while the next two chapters examine the economic and political environments of the 1980s and 1990s.

■ K. Hawkins, *British Industrial Relations 1945–1975*, Barrie & Jenkins, 1976. This book traces the development of British industrial relations up to the mid-1970s with particular emphasis on relations between trade unions and the government in the development of legislation and incomes policy.

■ References

1. A. Fox, *Man Mismanagement* (2nd edn), Hutchinson, 1985, p. 16.
2. R. Taylor, *Workers and the New Depression*, Macmillan, 1982, pp. vii and 199.
3. P. Nolan and J. Walsh, 'The structure of the economy and labour market', in P. Edwards (ed.), *Industrial Relations: Theory and practice in Britain*, Blackwell, 1995, table 3.2, p. 68.
4. P. Blyton and P. Turnbull, *The Dynamics of Employee Relations* (2nd edn), Macmillan, 1998, p. 44.
5. S. Bach and K. Sisson, 'Personnel management in perspective', in S. Bach and K. Sisson, *Personnel Management* (3rd edn), Blackwell, 2000, p. 27.
6. Nolan and Walsh, *op. cit.*, p. 68.
7. S. Kessler and F. Bayliss, Contemporary *British Industrial Relations* (3rd edn), Macmillan, 1998, p. 55.
8. R. Ellison, 'British labour force projections: 1994 to 2006', *Employment Gazette*, April 1994, pp. 111–121.
9. D. Deaton, 'Unemployment', in G. S. Bain (ed.), *Industrial Relations in Britain*, Blackwell, 1983, table 10.1, p. 239.
10. J. MacInnes, 'Why nothing much has changed: recession, economic restructuring and industrial relations since 1979', *Employee Relations*, vol. 9, no. 1, 1987.
11. Blyton and Turnbull, *op. cit.*, p. 46.
12. M. Daly, 'The 1980s – a decade of growth in enterprise', *Employment Gazette*, March 1991, pp. 109–131.
13. Nolan and Walsh, *op. cit.*, p. 66.
14. *Economic Survey of the United Kingdom*, OECD, June 1998.
15. Blyton and Turnbull, *op. cit.*, p. 45.
16. Deaton, *op. cit.*, p. 239.
17. J. Lawlor and A. White, 'Measures of unemployment: the claimant count and the LFS', *Employment Gazette*, November 1991, p. 618.
18. 'More to unemployment figures than meets the eye', *The Economist*, July 1995.
19. C. Denny, 'Black and Asian jobs at risk: minorities will take brunt of slowdown', *Guardian*, 16 April 1999.
20. A. Britton, 'Full employment in the industrialized countries', *International Labour Review*, vol. 136, no. 3, 1997, pp. 293–314.
21. A. Sen, 'Inequality, unemployment and contemporary Europe', *International Labour Review*, vol. 136, no. 2, 1997, pp. 155–172.
22. C. Denny, 'US runs out of workers as job boom peaks', *Guardian*, 3 April 1999.
23. I. Traynor, 'Bleakest midwinter on German jobs', *Guardian*, 10 February 1999.
24. R. H. Tawney, *Religion and the Rise of Capitalism*, Penguin, 1961, p. 239. Reprinted with permission of John Murray (Publishers) Ltd.
25. Sen, *op. cit.*
26. S. Milne and L. Elliott, 'How rich and poor must both pay the price of a workplace revolution', *Guardian*, 4 January 1999.
27. H. Wilkinson, 'Better balance between job and personal life is key demand of the new work ethic', *Guardian*, 6 January 1999.
28. W. Woodward, 'Greying of Britain will put children in the shade', *Guardian*, 29 May 1999.
29. 'Political and legal environments' (Unit 8B, *Industrial Relations*), Open University Press, 1976, p. 7.
30. C. Crouch, *Class Conflict and the Industrial Relations Crisis*, Heinemann, 1977; D. Strinati, *Capitalism, the State and Industrial Relations*, Croom Helm, 1982; C. Crouch, *The Politics of Industrial Relations* (2nd edn)), Fontana, 1982, p. 145.
31. Professor J. Griffith, 'The collective unfairness of laissez-faire', *Guardian*, 14 June 1990.
32. *Ibid.*
33. J. Berridge, 'Editorial: The industrial relations outcomes of the British General Election of 1997', *Employee Relations*, vol. 19, no. 3, 1997, p. 190.
34. J. Due, J. S. Madsen and C. S. Jenson, 'The social dimension: convergence or

diversification of IR in the Single European Market?', *Industrial Relations Journal*, vol. 22, no. 2, 1991, p. 88.

35. A. Flanders, 'Collective bargaining', in A. Flanders and H. A. Clegg (eds), *The System of Industrial Relations in Great Britain*, Blackwell, 1960, pp. 276–8.

36. K. Hawkins, *British Industrial Relations 1945–75*, Barrie & Jenkins, 1976, pp. 18–19.

37. A. Flanders, *Collective Bargaining: Prescription for Change*, Faber & Faber, 1967, p. 28.

38. Report of *Royal Commission on Trade Unions and Employers' Associations* (Donovan Commission), HMSO, 1968 (Chapter III).

39. *Ibid.*, p. 36.

40. Hawkins, *op. cit.*, p. 63.

41. *Ibid.*, p. 80.

42. *In Place of Strife*, HMSO, 1969, p. 5.

43. Hawkins, *op. cit.*, p. 82.

44. *Heaton Transport* v *T&GWU* (1973); *Midland Cold Storage* v *Turner* (1972); *Con-Mech (Engineering)* v *AUEW* (1973).

45. *Trade Union Immunities*, HMSO, 1981, p. 20.

46. J. McIlroy, *Trade Unions in Britain Today*, Manchester University Press, 1988, p. 9.

47. Report of the *Committee of Inquiry on Industrial Democracy* (Bullock), HMSO, 1977, p. v.

48. R. Taylor, 'The trade union "problem" since 1960' in B. Pimlott and C. Cook (eds), *Trade Unions in British Politics*, Longman, 1982, p. 206.

49. W. Brown and K. Sisson, 'Industrial relations in the next decade – current trends and future possibilities', *Industrial Relations Journal*, vol. 13, 1982, p. 20.

50. E. Rose, 'The "disorganized paradigm" – British industrial relations in the 1990s', *Employee Relations*, vol. 16, no. 1, 1994, pp. 27–40.

51. P. Beharrell and G. Philo, *Trade Unions and the Media*, Macmillan, 1977, p. ix.

52. *Ibid.*, p. 1.

53. *Ibid.*, p. 4.

54. J. Seaton, 'Trade unions and the media', in B. Pimlott and C. Cook (eds), *Trade Unions in British Politics*, Longman, 1982, p. 273.

55. Glasgow University Media Group, *Bad News* (1976); *More Bad News* (1977); and *More Bad News*, vol. 2 (1980), Routledge & Kegan Paul.

56. TUC Media Group, *A Course for Concern*, TUC, 1980, p. 29.

57. Beharrell and Philo, *op. cit.*, p. 7.

chapter three

Concepts and values in industrial relations

The perceptions, attitudes and behaviour of the participants within the industrial relations system are largely determined by their personal values (beliefs). By the end of this chapter, you should be able to:

- distinguish the different meanings of 'fairness' in the employment relationship;

- understand the differing nature of power, its relationship to authority and the process of its legitimisation;

- explain the underlying assumptions and potential tensions between 'individualism' and 'collectivism';

- identify the differences and interrelationship between 'rights' and 'responsibilities' in a social system such as industrial relations;

- appreciate the importance of integrity and trust in the maintenance and development of personal relationships in the conduct of industrial relations.

Definition

Industrial relations involves a range of concepts (abstract ideas) which require subjective, value judgements (based on moral or ethical principles and beliefs) for which there are no universally accepted criteria.

Key issues

While you are reading this chapter, you should keep the following point in mind:

- We all have different views of the world (in industrial relations, about the nature of capitalism, work and the employment relationship). Although these views may vary in the extent to which they are legitimised and/or accepted within society, we cannot easily say that another person's ideas are 'wrong', but rather that we 'disagree' with them.

3.1 Introduction

Industrial relations is not an 'objective' science. Indeed, it may be argued that there are no simple objective facts in industrial relations. For example, before it is possible to calculate the number of trade unions in the UK, it is necessary to define what organisational characteristics are appropriate for determining whether or not an organisation may be classified as a 'trade union', and the characteristics which are chosen will depend on what is *believed* to be the purpose and nature of a trade union. More importantly, as Hyman and Brough point out, 'the arguments of those involved in industrial relations are shot through with essentially moral terminology'[1]. Perhaps the most important issues and debates in industrial relations, apart from that concerning the conflictual/consensual relationship of the participants, centre around such concepts as fairness/equity, power/authority and individualism/collectivism. However, as Kerr and Siegal argued, these concepts 'are not subject to discovery by any purely technical explanation but must be defined by the exercise of value judgements'[2], and Ackers points out that 'there are both multiple perceptions of what reality is and more than one view of what is right and wrong in industrial relations'[3].

The inherent problem with any value-laden concept is trying to understand what is meant by the term and its limitations. Different individuals and groups have different perceptions of what is 'good/bad', 'right/wrong' or what power may be exercised legitimately and when. It is these differing perceptions which provide the underlying dynamic tension within industrial relations (see Box 3.1).

3.2 Fairness and equity

Although the concept of 'fairness' or 'equity' implicitly underlies the entire conduct of industrial relations, it is explicitly most frequently associated with considerations of pay and dismissals. However, there are many who would argue, perhaps cynically, that nothing in life is ever fair and therefore appeals to fairness are little more than attempts to provide a semblance of justification or legitimacy for actions and decisions which might otherwise appear to be simply expedient. Others, such as Brown, argue that the use of the concept is 'more

Box 3.1	Ethics and HRM

'Strategy involves setting missions and visions and defining core organisational values ... [which] cannot be done without considering ethical questions ... Corporate bodies cannot be made to act ethically by mission statements, ethical audits and codes of ethics alone ... Organisations are characterised by value plurality, and mission statements and core values are part of that plurality rather than the means of overcoming it ... Corporations, as legal fictions without consciences, will only act ethically when the people who are part of them are skilled at thinking about, and coping with, ethical issues and are supported by an organisational culture that encourages ethical awareness and debate.'

Source: C. Fisher and C. Rice, 'Managing messy moral matters: ethics and HRM', in J. Leopold, L. Harris and T. Watson (eds), *Strategic Human Resourcing: Principles, Perspectives and Practices*, FT Pitman, 1999, p. 311.

than an ideological whitewash, to be applied *ex post* to provide an appearance of rationality'[4] and certainly Hyman and Brough believe that 'the commitment of one side or the other to a particular notion of fairness often appears to exert a significant influence on the actual course of industrial relations'[5].

The use of the term is confused perhaps by its close association, in many people's mind, with the term **equality**. In this way anything which creates or sustains inequality may be perceived as being 'unfair'. However, the concept of 'fairness' or 'equity' does not automatically imply equality; equality is only one value or belief set that may be used to judge the existence and extent of fairness. There are many who would argue that the existence of social inequality is both inevitable and fair because of differences in individual personal attributes. Certainly there is no doubt that inequalities exist both within society and the organisation: for example, unequal distribution of wealth, incomes and ownership; variations in benefits such as job security, nature of work, status, education and health; differential access to power, authority and control. Indeed, the dominant values and ethos within a capitalist society, extolled through the virtues of individualism and competition, support the creation and maintenance of such inequalities and thereby legitimise their fairness. However, from a Marxist perspective based on more egalitarian values it is the existence of such inequalities at the macro level of society (the absence of 'social justice' in respect of the distribution of wealth, power, rights and duties) which renders the concept of 'fairness' at the micro level of the individual or organisation almost meaningless. Any notions of fairness held by the subordinate which differ from those of the dominant may be seen as destabilising and, if recognised and accepted, a threat to the dominant's position.

Zweig has suggested that 'the idea of fairness is linked strongly with the best customs and traditions and the best social rules'[6]. However, this more abstract approach immediately raises problems of how to identify what is 'the best'. The values to which one person attaches the highest priority and greatest concern may not be the same for other people. This has led many, consciously or unconsciously, to adopt a **utilitarian or democratic notion of fairness** (that which is in the interests of or acceptable to the majority) in the mistaken belief that it is demonstrably impartial and fair and will therefore dispel feelings of unfairness among the minority. However, the outcome of majority rule, even though it is legitimised by the nature of the process, will not automatically be considered to be 'right' or 'fair' by the minority, who have different values and expectations to the majority.

Some people might go even further to suggest that certain activities rise above personal values and provide an **impersonal technical notion of fairness**: for example, market forces, job evaluation or the legal process. However, even the proposition that 'the free interplay of market forces should be allowed to determine wage levels' is a value judgement. Similarly, any suggestion that it is the job-evaluation system which, independently and impartially, determines an individual's pay ignores the fact that it is people who, subjectively, both allocate the weightings in the scheme (i.e. determine which attributes are to attract the highest measure) and evaluate the individual's job against those criteria. So far as the legal process is concerned, again it is people who make, invoke, interpret and apply the law in the light of their values and notions of fairness.

Fairness is perhaps most usefully seen as a **relative and variable concept** with which to examine the conduct of human relationships. In this respect it may be used in three ways:

- It may imply, as Hyman and Brough suggest, that 'in an exchange there should be reasonable reciprocity or balance between the parties concerned'[7]. However, difficulties arise in determining what are the relevant criteria by which to judge the **reciprocity of the exchange** – should they relate only to the outcome (the costs/benefits to each party) or should they include some assessment of the quality of the process by which the outcome is achieved (joint determination versus unilateral imposition)? Ultimately, whether reciprocity exists can be determined only by reference to the values of the participants and their view of the nature and quality of their exchange. It is 'fair' if the participants consider it to be fair.

- In a wider context, fairness may imply that a particular exchange is **consistent with other exchanges** undertaken elsewhere. It is in this context that it is possible to have 'fair' inequalities, but this requires a wide measure of agreement regarding both the criteria for determining similarities and differences between situations and the evaluation of their relative importance. An exchange is only 'fair' if others, outside the direct participants, consider it to be fair in relation to themselves or other individuals and groups.

- Fairness may, particularly in respect of non-monetary exchanges, imply **equality of treatment and consideration** in the conduct of different relationships and within the same relationship over time. There is an expectation that the same types of criteria and standards of judgements should apply in similar circumstances; that relationships should be conducted, and therefore may be judged, according to an accepted code. It is 'fair' if it is consistent.

Finally, because fairness is relative, it is **not constant**. As situations and environments change, so the participants' notion of what is fair may change. For example, it is to be expected that during a recession management's notion of a 'fair' wage increase will decrease because its major reference point (reduced demand and increased competition affecting its ability to pay) changes while the employees' notion of a 'fair' increase may remain unchanged because their major reference points (cost of living, comparability, etc.) have not changed. Equally, if one group of employees perceives other groups to achieve better wage increases through the use of industrial action and/or they become more aware of their own industrial power, so they are more likely to perceive it as being 'fair' for them to seek the same levels and/or use the same means.

3.3 Power and authority

The concepts of 'power' and 'authority' occupy a central position in industrial relations, particularly with respect to its collective aspects. People frequently make value judgements regarding trade unions having too much or too little power in relation to management and government, or trade unions having too little authority or control over their membership, or management having too little authority within its own organisation. In practice the two concepts are inextricably linked: authority is achieved through power and vice versa.

There is no universally accepted definition of **power** (see Box 3.2). For Koontz and O'Donnell 'power implies force'[8]; for Hyman, it is 'the ability of an individual or group to control his [their] physical and social environment; and, as part of the process, the ability to influence the decisions which are or are not taken by others'[9]; while in purely operational terms, for example in negotiations, Magenau and Pruitt regard it simply as the 'capacity to elicit concessions from the other party'[10]. Clearly, therefore, power has different meanings and it is useful to differentiate between the following:

■ Power meaning the ability to **control** or impose, i.e. to direct or regulate a situation or person(s) despite any desire or attempt to influence from another individual or group. Certainly Kirkbride and Durcan argue that 'power ... is inherently entwined in the very fabric of social life and its processes ... "domination" is where there is an asymmetry of resources and one actor is thus much more "powerful" than the other', and power is 'not "a" resource, but instead resources are the means through which power is exercised and by which structures of domination are reproduced'[11].

■ Power meaning the ability to **influence** and thereby secure some modification in another party's decision or action. This may be subdivided between:

   ▎ the ability to force a change in the other party's decision, usually after it has been made, by the **explicit** expression or threat to express that power; and

   ▎ the ability to generate an **implicit** influence which will form an integral part of the environment which has to be taken into account by the other party in its decision-making process.

This latter distinction is recognised by Magenau and Pruitt when, in the context of negotiations, they distinguish between strategic power (which 'consists of all the elements of the situation that allow one party to influence the other') and tactical advantage (which consists of the 'successful use of distributive tactics for enhancing one's influence')[12].

Hyman argues that, while power is used for a purpose, which in industrial relations is 'primarily as a resource ... in the service of collective interests'[13], it can serve this purpose only if it is exercised over people. The employment relationship is inherently a 'power/authority' relationship. French and Raven[14] identified five major interrelated sources of power within the organisational relationship:

■ *Reward* – having control or influence over the achievement of some goal or benefit which is desired by another;

■ *Coercion* – having the ability to inflict some punitive measure against another (this may be linked to the denial of reward or the formal roles which the people hold);

■ *Legitimised* – occupying a role which is formally designated as containing a superior direction or regulation of others;

Box 3.2	The ambiguity of power

'... it is difficult to tie down exactly what the phenomenon is. We know that it has a great deal to do with asymmetrical patterns of dependence whereby one person or unit becomes dependent on another in an unbalanced way, and that it also has a great deal to do with an ability to define the reality of others in ways that lead them to perceive and enact relations that one desires. However, it is far from clear whether power should be understood as an interpersonal behavioural phenomenon or as the manifestation of deep-seated structural factors. It is not clear whether people have and exercise power as autonomous human beings or are simply carriers of power relations that are the product of more fundamental forces. These, and other issues – such as whether power is a resource or a relationship, whether there is a distinction between power and processes of societal domination and control, whether power is ultimately linked to the control of capital and the structuring of the world economy, or whether it is important to distinguish between actual manifest power and potential power – continue to be the subject of considerable interest and debate among those interested in the sociology of organization.'

Source: G. Morgan, *Images of Organization* (2nd edn), Sage, 1997, p. 199. © 1997 Sage Publications, Inc. Reprinted by permission of Sage Publications, Inc.

- *Referment* – having the personal attributes which lead others to defer in their decisions or opinions;
- *Expertise* – having particular knowledge or experience which is considered to be superior to that of others (this may be linked to the role occupied by the person or their personal attributes).

Morgan[15] identifies a range of more diffuse, implicit and pervasive sources of power derived from the 'dynamics of organisational life':

- Control of resources and technological systems;
- Control of knowledge, information and decision-making process;
- Use of organisational structures, rules and regulations;
- Control of alliances, networks, 'informal organisation' and counter-organisations.

More importantly, Magenau and Pruitt highlight that power can only exist and be exerted if there is a **reciprocal perception of power**. In the context of bargaining negotiations, they argue that 'when I feel stronger than you, this is no guarantee that you will feel weaker than me or, feeling weaker, that you will accept my contention that you should concede'[16]. From this they conclude:

- Perceived power equality between the parties provides for an easy agreement and high-value outcome;
- Perceived low power inequality provides for a difficult agreement and low-value outcome;
- Perceived high power inequality provides for an 'easy' agreement and high but biased value outcome.

This last situation equates to control or imposition through power and is always likely to be perceived as 'unfair' by the 'losing' party. It is because of the need to establish a reciprocal perception of power, and thereby determine the relative power relationship between the parties, that power needs to be demonstrated explicitly – at least occasionally.

At the same time, because of the collective nature of industrial relations, it is important to recognise that the concept of power over people has an **internal as well as external dimension**. Any collectivity, whether a work group, trade union or management, exercises internal power and authority over its individual members in the establishment and achievement of the collectivity's objectives. Without the exercise of such power and authority the collectivity lacks direction and control (i.e. is not a collectivity). It is the exercise of this internal power and authority which, to a large measure, provides the real source and extent of the power which the collectivity may direct towards influencing others and controlling their situation.

Authority is usually defined in terms of the legitimate use of power. Hence, Koontz and O'Donnell regard it as 'the right inherent in a position to utilize discretion in such a way that [organizational] objectives are set and achieved'[17], and Fox defines it as 'the right to expect and command obedience'[18]. If the concept of 'authority' rests on the **legitimisation** of power, then it is important to examine the basis of this legitimacy. An important part of legitimisation comes from the general process of **socialisation**. At the society level, Fox points out that 'as children we are urged to obey parents, teachers, policemen, and public officials simply because they are parents, teachers, policemen and public officials ... We also learn that if punished for transgression we are receiving no less than our just desert. These are lessons in the behaviours appropriate to subordination. ... By the time [the majority] take up employment they are trained to accept that they ... come under a generalized expectation that they will accept the orders of persons appointed to govern them'[19].

At the organisational level, this process of socialisation is reflected in the notion of **managerial prerogative**. Hyman regards this as a natural privilege or 'right accorded to management in capitalism to direct production and to command the labour force'[20], while Fox believes that 'in entering into a contract of employment, the employee legitimises the employer in directing and controlling his actions ... and legitimises, too, the employer's use of sanctions if necessary to maintain this obedience'[21]. In this way, Torrington and Hall argue, 'the individuals who become employees of the organisation surrender a segment of their personal autonomy to become relatively weaker, making the organisation inordinately stronger'[22].

Management's inherent authority is based, therefore, on society's infrastructure legitimising its role and power in the operation of the economic system – the employment relationship is an asymmetrical one. Consequently, it is argued, management has little need to utilise overtly coercive power in exercising this authority because the subordinates it seeks to control accept the values on which its power and authority rests. However, if necessary, the mechanism of coercion legitimised by society (the law) will support its authority. Certainly, Kelly believes that the employer's power is about more than 'influencing decisions', it is about the capacity to pursue direct coercive practices (such as repression, victimisation and blacklisting) supported by external factors (such as high unemployment, right-wing governments and anti-union laws)[23] – it is about control.

The notion of power being legitimised through authority has three important implications for industrial relations:

1. *Use of power is perceived to be unacceptable (wrong/bad), while the exercise of authority is acceptable (right/good).* This is often accompanied by a belief that power should not be used for sectional goals or purposes but only in the furtherance of 'society' goals (i.e. those determined by the dominant values within society). Hence, the existence of a belief that the trade union organisation, through its officials, should act responsibly and if necessary become a 'social police force' to ensure that its members' demands or actions do not threaten to disrupt society.

2. *There is a potential conflict of loyalty between the individual's role as an employee and a trade union member.* The process of socialisation induces an acceptance of orders from those appointed to 'govern' (i.e. those in superior social or organisational roles). For union representatives to be perceived as legitimate alternative 'authority' roles to management requires the legitimisation of the role of trade unions within both society and the organisation. Thus, Kelly argues that a union's 'key power resource' is its members 'willingness to act'.[24]

3. *The rights or entitlements of subordinates are closely bound up with the exercise of power and authority – or, more particularly, its control.* Some subordinate rights are formally legitimised by direct management acquiescence through the process of collective bargaining. Through this process the exercise of managerial power and authority becomes, in certain areas, subject to the subordinates' formal acceptance and agreement and may involve at least a partial accommodation between dominant and subordinate values. The precise nature and extent of these rights will vary depending on the power relationship between the parties involved in the negotiation. Other subordinate rights may be created and supported by society through the law imposing an external control on the exercise of managerial power and authority (for example, dismissals). Such rights are universal and not, as in collective bargaining, directly dependent on the power of subordinates to influence their management. However, they are dependent on the wider power of the subordinate groups as a whole to influence society's decision-making process (i.e. the government). Equally, of course, the law may maintain or extend managerial power and authority and even negate subordinate rights which have been obtained through collective bargaining (for example, the legislation to 'outlaw' closed shops/union membership agreements). Finally, other rights (such as the 'right' to strike) appear to rest, at least in part, on management's informal condonation of such actions by subordinates (i.e. the preparedness of management not to exercise their socialised or legal rights against such actions). Such a process requires no formal concession to the subordinates' values and continues only so long as the action does not present a serious threat to the dominant's position or values.

3.4 Individualism and collectivism

A frequently expressed value throughout much of a modern industrialised society is the importance of the individual. In the employment sphere this is reflected in a belief that people should not be lumped together simply as units of a factor of production or treated impersonally as a number on a clock card. Rather they should be seen as individual human beings each with his or her own aspirations, attitudes and attributes and each, in their own sphere of work, able to make a unique and significant contribution to the successful operation of the organisation. This philosophy appears to be at variance with the collective nature of much of industrial relations. Certainly, a number of very important aspects of industrial relations centre on the question of how much freedom should be allowed to the individual or how far the needs of a collective system should predominate.

In the UK context, waged work in industry was regarded in the beginning as little more than a continuation of the individual master/servant relationship associated with the earlier 'feudal' type agriculture and domestic work situation. It was in response to this harsh, coercive or, at best, paternalist-subordinated individual relationship that employees combined to redress the power imbalance and secure a less asymmetrical relationship. However, it would be too simplistic to equate the management/employee relationship with 'individualism' and the management/union relationship with 'collectivism'. It is important to realise that the inputs of both management and unions into the industrial relations system contain elements of both individualism and collectivism. It is this interrelationship between individualism and collectivism which lies at the heart of industrial relations. Perhaps the real issue in respect of the balance between the two is not one of an absolute freedom or constraint of the individual employee *per se* but, rather, the degree to which the individual is, or should be, (1) responsible and subordinated to, (2) regulated by, and/or (3) protected against either or both of the two collectivities with which he or she has dealings – the employing organisation and the union.

It is important to recognise that the terms **'individualism' and 'collectivism' may be used to refer to three different aspects of industrial relations**:

- Management is free to deal with its employees as *it* sees best without any intermediary constraint or filter of a trade union, *or* trade unions, as the collective representative of employees, regulate the work situation on an equal and joint basis with management;

- Employees are treated differentially, with individuals doing the same work receiving different pay dependent on their individual attributes abilities or performance (individual contract), *or* employees receiving the same terms and conditions of employment (common collective contract), irrespective of their individual attributes, abilities or performance;

- The individual perceives his or her economic or social well-being to be a matter for his or her own efforts independent of any peer group (the concept of egotism), *or* the individual perceives a bond with fellow employees and believes that individual needs can only be met via collective action (the concept of fraternalism).

These elements are at the centre of the dynamics of recent developments in UK industrial relations – 'human resource management' challenging 'industrial relations' (see Box 3.3). However, it is important to have regard to some of the underlying assumptions about the position of the individual in the institutions, processes and conduct of the employment relationship.

First, it has often been argued that the fundamental basis of a democratic society is the **freedom of the individual**: the freedom to choose and make decisions in respect of the conduct of the individual's life. However, there is no such thing in any society as total freedom to do as one wishes: 'individual freedom' is a relative not absolute concept. At the society level, it is generally accepted that the individual has freedom of action only where that action does not harm others or interfere with the 'rights' or 'freedoms' of others. However, from a Marxist perspective, it may be argued that these 'rights' or 'freedoms' are determined by the dominant values within society and, therefore, any change in the basis of society can be achieved only by actions which will be regarded as a challenge to those dominant values and harmful to or an interference with the existing 'rights' of others. At a lower level, whenever an individual joins an organisation – whether it is a company, trade union, political party or even a social club – he or she agrees, explicitly or implicitly, to abide by the objectives, rules and decisions of that organisation and, in so doing, relinquishes the 'freedom' to act independently for the period of membership. If at any time the decisions of the organisation or the restrictions placed on the individual's freedom are considered to be unacceptable, then he or she may choose between seeking change while remaining a member of the organisation or resigning from the organisation.

An important element of the debate regarding legislation to regulate the conduct of trade unions centres on **whether or not the act of joining an organisation and the associated relinquishing of individual freedom is**

Box 3.3	Individualism and collectivism: finding the balance

'The current state of affairs ... entails the new individualistically oriented employer-led initiatives being pursued alongside a collectivist/procedure-based system inherited from previous decades. It seems to us that few employers have worked out an effective articulation between these two systems.' (p. 230)

'So, what might be the way forward? This, we suggest, has to rest upon both individualism and collectivism. There is some truth in the message about empowerment, of the need to encourage individuals to identify opportunities and to pursue them; and there will be a need to build environments and cultures which encourage highly competent organizational members to excel above the norm ... But there is an equal danger in taking all this too far without paying due regard to the abuses, cynicism and arbitrariness which can too easily emerge under such conditions unless checked by some regulatory mechanism. The central issue then, is to find this balance.' (pp. 231–2)

Source: J. Storey and K. Sisson, *Managing Human Resources and Industrial Relations*, Open University Press, 1993.

voluntary. It has been argued that if trade union membership is not voluntary (i.e. if the individual is coerced into membership without the opportunity to exercise choice) then it is an unacceptable use of power and negation of individual freedom which requires legal intervention to restore and protect the individual's 'rights'. Indeed, some distinguish between the individual's relationship to the trade union (which may appear involuntary if there were a closed shop or pressure from work colleagues to join the union) and the individual's relationship to the employer (which appears to be voluntary, in that the individual may choose whether or not to work for a particular organisation). Yet, is an individual's acceptance or continuation of employment at a low wage during times of high unemployment when the employer 'can always get someone else' any more or less of a voluntary act, any more or less coerced, than an individual being required to join a trade union as part of his or her acceptance or continuation of employment? All decisions involve elements of freedom and coercion or pressure.

Second, it is important to recognise that a **collective basis to the employment relationship** exists because it meets certain needs of both management and employees. On the management side, a modern organisation encompasses a variety of tasks and roles which require to be integrated, co-ordinated and regulated to achieve the effective operation of the organisation. Thus, management defines the tasks and responsibilities of each role and plans its work arrangements. Each employee fits within this **systematised arrangement of tasks, roles and operations** as part of a particular department, category of employee or operational activity – whether process worker, technician, clerk or manager. The creation of groups of people with similar tasks/roles within the organisation has been generally accompanied, even without trade unions and collective bargaining, by similar treatment in respect of the reward system and other conditions of employment. Thus, management's own arrangement of its operations induced the development of a collective basis to the employment relationship. The collective basis is not created but only enhanced when, with the advent of trade unionism within the organisation, it becomes formalised through written agreements and procedures.

On the employees' side, the fact that the individual is a member of a group subject to the same controls and terms and conditions of employment means that, for most individuals, any **improvements in their personal situation can be achieved only by improving the group's situation**: individualism has to be replaced by collectivism. The individual, by combining with others, not only establishes the means to protect his or her interests and improve terms and conditions of employment but also increases his or her power *vis-à-vis* management and is able to secure a more favourable outcome than by acting alone. He or she is no longer one person who may easily be replaced by another person but part of a collectivity for which it is more difficult for management to find a substitute – certainly at short notice. However, the power and ability of the employees' collectivity to further the individual's interests rests largely on its internal **fraternalism/solidarity**: that is, the extent to which the individual members are prepared to subordinate personal aspirations to the collective needs, goals and decisions of the group. Deery and Walsh note that a 'collectivist work orientation' requires 'a belief that the most appropriate way of addressing industrial issues and achieving improvements in terms and conditions of work is through a union and by collective effort'[25]. Thus, the individual is free to dissent and oppose during the decision-making process, but once the collective decision has been made, he or she is expected to support it and, if necessary, display collective solidarity. The collectivity must ensure the organisation, control and compliance of its members.

The emphasis on collectivism in the determination of the employment relationship has been closely associated with the notion of **voluntarism**: that is, the freedom of the parties to organise themselves, to determine the nature and content of their relationship and to regulate it without governmental or legal intervention. Within this principle both management and trade unions, as the parties responsible for the conduct of collective relations, have an interest and responsibility to ensure that individuals on either side do not, through their actions, challenge or undermine the operation and authority of the collective system. There is certainly an expectation that individual managers and union members will comply with collective agreements made on their behalf. Thus, it may be argued, the foundation of 'voluntarism' in industrial relations is the control of individuals – if necessary by coercion.

Individual subordination to collective interests appears to clash with society's notion of 'freedom of the individual'. However, **the law** treats the employer/employee relationship differently from the trade union/member relationship. In the former, even though there has been some legislative restriction of management's exercise of control over its employees (e.g. unfair dismissal), the common law still supports the corporate power position of the organisation (management) by assuming the individual's contract of employment to be one made voluntarily between equals and by establishing an asymmetrical set of rights and obligations which clearly favour management over the individual. In the latter, particularly as a result of the 1980s legislation, the law is directed towards supporting individualism by allowing the individual to exercise freedom in respect of not joining a trade union or not taking part in industrial action. Such protection or advancement of the rights of the individual at the expense of the collectivity must weaken the solidarity, and therefore the power, of the trade union. Clearly, therefore, the issue of individualism versus collectivism is closely bound up with perceptions regarding what is the legitimate exercise of power and authority within the employment relationship.

3.5 Rights and responsibilities

A **'right'** is generally defined as 'a just or legal claim or title' or 'that which is due to anyone by law, tradition or nature' and appears to rest on two distinctive groups of concepts. First, there are concepts (such as 'freedom' and 'entitlement') which seem to imply a positive approach wherein the 'right' is regarded as being fundamental in nature and universally applicable to all – for example, a right to freedom of speech. However, such freedom may not be absolute and without constraint where it impinges on the right or freedom of others – for example, the constraints placed on freedom of speech in respect of libel, slander, incitement to racial hatred, etc. Second, there are concepts (such as 'privilege' or 'immunity') which suggest a negative approach wherein the 'right' is regarded as a special advantage not given to others or an exemption from a general obligation or duty – for example, the 'right to strike' in the UK is based on providing immunity from a tort claim for damages. It is important to recognise that such an immunity does not remove the 'wrong'; it is only the sanction for committing that 'wrong' which is waived. It is this latter notion which gives rise to the idea that a 'right' is something which has to be earned.

Perhaps one of the most fundamental 'rights' issues in industrial relations is that of **managerial prerogative** or **management's right to manage**. 'Prerogative' is often defined as 'an exclusive right or privilege held by a person or group especially an hereditary or official right'. Managerial prerogative has been characterised by Storey as representing 'an area of decision making over which management believes it should have (and acts as if it does have) sole and exclusive rights of determination'[26], and by Marsh as carrying with it 'the implication that there are actions or areas for action so essential to management that these must remain unilaterally the property of management if management itself is to continue to exist'[27]. The idea of the existence of a managerial prerogative has been derived, initially, from the pre-eminence given to management's agency relationship to the owner (provider of capital) within the capitalist system and, more latterly, from its perceived monopoly of expertise to make the right organisational judgements and decisions. Arguably, it is against this perceived fundamental right that the rights of employees have to be judged. Perhaps management needs no more than an acceptance of its general socialised 'right to manage', whereas employees need a myriad of specific legislated rights if there is to be any sort of balance.

The term **'responsibility'** is defined as 'a duty, obligation or burden' or 'having control over something'. Again, the definitions seem to imply two very different views of the effect of a 'responsibility' on the individual. On the one hand, it seems to imply a constraint on the individual's freedom to act (the concept of accountability – 'I have a responsibility to'), while on the other hand, it seems to imply having the freedom or discretion to make decisions and exercise judgement (the concept of control – 'I have responsibility for'). Responsibility *to* and responsibility *for* are often interlinked – a manager may have a responsibility *to* (accountable) his or her superior *for* (control) the effective and efficient operation of a part of the organisation, while trade union leaders have a responsibility *to* their members *for* protecting their interests, maintaining and improving their terms and conditions of employment and maintaining the integrity, continuity and strength of the union as an organisation. It is important to recognise that a 'responsibility' may be either internally generated from within the individual's own personal perceptions and beliefs, or arise from the external expectations of others in a positive way (*given* to the individual) or negative way (*forced* on the individual).

The 'rights' and 'responsibilities' within a social relationship are not determined by one role unilaterally (unless that role has power to impose its expectations on others) but rather result from an interaction between different role expectations. It is the range, balance and **interaction between 'rights' and** '**responsibilities**', and the extent to which these are implicitly or explicitly stated and accepted or challenged, which demonstrate the nature and quality of social relationships. They reflect our social values and beliefs about the way we expect people to behave and relate to each other, what degree of freedom and/or control they have and what degree of accountability we expect in return. Ideally, perhaps, there should be congruence between the perceptions the different roles have of their respective rights and responsibilities, but there is always bound to be potential conflict between the idea that 'I should have the right' and 'we allow you the right' and between the responsibility a person seeks and that which is expected of them. At the same time, the rights and responsibilities of one will impinge on the rights and responsibilities of others.

So far as industrial relations is concerned, the explicit statement of 'rights' and 'responsibilities' may be codified and enforced within the bipartite rule making of the industrial relations system as well as being set out in society's legislation. The employment relationship is more than just a simple individual wage/work exchange (economic) or contract of employment (legal): it is also about the power and authority relationship between groups within the workplace. The fact that the interaction is, at least in part, determined by the perceived relative power relationship means that **the existence of 'rights' and 'responsibilities' is inextricably linked to the concepts of 'power' and 'authority'**. It might be argued that the law is simply an impartial expression of accepted social expectations about human behaviour and that the legal underpinning of rights is a reflection, codification and demonstration of society's willingness to provide protection and enforcement for those whose right is being infringed or restricted by others. However, much of the law in industrial relations may not be universally or even widely accepted, but may result from the views of a sectional interest within society predominating within the political system. Therefore, the explicit statement of 'rights' and 'responsibilities' within legislation may be little more than the use of state power to impose the beliefs and expectations of one group on others.

There appear to be some **interesting perceptions of the relationship between 'rights' and 'responsibilities'**:

- *Must a 'right' carry with it some equal and opposite 'responsibility'?* For example, does the right to strike also imply a responsibility to exercise that right with discretion (in particular, not to inflict irreparable harm to the employer or harm 'innocent' bystanders) and should that responsibility be codified in law (so curtailing or redefining the right)? This view is based on the belief that the 'right' is a 'privilege' which can be withdrawn if the behaviour in exercising that right is deemed by others to be unacceptable.

- *Does the existence of a 'right' imply a responsibility on the part of others to ensure that the right can be exercised effectively?* For example, it can be argued that the basic right of employees to associate and organise can have real meaning and effect only if a responsibility is placed on the employer to recognise and bargain with the employees' association and the employees have the further positive 'right' to withdraw labour temporarily without fear of losing their jobs.

- *Can responsibility, in terms of accountability, be invoked only if there is the right to control?* For example, reference is frequently made to both management's *responsibility* to secure the future well-being of the organisation and management's *right* to manage the organisation. Does the same then also apply in respect of a union's leadership?

■ *Are references to 'rights' and 'responsibilities' used simply to help justify (legitimise) particular perceptions and beliefs?* For example, during the 1980s the UK government espoused the view that 'unions have a responsibility to represent the views and interests of all their members', that a union's leadership and policies do not reflect the wishes of the 'silent majority' (who do not participate in union affairs) and, therefore, the union leadership should moderate its demands in order to secure the future prosperity of the organisations for which its members work and so protect the long-term interests of its members – the government's perception of what is responsible union behaviour!

3.6 Integrity and trust

Although the phrase 'it's a matter of principle' is heard frequently in industrial relations, there are many who perceive it to be largely a matter of *ad hoc* expediency based only on the principles of subterfuge, opportunism and 'wheeler-dealing'. However, the conduct of the personal relations which underpin industrial relations is very much concerned with the values of integrity and trust – whether between employee and supervisor, between shop steward and member, full-time official or manager, or between negotiators.

Integrity must be defined in terms of the **individual acting in accordance with his or her personal values and beliefs (ethics)** rather than in terms of the individual acting according to some 'universally accepted' code of conduct. Thus, a Marxist union representative seeking through his or her actions to overthrow capitalism and managerial authority is acting with as much integrity as the manager seeking to maintain them. The essential quality of integrity (honesty) is that the individual's words and actions should be seen by others to coincide and express a consistent set of values. A problem may arise for the individual where personal values and beliefs do not coincide with the organisational demands placed on the individual's role. In such a situation the incumbent must, if he or she is to maintain integrity and cannot change the organisational demands, either refuse to meet those demands and face any consequences or resign. If personal integrity is compromised (i.e. present statements or actions conflict with the values perceived by others to underlie previous statements or actions) then the trust and respect of others will be lost. It may be argued that the only 'matter of principle' in industrial relations is the maintenance of personal integrity.

Trust may be established only between people rather than between organisational collectivities called 'management' and 'union': inter-organisational trust stems from interpersonal trust. At a general level, but equally applicable to the interpersonal level, Fox[28] differentiates between 'high-trust' employment relationships, in which management and employees are prepared to accept an informal 'give and take' basis to their relationship, and 'low-trust' relationships where there is greater formalisation of the control within the relationship. Interpersonal trust exists where the individuals have confidence in, and feel able to rely on, one another not to seek actively, or even passively, to harm each other. In industrial relations, 'trust' does not require that the individuals will be completely 'open and frank' with each other because within their relationship each recognises that the other may be seeking maximum gain in a situation where there are competing interests and objectives. Rather, the establishment of trust requires the individual not to seek to subvert the other's position or relationship with third parties; to keep his or her word and agreements; to keep confidences or 'off the record' information; and, above all, to accept the legitimacy of the other's role and objectives. Finally, it is important to remember that it is difficult to establish trust but easy to lose it, and that, because trust is based on interpersonal relationships between individuals, it is not automatically transferable to new role incumbents.

■ Summary proposition

■ Perceptions in industrial relations are individual and value laden: they are based primarily on a belief of what is 'right' in respect of 'fairness' and the exercise of 'power' and 'authority'.

Activity   Think of some current or past situation (either from your workplace, personal life or more generally) which you felt to be 'unfair', or where you felt you had little 'power to influence' a decision, or where you did not 'trust' someone. Try to identify the factors which might have influenced your feelings and response to the situation, and the same for any other people directly involved.

■ Further reading

■ R. Hyman and I. Brough, *Social Values and Industrial Relations*, Blackwell, 1975. This examines the role of values and ideologies in industrial relations and the notion of fairness (particularly in respect of wage bargaining).

■ A. Fox, *Beyond Contract: Work, power and trust relations*, Faber, 1974. This examines the nature of power and authority in industry and its effect on the employment relationship.

■ C. Fisher and C. Rice, 'Managing messy moral matters: ethics and HRM', in J. Leopold, L. Harris and T. Watson (eds), *Strategic Human Resourcing: Principles, Perspectives and Practices*, FT Pitman, 1999. This chapter discusses a range of ethical issues and principles and the way in which HRM specialists may approach them.

References

1. R. Hyman and I. Brough, *Social Values and Industrial Relations*, Blackwell, 1975, p. 1.
2. C. Kerr and A. Siegal, 'The interindustry propensity to strike – an international comparison', in A. Kornhauser, R. Dubin and A. M. Ross (eds), *Industrial Conflict*, McGraw-Hill, 1954, p. 204.
3. P. Ackers, 'Back to basics? Industrial relations and the enterprise culture', *Employee Relations*, vol. 16, no. 8, 1994, p. 40.
4. W. Brown, 'Social determinants of pay', in G. M. Stephenson and C. J. Brotherton (eds), *Industrial Relations: A social psychological approach*, John Wiley, 1979, p. 122.
5. Hyman and Brough, *op. cit.*
6. F. Zweig, *The British Worker*, Penguin, 1952, p. 194.
7. Hyman and Brough, *op. cit.*, p. 8.
8. H. Koontz and C. O'Donnell, *Essentials of Management*, McGraw-Hill, 1974, p. 36.
9. R. Hyman, *Industrial Relations: a Marxist introduction*, Macmillan, 1975, p. 26.
10. J. M. Magenau and D. G. Pruitt, 'The social psychology of bargaining', in G. M. Stephenson and C. J. Brotherton (eds), *Industrial Relations: A social psychological approach*, John Wiley, 1979, p. 197.
11. P. S. Kirkbride and J. Durcan, 'Bargaining power and industrial relations', *Personnel Review*, 1987.
12. Magenau and Pruitt, *op. cit.*
13. Hyman, *op. cit.*
14. W. L. French and S. Raven, 'The basis of social power', in D. Cartwright (ed.), *Studies in Social Power*, Michigan, 1959.
15. G. Morgan, *Images of Organization*, Sage, 1997, pp. 170–98.
16. Magenau and Pruitt, *op. cit.*, p. 198.
17. Koontz and O'Donnell, *op. cit.*
18. A. Fox, *A Sociology of Work in Industry*, Collier Macmillan, 1971, p. 34. Reprinted with permission of the publisher.
19. *Ibid.*, pp. 45–6.
20. Hyman, *op. cit.*, p. 97.
21. Fox, *op. cit.*, p. 40.
22. D. Torrington and L. Hall, *Human Resource Management* (4th edn), Prentice Hall, 1998, p. 545.
23. J. Kelly, *Rethinking Industrial Relations: Mobilization, collectivism and long waves*, Routledge, 1998, p. 129.
24. *Ibid.*, p. 52.
25. S. Deery and J. Walsh, 'The decline of collectivism? A comparative study of white-collar employees in Britain and Australia', *British Journal of Industrial Relations*, vol. 37, no. 2, 1999, p. 250.
26. J. Storey, *Managerial Prerogative and the Question of Control*, Routledge & Kegan Paul, 1983, p. 102.
27. A. Marsh, *Concise Encyclopaedia of Industrial Relations*, Gower, 1979.
28. A. Fox, *Beyond Contract: work, power and trust relations*, Faber, 1974.

part two

Participants

Trade union development and function

Learning objectives

Trade unions are a type of organisation unique to industrial relations. By the end of this chapter, you should be able to:

- identify the defining characteristics of a 'trade union';

- explain the development of trade unions in the UK: in particular, the different organising principles which have been adopted, the nature and impact of legal regulation and the development of political representation and influence;

- understand the role of trade unions as a source of collective employee power and their functions in providing membership benefits and services, seeking to regulate terms and conditions of employment, representing employees in organisational decision making, promoting 'labour' interests in economic, social and political developments and influencing government policy;

- explain the concept of 'unionateness' and appreciate the influence of social stratification and class ideology in determining the character of unionism.

Definition

A trade union is any organisation, whose membership consists of employees, which seeks to organise and represent their interests both in the workplace and society and, in particular, seeks to regulate the employment relationship through the direct process of collective bargaining with management.

Key issues

While you are reading this chapter, you should keep the following points in mind:

- Trade unions are more than inanimate organisations; they are social groupings of *people* combining together as a means to meet *their* needs and interests. Therefore, it is important that we understand why *people* join (or don't join) and what *they* expect a trade union to do for *them*.

- Trade unions have continuously been faced by both management and government strategies anxious to constrain, rather than support, trade unionism and to protect managerial prerogative, capitalism and the existing social order. We should not be surprised, therefore, if unions have been 'adversarial' in the past and some are suspicious of 'partnership' in the present.

■ The nature of trade unionism is varied and dynamic (across time, groups and countries), reflecting different views of the employment relationship. In assessing union strategies, whether through collective bargaining, providing membership services or supporting statutory employment rights, we should consider their relative effectiveness in protecting and advancing the interests of their members.

4.1 Introduction

It is easy to view trade unions as simply 'economic' organisations which negotiate pay and conditions of employment with management on behalf of their members. However, trade unions are more than this. As Roberts noted in the late 1950s, they are, in reality, 'an expression of the fundamental right of men and women to organise themselves in order to protect and promote their interests by collective action'[1], while Towers argued in the late 1980s that they are 'much more than engines for converting bargaining power into improved pay and conditions for their members ... they are an integral and important part of the system of checks and balances which compose capitalist, liberal democracies'[2]. The function and activities of a 'trade union' are not confined exclusively to workplace, or even employment, issues. Trade unions are concerned about a broad spectrum of economic, industrial and social matters and this requires them to participate in a range of 'political' activities outside the workplace if they are to represent their members' interests.

Three elements are crucial in **distinguishing 'trade unions' from other organisations**: the nature of their membership (those who rely on the sale of their labour to provide their livelihood), their purpose (to protect and represent *employees*, provide them with collective power and support, and regulate their terms of employment), and the means they employ to achieve their purpose (emphasis on direct negotiations with the employer). However, it is important to recognise that the term 'trade union' can encompass a wide variety of organisations – ranging from traditional 'unions' (of one type or another) through 'enterprise' or 'house' unions and 'staff associations' to some 'professional associations'. At the same time, these organisations may use quite different means (at different levels of action) in pursuit of their objectives. It is the combination of membership, purpose and means which determines the character or unionateness of the organisation and its members.

Significantly, the UK legal definition of a trade union makes no reference to 'means'; it simply defines a trade union as 'an organisation, whether permanent or temporary, which consists wholly or mainly of workers of one or more descriptions and whose principal purposes include the regulation of relations between workers of that description and employers or employers' associations' (S.1, TULR(C)A, 1992). Furthermore, the two gradations of trade unions recognised by the law reflect only the economic workplace perception of their role:

- **Independent trade union** – a union declared by the Certification Officer to be 'not under the domination or control of an employer' and 'not liable to interference by an employer ... arising out of the provision of financial or material support or by any other means' (S.5, TULR(C)A, 1992);

- **Recognised trade union** – a union which is recognised by management 'to any extent, for the purpose of collective bargaining' (S.178(3), TULR(C)A, 1992).

4.2 Trade union development

The development of trade unionism in the UK, in common with other older industrialised countries, may be seen as a **social response to the advent of industrialisation and capitalism** (see Box 4.1). The earlier, largely agrarian, semi-feudal society relied primarily on a 'benevolent' state[3] and trade guilds to provide limited protection for peasants and artisans. The development of a new society based on the principle of a paid contractual relationship between 'employer' and 'employee', the emergence of a range of industrially based wage-earning classes, together with the withdrawal of the state from the determination of the terms of the new relationship, required 'employees' to create new institutions for their collective protection. The drawing together of individuals, as 'employees', into similar circumstances within new industrial organisations provided the focus for their collective interest.

The development of trade unionism in the **newly industrialised and industrialising countries** (particularly Asia and Africa) has not only, generally, taken place over a shorter period of time but has also been subject to different influences[4]. First, the general lack of industrialisation during their colonial period, coupled with the use of migrant labour in the primary producing sectors,

Box 4.1	Trade union development

'It is concerned with the aspirations and the fears of ordinary people, with their endeavours and their struggles, with their modest successes and their setbacks.' (H. Pelling, *A History of British Trade Unionism* (3rd edn), Penguin, 1976, p. 9.)

'The development of organized labour is a complex process based on changes in the economy and the ways in which people, in historically determined circumstances, define and pursue their interests. The possibility of collective labour organization is imminent in capitalist relations of production, which simultaneously divorce the worker from the means of production, and make production dependent on the social organization of labour. Yet both the extent and the form of unionism has varied widely over time and between societies.' (J. Waddington and C. Whitston, 'Trade unions: growth, structure and policy', in P. Edwards (ed.), *Industrial Relations: Theory and practice in Britain*, Blackwell, 1995, pp. 151–2.)

resulted in limited development of unionism (primarily among permanent employees in the public sector, including docks and railways). Second, trade unions provided a significant nucleus for 'independence' movements, including those against Japanese occupation in Asian countries, which engendered more of an 'anti-colonial' (political) rather than 'anti-capitalist' (industrial) ideology (although the two exploitations were interlinked). Third, the adoption of a strong post-independence government role in planning and directing economic development, particularly in the Asian 'tiger' economies of Singapore, Malaysia, South Korea and Taiwan (ROC), has tended to include government policy 'to subordinate the labour movement and "guide" trade unionism to broader considerations of national economic development as defined by the ruling élite'[5] – more like the former Communist eastern European 'corporatist' or 'transmission' belt form of unionism than the 'capitalist' unionism of western Europe or the USA. However, the wave of industrial action to pursue sectional wage claims in South Korea following the introduction of democratic government in 1987 suggests that securing a 'fair' share of any economic gain still remains integral to trade unionism[6].

This section briefly examines British trade union development in three interrelated areas: organisational, legal and political (see Figure 4.1).

Organisational development

It is difficult to identify the precise origins of modern trade union organisation in the UK. Tannenbaum[7] argued that trade unions should be regarded as an extension and development of the medieval craft guilds because of their similarity of concern for industrial and employment matters (including pay) – albeit that they existed within quite differing social and technological environments. The Webbs[8], however, argued that it is the uniqueness of their membership being confined to employees which makes trade unions qualitatively different from the guilds and, therefore, a separate distinct organisational category.

The real beginnings of UK trade unionism lie in the **Friendly Societies** established by craftsmen in the late eighteenth century. Members contributed a small amount each week and were entitled to receive benefit in the event of sickness, unemployment, retirement or death – **mutual insurance**. These societies also provided a forum for discussing wages and other employment matters which, on occasion, led to the formulation of a 'wage claim', however, these were generally couched in a subservient manner and processed not through recognised channels of collective bargaining but in the form of a petition to the employer or Parliament. Sometimes these societies established a loose co-operation to provide assistance to members who were 'on the tramp' – providing lodgings, help in seeking work and finance to move on to the next town if work was not available. Less often the co-operation involved financial or other help to a society whose members were in dispute with their employers. Co-operation was not permanent and might be withdrawn because of a shortage of funds or the rivalries which existed between societies.

Following the repeal of the Combination Acts in 1824, workers could

Figure 4.1 Trade union development

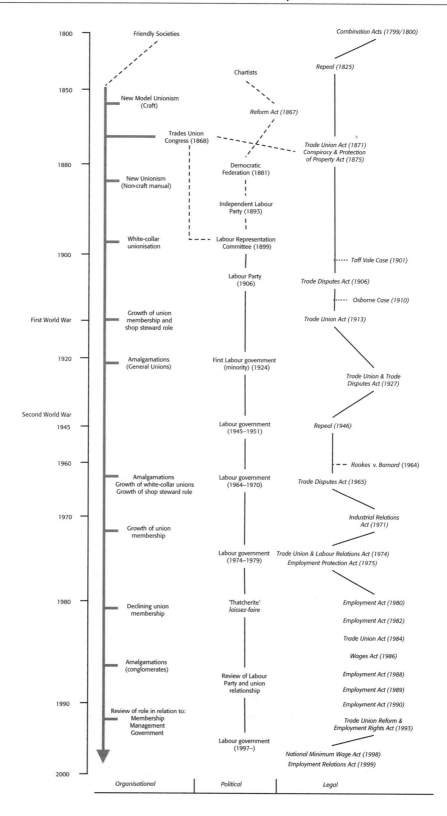

| Organisational | Political | Legal |

organise trade unions openly rather than under the guise of Friendly Societies. Attempts were made to establish trade unions on a more national basis and to widen their employment range. However, these organisations encountered many difficulties and often existed for only a few years. They relied on the officers of one of the member societies to provide the secretariat for the whole organisation, and were, therefore, subject to the rivalry, and even hostility, which existed between the local societies. Attempts were also made to establish **one consolidated trade union** to represent all workers irrespective of their trade or locality as part of a process of mobilising the 'working classes' on a collective basis to press for political and social reform. Perhaps the best-known example is the Grand National Consolidated Trade Union (1834). Organisationally, the GNCTU was a matrix federation of separate trade or industry sections linked together at the district level. Like similar organisations of the period, it lasted for only a short period because its limited funds were soon drained by a series of strikes.

In the mid-nineteenth century the first modern trade unions were founded among craftsmen – **new model unionism** (the Amalgamated Society of Engineers in 1851 – now AEEU). Apprentice-served craftsmen not only had the ability to read and write, which was essential for the development and maintenance of an organisation, and were better paid and in more regular employment than other workers, but, importantly, also had industrial strength derived from their possession of a scarce skill. The new 'model' involved an organisational hierarchy from national to branch level with a separate head office and full-time General Secretary, rather than relying on the officers of a dominant branch or society to carry out this function as in earlier attempts. Despite the apparent move towards a bureaucratic form of organisation, they relied heavily on their lay membership to administer and govern the union. As these unions achieved the permanency lacking in earlier national societies, so it became possible for them to secure recognition from employers and undertake collective bargaining.

See Chapter 5 – Trade union organisation and structure

During the second half of the nineteenth century **trade union co-operation** became established at the local and national levels, initially to represent the unions' views to government and seek reforms in legislation. Although trade unions had previously worked together on a transient basis, they now joined with other types of organisations which sought to represent the 'working classes' on a more formal, permanent basis in local **Trades Councils**. In 1868 a congress of Trades Councils representatives, called to discuss issues of concern to the trade union movement, laid the foundation for the present **Trades Union Congress** (TUC). Further congresses were held involving trade union representatives and, in 1871, a Parliamentary Committee with a full-time secretary was established as the executive body of Congress to provide a focus for political pressure (this committee became, in 1920, the General Council of the TUC). In 1895 Trades Council delegates were excluded and, from that point, the TUC's membership was confined solely to trade unions.

During the 1880s non-craft manual workers began to organise on a permanent basis – **new unionism** (gas workers' and dockers' unions were formed in 1889, the forerunners of the modern GMB and T&GWU respectively). These unions organised the semi-skilled and unskilled, poorer-paid workers and had to rely heavily on organising large groups as their source of industrial power because, as Lovell noted, 'it was only in times of exceptionally high employment that the mass of workers possessed any bargaining power'[9]. Cole noted that as a result they 'dispensed with friendly benefits altogether, and concentrated on the possession of funds for use in strikes and lockouts and in the expenses of organising and administration'[10]. Furthermore, because of their largely illiterate membership, they relied more heavily than the earlier craft unions on the use of outsiders to organise and run the union. At the same time **white-collar unionism** was also being established (National Union of Elementary Teachers in 1870 (now NUT); Clerks Union in 1890 (later APEX); and Municipal Officers Association in 1894 (later NALGO)).

By the end of the nineteenth century the foundations of the modern British trade union movement had been laid – permanent organisations representing a wide range of manual and non-manual employees with the TUC providing a focal point for co-ordination. However, the continuing development of unionism still required individuals to be prepared to take action at their workplace to secure and protect union 'rights' and 'principles', and in this they were often supported by the local community (see Box 4.2).

The increase in union membership and a change in management and government attitude towards trade unionism, in order to secure co-operation during the First World War, resulted in the increasing **appearance of shop stewards** who, as Pelling notes, 'had existed before the war, but they had received little general notice, and their activities were often curbed by intolerant employers'[11]. The period was closely associated with the political growth of the Shop Stewards Movement and syndicalism which, although confined to a small number of major engineering, shipbuilding and munitions factories, sought to mobilise the rank and file union movement to secure the workers' control of industry. Although the shop steward role declined during the interwar period,

Box 4.2	1919 – victory at Bodmin

'Southwest England was another area of militancy among asylum staffs, and yet again women figured prominently. The first strike at Bodmin asylum, Cornwall, resulted in a glorious victory. Five nurses, sacked for wearing union badges on duty, had been supported by thirty-four other nurses. The medical superintendent first dismissed the other thirty-four, then offered to reinstate all but the original five. Their reply was "All or none". They stayed out on strike for the rest of the week, while the men went to work on the male side. They even had the slogan "All or none" inscribed on a banner.

The strike caused a sensation in the town and sympathy was widespread among the public. The strikers – who were resident staff – were billeted and provisions in plenty were delivered to the picket lines. The town crier announced strike meetings and a Salvation Army band preceded the strikers as they marched through the town. The strikers won reinstatement, the right to wear union badges and, subsequently, a revision of their wages and conditions. The matron, Miss Hiney, later resigned "in view of medical opinion on the state of her heart".'

Source: M. Carpenter, *All for One: campaigns and pioneers in the making of COHSE*, COHSE, 1980, p. 23.

its re-emergence from the 1960s, as a consequence of full employment and the reform and formalisation of industrial relations at the organisational level, led Turner *et al.*[12] to adopt the phrase 'parallel unionism'. The workplace representative increasingly became the focal point for the members and industrial relations activity and, thereby, a potential threat and challenge to the formal, official union organisation.

While the **number of trade unions has declined** from a peak of 1,384 in 1920 to 234 in 1997, trade unions have become larger in size. At the peak of UK union membership (13.3 million in 1979), one-third were members of the three 'super' unions, each with over 1 million members (T&GWU with 2.1 million, AEU with 1.2 million and GMB with 1.1 million). In 1997, despite the decline in union membership, two-thirds of all trade union members were in the nine largest unions (each with 250,000+ members) and 82 per cent were in the 16 unions with 100,000+ members. The process of union amalgamations has resulted in the **evolution of 'open' general or conglomerate unions**. The consequent reduction in membership homogeneity engendered by this process led unions to reconstitute their internal organisation so as better to reflect and represent the differing needs and aspirations of diverse groups within their membership. The variety of sectional interests displayed in earlier periods by a multiplicity of trade unions is now reflected within the unions' internal organisational arrangements.

Since the early 1960s there has been not only a substantial 'up and down' in the number of trade union members in the UK but also a significant shift in the composition of the membership. The increase during the 1960s and 1970s (from 9.8 million in 1960 to 13.3 million in 1979) was primarily due to the **growth of non-manual employment and unionism**[13]. Similarly, the bulk of the decline in trade union membership since 1979 has been among manual employees in the manufacturing sector; so that, union membership is now significantly skewed towards non-manual and public sector employees[14]. Indeed, in 1997 the only 'super' union was the public services union UNISON with 1.2 million members and ten of the 16 unions with 100,000+ members could be regarded as primarily non-manual and/or 'public' sector oriented (see Table 4.3).

Changing industrial and employment structures during the 1980s and 1990s, combined with management 'labour flexibility' strategies, have required unions to develop their own counter-strategies to recruit more members among the private service industries, women, part-time employees, young people, ethnic groups, etc. to replace the decline in traditional male, full-time manual union members in the manufacturing sector. This has included the development of organisational arrangements to be more representative of these interests (for example, reserved places on the NEC and other committees for women, the establishment of 'black' sections, and more full-time officers specialising in equality issues and the problems of part-time members).

Legal development

The legal rights of trade unions reflect the attitude of the government of the day. However, even where legislation is established it has to be interpreted by the courts and while the trade union movement may be able to influence the nature and extent of legislation, its influence on the interpretation of that legislation by the courts is very limited.

The **Combination Acts (1799–1800)** were the last in a line of legislation (originating in the Statute of Artificers (1351)) which restricted the freedom of people to combine in organisations to further their interests because they might be used to subvert the process of government and act as a cover for rebellion. The combinations affected by these Acts were already illegal under both common law and other statutes and the penalties which could be imposed by the courts under these Acts were, in fact, less harsh: for example, the maximum penalty was two months' imprisonment compared to seven years' transportation given to the Tolpuddle Martyrs in 1834 under the Unlawful Oaths Act (1797).

The legal approach towards trade unions was founded on the **civil doctrine of restraint of trade** (any agreement which restricted trade or competition was void and unenforceable) and the **criminal offence of conspiracy**. These concepts have played an important part in the legal development of trade unions. The attitude of the courts was clearly seen in 1855, after the repeal of the Combination Acts, when it was argued that to treat a trade union as anything other than an illegal agreement in restraint of trade 'would establish a principle upon which the fantastic and mischievous notion of a "Labour Parliament" might be realised for regulating the wages and the hours of labour in every branch of trade all over the empire' with 'the most disastrous consequences'[15]. This restrictive approach was seen also in the individual employee's contractual position. Since 1351 employees had been guilty of a criminal offence if they failed to fulfil the terms of their contract of employment. Wedderburn noted that 'in 1854 over 3,000 workers were imprisoned for leaving or neglecting their work' while in 1872, despite revisions in the Master and Servant Act (1867), 'the figure reached 17,100 prosecutions and 10,400 convictions'[16].

The Combination Acts were repealed in 1824–5. However, Hawkins argued that the effect of this was to provide 'a legal freedom to organize but no corresponding freedom to pursue the objectives of trade unionism'[17]. Certainly, Wedderburn pointed out that even when the criminal offences relating to intimidation and threats were amended by the Molestation of Workmen Act (1859), so as to exclude peaceful persuasion of employees to strike from criminal liability, 'many of the judges' decisions scarcely registered this amendment'[18]. It was not until the 1870s that there were the beginnings of a real change in the legal status of trade unions.

The **Trade Union Act (1871)** and the **Conspiracy and Protection of Property Act (1875)** established that trade unions were not to be regarded as criminal conspiracies simply because their purpose was in restraint of trade and that two or more persons acting in contemplation or furtherance of a trade dispute could not be considered a criminal conspiracy unless the act undertaken would be criminal if committed by one person. At the same time, the Employers and Workmen Act (1875) removed criminal liability from the employee for breaching the contract of employment. However, the Conspiracy and Protection of Property Act maintained criminal sanctions for gas and water workers who, by striking, deprived consumers of their supply – this provision was extended in 1919 to include electricity workers and was not removed from these groups until the Industrial Relations Act (1971).

However, the legislation still left trade unions open to legal claims based on **civil, as opposed to criminal, liability for conspiracy**. In 1901 it was held that union officials organising a boycott amounted to a conspiracy to injure (*Quinn* v *Leathem*) and that damages could be enforced against the funds of a union (*Taff Vale Railway Co.* v *Amalgamated Society of Railway Servants*). This meant that if, during an industrial dispute, the union was successful in exerting economic pressure on the employer then the union or its officials could be liable to reimburse the employer's loss through a claim for damages. It is not surprising, as Vester and Gardiner pointed out, that the 1871 Act 'began to be regarded by many trade unionists as the most oppressive of all the oppressive legislation that had encumbered the growth of their unions, while some blamed the courts for having robbed them of the immunities Parliament had intended to give them'[19]. The position was remedied by the **Trade Disputes Act (1906)** which set the basis of the law relating to industrial action until the 1980s by protecting union funds from claims for damages, by providing immunity against claims based on civil conspiracy or inducing breach of the contract of employment and by making peaceful picketing lawful.

However, in 1910 a further omission came to light (*Osborne* v *Amalgamated Society of Railway Servants*) when it was held that it was unlawful for a trade union to raise funds for or contribute to a political party. This was a severe constraint on the unions' ability to further their members' interests by actively assisting in the development of the newly founded Labour Party. The position was reversed by the **Trade Union Act (1913)** which allowed trade unions to participate in political activities provided they established a separate political fund to finance such activities and individual members had the right and opportunity to opt out of contributing to such a fund.

Thus, by the beginning of the First World War trade unions had been removed from both criminal and civil liability for actions in pursuit of an industrial dispute and were free to support political parties. However, the interwar period was characterised by not only economic recession but also a regression in the legal status of trade unions. The **Trade Disputes and Trade Union Act (1927)** (following the General Strike in 1926) not only restricted sympathetic strikes and those which sought to 'coerce' the government but also declared various forms of industrial action to be illegal 'intimidation', required members to 'contract in' rather than 'contract out' of the union's political fund (reducing union affiliation to the Labour Party by about a third), prohibited Crown servants from joining trade unions which had political objectives or were affiliated to 'outside' bodies such as the TUC and prohibited local authorities and other public bodies from operating closed shops. Although, the Act was repealed in 1946 by the Labour government, it has many similarities with the legislation introduced in the 1980s.

The period from the end of the Second World War until the 1970s was virtually free of trade union legislation. However, in *Rookes* v *Barnard* (1964) it was held that a threat to induce a breach of contract by going on strike could amount to conspiracy to intimidate. Grunfeld pointed out that 'what startled the trade union world was that, after ... more than half a century of case law ... there still remained coiled in the common law the possibility of an action against union officials for crushing damages and costs for threatening strike action in breach of contracts of employment'[20]. The situation was quickly remedied by the **Trade Disputes Act (1965)**.

See Chapter 8 –
The government

Since 1971, as Lewis noted, 'successive governments representing different interests and ideologies have turned the legal framework of industrial relations into a political football'[21]. First, the Conservative government tried to balance some positive gains for trade unions (statutory recognition procedure, rights to disclosure of information, etc.) against greater statutory regulation of trade union activities (particularly, the closed shop and industrial action) – **Industrial Relations Act (1971)**. Although the Act existed for only two years, it provoked extensive hostility and active resistance from trade unions (many of whom refused to register under the Act) and resulted in court cases involving the imprisonment of shop stewards and the sequestration of union funds[22]. Then, in 1974–5, the Labour government not only restored trade union immunities to the pre-1971 position (**Trade Union and Labour Relations Act, 1974**) but also extended support for trade unions and collective bargaining by, in particular, confirming the union's right to disclosure of information and adding the right to be consulted in a redundancy, the right to time off for trade union activities and the right to refer a claim to the CAC that an employer was not observing the recognised or general terms and conditions (**Employment Protection Act, 1975**).

In marked contrast, following their election after the 1978–9 so-called 'winter of discontent', the **Conservative government's strategy during the 1980s**, based on a liberalist/*laissez-faire* ideology, was to curtail the perceived power of trade unions, allow management to re-exert its prerogative, promote 'responsible' trade unionism and protect individual members against union 'tyranny'. The legislation was introduced in stages – eight Acts in 13 years – and had three main elements:

- ▪ It restricted the scope of lawful industrial action, thereby reducing trade union power.
- ▪ It established what Lewis referred to as 'rights to disorganise' by establishing non-membership rights, thereby undermining the maintenance of collective relations.
- ▪ It intervened in the internal affairs of trade unions by promoting a representational democratic model, thereby reducing the influence of 'activists' on union decision making.

As in the 1920s, the introduction of this legislation coincided with adverse economic circumstances and management strategies which weakened trade unionism. Initially it was resisted by trade unions; including, as in the early 1970s, a number of major disputes where, through employer action to enforce these new rights, unions were fined for contempt of court and had their funds sequestrated. However, the defeat of the NUM in 1985 after a year-long strike (which divided the union and communities and involved confrontational mass picketing and large police operations to enforce the 'right to work'), coupled with the decreasing prospect of an early election of a Labour government, led to trade unions resigning themselves to having to work within this legal regulation. Most importantly, the 'new' Labour Party also made it clear in the early 1990s that, although it would aim to introduce some supportive legislation when elected, it did not intend to repeal much, if any, of this legislation.

Since its election in 1997, the Labour government has introduced two major pieces of employment legislation. Perhaps most importantly it has reintroduced a statutory procedure to support union recognition, established a new legal right for trade union officials to accompany members in grievance and disciplinary hearings, and begun to support the concept of a positive 'right to strike' by extending 'unfair dismissal' to protect employees undertaking a lawful strike (**Employment Relations Act, 1999**). In line with its theme of 'fairness and social justice' the government has also introduced, for the first time in the UK, a national minimum wage (**National Minimum Wage Act, 1998**).

Political development

The nineteenth century was a period of considerable political as well as industrial change. It started with two major political parties (Conservative and Liberal) and finished with the emergence of a third (Labour) representing the interests of the 'working classes'. In their early years, trade unions enlisted the support of radical members of existing parties to lead their agitation for industrial reforms and act as their voice within Parliament. Pelling notes that, even during the period of the **Chartists Movement**, 'which, confused and inchoate though it was, nevertheless had ambitious national aims based upon the belief in the identity of interests of the entire working class'[23], there were no formal direct links between Chartism and the developing trade union movement. Indeed, he suggests that, while the development of trade unionism was greatest in times of booming employment and among those groups of workers who were relatively unaffected by the industrial changes of the nineteenth century, the impetus for political reform and action came from those who were suffering the greatest effects of these changes and during periods of economic slump.

Even after the Reform Act (1867), which gave urban workers the vote, most trade union leaders supported the Liberal Party and favoured political action within the established political system rather than the creation of a new party. However, by the late nineteenth century organisations with socialist orientations had been formed to give political expression to the 'working-class movement'. Finally, in 1893, the **Independent Labour Party** was formed which sought to adopt a middle-of-the-road stance by both opposing collaboration with the Liberal Party and rejecting the revolutionary policies of the socialist parties. Although trade unions had already achieved representation in Parliament (11 union MPs in 1885), they either sat as Liberals or were prepared to co-operate closely with them. A reconciliation between the leadership of the major unions and the socialists concerning the approach and form of political representation was eventually achieved in 1899 when the TUC Parliamentary Committee agreed to convene a special congress of interested organisations to examine how to improve labour representation in Parliament. This resulted in the establishment of the **Labour Representation Committee (LRC)**. The initial response of the trade unions was mixed; less than half of the TUC's membership was represented at the special congress. In the 1900 general election the LRC managed to secure the election of only two MPs but in 1906 it won 29 seats and officially changed its name to the **Labour Party**.

During the twentieth century the Labour Party grew and not only replaced the Liberal Party as the viable alternative to the Conservative Party but also provided the UK government for over one-third of the postwar period. The **relationship between trade unions and the Labour Party** was, according to John Monks (TUC General Secretary), based on a 'set of shared values ... [which] included beliefs in the primacy of collective bargaining, in an expanding welfare state, and state intervention to promote economic growth and full employment'[24]. The trade unions accounted for 90 per cent of the Party's membership, 80 per cent of its annual income, sponsored almost 50 per cent of its MPs and had significant decision-making influence in the Annual Conference and NEC[25]. However, by no means do all trade unions affiliate to the Labour Party – in particular, most public sector unions have not affiliated to any political party, partly because of the wide spectrum of political views of their membership and partly because of their perceived relationship to government at the local and national levels. Similarly, the level of membership 'contracting out' of the political levy in some affiliated unions is 50 per cent or more and, during the 1980s, there was little doubt that 'a majority of trade union members no longer vote for the trade unions' party'[26].

The trade unions found, as early as 1924, that their 'special' relationship with the Labour Party did not necessarily result in a subservient Labour government; rather, there was 'a permanent difference in point of view between the government on the one hand and the trade unions on the other ... the trade unions had different functions to perform than the functions of government'[27]. When, in the late 1980s, the Labour Party leadership became increasingly concerned about their apparent unelectability, they set about constitutional and policy reforms aimed at modernising the party image – including **'loosening' the link between trade unions and the Labour Party**. Edwards *et al.* argue that both Party leaders and union leaders felt the move was desirable: 'the latter because many of their members, and particularly those groups that they wish to attract into membership, were hostile to the party; the former, because the charge that policy was dominated by the "union bosses" was seen as an electoral liability'[28]. Certainly, McIlroy believes that the Labour leadership was able to achieve this change largely because most union leaders shared their 'managerialist and consumerist approaches' which favoured 'top-down decision-making, plebiscitary democracy and marginalized activists'[29]. At the same time, the 'new' Labour Party made great efforts to appeal to management and the business community, including the preparation of a special Business Manifesto for the 1997 election. The result of these changes, according to Monks, is that 'trade unions are part of the coalition supporting Labour, but not the senior partners as of old'[30]. Certainly, the AEEU has expressed concern about the low level of 'manual working class' MPs in 'new' Labour[31], while the leader of the FBU has gone so far as to suggest that the trade unions should consider completely severing their link with the Labour Party[32].

It is important to recognise that the pattern of union development in each

Country profile 4.1   France – state supported unionism

French trade unions, like those in The Netherlands, Belgium and Italy, are divided on an ideological basis. At the beginning of the twentieth century there were two confederations: CGT (anarcho-syndicalist) which believed in the 'liberation' of workers through direct action, and the CFTC (Catholic) which espoused co-operation between labour and capital in line with Catholic doctrine. After two earlier splits, the CGT finally divided in 1948 over the issue of its strong link with the Communist Party, with the 'reformers' leaving to create the FO based on a more 'pragmatic socialism'. Similarly, the CFTC split in 1964 with the majority 'reformers' leaving to create the CFDT based on a 'democratic Christian socialism'. Each confederation has industry unions which compete with each other for the same members. In 1944, the CGC was created to represent supervisory, technical and managerial occupations across all industries.

All five of these central confederations have legal 'representative union' status at the national level, which gives them exclusive ('quasi-monopoly') rights in collective bargaining and the nomination of representatives at the workplace and to industrial tribunals. A sixth federation (UNSA, established in 1993, with most of its members in education and the police) has only limited recognition in parts of the public sector. The state has also, since 1936, legislatively supported the principle of national industry bargaining as the preferred structure and the minister can extend the terms of an agreement to make it binding on all employers in the industry – some 400 agreements each year are dealt with this way.

Not surprisingly, the unions have concentrated their attention on the 'socio-economic–political' forum at national level. They have not had to rely on securing recognition from individual employers in order to achieve the collective regulation of terms and conditions of employment or to provide the basis for their strength and influence in such collective bargaining. It has been sufficient, in the past, to rely on 'political activists' to mobilise sufficient demonstration of worker support to influence, in particular, the government. Hence, the general low level of union membership density – less than 10 per cent, although it is higher in some major manufacturers and parts of the public sector.

Over the past 20 years there have been developments in two directions. First, the Auroux report on 'Workers' Rights' led to legislation in 1982 which, in particular, required all organisations with union branches to undertake annual negotiations on wages and working hours – but there was no requirement to reach an agreement! In 1995, there were some 8,550 such company agreements covering about 3 million people (20 per cent of the workforce), although under half dealt with pay (most of the others dealt with working time).

Second, the unions have been involved in developing a series of multi-industry agreements on 'labour flexibility' – technological change, working time, equality, working conditions, fixed-term and temporary contracts and vocational training. Despite differences between the confederations (the FO and CFTC being reluctant to sign some of the agreements), this approach reflects a continuing use of traditional structures (where the unions are strongest) to seek to regulate the introduction of management labour flexibility strategies at the organisation level.

While mass 'political' mobilisation has not died out completely (as evidenced by the wave of industrial action against government policies in early 1995), nevertheless French unions seem to have moved towards a more 'social institutionalisation' approach to their role in industrial relations.

Federation	Membership	
	1976	1994
Confédération Générale du Travail (CGT)	2.1 million	480,000
Force Ouvrière (FO)	926,000	480,000
Confédération Française des Travailleurs Chrétiens (CFTC)	223,000	170,000
Confédération Française Démocratique du Travail (CFDT)	829,000	500,000
Confédération Générale des Cadres (CGC)	326,000	200,000
Union Nationale des Syndicats Autonomes (UNSA)	–	300,000

Source: J. Goetschy, 'France: the limits of reform' in A. Ferner and R. Hyman (eds), *Changing Industrial Relations in Europe*, (2nd edn), Blackwell, 1998.

See also Country profile 6.2 and Box 9.1.

Country profile 4.2   South Africa – political unionism

South African trade unionism has a complex history inextricably bound up with the socio-political legacy of *apartheid*. Its development has, because of the hostile environment, comprised a series of initiatives, shifting alliances and discontinuous organisation intertwined with the campaign for social and political change. In this sense, it is very reminiscent of the organising attempts of British trade unions in the nineteenth century. It is only since the mid-1980s, following the Labour Relations Act (1979) which gave legal recognition to trade unions representing black workers, that a degree of relative coherence and stability has existed.

In 1994, total union membership in South Africa was about 2.5 million workers (24 per cent union density). Trade union structure is characterised by political division, diverse organising principles and multi-unionism, which has resulted in a number of central trade union confederations (as well as 'independent' unions):

■ *COSATU* (Congress of South African Trade Unions) was established in 1985 but its antecedents, in attempts to support and organise black workers and belief in multi- or non-racial trade unionism, stretch back to the mid-1950s. It is by far the largest (1.5 million members in 19 unions) and, because of its close links with the African National Congress (ANC), the most important of the confederations.

■ *NACTU* (National Council of Trade Unions) was established in 1986 but, like COSATU, can trace a line of previous organisations supporting the principles of 'black consciousness'. It is the second largest confederation (330,000 members in 18 unions).

■ *FEDSAL* (Federation of South African Labour), established in 1985, is multi-racial and represents mainly non-manual employees (230,000 members in 17 unions). It seeks to provide an independent, moderate non-political union voice

and does not support the principle of industrial unionism.

■ *SACLA* (South African Confederation of Labour Associations) has the longest continuous history (established in 1957) but represents only white workers. It has about 80,000 members concentrated in mining and iron and steel.

■ *UWUSA* (United Workers' Union of South Africa) was established in 1986, claims to be a federation, but has only about 28,000 members and is closely linked with the Inkatha Party of Natal and Transvaal.

■ *FITU* (Federation of Independent Trade Unions) is a loose grouping of 'independent' unions to act as a voice at national level.

The fragmentation and potential competition between unions (both within and between federations and with the 'independent' unions) has led COSATU and NACTU, with some limited success, to encourage mergers and rationalisation within their respective federations. Both federations also support, in principle, greater unity through the merger of their federations, thereby increasing their influence at the national level. Significantly, COSATU, NACTU and FEDSAL are the only 'labour' representatives on the National Economic Development and Labour Council (set up by the government in 1995 to provide a forum for discussion and consensus on proposed policies and legislation).

The abolition of political *apartheid* by the election of a black majority government, while it has not removed the political dimension from trade unionism in South Africa, has provided an opportunity for them to concentrate more on the trade union issues that confront them and their members: the economic situation and management strategies at the workplace.

Source: S. Bendix, *Industrial Relations in the New South Africa* (3rd edn), Juta (Cape Town), 1996 (Chapter 7).

Country profile 4.3 Singapore – union and government symbiosis

Singapore is a 'young tiger' economy which has achieved a high rate of economic development and growth. Its initial emphasis on labour-intensive industries has been replaced by a drive towards high-technology, high value-added, capital-intensive industries and services. Its society and industrial relations are underpinned by a 'unitarist ideology and a strategy which seeks to mobilise the workforce to meet the economic objectives of the nation (city) state' (1:117). This finds expression in the 'symbiotic' relationship between the National Trade Union Congress (NTUC) and People's Action Party (PAP) – which has governed Singapore since it achieved independence in 1959 – 'which makes it difficult to distinguish government from unions in Singapore's industrial relations' (1:101).

Trade unions in Singapore, like those in many other developing countries, played an important part in the anti-colonial independence struggle. In 1961, three years after independence, there was a political 'schism' in PAP which was reflected in a break-up of the Singapore Trade Union Congress (STUC). The Singapore Association of Trade Unions (SATU) allied itself with the breakaway political left wing and had the majority of trade unions in the private sector. The NTUC allied with the ruling majority of PAP. In 1963 the STUC was banned and many of its union leaders, along with prominent leaders of the breakaway party, were arrested. Also, the discretion given to the Registrar under the law on trade union registration has been used on a number of occasions against non-NTUC unions or NTUC unions which have not conformed to NTUC policy (particularly on restructuring). There are few unions not affiliated to the NTUC.

The 'symbiotic' relationship between the NTUC and government can be seen in the following ways:

■ NTUC support for the government's strategies for economic development;

■ PAP MPs being trade union leaders and members of the NTUC NEC;

■ The NTUC General Secretary being a Cabinet Minister without Portfolio;

■ A formal NTUC/PAP liaison committee.

Singapore's trade union structure is mixed. In 1981 the NTUC decided to restructure two of its 'omnibus' unions (the Singapore Industrial Labour Organisation and the Pioneer Industries Employees' Union) into nine industrial unions. However, later in the year, following a report by the statutory National Productivity Board advocating the adoption of Japanese employment practices, the NTUC committed themselves to the development of enterprise unions. In 1999, about 40 per cent of the NTUC's 70 affiliated unions could be classified as 'enterprise' based. However, the majority of the NTUC's membership remains in a small number of larger industrial type unions.

Significantly, the labour legislation and the existence of a National Wages Council to provide general wage guidelines has 'reduced the collective bargaining power of unions ... [and] ... removes a major incentive for joining unions' (2:65). Over the years, the NTUC has built up a range of commercial organisations (supermarkets, insurance, taxis) for its members which, together with its workers' recreation and education activities, are managed by the Singapore Labour Federation. However, union density in Singapore has declined from just over 30 per cent in 1957 to about 15 per cent in 1999.

Sources:
1. C. Leggett, 'Singapore', in S. J. Deery and R. Mitchell (eds), *Labour Law and Industrial Relations in Asia*, Longman Cheshire (Melbourne), 1993.
2. Chew Soon Beng and R. Chew, 'The development of industrial relations strategy in Singapore', in A. Verna, T. A. Kochan and R. D. Lansbury (eds), *Employment Relations in the Growing Asian Economies*, Routledge, 1995.

See also Box 9.4.

See Country profiles
4.1, 4.2 and 4.3

country is unique and reflects the past and present socio-political circumstances and processes of that country. In some countries trade unionism may be fragmented and mirror the political divisions within the society (France and South Africa), it may play an important role in some wider socio-political struggle for change (Singapore and South Africa), it may come to rely on government support for its collective bargaining role (France) or it may, even, become the industrial 'wing' of the government (Singapore).

Trade union membership

A wide range of factors can influence the level of unionisation:

- **Macro-economic climate** (in particular, inflation and unemployment). While high rates of inflation may induce employees to unionise as a means of maintaining or improving their standard of living (positive effect), conversely, continuing high levels of unemployment may reduce membership as the unemployed relinquish their membership and those in employment become less prepared to join or organise because of fears for their jobs (negative effect)[33].

- **Structure of the labour force**. The level of unionisation may be affected by a variety of occupational, industrial and socio-demographic characteristics. Certainly, in the past, trade unionism has been particularly high among full-time male manual workers in relatively large manufacturing organisations or employees in the public sector. Female or part-time employment, particularly in smaller service industry organisations, has tended to be much less well organised. Clearly, any shift in employment within or between these areas is likely to affect the level of overall unionisation[34].

- **Social values** (as expressed through government policies and legislation). Governments can adopt strategies which suppress, tolerate or encourage unionism and collective bargaining. However, as Adams and Markey point out, 'the overall behaviour of government may have a greater effect on industrial relations than the specifics of any piece of legislation'[35].

- **Management strategies**. Open management hostility towards collectivism and unionism has always been a deterent to employees joining a union. Similarly, recent HRM strategies directed towards individualism and inculcating employee commitment to the organisation are also intended to weaken the employee's need or desire to seek union protection and representation.

- **Union character and strategies** (nature of the union's policies and its leadership). The primary role of a trade union is to represent the interests of its members, therefore, potential members must feel that the union is pursuing policies and objectives which will be of benefit to them if they are to be persuaded to join.

Aggregate union membership in Britain increased from 2.0 million (13 per cent density) in 1900 to 8 million (40 per cent density) in 1945 – despite the dramatic fall associated with the mass unemployment of the interwar period. Three distinct periods of changing membership levels can be identified since 1945 (see Figure 4.2):

1948–1968   Following an increase of 1 million in the two immediate 'postwar' years, membership grew relatively slowly – an increase of only 1 million over 21 years ($\frac{1}{2}$ per cent per annum) – and density declined from 45 per cent to 43 per cent. Membership increased slower than the workforce.

1969–1979   Membership increased by almost 3 million (2.5 per cent per annum) and density increased to 55 per cent. Membership increasing faster than the workforce; the most significant increases being among females (69 per cent), non-manual employees (68 per cent) and the public sector (42 per cent).

1979–1998   Union membership has declined by $5\frac{1}{2}$ million between 1979 and 1998 (an average decline of 2.2 per cent per annum), more than wiping out the gains made during 1968–79 and resulting in a union density of about 30 per cent. This decline has happened while the workforce has been increasing. Significantly, the fall in 1998 was the lowest since 1979 (only 10,000) and 'statistically too small to be considered as representing a decline'[36].

Price and Bain have argued that there was a 'duality' in the pattern of union growth during the 1970s: 'in the well organised sector [public services and man-ufacturing] economic factors, employer policies, and public support for union recognition combined to produce a major expansion and consolidation of union membership and organisation' while 'in the poorly organised sector [particularly

Figure 4.2 UK union membership (1900–98)

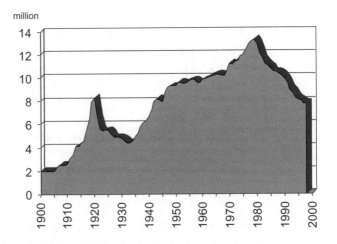

private services] neither economic factors nor public support for unionisation was sufficiently strong to overcome hostile employer policies and … unfavourable structural characteristics'[37]. Significantly, the union recognition gains made during the 1970s, principally for non-manual workers, did not 'act as a ratchet which will prevent union membership slipping away'[38]. Much of the reduction since 1979 has resulted from the substantial decline in manufacturing employment (particularly manual) and reductions in the size of establishments. This has been compounded by other changes in the composition of the workforce arising from increasing levels of female employment and employment in the service sector, by management strategies aimed at increasing labour flexibility (increased part-time working and temporary contracts)[39], by reduced inflation coupled with high and persistent unemployment[40], and by government legislation aimed at reducing trade union power[41].

The decline in **union density** has not been confined to the UK, but has been a common feature across most industrialised countries with the exception of the Scandinavian countries (see Table 4.1). In the past, union density has been defined as actual trade union membership as a percentage of *potential* union membership – this being those employed (excluding employers, self-employed and the armed forces) plus those unemployed[42]. However, as Kessler and Bayliss point out, in periods of high unemployment 'the measure of trade union density which best indicates the decline of union bargaining power is one which excludes the unemployed'[43] as well as the self-employed. In 1998, union density

Table 4.1 Trade union density (by country, %)

	1970	1980	1995
Sweden	68	80	83
Australia	52	50	33
UK	45	51	29
The Netherlands	37	32	29
Italy	36	49	38
Japan	35	31	24
Germany	33	37	30
USA	n/a	23	15
France	22	19	11
Taiwan (ROC)	10	15	35 (1992)
South Korea	n/a	20	14
Singapore	17	23	16

Sources: G. J. Bamber and R. D. Lansbury (eds), *International and Comparative Employment Relations* (2nd edn), Routledge, 1993 and (3rd edn), Sage, 1998.

S. J. Deery and R. J. Mitchell, *Labour Law and Industrial Relations in Asia*, Longman Cheshire (Melbourne), 1993.

A. Verma, T. A. Kochan and R. D. Lansbury (eds), *Employment Relations in the Growing Asian Economies*, Routledge, 1995.

as a proportion of *employees* was 33.3 per cent, compared to 30.7 per cent including the unemployed. Furthermore, there are some significant variations in union density within the workforce (see Table 4.2). Although there is now very little difference between male and female employees and between manual and non-manual employees, union density is significantly higher for full-time compared to part-time employees and for the public compared to private sector. Perhaps surprisingly, union density is high among professional and technical occupational groups but now relatively low in manufacturing. Similarly, union density in establishments with more than 25 employees is 37 per cent compared to 15 per cent in those under 25 employees[44].

The continuing decline in the number of unions through amalgamations has been associated with an **increasing concentration of union membership** in a relatively small number of large, often 'conglomerate', unions (see Table 4.3). However, in 1997 50 per cent of unions (127 out of 252) still had less than 1,000 members each and accounted for only 0.4 per cent of total UK union membership[45]. One important development for unions was the introduction of the requirement that union members had to sign fresh 'check-off' forms every three years if they were to continue to have their subscriptions deducted from their wages by the employer (S. 15, Trade Union Reform and Employment Rights Act, 1993). British Rail's withdrawal of its 'check-off' arrangement with RMT in 1993 resulted not only in a drop in membership but also a significant reduction in income[46]. Most unions were successful in 're-signing' the bulk of members and used the opportunity, wherever possible, to encourage members to change to direct debit payments[47]. The requirement to re-sign every three years was abolished by the new Labour government in 1997.

Table 4.2 UK union density (1998)

Category	(%)	Category	(%)
All employees	29.6		
Male	30.8	Full-time	32.8
Female	28.4	Part-time	20.2
Manual	29.8	Public sector	60.7
Non-manual	29.5	Private sector	19.2
Occupations:		*Industries:*	
Professional	49	Public administration	60
Associate professional and technical	44	Electricity, gas and water	58
		Education	53
Plant and machine operatives	38	Health	46
		Transport and communication	42
Craft and related	32	Financial services	31
Personal and protective	27	Manufacturing	30
Clerical and secretarial	24	Mining and quarrying	30

Source: P. Bland, 'Trade union membership and recognition 1997–98', *Labour Market Trends*, July 1999, pp. 343–51.

Table 4.3 UK largest
unions

Union	Membership (1999)	Finances (1997)	
		Income from members (£ m)	Total assets (£m)
UNISON – The Public Service Union	1,272 330	105.9	91.7
Transport and General Workers' Union	881 625	60.3	83.5
Amalgamated Engineering and Electrical Union	717 874	37.7	62.1
GMB	712 010	40.4	57.3
Manufacturing Science and Finance Union	416 000	23.5	21.3
Royal College of Nursing[1]	*312 141*	12.9	5.7
Union of Shop Distributive and Allied Workers	303 060	16.3	19.9
Communication Workers Union	287 732	25.2	31.2
Public and Commercial Services Union[2]	254 350	21.5	31.2
Graphical Paper and Media Union	203 229	18.5	42.8
National Union of Teachers	194 259	14.9	13.2
National Association of Schoolmasters and Union of Women Teachers	178 518	10.5	18.9
Association of Teachers and Lecturers	113 760	8.6	7.8
Union of Construction, Allied Trades and Technicians	111 804	4.1	2.0
Banking Insurance and Finance Union[3]	106 007	6.7	4.2
British Medical Association[1]	*104 344*	19.1	69.0
Total (for all trade unions)[1]	*7,801 315*	576.6	935.2

[1] Membership figures for RCN, BMA and Total are for 1997.

[2] The finances figures are the combined figures for the Public Services Tax and Commerce Union and the Civil and Public Services Association which merged in March 1998.

[3] BIFU merged with Barclays and Natwest Staff Associations to form UNIFI in January 1999; figures are for BIFU prior to the merger.

Sources: 1999 membership figures – *Labour Research*, August 1999, p. 3; 1997 figures – Certification Officer, *Annual Report* (1998), Appendix 4, pp. 48–9, HMSO.

4.3 Trade union function

An organisation's function is **the role or task it performs and the means used to carry it out**. However, it is difficult to consider the function of an organisation without, perhaps misleadingly, ascribing personal attributes to the organisation itself. Hyman emphasises that 'organisations do not perform actions or take decisions: rather, certain people decide and act in the name of the organisation' and ' "institutional" needs or interests makes sense only if interpreted as a metaphor for the considerations and priorities motivating those with power within organisations'[48]. The objectives, policies and actions displayed by trade unions derive from the leadership's perception of its function and may be at variance with the perception of individual members or distinct classes of membership. Those charged with leadership and decision making within the organisation may become as much concerned with maintaining an effective organisation, pursuing wider trade union principles and establishing political influence, as with ensuring that the policies and actions of the organisation serve the needs of the membership and fulfil the purpose for which the organisation was established.

It is possible to identify six distinct aspects of trade union function (see Figure 4.3).

- **Power** – to protect and support the individual by providing a collective strength to act as a countervailing force to the employer and a pressure group within society.

- **Economic regulation** – to maximise the wages and employment of their members within the framework of the wage/work contract of employment.

- **Job regulation** – to establish a joint rule-making system which both protects their members from arbitrary management actions and allows them to participate in decision making within the organisation for which they work.

- **Social change** – to express the social cohesion, aspirations or political ideology of their membership and seek to develop a society which reflects this view.

- **Member services** – to provide a range of benefits or services to the individual member.

- **Self-fulfilment** – to provide a mechanism whereby individuals may develop outside the immediate confines of their jobs and participate in decision-making processes.

Figure 4.3 Trade union function

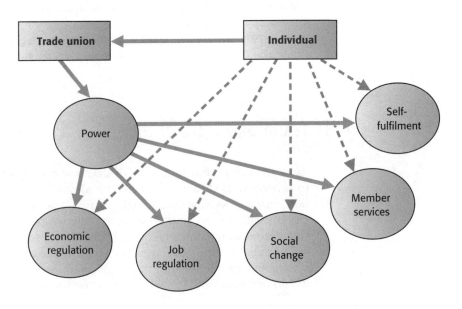

Power

Although the **power function of trade unions is a latent one**, manifest only in the exercise of its other functions, nevertheless Hyman argues that 'a trade union is, first and foremost, an agency and a medium of power'[49]. Without an organisation to represent them, individual employees are at a serious power disadvantage in their relationships with management. Not only do they lack resources in terms of knowledge and expertise to negotiate their terms and conditions of employment on an equal basis, but also the individual is one out of many potential employees who may, as a source of labour, be more easily substituted by management than he or she may substitute the employer as the source of wages. However, by employees acting in concert, management is less able to treat employees as individual, replaceable units of a commodity but rather is required to regard them as one collective and indivisible unit.

It is the acquisition of power through the collective strength of its membership which, to a large measure, determines the success of the trade union in carrying out its other functions. However, as Perlman pointed out, trade unionism is both '*individualistic* in the sense that it aims to satisfy the individual aspirations ... for a decent livelihood, for economic security and for freedom from tyranny on the part of the boss' and '*collectivistic*, since it aspires to develop in the individual a willingness to subordinate his own interests to the superior interests of the collectivity'[50]. While most employees join a trade union for instrumental reasons (protection and benefits from improved terms and conditions of employment), this can be achieved only through the power the trade union derives from the collective strength and solidarity of its membership. The power the trade union is able to exert externally in carrying out its economic and job regulation functions is dependent on its internal ability to secure concerted and controlled collective responses from its membership. This, in turn, is dependent on the preparedness of the members to forego their individual freedom and recognise the need for collective decision making and action. Hyman points out that 'it is only through the power *over* its members which is vested in the trade union that it is able to exert power *for* them'[51].

Bain and Price[52], in examining the level of union membership as an indicator of union power, suggested that trade unions seek to exercise power (influence) in three directions:

- **Within the labour movement**. Here a union's power may be related to its size relative to other unions, but other factors such as leadership 'quality' and alliances between unions are also likely to be important.

- **Towards government**. Here union power is not so dependent on the level of aggregate union membership as the government's perceived desire for or dependence on trade union support for the achievement of its policies (primarily a political/ideological decision, although changes in union membership levels may affect the government's perception).

- **Towards employers**. Here it is not the absolute level of membership but rather union density (completeness of organisation), enhanced or weakened by economic, technological and political factors, which provides the basis of union power.

The increasingly heterogeneous membership within many trade unions, with different interests and their consequent organisational segmentation, has **weakened the 'collective solidarity'** bond *within* unions. This has been compounded by changes in the members' work situation: increasing job insecurity, technological change and management strategies emphasising the individual rather than collective employment relationship (for example, individualised contracts and performance-related pay). At the same time, legislative changes made during the 1980s first restricted and then removed the ability to express wider union solidarity through sympathetic (secondary) industrial action. The weakening of solidarity was clearly seen in the mid-1980s when the TUC was unable to mobilise effective mass membership demonstration against the removal of union membership rights at GCHQ or to support the miners resisting pit closures – both of which could be regarded as matters of collective trade union 'principles'.

Economic regulation

Most people would emphasise the **collective negotiation of wages and other monetary terms of employment** (including hours and holidays) as a major, if not *the* major, function of a trade union. The importance of this function extends beyond the members who are the direct recipients of any improvements negotiated by a union (by setting benchmarks for other employers or by formal extension to all employers in the industry) and the level of wages resulting directly or indirectly from collective bargaining impact on the economic system.

Economists, such as Mulvey[53], argue that the **union's wage policy** can be expressed as seeking to maximise satisfaction (utility) in respect of wages and employment ($U_1, \ldots U_n$, for different levels of labour demand in Figure 4.4). However, because trade unions do not unilaterally determine wage levels but do so through the joint process of collective bargaining, the *actual* level of wages will be determined by the relative bargaining power of the parties involved. Nevertheless, Mulvey argues, the future wage policy of the union will still be closely linked to its utility function. This is depicted by line YXZ which links the union's maximisation points for different levels of demand. The change in angle at point X indicates 'that unions will vigorously resist wage reductions and trade away employment to do so when demand falls, whereas when demand rises they will tend to divide the demand increases more equally between wage increases and employment growth'[54]. The implication of the union's wage preference line (YXZ) being above the supply curve of labour (S-S) is that a union will always seek to maintain a level of wages (W_1) higher than the level that would result simply from the unrestricted interaction of supply and demand (W_2), even though if left to market forces the level of employment might be higher (E_2 rather than E_1).

Robertson and Thomas have gone further and suggested that the objective of trade union wage policy is 'to secure the maximum "real" wage consistent with full (or "high") employment of a union's membership ... and consistent with the members' leisure-income choice'[55]. The equation becomes more complex if the union's maximisation of wage and employment levels is to be consistent with

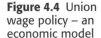

Figure 4.4 Union wage policy – an economic model

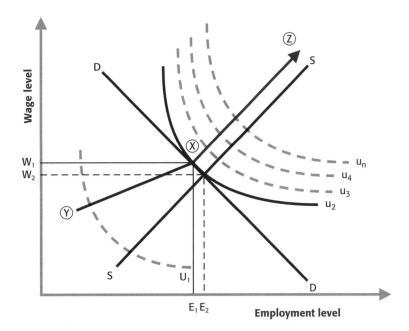

the minimisation of the working week, which economists assume to be inherent in the members' leisure–income choice. At the same time, it is necessary to consider whether it is the present or potential membership for which the union is seeking to maximise wage levels and employment, and whether it is seeking to do so in the short or long term.

On the other hand, there are those, such as Ross[56] as early as the 1940s, who emphasise the **political nature of the union's wage policy** and argue that it is the result of a reconciliation, by the leadership, of conflicting priorities among a generally heterogeneous membership. In their view, the policies and actions of trade unions in wage bargaining do not represent the results of rational economic decisions. Certainly, Mulvey accepts that in practice 'most trade unions formulate their wages policy with an eye to the wage policy they expect or observe other unions to follow'[57]. This may be due partly to the difficulties of applying an economic maximising approach and partly to the existence of perceived relationships between the wages of different groups of employees. These perceived relationships exist in two directions:

- **Comparability** or 'horizontal equity' between similar work in different organisations or industries;
- **Differentials** or 'vertical equity' between different work or levels within the same organisation or industry.

The effect of this may be to create and maintain a degree of rigidity in the general wage and salary structure which constrains variations that might otherwise arise from differences in industrial or economic circumstances (of organisations or industries) or the supply and demand for different categories of labour. Through this mechanism the bargaining strength of a few significant groups may determine the general wage level for the majority. Certainly, both government policy and management strategies since the early 1980s have been, in part, directed towards more wage flexibility linked to individual, group or organisational performance.

There are two different theories regarding the effect of the trade unions' economic function on **inflation and unemployment**:

- **Cost-push**. Wage increases are a direct primary cause of inflation and unemployment by increasing production costs and reducing profits, investment and competitiveness.

- **Demand-pull**. Higher wages lead to an expansion of demand, particularly in periods of full employment, which causes prices to rise (inflation) and leads to a lack of competitiveness and unemployment.

Trade union wage bargaining activity is primarily reactive, but, as Hawkins points out, this 'does not ... imply that particular wage agreements do not contribute to the upward movement of money wages' but rather that the trade unions' economic function is not 'an independent cause of inflation or unemployment'[58]. It is difficult to assess the **effect of the trade unions' economic function** in isolation from other factors such as changes in technology, productivity, demand for labour and government monetary and fiscal policies. Figures relating to the **distribution of national income** show that the overall share accruing to labour increased from 55 per cent during 1910–14 to 78 per cent in 1976[59]. However, Phelps Brown argued that 'the major cause of the rise in real wages ... has been the raising of productivity'[60] rather than trade union strength and that collective bargaining has been, in effect, 'between different groups of employees for the distribution of the national income between them as a whole and the inactive population'[61] – i.e. it achieved little more than an internal redistribution of labour's share of the national income. Furthermore, Stark[62] argues that the increasing inequality in wage and salary distribution seen during the 1980s resulted primarily from the shift in employment from middle-wage industries to either high- or low-wage industries.

See Chapter 9 –
Collective bargaining

The number of people directly covered by collective bargaining declined during the 1980s and 1990s. At the same time, the decentralisation of collective bargaining (away from industry-level multi-employer bargaining) has meant less opportunity for unions to extend 'gains' to those organisations where unionism is weak in the form of a 'common rate' across an industry – unlike France, where the government can extend collective terms across an industry. There is now greater pay variability between organisations as the pay bargaining which remains becomes more related to the economic performance of the individual organisation and its labour market conditions. However, it is management strategies intended to shift the emphasis of the 'reward system' within the organisation from a 'rate for the job' basis to an individual ability or performance related basis (including individual contracts for some staff) which has the greatest potential effect on the union's economic function. Certainly, some unions see a new 'wage bargaining' role in assisting such employees in their individual bargaining by providing information, advice and guidance.

However, protecting and, if possible, improving members' living standards and employment rights remains at the heart of a union's function (see Box 4.3).

| Box 4.3 | US reaps unhappy harvest of deregulation |

'Joe Vitali is an unhappy man. Across the Hudson from New York City, in the heart of Bruce Springsteen country, he stands by his machine in the textile mill and describes how the company is threatening to screw him.

As a thumbnail sketch of what the American-style deregulated labour market means in practice it's hard to beat. His employers, Westchester Lace, have announced new production targets for their workers, who produce material to be made into bras, wedding dresses and curtains.

"The company is setting me an impossible target. On my best day I can produce 100,000 yards. That's my very best day, without any problems. They want 120,000 yards, after which I will get an extra four cents for every extra 1,000 yards. If I don't make 120,000 yards I will get a warning."

"At the end of every month everybody will be waiting to see who is going to get the letter. It's just a way of exercising control over us. They want to put us in our place."

Joe is one of the lucky ones. His trade union, the Amalgamated Clothing and Textile Workers Union (ACTWU), is on the case, negotiating with Westchester Lace for more realistic targets.

Other workers in the US are not so fortunate. Trade union membership has fallen sharply over the past 15 years, and now stands at barely one-eighth of the workforce. Abuses are legion. Recently the *New York Times* documented the proliferation of illegal sweatshops in Manhattan and Brooklyn, using pictures of doors padlocked and chained to keep the workers in.'

Source: Larry Elliot, © *Guardian Weekly*, 26 February 1995.

See also Country profile 2.1 and Box 5.2.

Job regulation

The union's regulatory function covers much more than purely economic matters; it includes, as Flanders argued, the 'creation of a social order in industry embodied in a code of industrial rights'[63]. While management wishes to retain the maximum freedom of power, authority and decision making in managing the business, so employees wish to protect themselves against the adverse effects of such decisions. The trade union seeks, on behalf of its members, to limit management's power by making the latter's decisions and actions, wherever possible, subject to 'joint' regulation. In so doing, the power and authority structure within the organisation based on managerial prerogative is replaced by a system of jointly determined rules, particularly procedural, which regulate not only the individual relationship between employer and employee but also the organisational relationship between the company and the trade union.

The growth of 'informal' collective bargaining at the organisational level in the UK and, more importantly, its formalisation during the 1960s and 1970s provided the basis for an **expansion of the job regulation function**. Full employment coupled with expanding markets resulted in an increased preparedness on the part of management to negotiate enhanced payments and changes in working arrangements outside the framework of the then existing national-level negotiating machinery. In most organisations, a range of jointly agreed codified procedures were created covering recognition, the provision and scope of consultative and negotiating machinery and the handling of many workplace issues (grievances, discipline, redundancy, introduction of work study and work changes, safety, etc.). It is the strength of the trade union at the organisational level which determines the effectiveness of its job regulation function.

The job regulation role of the trade union has received only **limited support from legislation**: the requirements for management to disclose information for the purpose of collective bargaining and to consult recognised independent trade unions in a redundancy. In the past, British trade unions have generally preferred to secure such rights directly from the employer through their own efforts rather than being dependent on Parliament. Certainly, Flanders believed that 'a worker through his union has more direct influence in what rules are made and how they are applied than he can ever exercise by his vote over the laws made by Parliament'[64]. This is in marked contrast to other countries, such as Germany, where not only is there a division between the 'economic' role of the union in negotiating wages and conditions and the role of 'employee' representatives, elected by the whole workforce to a Works Council, in undertaking the 'job regulation' function at the workplace but also the role, rights and power of the Works Council are based in law.

The trade union's role as the representative of employees in jointly regulating the employment relationship has been **challenged and weakened by management** strategies to re-exert its authority and establish direct links between itself and its employees. It has sought to establish greater 'employee involvement', rather than 'union participation', within the workplace through strengthening direct communication, such as team briefings, and establishing 'employee councils'. However, trade unions have responded by seeking to expand the scope of job regulation into areas such as training (to ensure that their members are equipped to meet changes in work resulting from new technology) and, perhaps most important for strengthening their recruitment appeal among women, equal opportunities (such as maternity career breaks, childcare provisions, job sharing, equal rights for part-time employees, sexual harassment, etc.)[65].

Social change (political)

The trade union movement in the UK and Europe came into existence and experienced its initial phase of development at a time when the **segregation of society between 'capital' and 'labour'** was perhaps most marked and when the political aspiration of the working classes was first manifesting itself through the newly won rights to participate in the political system. Thus it is that van de Vall believes 'political action in the class war has always provided the union with latent macro-social functions'[66]. However, Anderson argues that from a radical perspective trade unions, because of their sectional approach to representing workers interests, 'do not *challenge* the existence of society based on division of classes, they merely *express* it'[67]. Certainly, van de Vall believes that because of changes in society 'societal class conflict has been reduced to a merely industrial, or microsocial, conflict' (**institutional isolation of social conflict**) and the early political, revolutionary approach displayed by some trade unions has given way to a more conservative approach based on evolution within the existing industrial and political system: 'the war between two industrial classes has gradually been succeeded by a system of labour–management accommodation'[68].

This accommodation does not mean, however, that trade unions no longer seek, through their policies and actions in both the industrial and political spheres, to attain a more egalitarian and socially just society.

Social change can only really be effected by influencing government policy, hence the need for unions to adopt **a 'political' role**. However, the way in which this role is carried out varies – in relation both to political parties and to the process of government. Trade unions in, for example, France, Italy and Belgium are divided on religious and/or political lines corresponding to the political parties and may be regarded as the 'industrial' wing of these parties. Germany and Sweden, with long periods of social democratic governments but without the same divisions or direct link between unions and political parties, established the concept of 'social partnership' between government, unions and employers which has given unions an extensive role in both society- and industry-level dialogues over a wide range of economic and social issues. In South Africa, until the unbanning of the ANC, the black trade union movement was the only quasi-legitimate method of expressing political as well as economic aspirations – hence its role in challenging the *apartheid* socio-political system (like the role of unions in supporting the independence struggle in colonial countries), the very close links between COSATU and the ANC and the division of the union movement based on different views of the racial issue. In Singapore, the trade union movement has been incorporated into the political process as a means of helping to secure the government's strategy for national economic development.

In the UK, the trade unions' **political role in relation to government** has undergone a significant shift over the postwar period. The 'consensus' or 'corporatist' political climate up to 1979 produced a number of government-supported institutions in the area of industrial and national economic planning, through which trade unions were able to be involved in and influence government economic and social policies (for example, NEDO, the MSC and ITBs, boards of nationalised industries as well as institutions associated with the operation of incomes policy). However, their involvement, even indirectly, in the process of national economic planning presented a **dilemma** – by entering into this accommodation they also shared, in varying degrees depending on the political party in power, in the responsibility for the decisions reached. These decisions, while arguably in the interests of society as a whole and wage/salary earners in particular, could, nevertheless, conflict with the sectional demands and interests of their members. Thus, trade unions had to balance directly protecting their members' interests, through their economic and job regulation functions in the collective bargaining process with management, with indirectly influencing government to adopt or modify policies which might equally affect their members' standard of living, job security, etc.

The period after 1979 saw the Conservative government abandon the previous 'consensus' or 'corporatist' ideology, severely diminishing the unions' potential influence. Indeed, the government no longer regarded the TUC as the body which had the exclusive right to nominate the 'employee' representatives to Employment Tribunals and ACAS. Perhaps, not surprisingly, this was accompanied by frustration among many trade unionists arising from a perceived lack of access to, let alone an inability to persuade, the government. Consequently, the trade unions began to view the social dialogue process within the EU as a more sympathetic and fruitful avenue within which to pursue their political function.

The trade union movement's **relationship to the Labour Party** has also undergone a substantial change in the 1990s. In the past, many regarded trade union involvement in the Labour Party as 'the only real counterweight to combat the negative extremism of the constituency rank and file'[69]. The Labour Party's reliance on the unions for membership and the 'political levy' to finance the party was reciprocated by their voting power at conference and in the election of the leader and NEC and their influence in policy making. However, following election defeats during the 1980s, the union relationship became perceived, certainly by the party leaders, as being a 'straight-jacket' or 'armlock' which was detrimental to electoral success. A series of constitutional changes during the 1990s reduced the unions' voting strength and thereby their role and influence within the party. McIlroy sees these changes as ones in which 'new Labour was to be an HRM organization, conflict-free, with one fount of authority – the leadership – legitimized by periodic referenda of the membership' and in which the leadership would 'insulate itself from union pressure ... rather than terminate the union link'[70]. While Labour encouraged unions to adopt a 'social partnership' approach to management at the organisational level, it was not prepared to offer a similar relationship at either Party or government level. Indeed, the 'new' Labour government has coined the phrase 'fairness not favours' to describe the unions' status which, Leopold believes, 'implies an end to the particular special relationship, with unions becoming one of many pressure groups seeking to influence the government'[71]. However, not all unions supported these changes because, arguably, it is easier and better to seek to influence the determination of policy within a political party *before* it is elected than it is to influence the policies of a government *after* it is elected.

Trade union political activity in Britain must be funded from a separate **political fund**. The **Trade Union Act (1984)** placed additional constraints on the procedure unions must follow to maintain a political fund:

1. Conduct a ballot of the members every ten years.

2. Have the rules for the ballot and notification of the members' right to be exempt from contributing to the political fund approved by the Certification Officer.

3. Conduct the ballot by postal voting (S.14, Employment Act, 1988) with independent scrutiny (S.5, Employment Act, 1990).

4. Where the majority of those voting do not support the maintenance of a political fund:

    (a) cease making payments from its political fund within six months;

    (b) cease collecting contributions from the members as soon as is reasonably practicable.

In addition, members who 'opt out' of the political contribution may, if their union subscriptions are deducted from wages by the employer, inform the employer not to deduct any contribution in respect of the political contribution. The member may seek a court order where the employer fails to comply with this or refuses to deduct only the 'normal' union dues (i.e. seeks to get the employee to make his or her own arrangements to pay union dues). Furthermore, any union member may apply for a court order where the union fails to comply with 4(b) above.

As Leopold pointed out, 'one of the few successes recorded by the trade union movement under recent Conservative governments was the campaign to retain political funds'[72] in 1985/6. All 38 unions which had a political fund obtained large majority votes in favour (averaging 84 per cent) as a result of a co-ordinated campaign emphasising that the ballot was about being able to undertake 'political' activities, not about affiliation to the Labour Party. Perhaps more significantly, the 1984 Act amended the **definition of 'political activity'** so that union campaigns against government policies (such as NALGO's campaign against public service cuts) could be construed as political activity, certainly if (as NALGO's campaign did) it coincides with an election. As a consequence, a number of public sector unions, which had generally sought to avoid any perception of being 'political', felt it necessary to establish political funds for the first time in order to safeguard their campaigning activities. All 17 unions which established a political fund for the first time (of which 12 were public sector unions) also gained a resounding 'yes' vote (averaging 78 per cent). The subsequent 1994/6 campaign was equally successful, despite all unions having to conduct it by postal vote (rather than the majority being conducted at the workplace as before) and there being more women and part-time members than in 1985/6. The postal voting appeared to affect the turnout which dropped from an average of 63 per cent in 1985/6 to 38 per cent in 1994/6 – ranging from 17 per cent in CATU to 57 per cent in the FBU. The average 'yes' vote remained high at 82 per cent of those voting, ranging from 93 per cent in ASLEF to 65 per cent in the NUM[73].

Member services

In their early days, before the advent of the welfare state, unions often provided a range of **mutual insurance** benefits not only to cover loss of pay during a strike but also in the event of the member's unemployment, sickness, injury or death. The emphasis was on the 'mutuality' of these benefits, in that they were provided from the subscriptions of the members themselves and unions would often call for an additional levy from working members to support others involved in a strike or during periods of prolonged unemployment. Thus, these benefits helped to strengthen the union's collective role by making members less dependent on their employer's 'benevolence'. During the course of the twentieth century these benefits, apart from strike benefit, generally became an insignificant aspect of the union's activity as the state took over the providing role. However, in some countries (such as Belgium, Sweden and Denmark) trade unions have played an important role in establishing and administering national unemployment insurance arrangements, which has been a significant factor in their high levels of union density[74].

In the last decade many trade unions have turned to the provision of more **modern 'member services'** (similar to the services provided by many companies to their employees) as part of their strategy to appeal to new potential recruits who do not have a 'tradition' of unionism. As Towers points out, such services have 'long been a feature of professional, managerial and white-collar unions'[75], but now most unions, with the support of the TUC, provide some form of package of discounted financial services (including insurance, mortgages and personal loans) as well as access to legal assistance for non-work-related matters[76]. It is the offer of credit cards by some unions as part of this package which has given rise to the term 'plastic card' unionism.

The term 'member services' may apply to 'any union facility which is of benefit to members *individually*'[77] (my italics) and it is the **individual basis** of these modern services which some believe may detract from the fundamental nature of trade unionism. Some unions which have adopted this strategy believe it is 'easier to appeal to a potential member's self-interest than to explain the more traditional industrial relations benefits associated with a union'[78], and Mason and Bain note that 'in some cases, advocates of services have been associated with the view that potential members are put off from joining unions by industrial action'[79], hence they regard it as an alternative to union 'militancy'. However, McIlroy argues that 'unless the unions can continue to effectively assert and extend their essential roles as successful wage bargainers, credit cards, Filofax and videos are unlikely to reverse their present decline'[80]. Certainly, if people join a union *only* or *primarily* for the personal benefits they gain from these services (as opposed to the alternative instrumental reason of gaining its protection in the workplace), they are likely to weaken the basis of the union's 'fraternalist' ideals and 'collective consciousness' and, thereby, its ability to carry out its economic and job regulation function.

Self-fulfilment

The importance of the trade union, in terms of the individual's self-fulfilment, lies primarily in its **role in decision making**, through which the member is able to participate in areas of decision making far removed from his or her immediate work situation. This operates within two important interrelated systems:

- The union's **internal system of government**, wherein the member is encouraged to attend the branch and participate in its activities and, from there, become involved in a range of roles throughout the union concerned with the development of union policy and decision making on a range of social and political issues as well as economic and industrial matters.
- The **collective bargaining system**, wherein members can participate in the determination of the terms of their contract (through the formulation of claims and responses to management proposals) and undertake representational roles which afford a direct opportunity to influence management decisions.

In their early years trade unions were, in the absence of educational, political or other opportunities, an important, and sometimes the sole, **vehicle for the advancement of those with ability**. Indeed, membership participation was frequently encouraged by fining members who failed to attend branch meetings or by operating a form of 'organic democracy' which required each member to take a turn in holding office within the branch or union and thereby actively sharing the responsibility for the government of the union. In the postwar period, however, the growth of educational opportunities coupled with greater job opportunities in the technical and managerial fields has created other avenues whereby the individual may achieve greater self-fulfilment and, as a result, has diminished the role of the union in this area.

See Chapter 6 – Representation at the workplace

Nevertheless, this aspect of trade unionism is still important in trying to understand why people become active within trade unions and are prepared to give up their own time, with the consequent social cost to themselves and their families, to attend meetings and to stand out from the mass and act as the representative of their fellow workers or union members. It is too simplistic to state that they have a desire for 'power' and that these roles within a trade union provide them with the opportunity to acquire and exercise such power. It is perhaps better to say that any 'activist' within a trade union, whether simply a member or a shop steward, branch official or other officer of the union, is active because of some social commitment to improving employees' working lives. Thus, by taking an active part within the union the individual achieves a generally more satisfying role in life than he or she would otherwise do.

4.4 Union character and strategy

Trade unions, in the UK and most other countries, have suffered from declining membership and influence since the early 1980s resulting from high unemployment and employment restructuring combined with the decollectivisation of employment relations and development of 'new individualism' strategies by management. Consequently, they have been faced with the need to reassess their functions, activities and methods (reconsider their *raison d'être*) and develop strategies to recruit new members as well as retain existing ones (see Box 4.4).

It often appears attractive to ignore the complexities of trade unions and try to categorise and compare them in a single phrase:

■ **Expression of class-consciousness** – emphasises the potential role for unions in mobilising sectional and incomplete interests within a 'revolutionary' political party to develop a 'socialist' society.

■ **Social responsibility** – displays an expectation that unions will exercise their role and activities in a way which is not detrimental to the existing capitalist economic, social and political system.

■ **Business unionism** – suggests an almost exclusive emphasis on securing members' interests within the economic/industrial system through direct negotiation of the employment relationship with employers (as in the USA).

■ **Welfare unionism** – indicates a broader outlook beyond the narrow economic, industrial and job regulation interests of their immediate membership and a concern with wider social, economic and political issues – a common view of British and European unions.

■ **Political unionism** – emphasises integration into the political processes within society and securing members' interests through political alliances, action and statutory regulation – a feature of politically differentiated trade unionism in some European countries.

Box 4.4	Unions face a clouded future

'For anyone concerned with the future of trade unions, three trends are critical. The first is the worldwide threat to jobs in industries which traditionally have been mass employers. The second is the rise of the knowledge worker in an information-driven global economy. The third is the dwindling membership of trade unions. Though the three trends have different origins and follow separate lines of logic, their convergence can turn organised labour into an anachronism as dated as the dungeon-like workplaces of the Industrial Revolution, in whose crucible the working class was moulded. This will warm some hearts. It should chill many more. Not for nothing, then, did concerns over the fate of trade unions in a changing world hang over the recent conference of the National Trades Union Congress.

Inexorable forces are at work. In parts of the world, labour-intensive industries dependent on the large-scale exploitation of natural resources – coal and steel are just two of many examples – face the sunset of structural change. As they retrench, forcing many workers into the ranks of the unemployable, they eat into the membership base of trade unions. Elsewhere, the changing nature of work takes its toll. Smaller enterprises contract out many of their functions, decimating the concentrations of labour needed to form viable in-house unions which can then link up with industry-wide unions and umbrella labour organisations.

Taking the place of industrial muscle, symbolised by the man in muddied overalls and hard hat, is the knowledge worker, one whose particular education and skills give him the ability to negotiate premium terms for himself. The knowledge worker is nothing if not mobile, for the borders of the economy he inhabits are coterminous, not with that of nations, but with the world's. He does not need unions – or thinks he does not need one – preferring, instead, to have his market worth written into a contract with the employer. Even others who are not quite part of the cognitive elite do not join unions, or they give up their membership, for a variety of reasons. Professionals have few bread-and-butter interests in common with the working class; parts of the working class graduate into the middle class; even those who stay back have few incentives for joining unions since benefits negotiated on behalf of members are available to all employees, more so in tight labour situations. Union membership then stagnates, or falls.

This can be harmful. The demise of collective bargaining, one of the great advances in modern industrial organisation, could hasten the approach of a world in which employers have less reason to be enlightened and are more likely to take what they can in the jungle of the market place. Keeping them in check is a job that would fall on governments. As much as anti-monopoly laws protect consumers from carnivorous businesses, employees need to be protected from exploitation by greedy bosses. But that is easier said than done because global economic change may pare the powers of the nation-state itself. The onus would fall then on workers to protect themselves. As always, the key to that lies in their organisation. Trade unions cannot replace the realities of the coming world; it would be misguided for them to try. But even in that world, they will matter, by negotiating minimum standards of employment and benefits; by giving workers a forum to which they can turn for redress; ultimately, by multiplying the power of each worker by the number of co-workers who unite with him. But whether they can do that, or whether they will go the way of artefacts of early industrialisation, is something that depends on workers themselves. Trade unions can remain viable only if people join them and participate in their deliberations. They are no more – and no less – than what workers make them.'

Source: Editorial, *The Straits Times* (Singapore), 2 November 1995.

Price described the concept of 'union character' as 'a shorthand phrase for conveying some of the differences between unions in goals, policies and activities'[81]. Such differences arise, in part, from differing perceptions of the nature of economic and social stratification within society and the role of trade unionism within that stratification (see Figure 4.5). Much of the discussion in the 1970s

Figure 4.5 Union
character

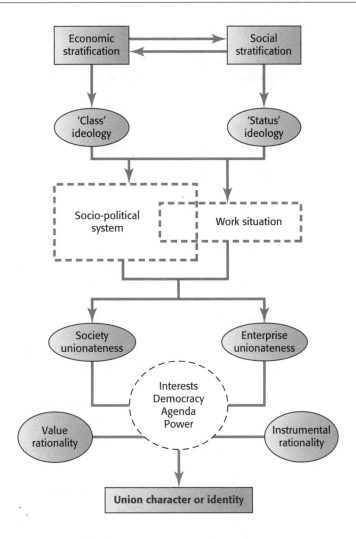

about union character in the UK was closely linked to the concept of 'unionate-ness' and comparisons between 'traditional' manual and the growing non-manual unionism. Blackburn defined **unionateness** as the extent to which an organisation 'is a whole-hearted trade union, identifying with the labour movement and willing to use all the power of the movement'[82]. The criteria for judging the unionateness of an organisation are based on two groups of factors:

■ *The organisation's ability and willingness to pursue its members' interests* – the extent to which it regards collective bargaining as its primary function, its degree of independence from employer influence and its preparedness to utilise industrial action.

■ *The organisation's commitment to the principles and ideology of a trade union movement* – whether it considers itself a trade union, works with other unions (e.g. affiliated to the TUC) and political parties representing workers interests (e.g. affiliated to the Labour Party).

However, both Bain *et al.*[83] and Price criticised this not only in terms of the ambiguity and relevance of the criteria, the difficulty of measuring them and the outcome variability (as much within manual and non-manual union groupings as between the groups), but also because it is based on an 'assumption that the manual union "ideal-type" ... is itself a measure of a class-conscious form of worker organization'[84]. Within a simple **class ideology** framework, white-collar employees are perceived to form part of a middle class distinct from the working classes of manual workers. This difference, it is argued, is reflected in the apparent reluctance of white-collar workers to join trade unions and to utilise the industrial action weapon or the development of a distinctive character to any organisation which they do join (the maintenance of a 'false class consciousness'). It has also been argued that non-manual union members have different attitudes:

- **Egotist/individual** behaviour (seek to improve their economic or social status by their own individual efforts) rather than **fraternalist/collective** (combine with others in a similar position to exert greater pressure to improve the position of the group as a whole – and thereby improve their own position)[85].

- **Instrumental reasons** for joining a union (the 'insurance policy' of support and representation in any problem with their employer which, as an individual, they cannot handle) and are wary of unions adopting what they see as a 'political' stance[86].

- A preference for **co-operation rather than conflict** with management, the integration of individualism with collectivism, and greater preparedness to be involved in management systems, such as job evaluation and performance-related pay, which allow for individual advancement within a collective framework.

Many believe that a class analysis is no longer valid within a modern industrial society. However, Prandy *et al.* believe that the underlying notions of 'class interest', 'class consciousness' and 'unionateness' *are* relevant to an understanding of the character of trade unionism, providing it is recognised that 'class consciousness varies ... in terms of the particularity or generality of interests'[87] which are identified and acted upon. They distinguish between **enterprise unionateness** (collective behaviour patterns *within* the workplace which seek change in the employment situation based on instrumental and sectional interest with no requirement for an ideological commitment) and **society unionateness** (collective behaviour patterns which recognise a commonality of interest with other groups and organisations *outside* the immediate work situation and a need to act at the society level to achieve the desired change, and which, therefore, contain an ideological element). The prime determinant of 'society unionateness' appears to be the social origin of the employee – in particular whether the employee's father was a member of a trade union – although unionateness is also stronger among lower-paid, longer-service employees. 'Enterprise unionateness', on the other hand, appears to be influenced by the employee's attitude to management (negative or positive) linked to the employee's degree of job attachment, promotion expectations and self-estrangement. Prandy *et al.* concluded that these are 'two different but related aspects, rather than totally distinct variables'[88].

Bain *et al.*'s approach to union character concentrated on the **status ideology** generated by social stratification, rather than the economic labour/capital division which underlies the 'class ideology' approach. In their view, 'status is concerned with a person's position in the hierarchy of prestige in the society at large' and 'the workers' position in the social stratification system generates a certain picture or image of industry and the wider society which shapes their attitudes to trade unionism'[89]. It may be argued that 'status ideology' also implies an acceptance of the hierarchical stratification and the authority structure it represents as being both valid and internally compatible. Thus, because of the inherent 'middle class' values of individualism associated with the higher social position, non-manual unionism will arise only when they perceive their social position to be threatened by activities within the industrial environment (relative deprivation). Further, it may be expected that white-collar unionism, when it does arise, will display different characteristics and have less in common with manual unionism.

The varying character of non-manual unionism has been reflected in the existence of not only trade unions but also **staff associations and professional associations**. While it may be argued that a staff association is a form of 'false class consciousness', it is important to note that a significant number, some created in the 1970s as a deliberate alternative to trade unions, have subsequently transferred their engagements to TUC-affiliated trade unions. At the same time, non-manual employees have become increasingly prepared to see industrial action as a legitimate and necessary means – for example, in 1995 the RCN finally voted to accept the use of industrial action. Both are indications, perhaps, of increasing unionateness. Certainly, the evidence of the 1980s and 1990s is that *both* non-manual and manual employees have been similarly affected: subject to the same management strategies aimed at re-exerting control over work, the same legislation aimed at weakening employee influence over employment relations and the common threat of increased job insecurity. Professional associations appear to epitomise a status ideology and represent the opposite 'class' to that of trade unions. Their involvement in industrial relations activities has arisen primarily because their membership, or substantial parts of it, have become employed rather than being self-employed. Significantly, this professional/union mix has also been sought, from the opposite direction, by some unions (particularly in education) seeking to enhance the perceived status of their members.

Poole[90], in seeking to explain the variation in 'social actions' pursued by unions in different countries, distinguishes between approaches based on **instrumental-rationality** (concentrating on economic objectives and job regulation in the immediate workplace) and those based on **value-rationality** (aiming to transform the nature of the employment relationship itself). The former is closely linked to the idea of 'business' unionism and 'enterprise unionateness'. The latter is closely linked to the concept of 'society unionateness' but may be underpinned by a variety of values (political, religious or nationalist) rather than a simple class ideology. Certainly, as Bean notes, in many European countries 'the major dividing lines have been less between the craft and industrial unionism dimensions [*to which may be added the divide between manual and* *non-manual*] than between, on the one hand, secular and confessional (generally Catholic) unionism, and reform-orientated (mainly socialist) or revolutionary (communist or syndicalist) unionism on the other'[91] (my italics). Value-rationality-based trade unionism, of necessity, requires unions to adopt strategies which require close involvement with the political system, which may range from differentiated party political allegiances, through 'social partnership' with governments to 'corporatist' control by government.

More recently, Hyman has suggested that trade union identity stems from an interaction between interests (the extent to which the members interests are exclusive or shared with others – whether inside or outside the workplace), agenda (the content and expression of those interests), democracy (the extent to which the membership is involved in and supports the strategy and actions) and power (the willingness of the members to act). He put forward four alternative union identities for the future, but cautioned that if a trade union sought to be exclusively one or other 'ideal' type, 'it would no longer remain a trade union as that institution has traditionally been understood'[92]:

- *Friendly society* – focus on the individual employee/member and the provision of services, advice and individual representation.

- *Company union* – focus on co-operation with management to enhance organisational performance.

- *Social partner* – focus on government and the improvement of 'social wage' elements through political exchange.

- *Social movement* – focus on mass support and campaigning on wider social and community issues (similar to the past 'class' politics approach).

One of the fundamental problems for trade unions has been the need to represent and service their existing members, while at the same time improving their appeal to those employees who have not traditionally been members. However, as Willman[93] points out, in the absence of an aggregate increase in union membership trade unions are essentially **competing for a share of two markets**: in the **membership market** they compete to provide representation, insurance and other services to individuals, while in the **employer market** they compete to become the bargaining agent and 'voice' of employees in the organisation. He argues that while the two 'markets' are normally interrelated – recognition usually depends on sufficient membership, and recruiting and maintaining membership depend on recognition – nevertheless the 'employer market' is to a certain extent independent of the 'membership market'.

Certainly, trade unions have had to **adapt to the development of HRM** and changes in the employment relationship at the workplace. Most unions have accepted that simple rejection or resistance are not viable, given the shift in the balance of power in favour of management; such strategies would result in little, if any, influence over the terms of HRM and give management complete freedom to 'suborn' employees' commitment on its terms. In the 1980s, some unions sought to make themselves more attractive to management by agreeing to 'single-union agreements' with no-strike clauses, employee councils, etc. and even, on some 'greenfield' sites, selling themselves to management in 'beauty contests' before employees had been recruited. More recently, trade unions have taken the initiative by offering management a more positive 'partnership' style of union relationship. Guest[94] suggests that trade unions may, as alternatives to a 'friendly society' strategy of individual services and representation, broaden the bargaining agenda in two ways:

- ■ *Quality of working life strategy*. Trade unions can draw on the content and approach of the European Social Chapter to promote health and safety, training and development, work redesign (including teamworking, employee empowerment and autonomy) and more flexible working patterns. They need to convince management that any improvements in the employees' quality of working life will also lead to improvements in organisational performance.

- ■ *HRM strategy*. Trade unions can encourage management to implement sound, effective and *fair* HRM strategies – particularly the 'soft' aspects – to ensure that other, more unpalatable alternatives are not adopted.

At the same time, trade unions have needed to **reassess their recruitment appeal**. In doing so, they have undertaken, with the support of the TUC, local labour market surveys and joint recruitment campaigns in particular localities[95] and targeted specific groups such as service organisations, women, part-timers and young people. At the same time, much has been made of the unions' enhancement of individual member services (such as legal advice, pension and insurance arrangement and credit cards) which it is believed will appeal to those employees who have no 'tradition' of unionism as well as those faced with individualisation of the employment relationship. However, Williams believes that a 'shift towards more explicit individualized representational and servicing function' makes unions 'more like organisations that have "consumers" of their services rather than active members'[96]. Similarly, Heery has noted that the GMB has moved towards a form of 'managerial unionism' – its stated objective is to be 'the best known and best respected union in Britain' and it adopts management techniques to 'research members' needs and design and promote attractive servicing packages in response'[97].

See Case study 4.1   Trade unions have become more conscious of the need to **move away from servicing and towards organising** – to mobilise its membership. In 1998 the TUC, following the example of the AFL-CIO in the USA and ACTU in Australia, established an Organising Academy which in its first year had 36 trainee organisers sponsored by 17 unions[98]. The purpose of organising is not just to recruit new members but to help them 'self-organise'. However, as Kelly points out, collective mobilisation and action requires, first of all, some perceived injustice[99]. He argues that an examination of social attitudes suggests that employees are 'increasingly dissatisfied with the amount of "voice" they can exercise over workplace decisions ... increasingly critical of the pay differentials between the highest and lowest paid groups' and there is a 'growing lack of trust in, and criticism of, management'[100]. Indeed, Deery and Walsh argue that HRM may actually contain the seeds of 'heightened collectivism, stronger union commitment and a significantly greater willingness to take industrial action'[101] wherever it is associated with work intensification, job insecurity, pay disparities, etc.

Significantly, Waddington and Whitston have found, from a sample of over 10,000 new members across 12 unions, that 'traditional collective reasons

Case study 4.1 ■ T&GWU – responding to the membership challenge

In the 1970s, the T&GWU was frequently seen as the epitome of the then 'new' unionism[1]:

■ Reduced reliance on members being 'serviced' by full-time officers in favour of more active participation in decision-making by the rank-and-file members (democratic control);

■ Developing better-trained and more self-reliant shop stewards to carry out the union's representational and negotiating roles at the workplace – accepted and institutionalised within formal recognition and procedural agreements with management (parallel unionism).

Significantly, however, the T&GWU believes that one reason for its drop in membership from 2.1 million in 1979 to 881,000 in 1999 lies in its failure to 'educate' its members: 'we did not explain why trade unionism was necessary and what it would be like without trade unions. We took it for granted that people joined and,

once they joined, we basically left them to it. We were reliant on employers and on the law – things that were not fundamentally our friends'[2].

The T&GWU has initiated two strategies over the past 15 years to stimulate membership recruitment[3]:

■ *Link-Up* was aimed initially at part-time and temporary employees within the workplace, but eventually broadened out into a more community-based approach (for example, Recruit-a-Mate and joint advisory schemes with the Citizens Advice Bureau). Unfortunately, many full-time union officers saw it as a 'top down' short-term 'campaign' to recruit *new* members, following which they would return to their 'normal' activity of servicing and negotiating on behalf of *existing* members.

■ *Organising for Strength* returns to the early roots of trade unionism. It emphasises the responsibil-

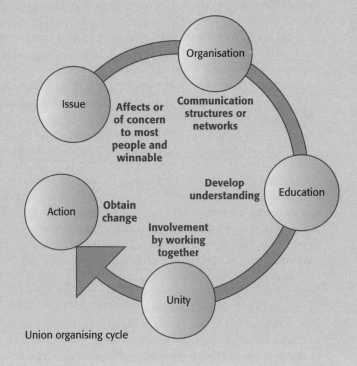

Union organising cycle

Case study 4.1 ■ T&GWU – responding to the membership challenge
(continued)

ity and role of rank and file members not only to recruit new members but also to organise themselves and determine their own agenda (self-organisation and the organising cycle). By building up union consciousness, or participative unionism, the union hopes to be better able to retain as well as recruit members.

Through this, the union has tried to redress the ideological 'battle' underpinning HRM (understanding and defending collectivism) as well as deal with the specific HRM strategies and actions which do not fit within the previous concept of a 'cash exchange' relationship but which still, nevertheless, exploit and intensify the labour process. By putting forward a

positive agenda (for example, training and equality issues), they believe HRM is 'now more likely to be seen as a set of negotiating issues rather than something completely new with a new philosophy'[2].

Sources:
1. E. Heery, 'The new new unionism', in I. Beardwell (ed.), *Contemporary Industrial Relations: a critical analysis*, Oxford University Press, 1996, pp. 180–3.
2. J. Fisher, 'The challenge of change: the positive agenda of the TGWU', *The International Journal of Human Resource Management*, vol. 8, no. 6, 1997, pp. 795–806.
3. P. Blyton and P. Turnbull, *The Dynamics of Employee Relations* (2nd edn), Macmillan, 1998, pp. 103–9.

See also Boxes 5.1 and 6.4 and Case study 6.3.

remain central to union joining'[102]. The top two reasons given for joining a union were 'support if I had a problem at work' (72 per cent) and 'improved pay and conditions' (36 per cent), with 'belief in trade unions' generally being ranked third just ahead of 'free legal advice' and 'most people at work are members'. Perhaps not surprisingly, new union members who were in the 'semi- or associate-professionals and technicians' category or health industry placed 'free legal advice' in second place as their reason for joining above 'improved pay and conditions', but 'managers, administrators and professionals' ranked 'belief in trade unions' more highly than other groups. Waddington and Kerr[103] found the same factors influenced members to remain in UNISON.

Wever argues that the past strength of trade unionism has been not only its awareness that social and economic welfare are inseparable but also its capacity to act in both spheres. Consequently, it must continue to demonstrate its ability to provide 'added value' not just to management but to society as a whole. Successful union strategies are those which 'anticipate change; articulate alternatives to employer strategies; rally community groups and other constituencies with common interests; strongly emphasize worker skills and participation in decisions about the organization of work, production and skill development; and embody flexibility, broadly defined'[104].

■ Summary propositions

- ■ Trade unions have developed from small localised organisations into complex national institutions which can play an integral and influential role not only in the workplace but also in society.

■ Trade union membership and influence in the UK has been affected by unemployment, changes in the composition of the labour force, management strategies aimed at marginalising them and, most importantly, the withdrawal of government support during the 1980s.

■ Trade unions have to balance their activities in direct pay and job regulation with management with their pursuit of economic regulation and social change at the society level through the political process.

Activity   See if you can get some 'primary' materials from a trade union – such as recruitment literature, member magazine, conference report, rulebook or constitution. You could phone or write to them locally or nationally, or browse their web site – most major unions have one. Once you've got some materials, try to identify the union's aims and objectives, what sort of issues are of concern to it, (debated at conference or covered in the members' magazine) and how these might reflect the different functions of a trade union. You could also look at how the union projects itself or appeals to potential members in its recruitment literature.

■ Further reading

■ H. Pelling, *A History of British Trade Unionism*, Penguin, 1976. A very readable account of the historical development of the trade union movement in Britain.

■ M. P. Jackson, *An Introduction to Industrial Relations*, Routledge, 1991. Chapter 2 examines the historical development of trade unions in the UK and elsewhere, while Chapter 3 discusses the problems of UK unions in the 1980s and 1990s.

■ B. Pimlott and C. Cook, *Trade Unions in British Politics* (2nd edn), Longman, 1991. Chapters 14, 15 and 16 examine the union-political relationship during the 1980s Thatcher government, in the revision of the Labour Party and in the growing importance of the EU.

■ R. Hyman and A. Ferner, *New Frontiers in European Industrial Relations*, Blackwell, 1994. Chapter 4 (J. Visser, 'European trade unions: the transition years') assesses the reasons and pattern of union decline, while Chapter 5 (R. Hyman, 'Changing trade union identities and strategies') considers the variety of union responses.

■ References

1. B. C. Roberts, *Trade Unions in a Free Society*, Institute of Economic Affairs, 1959, p. 1.
2. B. Towers, 'Trends and developments in industrial relations: derecognising trade unions: implications and consequences', *Industrial Relations Journal*, vol. 19, no. 3, 1988, p. 184.
3. For example, the Statute of Artificers (1563), which allowed JPs to fix wage rates in their locality.

4. R. Bean, *Comparative Industrial Relations* (2nd edn), Routledge, 1994 (Ch. 9 – Industrial relations in developing countries).

5. *Ibid.*, p. 219.

6. B. Wilkinson, 'The Korea labour "problem" ', *British Journal of Industrial Relations*, vol. 32, no. 3, 1994.

7. F. Tannenbaum, *The True Society: A Philosophy of Labour*, Cape, 1964.

8. S. and B. Webb, *History of Trade Unions*, Longman, 1896.

9. J. Lovell, *British Trade Unions 1875–1933*, Macmillan, 1977, p. 21.

10. G. D. H. Cole, *A Short History of the British Working Class Movement 1789–1947*, Allen & Unwin, 1966, p. 246.

11. H. Pelling, *A History of British Trade Unionism*, Penguin, 1976, p. 151. Reprinted by permission of Penguin Books Ltd. © Henry Pelling, 1963, 1971, 1976.

12. H. A. Turner, G. Clark and B. Roberts, *Labour Relations in the Motor Industry*, Allen & Unwin, 1967.

13. R. Price and G. S. Bain, 'Union growth in Britain: retrospect and prospect', *British Journal of Industrial Relations*, vol. 21, no. 1, 1983.

14. J. Waddington and C. Whitston, 'Trade unions: growth, structure and policy', in P. Edwards (ed.), *Industrial Relations: Theory and Practice in Britain*, Blackwell, 1995, tables 6.3 and 6.4.

15. *Hilton v Eckersley* (1855) quoted in K. W. Wedderburn, *The Worker and the Law*, Penguin, 1971, p. 86. © K. W. Wedderburn, 1965, 1971.

16. *Ibid.*, p. 76.

17. K. Hawkins, *Trade Unions*, Hutchinson, 1981, p. 40.

18. Wedderburn, *op. cit.*, p. 310.

19. H. Vester and A. H. Gardiner, *Trade Union Law and Practice*, Sweet & Maxwell, 1958, p. 11.

20. C. Grunfeld, *Modern Trade Union Law*, Sweet & Maxwell, 1966, p. 439.

21. R. Lewis, 'Collective labour law', in G. S. Bain (ed.), *Industrial Relations in Britain*, Blackwell, 1983, p. 392.

22. *Heaton Transport* v. *T&GWU* (1973); *Midland Cold Storage* v *Turner* (1972); *Con-Mech (Engineering)* v *AUEW* (1973).

23. Pelling, *op. cit.*, p. 42.

24. J. Monks, 'Government and trade unions', *British Journal of Industrial Relations*, vol. 36, no. 1, 1998, p. 126.

25. R. Taylor, *The Fifth Estate*, Pan, 1980, pp. 97–112.

26. J. McIlroy, *Trade Unions in Britain Today*, Manchester University Press, 1988, p. 56.

27. W. J. Brown (1925 TUC Congress) quoted in Pelling, *op. cit.*, p. 170.

28. P. Edwards, M. Hall, R. Hyman, P. Marginson, K. Sisson, J. Waddington and D. Winchester, 'Great Britain: still muddling through', in A. Ferner and R. Hyman (eds), *Industrial Relations in the New Europe*, Blackwell, 1992, p. 45.

29. J. McIlroy, 'The enduring alliance? Trade unions and the making of new Labour, 1994–1997', *British Journal of Industrial Relations*, vol. 36, no. 4, 1998, pp. 545 and 547.

30. Monks, *op. cit.*

31. L. Ward, 'Union fights for working class MPs', *Guardian*, 2 September 1998.

32. S. Milne and N. Watt, 'Call to break union links with Labour', *Guardian*, 14 September 1999.

33. G. S. Bain and F. Elsheikh, *Union Growth and the Business Cycle*, Blackwell, 1976; G. S. Bain and R. Price, 'Union growth; dimensions, determinants and density', in G. S. Bain (ed.), *Industrial Relations in Britain*, Blackwell, 1983; R. Disney, 'Explanations of the decline in trade union density in Britain: an appraisal', *British Journal of Industrial Relations*, vol. 28, no. 2, 1990.

34. F. Green, 'Recent trends in British trade union density: how much a compositional effect?' *British Journal of Industrial Relations*, vol. 30, no. 3, 1992.

35. R. Adams and R. Markey, 'How the State influences trade union growth: a comparative analysis of developments in Europe, North America and Australasia', *International Journal of Comparative Labour Law and Industrial Relations*, Winter 1997, p. 300.

36. 'Union decline bottoms out', *Labour Research*, August 1999, p. 15.

37. Price and Bain, *op. cit.*, p. 61.

38. Bain and Price, *op. cit.*, p. 33.

39. Green, *op. cit.*

40. J. Waddington, 'Trade union membership in Britain, 1980–1987: unemployment and restructuring', *British Journal of Industrial Relations*, vol. 30, no. 2, 1992.

41. R. Freeman and J. Pelletier, 'The impact of industrial relations legislation on British union density', *British Journal of Industrial Relations*, vol. 28, no. 2, 1990.

42. J. Kelly and R. Bailey, 'British trade union membership, density and decline in the 1980s: a research note', *Industrial Relatons Journal*, vol. 20, no. 1, 1989.

43. S. Kessler and F. Bayliss, *Contemporary British Industrial Relations* (3rd edn), Macmillan, 1998, p. 166.
44. P. Bland, 'Trade union membership and recognition 1997–8', *Labour Market Trends*, July 1999, table 5, p. 349.
45. Certificiation Officer, *Annual Report* 1998, p. 17.
46. 'Will trade unionists say "yes" to the union?' *IRS Employment Trends*, no. 559, 1994.
47. 'Signing up – a hard slog', *Labour Research*, September 1994.
48. R. Hyman, *Industrial Relations: A Marxist introduction*, Macmillan, 1975, p. 66.
49. *Ibid.*, p. 64.
50. S. Perlman, 'Labour's "home-grown" philosophy', in W. E. J. McCarthy (ed.), *Trade Unions*, Penguin, 1972, p. 28.
51. Hyman, *op. cit.*, p. 65.
52. G. S. Bain and R. Price, *Profiles of Union Growth: A comparative statistical portrait of eight countries*, Blackwell, 1980.
53. C. Mulvey, *The Economic Analysis of Trade Unions*, Martin Robertson, 1976.
54. *Ibid.*, p. 35.
55. N. Robertson and J. L. Thomas, *Trade Unions and Industrial Relations*, Business Books Ltd, 1968, p. 39.
56. A. M. Ross, *Trade Union Wage Policy*, University of California Press, 1948.
57. Mulvey, *op. cit.*, p. 42.
58. Hawkins, *op. cit.*, p. 22.
59. B. Burkitt and D. Bowers, *Trade Unions and the Economy*, Macmillan, 1979, table 5.2, p. 62.
60. E. H. Phelps Brown, *The Growth of British Industrial Relations*, Macmillan, 1960, p. 366.
61. E. H. Phelps Brown, 'New wine in old bottles: reflections on the changed working of collective bargaining in Great Britain', *British Journal of Industrial Relations*, vol. 11, no. 2, 1973.
62. T. Stark, 'The changing distribution of income under Mrs Thatcher', in F. Green (ed.), *The Restructuring of the UK Economy*, Harvester Wheatsheaf, 1989.
63. A. Flanders, *Management and Unions*, Faber & Faber, 1970, p. 43.
64. *Ibid.*
65. 'New bargaining agenda for unions', *IRS Employment Trends*, no. 479, January 1991.
66. M. van de Vall, *Labour Organizations*, Cambridge University Press, 1970, p. 54.
67. P. Anderson, 'The limits and possibilities of trade union action', in R. Blackburn and A. Cockburn (eds), *The Incompatibles*, Penguin, 1967, p. 264. Reprinted by permission of Penguin Books Ltd. © New Left Review, 1967.
68. van d Vall, *op. cit.*, p. 55.
69. Taylor, *op. cit.*, p. 100.
70. J. McIlroy (1998), *op. cit.*, p. 545.
71. J. W. Leopold, 'Trade unions, political fund ballots and the Labour Party', *British Journal of Industrial Relations*, vol. 35, no. 1, 1997, p. 35.
72. J. W. Leopold, 'Moving the status quo: the growth of trade union political funds', *Industrial Relations Journal*, vol. 19, no. 4, 1988, p. 286.
73. Leopold (1997), *op cit.*, table 1, p. 28.
74. P. B. Beaumont and R. I. D. Harris, 'The importance of national institutional arrangements: the case of trade union membership and unemployment', *The International Journal of Human Resource Management*, vol. 9, no. 6, 1998, pp. 1064–75.
75. B. Towers (ed.), *A Handbook of Industrial Relations Practice* (3rd edn), Kogan Page, 1992, p. 40.
76. 'Union services: the way forward?' *IRS Employment Trends*, no. 457, February 1990.
77. *Ibid.*, p. 6.
78. *Ibid.*, p. 12.
79. Mason and Bain, *op. cit.*, p. 37.
80. McIlroy (1988), *op. cit.*, pp. 220–1.
81. R. Price, 'White collar unions: growth, character and attitudes in the 1970s', in R. Hyman and R. Price, *The New Working Class? White Collar Workers and their Organizations*, Macmillan, 1983, p. 163.
82. R. M. Blackburn, *Union Character and Social Class*, Batsford, 1967, p. 18.
83. G. Bain, D. Coates and V. Ellis, *Social Stratification and Trade Unionism*, Heinemann, 1973.
84. Price, *op. cit.*, p. 166.
85. W. G. Runciman, *Relative Deprivation and Social Justice*, Routledge & Kegan Paul, 1966.
86. N. Nicholson, G. Ursell and P. Blyton, *The Dynamics of White Collar Unionism: A study of local union participation*, Academic Press, 1981.
87. K. Prandy, A. Stewart and R. M. Blackburn, *White-Collar Unionism*, Macmillan, 1983, p. 13.
88. *Ibid.*, p. 171.
89. Bain *et al.*, *op. cit.*, pp. 8–9.
90. M. Poole, *Industrial Relations: origins and patterns of national diversity*, Routledge & Kegan Paul, 1986, p. 68.
91. Bean, *op. cit.*, p. 19.
92. R. Hyman, 'Changing trade union identities and strategies', in R. Hyman and A. Ferner

(eds), *New Frontiers in European Industrial Relations*, Blackwell, 1994, p. 136.

93. P. Willman, 'The logic of "market-share" trade unionism: is membership decline inevitable?' *Industrial Relations Journal*, vol. 20, no. 4, 1989, pp. 260–70.

94. D. Guest, 'Human resource management, trade unions and industrial relations', in J. Storey (ed.), *Human Resource Management*, Routledge, 1995, pp. 110–41.

95. 'Unions respond to membership losses', *IRS Employment Trends*, no. 519, 1992.

96. S. Williams, 'The nature of some recent trade union modernization policies in the UK', *British Journal of Industrial Relations*, vol. 35, no. 4, 1997, p. 501.

97. E. Heery, 'The new new unionism', in I. Beardwell (ed.), *Contemporary Industrial Relations: A critical analysis*, Oxford University Press, 1996, p. 187.

98. 'Organise, activate and motivate', *Labour Research*, September 1998, pp. 13–15.

99. J. Kelly, *Rethinking Industrial Relations: Mobilization, collectivism and long waves*, Routledge, 1998, p. 64.

100. J. Kelly, 'The future of trade unionism: injustice, identity and attribution', *Employee Relations*, vol. 19, no. 4, 1997, p. 412.

101. S. Deery and J. Walsh, 'The decline of collectivism? A comparative study of white-collar employees in Britain and Australia', *British Journal of Industrial Relations*, vol. 37, no. 2, 1999, p. 262.

102. J. Waddington and C. Whitston, 'Why do people join unions in a period of membership decline?' *British Journal of Industrial Relations*, vol. 35, no. 4, 1997, p. 518.

103. J. Waddington and A. Kerr, 'Membership retention in the public sector', *Industrial Relations Journal*, vol. 30, no. 2, 1999, pp. 151–65.

104. K. S. Wever, 'Unions adding value: addressing market and social failures in the advanced industrialized countries', *International Labour Review*, vol. 136, no. 4, 1997, p. 465.

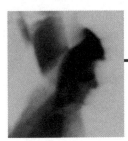

chapter five

Trade union organisation and structure

Trade unions, individually and as a movement, are there to represent employees' interests. By the end of this chapter, you should be able to:

■ explain the institutional arrangements of trade union organisation and the process of union government (in particular, the differences between 'participative' and 'representative' democracy and the nature of the union's 'leadership');

■ appreciate the diversity of trade union structure and understand the concepts of 'open', 'closed', 'sectoral' and 'conglomerate' unions in relation to the pattern and process of union mergers;

■ explain the function of the Trades Union Congress in regulating inter-union relations and supporting the development of trade unionism.

Definition

The term organisation refers to the internal institutions and processes which form the union's administrative, representative and authority systems, while the term structure refers to the different types of union based on their recruitment patterns or memberships' job territory.

Key issues

While you are reading this chapter, you should keep the following points in mind:

■ The power, influence and effectiveness of a trade union depends very much on the existence of committed active members both at the workplace and throughout the union organisation. We need to appreciate the inherent tensions within a trade union between *efficiency* (in organising and servicing their members) and *democracy* (being representative of, and ultimately controlled by, the membership).

■ No one structural principle has dominated the development of trade unions in the UK. Over recent years, the process of mergers has resulted in the development of a small number of conglomerate 'super-unions'. We need to consider whether this concentration, with its potential loss of identity and 'common interest' among the members, is the best way to represent 'labour'.

■ The TUC, despite declining union membership in the UK, is the only body which can claim to represent 'employees' as a whole. We need to consider whether the TUC should concentrate on reflecting and representing its members (affiliated trade unions), or 'network' and co-ordinate activities with other organisations to project a wider labour interest (employees or workers generally).

5.1   Introduction

Trade union 'organisation' and 'structure' should not be viewed simply as static institutional arrangements but rather as dynamic adaptive processes. Certainly, for the last two decades, UK trade unions have had to adjust to declining membership, more flexible and fragmented work patterns and government-imposed legislative controls on their decision making. However, trade unions

---

Box 5.1   The Transport and General Workers' Union

'Right from the start the Union was built on two fundamental principles. First and foremost, the rules and structure of the Union were designed to guarantee that control of the Union was in the hands of its members, that it was run and its policies made by their elected representatives and not by full-time employees of the Union. Democracy in the T&G means that decision-making rests with the elected committees and conferences of the Union, and these consist of ordinary men and women members still working at their jobs. The second principle is that within the multi-industrial make-up of the Union, there is room for each industry to have a say on matters which affect only or chiefly the industry itself. The structure of the T&G was geared from the outset to accommodate the interests of the different industries in which the union has members. It does this by means of a committee structure and a system of election to conference which reflects not just the wide geographical spread of members, but also the trades in which they work. Each member belongs not only to a Region of the union, but to a Trade Group as well – and has a right to representation on both counts.

The essence of the Union's structure and constitution is its flexibility. The T&G has always been able to adapt to changing circumstances, but without abandoning any of its principles. Obviously, during the last sixty years some industries have grown, while others have shrunk – and new industries have come into being. In 1922, for example, some 70 per cent of the Union's membership was connected with transport, whereas today the opposite is the case – over 70 per cent is employed in other industries. Indeed, the Union has grown vastly, and not only by recruitment. Many established unions have amalgamated with the T&G over the years – sometimes bringing to our Union members in trades the T&G had not previously covered, or had covered only to a small degree. The structure of the Union has had to be flexible and able to bend to accommodate new members. A rigid, over-formal constitution, however effective to begin with, would never have stood the strain of growth and change.

Good examples are found in the joining of the National Union of Dyers, Bleachers and Textile Workers and the National Union of Agricultural and Allied Workers with the T&G in the 1980s. The new influx of members brought about by the merging of the unions with our own meant change throughout the Union – at national and regional level, as well as locally. It has meant two new trade groups within the Union – the one representing textile workers, the other workers in agricultural and related industries – and adjustments to representation on committees within the regions too. To remain a strong and viable union in the 1980s and beyond, the Union has to be big enough and versatile enough to make the sort of changes modern conditions demand.'

Source: Your Union at Work – 1, TGWU Education Department, pp. 50–1.

See also Box 6.4 and Case studies 4.1 and 6.3.

still retain their unique quality as 'mutual' organisations (i.e. 'owned' by their members and run for their benefit). The principle of 'mutuality' impinges on both union organisation (democratic control, accountability and decision making) and union structure (the members' perception of the common interest which binds them together). This is clearly seen in the example of the T&GWU (see Box 5.1).

It is also important to recognise that 'organisation' and 'structure' are interrelated features of trade unionism. The way a union manages and governs itself is, partly, a reflection of its type of membership. For example, the old 'craft' unions were able to rely on an educated and literate membership to provide a cadre of part-time lay officials to manage the union, while the unions seeking to organise and represent semi-skilled and unskilled production workers and labourers tended to rely more on recruiting external full-time 'officers' to help run their union. Similarly, non-manual public sector unions tended to adopt a 'civil service' or 'local government' management model which differentiated lay elected 'councillors' (who decide policy and strategy) from appointed 'officers' (who carry out those decisions). Likewise, union mergers are, in part, the result of perceived notions of common interest, both industrial structure as well as political outlook, and may be facilitated (or otherwise) by the nature of the unions' organisational arrangements.

5.2 Trade union organisation

Although each union's organisation is unique, in terms of the interrelationship between members, officers, committees and conferences, nevertheless all unions display the same basic pattern of institutions (see Figure 5.1).

The branch

Despite an expansion and improvement in union communications and services direct to members, the branch still remains 'the primary unit of trade union organisation, and on it is based the whole pyramid of administrative and governmental structure'[1]. It is the formal institution for the **regular meeting of the rank and file membership** to participate directly in union affairs: conveying members' views upwards; disseminating union policy and instructions down; electing delegates to union committees and conferences; submitting resolutions on union policies and actions. Branches may vary in size (from a handful of members to several thousand), frequency of meetings (from once a fortnight to only once a year – the Annual General Meeting) and type (*geographical*: drawing membership from different industries or companies; *plant*: membership drawn entirely from a single employer).

A major problem facing trade unions is one of **low attendance at branch meetings**: often only 10–15 per cent. This is not new – the Webbs stated in the 1890s, 'only in the crisis of some great dispute do we find the branch meetings crowded'[2]. However, as Hyman points out, 'without membership participation

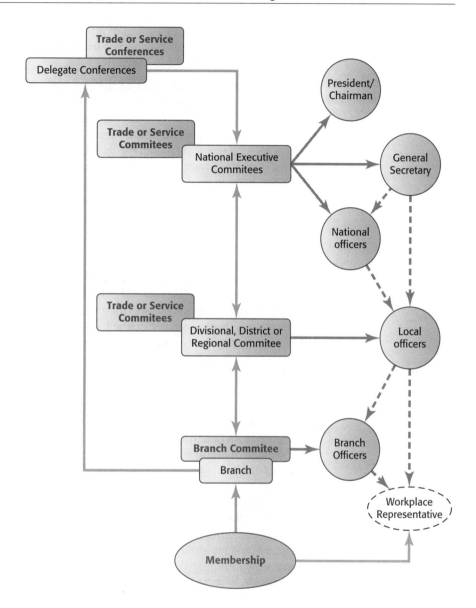

Figure 5.1 Trade union organisation

it is impossible to establish that the interests which trade unions represent (however "efficiently") are indeed those which members identify; and without active involvement, the capacity to mobilize collective resources – power – in support of these interests is constrained'[3]. It is possible to attribute low attendance to the following factors:

- People's general apathy and dislike of meetings;
- Timing and manner of conducting branch meetings;
- Specific factors relating to the membership pattern of the union (in particular women and part-time workers);

■ Most members no longer having to attend the branch meeting to pay their contributions but having it deducted from their wages by their employer or paying by direct bank debit.

Perhaps more significantly, part of the explanation also lies in the **changing pattern of collective bargaining**. The majority of members join a trade union for instrumental reasons relating to wage bargaining and job regulation. In the early local societies, the branch and union were one indivisible institution negotiating directly with local employers, with the membership directly participating in these decisions. With the advent of national unions and industry-wide bargaining, decision making became more distant from the members and centred on the national executive committee and full-time officers. The branch became, in the eyes of many members, simply concerned with the internal government of the union and of marginal value in determining the policies and actions of the union in those areas they consider to be most important. The subsequent shift in collective bargaining to the organisational level has reinforced the role of 'plant'-based branches but has produced a split between branch and workplace in 'geographical' branches – it is inevitable that members should place most importance on the relationship with their workplace representative (their representative to management).

Furthermore, the unions' increasing use of direct individualised communication to members at their home, attitude or market research surveys and postal balloting can easily reduce the role of the branch as a conduit for up and down communication. However, as Waddington and Whitson point out, 'local union organization underpins recruitment'[4]. Therefore, the maintenance of branch activity (and an active branch membership) must be an important element in the strategy to establish the infrastructure to recruit new members; certainly for plant-based branches, particularly in the public (or formerly public) sector, where workplace union organisation and branch organisation are co-terminous.

Most unions have some form of **intermediate organisation** variously entitled Area, District, Division or Region. In some, each branch automatically has its own representative (providing for direct participation and feedback between branch and 'regional' committee). In others, the committee is elected by the 'regional' branches/membership thereby resulting in no direct link for those branches who do not nominate a candidate or whose candidate is not elected. In some cases the intermediate level achieved relative power and autonomy through a conscious decision to create a system of power separation within the union's constitution (the Area 'unions' in the NUM) or through its role in negotiating 'district' agreements (the AEU's District Secretary and Committee). As Kessler and Bayliss point out, the decentralisation of collective bargaining has enhanced the need for 'regional' co-ordination and support of workplace bargaining and has resulted in some shift of unions resources from national to regional level – particularly those unions in the public (or formerly public) sector[5].

National executive committee (NEC)

In theory, the function of the NEC is to **administer and control the union between delegate conferences** and carry out the policies determined by the delegate conference. In practice, however, the division between policy making and implementation has not been so simple; the NEC cannot avoid being involved in **making policy**, at least in so far as it has to interpret and apply what is often a generally worded policy and respond to events and developments which occur between delegate conferences.

- **Size and type of NEC**. Some unions have relied on a large part-time NEC of lay members to better reflect the views of rank and file members but, because of their infrequent meetings, this may leave many, perhaps important, decisions in the hands of the full-time officers. Other unions have preferred a small full-time NEC to exercise control over full-time officers, but its members may lose contact with the rank and file and become part of the administrative establishment. This illustrates the essential dilemma between efficiency and democracy within union organisation. The AEEU's NEC has changed from a relatively small ten-person full-time executive (when it was the AEU) to a larger 48-person lay executive (16 elected on a geographic basis and 32 elected by industrial sectors). The larger NEC more easily facilitates provisions for ensuring representation of women.

- **Method of election**. In some unions, prior to 1984, the NEC was elected by the annual conference (or other body) thereby ensuring that it was accountable to that body and no other. However, the Trade Union Act (1984) and Employment Act (1988) have imposed one uniform system on all unions, which requires that all members of the union's principal executive committee, the General Secretary and President to be directly elected by the membership by secret postal ballot. This direct membership election has the effect of reducing the 'supreme' authority of the delegate conference; each segment of the union's organisation is able to claim the support of the same power base (the membership). It has also, in the case of the GMB, further reduced the power of Regional Secretaries by removing their *ex-officio* position on the union's Central Executive Council[6].

- **Special provision based on distinct interest groups**. Increasing membership and bargaining heterogeneity has led many unions to make provision for sectional groups (trade, industry or service) to be represented on the NEC. This has been supported by separate and distinct trade or service conferences, committees or advisory groups (at both national and intermediate levels) to discuss, co-ordinate and represent their differing sectional interests (particularly terms and conditions of employment). More importantly, many unions have, as part of a policy of positive discrimination to stimulate greater participation, established a proportion of 'reserved' places on the NEC for women. However, in 1997–8, only four of the top ten TUC unions achieved the same proportion of female NEC members as they had female membership (see Table 5.1), while the female membership in the two teaching unions were significantly under-represented on their NECs and the AEEU had none (although it has since changed its constitution to provide four reserved places for women).

Delegate conference

In their formative years trade unions were small enough to adopt a form of 'primitive' democracy (a meeting of the entire membership as the supreme policy-making body). As trade unions grew, this was replaced by a 'representative democracy' body, the delegate conference – the 'device of trade union government by which ultimate authority is returned to the members'[7]. Its function is to **determine the policy of the union** (debating and voting on resolutions from the branches or NEC) and to control the activities of the NEC and full-time officers. However, Hawkins notes that union conferences 'tend to discuss policy issues only in very general terms'[8], while McIlroy argues that the NEC can always 'interpret conference decisions to their own satisfaction, or argue that changed circumstances have rendered their realisation redundant and weather the storm at the next conference'[9].

Delegate Conferences vary in **size and type**. The T&GWU's Biennial Delegate Conference comprises some 700 delegates. However, its apparent opportunity for a substantial number of rank and file members to be part of the governmental process of their union at the highest level is reduced by the limited opportunity for any single delegate to contribute to the debate (there are only a limited number of speeches, many from the NEC or officers of the union, before delegates have to vote). The T&GWU has introduced proportionality for women in the election of delegates to the conference by its Regional Trade Groups and intends to introduce similar proportionality in respect of the election of Black and Asian ethnic minorities by 2002–3. The AEU, on the other hand, believed in a relatively small annual National Committee (92 members) which facilitated a more detailed discussion and scrutiny of union policy and actions and, also, could be convened quickly to authorise changes in union policy or actions in the light of developments during the period between normal conferences. However, since 1997, the new AEEU has adopted a twin structure of a union-wide biennial Policy Conference of some 600–700 branch delegates (elected two-thirds on an industrial basis and one-third on a geographical basis) supported by a series of biennial National Industrial Conferences with delegates drawn from workplace shop stewards.

The conference may also perform the function of a **Final Appeal Court** (to consider any claim by a member against disciplinary action, including expulsion, or complaint against the actions of the NEC or officers) or as a **Rules Revision Conference.**

Full-time officers

In 1991, according to Kelly and Heery[10], there were approximately 3,000 full-time officers in Britain – an average ratio of 1 : 3,229 members (worse than in other European countries), ranging from 1 : 1,919 members in UCATT to 1 : 15,476 members in UCW. The higher ratios appeared to be associated with more centralised bargaining in the public sector and/or strong workplace organisation of lay officers. About 15 per cent of the full-time officers were 'specialists' in areas such as journalism, PR, research, finance, education, legal, health and safety, equality and recruitment. Significantly, the number of 'health and safety' and 'recruitment' specialists had more than doubled since 1980 and the number of 'equality' specialists had nearly quadrupled – a reflection of the changed emphasis within unions. Waddington and Kerr found that 80 per cent of the UNISON members surveyed felt that 'contact with full-time officers' needed 'some' or 'much' improvement[11]. Certainly, the officers' workload had increased as a result of decentralisation of bargaining, while their numbers had reduced due to early retirements associated with the post-merger reorganisation of the union.

The number of **female full-time officers** is, generally, much less than would be justified by the proportion of female membership within the union (see Table 5.1). In 1984, SOGAT elected the first female general secretary, but in 1997 only six of the TUC's 73 affiliated unions had a female general secretary, and these were primarily small specialist professional unions (Association of Magisterial Officers, British Orthoptic Society, Community and District Nursing Association, National Association of Probation Officers and the Writers Guild) – the exception being the National Union of Knitwear Footwear and Apparel Trades (40,500 members)[12]. There are still significant perception and organisational barriers to increasing the proportion of female full-time officers at all levels[13] – most unions still retain aspects of a patriarchal culture. However, as Kirton and Healy identify in the case of MSF, women in senior positions within the union are trying 'to create a "woman-friendly" image, a union environment that reflects women's values, concerns and needs and to improve women's experiences of trade unions'[14].

While lay union officials are invariably elected to their posts and secretariat staff appointed, both methods are used in the selection of full-time officers with varying effects on union government. Where election is used, the method is defined in the union rulebook and subject to ultimate control by the membership through the Rules Revision Conference. It allows the membership to initiate a change in leadership style, policy and direction by nominating, supporting and/or selecting candidates prepared to challenge the current, established leadership. However, the apparent benefits for the election method may be

Table 5.1 Women in trade unions (1997–8)

Union	Female membership	Total membership	Females as proportion of		
			NEC	National full-time officers	Regional full-time officers
UNISON	1 016 661	78	65	38	24
GMB	258 912	36	41	8	13
T&GWU	173 588	20	13	4	8
USDAW	172 460	59	53	25	24
NUT	157 360	75	43	14	11
MSF	133 227	31	32	30	16
NAS/UWT	102 365	59	24	22	18
CWU	53 169	19	20	10	n.a.
AEEU	46 958	6	0[1]	0	2
GPMU	34 080	17	22	13	5

[1] Before change to 'lay' NEC and four reserved places for women.
Source: 'Are women out of proportion?', *Labour Research*, March 1998, p. 13.

distorted. Any incumbent office-holder has in-built advantages over a challenger by being better known and having legitimate access to the formal channels of union communication. The appointment method, on the other hand, is 'merely treated as a function of Executive authority'[15], relies heavily on the individual candidate desiring office and therefore initiating the process and contains the constant danger of the creation of a self-perpetuating, like-minded group of office-holders. Certainly, the merger of branches and the development of appointed branch-level full-time officers to organise and represent members, as part of the unions' organising drive, can represent a loss of democratic control by the membership and increased centralised control – a full-time officer, unlike a lay branch official, is part of the union's organisational hierarchy accountable to the General Secretary.

5.3 Trade union government

The popular view of unions displays a dichotomy regarding the expected relationship between the leadership and membership: too powerful and unrepresentative when calling on members to undertake industrial action, but exercising too little control when the rank and file press for action. Trade unions are complex organisations and, therefore, it is too simplistic to state that they are, or should be, always controlled either from the top or the bottom. Although, as Stein points out, trade unions are 'philosophically and traditionally a democratic institution which differs from other types of association ... in the degree to which it emphasises internal democracy'[16], Hyman argues that trade unions 'explicitly incorporate a *two-way system of control*. Union officials are accorded specific powers of leadership and of discipline; in appropriate situations they are legitimately entitled to exert control over the members. But at the same time they are the employees and servants of the members, who are thus in appropriate situations entitled to exert control over *them*'[17].

Certainly, many writers have argued in the past that too much emphasis on *democracy* may be at the expense of the **efficiency of the organisation in achieving its objectives**. Allen argued that 'trade union activity is to protect and improve the general living standards of its members and not to provide workers with an exercise in self-government'[18], while Taylor believed that 'the exercise in democratic self-government is only a by-product, a safeguard against an entrenched oligarchy ignoring rank and file opinion'[19]. Indeed, Hawkins argued that because the members regard their union as an instrumental collective 'they are not unduly disturbed if the union is led by individuals whose political outlook is at variance with their own'[20]. Therefore, the weakness, or even absence, of a democratic basis to the governmental process is not important so long as the leadership is able, overall, to satisfy the needs of the membership and protect their interests. After all, it can be argued, dissatisfied members always have the ultimate sanction of leaving what is, at its core, a voluntary organisation. Certainly, the 1980s saw the formation of several new 'alternative' unions which attracted some members of established unions who disagreed or were dissatisfied with their union's policies, action or leadership (for example, the creation of the Nationally Integrated Caring Employees in the Health Service). Significantly, some subsequently merged with EETPU (noted for its relatively right-wing political position) while it was outside the TUC.

Organisational democracy

Organisational democracy involves an interrelationship between **participative democracy** (membership involvement in policy formulation and decision making) and **representational democracy** (election of representatives to positions of 'government' or leadership). Bray noted, that the so-called right/left factions within unions perceive the basis of democratic government in different ways: to the right 'it is a representative process dependent upon an electoral technique designed to maximise the turnout of votes', while to the left 'it is the regular participation of members in the affairs of their union'[21]. The absence of substantial levels of participation either at branch meetings or in elections does not inevitably imply an absence of democracy but rather that many members do not exercise their democratic rights. Consequently, much of the debate on union democracy centred on the oligarchical nature of the governmental process and the importance of oppositional choices.

The **union's governmental process** involves an interaction between full-time officers, active and passive members within two subsystems: the representative (legislative) and administrative (executive) (see Figure 5.2). As Child *et al.*[22] pointed out, the organisational rationalities underlying each subsystem may conflict within the union's governmental process.

The function of the **administrative subsystem** is to ensure that the union operates efficiently and effectively (it is the *means*) and is founded on the following principles:

- There is a formal designation of decision-making roles with ultimate power, authority and control being vested in the formal leadership at the apex of the organisation.
- Decisions and instructions are communicated downward through a formal organisational hierarchy for implementation by the designated role holder at the appropriate level.
- Subordinates are accountable to the leadership for the successful achievement of the tasks set.

The function of the **representative subsystem**, on the other hand, is to ensure that policies and decisions of the union represent the wishes of, and are acceptable to, the membership (determination of *goals*). It necessitates the adoption of the following principles:

- Ultimate power, authority and control are retained by the rank and file membership itself.
- There is effective representative communication upward within the organisation.

Figure 5.2 Cycle of
union activity

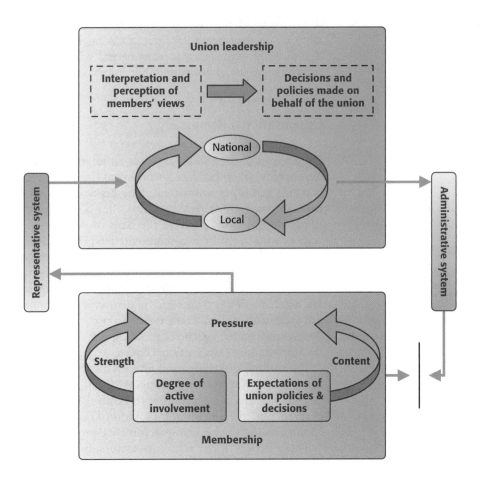

■ The decision-making process should be flexible and responsive to the varying needs of the multitude of subgroups within the union.

■ Decisions made in one part of the organisation may be challenged by the membership through other institutions within the organisation.

■ It is the leadership which is accountable to the membership for the successful achievement of the tasks set.

The nature of the **membership pressure** results from a combination of the membership's expectations of how the union will conduct its affairs on their behalf (*content*) and the extent of their active involvement in the union's management (*strength*). The varying interaction between these two elements was used by Child *et al.* to produce a typology of **membership attachment** which identifies four major types.

Among the smaller group of active membership:

■ The **stalwart**, for whom the union's policies, decisions and general approach are a reflection of his or her own aspirations and who therefore is prepared to maintain and uphold the *status quo* within the union, thereby legitimising the union's leadership;

▪ The **trouble-maker**, for whom there is a divergence from the union's approach on at least some, if not all, issues and who therefore seeks to influence the leadership and modify its policies and decisions.

Among the much larger group of inactive members are:

▪ The **card-holder**, for whom the union serves an instrumental function in respect of wage bargaining and job regulation and who therefore is content to remain passive so long as these needs are met;

▪ The **alienated member**, whose expectations of the union, in instrumental and/or ideological terms, diverge from the actual achievements of the union but who is not prepared to actively seek to change the union's approach.

It should be remembered that such a categorisation is dynamic. Once the trouble-maker has achieved the change in policy or approach, he or she is likely to become a stalwart, prepared to defend that policy or approach, while the original stalwart may become a trouble-maker seeking to reverse the decision and reinstate the previous policy or approach. Equally, the card-holder may, if the union no longer meets his or her instrumental needs, become an alienated member or possibly enter the trouble-maker category by actively seeking to change the policies and actions of the union.

The other crucial stage in the governmental cycle involves the **interpretation and translation of membership pressure into action** by the union's leadership. The term **leadership** is frequently used to imply that it is located exclusively at the national level or, indeed, is embodied in a small group (the NEC) or a single role (the General Secretary or President). However, in reality a trade union is not a monolithic entity with a single focal point of leadership. It is composed of an array of subgroups administered and represented, at national, regional and organisation levels, by a mixture of full-time officials and active lay members through the variety of organisational institutions (branches, committees, conferences, etc.). The leadership role within trade unions is therefore diffuse and includes all those roles which may be deemed, either individually or collectively, to have the power and authority to speak, make decisions and act on behalf of the union members (workplace representatives, branch officers, delegates to the various union committees and conferences as well as the General Secretary, NEC and full-time officers).

Within this wider definition of 'leadership', the representative subsystem should be viewed as a process of decision making *within and between* different segments of the leadership rather than a process of direct representation and control by the membership. For example, is the delegate conference really a meeting between the 'membership' and 'leadership' or rather a meeting of different elements of the leadership role? Certainly, Fox has cited examples where the membership has 'withdrawn legitimacy [*from union full-time officers*] and vested it in the unofficial leaders of low-level collectivities [*shop stewards*]'[23] (my italics). In these situations the membership is not withdrawing its support from the 'leadership' as such, but transferring the emphasis of its loyalty to that segment of the leadership role which is not only closest to them, and therefore likely to better understand their needs, but also subject to a more direct and immediate control by the membership.

Michels' *'iron law of oligarchy'*[24] concluded that all voluntary democratic organisations (including trade unions) will, because of the need to develop an effective system of internal administration, tend towards an oligarchical style of government involving a hierarchical bureaucracy with power and influence concentrated in the formal office-holders (particularly at the apex of the organisation). These roles have access to information, control of communication and decision making coupled with organisational and political skill. Turner[25] identified three major forms of union government: *exclusive democracy* (homogeneous membership with high active participation and a relatively small number of elected full-time officers); *aristocracies* (dominant membership group with a high participation, full-time officers drawn from that group and sometimes restrictions on the participation of other 'ancillary' groups); and *popular bossdom* (heterogeneous membership – generally unskilled or semi-skilled, low level of active participation and a 'professional' full-time officer group which acts as the organisational 'cement'[26]).

The model of organisational democracy developed by Edelstein and Warner accepts the **oligarchical nature of trade unions** but rejects any assumption that it inevitably means an undemocratic abuse of power. Rather, they view oligarchy as an organisational form of *decision making* which retains democratic principles as long as 'consistently effective opposition results from competition between equally powerful potential competitors and their supporters'[27]. Their notion of democracy rests on the twin concepts of (1) majority rule prevailing in both the formulation and implementation of policies and decisions as well as the selection of officials to govern the organisation, and (2) the right of the minority to organise opposition through formal and informal channels and, where substantial enough, to be represented within the decision makers. They identified a range of factors relating to the status hierarchy of officials, the existence of local centres of autonomy and the election or voting procedures which might allow the development and expression of opposition. They concluded from their survey of British and American unions that the formal union organisation could itself constrain any abuse of power from the development of oligarchy by stimulating competition within the union, particularly among the lower-level officials seeking to rise within the union hierarchy.

Many writers have emphasised the **opposition/choice elements** which are integral to any notion of democracy. As early as the 1950s Goldstein argued that 'an election, to have meaning to an individual in a free society, must provide an opportunity for making a choice. Choice, to have meaning, must imply the right of opposition. The right of opposition, to have meaning, implies the right and opportunity of a free exchange of and easy access to information and ideas that any member of the society might consider relevant to an informed discussion'[28]. Lipsett *et al.* argued that democracy could be institutionalised through the existence of organised and structured subgroups such as the 'party system' in the American International Typographical Union[29]. Dickenson has noted that, while the factions seen within British unions are more than simply a transient response to specific issues and may, particularly in the case of the left-wing factions, be based on a common ideological belief among their members, nevertheless they generally lack sufficient formal organisation to ensure their continuity[30]. However, Blackwell concluded from his study of three elections in the Bakers' union in the 1970s that 'entrenched, well structured groups are not invariably necessary for the exercise of democratic control and accountability by members. Less secure groups pursuing desired short- to medium-term goals may effect changes in methods, policy and personnel'[31]. Factionalism may be important in developing potential leadership ability, informing the membership, providing choice and making the current leadership more aware and possibly responsive to the membership. Certainly, Martin argued that the extent of democracy within the trade union organisation may be gauged by the degree to which there are 'constraints inhibiting union executives from destroying internal opposition'[32].

Taft, on the other hand, took the view that 'mutually warring factions are a luxury most unions cannot afford, and the result is a gradual elimination of open differences, and the growth of compromises between influential groups'[33]. Certainly, Dickenson recognises that factions tend to focus attention on the internal affairs of the union and, indeed, may provide the 'evidence' of both 'political motivation' among certain segments of the membership and polarisation within the union. However, Martin *et al.* argue that 'instability in specific unions is not the result of factionalism or of electoral procedures but of wider contextual factors (membership turnover, hostile employers, policy failures)'[34].

As a union increases in **size and diversity of membership**, the administrative subsystem is likely to become more formalised and bureaucratic, and the representative system will face increased difficulties in ensuring that the differing views of disparate groups are brought to bear on decision making. Many unions have sought to mitigate the effects of size and heterogeneity of membership by segmenting their membership into more homogeneous, almost autonomous, units based on the nature of the members' work and by decentralising certain aspects of the decision-making and policy-formulation process (particularly in relation to wages and terms and conditions of employment) to a series of mirror institutions at all levels – specialised branches, trade/service committees, conferences, etc. The complexity and variety of styles and methods of internal decision making within trade unions led Undy *et al.*[35] to develop an analytical framework which distinguished between (1) centralised and decentralised government, (2) diffused or concentrated decision making at each level and (3) decision making relating to bargaining and non-bargaining issues. They found, from their examination of a number of unions, that while external pressures may produce a downwards shift in bargaining decision making, non-bargaining decision making tended to remain centralised. However, this change did provide a stimulus for factionalism and a source of power for opposition to the national leadership.

Thus union government is, in practice, much more complicated than a simple relationship between a homogeneous mass of members and a single leader. On the one hand, the leadership role is dispersed throughout all levels and institutions of the union and, on the other hand, the nature of the membership's involvement in the management of the union is not constant. Van de Vall has suggested that trade unions are **polyarchic organisations**. The active membership and lay officials, 'by their two way communication within the organisation (controlling from members to leaders and informing from leaders to members), ... act as its democratic core. The larger and the more active this group, the closer the organisation approaches the ideal of the democratic theorists. The smaller its number and strength, the more the organisation moves towards the oligarchic pole'[36]. Hyman notes that 'experimentation with networks, working groups or discussion circles has become increasingly common: partly to meet the needs of more member-friendly organization, but also to rebuild a relationship between leaders, activists and ordinary members in ways which make strategic initiative effective because democratically developed'[37].

Legislated democracy

The only legislation, prior to the 1980s, affecting the unions' decision-making process was the requirement to ballot members on the initial establishment of a political fund (Trade Union Act, 1913) and amalgamations (Trade Union Amendment Act, 1876 as amended). However, during the 1980s the government gave statutory support to the **representational concept of democracy** in order to, in its terms, promote 'responsible' unionism, 'return the union to its members' and protect the individual member against union 'tyranny'.

■ *Public financial assistance for expenditure incurred in conducting secret ballots and elections* (Employment Act, 1980). Initially, TUC policy was not to take advantage of this offer; however, following a major confrontation with the AEU in 1985, the policy was abandoned and, in 1990, 74 unions (47 TUC affiliates) received £2.6 million for 557 elections/ballots[38]. Having sought to encourage the voluntary use of ballots by overcoming any argument against their use based on cost, the government proceeded to impose legal requirements for unions to conduct ballots for key national elections, industrial action and the maintenance of political funds – although in the case of ballots for industrial action, the union would not receive the money until any industrial action authorised (as a result of a 'yes' vote) had ended. However, this financial support ceased in 1996 (Trade Union and Employment Rights Act, 1993) leaving the unions and their members to bear the full cost of a system they did not seek – thereby diverting funds from providing other services to the members.

■ *Direct individual membership election*. The Trade Union Act (1984) required that the union's 'principal executive governing body' (the NEC) must be directly elected by the membership. This was extended (Employment Act, 1988) to include the union's General Secretary, President and any non-voting members of the NEC or officers in attendance for the purpose of contributing to policy formulation; gave candidates in all these elections the right to prepare an election address and have it circulated with the voting papers at no cost to the candidate; and, perhaps most importantly, required that elections must be conducted by postal voting and subject to independent scrutiny.

■ *Legal rights for individual members* (Employment Act, 1988). Union members were given the following rights:

  ▎ To inspect the union's financial records and to challenge expenditure from general funds for political or unlawful purposes or to indemnify a member or officer against court penalty for offence or contempt;

▮ To seek a court order restraining the union from proceeding with industrial action which might affect the member where it is not supported by a properly conducted ballot;

▮ To be protected against unjustifiable disciplinary action by the union (including where the member does not support industrial action even though it is lawful and supported by a majority in a properly conducted ballot);

▮ In limited situations, to apply to the court for a legal determination of a grievance the member may have with the union.

It has been suggested that **two themes** underpinned these changes. First, the encouragement of an 'individualistic (even consumerist) approach to union membership'[39]. Unions have had to establish direct communications (for the purpose of conducting ballots and elections) from the union's head office to each member which bypass the branch or workplace. At the same time, the individual member has been given the legal right to question, challenge and even ignore decisions which have been made by the active membership through the appropriate participatory democracy mechanisms. Second, the legislation has promoted a 'statutory constitutional template' involving the 'disfranchisement of activists'[40], 'abolished much of the historical particularity of union constitutions' and 'may strengthen the autonomy of a union's established leaders and legitimate a renewed "popular bossdom" style of government'[41]. The effect of this can clearly be seen in the case of NATFHE.

See Case study 5.1   Significantly, as Smith *et al.* note, the Trade Union Act (1984) left unions with discretion in the type of election process and many opted to utilise the branch or workplace as a focal point for the distribution of ballot forms and information. This strengthened the role of activists, and their relationship with the membership, through the need for them to administer the system, inform the membership and encourage them to participate (i.e. it maintained a collective element within the individual voting process). The government's 'suspicion' of the 'subtle pressure'[42] of branch- or workplace-based systems of ballots led them to introduce the requirement for postal elections and ballots in the Employment Act (1988). The underlying assumption was, as McIlroy noted, 'if the silent majority were able to participate through secret postal ballots, insulated from the "intimidation" of union meetings, the Conservatives felt that there would be a move to the right and improved industrial relations'[43]. However, he argued, 'if we are simply interested in increasing turnout then workplace ballots would appear to represent the best bet, as can be seen from the ballots in the NUM, which regularly passes the 70 per cent turnout mark'[44] and that 'members are in a better position to take decisions when they have listened to the arguments and made their own contribution'[45]. Certainly, Fatchett's examination of postal ballots during 1981/82 suggested that there was not a 'regular silent majority waiting to support moderate candidates'[46]. However, although the 'political fund' ballot turnout in 1985/6 averaged 63 per cent (with a concerted and co-ordinated campaign by the unions to encourage a positive vote for the maintenance of political funds), the average turnout in 1994/6 (with postal voting) dropped to 38 per cent [47].

Perhaps most significantly, the Employment Act (1988) also established a new **Commissioner for the Rights of Trade Union Members** (CRTUM) to assist members wishing to take legal proceedings against their union under their statutory rights. In deciding whether to provide assistance, the CRTUM could take into account whether the case raised a question of principle, involved a matter of substantial public interest and/or it was unreasonable to expect the individual union member to deal with the complexities of the case. The

Case study 5.1 ■ NATFHE* – union democracy?
* National Association of Teachers in Further and Higher Education.

Prior to the Trade Union Act (1984), NATFHE's representative system was based on indirect 'delegate' elections (see Diagram 1). The ordinary members, at their Branch AGM, elected representatives to a Regional Council; the Regional Council, at its AGM, elected representatives to the National Council, national Standing Committees and delegates to the Annual Conference; the National Council, in its turn,

elected the National Executive Committee (NEC). Only the Vice-President (who became President the following year) and the Honorary Treasurer were directly elected by the whole membership (conducted by postal voting). The General Secretary was a full-time employee of the union appointed by (and accountable to) the NEC.

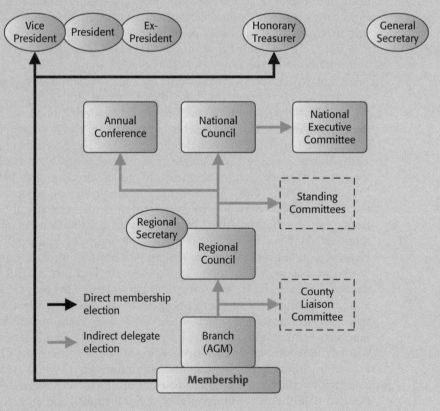

Case Study 5.1 (Diagram 1) Pre-1984

Case study 5.1 ■ NATFHE* – union democracy? *(continued)*

The Trade Union Act (1984) required all voting members of a union's *principal executive governing body* to be directly elected by a secret ballot of the union's membership. Initially, NATFHE concluded that its National Council was this body and should, therefore, be elected by postal ballot on a regional basis; and also decided that the Regional Secretary should be included as one of the region's National Council members (see Diagram 2). These changes had two important potential effects:

■ *They created a gap between the regional and national levels of the union.* National Council members were not automatically members of their Regional Council and, therefore, the only certain link, in terms of common membership between the two bodies, would be the Regional Secretary. Equally important, the Regional Secretary could become isolated from, and lose the confidence of, his or her own Regional Council – but they could do nothing to remove the person.

■ *National Council accountability was shifted.* The National Council could ignore the views of the active membership (as expressed at Regional Councils via Branch meetings), subject only to re-election the next year by the regional membership. Regional Councils could not, as under the previous arrangement, mandate or exert any sanctions on *their* National Council members who did not support regional policies and decisions within the deliberations of the National Council.

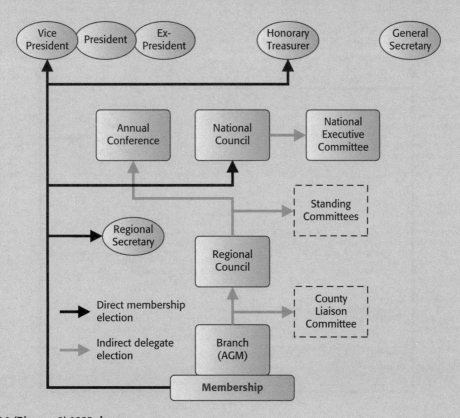

Case Study 5.1 (Diagram 2) 1985 changes

Case study 5.1 ■ NATFHE* – union democracy? *(continued)*

In 1987, following a member's complaint to the Certification Officer, it was held that NATFHE's *principal executive governing body* was the National Executive Committee. Consequently, NATFHE restored the pre-1984 position of Regional Council delegates electing the members of the National Council and introduced direct membership election of the NEC (see Diagram 3). While this removed the gap between regional and national levels and restored the National Council's accountability to Regional Councils, nevertheless it created a new division in control and accountability at the national level – between the National Council and NEC. To whom should the NEC be responsible (collectively and as individuals) – their electorate (the membership) or the National Council (the national level 'policy' body linked to the active membership)?

Later, the Employment Act (1988) required that the membership should also elect a union's General Secretary, President and all *non-voting* NEC members and officers in attendance for policy formulation. In the past, the National Council had been able, through its election of the NEC and powers to co-opt additional members, to ensure that important sectional interests were represented on the NEC. Direct election of the NEC by members cannot ensure this. NATFHE responded by establishing separate regional and national advisory bodies for its two main groups of members – higher and further education. Significantly, in NATFHE's first General Secretary election (under a single transferable voting system) the incumbent lost – although he had a majority of first preference votes!

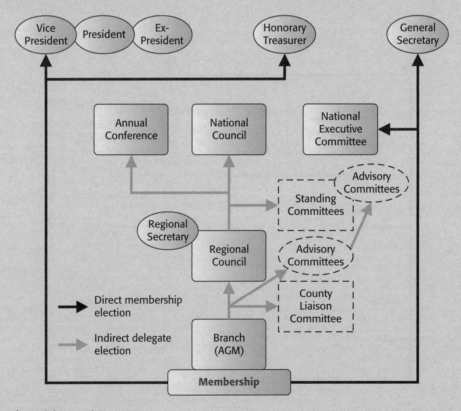

Case Study 5.1 (Diagram 3) Post-1988

CRTUM's assistance took the form of either bearing the costs of any advice or assistance provided by a solicitor or barrister or representing the individual in 'out of court' proceedings. The CRTUM could not directly represent the individual but was required, where proceedings resulted from its assistance, to indemnify the individual against liability for costs or expenses which might arise from a court judgment. The Employment Act (1990) extended the CRTUM's role to cover allegations of breach of the union's rulebook as well as the individual's statutory rights. Morris[48] notes that in 1991/2 CRTUM received 345 enquiries but only 64 formal applications for assistance and only 14 were actually assisted. Significantly, no similar statutory body was established to support employees in legal challenges to the actions of their employer. The Labour government has abolished the CRTUM, along with the Commissioner for Protection against Unlawful Industrial Action, but extended the role of the Certification Officer to adjudicate in such disputes between individual members and their union (S. 28, Employment Relations Act, 1999).

5.4 Trade union structure

Trade union structure is concerned with how trade unions, as independent and autonomous organisations, have been conceived and developed in order to promote the process of recruiting, organising and representing employees across the diverse range of industries and occupations that exist in an industrialised society. The recruitment pattern of British trade unions has been described as displaying 'baffling complexity and apparent lack of rationality'[49], and it has been claimed that 'only a classification with as many separate categories as there are major individual unions could do justice to the diversity which exists'[50]. Britain's trade union structure has often been criticised in the past for being outdated, lacking in industrial unions and, thereby, resulting in competitive multi-unionism and a conservative and reactionary trade union movement reluctant to accept technological change. The existence of **'multi-unionism'** (i.e. more than a single union in relation to the collective bargaining structure) has certainly presented a number of problems:

- *Competition between unions for both members and jobs* has resulted in job-demarcation disputes (involving institutional conflict between organisations as well as people); recognition disputes (which union(s) should be recognised to represent a particular group); and poaching disputes (where one union recruits people who are already members of another union or who are in a group of workers for whom another union is already recognised).

- *Complicated collective bargaining* by requiring reconciliation of differing union objectives into a common claim to management, institutionalising the problems of differentials and leading to comparability claims and leap-frogging wage negotiations.

- *Duplication and dilution of union efforts* to recruit, represent and service their members, diverting attention from their real purpose of confronting the employer.

■ *Creation of joint shop stewards' committees* to integrate the activities of the unions at the organisational level which could amount to an alternative parallel form and focus of union organisation.

See Chapter 6 – Representation at the workplace

However, the problem of multi-unionism has greatly diminished – partly through union amalgamations and partly through the development of a more proactive managerial strategy on trade union recognition (particularly the recent developments in 'single-table bargaining' or 'single-union agreement'). However, Hyman argued that 'the fact that multi-unionism may cause certain problems for managerial control should not be accepted as a valid base for criticism of union structure'[51] – trade unions exist to represent the diverse sectional interests of employees as they perceive them.

Structural classification

See Country profiles 5.1, 4.1 and 4.2

The membership recruitment interests of British unions has usually been delineated by **occupational and industrial boundaries**. In contrast, political and religious beliefs have formed important boundaries for union membership in countries such as Italy, France, Belgium, The Netherlands and South Africa. Trade union structure in the UK today is the result of not only, as Clegg noted, 'the state of technology and industrial organization at the time of their birth and growth'[52] - primarily the nineteenth and early twentieth centuries – but also, as Jenkins and Mortimer pointed out, an evolution 'in response to the needs and wishes of its members'[53]. Most trade unions have modified their recruitment patterns in response to changes in the industrial and technological environments and the associated changes in jobs, skills and occupations. The reduction in the number of unions and the consequent increase in size of many unions has resulted in greater heterogeneity of membership and a weakening of the 'simple' bond of common interest displayed by the early trade unions.

The approaches set out below should not be seen as identifying separate categories within which unions have to be fitted but rather concepts against which unions can be analysed (i.e. how far they comply with or deviate from one or more of these principles and the consequent influence on the union's ethos).

Simple classification

This is based primarily on the doctrinal debate between craft, industrial and general unionism that characterised the development of trade unions during the nineteenth and early twentieth centuries:

1. *Occupational unions (horizontal)*. It is the work performed by the individual and its location in the industrial hierarchy which provides the unifying force (common interest) with others spread across a range of industries:

   ▌ *Craft unions*. Their distinguishing feature has been 'exclusive identity' (concern to control entry into the trade and maintain their skill base). Most single-craft unions in the UK subsequently amalgamated to form 'multicraft' unions and/or become 'craft and allied occupation' or 'industrial' unions through the recruitment of less skilled employees and supervisory or managerial staff. Initially these groups were recruited to

Country profile 5.1   The Netherlands – changing social 'pillars'

Trade union structure in The Netherlands has, in the past, reflected the 'pillarised' organisation of the society seen in education, news media and political parties (as well as trade unions and employers' associations). Two of these pillars have centred on the Catholic and Protestant religions, the third focused around the 'socialist' political ideology (but lacking the integrative mechanisms of, obviously, a church or its own education) and the fourth a more diffuse 'liberalism'. However, this 'pillarisation' has become weaker since the 1970s.

At the same time, the neo-corporatist approach to industrial relations evident in The Netherlands has meant that trade unions have placed emphasis on the national level. They are involved in a variety of bipartite and tripartite arrangements concerned with wages, economic and social policies, while collective bargaining has been conducted primarily through strong multi-employer national agreements. This has resulted in less union emphasis on organisation in the workplace; consequently, they have been in a weak position to cope with recent managerial pressures for decentralisation and changes in working patterns. There has also been some competition between the federations in industry and company negotiations.

In 1981 the Socialist and Catholic trade union groups finally merged to form the FNV, while the Syndical Communist Federation withered away with some of its organisations and members transferring to the FNV. The FNV has a dominant position with 58 per cent of total trade union membership. The second major federation (CNV) still reflects the religious 'pillarisation', while the creation of the VHP in 1974 reflects the desire of middle managers to maintain their different status ideology base. The ACV, established in 1990, represents some groups in the public sector; although a number of its affiliated unions, accounting for almost half its membership, have recently moved over to the FNV.

All the federations have seen moves towards more co-operation and provision of joint services between affiliates, often as a prelude to more formal mergers. The most important merger has been in the FNV. In 1998, the largest FNV union *Industriebond* (manufacturing) amalgamated with three other unions (*Dienstenbond* (private services), *Vervoersbond* (transport) and *Voedingsbond* (food industry)) to create a conglomerate private sector union with a combined membership of about 500,000 members. Together with *AbvaKabo* (public sector) – the FNV's second largest union with a membership of just over 300,000 – they account for 70 per cent of FNV's total membership. These two organisations will dominate not only the FNV (and indeed call into question the relationship between the central federation and individual unions and even its continued existence as a federation), but also the employee side of national industrial relations.

Federation	Membership (1996)
Federation of Dutch Trade Unions (FNV)	1.2 million
Christian-National Union Federation (CNV)	348 000
Federation of White-Collar and Senior Staff (VHP)	160 000
General Union Federation (AVC)	104 000

Sources: J. Visser, 'The Netherlands: the return of responsive corporatism', in A. Ferner and R. Hyman (eds), *Changing Industrial Relations in Europe*, Blackwell, 1998, pp. 294–9; K. Schilstra and E. Smit, 'Union or commonwealth? The balance of power and the organisational structure debate in the Dutch Federation of trade unions', *Industrial Relations Journal*, vol. 25, no. 4, 1994.

protect the interests of the skilled membership from 'cheap' competition or secure their lines of promotion. However, the pre-eminence of the skilled group declined as the size of the other groups increased.

▌ *Semi-skilled/unskilled unions*. The 'new unionism' of the late nineteenth century concentrated on organising workers not catered for by the craft or promotion unions. Subsequently, some amalgamated to provide the nucleus for the creation of 'general' unions or combined with 'craft' or 'promotion' unions in the same industry to produce 'industrial' manual unions.

▌ *Non-manual (white collar) unions.* A significant feature of trade union structure has been the organisation of non-manual employees into separate unions (or, at least, virtually autonomous sections of manual unions, e.g. ACTSS within the T&GWU). Some recruit a single occupation (NUT), some are multi-occupational (IPMS) and others recruit across a range of non-manual employees in a variety of industries (ACTSS, MSF). An added complication is the existence of *professional associations* which, in addition to their role of maintaining professional standards, carry out collective bargaining on behalf of their members (BMA, RCN).

2. *Industrial unions (vertical).* The bond of common interest lies with em-ployees performing other work at different levels in the same organisation (industry) rather than with those applying the same craft, skill or occupation in other industries. Hughes[54] suggested that it would have the greatest appeal where the knowledge and skills required were industry-specific and not easily transferable, or where the uniqueness of the working environment isolated employees from those in other industries. Jackson[55] identified two types of industrial union: *monopoly industrial union* (one union organising all workers in a given industry) and *single-industry union* (a union which restricts its recruitment to one industry, but there might be more than one union in that industry). Originally, monopoly industrial unionism was seen in sociopolitical terms as a mirror of management organisation and a means to support the working classes taking control of both their workplace and society. In the UK there is no monopoly industrial union – unlike the 16 industrial unions established in Germany after the war. However, a number of unions can be classed as being, or have been, single-industry unions (e.g. COHSE, ISTC, NUM and NUR) but in all these industries there are other unions (often craft or general) also seeking to organise groups of workers.

See Country profile 5.2

Three major advantages have often been put forward in the past for restructuring UK unions on an industrial basis: it would strengthen the unity of trade union membership and organisation; simplify collective bar-gaining; and facilitate a greater sense of affinity between the trade union and the industry it represents. Perhaps not surprisingly, its greatest advocates have been those unions which had a clearly identified industrial base. However, the industrial system does not divide neatly into discrete indus-tries with clear boundaries and the boundaries themselves are constantly changing with new techniques, processes and industries. Certainly, a union based on a declining industry would suffer diminished influence and effec-tiveness at the very time when perhaps they are needed most. Furthermore, in the UK it would require major realignments of membership between existing unions (particularly unions such as T&GWU, GMB and MSF) and some groups might feel that their sectional interests are likely to be over-ridden by those of the majority.

3. *General unions.* The idea of a general union (without either occupational or industrial boundaries) predates even the craft unions of the mid-nineteenth century. However, it is important to differentiate the earlier politically inspired attempts to create a general union (the Grand National

Country profile 5.2   Germany – industrial unionism?

German trade union structure was rebuilt after the Second World War on the principles of 'one plant, one union' and industrial unionism (i.e. the integration of manual and non-manual employees in one union), together with no ideological fragmentation (political or religious) or formal affiliation to a political party. However, the DGB (which accounts for 84 per cent of all trade union members) has an ideological sympathy with the Social Democratic Party and believes in the social regulation of capitalism.

Although German trade unionism is dominated by the DGB, there are two other important central federations: DAG which represents non-manual employees (occupational horizontal across industries) and DBB which organises civil servants (*Beamte*, who do not have a legal right to collective bargaining or strike action). A fourth, much smaller, central federation (CGB) has sought to maintain a religious ideological basis. The membership of both DAG and DBB overlap with the membership of DGB affiliates – DAG has a large membership in banking and insurance while DGB has almost as many 'civil servants' among its affiliates as DBB.

Trade unionism grew steadily from 1950 apart from a small drop in the early 1980s. However, more recently, the DGB has been faced by two challenges. First, following reunification, its membership shot-up from 8 to 12 million in one year (1990–1) as the eastern German unions were dissolved and their members encouraged to join DGB affiliates. However, many of these people subsequently drifted away as they lost their jobs or their high hopes that the unions could achieve rapid improvements in their working and living conditions were not realised. Second, there has been a shift in membership as manufacturing has declined (traditional trade union membership stronghold) while non-manual and service employment has grown (the more difficult recruitment areas).

The DGB has been structured on an industrial unionism basis with sixteen affiliated unions. However, it has been dominated by just two – IG Metall with 2.9 million members and OTV (public services and transport) with 1.8 million members. Following a structural review in the early 1990s,

several mergers have taken place among DGB affiliates resulting in a shift towards larger 'multi-sector' or conglomerate unions: the construction union has merged with the agricultural union (1996), the mining and leather unions have joined the chemical union (1997) and two unions (textile and clothing; wood and plastics) have joined IG Metall (1998/9) – increasing its membership to some 3.3 million members (by far the largest single trade union in the world).

Internal organisation of the individual unions is firmly rooted in a delegate system (representative rather than participative democracy) with centralised policy making and national conferences being held only every four years. This reflects the 'dual' nature of the industrial relations system within Germany with trade unions conducting collective bargaining (pay and terms of employment) with employers' associations at industry or sector level, while Works Councils (based on employee representatives) deal with job regulation at the workplace level.

Union Federation	Membership	
	1970	1995
German Trade Union Confederation (DGB)	6.7 million	9.4 million
German Civil Servants' Federation (DBB)	721 000	1.1 million
German Salaried Employees' Union (DAG)	461 000	507 000
Christian Federation of Trade Unions (CGB)	304 000	304 000

Sources: O. Jacobi, B. Keller and W. Müller-Jentsch, 'Germany: facing new challenges', in A. Ferner and R. Hyman (eds), *Changing Industrial Relations in Europe*, Blackwell, 1998, pp. 200–4; F. Fürstenberg, 'Employment relations in Germany', in G. J. Bamber and R. D. Lansbury (eds), *International and Comparative Employment Relations* (3rd edn), Sage, 1998.

See also Country profiles 7.2 and 10.1.

Consolidated Trades Union of 1834) from the structurally evolved general unions which exist today. Unions which might today be classified as general (T&GWU, GMB) did not originate as such but developed by virtue of amalgamations between unions which themselves were organised on occupational or industrial lines. Each has tended to adopt the occupational and industrial pattern provided by the amalgamating unions as its major sphere of organisation, and each new amalgamation has produced a shift in that sphere of organisation.

4. *Federations*. The existence of multi-unionism combined with multi-employer industry-wide collective bargaining created a need for a structural mechanism within which trade unions could co-operate and co-ordinate their activities. The TUC recognised that a formal federation could provide 'a loose form of industrial unionism ... where the industrial, craft or general workers unions, who are concerned in any industry, may get together to pursue jointly the problems affecting the industry with which they are concerned'[56]. The federation may be viewed either as a structural form in its own right – halfway between autonomous unions acting independently and full amalgamation into an industrial union – or as a necessary prelude to industrial unionism. However, it inevitably raises issues about the balance of power and decision making between the federation and its individual constituent unions on such issues as wage bargaining and industrial action. For some unions the federation may occupy a central place in their thinking because the bulk, if not all, of their membership is within that industry; for others the federation is more marginal because only a small proportion of their membership come within the industry concerned. The erosion of multi-employer national bargaining and union amalgamations has reduced the role for federations. Although a Railway Federation of Unions was established in 1983 by the NUR and ASLEF, which it was hoped TSSA would eventually join, this did not happen and subsequently the NUR merged with the NUS to form RMT. At the same time, the change from BR into a number of distinct privatised operating units has resulted in a segmentation of bargaining arrangements.

See Country profile 6.1

5. *Enterprise unions*. Some unions confine their recruitment to the employees of a single organisation. While Japan, with its strong emphasis on internal organisation labour markets, is characterised by this form of union structure, such unions are primarily found in the UK among non-manual *staff associations* in the financial services sector. While enterprise unionism may have the advantage of focusing on the organisational commonality of interest and co-operation between employees and management, it also tends to isolate employees from wider industry and social issues and the trade union movement. Enterprise unions may be perceived as 'company' or 'house' unions, implying they are under the influence (or even domination or control) of management. While the establishment of staff associations in the UK financial sector in the early 1970s reflected the internal preoccupations and relatively benevolent and paternalistic nature of their employment relationship at that time, nevertheless they 'have evolved from largely employer-inspired bodies to function as independent trade unions'[57]. Certainly, with the

erosion of paternalism and introduction of redundancies in Barclays Bank in the early 1990s, the Barclays Group Staff Union changed its name to UNiFI in 1995, affiliated to the TUC in 1996 and, with 44,000 members, merged with BIFU (120,000) and the NatWest Staff Association (38,000) to form UNIFI in 1998[58].

More dynamic approach

The change in trade unions from the simple occupational and industrial concepts illustrates Hyman's point that trade union structure 'is not a fixed phenomenon but a process' involving constant adaptations to reconcile two contradictory forces: 'on the one hand towards breadth, unity and solidarity; on the other towards parochialism, sectionalism and exclusion. The one encourages unionism which is open and expansive; the other, unionism which is closed and restrictive'[59]. For Turner[60] 'closed' unions had the ability to restrict entry into the trade or occupation and as a result maintained an exclusive approach to their membership recruitment pattern. 'Open' unions, on the other hand, lacked the ability to control entry into the trade or occupation and therefore relied on the numerical strength of their membership to provide their bargaining power. Subsequently, the terms **'open'** and **'closed'** have been used simply to categorise unions on the basis of the scope and direction of their membership recruitment patterns and no longer necessarily imply a qualitative judgement in respect of a union's attitude towards controlling the labour supply. These concepts are important in analysing and understanding the *hybrid unions* which form the bulk of trade unions and the changes in a union's structural type which have taken place in the past and/or may take place in the future: open in certain directions and closed in others.

It has also become useful to adopt the wider concept of a **sectoral union** to replace the narrower concept of an industrial union. Hughes applied the term to those unions 'which are by historical origin or "principle" of organisation, concentrated in a particular section of the economy, but prone to take an "open" approach to the definition of that sector and ready to extend into "allied" fields'[61]. It denotes a union which is prepared, at least in part, to recruit from a significant range of occupations across a number of related industries.

However, Undy *et al.* believed that Turner's open/closed typology did not 'distinguish sufficiently between the various dimensions of development in union job territory'[62]. In their view, the full dynamics of changing union structure can only be understood if the relative openness of the union's recruitment boundaries is related to two other important factors:

- ■ **The membership market**: whether the union exists in an expanding or declining employment area and the degree of inter-union competition for membership within that area ('sheltered' or 'exposed' environment);

- ■ **Union orientation to recruitment**: whether the union adopts a *passive* policy and strategy towards recruitment, wherein membership expansion is not afforded a high priority, or a *positive* approach, where the union consciously seeks to expand its membership within its existing market and/or expand into new markets.

On this basis Undy *et al*. identified that the General and Municipal Workers Union (now GMB), while open in terms of its scope of recruitment and exposed in terms of inter-union competition for membership, nevertheless was passive in its orientation to growth. Its subsequent merger with the Boilermakers, APEX and others indicates a more active role. ASTMS (now MSF), on the other hand, while 'intermediate' in respect of both its scope and recruitment and inter-union competition for membership, was very positive in its policy towards growth and expansion of its membership.

Bridgford and Stirling believe that it is difficult to categorise trade unionism by a single dimension (i.e. the industrial and/or occupational mix of the unions' membership). They suggest that an analysis of **national trade union movements** requires membership patterns to be linked to two other dimensions: the degree of centralisation of collective bargaining and links to the political system. They identify a framework which ranges from highly centralised and cohesive with 'an industrial union structure, a single confederation linked to one political party and a centralised bargaining system' through to decentralised and fragmented with 'a diverse membership base, political divisions and fragmented bargaining arrangements'[63]. Germany come closest to the centralised and cohesive model with France (strong political divisions) and the UK (strong membership and bargaining divisions) coming towards the other end of the spectrum. However, they recognise that, at least in the past UK context, there have been significant variations between the public and private sectors in respect of both the degree of centralisation of collective bargaining and the diversity of membership within unions. Sweden provides an interesting example of the role of 'bargaining cartels' (federations) in bridging the gap between union structure and the collective bargaining arrangements.

See Country profile 5.3

Country profile 5.3   Sweden – Bargaining cartels

Swedish trade unionism has been characterised by:

■ *High union density* – over 80 per cent and uniformly high across all groups (male and female, private and public sectors, and manual and non-manual);

■ *Strong centralisation* – through long periods of Social Democrat government associated with neo-corporatist strategies of co-operation between government, unions and management;

■ *Structural division based on occupation* – since the 1940s there have been three central trade union organisations: the LO (manual workers), TCO (non-manual employees) and SACO (professionals).

However, its structure becomes more complex because, in addition to individual unions and their respective central confederations, there are also 'bargaining cartels' which are at the centre of the primary function of trade unionism (collective bargaining).

Until the 1970s, collective bargaining was dominated by the central 'framework' agreement negotiated between the LO and SAF (central employers' organisation) for manual workers in the private sector. This central agreement was supported by 'implementation' negotiations involving the individual trade unions at the industry/sector levels and subsequent company-level negotiations on specific issues. In the two segments of the public sector (national and municipal employees) a single LO union is the 'bargaining cartel' for manual workers – indeed, several LO unions amalgamated in 1970 to form SF to provide a single union 'cartel'.

The development of collective bargaining among non-manual employees has been more fragmented

Country profile 5.3   Sweden – Bargaining cartels *(continued)*

and has presented difficulties of co-ordination between the various groupings. In the private sector, a joint 'cartel' (PTK) was formed from among unions in TCO and, to a lesser extent, SACO to undertake centralised bargaining similar to that undertaken by LO for manual workers. However, in the public sector, each confederation formed its own 'bargaining cartel' for the national and municipal sectors.

Throughout the 1980s and 1990s, Sweden has faced 'zigzag' pressures for decentralisation and centralisation. For example, in 1983 VF (the engineering employers) broke away from the SAF nation-wide negotiations to conclude its own industry agreement with the support of Metall (the LO engineering union). Similarly, changes in the public sector in the 1990s led both TCO and SACO to replace their two cartels (based on the division between national and local government employment) with a number of smaller

'mini-sector' cartels – some of which are coterminous with the membership of a single union. Again, in 1997, the engineering unions were at the heart of a 'group of eight' which negotiated an agreement covering both manual and non-manual employees in manufacturing.

However, both employers and government have also been concerned at periods of economic crisis to maintain some form of central co-ordination. Indeed, between 1990 and 1995 there was a reversion to a centralised tripartite arrangement to co-ordinate collective bargaining to achieve wage restraint.

Sources: A. Kjellberg, 'Sweden: restoring the model?', in A. Ferner and R. Hyman (eds), *Changing Industrial Relations in Europe* (2nd edn), Blackwell, 1998, pp. 74–117; O. Hammarström and T. Nilsson, 'Employment relations in Sweden', in G. J. Bamber and R. D. Lansbury (eds), *International and Comparative Employment Relations* (3rd edn), Sage, 1998, pp. 224–48

Union Confederations

| **LO**
Swedish Trade Union
Confederation
(Founded 1898)
Manual (Private & Public)
1,890,000 members (1996) | **TCO**
Central Organisation of
Salaried Employee
(Founded 1944)
Non-Manual (Private & Public)
1,122,000 members (1996) | **SACO**
Swedish Confederation of
Professional Associates
(Founded 1947)
Professional (Private & Public)
310,000 members (1996) |

Individual unions

| *Examples:*
– State Employees Union
– Municipal Workers Union
– Metal Workers Union | *Examples:*
– Commercial Salaried Employees
– Local Government Officers
– Clerical & Technical Workers in Industry
– Supervisors Union | *Examples:*
– Teachers
– Graduate engineers |

Bargaining cartels

	Manual	**Non-manual**	
Private	LO	PTK Federation of Salaried Employees in Industry & Services *(1973)*	
Public *National*	SF State Employees Union *(1970)*	TCO – S *(1967)* TCO – OF Sector Cartels *(1990s)*	SACO – S *(1976)* Sector Cartels *(1990s)*
Municipal	**SKAF (Kommual)** Municipal Workers Union	KTK Federation of Salaried Local Government Employees *(1976)*	SACO – K *(1976)*

See also Country profile 9.1.

Role of the TUC

In spite of frequent debates within the TUC and the trade union movement regarding trade union structure, at no time has there been a significant conscious move to reform along one line as opposed to another. In marked contrast to other countries, **British trade unions have determined their own membership patterns without any systematic intervention from the TUC**. In Germany, for example, the trade union movement was reconstructed after the Second World War, under the auspices of the British TUC, on an industrial basis. In the USA, despite the clash of ideologies, both the AFL (craft) and the CIO (industrial) (and the combined AFL-CIO after 1955) delineated and, to some degree, controlled the occupational/industrial membership of individual unions by granting charters to their constituent unions.

A 1964 TUC report recommended that, instead of trying to draw up a comprehensive structural blueprint for the future, the TUC should consider 'how best to stimulate and guide the process of piecemeal and ad hoc developments by which changes have come about in the past'[64]. Its role has been to act as a catalyst to draw together unions with a common interest and be available if needed to aid the process of merger. Its role in the resolution of inter-union disputes (through the Bridlington principles) and the fear of fragmentation through breakaway unions[65] have, in general, militated against structural reform. Certainly, the TUC was not able to 'broker' a spheres of influence deal between ASTMS/MSF and BIFU over their competing recruitment and acquisition of staff associations in the financial services sector[66]. However, the TUC is concerned that the new statutory recognition procedure (Employment Relations Act, 1999) could lead to a 'new wave of competition between unions intent on gaining recognition' and, therefore, it would like to see 'fewer unions, desirably perhaps one union, in key sectors like public services, education, transport, private services and manufacturing'[67]. It recognises that many unions have membership in more than one of these sectors and it would be difficult to persuade unions (and possibly the members themselves) to transfer *existing* members, but this leaves open the possibility of agreeing organisational spheres of recruitment for *new* members.

Mergers and amalgamations

Buchanan[68] noted that changes in the **law relating to union amalgamations** have facilitated increased merger activity. There are legal differences between *merger by amalgamation* and *merger by transfer of engagement*: either may be used where two unions merge by one losing its identity within the other, but where they merge to form a totally new union only merger by amalgamation may be used. Under the Trade Union Amendment Act (1876) merger by amalgamation required the agreement of not less than two-thirds of the membership of each union. The Trade Union (Amalgamation) Act (1917) reduced this to (1) at least 50 per cent of the membership of each union voting and (2) those in favour exceeding those against by 20 per cent or more. This was followed by the first wave of mergers (including the creation of the T&GWU and GMWU).

However, as unions increased in size it became difficult, if not impossible, to achieve 50 per cent membership participation in the ballot. The Societies (Miscellaneous Provisions) Act (1940), which applied to mergers by transfer of engagements, required only the transferring union (often a small union) to undertake the ballot. The Trade Union (Amalgamation) Act (1964) relaxed the voting requirement still further to a simple majority of those voting in both types of merger. Legislation may also be used to discourage small unions and, thereby, encourage them to merge. For example, legislation in Ireland in 1990 increased the minimum size of union required to obtain a 'negotiating licence' (be recognised as a legally authorised trade union) to 1,000 members[69], while the government in Australia set the minimum size for federal registration (and access to the federal conciliation and arbitration service) at 1,000 members in the mid-1980s and increased it to 10,000 in 1991[70].

It is important to recognise that union mergers may be a **response to the need to maintain financial and/or organisational viability**. Buchanan[71] explained the increase in merger activity during 1963–79 not only in terms of legal relaxation and changing technology or employment affecting unions' recruitment patterns, but also because increasing inflation created financial difficulties for unions and, at the same time, emphasised the importance of maintaining union strength to be able to protect the members' interests through negotiation with employers or representation to government. Similar financial pressures have resulted from the declining union membership since 1979. Undy *et al.*[72] concluded, from an analysis of mergers during the 1960s and 1970s, that a decline in absolute membership or an increase in the demands on the union's services, resulting from such developments as more sophisticated bargaining, increased legislation or incomes policy, may prompt a **defensive merger** in which the union, usually the minor union in the merger, seeks organisational security by joining with a larger organisation. However, for the dominant union, the merger may be primarily a **consolidatory merger** which confirms its position as the dominant union in the industry. In contrast, they regarded the approach of both the T&GWU and ASTMS as primarily one of **aggressive mergers** wherein they 'generally outbid their competitors for the privilege of rescuing minor unions from extinction' and thereby 'make effective inroads into the minor merging unions' new and relatively unorganized job territories or, on the other hand, to prevent the better organized areas of job territory falling to some other competitor organization'[73]. All these approaches can be seen in the recent history of both the AEEU and MSF.

See Case study 5.2

The general pattern of UK mergers in the 1970s was primarily one of small (often non-TUC unions) being absorbed by established TUC unions. This was followed, in the early 1980s, by the merger of medium-sized unions (either among themselves or with large unions). This has resulted in a much wider recruitment base for many unions. Buchanan notes that from the late 1980s the merger process shifted towards relatively large unions combining to create 'super-unions' (i.e. large conglomerate unions) to retain their relative position in the trade union movement, resulting in an increased concentration of union membership[74].

A number of significant points arise from the studies of trade union amalgamations:

■ **Attitudes of the unions' leadership**. Undy *et al*. noted that while natural growth of a union's membership 'can be determined by factors outside the control of the national leaders', mergers and amalgamations 'cannot be experienced by the union without a positive act by the national leadership'[75]. It is they who determine the suitability of potential and actual merger partners, and suitability is measured not simply in terms of any objective industrial or occupational 'fit' of the respective unions' memberships, but involves other factors such as the proposed internal governmental arrangements for the new union (including arrangements for the existing officers of the merging union) and the 'political' stance of the unions.

■ **Not generally a simple 'once and for all' integration of two organisations**. As Hughes pointed out, amalgamations are 'a process involving structural changes, and changes in trade union organisation and attitudes extending over a number of years'[76]. In some cases internal organisational changes are a prerequisite for amalgamation to be acceptable, while in others they have been left to be dealt with after the amalgamation. At the same time, Undy *et al*. noted that the dynamic nature of union mergers had the potential to create a merger movement in so far as 'a merger stimulated by absolute size reasons disturbed other unions' relative size considerations' who then 'in turn, sought mergers in order to restore the status quo'[77].

■ **Some degree of loss of identity**. Upton has noted that union activists 'may be asked to merge with another union which has often been regarded as a nuisance, a rival or even a downright bogey'[78]. The extent of any loss of identity will depend on the organisational arrangements made for integrating the different sets of membership, officers and institutions. This problem has been eased to the extent that unions have developed internal organisational arrangements which allow a degree of separate identity through trade or service sections (amounting almost to internal 'federations'). Thus, when the NUAAW merged with the T&GWU in 1981 it, in effect, took over the T&GWU's existing agricultural section. However, as Upton points out, it is important to recognise that 'however much autonomy is promised within its own province a small union which goes in with a larger partner does have a lesser pull on the resources of the organisation and is only a minority sectional interest in the new union'[79].

Several trends can be identified in the **mergers in the 1980s and 1990s**:

■ *Strengthening of the industrial/sectoral basis* in some industries facing strong competition, declining employment and/or management rationalisation strategies:

  ▪ Printing (merger of NGA with SOGAT to form GPMU in 1990);
  ▪ Television (merger of ABS and NATTKE to form BETA in 1984 and its subsequent merger with ACTAT to form BECTU in 1991);
  ▪ Post and telecommunications (merger of CPSA (Post and Telecommunications Group) with POEU to form NCU in 1985 (a 'unique merger'[80] because it involved the transfer of only part of the CPSA's membership) and its subsequent merger with UCW to form CWU in 1995);

▎ Civil service (merger of CSU and SCPS to form NUCPS in 1988, followed by its merger with the IRSF in 1996 to form PSTCU and then its merger with CPSA to form PCSU in 1998).

▌ *Continued development of the large conglomerate unions.* The so-called 'general' unions (T&GWU and GMB) have now been joined by the AEEU (formed in 1992), MSF (formed in 1988) and UNISON (formed from the merger of COHSE, NALGO and NUPE in 1992).

▌ *Blurring of the public/private sector boundary.* This has resulted primarily from the 'forced' movement of substantial groups of union members into the private sector (gas, electricity, water, etc.) and the decision of traditional public sector unions, such as NALGO and NUPE, not to relinquish this membership; hence, at least in part, the choice of the word UNISON (emphasising unity) as the title for the merged COHSE, NALGO and NUPE, rather than a 'traditional' title identifying the coverage of the union's membership and interest. Similarly, the PCSU now encompasses both 'public' and 'commercial' services. Additional blurring of the divide has come from other mergers: the public sector Health Visitors' Association merged with MSF, while the private sector National Unilever Managers' Association merged with IPMS (formerly the Institution of Professional Civil Servants).

Case study 5.2 ▌ Two dynasties? Developments in UK trade union structure

The Amalgamated Engineering and Electrical Union (718,000 members in 1999) originated in the old strength of manual labour in manufacturing, while the Manufacturing, Science & Finance Union (416,000 members in 1999) represents the new strength of non-manual employment, service industries and new technology.

Over its first hundred years, the AEU expanded from a narrow occupational basis of engineers to an industrial basis of engineering to become a *craft and allied occupation* union. Although its membership was primarily skilled engineering craftsmen in a range of industries, it also included semi-skilled and unskilled workers and supervisory grades in the engineering industry.

Between 1967 and 1971, the AEU (1 million members) sought *consolidatory mergers* with smaller unions in its own sphere of activities which would create a dominant *sectoral/general union* in engineering. For the smaller unions involved (Union of Foundry Workers with 68,000 members and Constructional Engineering Union with 27,000 members), it provided a *defensive merger* giving

increased security and influence as part of a bigger organisation. Although the Draughtsmen and Allied Technicians Association (with 90,000 non-manual members) saw merit in closer collaboration with its manual counterparts it was unhappy at losing its independence and identity as a junior partner in the new union. To facilitate the merger process:

▌ The four unions were initially to retain their individual identity through separate sections (with internal self-government) within a federal union (the Amalgamated Union of Engineering Workers) which would eventually become a single unified organisation.

▌ The non-manual members of the original AEU were combined with the DATA membership and renamed Technical and Supervisory Section (TASS).

Unfortunately, no other unions in the engineering/metal sector were prepared to follow suit and merge with the AUEW. At the same time, TASS resisted attempts at final unification of the four

Case study 5.2 ■ **Two dynasties? Developments in UK trade union structure**
(continued)

sections because of differences with the AEU about the process of union government and political outlook. TASS even, unsuccessfully, resorted to legal action to try to stop the merger of the other sections. In 1984 the other sections formally united in one union and reverted to the name AEU. Now, instead of one sectoral/general union, there were two quite separate unions – with the AEU returning to primarily a *craft/allied occupation* union. However, TASS had exerted its independence by separately merging with unions which were, primarily, manual (the Patternmakers, NUSMWCH&DE and Tobacco Workers) and therefore was no longer purely a non-manual union.

Also in the late 1960s, the Association of Scientific,

Technical and Managerial Staffs (ASTMS) was formed from a merger between AScW (Association of Scientific Workers with 50,000 members) and ASSET (Association of Salaried Staffs, Executives and Technicians with 21,000 members). This opened the boundaries of the union and ASTMS subsequently adopted a strategy of *aggressive mergers* by outbidding competing unions to acquire, in particular, staff associations in insurance, building societies and other private sector companies. The union also increased by natural growth as the high-profile image of the union, and in particular its General Secretary (Clive Jenkins), attracted many of the new technical staffs, professionals, administrators and managers (71,000 in 1967, 147,000 in 1969 and 496,000 in 1979).

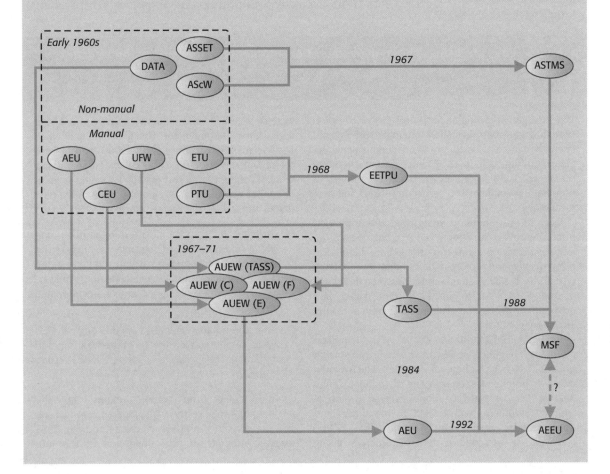

Case study 5.2 ■ Two dynasties? Developments in UK trade union structure
(continued)

However, the pressures of the 1980s affected even an aggressive recruiter and in 1988 ASTMS (390,000) and TASS (241,000) merged. Both unions were of the same 'type' (non-manual, mainly private sector), shared a similar 'political' outlook and for both it represented a *consolidatory merger* to become the premier union for non-manual employees in the private sector. Significantly the new name of Manufacturing, Science and Finance Union denoted a further opening of the union's main areas of recruitment interest. MSF has steadily built up its position based on technical, professional and managerial employment, service industries and new technology. It has also built up its membership in the public sector.

The 'divorce' of the AEU and TASS left the AEU without a base for potential membership growth (in particular, non-manual members). However, in 1992 the AEU (622,000) merged with the EETPU (Electrical, Electronic, Telecommunications and Plumbing Union with 357,000 members) – the EETPU being itself the result of a merger in 1968 of two 'craft' based unions (the electricians and plumbers). The EETPU's expulsion from the TUC in 1988 had left it free to 'absorb' a range of organisations (principally non-TUC affiliated

'management' or 'professional' associations) which had little if any relationship to its principal industrial base and whose merger with the EETPU appears to be more *'politically'* based (certainly some were 'breakaways' from other, TUC-affiliated, unions). The merger between the AEU and EETPU can itself be seen as both a politically motivated merger (both being 'right' wing in political terms) as well as justified in terms of any complementary nature of their respective memberships. Certainly, the merger allowed the trade union movement to more easily resolve the problem of a major union remaining outside the TUC. The AEEU has established a separate staff section – the Federation of Professional Associations – containing five distinct groups, each with its own governing body and control over its own internal affairs (the Electrical and Engineering Staff Association (EESA) – which is the biggest, Association of Managerial and Professional Staff (AMPS), British Transport Officers Guild (BTOG), Steel and Industrial Managers Association (SIMA) and the United Kingdom Association of Professional Engineers (UKAPE)).

As these trade unions move into the twenty-first century, there have been news reports of possible merger discussions between the AEEU and MSF.

5.5 Trades Union Congress

See Country profiles 5.1, 5.2. 5.3, 4.1 and 4.2

The Trades Union Congress (TUC) is the central co-ordinating organisation of the trade union movement in Britain. (*Throughout this section the terms TUC and Congress are used to refer to the complete organisation and the annual delegate conference respectively.*) The **power and authority of the TUC** lies in the fact that 'it has a near monopoly of representation'[81] and has 'been able to prevent the major rifts developing between sections of the union movement that are a characteristic of some other countries'[82] with potentially competitive central co-ordinating focal points for national trade union activity. Significantly, some 13 new unions joined the TUC between 1995–8 after it stopped 'allowing the objections of existing affiliates to block applications' and only required that new affiliates should be 'independent' unions and not a 'breakaway' from an existing union[83]. Although the majority of these were small unions, nevertheless the affiliation of the Association of Teachers and Lecturers (153,000 members) in

1998 means that only two major organisations are outside the TUC: the Royal College of Nursing (311,000 members) and the British Medical Association (104,000 members). There are a further four organisations with approximately 30,000–40,000 members each (National Association of Head Teachers, Professional Association of Teachers, Royal College of Midwives and Lloyds TSB Group Union). However, the TUC is often regarded as more than just the representative of its affiliates or even the trade union movement as a whole, but rather as the representative of all employees – whether they are unionised or not.

It is important to remember that, like employers' associations, the TUC is a **second-degree grouping** comprising organisations rather than individuals and is 'a loose confederation, not a centralized monolith'[84]. The TUC's role is limited by the fundamental principle that each union retains its independence to protect and pursue the interests of its members (particularly in carrying out its economic and job regulation functions) and is responsible ultimately only to its own members for its actions. The TUC's authority over affiliated members must 'be defined in terms of influence, not of power' derived from 'the willingness by unions, and by their members, to abide by decisions to which they are parties'[85]. Certainly, Kessler and Bayliss believe that the dispute in 1987 between the T&GWU and AEU over single-union recognition for a proposed new Ford plant in Dundee (which resulted in Ford pulling out) demonstrated that the TUC was 'of little account when two of its biggest affiliates fought each other and when their sectional interests were at stake'[86].

The General Council has the **power to suspend from TUC membership** (the power to expel is retained by Congress) any affiliated organisation which does not abide by TUC policies or whose activities are detrimental to the trade union movement. However, as Hawkins pointed out, the essential dilemma for the TUC is that 'if [it] ever found itself in the position of having to expel two or three major unions which have seats on the General Council, its own credibility as a representative body would be damaged'[87]. In 1985 there was a confrontation between the TUC and the AEU and EETPU, with potential expulsion and suggestions of forming an alternative 'TUC', regarding their acceptance of public funds to support the use of ballots which, at that time, was against the policy of the TUC. The issue was resolved by a change in TUC policy. Subsequently the EETPU was expelled in 1988, for failing to abide by a Disputes Committee decision to terminate two of its single-union recognition agreements, but any alternative focus of representation failed to materialise and it was readmitted following its merger with the AEU in 1992.

Organisation

The **annual Congress** determines TUC policy through its debates and votes on the annual General Council report and resolutions submitted by individual unions and the General Council. However, it would be wrong to regard Congress as an opportunity for rank and file members to participate in what may be considered the supreme policy-making body of the trade union movement. The union delegations are composed, primarily, of representatives with the authority to speak on behalf of, and commit, their organisation and include a significant proportion of senior full-time officers and NEC members (generally mandated on most issues by virtue of the policies and decisions previously determined by their own annual conferences). Furthermore, the General Council has significant influence on drawing up the agenda for Congress (it submits resolutions for debate) and its members are considerable, or even majority, contributors to the Congress debates. Indeed, Clegg commented that 'the council dominates Congress' and that 'unless the council is divided, it is not easy for Congress to initiate policy'[88]. However, Congress does have the power to 'refer back' sections of the Annual Report for further consideration and, in the past, this has generally been followed by some modification of policy.

Until 1983 the **General Council** was elected by Congress based on trade groups. While each union could nominate candidates only for their particular trade group, all unions were involved in the voting. The intention underlying this system was to produce General Council members who were responsible not to a particular union or trade group but to Congress as a whole. The arrangement was changed in 1983 to one based on an **automatic right of representation dependent on size** (more than 100,000 members) plus a number of seats allocated for smaller unions to be elected at Congress from within that group of unions. It is possible that this 'right' based on size has provided an additional stimulus for amalgamations. In 1989 the thresholds for additional seats were lowered, reflecting the decline in union membership, so that a union became entitled to a second seat if it had 200,000 members (previously 500,000) and, at the top, a union with more than 1.2 million members became entitled to six seats (previously 1.5 million members entitled a union to five seats). The number of seats for small unions was reduced from 11 to eight. Most importantly, unions entitled to two or more seats must nominate at least one female if they have more than 100,000 female members; this is in addition to the four seats reserved for women to be elected from unions with less than 200,000 members. Later, an additional three seats were reserved for black members (one female).

The effect has been to ensure that the General Council is more representative: more non-manual, more public sector, more women. Kessler and Bayliss believe that the change to 'representation by right' has had 'an effect on the political balance of the General Council in favour of moderation' and has 'reduced the power of the very large unions in that they no longer dominated the votes in the election of the members from the smaller unions'[89]. However, it also weakened the constitutional relationship between the General Council and Congress. Most General Council members are now clearly there to represent *their* union and are not, either individually or collectively, accountable to an electorate (the annual Congress). Further changes to the working of the General Council have been made as part of the 1994 'relaunch' in order to improve the process of decision-making. The General Council's standing committees have been scrapped, along with the TUC's industry committees, and replaced with more flexible and transient Industry Forums and Task Groups to develop policies on specific issues and whose membership is not confined simply to members of the General Council. The General Council now meets only four times a year, but a smaller Executive Committee has been established which meets every month.

These changes, Heery argues, demonstrate a 'greater preparedness on the part of the TUC to shake off the constraints of "pseudo-democratic structures"[90].

The **General Secretary** is perhaps the only role which may truly be said to **represent the whole TUC** and trade union movement. Unlike the members of the General Council (who are only part-time representatives of the TUC), the General Secretary is employed full-time on behalf of the TUC. Although the General Secretary's role may be regarded as an executive one subordinate to both the General Council and Congress, nevertheless it plays a significant part in influencing the direction of the TUC's affairs and policies. The General Secretary is a member of Congress, the General Council and often acts as the leader and chief spokesperson of TUC delegations. However, as Taylor pointed out, although the General Secretary 'symbolizes the TUC, acting as its collective spokesman to the outside world ... he has no big battalions to mobilize in his own support'[91] and can only exercise influence through persuasion.

Trades Councils have a longer history than the TUC and were instrumental in its establishment in 1868. Constitutionally they are not affiliated members of the TUC but simply registered with it. Their function is, primarily, to provide a focal point for trade unions in their locality and it is TUC policy, supported by many unions, to encourage union branches to affiliate to their local Trades Council. However, the TUC reported in 1980, at the height of trade union membership in the UK, that only about 30 per cent of union members were affiliated to Trades Councils[92]. Nevertheless, on many occasions Trades Councils have been able to play an important role in mobilising rank and file trade union support for both local and national issues.

The TUC has eight **Regional Councils** in England and a Welsh TUC whose functions are to represent and support TUC policy and activities at the regional level. The Regional Councils comprise officials (either full-time or lay) nominated by unions which have membership in the region with, in addition, 25 per cent of the members being appointed by the County Associations of Trades Councils (CATCs) within the region. The Welsh TUC, however, is structured more closely on the national institutions of the TUC itself with an annual delegate conference and a General Council. In addition, Scotland has its own, completely separate, **Scottish TUC** established in 1897, following the decision of the 'English' TUC to exclude Trades Councils from membership. Its organisational arrangements reflect the duality of its membership, although trade unions have the predominant position. It has some 80 affiliated unions (of which a few are exclusive to Scotland). In the past, the STUC has worked in close collaboration with the 'English' TUC but is the trade union movement's representative on Scottish employment, industrial, economic and social matters – particularly to government. Its role has been enhanced by political devolution under the Labour government and the re-establishment of a separate Scottish parliament.

Function

It is possible to distinguish between the TUC's internal functions *within* the trade union movement and its external function *on behalf of* the movement. Its **internal function** is primarily concerned with developing policy, co-ordinating the activities of its affiliated organisations and stimulating trade union activity in those areas and on those issues where it is needed. There are three areas in which the TUC can seek to support or constrain affiliates:

1. *Industrial disputes*. The TUC has rarely used the full extent of its powers to organise active support from affiliates for a member in dispute. The 1926 General Strike presented a major constitutional problem – who should control the conduct of the dispute and, most importantly, the negotiations? The TUC felt that the miners, in requesting active support to resist wage cuts, had effectively transferred responsibility for negotiations and determination of the settlement to the TUC – even though the final settlement included wage cuts and there was no miners' representative on the TUC Negotiating Committee. When similar situations arose in 1984 (GCHQ and mining disputes), the TUC's call for support was confined to an exhortation for moral and financial support from the trade union movement generally. The removal of legal immunity from secondary industrial action (Employment Act, 1990) means that any call for supportive industrial action would open the TUC, unions and their members to injunctions and possible claims for damages.

   In the 1960s and 1970s, the TUC played an active role in trying to resolve many major disputes (particularly in the public sector). During such initiatives, involving meetings with government ministers and chief executives in the public or private sector, the TUC sought not only to put the union's case more forcefully to the employer but also to conciliate between the two sides in order to reach a settlement without recourse to a strike. In this respect the TUC's efforts were often complementary to, and supportive of, the work of ACAS. However, Waddington and Whitston believe that the TUC's intervention 'was directed towards the restriction of any political damage arising from initiatives launched by individual affiliates rather than the co-ordination of actions'[93]. Certainly, changes in government and management strategies towards industrial relations since 1979 have marginalised this role.

2. *Inter-union disputes*. The TUC's approach to inter-union disputes about recruitment and recognition has been guided by the **Bridlington Principles** (established in 1939).

   ▪ These encouraged unions to develop arrangements on closer working and spheres of influence.
   ▪ They required a union, before taking applicants into membership, to 'clear' their standing with any previous union, which could decline to 'release' them if, for example, they were in arrears of contribution or in the process of being disciplined for a breach of the union's rules.
   ▪ They restricted a union's right to recruit employees at any place where another union already has members and negotiates terms and conditions.

   Elgar and Simpson[94] believe that the relatively rigid approach to regulating union competition in the early years (which favoured the existing organisation and recognition rights of the big unions) gave way to a more flexible approach in the late 1970s and 1980s with the growth of more open recruitment patterns among many unions and the development of 'single-union agreements'. The Bridlington Principles were amended in 1988 to require a union not to enter into a single-union agreement which might deprive other union(s) of existing recognition and/or negotiation rights without their agreement. Furthermore, a Code of Practice required a union to notify the TUC when it was 'in the process of making' a single-union agreement (irrespective of whether other unions had recognition or negotiation rights) so that the TUC could offer advice (taking into account whether another union had significant membership or was recognised elsewhere for a similar group of employees and/or the same employer). At the same time, the Special Review Body raised the possibility of introducing procedures 'whereby a union or group of unions wishing to organise a particular undertaking, establishment or grade could apply for sole organising rights for a period of one year' or 'under which particular industries or sectors could be accorded "protected status" with the result that access to them would be restricted to those unions already there'[95]. However, any TUC attempt to regulate the pattern of union recruitment has been effectively unworkable since 1993 by virtue of the legal right given to employees to join whichever union they wish (S.14, Trade Union Reform and Employment Rights Act, 1993). Kessler and Bayliss point out that in the subsequent revision of the 'Disputes Principles and Procedure' the TUC has introduced not only a 'binding commitment' on all affiliates that 'they will not knowingly and actively seek to take into membership the present or recent members of another union by making recruitment approaches (whether directly or indirectly) without the agreement of that organisation'[96] but also a moral obligation to compensate the organisation for loss of income if they do.

3. *Conduct of affiliated organisations*. The General Council has the power to investigate the conduct of any affiliated member whose activities may be detrimental to the interests of the trade union movement or contrary to the declared principles or policy of Congress. The most notable case was in 1961 when the ETU was expelled as a result of ballot rigging by Communist elements within the union[97]. There was an obvious reluctance on the part of the TUC both to become involved in the internal affairs of a member organisation and to proceed with the expulsion of a major union which could reduce its solidarity and representative nature. In 1976, in response to pressure concerning the power of trade unions to expel or refuse membership in a union membership agreement (closed shop) situation, the TUC established an Independent Review Committee to which an individual could appeal. However, the number of appeals was small (53 cases between 1976 and 1983 with 23 formal hearings) and there was no provision for any financial compensation to be awarded. The existence of the committee was not sufficient to avoid the introduction of legislation in the 1980s to restrict and then 'outlaw' the closed shop.

The **external function** of the TUC is to represent 'the movement to the government and other outside organisations, asserting the independence of the trade union movement and the right of trade unionists to a share in decisions which affect them, accepting the corresponding obligations and reminding unions of those obligations, and when necessary defending particular unions against external bodies'[98]. The TUC has **no direct collective bargaining role**; while Congress may adopt policies in respect of wages, hours, holidays, retirement age and general working conditions, it is up to the affiliated organisations to translate these policies into reality, through their negotiations with companies and employers' associations. This is in marked contrast to some other countries, such as Sweden, where the central union organisations have had responsibility for periodically negotiating national 'umbrella' agreements with the government and central employers' organisations. However, under the corporatist political ideology of the 1960s and 1970s the TUC did become 'increasingly involved in the actual administration of the industrial system, nominating representatives of the trade union movement to a great variety of public committees, councils, boards and other organisations'[99]. During the period of the 'social contract' (1974–7) the TUC agreed to, and supported, an incomes policy with the Labour government in return for their commitment to a range of economic and social policies and, as Hawkins points out, in the 1973/4 mining dispute which immediately preceded this, the TUC went so far as to make an offer to the Conservative government 'which committed the General Council to dissuade affiliated unions from quoting an exceptional miners' settlement, if such a settlement was allowed, in support of their own wage claims'[100]. However, the government's 'free market' ideology after 1979 precluded any continuation or development of such a role.

Much of the TUC's effort since the late 1980s, like that of unions in other countries, has been directed towards **reducing the decline in trade union membership**. Part of the TUC's Special Review Body report in 1988 was concerned with examining how the TUC might support and co-ordinate individual trade union activity in a number of areas. For example:

- Pooling resources to undertake local labour market surveys and joint recruitment campaigns in particular localities;
- Improving recruitment literature and strategies aimed at particular groups such as women, young people, part-timers, etc;
- Developing joint services for individual union members (e.g. legal advice, pension and insurance arrangements and credit cards);
- Creating a positive image for trade unionism.

More importantly, 1994 marked **the relaunch of the TUC** and its 'attempt to generate a new ethos and sense of mission'[101]. In addition to streamlining its decision-making processes, Heery identifies two other major strands in the 'relaunched' TUC (similar to the strategies developed in the USA and Australia – see Boxes 5.2 and 5.3):

- **Networking organisation**. The TUC is seeking to project and represent a more 'broadly conceived labour interest' which involves:
    - Identifying 'world of work' issues which have relevance and appeal to the broad range of employees who are not current union members.
    - Establishing campaign alliances with other community-based agencies and groups.

| Box 5.2 | USA – Labour looks to grow from grass roots |

'... Using a populist, grass-roots approach to politics and organizing, [John Sweeney, new head of the AFL–CIO] hopes to revive an institution long in decline and struggling to deal with the forces of global competition and technological change ... starting with a top-to-bottom reorganization of the AFL–CIO's marble and granite headquarters ... Several members of the longtime staff are on their way out.

In their place is a cadre of "fortysomething" activists, many of whom came to the labor movement from a background of civil rights, community and anti-war organizing.

The Sweeney team is refocusing labor's spending with plans to increase political spending sevenfold, to $35 million this year ... It also plans to raise another $20 million for organizing new members.

Part of the money will go into recruiting 1,000 young activists from college campuses and union halls for what they'll call Union Summer, a community and labor organizing campaign modeled after the civil-rights movement's Freedom Summer.

It's a deliberately different image from Bal Harbor, Florida, where labor leaders this week will have their last chance to lounge in pool-side cabanas at a resort hotel during the labor federation's annual winter meeting. Sweeney doesn't know where next year's meeting will be, but he's pushing for something decidedly less opulent and in a region where labor is running an organizing campaign ...

The AFL–CIO is not a union itself. It is a trade association for unions created in 1955 by a merger of the American Federation of Labor and the Congress of Industrial Organizations.

Back then labor was powerful not only in politics and the workplace, but also in communities. An explosion of union organizing in the nation's basic manufacturing industries in the mid-1930s had helped propel a largely unskilled, blue-collar work force into the economic middle class.

Industrial unions had helped create good wages, job security and such benefits as pensions, paid vacations and health insurance that are taken for granted by many workers today.

But in recent decades, the nation's economic base shifted away from manufacturing to service and high-tech industries in which unions were weak. Labor leadership, with some notable exceptions, was slow to catch up to those changes and to adjust to the needs of women, Asians, Hispanics and blacks.

Today, AFL–CIO membership stands at 13 million, the lowest level since 1969 and barely more than the 12.6 million members it had when the federation was founded in 1955.

The answer, say the new union activists, is to take the labor movement outside the Capital Beltway and into the streets. "We're up to here in Washington-think. What we need now is a grass-roots base," said a Sweeney aide.

That means refocusing labor's image, resources, spending and politics. "The clout can't come from the money," said the AFL–CIO's new political director, Steve Rosenthal, 43, a former top aide to Labor Secretary Robert B. Reich. "The centerpiece is really the notion of rebuilding our activist base."

At the heart of change in the AFL–CIO is the newly created Organizing Department. Headed by Richard Besinger, 45, an activist with 15 years' organizing experience, the department will first have to persuade the majority of the AFL–CIO's 78 member unions that organizing is the key to their future.

The new approach to organizing ... will be on display during this Union Summer. Alinsky organized the economically oppressed in cities across America with tactics that included sending black picketers to the suburban homes of white slum-lords and dropping dead rats on the steps of city hall.

The AFL–CIO hopes to build a cadre of activists across the country to register voters, work for legislation and organize workers at job sites. "Our members are participants in a broader community. Community issues are labor issues, too," said Sweeney.

Besinger sees attracting young people to the cause as the key to effective organization. It is also the seed of the budding social movement Sweeney wants to build.

The AFL–CIO is coordinating some of its political organizing efforts with such groups as abortion-rights advocates and environmentalists ...'

Source: Frank Swoboda and Martha M. Hamilton, © *Guardian Weekly*, 25 February 1996.

See also Country profile 2.1 and Box 4.3.

▌ Broadening its links with all political parties (particularly in the new devolved political institutions) and a range of organisations which represent management in one way or another (and not just the CBI).

■ **Encompassing unionism**. Heery argues that one way in which the TUC is developing its 'encompassing' strategy is by offering itself, through its networking, as an 'authoritative social partner engaged in the co-operative management of the economy with government and employers and pursuing full employment, minimum standards and a favourable framework of employment law in return for wage restraint and union co-operation with economic modernization'[102]. However, to do this the TUC must be able to control (or at least co-ordinate) the bargaining of its affiliates. The second element of the 'encompassing' strategy has been to co-ordinate union membership recruitment through its New Unionism Task Group and the establishment of an Organising Academy to train the new breed of union 'organisers' and use the trainees in specific recruitment campaigns.

The TUC's external role is not confined to Britain. The TUC also plays a very active and important part at the **international level** in both trade union and 'state' organisations. It is a member of the **European Trade Union Confederation** (formed in 1973) which covers 29 countries, 67 affiliated confederations and some 60 million trade unionists both inside and outside the EU and has representatives on the Economic and Social Committee of the EU and a range of specialist advisory committees. The role of the ETUC is becoming increasingly important for UK employees as more employment and labour market decisions are taken at EU rather than national levels. Certainly, the two main issues confronting the ETUC are the extent to which it should continue and extend the 'social dialogue' process of determining European-wide minimum standards and what role could (and should) it play in economic policy matters given that the majority of EU countries have adopted the common euro currency[103].

At the world-wide level the TUC was instrumental in the formation of the International Confederation of Free Trade Unions (ICFTU) in 1949 (as an alternative to the Communist-dominated World Federation of Trade Unions) and provides the UK's worker representative to attend the annual conference of the International Labour Organisation (UN agency) as well as being represented on a number of its industrial committees. At the same time, the TUC has encouraged its affiliated members to play an active part in international affairs through their own industry-based international federations. One of these federations, the International Transport Workers' Federation (ITF) covering 5 million members in 120 countries, has been able through the threat (and use) of industrial action to secure what amounts to a virtual world-wide minimum wage for shipping[104].

Throughout its international activities the TUC has sought not only to represent and pursue the interests of British trade unionists and workers but also to aid and support trade union organisations and workers in those countries where trade unionism is weak or under threat from either employers or government. A major task has been to resist directly (by encouraging trade union co-operation

| Box 5.3 | Australian trade unions in bid for new members |

'... In the past five years, almost 500,000 workers have quit unions, leading the ACTU [Australian Council of Trade Unions] to launch a radical plan to recruit new members and lure old members back.

ACTU membership was 2.7 million five years ago. It is now between 2.2 and 2.3 million despite a growth in the jobs market.

Speaking at an ACTU congress last week, the council's secretary, Mr Bill Kelty, said part of the plan was to use the council's existing funds to set up a "bank" of sorts which would be tapped by affiliates for recruitment purposes. The ACTU has assets of about A$17 million.

Mr Kelty said the idea was to shift resources back to unions so that they could establish a stronger presence in individual workplaces.

He said that the council had recently completed a restructuring of the various unions under its umbrella, which had seen the total number of unions reduced, mainly through mergers, from 140 to about 40.

He said the next stage in the plan was to focus on recruitment with a stronger presence in the workplace.

He outlined several ways this would be done including:

■ Training 300 new union organisers and 20,000 shop stewards, who would operate at the local level.

■ Focusing on the needs of unions in country towns.

■ Using enterprise bargaining as a tool to recruit new members. Members would be shown how they could gain higher wage rises through the collective strength of a union.

■ Providing incentives like discounts on home loans, telephone services, credit cards, travel insurance and certain retail products.

... One problem Mr Kelty and his colleagues will face in swelling their ranks is that much of the recent growth area in the country's economy in terms of jobs has been in the service industry, retail, tourism and finance, areas largely not unionised.

But one factor which the ACTU will be counting on, especially where women workers are concerned, is the appointment of Ms Jennie George as the new president-elect of the ACTU.

Ms George is the first woman in the history of the ACTU to be appointed president and she is an ardent champion of women's rights. The ACTU hopes that she will be able to encourage more women into the union movement ...

There is one area though where the ACTU will have great difficulty recovering the ground it has lost. The outgoing ACTU president, Mr Martin Ferguson, ... said organised labour had failed to capture the "hearts and minds of a new generation" and that unions should look at the belief that organised labour "was out of touch". He revealed, significantly, that union research showed the movement had not made headway with younger workers.

"The ordinary workers, the sole parent, the retired worker, the recent school leaver, the new parent, know little of the union movement's role in the improvements in their standards of living", he said.

He then touched on what many in Australia feel is the problem with the ACTU and why they are disillusioned with it.

"We must show that we stand for real issues, that unions are not just being run by the best technocrats."

"If we have no heart, we are no better than the average salesperson moving from company to company plying our wares or results based on what has the best-selling pitch or the most competitive rate. That's not what the union is about, nor should it be." '

Source: Surinder Singh, *The Straits Times* (Singapore), 5 October 1995.

See also Country profiles 8.2, 9.2 and 12.1.

at company, industry and national levels) and indirectly (through influencing governments) the ability of multinational corporations to move their production and investment to those areas where wage costs are low and trade unionism weak. Certainly, western trade unions have supported moves to include 'social clauses' in trade agreements, particularly with Asian countries, to limit 'unfair' trade competition derived from lower labour standards and restrictions on trade union activity.

Waddington and Whitston[105] believe that, since 1979, the TUC's functions which gave it 'authority' over affiliates (regulating union competition and providing a 'conduit' to government to influence public policy) have been, at best, eroded or, at worst, lost. As a consequence, since the late 1980s, it has sought to establish a 'new' role in supporting affiliates in improving and extending membership recruitment (particularly among women, part-time and temporary workers and ethnic minorities) and emphasising its role in representing UK unions within the EU's social dialogue process. The TUC sees the development and strengthening of the 'social dimension' within the EU as an important counter-balance to the free-market deregulation approach of the UK government. However, Willman and Cave suggest that the creation of a small number of 'super-unions' coupled with their potential to develop a variety of bi- or multi-lateral collaborative, expertise-sharing arrangements may raise important and fundamental issues for their future relationship with the TUC and, indeed, the role of the TUC itself[106].

■ Summary propositions

- Trade unions are primarily oligarchic organisations in which control and accountability are exercised through an interrelationship of participative democracy (membership involvement in decision making at the branch and through ballots) and representative democracy (membership election of representatives to positions of leadership), with diffuse, and potentially opposing, focuses of 'leadership' at national, regional and local levels.

- Union amalgamations are driven by a variety of considerations ('political', organisational survival, as well as, industrial structural logic) and therefore have not resulted in the predominance of any one form of trade union but have created, and are likely to continue to create, larger more 'open' conglomerate unions with a diversity of membership interests which have to be accommodated and reconciled within the internal organisation of the union.

- The traditional role of the TUC has been brought into question by declining trade union membership and influence, the concentration of membership in a small number of 'super-unions' and the decentralisation of collective bargaining away from 'national' industry-wide agreements. It has relaunched itself as a campaigning 'networking' organisation within a more encompassing concept of the labour interest.

Activity If you have been able to get some 'primary' materials from a trade union (as suggested in Chapter 4), you could see what they say about the union's formal organisational arrangements. In particular, try to identify how the union's NEC is elected (and what provisions, if any, are made for the separate election of women and other special groups); whether there are separate committees or conferences for different sectional interest groups (and what power/authority they have); what organisational issues (if any) have been discussed at the union's annual conference; and any indications of union efforts to encourage members to actively participate (attend branch meetings, become representatives, etc.).

Further reading

- *TUC Reports.* The annual reports of the TUC (and other special reports and consultative documents) provide an up-to-date insight into the range of work carried out by the TUC and the policy debates of the annual Congress.
- A. Ferner and R. Hyman (eds), *Changing Industrial Relations in Europe*, Blackwell, 1998; G. J. Bamber and R. D. Lansbury, *International and Comparative Employment Relations*, Sage, 1998; S. J. Deery and R. J. Mitchell, *Labour Law and Industrial Relations in Asia*, Longman Cheshire (Melbourne), 1993. All these books provide useful comparative information on trade unions in a variety of different national contexts.

References

1. B. C. Roberts, *Trade Union Government and Administration*, Bell, 1956, p. 80.
2. S. and B. Webb, *The History of Trade Unionism* (1920 edn), Longman, p. 465.
3. R. Hyman, 'Changing trade union identities and strategies', in R. Hyman and A. Ferner (eds), *New Frontiers in European Industrial Relations*, Blackwell, 1994, p. 123.
4. J. Waddington and C. Whitson, 'Why do people join unions in a period of membership decline?' *British Journal of Industrial Relations*, vol. 35, no. 4, 1997, p. 530.
5. S. Kessler and F. Bayliss, *Contemporary British Industrial Relations* (3rd edn), Macmillan, 1998, p. 175.
6. E. Heery, 'The new new unionism', in I. J. Beardwell (ed.), *Contemporary Industrial Relations*, Oxford University Press, 1996, p. 182.
7. Roberts, *op. cit.*, p. 160.
8. K. Hawkins, *Trade Unions*, Hutchinson, 1981, p. 112.
9. J. McIlroy, *Trade Unions in Britain Today*, Manchester University Press, 1988, pp. 135–6.
10. J. Kelly and E. Heery, *Working for the Union – British trade union officers*, Cambridge University Press, 1994.
11. J. Waddington and A. Kerr, 'Membership retention in the public sector', *Industrial Relations Journal*, vol. 30, no. 1, 1999, table 3, p. 161.
12. 'Are women out of proportion?' *Labour Research*, March 1998, p. 14.
13. E. Heery and J. Kelly, 'A cracking job for a woman – a profile of women trade union officers', *Industrial Relations Journal*, vol. 20, no. 3, 1989; S. Ledwith *et al.*, 'The making of women trade union leaders', *Industrial Relations Journal*, vol. 21, no. 2, 1990.
14. G. Kirton and G. Healy, 'Transforming union women: the role of women trade union officials in union renewal', *Industrial Relations Journal*, vol. 30, no. 1, 1999, p. 43.

15. J. Hughes, 'Trade union structure and government', Research Paper 5 (2), *Royal Commission on Trade Unions and Employers' Associations*, HMSO, 1968, p. 45.
16. E. Stein, 'The dilemma of union democracy', in J. M. Shepheard (ed.), *Organisational Issues in Industrial Society*, Prentice Hall, 1972.
17. R. Hyman, *Industrial Relations – A Marxist Introduction*, Macmillan, 1975, p. 73.
18. V. L. Allen, *Power in Trade Unions*, Longman, 1954, p. 15.
19. R. Taylor, *The Fifth Estate*, Pan, 1980, p. 196.
20. Hawkins, *op. cit.*, p. 115.
21. M. Bray, 'Democracy from the inside: the British AEUW(ES) and the Australian AMWSU', *Industrial Relations Journal*, vol. 13, no. 4, 1982, p. 91.
22. J. Child, R. Loveridge and M. Warner, 'Towards an organizational study of trade unions', *Sociology*, vol. 7, no. 1, 1973, p. 78.
23. A. Fox, *A Sociology of Work in Industry*, Collier Macmillan, 1972, p. 123. Reprinted with permission of the publisher.
24. R. Michels, *Political Parties*, Free Press, 1966.
25. H. A. Turner, *Trade Union Growth, Structure and Policy*, Allen & Unwin, 1962.
26. H. A. Clegg, *General Union*, Blackwell, 1954, p. 342.
27. J. D. Edelstein and M. Warner, *Comparative Union Democracy*, Allen & Unwin, 1975.
28. J. Goldstein, *The Government of a British Trade Union*, Allen & Unwin, 1952.
29. S. M. Lipsett, M. A. Trow and J. S. Coleman, *Union Democracy*, Free Press, 1956, p. 15.
30. M. Dickenson, 'The effects of parties and factions on trade union elections', *British Journal of Industrial Relations*, vol. 19, no. 2, 1981, p. 198.
31. R. Blackwell, 'Parties and factions in trade unions', *Employee Relations*, vol. 12, no. 1, 1990, p. 31.
32. R. Martin, 'Union democracy: an explanatory framework', *Sociology*, vol. 2, 1968, p. 205.
33. P. Taft, *The Structure and Government of Labor Unions*, Harvard University Press, 1954.
34. R. Martin, P. Smith, P. Fosh, H. Morris and R. Undy, 'The legislative reform of union government 1979–94', *Industrial Relations Journal*, vol. 26, no. 2, 1995, p. 153.
35. R. Undy, V. Ellis, W. E. J. McCarthy and A. M. Halmos, *Change in Trade Unions*, Hutchinson, 1981, p. 119.
36. M. van de Vall, *Labor Organizations*, Cambridge University Press, 1970, p. 153.
37. Hyman (1994), *op. cit.*, p. 124/5.
38. *Annual Report of the Certification Officer 1990*, Appendix 9.
39. Martin *et al.*, *op. cit.*, p. 148.
40. P. Smith, P. Fosh, R. Martin, H. Morris and R. Undy, 'Ballots and union government in the 1980s', *British Journal of Industrial Relations*, vol. 31, no. 3, 1993.
41. Martin *et al.*, *op. cit.*, p. 152.
42. *Trade Unions and their Members*, HMSO, 1987, p. 25.
43. McIlroy, *op. cit.*, p. 150.
44. *Ibid.*, p. 153.
45. *Ibid.*, p. 154.
46. D. Fatchett, 'Postal ballots – some practical considerations', *Industrial Relations Journal*, vol. 13, no. 4, 1982, p. 15.
47. J. W. Leopold, 'Trade unions, political fund ballots and the Labour Party', *British Journal of Industrial Relations*, vol. 35, no. 1, 1997, table 1, p. 28.
48. D. Morris, 'The Commissioner for the Rights of Trade Union Members – a framework for the future?', *Industrial Law Journal*, vol. 22, no. 2, 1993.
49. Hawkins, *op. cit.*, p. 107.
50. J. D. M. Bell, 'Trade unions', in A. Flanders and H. Clegg (eds), *The System of Industrial Relations in Great Britain*, Blackwell, 1960, p. 138.
51. Hyman (1975), *op. cit.*, p. 59.
52. H. Clegg, *Trade Unionism under Collective Bargaining*, Blackwell, 1976, p. 39.
53. C. Jenkins and J. E. Mortimer, *British Trade Unions Today*, Pergamon Press, 1965, p. 1.
54. J. Hughes, 'Trade union structure and government', Research Paper 5 (1), *Royal Commission on Trade Unions and Employers' Associations*, HMSO, 1967.
55. M. P. Jackson, *Industrial Relations* (2nd edn), Croom Helm, 1982, p. 49.
56. TUC, *Report on Trade Union Structure and Closer Unity*, 1947.
57. 'Staff associations: independent unions or employer-led bodies?' *IRS Employment Trends*, no. 575, January 1995, p. 6.
58. 'Banking on union merger', *Labour Research*, January 1998, pp. 11–13.
59. Hyman (1975), *op. cit.*, p. 41.
60. Turner, *op. cit.*
61. Hughes (1967), *op. cit.*, p. 6.
62. Undy *et al. op. cit.*, p. 74.
63. J. Bridgford and J. Stirling, *Employee Relations in Europe*, Blackwell, 1994, p. 94.
64. TUC *Annual Report*, 1964.
65. S. W. Lerner, *Breakaway Unions and the Small Trade Union*, Allen & Unwin, 1962.
66. J. Waddington and C. Whitston, 'Trade unions: growth, structure and policy', in P. Edwards (ed.), *Industrial Relations:*

theory and practice in Britain, Blackwell, 1995, p. 184.

67. 'TUC wants one industry, one union', *Labour Research*, June 1999, p. 9.
68. R. T. Buchanan, 'Merger waves in British unionism', *Industrial Relations Journal*, vol. 5, no. 2, 1974.
69. P. Gunnigle, G. McMahon and G. Fitzgerald, *Industrial Relations in Ireland*, Gill & Macmillan (Dublin), 1995, p. 60.
70. J. T. Campling and G. Michelson, 'Trade union mergers in British and Australian television broadcasting', *British Journal of Industrial Relations*, vol. 35, no. 2, 1997, p. 222.
71. R. Buchanan, 'Mergers in British trade unions 1949–79', *Industrial Relations Journal*, vol. 12, no. 3, 1981, Table 1, p. 41.
72. Undy *et al.*, *op. cit.*, p. 74.
73. *Ibid.*, p. 215.
74. R. T. Buchanan, 'Measuring mergers and concentration in UK unions 1910–88', *Industrial Relations Journal*, vol. 23, no. 4, 1992.
75. Undy *et al.*, *op. cit.*, p. 61.
76. Hughes (1967), *op. cit.*, p. 6.
77. Undy *et al.*, *op. cit.*, p. 216.
78. R. Upton, 'Trade union marriages – the reasons and the rites', *Personnel Management*, September 1980, p. 39.
79. *Ibid.*, p. 38.
80. P. Blyton and P. Turnbull, *The Dynamics of Employee Relations* (2nd edn), Macmillan, 1998, p. 130.
81. J. Sinclair, 'Trade unions', in G. Hollinshead, P. Nicholls and S. Tailby (eds), *Employee Relations*, FT Pitman Publishing, 1999, p. 147.
82. M. Jackson, *Trade Unions*, Longman, 1982, p. 4.
83. 'TUC – increasingly the place to be', *Labour Research*, December 1998, pp. 17–18.
84. Taylor, *op. cit.*, p. 71.
85. 'Trades Union Congress Structure and Development', *Interim Report of the General Council*, TUC, 1970, p. 2.
86. S. Kessler and F. Bayliss, *Contemporary British Industrial Relations*, Macmillan, 1992, p. 165.
87. Hawkins, *op. cit.*, p. 102.
88. H. A. Clegg, *The Changing System of Industrial Relations in Britain*, Blackwell, 1979, p. 336.
89. Kessler and Bayliss (1998), *op. cit.*, p. 185.
90. E. Heery, 'The relaunch of the Trades Union Congress', *British Journal of Industrial Relations*, vol. 36, no. 3, 1998, p. 352.
91. Taylor, *op. cit.*, p. 78–9.
92. 'The Organisation, Structure and Services of the TUC', *TUC Consultative Document*, 1980, p. 8.
93. Waddington and Whitston (1995), *op. cit.*, p. 175.
94. J. Elgar and B. Simpson, 'A final appraisal of "Brindlington"? An evaluation of TUC Disputes Committee decisions 1974–1991', *British Journal of Industrial Relations*, vol. 32, no. 1, 1994, pp. 47–66.
95. 'TUC special review body reports', *Industrial Relations Review and Report*, no. 420, July 1988, p. 9.
96. Kessler and Bayliss (1998), *op cit.*, pp. 191–2.
97. See C. H. Rolph, *All Those in Favour? The ETU Trial*, André Deutsch, 1962.
98. TUC (1970), *op. cit.*, p. 2.
99. Hawkins, *op. cit.*, p. 100.
100. ACAS, *Industrial Relations Handbook*, HMSO, 1980, p. 44.
101. Heery (1998), *op. cit.*, p. 339.
102. *Ibid.*, p. 351.
103. 'Euro unions debate way forward', *Labour Research*, June 1999, pp. 21–2.
104. A. Breitenfellner, 'Global unionism: a potential player', *International Labour Review*, vol. 136, no. 4, 1997, p. 545.
105. Waddington and Whitston (1995), *op. cit.*
106. P. Willman and A. Cave, 'The union of the future: super-unions or joint ventures', *British Journal of Industrial Relations*, vol. 32, no. 3, 1994, pp. 395–412.

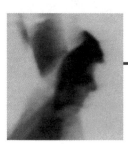

chapter six

Representation at the workplace

Learning objectives

Without representation, employees are essentially powerless to influence workplace decisions. By the end of this chapter, you should be able to:

■ appreciate the ways in which employee representation may take place within non-union organisations;

■ understand the process of trade union recognition, its legal regulation and, in particular, the nature of single-union agreements, single-table bargaining arrangements and union membership agreements within the recognition framework;

■ explain the role of the representative at the workplace in relation to the union, members/employees and management;

■ appreciate why people become workplace representatives and the types of leadership they may display.

Definition

The term representation refers to the formal designation of certain organisational institutions and processes as the means whereby employees can, on a collective basis, enter into a dialogue with management, express their views and seek to influence management decision making.

Key issues

While you are reading this chapter, you should keep the following points in mind:

■ An employee's 'right to join' a union is of little real value without an associated 'right to representation' (union recognition by the employer). So, if the employee's right to be a member of a union is guaranteed by society (through legislation), shouldn't we also require management to recognise unions and bargain 'in good faith'?

■ HRM strategies and the impact of EU legislation have introduced a new dimension into UK workplace representation – 'employee' representatives alongside, or instead of, 'union' representatives. We need to be aware that the different natures of the two types of role have a differential impact on the regulation of the employment relationship (particularly in respect of managerial authority relations).

■ We need to appreciate that workplace representatives are primarily intermediaries, but subject to a high level of role-conflict. They have to act as both initiators and responders in relation to the people they represent (employees and/or members and union) as well as co-operate with management in resolving organisational problems (while maintaining their independence from management).

6.1 Introduction

Morgan points out that in a democratic society there is an inherent conflict between an individual's rights as a citizen and as a paid employee. As a citizen he or she is 'free to hold his own opinions, make his own decisions, and be treated as an equal', while as an employee 'he is expected to keep his mouth shut, do what he is told, and submit to the will of his superior'[1]. Equally importantly, a democratic society embodies the 'right of representation' through organised political parties, with differing views and interests, which periodically seek popular support for the opportunity to be the government within society. Indeed, the phrase 'no taxation without representation' was the principal slogan of the American Revolutionary War of Independence from Britain (1775–83).

Discussion about the rights and nature of employee representation within the workplace is not new. In the 1960s a central part of Flanders' analysis of UK industrial relations was the *challenge from below* wherein 'employees are claiming a greater influence on managerial decisions'[2], while in the 1970s McCarthy and Ellis emphasised the need to adopt a *management by agreement* approach in which 'no area of management decision-making is beyond the rightful concern of employees'[3]. Certainly, Lumley argued that without some 'organised countervailing force outside an organisation's managerial hierarchy to provide a check on unilateral management decision making' the employment relationship is little more than a set of administrative procedures[4] – a key element being the 'organised' nature of the countervailing force. However, as Hyman points out, 'employee representation' is very much about the 'representation of *interests*' and, as such, needs to be judged in terms of autonomy (independence from management), legitimacy (its representative nature) and efficacy (degree of success or achievement)[5].

6.2 Non-union representation

The extent of trade union recognition at the workplace in the UK has declined since the early 1980s, in line with the decline in the level of trade union membership (see Figure 6.1). In 1984 about one-third of establishments did not recognise a union, whereas in 1998 the proportion had increased to over a half. This increase in non-unionism may appear to be simply the result of the **emphasis placed on individualism** within the new HRM strategies and its incompatibility with collectivism. However, Legge argues that this ignores the strong element of collectivism which also exists in HRM strategies – namely, the development of a team ethos, commitment to the organisation and strong corporate culture which exert 'unobtrusive collective controls on attitudes and behaviour'[6]. Thus, McLoughlin and Gourlay suggest that it is the 'form of collectivism which is embodied in the independent representation of employee interests by trade unions and collective bargaining that is being called into question'[7], not necessarily collective employee representation itself.

Union density, and therefore union recognition and representation, among **small firms in the private sector** has always been low – in 1998 union density was only 8 per cent in establishments with less than 25 employees (as opposed to 26 per cent in establishments with more than 25 employees), while in public sector establishments union density was 51 per cent and 63 per cent respectively[8]. Since the 1980s, small firms have been seen by some people as the epitome of employee relations in the new enterprise culture: better and more open communications, more personalised 'human' relations and more opportunity for employee commitment and involvement. However, this apparent supportive climate for *employee representation* has to be set against the constraining management style which appears to exist in small firms. Blyton and Turnbull describe the prevailing style as 'a mixture of unitarism, paternalism and authoritarianism' which contains an 'over-riding desire to perpetuate managerial authority' because of the owner/manager's 'possessiveness'[9]. In such an environment, there will be little, if any, likelihood that the employees' right to representation and influence over management decision making will be voluntarily acknowledged – let alone encouraged; indeed, the employees' 'voice' is perhaps inevitably 'more circumscribed, irregular and informal'[10].

As Blyton and Turnbull point out, it is important to distinguish between organisations which are ***anti-union*** (**suppression**) and those which are ***non-union*** (**substitution**)[11] – although whose which are non-union may also display anti-union traits when their non-union strategies are challenged. They suggest that among the larger 'sophisticated paternalist' non-union organisations (such as Marks & Spencer) 'management recognises the need to manage employee relations *as if* the workforce has divergent interests [so that] management is able to identify concerns, allay fears, satisfy workers' aspirations and *stay non-union*'[12]. Consequently, such organisations see nothing incongruous in establishing internal mechanisms which include *collective* employee representation as part of their strategy to avoid unions. It may be that their size inevitably induces greater formalisation and collectivisation of the employment relationship at the workplace. However, Flood and Toner[13] argue that the rationale of a union avoidance policy for large organisations is premised, in part, on replacing the union with sophisticated organisational communication mechanisms (including a good complaints procedure) which can be used both to promote a unitary culture among employees and to restrict 'radicals' in projecting a distinct 'employee' adversarial interest. The employee 'interest' represented through such an approach is conditioned by and focused on organisational needs.

Significantly, Terry argues, **recent legal developments** might 'constitute the single most important reason for believing that non-union forms of employee representation may come to assume increasing significance'[14]. First, in 1994 the European Court of Justice held that UK legislation did not comply with the EU Directives by restricting consultation rights, on both redundancies and the transfer of the undertaking, to representatives of 'recognised unions' rather than representatives of the 'workforce' – thus, the right of employees to be *collectively* consulted should apply to all (whether unionised or not). The amended regulations[15] now allow management to choose between consulting recognised unions or 'elected representatives of the affected employees' (even where unions are recognised). Thus, even in non-union organisations management will have to ensure at least *ad hoc* collective employee representation if or when these matters arise. In 1996, employees in non-union organisations were also given the right to health and safety representatives and consultation on a continuing basis[16]. A further development has been the recent creation, alongside the right to be accompanied by a recognised union representative, of a right for an employee to be accompanied by a 'fellow worker' during disciplinary or grievance hearings which deal with 'serious matters' (Employment Relations Act, 1999).

See Case study 6.1

The second main development has been in the area of more **general information and consultation**. Not only has the UK ended its 'optout' of the European Works Council Directive, but there is also a possibility of a further EU Directive which would require organisations to establish a national 'works council' or similar body with a legal right to receive information and be consulted. There have already been moves in this direction by some organisations (some unionised, some not) with the introduction of 'company councils' which 'represent a compromise between the need for employee participation and the desire to steer clear of collective bargaining' and are 'one manifestation of a partnership approach to employee relations'[17]. However, such bodies lack any legal support for their existence or legal rights in their operation. Terry suggests, from an examination of the operation of such 'company councils', that employee representatives may be seen as 'less able, trained, expert, or more nervous than their union counterparts (and hence less likely to press management) and/or that management takes less seriously representatives who lack the potential sanctions of trade unionists'[18].

See Chapter 10 – Employee involvement and participation

The development of 'company' or 'works' councils, alongside union recognition and other forms of direct employee participation initiated by management, creates a combination of 'single, dual and triple' channels of representation which, Hyman argues, has 'significant implications for the struggle for representative autonomy, legitimacy and efficacy'[19] within an organisation's employee relations system and processes. Certainly, Terry suggests that, in the absence of legal support, employee (as opposed to union) representation can only be partial and if it proves to be ineffective or weak then the only alternative to its demise is to become transformed into a union based representation mechanism[20]. The establishment of 'company councils' by management as part of a non-union (substitution) strategy may well, therefore, follow the 'independent' staff associations management supported and helped their staff establish in the 1970s – become part of main stream union representation mechanisms.

Case study 6.1 ■ Bristol & West – partners' councils

The Bristol & West employs about 2,500 people in financial services, has no 'recognised' unions and introduced 'partners' councils' at Divisional and Group levels in 1994. The objective of these councils is 'to act as the representative body for staff on corporate Human Resources policy, procedure and performance issues'. The company reviews all its HR policies (including pay) annually and employees are invited to make an input through the partners' councils.

There are seven divisional councils, each comprising 15 annually elected employee representatives. In order to avoid a two-sided adversarial image, there are no appointed 'management' members (i.e. the councils are not joint employee/management bodies), although 'the company tries to make sure that there is at least a professional, technical and managerial presence on each council'. On major issues, such as pay, working time and redundancies, a senior manager or member of the Group HR may make a presentation to the divisional councils before they consult the other employees. Recommendations from the divisional councils are sent to Group HR, but a manpower planning and development committee (comprised of senior managers) makes the formal decision on any change. Although two of the chairs of the divisional councils also attend, in rotation, this committee is 'the stage beyond consultation'.

The Group partners' council comprises the seven chairs of the divisional councils plus three senior managers (one of which is the Managing Director who also chairs the meeting). It meets twice a year and its role is to oversee the work of the divisional councils and act as the consultation body on 'high-level business information'. In addition, the company has an annual day-long forum for the divisional council representatives where individual directors make presentations and answer questions.

Source: IDS Study 672, *Company Councils*, July 1999.

6.3 Trade union recognition

Trade unionism at the workplace relies on the union being able to act in support of its members' interests. To do this the union must be 'recognised' and have resources available at the workplace to act as the representative of its members. Through the recognition process **trade union(s) are formally accepted by management as the representative of all, or a group, of employees for the purpose of jointly determining their terms and conditions of employment**. It is perhaps the most important development in an organisation's industrial relations system involving both a change in the *intra-organisational* relationship between management and employees and the introduction of a new *inter-organisational* relationship between the organisation and union. It confers legitimacy and determines the scope of the trade union's role. Torrington and Hall argue it delivers 'collective consent to a general framework of rules and guidelines within which management and employees operate' and symbolises 'a highly significant movement away from unilateral decision making by the management'[21]. Similarly, Towers argues, in the context of the debate about derecognition, that 'trade union rights to oppose, to bargain, to organise – even to exist – are at stake should a derecognition movement prosper'[22].

The **focus of the recognition issue has shifted** since the 1970s. At the core is the issue of whose interests should predominate in determining the shape of employee representation and, through that, collective bargaining. During the 1970s, the emphasis was on developing a codified and coherent approach to the recognition process at the organisational level to support the development of collective representation and bargaining with, if necessary, statutory support for unions encountering management resistance to granting recognition. The initial recognition of a union was regarded as a starting point for a continuing process of enhancement as the relationship between management and the union(s) developed with subsequent extensions of the scope of collective bargaining and involvement of the union and/or employees in joint decision making with management. Since the early 1980s, the emphasis has been on management strategies aimed at fostering a more co-operative and flexible industrial relationship to support the achievement of greater organisational performance and flexibility. This has included redefining or rationalising recognition and bargaining arrangements (including single-table bargaining and single-union agreements) or even removing recognition, while the union membership agreement (closed shop) has been made inoperable by legislation.

Extent of trade union recognition

There is no doubt that there has been a **decline in union recognition** in the UK since the 1970s. Overall, the proportion of establishments with recognised unions has dropped from just under two-thirds in 1984 to just over 40 per cent in 1998 (see Figure 6.1). However, the percentage of establishments *with* union members which recognise a union remains high at 85 per cent – clearly, recognition depends on the existence of union membership within the organisation. While recognition has remained high in the public sector, private manufacturing has experienced a relatively dramatic decline.

Figure 6.1 Trade union recognition

Sources: N. Millward *et al., Workplace Industrial Relations in Transition,* Dartmouth, 1992; Cully *et al., The 1998 Workplace Employee Relations Survey: First Findings,* Department of Trade and Industry, 1998.

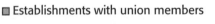

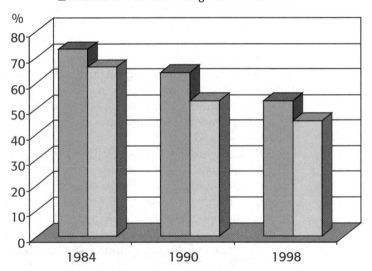

Changes in the structure and pattern of employment in the UK have been major contributors to this decline in union recognition: decreases in male employment, the manufacturing sector, manual work and large organisations and increases in female and/or part-time employment, the private service sector, non-manual work and smaller organisations. These latter employment growth sectors are also the very sectors which traditionally have been more difficult for trade unions to organise and, therefore, trade unions have not been able to convert this employment growth into any substantial growth in union membership and recognition. At the same time, the growth of 'greenfield site' developments (such as new business parks, out-of-town retail and distribution centres, etc.) present management with an opportunity to establish new approaches to employee relations (including non-unionism), particularly if it does not involve the transfer of staff from existing, possibly unionised, sites.

Certainly, Millward and Stevens believed that the decline in union recognition in private manufacturing in the early 1980s 'appears to be predominantly a structural change arising from the disproportionate rate of closure of large manufacturing plants'[23], which generally had high union membership and recognised unions, rather than from any sustained management campaign in manufacturing industries to withdraw from union recognition. Furthermore, the abandonment of centralised multi-employer bargaining in industries such as engineering may also have reduced recognition at the organisational level – particularly among smaller companies. Visser[24] points out that, in countries like Sweden, Germany and The Netherlands, the extension of multi-employer agreements across an industry or sector (either by custom or law) coupled with a relatively small wage differential between unionised and non-unionised organisation provides little incentive for an organisation not to recognise unions.

Significantly, only three out of the top 44 UK private sector organisations employing more than 25,000 people do not recognise unions – Marks & Spencer, John Lewis Partnership and McDonald's[25]. However, Bassett[26] notes that **union recognition and non-unionism often exist side by side**. Thus, it has been quite common for manual employees to be represented by unions while non-manual employees are non-unionised. In addition, organisations which span a range of industrial settings may have quite diverse recognition situations. In the 'hospitality sector', for example, Whitbread, Bass and Scottish & Newcastle have recognised unions in their brewing and distribution operations for a long time but are generally non-unionised in their pubs, restaurants and hotels. Similarly, at an international level, organisations like IBM and Marks & Spencer (which are generally regarded in the UK as a culturally non-union organisations) may, nevertheless, be unionised in countries which provide statutory support for recognition.

Legal intervention

Traditionally, British trade unions have sought to secure **recognition through direct representation to management** based on their own efforts and ability to recruit sufficient members in the workplace to be able to demonstrate, if necessary by industrial action, the desire of the employees to be represented by a trade union. However, during the 1970s (under the Industrial Relations Act (1971) and the Employment Protection Act (1975), but repealed in 1980) a **statutory procedure** existed which could be invoked by trade unions as an alternative to industrial action when management was not prepared to grant recognition voluntarily. It was intended only to be used as a last resort. Nevertheless, during 1976–9, ACAS handled 2,066 recognition cases under its voluntary conciliation machinery and 1168 under the statutory procedure – granting some form of recognition in 1,524 cases covering approximately 133,000 employees[27].

During the existence of the statutory procedure, the CIR and later ACAS sought to develop a **systematic approach** to determining trade union recognition and collective bargaining arrangements at the workplace that minimised, as far as possible, multi-unionism and inter-union disputes. This involved consideration of three inter-related aspects: bargaining unit, bargaining agent and the degree of recognition (see Figure 6.2):

Bargaining unit. This comprises the group, or groups, of employees who might ultimately be represented by the union(s) and be covered by jointly negotiated terms and conditions of employment. A number of factors can be used to establish the degree of **common interest** (internal homogeneity) among employees and therefore the boundary of a bargaining unit[28]:

 ▪ Characteristics of the workgroup (job skills and content; training, qualifications and experience; payment systems and other conditions of employment; patterns of recruitment, promotion and transfer of employees);
 ▪ Existing trade union membership and collective bargaining arrangements (including attitude towards collective bargaining, employee preference of association and existence of consultative committees);
 ▪ Management structure and authority.

Bargaining agent. The union(s) seeking recognition should be independent (not under the influence or control of management), appropriate (capable of taking into membership all employees likely to comprise the bargaining unit), effective (having sufficient resources) and representative (to be determined through the final ballot).

Degree of recognition. There are two possible levels of recognition:

 ▪ *Procedural recognition* does not give the union any right to be involved in the initial determination of terms and conditions of employment nor is it accepted as the representative of the entire bargaining unit, but it may make representations to management when its members, individually or collectively, have a complaint regarding the application of managerially determined terms and conditions or when management's actions are considered to be unfair or unreasonable.
 ▪ *Negotiating recognition*, which is the ultimate objective, gives the right to joint determination of the terms and conditions of employment which will apply to all employees in the bargaining unit. Negotiating recognition may be given on an exclusive basis or jointly with other unions.

Figure 6.2 Trade
union recognition
process

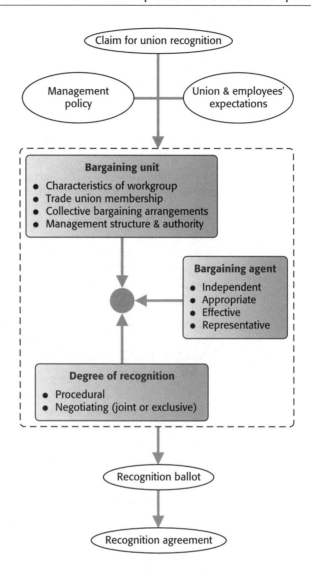

Attention has refocused on each of these elements with decentralisation of collective bargaining and the development of single-table bargaining or single-union agreements. It has necessitated not only a technical redefinition of the boundaries of the bargaining unit(s) but also a more fundamental reassessment of the importance attached to the various common interest factors (often in favour of organisational performance and flexibility factors) and a reappraisal of which union (and how many) should be recognised and for what purpose.

Ballot. The critical question to be determined by the ballot is not how many employees are members of the union(s) but rather how many wish the union(s) to represent them in the joint determination of their terms and conditions of employment [29]. Neither the law, the CIR nor ACAS was prepared to define a precise threshold level of support to determine whether or not recognition should be granted. Some management argued that there should be a substantial majority (66–75 per cent of the total employees) before being expected to make such a fundamental change in the employment relationship. However, both the CIR and ACAS recommended recognition where the support for the union was less than 50 per cent of those voting, partly because it is clear that the degree of support, including trade union membership, normally increases once the union is recognised and able to demonstrate its ability to represent the interests of the members of the bargaining unit.

The recognition agreement. The agreement should, assuming that it is for full negotiating rights, cover three main areas:

■ The rights of management (to manage the affairs of the organisation in the most efficient, productive and profitable manner) and the rights of the union(s) (to represent its members' interests, to negotiate and jointly agree terms and conditions of employment and to be consulted on changes in the organisation or working arrangements);

■ Scope and institutions of collective bargaining (those issues which will be subject to formal joint negotiation, such as wages, hours, holidays, other benefits and working arrangements, and the machinery for negotiation, consultation and the resolution of any disputes);

■ Role of workplace representatives (number and constituencies, qualifications required to be eligible to become a representative (e.g. length of service), method of election and accreditation, period of office, how he or she should carry out the role, and what facilities will be afforded by management).

The **inadequacy of the 1970s statutory procedure** to deal with an employer who was determined not to grant recognition was clearly demonstrated in the Grunwick case (1977) where, despite Lord Denning's statement that 'this statute makes great powers available to trade unions ... they can bring immense pressure on an employer who does not wish to recognise a trade union'[30], Torrington and Chapman noted that 'the management not only refused union recognition, but also dismissed all of a substantial number of employees who took strike action, refused to co-operate with an ACAS ballot of employees' opinion, refused to accept the recommendation and ... despite every form of persuasion, including mass picketing and union attempts at blacking supplies, ... remained firm in refusing to recognise and in the end the state agencies were as powerless as the trade union movement'[31]. Rather than reform and strengthen the statutory procedure to overcome these problems, the Conservative government abolished it in 1980.

See Case study 6.2

Nevertheless, throughout the 1980s and 1990s, ACAS continued to handle some 100–200 collective conciliations each year dealing with recognition. In 1995, the TUC proposed the introduction of statutory rights to recognition on a step-by-step basis:

■ Any union member should have the legal right to individual union representation without any requirement for the employer to recognise the union.

Case study 6.2 ■ Recognition at ADT Fire and Security

'ADT Fire and Security had been formed following a merger of ADT with Thorn Security and Modern. The AEEU had a collective bargaining agreement at Thorn in respect of categories of engineering staff, but no similar arrangement with any union existed at ADT and Modern. The newly merged company decided to de-recognise the union for collective bargaining, and gave notice. The AEEU balloted for industrial action.

ACAS involvement began following an invitation to the parties in June 1998 to attend informal joint talks. Following this meeting, ACAS continued to assist the parties in producing an agreed basis for resolving their differences. The outcome was an agreement that they would make use of the balloting procedures and arrangements for statutory trade union recognition as set out in the Government's *Fairness at Work* White Paper, published in May 1998. The White Paper proposed a statutory procedure which would lead to the award of recognition if a majority voted for it in a ballot, and if that majority represented at least 40 per cent of those eligible to vote.

The parties also agreed to the detailed basis for conducting this process, including: definition of the bargaining unit; arrangements for access by the union to the company's employees in the bargaining unit; wording of the ballot question; and various other arrangements for the ballot, including such matters as dates and content/layout of the ballot paper. The parties agreed to abide by the result.

The ballot was held between 16 and 30 October 1998 and conducted by Electoral Reform Ballot Services (ERBS). The result was that out of 1,697 staff eligible to vote, 1,142 voted for recognition of the union and 71 against. The 'yes' votes represented 67.3 per cent of those eligible to vote. Therefore the union had exceeded the 40 per cent required for achievement of recognition, and the parties entered into direct discussions on a new agreement.'

Source: ACAS, *Annual Report 1998*, pp. 47–8.

■ Where a union had more than 10 per cent *membership* in a bargaining unit, it should be given the legal right to be consulted.

■ Where it could win more than 50 per cent *support* from the employees in the bargaining unit, it should have a legally enforceable right to collective bargaining.

The new Labour government has reintroduced a statutory recognition procedure (Schedule 1, Employment Relations Act, 1999) which can be divided into four main segments:

■ **Voluntary negotiation**. Once a union (or group of unions) has presented a claim for recognition for a particular bargaining unit, the employer has ten days to respond (agree, reject or state willingness to negotiate) and, if the latter, a further 20 days in which to agree the composition of the bargaining unit and level of support for the union (prior to a formal ballot).

■ **Statutory validation**. If the employer rejects the union's claim or the parties cannot agree on the composition of the bargaining unit, the matter may be referred to the Central Arbitration Committee (CAC) which will:

▌ *Check that the claim is 'valid'*. The CAC has to ensure that the organisation employs more than 21 people, that the union is independent, and that its claim has been submitted in writing, states the claimed bargaining unit and has been received by the employer.

- *Assess that the union has support*. The CAC has to be satisfied that at least 10 per cent of the employees in the bargaining unit are members of the union and there are no other unions with membership among the same group.
- *Determine the boundary of the bargaining unit*. The factors to be taken into account are similar to the ones used under the previous statutory procedure but with the significant addition of ensuring its 'compatibility with effective management'.
- *Automatic recognition*. If the CAC decides that the union already has 50 per cent plus of the employees in membership, it can issue a declaration that the union should be recognised. However, some believe[32] that the CAC is more likely, at least initially, still to go to a ballot; using its powers to require a ballot where it believes it would be 'in the interests of good industrial relations' or it has doubts, because of the circumstances in which people joined the union or their length of membership, that a 'significant' number of employees want collective bargaining – which 'could potentially drive a wedge between a union and its members'[33].

- **Ballot**

  - *Mechanism*. The procedure provides for independent oversight of the ballot, a union right of access to employees prior to the ballot and the costs of the ballot to be split 50–50 between the union and employer.
  - *Result*. Recognition will be awarded if a majority of those voting, and at least 40 per cent of the total electorate, vote in favour of union recognition. The right to recognition will exist for three years but, equally, if the union loses the ballot, it is precluded from making a further claim for recognition for three years.

- **Determination of collective bargaining procedure**. If the union wins the ballot, the employer has 30 days in which to negotiate a collective bargaining procedure agreement with the union. If it fails to do so, the CAC can impose a legally binding contract to negotiate on mandatory items of pay, hours and holidays. Significantly, the Secretary of State has power to specify the *method* by which collective bargaining is to be conducted and this could include the inclusion of 'no strike' or compulsory arbitration clauses.

The procedure also allows for **termination of the recognition agreement** (derecognition). Termination can only take place during the first three years if the employer can show that the bargaining unit has ceased to exist or is no longer appropriate by virtue of changes in the organisation's structure or activities or 'substantial' changes in the number of employees within the bargaining unit. The CAC can decide, in the circumstances, that a new bargaining unit would be more appropriate. However, after three years has elapsed, either the employer or a group of employees can request an end to the union's recognition and, in the absence of the union's acceptance, the CAC can undertake a procedure similar to that for granting recognition which can also culminate in a ballot of the employees. Whether this will lead, eventually, to widespread ballots every three years to retain recognition (similar to the unions' ten yearly ballots to retain political funds) remains to be seen.

Each year in the USA there are some 3,000 recognition ballots (with the unions winning about half) and 400 derecognition ballots (with the unions losing two-thirds)[34]. Wood and Godard believe that an examination of their statutory recognition procedure shows not only that it is very legalistic and lengthy but also that it generates an 'adversarial culture' because recognition claims are perceived as 'a potential vote of no confidence in management'[35]. They point out that the objective of the new UK statutory recognition procedure appears to be 'to foster a fresh partnership model rather than to promote collective bargaining *per se*'[36], and that at every step the parties are given the opportunity to reach their own voluntary agreement with the specified time limits being there to maintain the negotiating momentum. Certainly, the procedure is not intended to be used to settle inter-union competition over membership or recognition; where there are two or more unions, they are expected to demonstrate that they are willing to co-operate within a single-table bargaining arrangement. Similarly, the procedure ensures that ACAS's voluntary conciliation role is clearly distinguished from the CAC's more legalistic arbitration role. Significantly, some employers (not least in the media sector) have already begun trying to forestall possible claims for union recognition by writing to employees to 'warn them of the dangers'[37], expanding the role of existing consultative company councils[38] or considering 'US-style union-busting' strategies[39].

Trade union members, and potential members, are afforded a degree of **legal protection** against actions by the employer designed to discourage trade union membership or activity:

■ It is unfair to **discriminate in recruitment or in employment terms or to discipline or dismiss** an employee because he or she is, or intends to become, a member of a trade union or takes part, or intends to take part, in its activities at an appropriate time (S.137, S.152 and S.146, TULRCA, 1992; S.2 Employment Relations Act, 1999). However, without an agreement or the consent of the employer, 'appropriate time' has been confined to outside the employee's normal working hours. Nevertheless, it is now unfair to dismiss an employee for 'campaigning about union recognition' (S.6, Employment Relations Act, 1999) and an employee going on strike to secure recognition is, as with any lawful industrial action, protected during the first eight weeks (S.16, Employment Relations Act, 1999).

■ Employees who are lay officials of an independent recognised union have the right to **'reasonable' time off from work without loss of pay** to carry out duties related to the matters for which the union is recognised (thus, the importance of the actual scope of recognition) and for training approved by the TUC or his or her union (S.168, TULRCA 1992). In addition, any trade union member has the right to 'reasonable' time off, but not necessarily with pay, to participate in any union activities (both within the workplace and within the wider union organisation (e.g. delegate to committees or conferences) (S.170, TULRCA 1992).

■ Individual employees now have the **right to be 'accompanied' by a union lay official** in 'serious' disciplinary or grievance hearings (S.10, Employment Relations Act, 1999). However, the union has to 'certify' that the lay official has experience or received training in this role and the lay official can only address the hearing and confer with the worker (not answer on their behalf) – therefore, it is not full representation rights. Nevertheless, union officials can carry out this role on behalf of non-union employees and, in so doing, seek to boost union recruitment[40].

Union derecognition

Claydon defines derecognition as 'a decision to withdraw from collective bargaining in favour of other arrangements for regulating employment relations'[41]. This does not include situations where, as part of a management strategy to simplify or rationalise recognition and collective bargaining arrangements, one or more unions lose negotiating rights in favour of another union (most notably the introduction of a single-union agreement). Claydon provides a useful framework for examining derecognition by reference to both the **breadth and depth of derecognition**:

■ **Breadth** – the proportion of the organisation's workforce affected by derecognition:

▮ **General** – derecognition of unions for all employees throughout the organisation or discrete business unit;
▮ **Grade-specific** – derecognition of unions for a specific grade or class of employees across the whole organisation or business unit;
▮ **Plant-specific** – derecognition of unions at one plant or unit while unions remain recognised elsewhere in the organisation.

■ **Depth** – the extent to which unions retain elements of a collective representational relationship with management:

▮ **Partial** – unions retain some negotiating rights over non-pay issues and may be consulted over pay;
▮ **Derecognition as bargaining agent** – unions retain the right to be consulted on collective issues and to represent members on individual matters;
▮ **Collective derecognition** – unions retain the right to represent members only on individual issues;
▮ **Complete derecognition** – unions are only able to provide members with minimum legal advice and services (e.g. injury at work, unfair dismissal, etc.) and management may or may not discourage union membership;
▮ **Deunionisation** – unions have no rights or facilities and union membership is discouraged.

Formal union derecognition during the 1980s 'remained rare'[42] and **primarily in the private sector** (despite the very emotive government action at GCHQ in 1984). Claydon's survey showed that nearly half of the 56 cases of derecognition up to 1988 took place in two industries (shipping, and newspaper and book publishing), each of which experienced long, bitter and well-publicised derecognition disputes (News International and P&O/NUS) which set the trend for other organisations in those industries. By far the biggest group involved the withdrawal of all collective union rights on a 'grade-specific' basis for some or all non-manual employees, which indicated that 'derecognition may have been a reversal of a pragmatic decision to recognise white collar workers in earlier years'[43]. In only a small number of cases did management refer to poor industrial relations or previous disputes as a reason for derecognition, but in 14 cases there was a change in either the ownership or senior management of the organisation which led to a significant change in attitude towards unions and collective bargaining.

A later survey by Gall and McKay suggests that 'derecognition should not yet be seen as the major problem facing the majority of trade unions ... since the number of workers affected is still quite small'[44]. However, they identified 391 cases of derecognition between 1988 and 1994 affecting an estimated 150,000 employees. There appears to have been a trend towards more derecognition among manual workers in manufacturing but, perhaps more significantly, there were as many cases in the private service sector (shops and hotels, banking and insurance, and general services) as in manufacturing (despite its initial lower level of recognition). In addition, the public sector (particularly hospitals and water) accounted for approximately 10 per cent of the cases – an indication of the impact of privatisation, deregulation and decentralisation of collective bargaining. However, as they note, 'in the NHS some trusts maintain that they have not derecognised trade unions by refusing to agree to collective bargaining, for they previously had recognition agreements covering only representational rights at the local level'[45].

Derecognition does not appear to have been a universal or even common element of management strategies. Claydon believed that derecognition would 'remain limited, if more common than in the past' and 'be piecemeal and possibly temporary'[46], while Gall and McKay[47] argued that derecognition could only become 'a truly significant part of industrial relations' if major, well-unionised companies adopt it as a clear part of their HRM policy throughout the whole organisation. However, Claydon's examination of derecognition during the early 1990s concludes that there has been some shift from a 'reactive' management approach to a 'purposive' one and, in the petroleum and chemical sector, the 'ominous' development among some major companies (such as Esso, BP, and Shell) which have used 'gradualist strategies of union exclusion leading ultimately to general derecognition of unions'[48].

The **union's** ability to withstand any management challenge or questioning of recognition will be reduced in the following circumstances:

- Where there is a low density of unionisation within the organisation or group of employees affected which allows management to question the representative nature of the union (e.g. significantly below 50 per cent density);

- Where the employee group affected has only a 'marginal' interest in the collective bargaining process (such as senior or middle managers or professional groups);

- Where there is limited membership support for the union (i.e. the employees within the affected group display a high degree of individualism as a result of their work situation, e.g. researchers, journalists);

■ Where the link between the workplace and any national bargaining arrangement is weak (decentralisation of collective bargaining – particularly the removal of any multi-employer national agreement – isolates the employees at the organisation level and reduces the availability of wider union support to resist attempts to derecognise).

It is also important to recognise that the 1980s and 1990s have not been a period of all one-way traffic for unions. **Union gains in recognition** must be put alongside derecognition. For example, in 1998 ACAS provided collective conciliation in 131 claims for recognition or proposals to de-recognise; of which 62 resulted in full or partial recognition and only six involved full or partial derecognition[49]. Similarly, one survey shows that over the period 1989–98 there were 644 reported cases of recognition compared to 494 cases of derecognition[50].

Single-union agreements

A 'single-union agreement' (SUA) is a situation in which **management formally grants one union sole and exclusive recognition rights within the organisation**. It is a formal declaration by management that part of its industrial relations strategy is (1) to have only one bargaining unit and (2) to recognise only one union within the organisation. However, the development of SUAs during the 1980s is about more than just rationalisation of recognition and bargaining arrangements – recognition was only one element of a **package of strategic industrial relations developments**. Indeed, Bassett described them as a 'radical industrial relations package' which 'hold out ... the prospect of stable, consensual industrial relations, and so stable company performance, allowing companies to concentrate on production, not on *ad hoc* solutions to keep it going'[51], while Gennard noted that employer interest in SUAs lies in their perceived advantage in 'providing a greater opportunity ... to secure a more flexible, co-operative and less conflict-prone workforce' and as 'a necessary pre-condition for the development of a managerial philosophy embodying teamwork, quality consciousness and flexibility'[52].

See Chapter 14 – Pay and working arrangements

The **SUA package** may include a number of elements in addition to 'exclusive recognition':

■ **Labour flexibility**. SUAs may involve the removal of traditional job boundaries and introduction of functional flexibility, requiring employees to transfer between jobs and/or undertake whatever task is required and within their capabilities based on increased training.

■ **Single status**. The harmonisation of terms and conditions of employment is necessary not only to support the achievement of labour flexibility but also 'to secure co-operative attitudes and some degree of common purpose and commitment from the workforce'[53]. However, as Bassett pointed out 'the Japanese in particular are highly status-conscious, and clearly regard *single* status as unthinkable', they 'prefer to describe their initiatives as "common terms and conditions"'[54].

See Chapter 10 –
Employee
involvement and
participation

■ **Employee participation**. Most SUAs provide for the establishment of some form of joint management/employee council which discusses a wide range of employee-related issues (including terms and conditions of employment). In some, it is purely 'advisory' to management and in others it replaces 'traditional' negotiations. Consequently, the right to union representation varies considerably (see Box 6.1) and only if the council is unable to reach a consensus is the union involved in direct negotiations with management and then, if necessary, arbitration. While Bassett is able to argue that 'the strong moral force of decisions reached in this way certainly predisposes the company to accept them', nevertheless he recognises that 'the unions have only a tangential impact on a structure such as this'[55]. Certainly, the emphasis on 'employee' not 'union' representatives is significant. Where such councils determine terms and conditions of employment, the absence of a strong union presence, in effect, negates the objective of recognition (negotiating terms and conditions of employment).

See Chapter 12 –
Conciliation and
arbitration

■ **Pendulum arbitration/'no strike' provision**. Most SUAs seek to remove the *need for* resort to industrial action by providing for the automatic use of arbitration to resolve such disputes. However, it is the inclusion of an additional 'no strike' clause in some SUAs (by which the union forgoes *in advance* the use of industrial action) which is regarded by some as an abandonment of a fundamental trade union principle – the right to withdraw labour.

The fact that trade unions accepted such SUAs may be as much a reflection of their weakened position during the 1980s and their desire to secure or maintain

---

Box 6.1	Union involvement in councils

■ No reserved seats for union representatives (Nissan – AUEW (1985) car manufacture).

■ Senior steward co-opted if not elected as normal employee representative (Toshiba – EETPU (1981) television manufacture).

■ Local full-time officer attends meetings *ex-officio* (Komatsu – AEU (1987) construction equipment manufacture).

■ One automatic seat for senior shop steward (Bowman Webber – EETPU (1985) Glass product manufacture).

■ A minimum number of union members (either elected or co-opted) have to be present for discussion on terms and conditions of employment (Optical Fibres – EESA (staff section of EETPU) (1983) fibre-optic production).

■ Equal numbers of management, union-accredited representatives and non-accredited employee representatives (BICC Optical Cables – MATSA (staff section of GMB) (1987) fibre-optic production).

■ Monthly representative forum between management and union representatives to discuss common issues (Anacomp – EETPU (1984) computer media manufacturer).

■ No council – regular six-monthly consultation meetings between ISTC General Secretary and UMD's chief executive (United Merchant Bar – ISTC (1985) steel manufacture).

Source: 'Single-union deals in perspective', *IRS Employment Trends*, no. 523, 1992.

membership as it is of any real change in industrial relations philosophy. There is little doubt that, in some cases, trade unions have accepted the inevitability of a SUA as an alternative to no union at all. However, as Gennard identifies[56], the proposed introduction of a SUA may **heighten competition and introduce conflict between unions** by affecting traditional patterns of recruitment or representation, particularly in the following circumstances:

- Where other unions already have membership or negotiating rights within the establishment, which will be lost;
- Where other unions are represented and/or have negotiating rights at other establishments of the organisation and therefore might reasonably expect a similar pattern in any new establishment;
- Where another union has been recruiting and seeking recognition from the employer but has not been selected for 'sole recognition'.

Perhaps the most important concern, however, relates to the **'beauty contest' approach** which may be adopted in granting sole recognition and the implications this has for the management/union/employee relationship (see Box 6.2). It may be little different from management determining which agency should have its advertising contract. It becomes virtually a commercial contract between management and a 'labour agent', decided on the basis of which agent will meet *management's* requirement, and the continuation of the contract is dependent on the agent maintaining management support – perhaps the ultimate in management sponsorship! It is the antithesis of the traditional process of recognition, which requires the union first to secure the backing of the employees by recruiting them as members before seeking the right to represent them (i.e. it is the employees who 'contract' with the union; it is *their* organisation, and it is *their* support which is essential for the continued existence of the union within the organisation). Indeed, where the SUA is being concluded for a 'greenfield site' even before employees have been recruited, the employees will have no opportunity to express their views regarding which union they want. One survey found that two-thirds of the SUAs had union membership levels of over 70 per cent, but a small minority had less than 25 per cent [57].

The **TUC sought to regulate the introduction of SUAs** by amending the Bridlington principles in 1988 to require a union not to enter into a SUA which might deprive other union(s) of existing recognition and/or negotiation rights without their agreement. In addition, unions should not agree to a 'no-strike' clause, but this does not preclude accepting a term requiring automatic arbitration of any dispute. Perhaps most significantly, the TUC has accepted a relaxation of the principle in respect of a union seeking to organise where another union is recognised but has only a small number of members. As Gennard notes, this could be 'significant for unions in the context of the reputedly low level of membership ... from the single-union agreements'[58]. However, another union can only challenge the 'recognised' union if management is prepared to review its stance and accept that union recognition should be determined primarily by the wishes of the employees rather than the needs of management.

Despite the focus given to the development of SUAs during the 1980s (not least because of the publicity given to the 'no-strike' element and the friction, if

Box 6.2	The beauty contest at Pirelli

In 1985 Pirelli General built a new computer-integrated manufacturing unit at Aberdare, South Wales. The management decided that multi-unionism would not be conducive to the achievement of flexibility and single status, and a policy of non-unionism would be antagonistic in the unionised setting of South Wales and to the unions Pirelli recognised at its other factories.

'... a decision was taken to approach five unions in South Wales with which the company had previously or currently had agreements ... the company outlined in some detail its proposed personnel philosophy and policies for the new factory, and each union was asked whether it wished to be considered for single recognition on these broad terms. All five unions approached responded positively and enthusiastically. The prize ... was the creation of new jobs and new union recruits in an area of very high unemployment.' The management 'held meetings with full-time officers of each union, at which the latter made detailed and in some cases highly professional presentations – including the use of videos – on their approach to employee and industrial relations ... As a result, two unions were shortlisted for further, more detailed discussions ... MATSA [Managerial, Administrative, Technical & Supervisory Association of the GMB] was ultimately selected because it was felt it had the approach to relations between managers and employees and between companies and unions which was most compatible with the personnel philosophy and policies for the new unit.'

Source: D. Yeandle and J. Clark, 'Growing a compatible IT set-up', *Personnel Management*, July 1989, pp. 36–9.

not hostility, between unions over SUAs), their **introduction appears to have been limited**. Although initially SUAs were regarded as a feature of foreign-owned, particularly Japanese, electronics companies setting up on a 'greenfield site' (where management wished to introduce a new philosophy of industrial relations), their introduction has extended into a much wider range of industries and situations. Similarly, while their introduction was primarily associated with the EETPU (and indeed was the reason for its expulsion from the TUC), now most of the major unions have concluded SUAs. Gall[59] reported that the introduction of new SUAs declined from the 106 concluded between 1985 and 1989 to only 14 between 1990 and 1992. He attributed this decline to a decrease in inward investment (particularly Japanese) and creation of new 'greenfield' sites, the possibility of reforming recognition and bargaining arrangements through alternatives (such as single-table bargaining), the achievement of labour flexibility through other HRM strategies and the increasing dissatisfaction of unions with SUAs. Furthermore, he argued that the number of employees covered by such agreements was 'negligible'. Some 75 per cent of the 218,000 employees covered by such agreements for which information was available worked for four organisations (Tesco and Asda supermarkets and the Midland and TSB banks – all long-standing recognition agreements). However, ACAS has pointed out that, so far as new recognition is concerned, 'where recognition was achieved single union arrangements almost always proved the way forward'[60].

See Country profile 6.1

Clearly, there is always a danger that the development of single-unionism could produce a form of **enterprise unionism**, similar to that in Japan, where employee and union 'commitments, loyalties and resources effectively extend no further than the enterprise itself'[61].

Single-table bargaining

The distinction between manual and non-manual groups has tended to be strong within organisations and has been closely associated with differences in their status and terms and conditions of employment and, therefore, different

Country profile 6.1   Japan – enterprise unionism

Japanese trade unions originated with its industrial revolution in the late nineteenth century and, like their counterparts in Europe and the USA, initially developed as craft and subsequently industrial unions. However, like Germany, the Second World War and immediate postwar occupation had a significant effect. As part of the reconstruction, 'enterprise' unionism became clearly established. Several factors have been put forward for this development:

■ Quickest way for US occupation officials to re-establish trade unionism;

■ Built on the 'product support organisations' that had been created during the war to enhance the war effort;

■ Support from the left-wing who saw workplace-level activists providing a counter-balance to the right-wing union leadership outside the enterprise;

■ Conforms with Japanese culture and other social structural relationships.

Japan has approximately 71,000 'enterprise' unions (the highest number of unions in any country) encompassing both manual and non-manual employees in a particular company or establishment. However, their membership is limited to 'regular' employees (part-time or temporary workers are not entitled to join) and the level of unionisation in small organisations is low. Consequently, trade unionism is associated with the élite of permanent employees in larger organisations (core employees) – about one third of total employment in Japan. The law prohibits employer domination of unions and does not provide any mechanism for granting *exclusive* recognition – this has arisen from the employers' willingness to agree to a 'union shop'. Unions are dependent, to some degree, on the privileges and facilities provided by the management (including, in some cases union officials being 'seconded' on full pay by the company to undertake their duties). While this may lead to some unions becoming 'incorporated' into the man-

agerial process, others are clearly 'independent' of management.

The unions have been willing to co-operate with management work strategies because their membership is largely insulated from much of their effects by the surrounding non-unionised, marginal, peripheral workers. Enterprise unionism has, up to now, been supported, at least in part, by the concept of strong internal labour market and 'lifetime employment'. If, as seems possible because of the change in Japan's economic position, employers draw back from this commitment it may erode the barrier between 'permanent' employees and others in the organisation (they may see themselves having more in common). At the same time, employee attachment to a single organisation may decline if they have to consider moving to look for a new job. This may have the effect of shifting attention more to the inter-enterprise aspects of trade unionism.

It is a misconception that Japanese trade unionism is confined only to the enterprise level. Most 'enterprise' unions belong to one of 100+ national industrial federations. While the enterprise union has a high level of autonomy and is self-supporting and financially independent, nevertheless the industrial federation has a role in co-ordinating their bargaining activities, dealing with common industrial problems and acting as a political pressure group. In addition, there are a limited number of unions which organise on a craft, occupational or industrial level, for example, *Kaiin* (the Seamen's union).

There are three central trade union confederations: Rengo (the largest with 60 per cent of all trade union members and covers all sectors), Zenroren (covering the public sector) and Zenrokyo (covering the service sector).

Sources: Y. Kuwahara, 'Employment relations in Japan', in G. Bamber and R. Lansbury (eds), *International and Comparative Employment Relations* (3rd edn), Sage, 1998; J. Benson, 'Japanese unions: managerial partner or worker challenge?', *Labour and Industry*, vol. 6., no. 2, 1995; D. H. Whittaker, 'Labour unions and industrial relations in Japan: crumbling pillar or forging a "third way"?', *Industrial Relations Journal*, vol. 29, no. 4, 1998.

See also Country profiles 2.2 and 7.1.

bargaining units. The term 'single-table bargaining' (STB) refers to the situation where **a single bargaining unit is established with one negotiation covering both manual and non-manual employees while still recognising more than one union** – in contrast to a single-union agreement, which involves not only a single bargaining unit but also a single union. (However, most SUAs and STB arrangements still exclude managers above a defined level and, therefore, rarely cover *all* employees within the organisation.) It is important to recognise, according to Marginson and Sisson, that such a unification of bargaining arrangements is 'underpinned by a common pay and grading system for both manual and non-manual workers' and 'it is usual for all staff, whether manual or non-manual, to receive an annual salary paid monthly and to have the same hours, holidays, and pension and sick-pay entitlements'[62]. Clearly, STB is **closely interrelated with the development of single status and harmonisation** in terms and conditions of employment.

Gall[63] notes that the pace of introducing STB increased in the early 1990s (some 80 cases covering 380,000 employees). He points out that STB, SUAs and derecognition may be viewed as complementary management strategies rather than as alternatives: the introduction of STB may be used as an opportunity to derecognise some unions (generally those with low membership) or an organisation may adopt STB at one plant and SUA or even derecognition at another. Certainly, it has been suggested that 'STB may be a collective bargaining arrangement which has yet to reach the peak of its popularity'[64] particularly because of possible developments in local authorities and the health service (see Box 6.3).

| **Box 6.3** | Single-table bargaining at Manchester Hospital Trust |

Manchester Central Hospitals NHS Trust (MCH) was one of the 'first-wave' NHS trusts established in 1991 with 6,000 employees. One of management's objectives was to establish a single job-evaluation-based pay spine to cover both medical and non-medical employees.

Management believed this could only realistically be achieved by replacing the existing 14 national 'functional' Whitley Councils with a single bargaining arrangement. The 22 unions and staff associations already recognised for 'information and consultation' purposes were given an undertaking that there was no intention of derecognition. A Joint Negotiating and Consultation Committee (JNCC) was established which was to comprise 12 union representatives; the allocation of seats to be decided by the unions themselves. The result was two seats each for NUPE, NALGO and the RCN, one seat each for MSF, COHSE, BMA and RCM and one seat each for a 'federation' of craft workers and smaller professional organisations. It was agreed that FTOs from any of the unions could attend committee meetings as non-voting members.

Initially the JNCC concentrated on developing common procedures on grievances, discipline and flexible working. The next step was to harmonise non-pay terms and conditions of employment across all groups. At the same time, discussion were held to discuss a new job evaluation scheme intended to reform pay structures as the prelude to local pay negotiations. Management hoped that the JNCC could also be used as a forum to discuss wider strategic business issues.

Source: 'Single-table bargaining and job evaluation at Manchester Hospitals Trust', *IRS Employment Trends*, no. 518, 1992.

Both Marginson and Sisson and Gall's surveys identified **three main reasons for management wishing to move to single-table bargaining:**

■ To make the bargaining process more efficient (particularly as part of the process of decentralisation), remove potential sources of conflict within the organisation and create greater co-operation and trust both between unions and between management and unions;

■ To support changes in working practices – particularly those associated with demarcation and labour flexibility;

■ To achieve greater intra-organisational consistency and, eventually, single status or harmonisation (either as a matter of philosophy/policy or as a more pragmatic aspect of achieving changes in working practices).

However, Gall also notes that some managements prefer to remain with two-table bargaining because they feel that STB increases trade union strength and unity and allows subordinates, through their representatives, to influence the determination of terms and conditions of professional and supervisory staff. Significantly, he reports also at least one T&GWU officer expressing concern that harmonisation associated with STB could 'decollectivise' the determination of manual employees' terms and conditions of employment.

Marginson and Sisson believe that the pressure to remove the distinction between manual and non-manual employees, thereby increasing the possibility and even need for single-table bargaining, will continue as a consequence of several factors:

■ The impact of both UK and European legislation on harmonisation of non-pay aspects of conditions of employment; and 'equal pay for work of equal value' requiring a single, integrated and coherent pay and grading system within organisations;

■ Technological developments blurring the traditional boundaries between manual and non-manual work;

■ The increasing management emphasis on securing employee involvement and commitment among all employees;

■ The continuing union amalgamation trend, perhaps inevitably, not only reducing the number of unions in organisations but also increasing the likelihood of manual and non-manual employees being members of the same union.

For their part, trade unions have been prepared to consider such a rationalisation of bargaining arrangements, particularly if it is perceived as the only alternative to a single-union arrangement (involving union competition for 'sole' recognition and consequent loss of recognition for some unions) or even, perhaps, non-unionism. Indeed, faced with the need to strengthen their position as bargaining has been decentralised, the unions have, in some cases[65], been the instigator of the move towards STB.

It may be argued that the creation of a single body at the organisation level allows the **development of a 'broader strategic perspective'** beyond the simple negotiation of pay and conditions. Certainly the terms of reference for the STB body are generally couched in broad terms ('all matters affecting employees at work') and therefore also provide 'employers with a forum to inform and consult union representatives on company plans and performance'[66] (i.e. potential integration of the processes of negotiation and consultation). Consequently, the development of STB may aid unions in extending their participation and influence into a wider range of organisational issues through more information and involvement in discussions relating to business policy and strategic issues.

With multiple bargaining units, the unions are able to represent the distinct interests of the employees within each separate bargaining unit, leaving management, through co-ordinating its responses to the various negotiations, to ensure that consistency is maintained within the organisation as a whole. However, single-table bargaining involves a transfer of 'responsibility for reconciling the different interests within a workforce from management to unions'[67] as they seek to present a united front to management. Thus, the way in which **representation among the various unions on the STB body** is to be determined or allocated may become important. Clearly, if representation is allocated pro rata to the unions' membership then the union with the largest membership is likely to dominate and the interests of smaller groups of employees may be submerged or lost. Conversely, if all the unions have equal representation irrespective of the level of their membership, it may be perceived as giving undue weight, in terms of decision making, to the smaller unions. While some STB arrangements have simply opted for one or other of these approaches, others have left it to the unions to decide how to split up the seats and some have established a 'checks and balances' arrangement of having a Joint Negotiating Committee with equal union representation but accountable to a Joint Negotiations Advisory Committee whose composition is pro rata to the union's membership level[68].

Marginson and Sisson note that 'the key significance of single-table bargaining is not that it replaces existing arrangements but that it adds a "top" tier where matters affecting all employees ... can be discussed' and that 'failure to maintain levels of negotiation which are specific to particular groups, and which take place below the single bargaining table, can lead to frustration'[69]. Single-table bargaining should not be seen as simply a process of abolishing existing separate bargaining arrangements and replacing it with one, all encompassing body. In a number of cases it involves a tiered approach, with the STB body acting as the forum for negotiation, consultation and discussion of issues affecting all employees and setting general parameters for any negotiations to be conducted in relation to specific groups of employees, with this lower-level negotiation being conducted as a 'sub-committee' and, therefore, accountable to the STB body.

Union membership agreement

The **closed shop** was defined by McCarthy in 1964 as a situation 'in which employees come to realise that a particular job is only to be obtained and retained if they become and remain members of one of a specified number of trade unions'[70]. This reflected the relative informality at that time. Subsequently, through legislation and greater formality, the term **union**

membership agreement (UMA) became more common: an agreement which 'has the effect of requiring the terms and conditions of every member of a specified class of employee to include a condition that he must be or become a member of the union(s) who are parties to the agreement' (S.30, Trade Union and Labour Relations Act, 1974). There were two main types based on the point at which they operated in the recruitment/selection process:

- **Post-entry**: required an employee to join the designated union(s) within a specified period after commencing work;
- **Pre-entry**: required that a potential employee already be a member of the designated union(s) before being offered employment.

The closed shop invoked strong, and often emotive, opinions. As Hanson *et al.* pointed out, 'those who dislike the closed shop in principle may prefer to use the term "compulsory unionism", emphasising the coercive element of the closed shop, while those who see it as a perfectly reasonable way of enabling trade unions to achieve some degree of organisational strength may prefer to talk about "union security" '[71].

The main **arguments against** the closed shop or UMA centred on its effect on the individual employee as well as management. Many believed it not only restricted management's ability to recruit and select whom it wished (and, as a consequence, reduced organisational performance), but it also infringed individual liberty and the use of coercion on employees was contrary to the principle of voluntary association[72]. However, the requirement to join a trade union, certainly for new employees, could be argued to be no more than a further contractual term which the employee must consider, along with all the other terms, when they decide whether to accept the offer of employment. People also argued that it increased trade union power. However, trade union power depends not just on the extent of its membership but also on the product and technology of the organisation and the position of the union's membership within the production or service process. It was also felt that the closed shop or UMA allowed the union to take its members for granted and employees might lose their job if they openly disagreed with union policy or alienated its officials. Certainly, Allen believed that compulsory unionism could 'remove the one check on the authority of trade union leaders which operates automatically and which ensures that the democratic mechanism in trade unionism is used to the best advantage'[73] – namely, to leave the union.

The **arguments in favour** of the closed shop or UMA were based, Hanson *et al.* argued, on a belief in 'the social utility of strong labour unions'[74] – it was an instrument for trade union security. Dunn suggested that the closed shop or UMA was, in reality, 'inconsequential', the 'final piece of the jigsaw' or a 'kind of ritual' which could be reconciled within a framework of 'mature industrial relations' in which it became 'the joint property of management and unions, its growth stimulated by values shared by trade union officials and industrial relations managers concerning order and conformity to which shopfloor and individual values should be subjugated'[75]. The union's 'power' may then be exercised to ensure that the membership observe the terms of any agreement made on their behalf with management. At the same time, it removes, what is often referred to as, the 'free rider': an employee who is not a member of the union, and therefore does not contribute to it, but nevertheless receives the improvements in wages and conditions negotiated by the union.

It has always been difficult to assess the precise **extent of the closed shop or UMA**: in 1964 McCarthy estimated 3.75 million employees; in 1978/9 Gennard *et al.*[76] estimated 5.2 million, but in 1989 Stevens *et al.* estimated 2.6 million employees[77]. Its decline can be attributed, to a significant extent, to the **legislation of the 1980s**. Although the Industrial Relations Act (1971) had sought to regulate what were then termed 'agency shops' or 'approved closed shops', the main impetus for legislation was provided by three British Rail employees who, having been dismissed in 1976 following the introduction of a UMA, eventually obtained a ruling from the European Court of Human Rights that their dismissal had been contrary to the European Convention on Human Rights. The 1980s legislation initially deemed it 'unfair' to dismiss an employee for not being a member of a trade union where the employee genuinely objected on grounds of conscience or other deeply held personal conviction or had not previously been a member of a trade union (Employment Act, 1980) or where the UMA had not been approved by 80 per cent of the employees in a ballot (Employment Act, 1982).

The accompanying Code of Practice encouraged an 'anti-UMA' approach by stating that 'employers are under no obligation to agree to the introduction or continuation of a closed shop, notwithstanding that it has been endorsed in a ballot of employees'[78] and that the legally specified minimum level of support for the approval of a UMA 'does not prevent an employer from deciding that the required majority should be higher ... or that there must be minimum percentage turnout'[79]. Perhaps not surprisingly, ACAS declined to be involved in drawing up this Code of Practice on the grounds that it would impair its impartiality.

Finally, the Employment Acts (1988 and 1990) made the closed shop or UMA unenforceable by introducing an automatic and blanket presumption of unfairness to dismiss an employee for non-membership of a trade union and making it unlawful to refuse employment on the grounds that the person is not a member of a union or is unwilling to become a member of a union.

6.4 Union workplace representative

The union's representative at the workplace may go under a variety of titles; the most common being 'shop steward' (manual unions) and 'staff' or 'departmental representative' (non-manual unions). The position is further complicated by the fact that branch officers may carry out the role (particularly among non-manual employees or in the public sector)[80]. A steward is **an employee who is accepted by both management and union as a lay representative of the union and its members with responsibility to act on their behalf in industrial relations matters at the organisational level.** Moore[81] noted that the uniqueness of the steward role lies in the individual being employed by one organisation but acting as an officer and representative of another organisation; consequently, the individual occupies a dual status role of employee (low status) and union representative (high status). (*This section will use the term 'steward' to avoid confusion with 'employee representatives' for non-union employees.*)

See Country profile 6.2

Any comparative examination of 'union workplace representatives', certainly in a European context, quickly identifies the relative uniqueness of the UK 'steward' system. In most other European countries there is a 'dualism' of representation at the workplace: 'employee representatives' elected by all workers to some form of 'Works Council' (generally with a consultative role) and 'union representatives' elected by union members to undertake a collective bargaining role. They also differ from the UK in that generally the right to 'employee' representation, and in some countries the right to 'union' representation, is founded on legislation – indeed, Bridgford and Stirling note that in Finland 'except in cases of serious misconduct or redundancy, termination of a union agent's employment requires the consent of the majority of employees he or she represents'[82]. They also point out that 'in much of the rest of Western Europe, employee participation systems or centralized bargaining arrangements can significantly reduce the role of the union representative as a workplace bargainer'[83] – factors which are also important in the changing role of the UK steward.

The **development of the steward role** in the UK has been closely associated with periods when the workplace has become the focus of collective bargaining and industrial relations activity. In the mining industry, the Coal Mines Regulation Act (1887) allowed miners to elect and pay a 'checkweighman' to check the weight of each miner's output (of vital concern because of the piecework payment system) and, in the engineering industry, stewards appeared in the 1890s at a time of 'change in industrial techniques and workplace management, especially the introduction of piece rate, incentive schemes, and high speed machine tools'[84]. The first major impetus for a more general development of the steward role came during the **First World War** when government and employers were anxious to maximise the war effort by changes in working methods and the dilution of labour. They needed union representatives who were familiar with working methods and had the direct support of the employees involved. The importance of the steward role was recognised when the Whitley Committee Report (1917) recommended the establishment of joint committees at the workplace and the Engineering National Agreement accepted stewards and work committees as the first level of negotiation. During this period, the steward role also provided an alternative focus of industrial activity and power to the official trade union organisation. The **Shop Stewards Movement**, in addition to co-ordinating trade union activity at the workplace to deal with dilution of labour, new working arrangements, etc., sought to mobilise the rank and file of the trade union movement to demand increased industrial democracy through the workers' control of industry. Its strength declined with the end of the First World War and the steward role reverted to one of 'minimum' union administration.

Terry argues not only that the **growth of the steward role from the 1960s and through the 1970s** resulted in the development of 'widespread decentralized, relatively autonomous structures at workplace level' but also that they 'lost

Country profile 6.2 Workplace representation – France

Workplace representation is statutory based and involves three different types of representatives.

Employee delegate (all organisations with ten or more employees). The *délégation du personnel* represents the individual interests of employees by monitoring the implementation of existing regulations (both legal and collective agreements). They are elected every two years from a list presented by representative unions (only if insufficient are elected can independents then stand). They have no bargaining power, although the employer must meet with them collectively each month, and are allowed ten hours paid time per month to carry out their duties.

Trade union delegate (organisations with more than 50 employees). The *délélgués syndicaux* are designated by the recognised union and must have been employed in the organisation for one year. Their number is limited to one for an organisation between 50 and 999 employees up to five where there are over 10,000 employees. They alone are empowered to negotiate collective agreements, may not be dismissed or transferred without the agreement of the labour inspectorate and are entitled to up to 20 hours per month for union duties (for an organisation with more than 501 employees) and, during bargaining, up to a further 15 hours per year (for an organisation with at least 1,000 employees.

Works committees (organisations with more than 50 employees). The *comité d'entreprise* is elected by the employees (from union lists) and the delegates have 20 hours paid time per month for their work. The Committee receives regular information from management on employment, finance, production and the general running of the organisation. It must be consulted before any decision is taken concerning the structure and activities of the undertaking, on working conditions, the introduction of new technology and any collective redundancies and it has to agree profit-sharing arrangements and changes in working hours. In 1982, the law allowed the establishment of *comités de groupe* to be involved in corporate decision making.

Organisations of over 50 employees must also have a health and safety committee and those with more than 300 employees must have a training committee.

A government inquiry in 1990 found that 64 per cent of organisations between 11 and 49 employees had no staff delegates; 30 per cent of organisations with between 50 and 100 employees had no works council and 60 per cent had no union delegates. The report recommended the merger of employee delegates, health and safety committees and works councils into one body. In 1993 the law was amended to help small organisations; in particular, organisations with between 50 and 199 employees were allowed to adopt a single representative structure by the employee delegates taking over the work of the works committee.

Sources: J. Goetschy, 'France: the limits of reform', in A. Ferner and R. Hyman (eds), *Changing Industrial Relations in Europe*, Blackwell, 1998, pp. 385–6; J. Goetschy and A. Jobert, 'Employment relations in France', in G. J. Bamber and R. D. Lansbury (eds), *International and Comparative Employment Relations*, Sage, 1998, pp. 179–82.

See also Country profile 4.1 and Box 9.1.

much of their unofficial, almost clandestine, status and became accredited union officials, with defined rights and responsibilities'[85]. This may be attributed to four main factors:

- 'Full employment' and a shift in the emphasis of collective bargaining away from the national level (full-time officers) and to the workplace;

- The formalisation of organisational-level industrial relations through the development of written policies, procedures and agreements;

- The growth in the size of trade unions and positive attempts to decentralise power and authority to the workplace (where most members have the greatest interest);

■ State support both through the work of the CIR and ACAS in supporting recognition and the development of collective bargaining and, from the mid-1970s, through legislation (e.g. time off).

In the 1980s, the steward role once again came under pressure. Recession and job losses/threats, declining union membership, hostile legislation and management demands for greater labour flexibility in a cost/quality competitive world substantially reduced the industrial power of employees and, therefore, the power of stewards. At the same time, management introduced strategies aimed at greater *employee* identification with, and commitment to, the interests and objectives of the organisation; reducing the status of the union within the organisation by consulting rather than negotiating wherever possible; and reducing its support for the steward role by restricting and regulating time off for union activities (particularly stewards who previously were 'full-time'). As Terry points out, the reduction in activities and influence of stewards has been 'most marked over issues of managerial relations ... an area in which management had been reluctant to concede formal bargaining rights to stewards in the 1970s'[86]. However, these very same factors also heighten the importance of the steward role as a focus for the maintenance and mobilisation of trade unionism among employees. Terry concludes that 'British trade unions have no feasible alternative to the shop steward model'; they 'continue to rely on stewards for their basis – to recruit, organize and represent the membership' and 'steward systems will continue to be found wherever unions are found'[87].

In examining the steward's role, it is useful to follow the approach adopted by Warren[88] and consider its relationship to the union, the rank and file members who form the steward's 'constituency' and the management with whom the steward has to deal (see Figure 6.3). As Darlington[89] points out, the steward's role displays contradictory tendencies in each of these relationships: from independence to dependence (union), from democracy to bureaucracy (members) and from resistance to accommodation (management). In addition, as Warren points out, 'for any focal person, there is not only a sent role, but also a received role'[90] consisting of the individual's perceptions and understanding of what was sent, and the role itself.

Relationship to union

There are two sources for the **expectations placed on the role**: *formal* expectations expressed in the rule book, policies and other official documents (see Box 6.4) and, superimposed, *informal* ones derived from the particular full-time officer(s) with whom the steward deals. It is important to recognise that the steward role has not, in most unions, been created as part of a conscious organisational arrangement but has evolved over a period of time to fill a gap made apparent by the shift in emphasis of collective bargaining to the workplace level.

While the steward epitomises the primary trade union function of protecting and furthering the interests of the members in their relationship with management, there is, nevertheless, an inherent dilemma within the role – *representative of members* to management and union, and *representative of union* to members

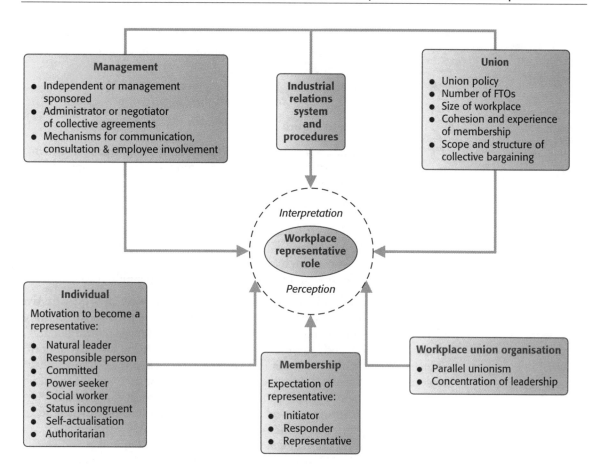

Figure 6.3 Influences on workplace representative role

and management. Although the prerequisite for a steward is to be elected by the members at the workplace, the official status of the role is dependent on the steward being formally accredited as such by the union and accepted by management. The steward's **administrative role** on behalf of the union is fairly universal: recruitment of new members, collection of subscriptions (or ensure member pays via a check-off arrangement or bank direct debit), inspection of union cards, ensuring that collective agreements are applied at the workplace and acting as a communication link between the union and its membership. However, it is more difficult to specify the precise nature and authority of their **representative role** given the variety of managerial and industrial relations situations within which the role is carried out.

In their examination of the **relationship between the steward and the full-time officer** Boraston *et al.* concluded that there are 'varying degrees of interdependence ranged along a continuum, approaching complete independence at one end and verging on complete dependence at the other'[91]. They identified a number of factors which might affect the degree of steward independence from, or reliance on, the full-time officer:

■ The union itself

■ *Policy of the union* towards the concept of steward independence and the level of training and support provided.
■ *Lack of sufficient full-time officers* may require the stewards at better-organised workplaces to rely more on their own resources.

■ The workplace and nature of the collective bargaining system

■ *The larger the size of the workplace*, the greater the delegated management authority, the more issues to be resolved and the greater the opportunity for stewards to gain experience in handling industrial relations situations.
■ *Cohesion, commitment and union experience among the union's membership* is likely to increase pressure for management's actions to be subjected to immediate and direct trade union scrutiny and agreement.
■ *The structure of collective bargaining* (with its emphasis on either workplace or national level) may increase or decrease the scope for stewards to develop an independent collective bargaining role.

However, steward independence is a **qualitative as well as a quantitative** issue. It is not just a function of how often they, as opposed to the full-time officer, act as the union's representative in meetings with management but also a function of the type and importance of the issues over which they have authority to reach agreement with management without reference to the full-time officer. However, the fact that the full-time officer is not present does not automatically mean that stewards are acting independently, for they may already have consulted with the full-time officer and may indeed be following instructions.

Certainly, the workload of full-time officers has increased substantially[92] as a result of management strategies aimed at decentralisation of collective bargaining, greater flexibility (in both working practices and pay) and challenging the role of the union within the workplace. More time is now spent in providing information and support to stewards to undertake their own negotiations. However, while some officers reported that stewards were becoming increasingly able to conduct negotiations, others said that stewards seemed reluctant to accept more responsibility (particularly in pay negotiations), that they often lacked the confidence to respond to 'tough' management and that, therefore, an important part of their role was to maintain stewards' morale. The amount of training required, given the turnover rate of stewards, is quite high; for example, Crofts reported that during 1990–93 the GMB sent 10,500 of its stewards on a two-day course and 5,200 subsequently completed a five-day course[93]. Certainly, Lloyd argues, from her examination of decentralisation of collective bargaining in the NHS, that the development of effective steward organisation and representation depends on 'supportive rather than dominant officers and a managerial approach which encourages a wider range of stewards to participate'[94].

In the 1970s, Goodman and Whittingham argued that a major factor in the relationship between stewards and their full-time officers was 'the nature of relationships *between* stewards and the influence of the organisations they have formed'[95]. The creation of single-union **Shop Steward Committees**, Joint Shop Stewards Committees (JSSCs) (to provide inter-union co-ordination in

Box 6.4	T&GWU – shop steward

'The steward's is never an easy task. As the pace of change at work quickens and management techniques sharpen, the job becomes daily more and more demanding. Broadly, the steward's work can be summarised under the following headings:

- **Recruitment** – talking to new employees about the Union; informing them of the merits and benefits of not only T&G membership, but active T&G membership; signing them up as Union members (in many well-organised workplaces, the stewards have immediate and unlimited access to new entrants; in others, they contribute to the induction programme for new workers; in the worst organised they'll be lucky even to get the names of starters).

- **Collecting members' contributions** – a far less prominent feature of the steward's role today in the great majority of organised workplaces, where the employer, by agreement with the Union, will usually deduct members' dues at source, from the wage packet (a bonus for union organisation, as long as it doesn't reduce the contact between a steward and his or her members).

- **Grievance handling** – talking to members about their day-to-day problems, raising them with management where appropriate, getting a speedy resolution of matters in the member's favour and reporting the result back as quickly and accurately as possible.

- **Defending members** – both individuals where disciplinary problems arise and groups of members where their terms and conditions are under attack (from the driver warned for lateness, to the cleaners whose job the firm is threatening to put out to contract).

- **Negotiating on wages and conditions** – to maintain, improve and extend them (from the basic hourly rate to the company pension, from maternity leave to time-off for public duties, from company-provided work-wear to a subsidised canteen, from full disclosure of the company accounts and finances to an increased say in the running of the company itself).

- **Protecting members' health and safety at work** – many shop stewards are also safety reps, monitoring the hazards of work and making sure the employer takes the appropriate steps to eliminate them (from blocked fire-doors to unroadworthy vehicles, from back strains to toxic gasses).

- **Turning passive card holders into active trade unionists** – convincing members of the need for them to take part in the work of the Union at shop floor level, by discussion and encouragement, and leading by example (perhaps the most difficult and most vital job of all).

At the end of the day, the effectiveness of the Union at each workplace depends upon the workers there acting in unity ... Workplace unity means taking joint action with a common aim in mind: fighting for the best of terms and conditions, while bearing in mind the Union's policy and the need for loyalty to the wider labour movement. It's the steward's role to forge that unity, resolving the different pressures of being, at the same time, a representative of his or her members, an officer of the Union, and a company employee.'

Source: Your Union at Work – 1, TGWU Education Department, pp. 53–4.

See also Box 5.1 and Case studies 4.1 and 6.3.

multi-union situations) and Combine Committees (bringing together stewards from different sites in a multisite organisation) not only provides the forum for discussing issues and collectively deciding strategies at the workplace but also offers a system of mutual support to stewards who otherwise might be weak and isolated as individuals and facilitates the mentoring and development of new stewards by more experienced or senior stewards. Schuller and Robertson identified that stewards spent more time talking to each other than talking to their constituents. They suggest that this could arise from a strategic concentration of leadership as part of a strong union presence within the organisation or from a defensive cohesion as stewards take 'refuge in each other's company in the face of member apathy or even hostility'[96]. Terry[97] noted the development of a *key steward's role* among the often fragmented and dispersed workforce in local government. The individuals who occupy the role are mobile and have access to a range of both membership and management but generally lacked support from a strong steward committee or organisation.

Certainly, JSSCs and, to a lesser extent, Combine Committees played an important role in the development of trade union activity and collective bargaining at the workplace in the 1960s and 1970 – particularly among manual employees in manufacturing[98]. However, such committees present problems for union control: their membership and activities cross the traditional intra-union boundaries of geographical or industrial areas as well as inter-union boundaries. The institutionalisation of the steward's autonomy and power through such committees may reach the stage of what Turner *et al.*[99] termed **parallel unionism** (semi-independent of the union organisation). With the continuing decentralisation of collective bargaining, shop steward committees remain important in supporting and co-ordinating (together with FTOs) union activity at the workplace, yet the need for JSSCs may be reduced as a result of union mergers.

However, these committees are also subject to the same internal pressures as the official union organisation: 'senior stewards, like the full-time officials before them, are forced to assume something of the role of buffer between the employer and the operatives' and 'its leaders are obliged to balance a variety of group interests against the particular sectional claims with which they are confronted'[100]. England[101] believes that union attempts to incorporate the steward role within its policy-making arrangements and thereby to secure their active commitment to the achievement of such policies is made more difficult by management attempts to incorporate the role within its labour strategies at the organisational level.

Relationship to members

The workplace link between steward and union members is crucial given the apathy among rank and file members in attending branch meetings. Although this apathy has carried over into the workplace, in that most stewards take up their position unopposed, nevertheless the steward is, in theory at least, **elected by the union members at the workplace** and, Warren argued, 'remains accountable to those who have elected him ... since without their support, even if it is expressed merely as apathetic non-opposition, he is impotent'[102]. Certainly, Schuller and Robertson[103] believe that the absence of a formal contested election does not indicate the absence of membership involvement in the selection process: the selection may be made informally by the members so that there is only one nomination for the official election. The essential quality of the steward role, and the real source of its power and influence, lies in the steward being a **lay official** who continues to work among, and experience the same day-to-day problems as, the people who elected him or her.

Stewards represent not only their constituents to both management and the union but also the union, and the trade union movement as a whole, to constituents and management. Consequently, the role is crucial in the development and maintenance of unionateness among the membership. However, Nicholson *et al.*'s 1980 survey of NALGO stewards found that the more politically 'conservative' stewards (about one-third) 'tend to espouse the "spokesman" rather than the "leader" role for stewards', 'had fewer close links with their fellow stewards either within or outside their own departments' and adopted 'a less committed and more oppositional stance towards [the union]'[104]. In marked contrast, Darlington found that the 'overtly ideological and solidaristic, rather than instrumental and individualistic, commitment to trade unionism' among left-wing Merseyside Fire Brigades Union stewards, in the early 1990s, 'clearly played a crucial role in translating shopfloor discontent into a sense of injustice, which has then enabled them to mobilise workers for collective action against management'[105].

Stewards can only exercise a **leadership role** through argument and persuasion because they have no sanction which may be applied against the members collectively. The members, on the other hand, may apply the ultimate sanction of removing stewards from office if they fail to respond to their wishes. Thus, stewards have to conform to the broad expectations of their members, although they have some freedom to interpret these in the light of union policy or their own assessment of the situation. Pedler[106] suggested that the steward performs three functions in relation to union members (these may vary with the issue and the work group involved):

- ■ **Initiator** – to identify problems and issues of concern to the group, to formulate ideas and possible solutions and, if necessary, to provide a lead to the group;
- ■ **Responder** – to be aware of, and to take account of, the collective aspirations and feelings of the members and to seek to attain their goals wherever possible;
- ■ **Representative** – to act as their spokesperson in any dealings with management, union or other workgroups.

Batstone *et al.*[107] put forward a **steward typology** which combines the steward's role in formulating decisions (from 'acts on membership instructions' to 'determines decisions') with the steward's objective (from 'pursuit of trade union principles' to 'pursuit of sectional interest'). A 'leader' adopts a positive initiator role in decision making and seeks to achieve decisions and strategies which are supportive of trade union principles. Such a role is closely associated with the development of steward 'networks' and possible élitism. Thus, it may be argued that 'leadership' is a function of not only individual personality but also the degree of authority afforded to the role by the structure and institutions of the industrial relations system. Both the 'popularist' and 'cowboy' place greater emphasis on the pursuit of sectional interests but, whereas the 'cowboy' adopts a positive initiator role in identifying and supporting situations or strategies which will enhance this objective, the 'popularist' acts only in response to direct expressed membership wishes.

However, Willman[108] suggests that this approach suffers from two major weaknesses. First, the definition of 'trade union principles' in terms of generalised subjective value concepts such as 'justice' and 'fairness' cannot easily be related to the specific actions or policies adopted by stewards and success in leadership requires to be judged in relation to the achievement of more specific issue-related policies. Second, it does not allow for the impact which management may have had through promoting the steward role. He suggests that 'management sponsored' and 'independent' steward organisations may display quite different policy characteristics and as a consequence 'an apparent "cowboy", in a management sponsored organization, might be pursuing policies convergent with a "leader" in a different independent one: he may simply be in "opposition" rather than "government" within the organization'[109].

Recent developments illustrate the dilemma for stewards. The acceptance of part-time working, temporary contracts, flexible hours, etc. may adversely affect 'job security' (a union principle) but at the same time may be the only alternative to job losses and may even be positively supported by some or all of the stewards' members (sectional interest). The same dilemma often confronts stewards when management offers relatively generous voluntary severance or early retirement packages to achieve an easy reduction in the labour force. Compulsory competitive tendering in the public sector presented a more fundamental challenge to stewards. In order to keep the work 'in house', maintain membership and some control over the work, stewards have had to 'collaborate' with management to the extent of agreeing to reduce the numbers employed, change working arrangements and renegotiate (reduce) established terms and conditions of employment in order to be competitive with outside organisations (often non-union).

Relationship to management

The development of the steward role took place largely outside any organised framework of management policy on industrial relations. Flanders, referring to the growth of the steward's role during the 1960s, suggested that 'by making ad hoc concessions to pressure, when resistance proved too costly, [management] fostered guerrilla warfare over wages and working conditions in the workplace and encouraged aggressive shop-floor tactics by rewarding them'[110]. Hyman, seeing the development more in terms of strong workplace organisation than weak management, believed that 'sophisticated and inventive workplace representatives have been able to exploit the discontinuities between the individual firm and its employer's association, play on the internal divisions and weaknesses of management, and generalise concessions won in positions of strength'[111].

It is evident that the growth of the role has been due, at least in part, to management's willingness to allow or even encourage such a development. Despite the popular perception of stewards being active militants as compared to the responsible approach of union full-time officers, managers have (in the past) preferred to negotiate with stewards because they are 'employees of the firm, they know how their members are likely to react to a particular proposal, they are likely to have detailed knowledge of problems on the shop floor, and they have to maintain an effective, day-to-day working relationship with management'[112]. Certainly, the involvement of the full-time officer may present the appearance of intervention by an external body (the union organisation) in the affairs of the firm and a challenge to the process of management, while reconciling issues and differences with stewards (the employees' representatives) may be seen as part of the 'normal' process of management.

The extension and formalisation of collective bargaining at the organisation level in the 1960s and 1970s resulted in a greater codification of the steward's role and authority. The role tended to move away from being a passive guardian of the *union*'s collective agreements negotiated at the national level to one of direct negotiations with management. In addition, stewards provided the focal point for consultation by management on a range of wider issues relating to changes in work arrangements, the state of the business, future orders, etc. However, Schuller and Robertson concluded that most stewards remained **primarily administrators rather than negotiators of collective agreements** in that the majority 'did not engage in negotiation in the sense of taking part in the making of agreements'[113]. Negotiation (making agreements) was conducted either outside the organisation at national or company level by full-time officers or at the organisational level by full-time officers but often supported by convenors or senior stewards who could play a more significant role in negotiations. Nevertheless, the ordinary steward is likely to be involved, and even influential, in the determination of claims, strategy and outcomes through participation in the stewards' committee.

While the close involvement of stewards with management in resolving organisational problems may be desirable, it also presents certain dangers. The day-to-day interaction between stewards and managers may allow them to develop a better understanding of each other's attitudes and views, but it may also present the appearance, to the union members, of the steward becoming **socialised into an acceptance of management's views**. Stewards may, through their involvement with management in the implementation of agreements, take on a quasi-managerial responsibility in ensuring their members' compliance with the provisions of such agreements. Full-time convenors, in particular, may easily become divorced from both union members and other stewards. Catchpowle *et al.* note that in post-*apartheid* South Africa stewards have had to adjust from a political role of confrontation and disruption at the workplace to one of compliance and co-operation with management in implementing workplace changes and this can lead to 'resentment and feelings of betrayal amongst rank and file members'[114].

Importantly, Willman differentiated between **independent** and **management-sponsored** steward organisations[115]. An independent steward organisation arises from the employees'/union's bargaining power and is characterised by an emphasis on policies, decisions and actions which maintain employee control over the work situation and extend employee influence over management decision making. Management-sponsored steward organisations, on the other hand, develop with the direct or indirect support of management and are characterised by the pursuit of policies allied to 'the rationalisation of personnel administration' within the organisation. Certainly, Willman believed that the differences displayed by these two types of steward organisation distinguish, in the common perception, between militant and moderate steward behaviour – for example, he notes that with independent steward organisations 'restrictive practices may be protected, rather than sold under productivity bargaining, and allegiance to the technology upon which job control practices rely may encourage opposition to technological change'[116]. He suggested that the development of management sponsorship of stewards may be related, at least in timing, to the development of regulatory legislation (dismissals, health and safety, equal pay, maternity rights, etc.) and management efforts aimed at labour rationalisation and efficiency, hence the involvement of stewards in management systems and procedures such as work study, job evaluation and TQM.

In the 1960s and 1970s management sought to incorporate stewards, first, into the management of industrial relations through greater formalisation of the organisational system, and then into managing work changes through productivity bargaining. Both were aimed at restoring order and management control within the organisation and involved extensive discussions between management and stewards in working parties, etc., outside formal negotiations, as the means for resolving issues in a co-operative approach – the outcome of which stewards 'sold' to their members. In the 1980s and 1990s, it may be argued,

See Case study 6.3

many have continued to seek to incorporate stewards ('get them on our side' rather than outright confrontation) into the development of more flexible working arrangements and a variety of forms of employee involvement – again, using working parties, visits to other organisations to see how a system works before it is introduced, etc. This time, as Terry points out, there is an 'absence of a clear-cut set of arguments to resist such managerial innovation; put crudely, stewards who for years criticized managers for failing to listen to the shopfloor expertise of their members found it difficult to argue against initiatives (team working, quality circles) that claimed to achieve just that'[117]. However, such arrangements may contain the seeds for a further weakening of unionism at the workplace and the role of the steward because they are inherently less susceptible to collective employee or union control (or even influence).

An individual

In view of the nature and vagueness of the various expectations placed on the steward, it is perhaps not surprising that the role suffers from both role ambiguity and role conflict. The steward, as an individual, also has expectations of the nature of the role. Moore[118] identified eight reasons which are frequently put forward to explain the **motivation of individual members to become stewards**:

- **Natural leader** – inherent 'leadership' qualities are evident in the normal working relationships;
- **Responsible person** – feels a responsibility to take on a role which no one else will do or perceives the only candidate(s) to be poorly qualified for the role;

Case study 6.3 ■ Ford Halewood – T&GWU shop stewards in action

The T&GWU had about 80 stewards in the Body and Assembly plants at Ford Halewood in the early 1990s. Each plant had its own stewards' committee with a convenor, deputy convenor and five senior stewards.

1970s to early 1980s

Industrial relations at Ford during the late 1960s and early 1970s was characterised by a shopfloor struggle between an 'authoritarian reassertion of management control' and resistance by a 'highly confident, active and combative shopfloor union membership' resulting in frequent spontaneous sectional and plant-wide disputes over working arrangements, discipline, etc. Stewards, continually subject to direct 'democratic accountability and the challenge of alternative ideas and personalities' from the member, both responded to and led the members in challenging management actions and, in so doing, built up a 'relatively powerful plant-wide collective stewards organisation'.

In the early 1970s management adopted a policy of 'accommodating to, if not trying to incorporate, a layer of senior shop stewards' while still seeking to achieve high output through work intensification and management control of working arrangements. Plant convenors were included on the Ford National Joint Negotiating Committee (previously only national full-time officers); post-entry closed shop and check-off arrangements were established; and, at Halewood, 15 senior stewards became full-time on union activities and provided with office facilities in order to play a larger role in resolving disputes. Despite this apparent 'incorporation' (a core of senior stewards no longer working alongside the members on-the-job, more frequent contact between convenors and senior Ford UK managers and the FTOs' expectation that convenors would ensure their members supported agreements made at the NJNC and resist sectional disputes), the ordinary stewards still maintained a close relationship with the members and played an active part in the sectional and plant disputes which continued (although declining) throughout the 1970s – sometimes at variance with the plant-wide strategy of the stewards committee.

Early 1980s to early 1990s

Management responded to the severe international competition in the early 1980s by presenting the stewards with Halewood's poor productivity and industrial relations compared to its Continental plants and the threat of the plant's closure without radical changes in working arrangements, greater flexibility and an end to persistent industrial action. Under pressure from FTOs, the stewards accepted the need to change – 'fighting the competition instead of each other'.

At the same time, management introduced an Employee Involvement strategy which sought to replace confrontation with dialogue with unions and employees (although on occasions it still exerted its managerial prerogative). Some physical working conditions were improved, video presentations made to small groups, open days arranged for families and workers flown to continental plants to 'see for themselves' how they did things. Stewards were further 'incorporated' by shifting the convenors' offices away from the shopfloor and alongside the plant managers and more stewards became 'full-time' to be more easily available to resolve problems and participate in 'action groups' with management. Stewards were less available on the shopfloor to members, had fewer meetings with members and, because the economic climate and resultant job losses also reduced member 'militancy', there were fewer challenges to stewards.

The degree of 'accommodation' achieved is indicated by the stewards' decision in 1990 to recommend production workers cross an EETPU picket line during a craft strike and later the issuing of a leaflet which used unitarist phrases more associated with management: 'We are all in the same boat. We all need to pull together'! While management achieved the work changes, improvements in productivity and decline in strikes it wanted, the new relationship between stewards and management 'had the effect of demobilising their members self-activity, routinising workplace trade unionism and undermining the vitality and strength of the stewards' organisation'. However, the limits to 'accommodation' was seen in 1991, on the day before Ford's European Vice-President was due to visit Halewood, when workers

Case study 6.3 ■ **Ford Halewood – T&GWU shop stewards in action**
(continued)

threatened to strike over the abusive attitude of a manager towards an operator and stewards organised mass meetings which halted production after discussions with the departmental manager failed to resolve the issue.

In 1992, management withdrew 'full-time' status from sectional stewards. A further threat to the steward role came from the development of team working with 'team leaders' drawn from the operators, responsible for organising the team's work and with the potential to 'represent' them to management.

Source: R. Darlington, 'Shop stewards' organisation in Ford Halewood: from Beynon to today', *Industrial Relations Journal*, vol. 25, no. 2, 1994.

See also Case studies 4.1, 7.2 and 11.2 and Boxes 5.1 and 6.4.

- **Committed individual** – is committed to opposition to the capitalist/management system and regards the role as a means of expressing/furthering that opposition;
- **Power-seeker** – accepts a role because of the power contained in that role;
- **Social worker** – wishes to serve the needs of others;
- **Status incongruent** – seeks to enhance his or her status by occupying a role of higher status than the one currently occupied;
- **Self-actualisation** – regards the role as an opportunity to utilise and develop his or her abilities and so enhance job satisfaction;
- **Authoritarian** – regards the role as providing a position of authority over others.

Moore found from his survey of stewards that none of these explanations were satisfactory. He concluded that 'perhaps the greatest single characteristic ... underlying the motives of the respondents in becoming shop stewards, was the inability to stand the stress of the disorganisation that results from ineffective or non-existent shop-floor leadership' linked to 'a sense of responsibility mainly to self, but partly to others' and 'a desire to have some measure of control over the matters which are of immediate personal concern in the workplace'[119]. It would appear, therefore, that the main motivation to become a steward is that the individual is simply a committed trade unionist.

■ Summary propositions

- Trade union recognition is not a single event but a dynamic process of change in an organisation's employment relationship.
- The 1980s and 1990s have seen a shift in the emphasis of recognition from supporting collectivism and union power (including maintaining union membership agreements) to supporting organisational change, flexibility and co-operation (through partial derecognition, single-table bargaining, and single-union agreements).

- Although recent management HRM strategies and EU legislation have favoured 'employee' as opposed to 'union' representation, the re-introduction of a statutory union recognition procedure may afford unions an opportunity to regain some ground (particularly among hostile employers).
- The steward role is under threat from management HRM strategies aimed at flexible individual work arrangements and employee involvement mechanisms which are less susceptible to external collective influence or control.

Activity   If you have been able to get some 'primary' materials from a trade union (as suggested in Chapter 4), try to identify what they say about the union's workplace representative, what training is provided by the union for them and what links do they have to other institutions within the union organisation (e.g. branch, regional committee, etc.).

Further reading

- I. McLoughlin and S. Gourlay, *Enterprise without Unions*, Open University Press, 1994. This book examines the 'benign image of non-unionism' as it operates in the high-technology sector.
- P. Ackers, C. Smith and P. Smith, *The New Workplace and Trade Unionism*, Routledge, 1996. This examines not only developments in trade unionism at the workplace but also the impact of changes in work organisation.
- P. Bassett, *Strike Free: New industrial relations in Britain*, Macmillan, 1987. This provides a useful examination of both the background and nature of single-union agreements.
- P. Fosh and E. Heery (eds), *Trade Unions and their Members*, Macmillan, 1990. Useful chapter by E. Heery and J. Kelly on the relationship between stewards and FTOs.
- R. Darlington, *The Dynamics of Workplace Unionism*, Mansell, 1994. This provides a detailed examination of shop stewards in three Merseyside organisations.

References

1. G. Morgan, *Images of Organization* (2nd edn), Sage, 1997, p. 153.
2. A. Flanders, *Industrial Relations: What is wrong with the system?* IPM, 1965, p. 44.
3. W. E. J. McCarthy and N. D. Ellis, *Management by Agreement*, Hutchinson, 1973, p. 4.
4. R. Lumley, 'A modified rules approach to workplace industrial relations', *Industrial Relations Journal*, vol. 10, no. 3, 1979, p. 49.
5. R. Hyman, 'The future of employee representation', *British Journal of Industrial Relations*, vol. 35, no. 3, 1997, pp. 310–11.
6. K. Legge, 'Human resource management: a

critical analysis', in J. Storey (ed.), *New Perspectives on Human Resource Management*, Routledge, 1989, p. 36.

7. I. McLoughlin and S. Gourlay, *Enterprise Without Unions: Industrial relations in the non-union firm*, Open University Press, 1994, p. 35.

8. P. Bland, 'Trade union membership and recognition, 1997–98', *Labour Market Trends*, July 1999, table 5, p. 349.

9. P. Blyton and P. Turnbull, *The Dynamics of Employee Relations* (2nd edn), Macmillan, 1998, p. 269.

10. McLoughlin and Gourlay, *op. cit.*, p. 153.

11. Blyton and Turnbull, *op. cit.*, p. 267.

12. *Ibid.*, p. 268.

13. P. Flood and B. Toner, 'Large non-union companies: how do they avoid a Catch 22?' *British Journal of Industrial Relations*, vol. 35, no. 2, 1997, figure 1, p. 268.

14. M. Terry, 'Systems of collective employee representation in non-union firms in the UK', *Industrial Relations Journal*, vol. 30, no. 1, 1999, p. 19.

15. *Collective Redundancies and Transfer of Undertakings (Protection of Employment) (Amendment) Regulations*, 1995.

16. *Health and Safety (Consultation with Employees) Regulations*, 1996.

17. 'Company Councils', *Incomes Data Services Study*, no. 672, July 1999, p. 1.

18. Terry, *op. cit.*, p. 25.

19. Hyman, *op. cit.*, p. 315.

20. Terry, *op. cit.*, p. 27.

21. D. Torrington and L. Hall, *Human Resource Management* (4th edn.), Prentice Hall, 1998, pp. 510 and 512.

22. B. Towers, 'Trends and developments in industrial relations: derecognising trade unions: implications and consequences', *Industrial Relations Journal*, vol. 19, no. 3, 1988, p. 5.

23. N. Millward and M. Stevens, *British Workplace Industrial Relations 1980–1984*, Gower, 1986, p. 64.

24. J. Visser, 'European trade unions: the transition years', in R. Hyman and A. Ferner (eds), *New Frontiers in European Industrial Relations*, Blackwell, 1994, pp. 97–8.

25. 'Big business: unions make inroads', *Labour Research*, September 1999, pp. 11–13.

26. P. Bassett, 'Non-unionism's growing ranks', *Personnel Management*, March 1988, pp. 44–7.

27. R. Price and G. S. Bain, 'Union growth in Britain: retrospect and prospect', *British Journal of Industrial Relations*, vol. 21, no. 1, 1983.

28. CIR, *Trade Union Recognition: CIR Experience*, HMSO, 1974.

29. CIR, *Ballots and Union Recognition: A guide for employers*, HMSO, 1974, p. 8.

30. Quoted in K. Hawkins, *A Handbook of Industrial Relations Practice*, Kogan Page, 1979, p. 52.

31. D. Torrington and J. Chapman, *Personnel Management* (2nd edn.), Prentice Hall, 1983, p. 156.

32. *The Employment Relations Act 1999 – a guide for trade unionists*, National Union of Journalists, November 1999, p. 11.

33. A. Arkin, 'Political spotlight falls on dormant recognition body', *People Management*, January 1999, p. 9.

34. 'US recognition law fails unions', *Labour Research*, May 1998, pp. 11–13.

35. S. Wood and J. Godard, 'The statutory union recognition procedure in the Employment Relations Bill: a comparative analysis', *British Journal of Industrial Relations*, vol. 37, no. 2, 1999, p. 205.

36. *Ibid.*, p. 236

37. S. Milne, 'Question time for press barons', *Guardian*, 14 December 1998.

38. J. Walsh, 'Murdoch papers "trying to head off return of unions"', *People Management*, February 1999, p. 12.

39. 'Bosses try to avoid fairness', *Labour Research*, March 1999, p. 25.

40. 'Represent and recruit!', *Labour Research*, September 1999, pp. 15–16.

41. T. Claydon, 'Union derecognition in Britain in the 1980s', *British Journal of Industrial Relations*, vol. 27, no. 2, 1989.

42. ACAS, *Annual Report 1990*, pp. 11–12.

43. Claydon, *op. cit.*

44. G. Gall and S. McKay, 'Trade union derecognition in Britain 1988–1994', *British Journal of Industrial Relations*, vol. 32, no. 3, 1994, pp. 433/4.

45. *Ibid.*, p. 439.

46. Claydon, *op. cit.*

47. Gall and McKay, *op. cit.*, p. 443.

48. T. Claydon, 'Union derecognition: a re-examination', in I. Beardwell (ed.), *Contemporary Industrial Relations: a critical analysis*, Oxford University Press, 1996, p. 163.

49. ACAS, *Annual Report 1998*, p. 42.

50. 'Climate warms to union deals', *Labour Research*, June 1999, pp. 19–20.

51. P. Bassett, *Strike Free: new industrial relations in Britain*, Macmillan, 1987, p. 90.

52. J. Gennard, 'Motives for and incidence of seeking Single-union Agreements', in B. Towers (ed.), *Handbook of Industrial Relations Practice*, Kogan Page, 1989, p. 248.
53. Bassett, (1987), *op. cit.*, p. 101.
54. *Ibid.*, p. 100.
55. *Ibid.*, pp. 102–3 and 105.
56. Gennard, *op. cit.*, p. 248.
57. 'Single union deals', *IRS Employment Trends*, no. 442, June 1989, pp. 5–11.
58. Gennard, *op. cit.*, p. 258.
59. G. Gall, 'What happened to single union deals? – a research note', *British Journal of Industrial Relations*, vol. 24, no. 1, 1993.
60. ACAS, *Annual Report 1986*.
61. W. Brown, 'Britain's unions: new pressures and shifting loyalties', *Personnel Management*, October 1983, p. 48.
62. P. Marginson and K. Sisson, 'Single table talk', *Personnel Management*, May 1990, p. 46.
63. G. Gall, 'The rise of single table bargaining in Britain', *Employee Relations*, vol. 16, no. 4, 1994.
64. 'Single-table bargaining: an idea whose time has yet to come?' *IRS Employment Trends*, no. 577, 1995.
65. 'Single-table bargaining – a survey', *IRS Employment Trends*, no. 463, May 1990.
66. *Ibid.*, p. 10.
67. *Ibid.*, p. 5.
68. *Ibid.*, p. 9.
69. Marginson and Sisson, *op. cit.*, pp. 48 and 49.
70. W. E. J. McCarthy, *The Closed Shop in Britain*, Blackwell, 1964.
71. C. Hanson, S. Jackson and D. Miller, *The Closed Shop*, Gower 1982, pp. 8–9.
72. *Trade Union Immunities*, HMSO, 1981, p. 66.
73. V. L. Allen, *Power in Trade Unions*, Longman, 1954, p. 59.
74. Hanson *et al.*, *op. cit.*, p. 9.
75. S. Dunn, 'The growth of the post-entry closed shop in Britain since the 1960s: some theoretical considerations', *British Journal of Industrial Relations*, vol. 19, no. 3, 1981, p. 293.
76. J. Gennard, S. Dunn and M. Wright, 'The extent of closed shop arrangements in British industry', *Department of Employment Gazette*, January 1980, pp. 16–22.
77. M. Stevens, N. Millward and D. Smart, 'Trade union membership and the closed shop in 1989', *Employment Gazette*, November 1989, pp. 615–23.
78. Department of Employment, *Code of Practice – Closed Shop Agreements and Arrangements*, HMSO, 1983, p. 11.
79. *Ibid.*, p. 17.
80. I. Kessler, 'Shop stewards in local government revisited', *British Journal of Industrial Relations*, vol. 24, no. 3, 1986.
81. R. J. Moore, 'The motivation to become a shop steward', *British Journal of Industrial Relations*, vol. 18, 1980, p. 91.
82. J. Bridgford and J. Stirling, *Employee Relations in Europe*, Blackwell, 1994, p. 100.
83. *Ibid.*, p. 101.
84. J. F. B. Goodman and T. G. Whittingham, *Shop Stewards*, Pan, 1973, p. 28.
85. M. Terry, 'Trade unions: shop stewards and the workplace' in P. Edwards (ed.), *Industrial Relations in Britain: Theory and practice*, Blackwell, 1995, pp. 204 and 206.
86. *Ibid.*, p. 215.
87. *Ibid.*, pp. 224/5.
88. A. Warren, 'The challenge from below: an analysis of the role of the shop steward in industrial relations', *Industrial Relations Journal*, Autumn 1971, pp. 52–60.
89. R. Darlington, 'Shop stewards' organisation in Ford Halewood: from Beynon to today', *Industrial Relations Journal*, vol. 25, no. 2, 1994.
90. Warren, *op. cit.*, p. 54.
91. I. Boraston, H. Clegg and M. Rimmer, *Workplace and Union*, Heinemann, 1975, p. 153.
92. 'The changing role of trade union officers 1: the devolution of pay bargaining', *IRS Employment Trends*, no. 526, December 1992; 'The changing role of trade union officers 2: collective bargaining and working practices', *IRS Employment Trends*, no. 527, January 1993.
93. P. Crofts, 'Setting a new standard for union officials', *Personnel Management*, September 1993, pp. 46–9.
94. C. Lloyd, 'Decentralization in the NHS: prospects for workplace unionism', *British Journal of Industrial Relations*, vol. 35, no. 3, 1997, p. 443.
95. Goodman and Whittingham, *op. cit.*, p. 126.
96. T. Schuller and D. Robertson, 'How representatives allocate their time: shop steward activity and membership contact', *British Journal of Industrial Relations*, vol. 21, 1983, p. 340.
97. M. Terry, 'Organising a fragmented workforce: shop stewards in local government', *British Journal of Industrial Relations*, vol. 20, 1982, pp. 1–19.
98. S. W. Lerner and J. Bescoby, 'Shop steward combine committees in the British engineering industry', *British Journal of Industrial Relations*, vol. 4, 1966, p. 137; P.

Willman, 'The growth of combine committees: a reconsideration', *British Journal of Industrial Relations*, vol. 19, no. 1, 1981, pp. 1–13.

99. H. A. Turner, G. Clack and B. Roberts, *Labour Relations in the Motor Industry*, Allen & Unwin, 1967.
100. *Ibid.*, p. 222.
101. J. England, 'Shop stewards in Transport House: a comment upon the incorporation of the rank and file', *Industrial Relations Journal*, vol. 12, no. 5, 1981, pp. 16–29.
102. Warren, *op. cit.*, p. 57.
103. Schuller and Robertson, *op. cit.*, p. 333.
104. N. Nicholson, G. Ursell and P. Blyton, 'Social background, attitudes and behaviour of white-collar shop stewards', *British Journal of Industrial Relations*, vol. 18, 1980, p. 236.
105. R. Darlington, 'Workplace union resilience in the Merseyside Fire Brigade', *Industrial Relations Journal*, vol. 29, no. 1, 1998, p. 70.
106. M. J. Pedler, 'Shop stewards as leaders', *Industrial Relations Journal*, Winter 1973, pp. 43–60.
107. E. Batstone, I. Boraston and S. Frenkel, *Shop Stewards in Action*, Blackwell, 1977.
108. P. Willman, 'Leadership and trade union principles: some problems of management sponsorship and independence', *Industrial Relations Journal*, vol. 11, no. 4, 1980, pp. 39–49.
109. *Ibid.*, p. 44.
110. A. Flanders, *Management and Unions*, Faber, 1970, p. 196.
111. R. Hyman, *Industrial Relations – A Marxist Introduction*, Macmillan, 1975, pp. 154–5.
112. Hawkins, *op. cit.*, pp. 183–4.
113. Schuller and Robertson, *op. cit.*, p. 339.
114. L. Catchpowle, J. Stanworth and J. Winters, 'Paradise postponed: dilemmas facing shop stewards in the new South Africa – accommodation or resistance?' *Industrial Relations Journal*, vol. 29, no. 4, 1998, p. 278.
115. Willman, *op. cit.*
116. *Ibid.*, p. 45.
117. Terry (1995), *op. cit.*, p. 223.
118. Moore, *op. cit.*, p. 92.
119. *Ibid.*, p. 97.

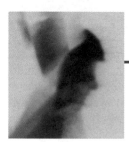

chapter seven

Management

Management is both a process and a distinct group of roles within the organisation. By the end of this chapter, you should be able to:

■ understand the process of developing management strategies in industrial relations and, in particular, the interaction between 'constraints' and 'choices' and the tension between maintaining 'managerial prerogative' and 'managing by consent';

■ identify the variations in management style derived from the inter-relationship between 'individualism' and 'collectivism' and their impact on organisational industrial relations;

■ distinguish the nature and impact of different management strategies in industrial relations, in particular, recent developments in 'human resource management' and 'partnership';

■ explain the changing role and function of employers' associations and the Confederation of British Industry

Definition

The characteristic which delineates management, as a group, from other roles in the organisation is that, through the formal authority structure of the organisation, they represent, make decisions and act on behalf of the organisation as an entity.

Key issues

While you are reading this chapter, you should keep the following points in mind:

■ Management styles and strategies in industrial relations result from managers' choices. We must remember that while the situations, constraints and issues to be dealt with may result from external structural factors, *how* they are dealt with involves some measure of personal value choices.

■ Human resource management appears to emphasise individualism, flexibility, commitment and co-operation – which are frequently seen as the antithesis of trade unionism (collectivism). We need to consider how far this can be integrated with the right of employees, as a group, to participate with management in organisational decision making (a genuine equal partnership).

■ A significant element of management strategy has been to diminish the role of joint regulation through collective bargaining, particularly multi-employer national agreements, and re-establish its freedom and 'prerogative' to determine terms and conditions of employment. However, we need to view any such gain against the increasing regulation of employment from national and European legislation (determined not by collective bargaining but within the political system).

7.1 Introduction

Frequently, management is, from a legalistic or labour/capital frame of reference, perceived to be 'the employer'. Conversely, managers are often at pains to point out that they are employees like anyone else in the organisation. However, both these views are too simplistic; few managers are either major owners of capital (although they are generally perceived by many to represent that interest) or the personal employer of other people. In terms of its role in organisational decision making, management as a group is distinct from the owner (shareholder), employer (the impersonal organisation) and, certainly, other employees. However, the extension of more significant levels of share ownership among managers and management 'buy-outs' in organisations may well create a greater personal feeling of being the owner and employer among the managers concerned.

Similarly, the traditional hierarchical division of management, with inherent differentials in authority and scope for decision making, led some to limit the term 'management' to those at the top of the organisation (directors and senior management), who may be perceived as the appointed agents of the owner/employer, while those at the bottom of the hierarchy (supervisory management) were regarded as little more than a subgroup of employees because of their virtual removal from the organisation's decision-making process. The tendency in the 1970s for supervisory, junior and even middle levels of management and the technical or professional groups to become organised, whether through trade unions or other bodies such as staff or professional associations, was seen as evidence to further justify the exclusion of these groups from both the managerial decision-making process and the group termed 'management'. Fox believed that the development of a collective consciousness among such groups and their 'pursuit of some degree of collective security by imposing discretion-reducing rules or understandings, upon top management'[1] demonstrated the existence of a 'low-trust' relationship within the management structure. Since then, most organisations have delayered the managerial hierarchy, enhanced the role of managers, increased their power and authority and drawn them into the organisational decision-making process.

The perceived basis of management's legitimacy to manage has tended to move away from the 'agency' principle, where its authority stems solely from it being the appointed representative of the organisation's owners, in favour of the 'possession of expertise' principle, where its authority derives primarily from a belief and acceptance that it has the requisite knowledge and ability to direct the affairs of the organisation. This **growth of managerialism** has reached the point where it is possible to see management as a distinct group not only within the organisation but also within society. It has been argued that the traditional role and authority of the 'line' or 'general' management was eroded not only by the growth of trade unions but also by the increased complexity and sophistication of modern organisations based on 'functional specialisms' – research and development, marketing, finance, production control and, perhaps most importantly in the industrial relations area, management services (work/method study) and personnel. The organisational division between functional specialist and line management roles remains an important one despite the trend towards greater flexibility in individual manager career development, both between different specialisms and between specialisms and line management. The line management group is often regarded as the only group within management responsible for the organisation in some holistic sense; while the 'functional specialist' is responsible only for narrow technical decisions or advising line management in the exercise of wider responsibilities.

Sisson and Marginson, focusing on the 'responsibility for managing the relationship with employees'[2], put forward three possible **management models**:

- *Systems actor*. Management, in common with the other actors in the system (unions and government), seeks to maintain a stable system of industrial relations (institutions, processes and rules) through which the organisation may respond to pressures from the environments (economic, market, technology, etc.).

- *Strategic actor*. Management can exercise purposeful discretion or choice in making decisions (both goals and strategies) not only in industrial relations but also in determining the organisation's business strategy.

- *Agent of capital*. Management is bound by the 'market laws' of the capitalist system which constrains them to view labour in terms of a factor of production, cost and efficiency. The method of legitimising its authority to the workforce will vary according to 'market circumstances' (direct control, joint determination of rules or responsible autonomy).

7.2 Process of strategy development

In analysing the role of management in industrial relations it is useful to examine the following (see Figure 7.1):

- The interrelationship between 'constraints' and 'choices' which, it is argued, shape managerial strategy in industrial relations;

- Managerial objectives and alternative styles of industrial relations management;

- Aspects of the organisational and industrial relations system which impinge on the development and execution of managerial strategies;

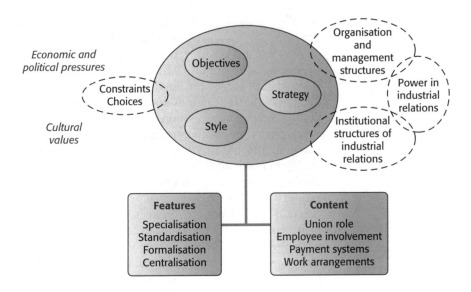

Figure 7.1
Development of management strategies

'Constraints' and 'choices'

Poole suggested that management's decisions and actions in industrial relations can only be appreciated fully if it is recognised that they result from an **interaction between constraints and choices**. The constraints which surround management, stemming from economic and political pressures within the organisation's environment, 'set boundaries to the probable strategic choices', 'place certain identifiable limitations upon the total amount of control vested in members of the enterprise' and 'tend to direct choices along particular channels while curtailing other modes of initiative'[3]. However, Poole argued, it would be wrong to adopt a purely deterministic view of management decision making and strategy development – to do so would mean that the 'crucial role of choice in the formulation of strategy tends to be "organised out" when 'the very conception of strategy incorporates at root the idea of an overall design within social action and a considerable measure of rationality and calculus'[4] in its determination and achievement. Thus management's strategies and decisions in industrial relations are not simply imposed by circumstances but are the result of conscious choices.

Poole identified two major **environmental constraints** which appear to have a significant influence on management's strategy formulation:

■ Both Marxists and capitalists often argue that the **free enterprise market ideology** imposes a fundamental limitation on managerial discretion, which mitigates against the implementation of policies and strategies which are employee-centred rather than business-centred (i.e. meeting the needs and aspirations of employees in preference to satisfying the economic and productive needs of management). The predominance of the capitalist ethos within society directs management towards policies which will minimise the organisation's wage costs and maintain output. At the same time, the changeable and unpredictable nature of the organisation's market environment 'induces an excessive caution in the formulation of advanced labour policies'[5].

See Chapter 8 –
The government

■ **Governmental policies and strategies** for the management of the economy (including the labour market), whether directly through a corporatist political ideology or indirectly through a *laissez-faire* one, may constrain managerial freedom and initiative at the organisational level. In industrial relations this has been expressed in concern for order (through the control of wages, industrial action and industrial power), unity (through increased co-operation between management and employees) and, more recently in the UK, flexibility (through continuous adaptation to changing environments).

Despite these constraints, **management is able to exercise some choice** in how it responds to these general pressures and the more specific pressures resulting from the organisation's particular market and technological position. Poole suggested that there are **three types of rationality** which may, individually or in combination, determine management's perception and choice of strategies:

■ Rationality based on **material interest**, which will tend to favour those strategies and decisions which are perceived to best serve management's economic, productive and power interests, for example, strategies intended to minimise wage costs and maximise productivity;

■ Rationality based on **moral idealistic values**, which regards certain issues to be 'a matter of principle' and a particular strategy to be intrinsically 'right' in terms of achieving an ideologically based goal, for example, strategies to avoid, resist or remove trade union recognition or the expansion of collective bargaining and thereby support management's 'right to manage';

■ Rationality derived from **technocrat values**, which support the adoption of strategies which appear to take account of all variables and provide a satisfactory outcome with the least harmful repercussions, for example, strategies based on an algorithmic approach which satisfy the criterion of logical reasoning.

It is the element of choice which, arguably, accounts for the variation in management's business and industrial relations responses to the same set of external environments. However, the choice is not unlimited; the interaction between 'constraints' and 'choices' produces **constrained choices**. In reviewing the attractiveness of the 'strategic' human resource management concept, Colling notes that 'the nature, direction and speed of change are seen as being at the discretion of management subject to *internal* considerations such as the traditions and culture of the firm'[6] (my italics). Morishima, in examining the changes in human resource management in Japan, suggests that management's choices are also limited by public policy 'designed to impose constraints which may be beneficial for the community at large as well as for individual firms'[7]. In implementing change, he argues, 'management evaluates the institutional context and examines the element or elements of the HRM system that are most *conducive* to change'[8] (my italics). Similarly, Drumm noted that the introduction of the new HRM paradigm in Germany during the 1980s viewed human resources as having 'to be used effectively, as well as responsibly, according to social targets and norms'[9] – indeed, in 1986 changes were made in the legal constitution of the firm to require firms with over 2000 employees to include HRM as an obligatory function of top management.

Wilson suggested that **social responsibility**, which is 'a concept involving consideration of ethics ..., power and authority'[10], is a crucial area in which 'constraints' and 'choices' have to be reconciled by management. It implies that management should give consideration, within its decision making, to the values, expectations and interests of the external society. Social responsibility may be incorporated into managerial decisions for different reasons:

- There may be a **tradition or custom** within the management of the organisation, based on ideological values, which accepts the notion of social responsibility (for example, in the nineteenth century a number of Quaker companies recognised and implemented social responsibility through the medium of employee welfare).

- It may be incorporated purely out of **management self-interest** – by appearing to accommodate a measure of social responsibility within its actions and decision making, management can more easily gain acceptance of its actions and achieve its primary economic and productive goals.

- Management may incorporate it simply because it is required to do so, to varying degrees and on some issues, by **external conventions or law** emanating from society itself (i.e. social responsibility is an externally imposed constraint).

The latter two may be interrelated – only by incorporating social responsibility into its decision making can management limit external imposition by law and so maintain the greatest discretion in its authority and control.

Management's social responsibility may be applied in two distinct directions dependent on whose interests it is believed should be taken into account:

- **Internal responsibility**, which is directed towards accommodating the interests, expectations and satisfaction of the organisation's employees;

- **External responsibility**, which is directed towards accommodating the needs and expectations of the surrounding community and society.

While the former has been the focus of much of industrial relations and personnel thinking for some considerable time (extending management accountability through employee participation and involvement), the latter has achieved prominence only more recently. It has become an increasing focus of attention primarily because the scale of organisations and the interrelated complexities of industry and society have meant that decisions made in one organisation have significant effects outside the organisation – both in other organisations and in society itself. Consequently, it has been argued, management must take a less parochial perspective and consider the results of their strategies and decisions in a wider setting. Those who adopt a radical perspective might argue that in a modern industrial society management's authority and legitimacy is dependent on not just the employees' acceptance of management's role and strategies but also society's acceptance.

Case study 7.1 ■ British Airways: Interrelationship of business and HRM strategies

British Airways (BA) was formed in the early 1970s from the merger of the two UK state-owned airlines – British Overseas Airlines Corporation (BOAC) and British European Airlines (BEA). Since the late 1970s BA's business and HRM strategies have been influenced by three important factors:

■ Privatisation (announced by the in-coming Conservative government in 1979 but not implemented until 1987);

■ Recession and increasing costs;

■ Increasing competition and, in particular, the deregulation of civil aviation in Europe.

The 1980s

Business strategy

BA's initial 'survival plan' to counter the recession of the early 1980s centred on cutting costs, including the sale of aircraft and buildings and the rationalisation of unprofitable routes. Subsequently, the emphasis shifted to securing the future by developing and marketing 'added-value' business and improving the quality of customer service (new image, investment in new aircraft and other facilities). The organisation was restructured around major market route groupings (domestic, European, North Atlantic, etc.) to support a more focused approach to business development. BA's business strategy benefited from the fact that civil aviation, generally, was a highly regulated market dominated by 'national flag carriers' and with routes and market share largely determined by bilateral agreements negotiated between governments or airlines. Significantly, BA was able to persuade the government that it should remain as a single entity when privatised.

HRM strategy

Improvements in *labour productivity and costs* were achieved through a substantial reduction in the number of employees (from 55 000 in 1980 to 35 000 in 1984) coupled with changes in working patterns and practices. These were implemented through generous voluntary severance terms, redeployment, a commitment on job security for remaining employees and being prepared to 'pay for change' when resistance was encountered. At the same time BA introduced a series of *developmental or mutual commitment* human resource approaches:

■ Bringing staff together on a 'cross-functional' and 'cross-grade' basis for customer service training and development;

■ Strengthening the union consultative mechanism through regular monthly meetings to discuss financial information and business developments on an 'open book' basis;

■ Team briefings and, in some areas, teamworking;

■ Profit-related pay scheme;

■ Management performance appraisal to include 'behaviours' (management style), partly based on subordinate input, alongside performance in job 'key result areas'.

The 1990s

Business strategy

The 1990s saw increased competition for BA from deregulation in Europe, from US airlines flying into UK regional airports and from the development of other UK carriers. Again, BA instigated an immediate cost-saving programme in 1991. More importantly, its business strategy concentrated on the creation of a 'global' company through buying into other airlines and a variety of other joint ventures. This was accompanied by the creation of and differentiation between 'business units'. While the 'added-value' approach was retained for BA's core of intercontinental services from Heathrow, its Gatwick operations concentrated on 'low-cost, low-fare' European services and, in 1997, it set up its own 'no-frills low-price' airline (Go) operating from Stanstead. While some ancillary services (such as catering) were contracted out, others (such as engineering and maintenance support services) remained as separate profit centres but able to seek business from other airlines.

Case study 7.1 ■ British Airways: interrelationship of business and HRM strategies *(continued)*

HRM strategy

Again, part of BA's HRM strategy focused on *reducing labour costs*, including reducing the number of employees by 5,400 (15 per cent) between 1990 and 1993. Although BA management appeared to be still committed to a *mutual commitment* strategy (including a union based collective relationship), nevertheless there were two significant developments:

■ The creation of 'business units' and devolution of management authority, coupled with differences in the nature and impact of competition on each unit, resulted in increasing variation in pay, terms and conditions of employment and working practices (particularly between BA's intercontinental and European operations), thereby undermining the role, or even continuation, of 'company' bargaining.

■ The 'participative' approach of management appeared to become weaker and the 'behaviours' element of manager appraisal was perceived to be only of secondary importance to job performance (if not eliminated altogether).

In 1997, BA was involved in a major dispute with the T&GWU when it sought to impose a pay restructuring package on cabin staff, including a 'mass sickie' which

grounded aircraft when BA threatened to dismiss employees if they went on strike. The final agreement included a provision to set up a joint working group to develop a 'shared vision' of future long-term relations. Three years later, despite a rolling programme to cut a further 6,000 jobs, BA had an established partnership agreement with the AEEU and was in the process of developing similar agreements with the T&GWU and Balpa (airline pilots) in order to keep employees and unions 'in tune' with business needs and plans.

The experience of BA suggests that strategic HRM is likely to encompass both elements of labour cost reductions as well as elements aimed at developing mutual commitment within the organisation and that the balance between the two will depend on the nature and content of the organisation's external environment and the extent to which the organisation is able to influence that environment. BA's increasing global business perspective and strategy may eventually strengthen the arguments for locating at least some parts of its operations outside the UK.

Sources: T. Colling, 'Experiencing turbulence: competition, strategic choice and the management of human resources in British Airways', *Human Resource Management Journal*, vol. 5, no. 5, 1995, pp. 18–32; J. Walsh, 'Chastened BA lands deal with its unions', *People Management*, September 1997, p. 11; D. Gow, 'BA makes strike union a partner', *Guardian*, 21 January 2000.

See also Case study 14.4.

Management objectives

See Case study 7.1

So far as management is concerned, the **primary purpose of industrial relations is to support its strategies aimed at maintaining efficient and effective operations and improving organisational performance**. Gospel argued that within this there is a further implicit objective of maintaining **managerial security**, which 'is concerned with the distribution of power, control and decision making'[11] within the organisation. Such security may be achieved through two basic, but very different, approaches: safeguarding, and if possible extending, 'managerial prerogative' *or* including employees (and, where appropriate, their representatives) in the decision-making process and 'management by agreement'.

The notion of **managerial prerogative** or the 'right to manage', whether derived from management's agency relationship to the owners or its perceived monopoly of expertise to make the 'right' organisational judgements and decisions, is deeply ingrained in the thinking and behaviour of management. Storey argued that it represents 'an area of decision making over which management believes it should have (and acts as if it does have) sole and exclusive rights of determination and upon which it strenuously resists any interference'[12]. Despite an apparent acceptance of the pluralistic perspective, many managers may be irritated by what they regard as restrictions placed on 'their ability to do their job' by trade unions, collective bargaining and the industrial relations system. The requirement to consult or negotiate about organisational changes is often perceived as an imposition which diverts time and attention away from their primary task of maintaining the productivity and efficiency of the organisation. Consequently, it may be argued that there is a constant underlying pressure within management both to resist any extension of joint regulation and to restore unilateral regulation wherever and whenever circumstances allow.

However, McCarthy and Ellis believed that management's 'pursuit of what might be termed a "hard line", insisting on their so-called managerial prerogatives, would involve them in using their economic power to the full'[13] and would, in a context where trade unions and collective bargaining are already established, create deep-seated conflict. The confrontational attitudes engendered by the forceful re-exertion of managerial prerogatives cannot realistically provide a foundation for the creation of a long-term co-operative relationship between management and employees. The **management by agreement** approach is founded on the principle that management can only effectively manage the organisation's operations by sharing power, authority and decision making through the joint regulatory processes of the industrial relations system.

The potential clash between management seeking to maintain its prerogative and employees or unions seeking more management by consent is clearly demonstrated in Perline and Poynter's survey of union research directors and corporate executives in charge of labour relations in the USA[14]. This showed that while there was broad agreement between both sets of respondents that a range of corporate policy or strategic decisions should be regarded as managerial decisions there was also wide disagreement over many other issues. On ten items relating to significant areas of work control (including 'business location', 'size of workforce', 'means of manufacture', 'quality' and both 'scheduling of operations' and 'scheduling of shifts') over 75 per cent of the managers felt these should be management decisions while, in all items except one ('discharge of employees'), a clear majority of the union respondents felt these should be joint decisions. Overall, while there appeared to be substantial union agreement with management's assertion that a range of corporate strategic decisions were a matter for managerial decision making, there was little management agreement with the union's assertion that a broad range of operational decisions should be subject to joint decision making: clearly indicative of a management concern to maintain and protect its managerial prerogative.

The **newer HRM approaches**, developed in the 1980s, emphasise individualism (rather than collectivism), unitary (rather than pluralism), consultation (rather than negotiation and agreement), flexibility (rather than uniformity), employee commitment (rather than simple compliance) and empowerment and 'responsible' autonomy (rather than direct control). This can be seen as a reassertion of managerial prerogative (albeit under an apparently more positive, developmental and humane guise), particularly in so far as employees are expected to be committed to *management's* organisational objectives; the limits of flexibility, empowerment and autonomy are delineated by *management* and are task related; the primary relationship is between *management* and *its* employees; and the process of regulation emphasises consultation which provides greater *management freedom* to 'set the agenda' and make decisions.

Management styles

Marsh suggested that 'the style in which a company approaches its employee relations activities is related to policy and to its philosophy of management'[15]. Purcell defines **management style** as 'the existence of a distinctive set of guiding principles, written or otherwise, which set parameters to and signposts for management action in the way employees are treated and particular events handled'[16]. It is important to recognise that 'management' style is not necessarily synonymous with 'organisational' style. While there is little doubt about the significance or importance of managerial style in determining the organisation's style of industrial relations, nevertheless, as Purcell points out, 'an important analytical distinction must be drawn ... between classifications of the outcome of the interaction of management and labour and the attitudes, beliefs or frames of reference of the parties, most notably management, in determining the style that they wish to pursue'[17]. Poole took a similar approach in recognising that the development of managerial styles and strategies in industrial relations both influence the industrial relations system and are influenced by it. Therefore, 'management *intended* style' should be seen as one input into the organisation's industrial relations system from which 'organisational style' is the output.

Purcell suggested that **management style in industrial relations can be related to two dimensions – individualism and collectivism** (see Figure 7.2). He defined the **individualism dimension** as 'the extent to which personnel policies are focused on the rights and capabilities of individual workers'[18] and in particular 'the extent to which the firm gives credence to the feelings and sentiments of each employee and seeks to develop and encourage each employee's capacity and role at work'[19]. He identified three stages along this dimension:

1. **Commodity status (labour control).** The employee is regarded as an individual unit of production to be hired and fired in the light of operational requirements (reliance on external labour market) and therefore has low job security; the managerial focus is on cost minimisation, the achievement of surplus value (profit) and direct overt control of the employee (negative discipline sanction).

2. **Paternalism.** The employee is regarded as a natural subordinate deferential role whose freedom is limited by 'well-meant' regulation; management accept a degree of 'social responsibility' to provide benevolent welfare care for *its* employees.

3. **Resource status (employee development).** The employee is regarded as a potential resource to be developed and nurtured (reliance more on internal labour market, implying the existence of careful selection, training and development programmes, career development strategies and a good reward

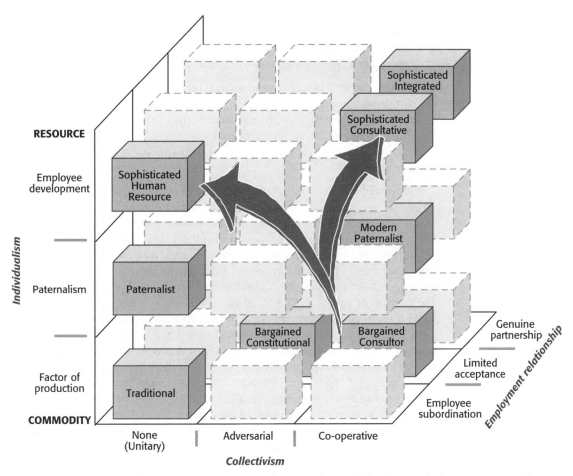

Source: Derived from J. Purcell, 'Mapping management styles in employee relations', *Journal of Management Studies*, September 1987, p. 541.

Figure 7.2 Typology of management styles

package but linked to individual performance and appraisal, etc.); the managerial focus is on communication and employee involvement to secure commitment.

The **collectivism dimension** is defined as 'the extent to which management policy is directed towards inhibiting or encouraging the development of collective representation by employees and allowing employees a collective voice in management decision-making'[20]. This dimension, Purcell argued, is reflected in two ways; first, the existence of democratic structures through which employee interests may be expressed and pursued (this may be based on independent trade unions or other forms of employee representation such as Works Councils and may range from consultation through bargaining to full participation, including worker-directors); and second, the degree to which management opposes or accepts, and thereby gives legitimacy to, the collective processes. Again, Purcell identified three stages along this dimension:

1. **Unitary**. Management overtly or covertly opposes collective relationships.

2. **Adversarial**. The managerial focus is on stability, control and institutionalisation of conflict; containment of collective relationships to limited and clearly identified areas of operational decision making; and reluctance to concede or compromise even within these areas of bargaining.

3. **Co-operative**. The managerial focus is on 'constructive' relationship beyond simple bargaining of terms and conditions of employment; greater incorporation of employees and their representatives into organisational structures and discussions, including aspects of strategic management; and greater openness and preparedness to modify plans/decisions in light of those discussions.

Purcell argued that the interrelationship between individualism and collectivism within management style is complex and not, as might be expected, a simple conflict between the two (i.e. that increased emphasis on individualism must automatically imply a reduction in collectivism). He believed that there is no intrinsic reason why the development of an HRM individualistic approach must inevitably imply a move away from collectivism and that it is possible to integrate both 'employee development' and 'co-operative collectivism'. Developments in the UK during the 1980s such as the introduction of the human resource management concept (incorporating greater attention to selection, training, labour flexibility, individualised reward system, etc.) and management interest in non-union organisation, derecognition and reduced status for the union and shop stewards may be seen as strategies aimed towards greater individualism. Equally, management strategies directed towards the decentralisation of collective bargaining, creating a stronger link between organisational performance or flexibility and improvements in terms and conditions of employment, and the development of single-union or single-table bargaining arrangements (which may include harmonisation, an Employee Council and the 'no-strike' pendulum arbitration clause) could be regarded as moves towards reduced adversarial and increased co-operative collectivism.

However, the **apparent values which underlie the definition of the two axes** in Purcell's model are open to question. On the **individualism axis** Purcell only refers to management giving 'credence to the feelings and sentiments of each employee' (i.e. the degree to which management *think* about or *believe* they should meet the individual needs of employees). There is no inclusion of the extent to which management accepts the employee's 'right' (even as an individual employee) to express views or, more importantly, seek to modify or influence management policies or decisions. In all three degrees it appears that it is management rather than the employee who identifies which employee needs or wants are to be satisfied – 'We know what is best for you'. The higher-order degrees may be more 'employee-centred' in respect of the material well-being and 'technical' development of the employee but appear to involve little advancement in terms of employee participation in and influence on management decisions. Indeed, it could be argued that the investment or employee resource development approach is simply the seduction of employees to management goals through responsible autonomy (i.e. management values and objectives become an integrated element within the employee's role). Marchington and Parker[21] argue that it is important to recognise on the individualism axis that all employers will seek to control labour costs and therefore it is a constant throughout the dimension and not just a feature of the 'commodity status' end, as implied in Purcell's model. They suggest that the development orientation at the higher levels of this dimension is indicative only of management's 'investment orientation' towards labour, which arises from an increasing management concern about the organisation's competitive position, product quality and/or customer satisfaction, and therefore, by implication, is the result of economic and technological factors rather than a statement of management value choice.

In defining the **collectivism axis**, Purcell refers to the *'right'* of employees to have a say in *those* aspects of management decision making which concern them, uses the term 'constructive' (in inverted commas) to signify an apparently important aspect of the co-operative relationship and refers to the incorporation of employee organisations into the 'organisational fabric'. This begs a number of questions. On whose terms and values? Who defines what is, or what is not, 'constructive'? Does 'constructive' mean behaviour which is reasonable only in management's eyes and that situations should be evaluated and reacted to from a management perspective and with management values? Similarly, Marchington and Parker argue that to see the creation or continuation of relations with unions as evidence of management *commitment* to 'collectivism' is wide of the mark and that the definition should be replaced with management attitudes and behaviour towards trade unions in the workplace and the degree to which a 'partnership orientation' is pursued.

Both axes could be interpreted as a spectrum of management intention from 'coercion' to 'seduction' of employees to management perspectives and values (one as an individual employee and the other through suborning the employees' organisation). This would suggest that management is only prepared to accept challenge by employees in an adversarial mode with limited collective joint regulation – and certainly little influence in the strategic areas of managerial decision making. It could be, of course, that this is the reality of management's 'intended' style: that it simply reflects management's inherent desire to manage with the minimum challenge to its authority and decisions and that this will be modified in the organisation's industrial relations style in the light of any employee reaction and power. If the model is to accommodate an intended 'partnership' management style which integrates 'employee development' individualism with *independent* collectivism, it is useful to add a third dimension – **management's attitude towards the underlying employment relationship**. This may range from 'employee subordination', where the maintenance of managerial prerogative is pre-eminent, through a 'limited acceptance' of the right of the employee to decide jointly with management on a range of largely operational decisions, to 'genuine partnership', where all organisational decisions are open to employee participation and influence.

It is possible to locate the earlier Purcell and Sisson[22] and later Purcell and Ahlstrand[23] typologies of management styles within this amended model:

1. **Traditional**. The employee is regarded as a factor of production to be employed and discarded as necessary and whose cost to management should be minimised (low pay and little sense of job security). The subordinate

position of the individual in the employment relationship is regarded as part of the 'natural order' and any attempt to collectivise the relationship is resisted. It is very clearly based on a belief in management's right to manage and is associated closely with authoritarian management, open hostility towards trade unions (including refusal to recognise or negotiate with them) and reliance on legal rights and protection to support their interests and actions.

2. **Paternalist**. Here there is a continuing belief in the 'natural order' (hierarchy and grade structures) with an emphasis on employee loyalty supported by limited downward communication and, above all, a 'welfare caring image ... which focuses on the employee's place in the firm'[24].

3. **Sophisticated human resource**. Management, by adopting positive personnel policies on recruitment, pay, welfare, consultation, etc., seeks to create an organisational climate which ensures 'that individual aspirations are mostly satisfied, that collective action is seen as unnecessary and inappropriate'[25]. The employee is regarded as a flexible organisational resource to be developed and rewarded in the light of his or her abilities or attributes. The emphasis is on communication and involvement to develop employee loyalty and commitment to the organisation with the intention of making collectivism and trade unions both unnecessary and unattractive. Thus management seeks to establish a direct relationship with its employees within a strong internal labour market, without the intervention of trade unions, and its intention in so doing may range from 'sophisticated' employee subordination through to genuine partnership in decision making.

4. **Sophisticated modern (bargained)**. This style of management recognises that managerial prerogative is diminished by the existence of trade union power. It seeks to regulate the situation by establishing joint institutions and procedures to minimise and institutionalise conflict (while maximising the notion of common interest through joint consultation) and concedes limited acceptance of the employee's right to and role in decision making. Purcell and Sisson subdivide this group into two:

   ▮ **Constitutionalist**. The basic value structure of management is similar to that of the traditionalist and the importance of managerial control is emphasised in order to minimise union influence or constraints. The relationship is restricted to conflictual 'terms and conditions of employment' and 'the limits on collective bargaining are clearly codified in the collective agreement'[26].
   ▮ **Consultor**. The interdependent relationship is formalised primarily with interest groups represented through trade unions but 'every effort is made to minimise the amount of collective bargaining especially of a "conflictual" or "distributive" kind' and 'great emphasis is placed on "co-operative" or "integrative" bargaining; "problems" have to be solved rather than "disputes" settled'[27].

In the latter typology, the 'consultor' sub-classification is omitted because of the potentially inherent instability of seeking to pursue a co-operative relationship with employees collectively while still maintaining a cost-minimisation, factor of production approach to employees individually, therefore, it is elevated on the individual axis (and re-titled, 'modern paternalist'), i.e. a recognition that it involves a more 'human relations' view of the individual.

5. **Modern paternalist**. This involves formalised relationships (both market and managerial) and an 'emphasis on "constructive" relationships with trade unions with extensive information provided and a network of consultative committees within the context of a caring welfare image'[28] (however, the precise nature of what is 'constructive' is largely determined by management).

6. **Sophisticated consultative**. Here the emphasis is on the commitment, flexibility and adaptability of the individual (involving empowerment, autonomous responsibility, teamworking, etc.), provision of information and discussions about strategic (as well as operational) decisions – often within new joint regulation bodies such as Employee Councils – 'but the "right of last say" rests with management'[29].

A further category may be added: **sophisticated integrated**. This combines the existence of a genuine equal collective based partnership with the development of individualism in terms of enhancing the individual's potential contribution to the organisation, rewarding individuals on the basis of their attributes or abilities and, above all, meeting the individual's personal needs for satisfying work, a sense of commitment and identification with the organisation, etc. The primary difference between this style and the 'sophisticated consultative' is the abandonment of the notion of 'managerial prerogative' and acceptance of the right of employees, through a variety of collective and individual forms, to participate *with* management in decision making (see Box 7.1). Through accepting an equal collective partnership, all parties (the individual and union as well as management) can be considered as having an equal responsibility to create and maintain an organisation which is not only efficient, responsive, adaptive, productive and profitable but also one which provides job security, satisfying work, and an improving standard of living and quality of life.

Kessler and Purcell[30] suggest that the 'traditional' style can be seen in many labour-intensive service organisations (such as retail, hotels, catering, etc.), while the 'bargained constitutional' style is often associated with the public sector or manufacturing organisations with a high proportion of manual workers (generally unskilled or semi-skilled) and the 'consultor' or 'modern paternalist' is more likely in relatively stable process industries (such as oils, chemicals) which are more capital-intensive and rely more on skilled, technical workers. On the other hand, the 'sophisticated human resource' and 'sophisticated consultative' styles are both more typical of high technology and/or greenfield sites (differentiated only by whether or not trade unions or other forms of employee representation are accepted) but the 'sophisticated consultative' style can also be found among some more traditional organisations which have sought to undertake strategic change in business objectives, organisational structures and employment relationships.

However, most organisations do not fit neatly within one or other of these 'ideal' types. Purcell and Sisson identified the **standard modern** as the predominant 'style' of industrial relations management: essentially pragmatic and reac-

Box 7.1	AT&T (USA): workplace of the future

An agreement was concluded in 1992 between AT&T, CWA (Communications Workers of America) and IBEW (International Brotherhood of Electrical Workers) which seeks to replace adversarial relations with co-operation and collaboration.

'The new framework has four levels, which differ by focus and time frame:
1. The *Workplace Models* develop new ways to manage change. They encourage union officers and AT&T managers to identify and develop new approaches to managing change in the local workplace. Their focus will be on quality, customer satisfaction, quality of working life and competitiveness. They may involve self-managed or self-directed teams, continuous quality-improvement efforts, flexible work environments, union involvement in the development of new systems of work organizations and other initiatives.

2. The *Business-unit/Division Planning Councils* involve unions in key business-unit decisions, such as the assessment of market conditions, the deployment of new technology and future workforce requirements. They influence decisions that determine production technology, work organization, job content and employment, worker education and so on.

3. The *Constructive Relationship Council* (CRC) reviews existing and pilot programs that relate to national contract agreements. The existing Council comprises two management and two union representatives from each of the national bargaining committees. It also oversees the Workplace Models and the Business Councils.

4. The *Human Resources Board* reviews AT&T's worldwide HR issues and provides input to the firm's senior management. On the board are three AT&T executives, two union officials and two outside HR experts, agreed to by both the company and the union. The Board's mission is to address a broad range of strategic issues that affect employees. It makes recommendations directly to the executive committee of AT&T in areas that include all aspects of working conditions that impact employees, including education and training, future work force needs and benefits problems, like health care.'

Source: P. Stuart, 'Labor unions become business partners', *Personnel Journal*, August 1993, pp. 54–63, © ACC Communications Inc./Workforce, Costa Mesa, CA. Used by permission. All rights reserved.

tive in character, the approach adopted or the emphasis placed on industrial relations considerations at any particular point in time varies depending on the values and attitudes of the managers involved and the nature and extent of the pressures they perceive being exerted on them. Furthermore, many organisations are **hybrids** which combine elements of different styles:

■ *Continuity and change*. No organisation can change something so fundamental as its management style overnight. Consequently, recent changes in organisations entailed 'new individualistically oriented employer-led initiatives being pursued alongside a collectively/procedure-based system inherited from previous decades'[31].

■ *Organisation decentralisation*. The devolvement of managerial authority and responsibility to autonomous or semi-autonomous business units is likely, as a result of that autonomy, to produce different management styles within the same organisation. Such differentiation may be based on technological and production factors or the choice of the managers of those business units.

■ *Labour segmentation*. Different management styles may be applied to different segments of an organisation's labour force. It is easy to see how management may apply a 'sophisticated human resource' style to its relatively non-unionised technical and managerial groups while pursuing a 'bargained constitutional' style towards its unionised manual workers. Similarly, the 'flexible firm' model implies a strong 'sophisticated human resource' or 'sophisticated consultative' management style for the core workers within an internal labour market and a 'traditional' style towards the peripheral workers linked to the external labour market.

Since the 1980s many organisations, to a lesser or greater degree, have sought to shift from 'adversarial' to 'co-operative' on the collectivism axis (thereby integrating any union with organisational decision making), while evolving elements of 'employee development' along the individualism axis (thus increasing the employee's understanding of management's position and his or her commitment to the well-being of the organisation). Such developments have been intended to strengthen management's scope and ability to improve the organisation's performance, flexibility, competitiveness, quality, etc. In so doing, it may be argued that management has retained, if not strengthened, its managerial prerogative.

The industrial relations system

Any change in the **relative power relationship** between management and trade unions is likely to provoke (or allow) a modification of management style and strategy. This was seen clearly in the UK in the transition from the 1960s and 1970s to the 1980s, with economic conditions and government limitations on trade union power affording the opportunity for management to adopt new (and possibly tougher) styles and strategies. Marsh found that, during the 1970s, companies had become 'less autocratic and paternalistic and more participative and consultative ... more "formal" and more "negotiating" in their approaches to employee relations'[32]. However, Purcell and Sisson believed that the change in management attitude in the 1980s, at least among the 'standard moderns', was not 'simply a matter of "macho" managements taking advantage of large-scale unemployment and a government which is hostile to trade unions to settle old scores'; rather, 'the case for tough policies' became 'increasingly unanswerable', 'largely unchallenged' and 'portrayed as "common sense" and the "economic facts of life"'[33]. The absence of effective employee pressure in the 1980s gave management an increased opportunity to exercise choice, although, only some appear to have made a deliberate strategic choice to establish a more permanent and enduring style of management directed towards the more sophisticated 'human resource' or 'consultative' styles. Similarly, the movement towards a more partnership approach in the late 1990s may be indicative of shifts in the economic environment (particularly the labour market) and the ideology and strategies of the new Labour government.

The hierarchical character of management, with strategic authority vested in the most senior positions, means that it is the values, attitudes and perceptions of **directors and senior management** which predominate in the determination of style and strategy. In the 1970s Winkler[34] found that directors, and by implication senior managers, had little direct contact with either employees or their representatives and usually became involved in industrial relations matters only when an issue had reached the stage of a problem or even crisis for lower levels of management. Consequently, they tended to perceive employees and trade unions as a 'problem' or 'cost' – to many directors 'the strike or negotiation was an outside event, beyond their control or participation, roughly analogous to a revolution in a country which supplied their raw material'[35]. It is significant, perhaps, that during the 1980s and 1990s it is these senior managers, with their strategic concern for the competitive performance of the organisation, who have been the major impetus for changing the style of industrial relations management, developing HRM strategies and linking these changes directly with the achievement of business objectives. However, Batstone *et al.*[36] observed that, where trade union power was strong in the 1970s, **operational management** often maintained a 'bargained' relationship with 'strong' shop stewards (who not only represented but also led and controlled their membership) in order to reduce operational uncertainties and secure their 'managerial authority'. This could, of course, run counter to the expressed managerial policy at the strategic level to reduce trade union power. The development of a stronger organisational performance culture during the 1980s and 1990s (including devolution of authority, responsibility and accountability) has tended to bring operational management more in line with the business outlook of senior management.

There is little doubt that the role of the **functional specialist** (industrial relations, personnel, human resource management) has changed. Tyson and Fell[37] developed a typology, using the construction analogy, which differentiated the following:

- *Clerk of works* – routine administration of personnel systems;
- *Contracts manager* – making and interpreting agreements and procedures, resolving day-to-day problems, developing short-term policies and strategies;
- *Architect* – business oriented, integration of human resource and organisation design, developing long-term strategic designs.

It is often assumed that, with the development of the strategic human resource management concept, the role of the functional specialist has tended to shift from being a 'contracts manager' (1960s and 1970s) to being an 'architect' (1980s and 1990s). However, Storey[38] utilised a two-dimensional framework, based on the degree of intervention in policy development and whether that intervention is strategic or tactical, to provide four types of specialist role:

- *Handmaidens* (non-interventionary, tactical): a subservient, attendant, service-provider to the line management; an imposed, internal contractor role;
- *Advisers* (non-interventionary, strategic): internal consultant; monitor external human resource developments; integration of business change with organisational and human resource changes;

- *Regulators* (interventionary, tactical): formulate and monitor employment policies, procedures and rules; "managers of discontent", seeking order through temporary, tactical truces with organized labour[39];

- *Changemakers* (interventionary, strategic): integration of specialist 'human resource' expertise with general business concerns; seeking new directions for managing people based on employee commitment and responsible autonomy.

It can be argued that the 1980s saw the role of the functional specialist shift primarily from 'regulator' to 'handmaiden' (as line management has been given more responsibility for managing their human resource within their own budget) and only in a limited number of organisations has it really become a 'changemaker'. Significantly, Storey[40] believes that being seen to be a good 'general business' manager often overrides 'human resource specialist' concerns and expertise within the 'changemaker' role (thereby losing its specialist contribution) and notes that direct communication to employees is, in some organisations, seen as a matter for public relations rather than human resource specialists.

The **institutional structure of industrial relations** is closely interrelated with management strategies in industrial relations. Clegg observed that because 'collective bargaining has its regulatory effect by restricting and controlling managerial decisions ... it has its best chance of being effective when it operates at the points where managerial decisions are taken'[41]. At the same time Purcell and Sisson pointed out that management is able to 'use the levels at which collective bargaining takes place to control the activities of trade unions'[42]:

- Bargaining within a **multi-employer framework** through employers' associations may minimise the role of trade unions and shop stewards at the organisational level. The policy of both management and shop stewards is primarily directed externally towards influencing their representatives at the national level.

- Bargaining at the **corporate level** affords management the opportunity not only to avoid competitive comparisons between different sites but, in so doing, also to strengthen the role of union full-time officials *vis-à-vis* shop stewards and to absorb and weaken potential militancy at any one particular site.

- Bargaining at the **organisational level**, while potentially strengthening the role of shop stewards, offers management the opportunity to retain control of operational decisions and to minimise wage costs through productivity improvements by demanding that each organisation justify itself financially. It also has the effect of not affording 'the trade union any role in the determination of broad company policy' and 'leaves divisional and corporate management free to develop policy unbothered with the need to justify their decisions to trade unions, let alone bargain over them'[43].

However, it is not only the organisation's own institutional structure which may hinder or facilitate management strategies but also the **wider national 'culture'**. Sisson and Marginson[44] point out that the UK's past voluntarist approach, with minimal legislative intervention to establish uniform labour standards, provided management with significant latitude to develop its own style, approach and terms and conditions of employment which met their particular circumstances. Other European countries have relied more on detailed regulation through legislation or strong multi-employer industry or sectoral agreements which, in particular, include provisions relating to the conduct of the relationship (through, for example, Works Councils). Consequently, this makes it more difficult for management in any particular organisation to develop a contrary style or strategy. Similarly, Crouch comments that in those countries 'where new-right governments encouraged and supported employers in moves to neo-liberal policies, in macroeconomic policy, in their own relations with unions and in changing the legal framework, employers were more likely to connive at undermining central structures' (United Kingdom; Belgium, Denmark, Germany, Ireland and The Netherlands in the early 1980s; Sweden in the early 1990s) but 'where governments of any colour had anxieties about the stability of the social order, they were likely to reinforce rather than demolish national bodies for industrial relations conciliation, and this in turn inhibited employer militancy' (Italy, Spain and, to some extent, France and Germany)[45].

Finally, Gill and Concannon[46] suggested that **organisational differences in the form and approach to industrial relations**, and the managerial process which develops them, can be attributed to four factors:

- The authority relationship between line management and specialist staff for the conduct of industrial relations (specialisation);
- The extent to which consistency in decision making and action is being sought (standardisation);
- The codification of policies, procedures and practices in formal written documents (formalisation);
- The degree to which the organisation has autonomy in its industrial relations decision making (centralisation).

7.3 Management strategies

The desirability for management to be proactive rather than reactive and to identify and pursue an overall integrated style and approach to industrial relations has been written about, discussed and, in some of the more progressive organisations, practised since the early 1970s. However, while much of the consideration of style, strategy and policy in the late 1960s and 1970s was within a 'corporatist' (collective) environment and therefore emphasised the management/union relationship, its implementation in the 1980s within an 'individualist' environment emphasised the management/employee relationship.

Accommodation and institutionalisation

Management's apparent strategy up to the 1960s has been characterised as a continuation of its previous pre-war strategy: namely, a reliance on employers' associations and national agreements. The CIR pointed out that for many organisations 'the main industrial relations policy decision had been to join their employers' association and observe the agreements on basic terms and conditions which it negotiates with relevant trade unions'[47]. However, below the surface of this formal system there grew up, in much of industry, an array of informal and fragmented organisational 'bargaining' and practices.

The **Donovan Commission Report (1968)** concluded that Britain had two systems of industrial relations: the formal system embodied in official institutions, which had as its keystone the industry-wide collective agreement, and the informal system at the organisational level, which was conducted on a piecemeal basis and lacked any comprehensive and well-ordered strategies or agreements. This led the Donovan Commission to observe that 'at present boards can leave industry-wide agreements to their employers' association, and the task of dealing with workers within those agreements to their subordinate managers'[48]. In their view this did not provide a sound basis for the development of effective industrial relations. The prevailing philosophy of the Donovan Report towards reform was 'that collective bargaining is the best method of conducting industrial relations' and that there was wide scope for 'extending both the subject matter of collective bargaining and the number of workers covered by collective agreements'[49].

Their central recommendation was to support the development of 'effective and orderly collective bargaining' and the 'extension of collective bargaining' at the organisational level. They recommended that management, particularly boards of directors, should review industrial relations with the objective of developing formal substantive and procedural agreements at factory and company levels. They sought to encourage management to accept greater responsibility for a 'positive' response to their internal industrial relations problems, rather than adopting their more traditional response of joining an employers' association and relying on 'external' industry agreements and decisions to regulate their industrial relations. The problem was compounded, from a management perspective, by the trade union power at both national and organisational level engendered by a strong economy, full employment and a supportive Labour government (1964–70). Purcell and Sisson believe that for management 'the overriding need was to gain control of industrial relations in the workplace'[50] and, in Storey's terms, 'the challenge from below met a challenge from above'[51].

Purcell and Sisson identified three **lines of reform** by which management sought to regain control during the 1960s and 1970s:

- **Institutionalising and formalising the organisational-level industrial relations system** through the establishment of jointly agreed institutions and procedures – in particular, trade union recognition and the role of shop stewards; collective bargaining arrangements; and procedures relating to grievances, disputes, discipline, etc. This had the effect of regularising and legitimising the authority and status of both management and trade unions.

- **Reforming wage and salary structures** to regain control of wage costs – including removing the process of pay determination from the immediate 'point of production' management; establishing wage and salary systems based on formal work study and job evaluation; and linking pay and production through various forms of productivity bargaining. These arrangements were intended to remove anomalies and leap-frogging wage claims and to promote greater order and consistency.

■ **Emphasising and revitalising communication and joint consultation** as a means of promoting the notions of co-operation and problem solving between management and employees.

These strategies were closely associated with the development of the 'bargained constitutionalist' and 'bargained consultor' styles of management (both involving the acceptance of trade unions as an integral part of managing the human aspect of the business). It is a significant measure of the changes that had taken place in British industrial relations since the 1960s that in 1980 Marsh found that a substantial proportion of establishments had 'become more formal, either institutionally, procedurally or in relation to the setting down of rules'[52]. At the national level, the 1960s and 1970s was also a period of a corporatist ideology with attempts at government regulation of wages through incomes policy and debates about formal employee participation in organisational strategic decision making (Bullock Committee on Industrial Democracy, 1977).

However, Purcell and Sisson believe that by the early 1980s management saw its main problem as being one of flexibility – 'if the fault with unfettered sectional bargaining was its lack of control and excessive flexibility, reformed bargaining and pay structures can be seen to be unduly inflexible'[53]. Since the early 1980s management strategy has shifted: away from the apparent constraint of formalised joint regulation codified in collective agreements and towards greater organisational flexibility, individualism and a reassertion of managerial prerogative. For a significant number of organisations in both the private and public sector (but by no means all), this shift has been the product of a strategic review by management of its industrial relations style, objectives and the effectiveness of the industrial relations system to meet external pressures and constraints (in particular its economic environment) and, not least, to support and integrate more closely with its business objectives (see Box 7.2).

Direct challenge

In the early 1980s a combination of rapid economic recession, rising unemployment and increasing international competition together with a newly elected Conservative government, committed to reducing trade union power through legislative controls and enhancing market individualism, dramatically altered the balance of power between management and unions both nationally and at the organisational level. This provided the opportunity for management to adopt what has been termed **macho management**. Purcell described it as 'a new breed of tough managers, almost contemptuous of union and negotiating procedures' believing in 'the divine right of managers to manage, to broach no

| Box 7.2 | Industrial relations policies: Early 1980s |

■ To maintain good employee and industrial relations through good communications, procedures and agreements with trade unions.

■ To encourage a participative, open environment.

■ Ultimately sound industrial relations depends upon strong and purposeful line management working within proper controls, procedures and disciplines. Without pursuing a policy of confrontation, the company recognises its responsibility to initiate and implement change, to exercise and, where necessary, to regain control of the management function.

■ To maintain the identity of interest between the company and its employees. To provide for equality of opportunity, for the development of individual ability, and for constructive relations with the recognised trade unions.

■ To ensure that the necessary human resources are available, trained, utilised and motivated so as to fulfil the company's long- and short-term requirements.

■ To provide fair rewards for a fair day's work; reasonable working conditions and terms of service; work that satisfies the individual's needs for involvement and the full use of abilities and skills; and opportunities for advancement and self-realisation. This policy should lead to the employment of the minimum number of people commensurate with the efficient running of the business.

■ To respect, understand and develop the need for harmonious industrial relations through communication, participation and joint consultation.

■ Know all employees – don't let trouble makers start – get rid of them at any price – never a strike – virtually no industrial action. *(An organisation of under 200 employees.)*

Only five of the 69 statements quoted by Marsh referred to trade unions and only one included the encouragement of trade union membership. The emphasis of most organisational philosophies on industrial relations appeared to centre on the direct relationship between management and its employees.

Source: A. Marsh, *Employee Relations Policy and Decision Making: a survey of manufacturing companies carried out for the CBI*, Gower, 1982, Appendix 3, pp. 238–42.

argument and get on with the job of directing, controlling and enforcing order'[54]. The approaches used included the following:

■ A greater preparedness on the part of management to 'stand firm' in the face of employee or union opposition and less preparedness to compromise in negotiations (including, perhaps, less inclination to use conciliation or arbitration to settle disputes);

■ More emphasis on direct links with employees (including appealing directly to employees over the heads of shop stewards and full-time officials in the form of ballots and even, in some cases, the withdrawal of union recognition);

■ An increased preparedness to use rights established by legislation (including the dismissal or threatened dismissal of strikers and obtaining injunctions and damages against unions).

These strategies are closely associated with a shift towards a 'traditional' style of management and in some organisations (notably, News International at Wapping, the NCB and P&O) they resulted in major, long-running confrontations as management sought to impose major organisational, technological and/or production changes involving large-scale rationalisation and redundancies. However, most organisations, while becoming firmer in their dealings with trade unions, sought to do so without such open confrontation but rather relied on emphasising communication, consultation and employee involvement to introduce work changes and productivity improvements without the financial incentives associated with much of the productivity bargaining of the 1960s and 1970s. Edwards noted that, far from 'macho-management' being the prevailing trend in British industrial relations, 'a more subtle process seems to have been taking place in which firms have certainly been trying to change working practices but in which co-operation and involvement have been seen as important'[55].

See Case study 7.2

Human resource management

The term 'human resource management', which has become increasingly used in the UK over the past two decades, has been applied to a diverse range of management strategies and, indeed, sometimes used simply as a more modern, and therefore more acceptable, term for personnel, employee or industrial relations (i.e. 'old wine in a new bottle'). However, the importance of the 'new wine' aspect of HRM lies in its association with **a strategic, integrated and highly distinctive managerial approach to the management of people**. The distinctiveness lies in labour being seen 'not so much as a cost but as an asset or resource, which needs to be developed to its maximum ability, so that emphasis is on the individual employee and on his or her motivation, training and development'[56].

The development of HRM strategies in the UK during the 1980s was clearly **a response to a combination of external and internal pressures**. A significant change in the overall business environment, primarily related to an increasingly competitive national and international marketplace, produced a consequent need for organisations not just to become more productive but also to become more conscious of technology, quality, design and customer service/satisfaction. At the same time, many organisations instigated internal changes: company mergers, changes in top management, major redundancies, decentralisation of 'people management' activities to line management and attempts to establish a clearer performance-related organisation culture (directed towards change, product quality and/or customer satisfaction). Similar pressures were to be seen in the public sector as government privatised some parts and introduced quasi-market forces in others. Indeed, the process of privatisation provided an opportunity (and, perhaps, even required) a major review and reform of industrial

Case study 7.2 ■ Ford (UK): Changing management industrial relations strategy

'Fordism' has been synonymous with closely supervised, deskilled mass production labour. Certainly, the industrial relations management style of Ford (UK) in the 1960s and 1970s was *bargained constitutional* with an emphasis on 'maximising control rather than eliciting consent' (1:93). It was characterised by maintaining managerial prerogative through direct work and supervisory control, production based incentive payment systems to secure 'motivation' and low trust (adversarial) relations.

In the early 1970s, Ford (UK) adopted a strategy of *accommodation* or *incorporation* in reforming its bargaining institutions. Plant convenors were included alongside national union officials on the company National Joint Negotiating Committee, senior stewards at plant level became 'full-time on union duties' (with office facilities alongside plant management) and there was more frequent formal and informal contact between managers and union representatives at all levels (4 : 140). This strengthened the process of securing 'employee consent' to agreements but, in return for their enhanced relationship with management, convenors and stewards were expected to 'police' their members to ensure compliance.

In the 1980s, Ford pursued a twin-track business strategy of improving product design and quality while at the same time reducing costs and increasing efficiency by 'moving towards single sourcing of components in a tightly integrated European production system, coupled with the reduced stocks of components which come with JIT production and supply' (3:19). It introduced *quality circles* throughout its European operations, as a first step towards a more Japanese management approach, not only to improve product quality and productivity but also to increase employee motivation through greater 'involvement' and provide a non-adversarial link between management and employees. However, quality circles met with strong union resistance from manual unions in the UK because they 'threatened to by-pass existing bargaining institutions by subsuming work organisation issues far beyond quality improvements' (1:96).

Ford (UK) management recognised that it needed to adopt a more gradual process of organisational culture change and 'long-term renegotiation of the psychological contract between the individual worker and the company' (1:99) – the change from a low-trust to high-trust relationship could take 10–15 years. However, during this transition, the introduction of initiatives to establish a new culture for *future* competitiveness (change) proceeded alongside the maintenance of managerial prerogative to introduce rationalisation and improvements in efficiency considered necessary for *present* competitiveness (continuity).

There were four main elements to Ford (UK) industrial relations strategy:

1. *Pay & Working Practices Agreement.* Ford's aim was to reduce demarcations and increase labour flexibility. The agreements:

    ■ reduced the number of job classifications (from over 500 to 52) and expanded the tasks, roles and responsibilities within each classification to include repairing defects and quality assurance;

    ■ introduced craft flexibility, along with responsibility for preventative maintenance and mobility across operations;

    ■ introduced team working with team leaders taking over from supervisors the task of organising the team's work, breaks and maintainence of quality assurance;

Longer term, the company wished to introduce single-table bargaining, harmonisation of terms and conditions of employment and further simplification of the pay structure.

2. *Employee involvement.* The primary focus was on developing quality assurance through constantly monitoring and improving quality standards of design and manufacture aimed at achieving zero-defects (the responsibility of all employees and involving the establishment of quality discussion groups).

3. *Participative management.* The objective was to reduce inflexibility in both organisational structures and managerial attitudes. This involved simplifying control systems as well as devolving operational authority, responsibility and accountability (including some 'delayering' at the supervisory level) and the use of matrix forms of

Case study 7.2 ■ Ford (UK): Changing management industrial relations strategy *(continued)*

organisation to break down managerial functional barriers, to integrate design and marketing with manufacture and to focus on customer quality.

4. *Employee Development and Assistance Programme.* This provided an opportunity for employees to undertake, with company financial support, personal development and training which, although vocationally orientated, was outside strictly job-related training needs. In the first year 30 per cent of the workforce 'signed-up' (against the estimated 5 per cent) – the majority for languages, skills (woodwork, car maintenance and bricklaying) or health assistance programmes (aerobics, weight-loss, stress reduction or non-smoking). The programme provided a mechanism for local management and unions to come together in a non-adversarial relationship 'to benefit employees, not for any task orientated function but solely to provide individual employees with development or self-actualisation opportunities' (2:313).

Many of the labour flexibility changes also featured in Ford's operations elsewhere in the world – Belgium,

Germany, Spain, Australia and the USA. In the USA, for example, team leaders are elected and the teams have a role to play in establishing criteria for promotion and applying pay structures based on qualification, skill and ability (3:18). However, these changes have not always been received positively by the employees concerned. In Belgium, Germany and the UK there has been some resentment at the concept of 'Japanisation' and, certainly in the UK, increased flexibility and expanded tasks have been seen as simply means of work intensification.

In 1988, Ford (UK) experienced its first strike for ten years (the primary causes were proposed changes in working practices and the intention to use temporary workers) which lasted two weeks and demonstrated the vulnerability of Ford's integrated European production system based on JIT principles. Workers in Belgium and Germany were laid-off within a few days of the commencement of the strike in the UK, demonstrating 'the problem of adopting a set of arguably efficient (but inherently vulnerable) production arrangements in a situation where there is a tradition of adversarial relationships' (3:21). Significantly, Ford (UK) management accepted a 'non-imposition' clause

Elements of Ford's business strategy

Elements of Ford's IR strategy

Elements of Ford's business strategy		*Elements of Ford's IR strategy*
1. Improved standards of product quality and design 2. Improved cost and labour efficiency 3. Single sourcing of components 4. Integrated European production system 5. JIT production (reduced component stocks)	*Pay and Working Practices Agreement (1985 and 1988)*	Enabling framework for work re-organisation – Reduction in grades and demarcations – Increase in skills and job scope – Teamworking
	Employee involvement	Quality assurance programme
	Participative management	Simplify management structures and control Devolve authority, accountability and responsibility
	Employee Development and Assistance Programme	Self-selected vocational personal development and training outside strictly job-related needs

1980s business and industrial relations strategy

Case study 7.2 ■ Ford (UK): Changing management industrial relations strategy *(continued)*

– changes in working practices accepted in principle in the agreement would only be introduced with further agreement at the plant level.

In early 2000 Ford Europe announced plans to restructure its European operations and reduce over-capacity. Having complained about poor productivity and industrial relations at Dagenham (there had been a number of disputes, strikes and 'unofficial walkouts' over pay, discipline and racism) and described the employees as 'backward looking', 'insular', 'aggressive' and 'failing to support the company while the unions resist change' (5), the company announced that it was stopping car production at the site, although engine building and body work would continue.

Sources:
1. K. Starkey and A. McKinlay, 'Beyond Fordism? Strategic choice and labour relations in Ford UK', *Industrial Relations Journal*, vol. 21, no. 1, 1990, pp. 93–100.
2. K. Mortimer, 'EDAP at Ford: a research note', *Industrial Relations Journal*, vol. 21, no. 4, 1990, pp. 309–14.
3. B. Wilkinson and N. Oliver, 'Obstacles to Japanisation: the case of Ford UK', *Employee Relations*, vol. 12, no. 1, 1990, pp. 17–21.
4. R. Darlington, 'Shop stewards' organisation in Ford Halewood: from Beynon to today', *Industrial Relations Journal*, vol. 25, no. 2, 1994, pp. 136–49.
5. N. Bannister, 'Workers are insular, Ford tells minister', *Guardian*, 29 March 2000.

See also Case study 6.3.

relations and human resource management as an indication of the new status of the privatised industries (telecommunications, airways, electricity, gas, water, etc.).

Hendry *et al*. argue that these changes in both the private and public sectors 'created needs for new operating structures and systems, and new skills, knowledge and capability from staff'[57]. Therefore, in their view, the focus has been on the **strategic nature of HRM** and the organisation's 'ability to take, and implement, a strategic view of the whole range of personnel practices in relation to business activity as a whole'[58] in order to meet an identified business and skill performance gap and achieve technical change and product market development. At the same time, as Sisson and Marginson point out, management both supported and were supported by government policies and legislation aimed at 'deregulation of the labour market and rolling back the influence of trade unions'[59] – in the UK, at least, there was a perceived synergy between management and government aims.

In addition to the strategic characteristic of the HRM model (i.e. 'internal' integration of personnel policies, procedures and practices one with another and their 'external' integration with business policy and strategy), the other major characteristic relates to the development of **high mutual commitment** (see Box 7.3). Wood defines 'high commitment management' as being 'associated with recruitment practices which aim to attract and select highly committed and flexible people, internal labour markets which reward commitment and training with promotion and job security, and methods of direct communication and involvement such as team briefing, team working and quality circles' which, when used together in an integrated fashion, can be 'assumed to reflect an underlying commitment on the part of employers to their employees which is rooted in a conception of them as assets or resources and not simply as a disposable factor of production'[60]. This approach of 'mutuality or reciprocal dependence' is, as Torrington and Hall argue, based on accepting the principle that 'only by satisfying the needs of the individual contributor [*employee*] will the business obtain the commitment to organizational objectives that is needed for organizational success, and only by contributing to organizational success will individuals be able to satisfy their personal employment needs'[61].

Box 7.3	Strategic HRM and mutual commitment

'The central objective of HR policy is to secure the commitment of employees to innovation and continual improvement of product quality. Some measure of employment security and considerable investment in training and development are seen as essential supports for management effort in this area. Equally, the recruitment and retention of competent and committed staff is supported by competitive pay and reward structures which are perceived as fair. At the level of the workplace, these strategies require significant change in management behaviour. The crude assertion of managerial prerogative, associated with short-term low-cost approaches, is eschewed in favour of employee involvement in problem solving and the fostering of a climate of co-operation and trust.'

Source: T. Colling, 'Experiencing turbulence: competition, strategic choice and the management of human resources in British Airways', *Human Resource Management Journal*, vol. 5, no. 5, 1995, pp. 19–20.

High–commitment practices

- trainability and commitment as major selection criteria
- career ladders and progression possible for all employees
- long-term training budgets
- teamworking the predominant system
- regular quality circles
- flexible job descriptions
- jobs explicitly designed to utilise full range of employee skills and abilities
- quality responsibility integrated into the individual's job
- regular briefing groups throughout the organisation in work time
- annual formal assessment
- harmonisation or single status
- some element of pay linked to individual performance
- profit sharing
- temporary employees used primarily to protect job security of core workers
- expectation that organisation will provide permanent life-time employment
- no compulsory redundancy policy

Source: S. Wood, 'The four pillars of HRM: are they connected?' *Human Resource Management Journal*, vol. 5, no. 5, 1995, p. 52.

While the strategic business element (which emphasises labour cost consciousness) may be seen as the 'hard' HRM approach, the mutual commitment element (which emphasises employee commitment, adaptability and continuous improvement) is often seen as the 'soft' HRM approach. However, it is clear that these two elements are not necessarily mutually exclusive but generally co-exist with different priorities at different times. As Colling[62] suggests, it is the combination of the 'strategic' and 'commitment' elements which provides the basis for western organisations to develop competitive strategies in the international market based on value-added, quality and flexibility rather than based on simple cost-competition. However, while Sisson and Marginson recognise that 'managers see themselves engaged in the delicate exercise of simultaneously cutting costs and manufacturing yet greater consent'[63], they also question the extent to which management will be able to fulfil its part of the reciprocal commitment (particularly in relation to job security); certainly, even in Japan continuing job security is being questioned.

See Country profile 7.1

Beaumont[64] identified five main elements of the HRM package:

- A strong internal labour market providing training, development and promotion;
- Flexible organisational and work systems;
- Pay related to organisation performance or individual acquisition of skills and competences;
- Developed mechanisms of employee and group involvement in task decisions;
- Extensive communication from management.

However, as Morishima[65] points out, it is the synergistic integration of the HRM elements, and their location within a wider organisational context and strategy, which leads to its institutionalisation as a system of HRM. Guest[66] suggests that there are four components to **a distinctive HRM strategy model** (see Figure 7.3):

- An integrated package of HRM policy goals or outcomes comprising:
  - strategic and coherent integration of HRM into both strategic organisational planning and the everyday activities of line managers;
  - securing the commitment of employees to the goal of high organisational performance;
  - an adaptive, receptive and flexible organisational structure through 'job design' based on the principles of enriching the individual's work, establishing autonomous workgroup arrangements and creating a 'multiskilled' workforce; and
  - high-quality employees and management as well as high-quality production (goods and services).

- The implementation of a range of specific 'personnel' policies and practices (job design, selection, appraisal, development, reward, communication, etc.) directed specifically towards supporting the achievement of the overall HRM policy goals.

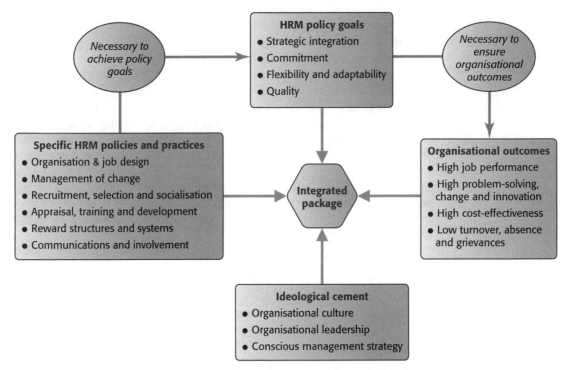

Source: Derived from D. Guest, 'Personnel and HRM: can you tell the difference?' *Personnel Management*, January 1989, figure 2, p. 49.

Figure 7.3 A model of HRM

■ An 'ideological cement' of a strong organisational culture, support from the organisation's leaders and a conscious management strategy that organisational success requires the effective utilisation of human resources.

■ The desired organisational outcomes which provide the criteria by which to judge the success of HRM (increased organisational ability to innovate and respond to change, greater cost effectiveness, improved employee job performance, etc.).

In addition to any favourable contingency factors relating to organisational structure (centralised, single product), technology (exercise of employee discretion and autonomy), ownership (American or Japanese) or site (greenfield, non-union or co-operative union), Storey[67] identified three **behavioural conditions** which appeared to be linked to the successful introduction and development of HRM: senior management commitment, mobilisation around a unifying 'change programme' and a post-crisis situation. However, Storey and Sisson[68] noted two major **limiting factors**: the short-termism of much UK management planning and decision making (particularly compared to Germany or Japan) and the dominance within most UK organisations of 'accountancy logic and accountancy-driven managerial control systems'.

It is clear that the creation of a **corporate culture** is a fundamental part of the HRM approach. Armstrong describes corporate culture as encompassing 'the company's goals and dominant ideologies ... expressed in company *values* – what is good for the organisation and what should or should not happen;

organisational *climate* – the working atmosphere of the organisation as perceived and experienced by its members; and management *style* – the way in which managers behave and exercise authority'[69]. However, writers differ in respect of the kind of culture that is required to underpin HRM – particularly in relation to the individualism and collectivism axes of Purcell's model. Guest believes that 'the values underpinning ... HRM are predominantly individualist and unitarist'[70] and, consequently, **challenge collectivism and the role of trade unions** in the process of managing people within the organisation: industrial relations is no longer perceived, by management, as a central activity.

Potential elements within the HRM strategy which accord with this view may range from shifting the emphasis of the collective relationship away from negotiation and agreement and towards consultation, bypassing the shop steward role by establishing or strengthening direct lines of communication and involvement with employees, or more 'macho' elements such as threatening derecognition if a union resists changes in work practices. The whole thrust of such strategic HRM is not, as has been argued for in the past, one of an upward direction of introducing and strengthening the 'people' factor in top-level management decision making, but rather a downward direction of ensuring that the 'human resource' (people) conforms to the business needs of the organisation. Fowler has described this approach to HRM as 'the complete identification of employees with the aims and values of the business – employee involvement, but on the company's terms', and questions whether it is 'genuinely concerned with creating a new, equal partnership between employer and employed, or ... offering a covert form of employee manipulation dressed up as mutuality?'[71]. These strategies represent a shift towards a 'sophisticated human resource' style of management (an increased investment oriented individualism coupled with decreased collectivism).

However, other writers believe that the adoption of HRM strategies does not necessarily imply abandoning collectivism but, rather, **a shift from an adversarial to co-operative style of collectivism**. Armstrong, for example, believes that although integration 'in the sense of getting members of the organisation working together with a sense of common purpose' is one of the fundamental principles underlying HRM, nevertheless 'this must take account of the fact that all organisations are pluralist societies in which people have differing interests and concerns which they may well feel need to be defended collectively'[72]. Similarly, Miller argues that in a 'mature' business (i.e. one which already has established collective bargaining structures and relationships) the achievement of the strategic element of HRM probably requires changes to improve organisational performance and efficiency to be agreed 'through negotiation with a representative body of employees'[73]. The inclusion and maintenance of collectivism within HRM strategies therefore implies a shift towards a 'sophisticated consultative' style of management.

Lucio and Weston identified three different types of **trade union response** to the introduction of HRM:

■ *Progressive social partnership*. This is represented by the 'positive engagement' with HRM shown by the AEU and EETPU (now merged into the AEEU) and their adoption of policies 'to attract inward investment and to complement new management initiatives ... to tie the union more closely to the

See Chapter 6 – Representation at the workplace; Chapter 9 – Collective bargaining; Chapter 10 – Employee involvement and participation

strategic considerations of the company ... even though this meant the union would no longer be considered the single channel of workers' interests'[74].

- *Making Donovan work*. This is represented by the GMB's strategy of seeking to extend the scope of collective involvement into the new HRM areas being developed by management (such as employee training and development, and equal opportunities) as well as aspects of quality management.
- *Holding on to independence*. This is represented by the T&GWU which shifted from initial outright opposition to HRM developments to a qualified accommodation subject to a guarantee of the union's independence.

Although many organisations have undertaken extensive and far-reaching changes in a wide variety of different aspects of industrial relations and human resource management (union recognition and bargaining structures; work and reward systems; communication and consultation, etc.), there is little evidence of a widespread shift in the managerial paradigm, adoption of an integrated strategic approach to HRM or management being a *strategic* actor. In the view of Sisson and Marginson, 'the notion of managers making strategic choices from a menu of options seems far removed from reality. They are taking advantage of the political context to reassert their control, but their use of it, and their response to business conditions, remains largely ad hoc and pragmatic'[75]. The picture is complicated by the extent to which organisations adopt different approaches for different groups of workers. As Boxall points out 'within each internal labour market or workforce segment, HRM incorporates a range of sub-functions and practices including workforce governance, work organisation, staffing and development and reward systems, some of which are individually-oriented, some collectively-oriented and yet others a blend of both'[76].

However, HRM should be viewed within a broader social context as well as the economic, market or production contexts (see Box 7.4). Certainly, Lees argues that management's strategies need to be judged not only in relation to production and labour market requirements, where they have to satisfy internal organisational efficiency criteria, but also in terms of the 'legitimacy market', where they will need to conform to and support external social and cultural expectations regarding the management of people (particularly as exemplified through legislation and government policy). He suggests that within the 'legitimacy market' there is 'competition between different value systems around the desirability and acceptability and morality of management concepts and practices' and within the workplace 'matters of social redistribution and justice are enacted and bargained, issues of social obligation and legitimacy and ethics assume supremacy over the economic agenda'[77]. Thus, it can be argued, management has only been successful in applying HRM strategies because the surrounding socio-cultural environment has allowed and supported it.

It is significant that there appears to be little, if any, correlation between HRM and **non-union organisations**. Most surveys show that the practices associated with both 'strategic' and 'mutual commitment' approaches to HRM are more a feature of unionised than non-union workplaces. Guest and Hoque[78] examined 119 non-union organisations established since 1980 (the beginning of the so-called 'new realism' in industrial relations) and have put forward a

| Box 7.4 | HRM and its social context |

'In the transition from industrial relations to human resource management (HRM), we have lost three important perspectives in the field of industrial relations. First, we no longer think in terms of interdependent actors with some balance among the parties ... Second, we seem to have forgotten that HRM is a system of interdependent parts that interact to produce a set of outcomes ... Finally, and most importantly, the social embeddedness of the HRM system has been lost in the transition to a view that HRM is something that is designed and implemented by individual firms alone.'

Source: M. Morishima, 'Embedding HRM in a social context', *British Journal of Industrial Relations*, vol. 33, no. 4, 1995, p. 617.

'HRM has ... been dependent upon the changing economic circumstances of the past decade. It grew in the boom of the last half of the decade, when "attachment", "commitment" and "development" were the watch-words. It faces its sternest test in the severe recession of the first half of the 1990s with its emphasis on restructuring, "downsizing" and a big reduction in both employee and managerial confidence in the prospects for renewed growth. For this reason HRM is now tinged with suspicion and a certain hostility as to its role in organisations. The difficulty for HRM is to establish its credentials as a central part of employee management in economic conditions that make the expansionary and developmental aspects of the approach extremely difficult to sustain. Is HRM recession-proof? While it has proved possible for traditionally conceived industrial relations and personnel management procedures to have endured economic cycles, even though the managerial strategies underlying them reflected the realities of the labour market, HRM has still to demonstrate that it has the robustness to move beyond generalised managerial prescriptions as a sustainable model of management. In this sense, the 1990s will be the testing ground for the idea of HRM as a consistent and integrated approach, as opposed to a fragmented and opportunistic set of interventions.'

Source: I. Beardwell and L. Holden, *Human Resource Management: a contemporary perspective*, Pitman, 1994, pp. 685–6.

'In the absence of supportive legislation and policy frameworks at the level of the local, national and now supra-national state, individual companies facing intensifying international competition may be unable to sustain strategic perspectives on their employment relationships, even where they have previously demonstrated the will to do so. At a time when the vision of a Social Charter appears to be giving way to British style "flexibility" across Europe, it might be opportune to reflect on the merits of relying on company level strategic choices as a path to national competitiveness.'

Source: T. Colling, 'Experiencing turbulence: competition, strategic choice and the management of human resources in British Airways', *Human Resource Management Journal*, vol. 5, no. 5, 1995, p. 3.

typology based on whether or not they have a HRM strategy and the extent of usage of HRM practices:

- *Good* (clear strategy; extensive use of HRM practices) – reflects high involvement management and employee commitment aspects of HRM;
- *Lucky* (no clear strategy; extensive use of HRM practices) – adopted innovative practices;
- *Ugly* (clear strategy; little use of HRM practices) – deliberate strategy to minimise employee rights and benefits;
- *Bad* (no clear strategy; little use of HRM practices) – human resource issues not really considered.

Of the 119 organisations, 47 per cent were classified as 'good', 23 per cent as 'lucky', 24 per cent as 'bad' and only 7 per cent as 'ugly'. In assessing the impact of these different styles on human resource management, employee relations and performance outcomes, Guest and Hoque concluded that 'the results demonstrate that strategic HRM pays off' in that the 'good' came out best and the 'bad' worst on all three sets of outcome measures[79]. However, Sisson and Marginson believe that the survey evidence of non-union organisation indicates that 'the model of Bleak House is more appropriate than HRM'[80] because of their generally lower pay, lack of employment security and little opportunity for employees to express their views or influence decisions. The position on the latter element may be alleviated, albeit in a limited way, by the recent legal changes requiring all employers to consult with *employee* representatives in the event of a transfer of the undertaking or a collective redundancy and to allow individuals to be accompanied by a 'fellow worker' during grievance or disciplinary hearings.

Workplace partnership approach

The 'workplace' partnership approach, which has achieved some prominence in the late 1990s, is intended to provide a 'new start' in improving organisational performance by 'establishing constructive employment relationships, where consensus replaces confrontation'[81]. **Support for the development of a 'partnership' approach** has come from three directions. First, as Claydon points out[82], trade unions and the TUC have taken the initiative in offering such an approach, in response to the changed market and employment contexts, as a means of recasting the union's 'alliances' with employees, management and government to one based on common concerns (for example, training, equal opportunities, and health and safety). Second, Ackers and Payne argue that, despite 'a decade of virtually unrestrained management prerogative'[83], management HRM strategies based on individualism, *employee* involvement and the marginalisation of unions do not appear to have significantly enhanced employee commitment, nor have they provided a sound basis for maintaining the 'organizational order and cohesion' that management need. Third, the political climate has changed with the election, in 1997, of a new Labour government committed 'to replace the notion of conflict between employers and employees with the promotion of partnership'[84].

Hollinshead notes that the **concept of partnership** appears to encompass not only 'the *substance* of the employment relationship, particularly in the fields of pay, deployment and staffing, and job security, but also the *mode of interaction* between the parties ... [which] purports to emphasise collaboration and trust building rather than "old style" adversarial methods'[85]. However, while Tailby and Winchester agree that the partnership approach has been 'hailed as an innovative and progressive development', they point out that the substantive elements of such agreements 'embrace a fairly familiar checklist' and that, in particular, the job security 'guarantee' which is offered to employees as evidence of this new approach to the employment relationship is, in reality, little more

Country profile 7.1   Japan: changing strategies of HRM

Many organisations and countries have regarded Japanese HRM practices as an important element in its economic success. However, the HRM practices that organisations have sought to emulate are themselves undergoing re-evaluation and change in Japan – particularly in non-manual areas where productivity has lagged behind that of most western countries. Morishima argues that 'the Japanese model of HRM is premised on the assumption that firms recruit candidates with the largest learning potential, provide them with continuous training opportunities, and reward them according to the degree to which they have acquired internally relevant job-related skills' (1:625).

1. *Educational credentialism.* Success in higher education, through limited highly competitive access, is assumed to guarantee the ability and characteristics of future employees (schools and universities compete to select the 'best'). This is often supported by a strong relationship between individual organisations and certain educational institutions (a dependence on and trust in the recommendations from those educational institutions). Consequently, there is a reliance on the educational system, rather than the organisation, to make the 'right' initial selection of people.

2. *Long-term employment.* The concept of 'lifetime employment' (from school or university to retirement with one organisation) has frequently been perceived as a central plank of Japanese HRM practice. Long-term employment (job security) is supported not only by management values and HRM practices but also by the following:

   ■ Legal protection which inhibits redundancy among 'regular-status' (core) employees without the employees' or union's agreement;

   ■ Government policy supporting job security by subsidising up to two-thirds of the wages of employees laid-off temporarily rather than made redundant;

   ■ Trade union policy of accommodation (particularly on wage issues) in return for 'job security'.

Estimates of the consequent 'overstaffing' or 'hidden unemployment' range from 1 to 5 million employees and affect nearly 75 per cent of organisations (1:626). At the same time, demographic factors have produced a bulge in the middle management ranks resulting in a 'career collision' between the early career plateau of many older managers and the lack of promotion opportunities for younger aspiring employees.

3. *Embedded organisational training.* Once recruited, employees are expected to undertake extensive, continuous specific 'on-the-job' training and development activities interspersed with periods of more general 'off-the-job' training at progression points in their career development. An occupational category may contain seven or eight skill grades within each of which an employee may take three to four years to demonstrate his or her competence before moving up to the next grade – a total of 20–30 years.

4. *Assessment and reward.* Pay and promotion is closely tied into the 'skill-grade' system of progression and reflects *capability* and *seniority* (skill acquisition derived from programmed on-the-job training) rather than *performance* (individual ability and contribution). The effect of this has been to limit the wage gap between people in the same category (or cohort of entrants) and to establish a strong link between an individual's wage level and his or her length of service with the organisation. The underlying concept of pay fairness is based on 'giving a piece of the cake, big or small, to all members of the group who took part in the collective undertaking' (2:618) with only limited recognition of variability in the individual's performance or contribution; an important element in the integration of individual and corporate objectives.

5. *Information participation.* Japanese work practices are often based on the decentralisation and devolution of decision-making responsibility. This requires not only sharing information (between different levels and parts of the organisation) but also the individual employee exercising judgement. The model also encompasses the concepts of continuous improvement (of product, individual and organisation), the integration of quality assurance into all aspects of work and teamworking involving consensus or collective decision making.

However, now 'a worldwide competitive environment requires a shift of Japanese industry from an

Country profile 7.1 Japan: changing strategies of HRM *(continued)*

enterprise-centred to a more market oriented approach' (2:617). This presents a dilemma for HRM practices: while some believe that "it is precisely during hard times that companies have to act responsibly *vis-à-vis* the workers, i.e. in respecting the unwritten personnel obligations of job and career security", others see the future lying in "radical change" through "the development of a pay for performance system for managers without any guarantee of job security in case of underpar performance" (2:618).

Two different change strategies can be identified:

1. *Externalisation of employment.* Within the legislative constraints, the concept of 'job security' has moved away from the simple 'employment with the same organisation until retirement', first, to transfer placement to a related organisation and, then, to transfer placement with an unrelated organisation (i.e. outplacement guarantee). Perhaps more importantly, some organisations have started to recruit contingent mid-career employees. These tend to be specialists introduced into the organisation as 'innovators and pace-setters of new management practices' (on fixed term contracts with clear performance reward criteria) and represent an *ad hoc* response to competitive pressures. The creation of this third

'specialised abilities' group within the Japanese labour market (between the long-term core and short-term flexible peripheral groups) has been acknowledged by Nikkeiren (Japanese Employers' Federation) (3:297).

2. *Competitive appraisal and reward.* Japanese organisations have introduced a number of changes aimed at assessing and recognising individual performance. The introduction of management by objectives has been linked to increasing the range of reward variability (within any given hierarchical level) dependent on the individual's performance in meeting his or her objectives. Similarly, promotion based on 'seniority' may no longer be guaranteed and younger people (with shorter length of employment) may be promoted over longer service employees. In the opposite direction, some organisations have introduced systems of 'status destitution' for poor performers. (2:619)

Morishima's survey of 1600 organisations in the early 1990s (1:635) showed that while 57 per cent appeared to be following the 'traditional' pattern of HRM, 33 per cent had sought to introduce a more competitive appraisal and reward strategy (these tended to be the larger, unionised, manufacturing

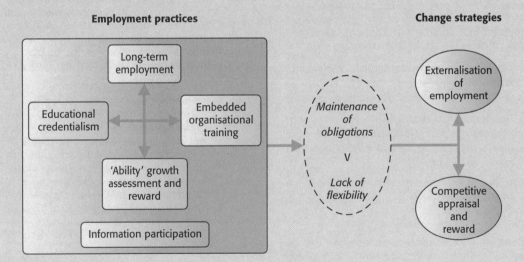

Japanese employment practices and strategies for change

Country profile 7.1   Japan: changing strategies of HRM

organisations) and 11 per cent had sought to introduce both strategies (these tended to be smaller, less unionised, service organisations).

These developments in HRM introduce a degree of uncertainty into the relationship between management and unions. The previous integration of the enterprise-based union with the organisation was based on the management guaranteeing job security and investment in training and development in return for the union ensuring co-operation by their members. Greater individualisation of the employment contractual relationship is leading more middle managers to organise to defend their interests and seek increased codification and standardisation of HRM practices: 'they do not accept or do not consider relevant anymore the complex rites of interaction, the

unwritten, informal and diffuse rules governing the appraisal, promotion and reward system that were traditionally the cement of the management system and of the cohesion of Japanese firms' (2:620).

Sources:
1. M. Morishima, 'Embedding HRM in a social context', *British Journal of Industrial Relations*, vol. 33, no. 4, 1995, pp. 617–40.
2. P. Debroux, 'Recent changes in human resource management practices in Japan', Conference proceedings: *Creating management synergy in Asian economies*, Asian Academy of Management, Penang, December 1995, pp. 616–35.
3. T. Grønning, 'Whither the Japanese employment system? The position of the Japan Employers' Federation', *Industrial Relations Journal*, vol. 29, no. 4, 1998, pp. 295–303.

See also Country profiles 2.2 and 6.1.

than 'relatively limited management commitments to avoid the use of compulsory redundancy as a means of labour shedding'[86]. Furthermore, they believe that management has only been prepared (or able) to make this gesture because of the general declining unemployment, strengthening labour market and a skills shortage. Indeed, in some organisations management has introduced a partnership agreement only *after* it has reduced its labour force. Nevertheless, Tailby and Winchester believe that the process of developing, negotiating and gaining acceptance of partnership agreements within the organisation does seem to have some 'distinctive features' which 'imply an ideological break with past practice', in particular, a long-term view of the organisation and employee relations, a language which reflects 'soft' HRM (plus some emphasis on 'jointism', openness and trust) and a 'considerable investment of time and resources in joint union-management presentations, publicity videos and roadshows designed to proselytize the benefits of partnership agreements to shop stewards and employees whose initial, enthusiasm has often been limited'[87].

Marks *et al.* point out that **management's partnership strategy** involves 'formal change programmes with an emphasis on "cultural transformation"; work reorganization, including both dismantling "restrictive practices" and harnessing employee innovation through teamworking regimes; and the reconstitution of entrenched adversarial industrial relations systems'[88]. Similarly, Coupar and Stevens (Involvement and Participation Association) distinguish three main features of the partnership approach:

1. a commitment to working together to make the business more successful;

2. understanding the employee security conundrum and trying to do something about it;

3. building relationships at the workplace which maximise employee influence through total communication and a robust and effective employee voice.[89]

However, it is important to recognise that the strategy appears to be based on an implicit unitarist business ideology epitomised by company literature such as 'We're in this together' (Co-operative Bank) and 'Working better together – a real partnership' (Tesco). Although, as Kelly points out, 'labour–management co-operation has been at the centre of trade union agendas for the past fifteen years across the capitalist world'[90], nevertheless it has been opposed, Claydon claims, not only by those on the management side who see partnership as 'another union Trojan horse' which will undermine the drive towards a 'free' labour market and the individualisation of the employment relationship but also by those on the union side who are 'sceptical of the possibility of genuine partnership'[91]. Certainly, there is little doubt that like other past 'co-operative' approaches, be it productivity bargaining in the 1960s and 1970s or the new style single-union agreements of the early 1980s, the development of a partnership approach contains the potential for subverting the union's role by its 'incorporation' into management because, it is argued, unions have little choice but to accept 'a role within the organisation which has been defined by management'[92]. How far the adoption of a co-operative partnership stance will also be a conditional requirement of the new statutory recognition procedure remains to be seen.

The confusion which appears to exist over the concept and nature of 'partnership' is perhaps exemplified by one survey[93] which reported that 44 and 27 respectively out of the 50 organisations surveyed 'sometimes or always' used *partnership* ('the organisation involves employees in the drawing up and execution of policies, but retains the right to manage') or *power sharing* ('employees are involved in day-to-day and strategic decision-making'). However, this survey did highlight a number **of problems associated with the introduction of 'partnership'**. First, most of the representative bodies or partnership mechanisms did not have any real decision-making powers – their role was primarily a communication one. Second, the respondents generally reported that their employee relations policies had only a 'marginal' impact on their 'moderate success' in securing employee commitment. Third, the organisations reported problems stemming from employee suspicion, mistrust and fear of change, while management felt insecure with the new approach and often feared the loss of their 'right to manage'. In two organisations, Marks *et al.* identified that managers encountered significant problems in having to cope with 'defining the limits of empowerment' and balancing their own 'discretion and inconsistency'[94].

It appears that, as with previous 'new' management strategies that were forecast to change fundamentally the nature of employment relations, only a small number of well-publicised organisations have sought to implement 'workplace partnership' as a coherent 'new-start' strategy. Certainly, Hollinshead believes that the 'durability of such arrangements' can be questioned if, as he suggests, most partnership arrangements are pragmatic responses within a 'standard modern' style of management[95]. Similarly, Tailby and Winchester point out that the relatively small number of these partnership arrangements in the UK is compounded by the fact that they 'exist in an institutional vacuum' within the wider society – *workplace* partnership is not being complemented by *social* partnership at the national level[96].

See Case study 7.3

Case study 7.3 ■ Blue Circle Cement – the 'way ahead'

Blue Circle Cement (BCC) concluded its 'way ahead' partnership agreement with the AEEU, GMB and T&GWU in 1997.

BCC had already introduced, in the late 1980s, an 'integrated working' package of changes. This included annual hours (to reduce overtime), simplified pay structure (four instead of 14 grades), expansion of the individual's job skills and the abolition of local pay negotiations and bonuses. These changes were accompanied by extensive voluntary redundancies, reducing the number of employees by three-quarters. The changes took six years to implement because of union resistance at each site.

However, by the late 1990s, BCC management believed that another 'step change' in performance was required, but this time it involved the unions right from the start. The initial step in the *process of creating an agreement* was the establishment of a 'think-tank' of managers and union representatives to identify the issues which needed to be addressed. This was followed by a 'company-wide action team' (CWAT), comprising managers, shop stewards and staff employee representatives, responsible for articulating the management and employee objectives to be incorporated in the agreement, translating these into a draft agreement and then briefing all employees about the spirit and content of the proposed agreement. Finally, the agreement was approved by a conference of the union delegates and accepted by the employees in a ballot.

The *agreement content* centres on an expectation that employees will support BCC's business strategies aimed at achieving 'excellence' through continuous personal training and development, flexible working and co-operating with voluntary redundancy and/or redeployment. It also includes a three-year pay deal

(based on 0.25 per cent above the Retail Price Index and extra pay for gaining additional skills), the abolition of clocking, harmonisation of terms and conditions (including shift allowances) and the intention to move towards a 37-hour week (at no additional cost). Significantly, the agreement expects employees to adopt a responsible and committed attitude and unions to represent their members' interests 'within viable solutions'. Similarly, the employment security commitment may be suspended or 'open to further debate' in 'exceptional circumstances', such as the closure of a site, significant changes in capital investment or market conditions or any fundamental breach of the spirit or terms of the agreement (including the use of industrial action).

The *process of maintaining the agreement* involves the CWAT continuously reviewing its operation and considering improvements or changes. Each site has its own local action team (LAT) which reviews the operation of the agreement, develops business improvement plans and deals with any problems which arise. The link between the two levels is provided by each LAT having a member on the CWAT, the creation of two 'Way Ahead facilitators' (one manager and one senior steward) who have been seconded to act as the secretariat for the CWAT and to provide LATs with advice, guidance and interpretation of the agreement, and twice yearly visits to each site by a mixed group of managers and stewards.

Source: 'Partnership agreements', *Incomes Data Services Study*, no. 656, October 1998, pp. 9–13.

Two innovative developments can be seen in other European countries. First, in Italy, the 20 sub-contracting firms supplying a Fiat subsidiary have introduced a cross-company partnership agreement[97] which aims to establish a 'common participatory system of employee relations', including inter-company consultative committees which bring together representatives of the individual company management, local employer's association and unions. Second, in Ireland, a new partnership framework agreed between Aer Lingus and SIPTU (the Services Industrial Professional and Technical Union) includes provision for either side to request the assistance of the 'facilitator' to help mediate a resolution to an issue or, if it cannot be resolved, process the issue on to the Labour

Court (both sides retain their freedom whether or not to accept any Court recommendation)[98].

Internationalisation

There is little doubt that industrial relations in the UK, like most other countries, has become more subject to an international dimension through the globalisation of organisations. Certainly, the so-called **Japanisation** of organisational industrial relations received considerable publicity in Britain during the 1980s and, for some, represented an ideal to be pursued. Ackroyd *et al.* argue that this 'Japanisation' came about in three different ways:

- *Direct* through the introduction of Japanese firms into the British economy and industrial relations system (but 'Japanese subsidiaries are not major employers of UK labour'[99]);

- *Mediated* by British organisations copying Japanese policies and practices to a greater or lesser extent (but 'such initiatives ... are likely to be mediated by the orientation of British management and therefore less straightforward in their effects'[100]);

- *Permeated* through the development of the British system to emulate Japanese structures and practices (but 'the evidence ... is very slight'[101]).

Oliver and Wilkinson[102] observed that 'Japanisation' strategies are based on an integration between personnel and industrial relations practices and new manufacturing methods and working practices – with the former supporting the latter. Certainly this has been most often linked in people's minds with non-unionism or the introduction of single-union agreements, which were portrayed as a package of measures designed around a new and integrated approach to organisational industrial relations. There were two main ingredients:

- A single union but with employment relations issues being handled through an Employee Council or Advisory Board (with 'employee' as well as 'union' representation and seeking to adopt a 'consensus' solution approach), coupled with open communication and employee involvement;

- Job flexibility and teamworking (linked to just-in-time production systems and an emphasis on quality), coupled with single-status and common terms and conditions of employment for all staff.

See Country profile 7.1

However, it is important to recognise that the 'Japanese style of management' may not be all it appears and it certainly has to be related to its own specific national culture. Certainly, Briggs believes that the public images of Japanese management, where 'workers are seen as secure in their jobs, protected by the paternalistic attitudes of their employers; management and shop floor workers dress in similar style, and both make valuable contributions to the running of the company; the workers strive for the same goals as the management, having adopted the values of the company wholesale; and contentment reigns – apparent from the workers' dedication and their reluctance to take industrial action', are 'misguided utopian illusions'[103]. She found from an examination of Japanese management in Japan that only the large firms and, therefore, a minority of employees have lifetime employment; employees 'conform' because of labour control systems rather than because they are committed; they 'endure' the work situation rather than being happy with it; and there is a subtle but very distinct hierarchy status relationship. She concludes that 'in human terms it is acceptable to the Japanese because it is consistent with their own cultural values, but the cost to the workforce in terms of quality of working life is dear'[104].

See Case study 7.2

Therefore, the simple introduction of 'Japanisation' into British industrial relations presents a clash between two very different cultures and may require modification if it is to succeed – as Ford's experience in the early 1980s showed. Certainly, Elger and Smith found that, among a small group of non-union Japanese 'transplants' in one area of the UK, there was little 'functional fit' between the organisations' policies and the local labour market conditions. They concluded that 'on the one hand, promotion opportunities, promises of job security or support in times of personal difficulty have reinforced the loyalty of some workers, while on the other hand, gaps between management rhetoric and practice, increased management stringency and perceived unfairness have eroded the commitment of others'[105]. Interestingly, Shadur and Tung note that a reverse process is now taking place in which many of the south-east Asian countries are 'adopting HRM policies and practices which are more characteristic of the western world'[106].

More significant for industrial relations, not only in the UK but throughout the world, is the role of **multinational enterprises** (MNEs). Their importance lies not just in their sheer size (volume of sales, investment and employment) in an international and any national context but rather in their 'transnationalism' – the integration of their activities, to some degree or other, across national boundaries and, therefore, their participation in more than one industrial relations systems. The increasing globalisation and freeing up of trade (whether within regional blocks such as the EU, ASEAN, NAFTA, or within the broader world reductions in tariff barriers through GATT and WTO), coupled with the variety of inter-organisational mergers, partnerships and joint ventures, has increased the scope for transnational operations. All countries in the 'old' industrialised world (Europe and North America) and the 'newer' industrialised countries (Japan and south-east Asia) are both 'source' and 'host' countries for MNEs.

Bean[107] outlines a number of **industrial relations implications** presented by the existence and growing power of MNEs. First, they are able to transfer managerial and industrial relations ideologies, policies and practices more easily between, and have less commitment towards, the different national industrial relations systems within which they operate. Second, trade unions are concerned about the MNEs' ability to transfer operations (with consequent 'social dumping' implications for employment and job security) or to threaten such moves to pressure trade unions to accept management strategies for change in the workplace. At the same time, the locus of major strategic decisions may well be outside the particular national system(s) affected and remote from potential union influence. Third, governments, particularly in developing economies, may rely on MNEs for economic development and, therefore, be more prepared to implement policies and legislation which support management and restrict trade unions. As a consequence there has been limited government action at either national or international level to establish a regulatory framework to cover the management of MNEs.

Perlmutter[108] classified MNEs as follows:

- *Enthocentric* – implements the parent company values and policies regardless of environmental differences in operating countries;
- *Polycentric* – accepts the environmental differences between countries and has a deliberate policy to maintain local identities;
- *Geocentric* has a 'global' outlook which seeks to select the 'best' and has universal standards as well as local variations.

He believed that, over time, organisations would shift towards the geocentric model, which implies the MNE rising above and being independent of individual national systems. However, Drumm notes (in the context of Germany) that 'international corporations are increasingly replacing their ethnocentric strategies by polycentric policies and concepts of management'[109] because strong sociocultural variables hindered their adoption, while Turner *et al.* found little or no evidence to suggest MNE 'dominance' overriding the 'host country effect' in Ireland[110]. Nevertheless, Coller and Marginson point out that 'co-operative competition' based on inter-plant (international) competition and 'the battle for survival' can induce employees to accept 'the logic of the management system' and thereby lead to a more homogeneous approach across the MNE[111].

Marginson and Sisson[112] offer an alternative view based on the **nature of corporate governance**. They identify two main models. The first is the *outsider* (likely to be found in MNEs originating from America, Britain, Ireland and Australia), characterised by a dispersed network of shareholding and financial interests and by investments judged primarily on shorter-term financial criteria. Within this framework, labour tends to be regarded more as a liability and cost to be minimised, and decision making about HRM is likely to be decentralised. The second model is the *insider* (likely to be found in MNEs originating from Europe, Scandinavia and Japan), characterised by an interlocking of shareholding and investments judged more in terms of the longer-term strategic development of the organisation. Within this framework, labour is seen more as an asset to be developed as a source of competitive advantage and HRM decision making is more likely to be viewed strategically and centralised.

7.4 Employers' associations

The main focus of an employers' association is the regulation, directly or indirectly, of employment relations. It is important to distinguish employers' associations from purely trade associations, which exclude labour affairs and confine themselves to trade matters such as marketing, pricing and technology – although the majority of associations do combine both labour and trade functions. However, as Bean[113] notes, there is a commonality throughout much of Europe whereby industries such as building, where the need for regulation of contract tendering cannot be easily separated from a desire to avoid labour wage-cost competition, integrate the employer and trade functions, while industries such as engineering tend to separate the functions with one main employers' association and a variety of specialist trade associations. It is also important to recognise that employers' associations are **second-degree groupings** (i.e. associations of corporate bodies rather than individuals) and therefore their existence reinforces, rather than creates, the collective power of the organisations which are its members.

Development

The development of employers' associations in most countries has been closely related to the development of trade unionism and collective bargaining. While there is evidence of transient local combinations of employers in the UK from the early nineteenth century, it was not until the 1890s that more permanent organisations were established – largely as a reaction to the increasing membership and stability of trade unions. Indeed, van Waarden refers to them as 'combat organizations ... designed to fight strikes, wage drift, trade unions, state measures or suppliers' cartels'[114]. Their primary objective was to **protect management's prerogative and resist the development of trade unionism** – in some cases by providing financial support to members resisting a union claim and faced with either a strike or lockout. Thus, there was a clear inducement to join an employers' association; the organisation which was not a member could not call on any support, if it was needed.

By the end of the First World War, employers' associations had become **institutions of collective bargaining** seeking, on behalf of their members, to regulate terms and conditions of employment on a district or national basis through negotiated agreements with trade unions. Such an arrangement meant that one collective agreement could be negotiated for all member organisations rather than individual organisations being picked off one by one: complete organisation (i.e. ensuring that as many employers as possible were members of the employers' association) became important. The non-federated organisation presented a constant potential threat to both other employers and trade unions by paying lower wages and therefore being able to undercut prices. Trade unions saw an expansion of employers' association membership not as a threat to themselves but as a means to extend the coverage of collective agreements and establish a common rate throughout the industry.

The more recent emphasis in the UK on **organisational-level bargaining**, brought about initially by full employment in the 1960s and the desire among many managements to undertake productivity bargaining which linked pay increases to work changes, reduced the regulatory effect of national agreements in much of the private sector. At the time, a number of organisations felt it necessary to leave their employers' association in order to have greater freedom to determine their own strategies. They were supported by their trade unions because it was seen as a way of increasing their members' wages. The pace of this development was accentuated during the 1980s and 1990s as management has sought to decentralise collective bargaining (away from, or reducing the role of, multi-employer national agreements) in order better to link the negotiation of terms and conditions of employment with the profitability, productivity and working arrangement needs of the organisation, as part of its strategy to improve competitiveness and flexibility (see Box 7.5). As a consequence, Beaumont[115] notes that trade unions have lost their 'natural allies' in supporting union recognition and the maintenance of industry level collective bargaining. In contrast, the employers' association role in negotiating industry- or sector-level agreements still remains strong in most other European countries.

See Country profile 7.2

Structure and organisation

The number of employers' associations in the UK declined from some 1,350 in 1968 to 210 in 1997. Most of this decline has been due to the demise of small local associations and the amalgamation of others within larger national associations – however, two major associations became redundant in the iron and steel industry (1967) and shipbuilding (1977) when nationalisation created a single-employer situation. The size of employers' associations, in terms of the number of members, ranges from 127,000 in the case of the National Farmers Union to eight in the Construction Confederation (see Table 7.1). Employers' associations are also to be found in the public sector representing local authorities, educational establishments, etc.

Box 7.5	Consequences of the decentralisation trend for employers' associations

'In the history of industry and employers' associations, the dominant interest of business has fluctuated with some regularity. Businesses have always had an interest in flexibility, in individual freedom to make the most of their advantages in the competitive struggle. However, they also had an interest in regulation, in controlling competition so as to prevent it from becoming too cut-throat. These two needs, the need for freedom and for regulation, have alternated throughout history and have vied for dominance. The urgency of each one depended on the business cycle, that is, on the intensity of competition ...

Some authors ... argue that the pressure to achieve greater flexibility is now arising from the internationalization of markets and the opening up of domestic economies. The resulting increased competition is forcing businesses to become more flexible, and the very process of internationalization is undercutting the national systems of regulation. The alternatives seem to be either completely open markets and competition, or interest organization and regulation at the international level, for example that of the EU.

However, those who present such arguments overlook the fact that the most highly developed and centralized systems of employers' associations and the most highly regulated economies were and are to be found precisely in those small countries like Austria, Sweden and The Netherlands which have been open to foreign markets or exposed to foreign competition through their sizeable export industries for a long time. Organization and regulation were precisely the strategies employed by these countries to increase the competitive position of industry, and not without success.'

Source: F. van Waarden, 'Employers and employers' associations', in J. van Ruysseveldt, R. Huiskamp and J. van Hoof (eds), *Comparative Industrial and Employment Relations*, Sage 1995, pp. 103 and 104, reprinted by permission of Sage Publications Ltd.

Table 7.1 UK major employers' associations, 1997

Employers' Association	Membership	Income from members (£m)	Total funds (£m)	Total assets (£m)
Construction Confederation	8	1.4	5.9	12.0
Paper Federation of Great Britain	57	1.3	1.2	1.9
Chemical Industries Association	175	4.2	0.2	2.4
Newspaper Society	216	2.9	1.7	3.8
Heating & Ventilating Contractors Association	1 159	1.6	6.2	8.8
Electrical Contractors Association	1 970	2.2	35.3	49.6
British Printing Industries Federation	2 971	3.8	1.7	4.5
Engineering Employers Federation[1]	5 058	10.8	35.5	45.6
Road Haulage Association	9 687	1.9	3.9	5.4
Retail Motor Industry Federation	11 424	3.4	3.9	8.3
Freight Transport Association	11 767	2.6	4.4	8.2
Federation of Master Builders	14 830	2.5	2.3	4.4
National Federation of Retail Newsagents	24 886	4.7	3.5	5.2
National Farmers Union	127 024	21.3	45.1	56.1
Total (for all employers' associations)	273 837	99.4	201.4	297.0
Number of employers' associations	210			

[1] Combined figure for EEF and its 13 regional associations.
Source: Certification Officer, *Annual Report (1998), HMSO.*

The **structure of employers' associations** varies between the following:

■ **National associations or federations** covering a whole industry – for example, the Chemical Industries Association with just over 170 organisations in direct membership.

■ **Specialised associations** which represent a distinct segment of an industry – for example, within the printing industry there is not only the British Printing Industries Federation (periodicals and general printing) but also the Newspaper Society (provincial newspapers) and the Publishers' Association (book publishing). Significantly, the employers' association in the national newspaper segment of the industry (Newspaper Publishers' Association) was disbanded together with multi-employer bargaining in the 1980s at the time of the introduction of new computer-based technology requiring significant changes in working practices.

■ **Local associations** representing geographically restricted industrial interests – for example, the West of England Wool Textile Employers' Association or South Western Provincial Employers' Association (local authorities). As van Waarden notes, both Germany and Italy have a very large number of locally based employers' associations in the construction industry (791 and 294 respectively), reflecting its handicraft tradition and predominance of small size organisations; and the *Länder* (regional) based employers' associations in the German metalworking industry are important because of their collective bargaining role[116].

The variations in current structure can be related to the number and relative size of the organisations within an industry (Chemical Industries Association) or the distinctively different interests and situations which exist within sub-segments of the industry (associations in the printing industry). Nevertheless, the one uniform factor in their development was the employers' acceptance that an industry basis, whatever its form, provided the main focus of their common interest and representational needs. However, while such a situation can serve the interests of single-industry organisations (whether small or large, single or multisite) it can present problems for multi-industry organisations. Sisson points out that the increased emphasis on decentralised organisational bargaining, rather than multi-employer industry-level bargaining, led some to contemplate 'a restructuring of employers' organisations based on the CBI and a number of multi-industry regional organisations with internal committees to represent particular industries or sectors; these committees, in turn, might carry out the bargaining agency functions of the existing national employers' organisations'[117]. However, such a change would have required not only a major restructure of employers' associations but also a major redirection in the role of the CBI.

It is important to recognise that there is a potential conflict for all organisations between the requirement to accept and abide by policy decisions of the association and the more basic principle that an organisation, when it becomes a member of the association, does not relinquish any of its rights or responsibilities to determine its own affairs and to act in its best interests. It is this conflict which has found expression in the desire of some organisations not to be bound by the decisions and agreements made by their association and to be free to pursue their own strategies in industrial relations at the organisational level. This led some employers' associations in the 1970s to establish a category of **non-conforming member** in order to ensure that such organisations could remain members of the association and so maintain the association's strength and influence both within the industry and outside. Thus, employers' associations appear to require less from their membership in terms of 'collective solidarity' than trade unions. Certainly, if large organisations opt out of their employers' association completely then the employers' association can easily become unrepresentative of the industry as a whole. One survey[118] showed that a majority of employers' associations are composed of relatively small organisations (less than 500 employees), but this is primarily a reflection of the normal size of organisations in the industry (e.g. National Association of Shopfitters) rather than a reflection of large employers opting out.

The **internal organisation** of employers' associations normally vests ultimate authority in a general meeting of its members. However, in practice, the primary responsibility for policy and decision making rests with a general council or executive committee (elected by the membership) and a number of specialist committees which may include co-opted members with particular expertise or interests to represent. These committees usually comprise directors or senior managers and, wherever possible, seek to arrive at decisions on a consensus rather than voting basis so as to avoid splits or factionalism within the membership. Certainly, in view of the likely differences in industrial relations thinking and strategy between larger and smaller organisations and the fact that the voting arrangements in most employers' associations (like that of the TUC) relate size of organisation to value of vote cast, any significant reliance on voting could easily foster a perception of large organisation domination. Nevertheless, the larger organisations do tend to dominate in the membership of the various committees. However, as a consequence of the consensus approach, the policies and decisions of an employers' association are likely to be more 'reactionary' in nature because they have to be founded on the lowest common denominator which will unite the membership. Only a small proportion of associations have a substantial number of full-time staff, many of the smaller associations being run by firms of accountants or solicitors or member organisations. However, this apparent lack of resources, as compared with trade unions, understates the real position in that employers' associations do not need to maintain funds to support industrial action or provide friendly society benefits. Much of the association's industrial relations resources and expertise lies in the members of its committees and the management of the organisations it represents.

Functions

The primary function of an employers' association is to support and promote the commercial objectives of its members. Its major activities can be divided into four categories:

- The direct negotiation of collective agreements with trade unions;
- Assisting its members in the resolution of disputes;
- Providing general help and advice to its members on industrial relations matters;
- Representing its members' views and interests to government and other agencies.

See Chapter 9 –
Collective bargaining

The relative importance attached to each of these activities, in particular the collective bargaining role, will depend on the perceived homogeneity and common interest among the members. As Bean points out, even in the USA, which is perhaps more noted for the predominance of organisational-level bargaining (where it exists), nevertheless there is a 'prevalence of multi-employer (association) bargaining in ... trucking, construction and retailing which are characterised by a large number of small or medium-sized firms operating in highly competitive and often localised markets'[119].

So far as management is concerned, negotiations should centre on the ability of the organisation to fund a pay increase and, in particular, the linking of pay increases to improvements in productivity. Such individual organisational factors cannot be taken into account adequately within the framework of a multi-employer collective agreement negotiated by an employers' association. By the early 1980s, Sisson argued, 'most managements are already non-conforming members of their employers' organisation in practice if not in name'[120], through 'topping up' national agreements. The process continued during the 1980s with the demise of a number of multi-employer collective

bargaining arrangements, including major ones such as the engineering industry. Nevertheless, membership of an employers' association remains important
in those industries which have retained multi-employer bargaining (such as,
construction, printing and electrical contracting).

The continuing process of decentralisation of collective bargaining has
further emphasised the employers' association role of **providing advisory and
consultancy services** and co-ordinating management strategies and bargaining
at the organisational level. Employers' associations provide a range of specialist
advice on law, recruitment, education and training, performance and quality
management, equal opportunities, health and safety, etc. as well as the more
traditional industrial relations issues of union recognition, collective bargaining, dismissals, redundancy, etc. Significantly, the greatest utilisation appears
to be among the larger (rather than smaller) member organisations. Certainly,
Sisson believes that 'employers' organisations probably exert more influence on
workplace industrial relations through the performance of these functions than
they did through multi-employer bargaining'[121]. However, the areas in which
advice is sought has changed as industrial relations and human resource management has changed. A major growth area has been advising members on the
impact of EU legislation and lobbying into the EU on behalf of British
employers[122].

Employers' associations may also **assist their members to resolve disputes**
by negotiating and operating on their behalf a disputes procedure with recognised unions. Originally the procedure was intended to allow 'the whole power
of the associated employers to be deployed on behalf of a member should that
be necessary'[123] – a dispute in one organisation could become a dispute in all by
the employers' association instigating a lock-out throughout its member organisations. However, the role of the procedure changed with the growth of trade
union power and organisational level bargaining. It became primarily a conciliation or arbitration forum in which, Munns suggested, the role of the employers' association is 'to seek the reconciliation of opposing views bearing in mind
the interests of the employers generally'[124]. Clearly, such a role presents a conflict for the employers' association between, on the one hand, representing the
interests of its individual member organisation and negotiating on its behalf
and, on the other, seeking to conciliate between its member and the trade
unions with whom it is in dispute.

Finally, employers' associations, like trade unions, undertake a **representational role** on behalf of their members. Unlike trade unions, however, employers' associations do not have formal direct links with any particular political
party. Nevertheless, member organisations may make financial contributions
to the Conservative Party and both employers' associations and their members
may support other bodies (e.g. Aims of Industry) which seek the maintenance
of free enterprise and a reduction in trade union power. Employers' associations seek to project the individual and collective interests of their members to
trade unions, government (and increasingly the European Commission) and
the general public primarily through publicity campaigns and direct lobbying.
In addition, they also present evidence to governmental inquiries and provide
the employers' representatives on a range of bodies such as Employment
Tribunals and ACAS.

Country profile 7.2   Germany: three pillars of multi-employer organisation

As Jacobi *et al.* point out. 'German business has long been highly organised' and 'most companies remain loyal to their associations' (2:204). There is a clear differentiation between three types of employers' organisation: chambers of industry and commerce, business (or trade) associations and employers' associations.

Chambers of industry and commerce. These are legally established, locally based bodies and all eligible organisations are required to join (i.e. membership is compulsory). They are primarily concerned with public policy affecting business community interests. Their activities include licensing and regulating trade practices, apprenticeship training and providing advice on business matters. The central body (DIHT) is mainly concerned with general national economic policy and foreign trade issues.

Business or trade associations. These associations are concerned mainly with product market issues (technology, marketing, research, etc.). The BDI represents private industrial organisations organised through a variety of regional and sectoral trade associations. For example, the VDMA (Association of German Machine and Systems Builders) has 3,000 organisations in membership (55 per cent of eligible companies) with 1 million employees and 80 per cent of sales in the

sector. It is divided on both a regional basis and sub-industry basis (machine tools, print equipment, wood product machinery, etc.). Although there are similar trade associations in the service sector, there is no central organisation similar to the BDI.

Employers' associations. Collective bargaining is carried out on a multi-employer basis at the sector level – the national employers' association negotiates a framework agreement on non-wage issues (hours, holidays, etc.) and co-ordinates the wage bargaining of its regional associations. Single employer bargaining is very much the exception with organisations having to leave their association or face expulsion. By far the largest employers' association is *Gesamtmetall* (Metalworking Industry) with some 7,500 firms in membership (43 per cent of eligible organisations) employing 2.5 million people (65 per cent of the industry's total employment). The BDA only covers the private sector (both industry and service sectors); public sector organisations have their own employers' associations. Similarly, the iron and steel employers' association has been excluded from the BDA because it is felt that the Codetermination Act for the Coal, Iron and Steel Industries (1951) requirement for employee/union election of the personnel director (who has the duty of representing the organisation in

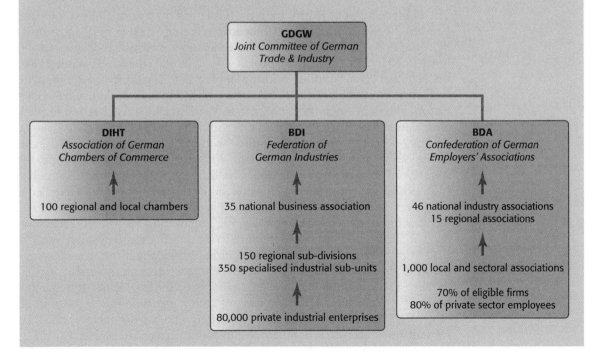

Country profile 7.2   Germany: three pillars of multi-employer organisation
(continued)

the employers' association) is incompatible with the work of an employers' association. The main function of the BDA is to represent and lobby for the employers' interests on social and labour policy issues to government (at national, European and international level). Like the DGB (German union confederation) it is represented on various committees within the Ministry of Labour and Social Affairs and is involved in drafting proposed legislation.

The three pillars of employer organisation are linked together through the GDGW (Joint Committee of German Trade & Industry) which provides a forum for discussion and co-ordination. Solidarity within the employers' associations has been facilitated by the existence of funds to support organisations involved in industrial action; indeed, 'the extensive use of the lock-out distinguishes German employers' associations from most of their counterparts in other European countries' (1:26). Similarly, the BDA has

issued guidelines to firms not to take advantage of other firms involved in industrial action by taking over their orders and not to hire strikers or employees locked out by their employer. However, as Jacobi *et al.* point out, recently there has been tension between the three 'pillars' with the DIHT and BDI advocating reductions in labour costs and decentralisation of collective bargaining to the organisation level and, in 1996, jointly opposing the nomination of the BDA's president for the post of president of UNICE (2:206).

Sources:
1. 'West Germany: Employers' organisations', *European Industrial Relations Review*, no. 188, September 1989, pp. 25–7.
2. O. Jacobi, B. Keller and W. Müller-Jentsch, 'Germany: facing new challenges', in A. Ferner and R. Hyman (eds), *Changing Industrial Relations in Europe*, Blackwell, 1998, pp. 190–238.

See also Country profiles 5.2 and 10.1.

The Confederation of British Industry

The Confederation of British Industry (CBI) was formed in 1965 as a merger between the British Employers' Confederation (established in 1919 and primarily concerned with labour affairs), the Federation of British Industries (established in 1916 and primarily concerned with trade and commercial matters) and the National Association of British Manufacturers (primarily concerned with small manufacturing organisations). Its **membership** includes individual organisations as well as employers' and trade associations and, directly or indirectly, it represents some 250,000 organisations with a combined employment of some 10 million people. Most importantly, the creation of the CBI resulted in an expansion of membership, beyond that of the former BEC, into retailing, the commercial sectors of banking and insurance and, above all, the then public (now privatised) corporations. However, at the time of its creation, a number of employers' associations expressed concern about allowing direct organisational membership of the CBI. For example, the Engineering Employers' Federation felt that 'if companies paid subscriptions to the new body ... they might not also wish to pay to their employers' organisation, particularly if they could exercise influence through the labour committee' and 'considered it unsatisfactory that the largest federation should have only one vote on the "unwieldy" 400-member council'[125]. Nevertheless, the inclusion of such a provision in the constitution of the CBI has meant that large organisations who are not members of their relevant employers' association are able to play an active role within the CBI.

The **objectives** of the CBI reflect its combined employer and trade functions:

- To formulate and influence policies in respect of industrial, economic, fiscal, commercial, labour, social, legal and technical issues;
- To provide a focal point for those seeking the views of British industry;
- To develop the contribution of British industry in the creation of wealth within a free-enterprise market situation.

In seeking to meet these objectives, Grant and Marsh argued, 'the CBI must not only be concerned with giving its members an opportunity to voice their opinions; it must also ensure that these opinions are aggregated into a policy which is well informed as well as representative of industrial opinion'[126]. The **organisational arrangements** within the CBI appear to emphasise 'managerial expertise' rather than 'representativeness and democracy'. The ultimate governing and decision making body is the Council which meets every month and comprises 400 representatives from each of the CBI's main categories of membership. The function of this Council is to provide guidance to the CBI's various officers and standing committees and to approve any policy proposals made by them. However, effective power and decision making rests with the CBI's two major officials, the President (elected on a part-time basis) and the Director General (appointed on a full-time basis), and various standing committees (whose members are appointed by the President and the Director General). At the local level, the CBI's Regional Councils co-ordinate its activities within the region, act as a communication channel between the membership and the CBI centrally and provide a sounding board for proposed policies. In 1977 the CBI introduced its first National Conference, open to attendance by any member and intended to provide a wider public forum to discuss issues of concern and project the employers' interests. However, unlike the TUC's Annual Congress, it is not the prime governmental body within the CBI and may only make recommendations to the Council. Its primary function is to provide publicity for employers' views.

The creation of the CBI in 1965 arose from a perceived need on the part of management to have a single focal point to represent their interests to government at a time of increased emphasis on economic planning and to act as a counterweight to the growing influence of the TUC. However, it is important to recognise that the CBI is not the only representative of employer or management interests. There is also the Institute of Management (with a membership of 80,000 managers and 600 companies with 3 million employees), the Institute of Directors (with 40,000 individual members) and the Institute of Personnel and Development. Indeed, there is a sense in which the IoD may be seen as representing 'employers' while the CBI, IM and IPD are representing 'organisational management', and, some would argue, the IoD, which is more representative of smaller companies than the CBI, exerted a much greater influence than the CBI on government policy and legislation during the 1980s. Similarly, in the current debates about the social partnership model, the IoD not only believes that the model is 'alien' to the UK but also challenges the CBI's assertion to be the sole, or at least primary, representative of employer/management interests in any discussions with TUC and government[127].

Summary propositions

■ Management's approach to industrial relations is the result of constrained choices aimed at maintaining managerial security and authority within the organisation's decision-making processes.

■ Management style in any organisation reflects a balance between management's desire to maintain its prerogative and promote individualism and its preparedness to accept collectivism and management by consent.

■ Management strategies over the past two decades have been directed towards reducing constraints on its decision making, emphasising the importance of the individual employee and developing organisational flexibility and competitiveness.

■ The role of most employers' associations has become one of supporting members with advice and representing their interests to government rather than negotiating collective agreements on their behalf.

Activity

See if you can obtain some 'primary' materials from the organisation you work for or another local or national organisation: any mission or HRM objectives statement; copies of employee magazine(s), employee reports or other materials given to employees (including recruitment or induction literature); public minutes of consultative committees (if any); copies of collective agreements (if any); etc.

You can then examine this material and try to identify what image the organisation is trying to project to its employees, how you would classify its management style and what is management's strategy towards, for example, trade unions and collective bargaining, employee involvement or participation and labour flexibility.

Further reading

■ M. Poole and H. Mansfield (eds), *Managerial Roles in Industrial Relations*, Gower, 1980; K. Thurley and S. Wood (eds), *Industrial Relations and Management Strategy*, Cambridge University Press, 1983; J. Storey, *Managerial Prerogative and the Question of Control*, Routledge & Kegan Paul, 1983.
These books present a range of thinking relating to managerial strategy in industrial relations and the nature of managerial prerogative.

■ J. Storey, *Developments in the Management of Human Resources*, Blackwell, 1992; J. Storey (ed.), *Human Resource Management: a critical text*, Routledge, 1995; P. Sparrow and M. Marchington, *Human Resource Management: the new agenda*, FT Pitman, 1998. These books examine the nature of strategic HRM change, its application in various organisations and its impact on employees and unions.

References

1. A. Fox, *Beyond Contract: Power, work and trust relations*, Faber, 1974, p. 239.
2. K. Sisson and P. Marginson, 'Management: systems, structures and strategy', in P. Edwards (ed.), *Industrial Relations: Theory and practice in Britain*, Blackwell, 1995, p. 89.
3. M. Poole, 'Management strategies and industrial relations', in M. Poole and R. Mansfield (eds), *Managerial Roles in Industrial Relations*, Gower, 1980, p. 40.
4. *Ibid.*, p. 44.
5. *Ibid.*, p. 42.
6. T. Colling, 'Experiencing turbulence: competition, strategic choice and the management of human resources in British Airways', *Human Resource Management Journal*, vol. 5, no. 5, 1995, p. 20.
7. M. Morishima, 'Embedding HRM in a social context', *British Journal of Industrial Relations*, vol. 33, no. 4, 1995, p. 618.
8. *Ibid.*, p. 619.
9. H. J. Drumm, 'Theoretical and ethical foundations of human resource management: a German point of view', *Employee Relations*, vol. 16, no. 4, 1994, p. 35.
10. K. Wilson, 'Social responsibility: a management perspective', in M. Poole and R. Mansfield (eds), *Managerial Roles in Industrial Relations*, Gower, 1980, p. 60.
11. H. F. Gospel, 'An approach to a theory of the firm in industrial relations', *British Journal of Industrial Relations*, vol. 11, 1973, p. 218.
12. J. Storey, *Managerial Prerogative and the Question of Control*, Routledge & Kegan Paul, 1983, p. 102.
13. W. E. J. McCarthy and N. D. Ellis, *Management by Agreement*, Hutchinson, 1973, p. 94.
14. M. M. Perline and D. J. Poynter, 'Union and management perceptions of managerial prerogative', *British Journal of Industrial Relations*, vol. 28, no. 2, July 1990, p. 179.
15. A. Marsh, *Employee Relations Policy and Decision Making: A survey of manufacturing companies carried out for the CBI*, Gower, 1982, p. 201.
16. J. Purcell, 'Mapping management styles in employee relations', *Journal of Management Studies*, vol. 24, no. 5, 1987, p. 535.
17. *Ibid.*, p. 534.
18. *Ibid.*, p. 533.
19. *Ibid.*, p. 534.
20. *Ibid.*, p. 533.
21. M. Marchington and P. Parker, *Changing Patterns of Employee Relations*, Harvester Wheatsheaf, 1990.
22. J. Purcell and K. Sisson, 'Strategies and practice in the management of industrial relations', in G. S. Bain (ed.), *Industrial Relations in Britain*, Blackwell, 1983, pp. 112–18.
23. J. Purcell and B. Ahlstrand, *Human Resource Management in the Multi-Divisional Firm*, Oxford University Press, 1994.
24. I. Kessler and J. Purcell, 'Individualism and collectivism in theory and practice', in *op. cit*, p. 348.
25. Purcell and Sisson, *op. cit.*, p. 114.
26. *Ibid.*, p. 115.
27. *Ibid.*
28. Kessler and Purcell, *op. cit.*, p. 349.
29. *Ibid.*, p. 348.
30. *Ibid.*, pp. 348–9.
31. J. Storey and K. Sisson, *Managing Human Resources and Industrial Relations*, Open University Press, 1993, p. 230.
32. Marsh, *op. cit.*, p. 203.
33. Purcell and Sisson, *op. cit.*, p. 117.
34. J. T. Winkler, 'The ghost at the bargaining table: directors and industrial relations', *British Journal of Industrial Relations*, vol. 12, no. 2, 1974.
35. *Ibid.*, p. 196.
36. E. Batstone, I. Boraston and S. Frenkel, *Shop Stewards in Action*, Blackwell, 1977.
37. S. Tyson and A. Fell, *Evaluating the Personnel Function*, Hutchinson, 1986.
38. J. Storey, *Developments in the Management of Human Resources*, Blackwell, 1992, pp. 166–85.
39. *Ibid.*, p. 169.
40. *Ibid.*, p. 185.
41. H. Clegg, *Trade Unionism under Collective Bargaining*, Blackwell, 1976, p. 10.
42. Purcell and Sisson, *op. cit.*, p. 109.
43. *Ibid.*, p. 110.
44. Sisson and Marginson, *op. cit.*, pp. 97–100.
45. C. Crouch, 'Beyond corporatism: company strategy', in R. Hyman and A. Ferner (eds), *New Frontiers in European Industrial Relations*, Blackwell, 1994, p. 219.
46. C. G. Gill and H. M. G. Concannon, 'Developing an explanatory framework for industrial relations policy within the firm', *Industrial Relations Journal*, vol. 7, no. 4, 1976/1977.

47. 'The role of management in industrial relations', *CIR Report*, no. 34, HMSO, 1973, p. 5.

48. *Report of Royal Commission on Trade Unions and Employers' Associations* (Donovan Commission), HMSO, 1968, p. 4l.

49. *Ibid.*, p. 50.

50. Purcell and Sisson, *op. cit.*, p. 102.

51. Storey (1983), *op. cit.*, p. 184.

52. Marsh, *op. cit.*, p. 187.

53. Purcell and Sisson, *op. cit.*, p. 107.

54. J. Purcell, 'Macho managers and the new industrial relations', *Employee Relations*, vol. 4, no. 1, 1982, p. 3.

55. P. Edwards, 'Myth of the macho manager', *Personnel Management*, April 1985, p. 35.

56. S. Kessler and F. Bayliss, *Contemporary British Industrial Relations* (3rd edn), Macmillan, 1998, p. 112.

57. C. Hendry, A. Pettigrew and P. Sparrow, 'Changing patterns of human resource management', *Personnel Management*, November 1988, p. 38.

58. *Ibid.*, p. 41.

59. Sisson and Marginson, *op. cit.*, p. 96.

60. S. Wood, 'The four pillars of HRM: are they connected?' *Human Resource Management Journal*, vol. 5, no. 5, 1995, pp. 49–58.

61. D. Torrington and L. Hall, *Human Resource Management* (4th edn), Prentice Hall, 1998, p. 20.

62. Colling, *op. cit.*, pp. 18–32.

63. Sisson and Marginson, *op. cit.*, p. 110.

64. P. B. Beaumont, 'Trade unions and HRM', *Industrial Relations Journal*, vol. 22, no. 4, 1991, pp. 300–8.

65. Morishima, *op. cit.*, pp. 617–40.

66. D. Guest, 'Personnel and HRM: can you tell the difference?' *Personnel Management*, January 1989.

67. Storey (1992), *op. cit.*, pp. 41–45.

68. Storey and Sisson, *op. cit.*, pp. 76–7.

69. M. Armstrong, 'Human resource management: a case of the emperor's new clothes?' *Personnel Management*, August 1987, p. 33.

70. Guest, *op. cit.*, p. 50.

71. A. Fowler, 'When chief executives discover HRM', *Personnel Management*, January 1987.

72. Armstrong, *op. cit.*, p. 33.

73. P. Miller, 'Strategic HRM: what is it and what it isn't', *Personnel Management*, February 1989, p. 51.

74. M. M. Lucio and S. Weston, 'The politics and complexity of trade union responses to new management practices', *Human Resource Management Journal*, vol. 2, no. 4, 1992, p. 80.

75. Sisson and Marginson, *op. cit.*, p. 113.

76. P. Boxall, 'Building the theory of comparative HRM', *Human Resource Management Journal*, vol. 5. no. 5., 1995, p. 6.

77. S. Lees, 'HRM and the legitimacy market', *The International Journal of Human Resource Management*, vol. 8, no. 3, 1997, pp. 234 and 236.

78. D. Guest and K. Hoque, 'The good, the bad and the ugly: employment relations in new non-union workplaces', *Human Resource Management Journal*, vol. 5., no. 1, 1994, pp. 1–14.

79. *Ibid.*, p. 11.

80. Sisson and Marginson, *op. cit.*, p. 111.

81. 'Partnership agreements', *IDS Study*, no. 656, October 1998, p. 3.

82. T. Claydon, 'Problematising partnership: the prospects for a co-operative bargaining agenda', in P. Sparrow and M. Marchington (eds), *Human Resource Management: The New Agenda*, FT Pitman, 1998.

83. P. Ackers and J. Payne, 'British trade unions and social partnership: rhetoric, reality and strategy', *The International Journal of Human Resource Management*, vol. 9, no. 3, 1998, p. 531.

84. *Fairness at Work*, HMSO, May 1998.

85. G. Hollinshead, 'Management', in G. Hollinshead, P. Nicholls and S. Tailby (eds), *Employee Relations*, FT Pitman, 1999, p. 88.

86. S. Tailby and D. Winchester, 'Management and trade unions: towards social partnership?', in S. Bach and K. Sisson (eds), *Personnel Management* (3rd edn), Blackwell, 2000, p. 383.

87. *Ibid.*, pp. 383–4.

88. A. Marks, P. Findlay, J. Hine, A. McKinlay and P. Thompson, 'The politics of partnership? Innovation in employment relations in the Scottish spirits industry', *British Journal of Industrial Relations*, vol. 36., no. 2, 1998, p. 210.

89. W. Coupar and B. Stevens, 'Towards a new model of industrial partnership', in P. Sparrow and M. Marchington (eds), *Human Resource Management: The New Agenda*, FT Pitman, 1998, p. 157.

90. J. Kelly, 'Union militancy and social partnership', in P. Ackers, C. Smith and P. Smith (eds), *The New Workplace and Trade Unionism*, Routledge, 1996, p. 101.

91. Claydon, *op. cit.*, p. 181.

92. *Ibid.*, p. 187.

93. 'Partnership at work: a survey', *IRS Employment Trends*, no. 645, December 1997, pp. 3–24.

94. Marks *et al., op. cit.*, p. 224.
95. Hollinshead, *op. cit.*, p. 89.
96. Tailby and Winchester, *op. cit.*, p. 385.
97. 'Partnership deal for Fiat suppliers', *European Industrial Relations Review*, no. 296, September 1998, pp. 25–6.
98. 'Aer Lingus workers agree IR framework and gain 5.5 per cent award', *European Industrial Relations Review*, no. 290, March 1998, pp. 20–2.
99. S. Ackroyd, G. Burrell, M. Hughes and A. Whitaker, 'The Japanisation of British industry?' *Industrial Relations Journal*, vol. 19, no. 1, 1988, p. 16.
100. *Ibid.*, p. 17.
101. *Ibid.*, p. 20.
102. N. Oliver and B. Wilkinson, 'Japanese manufacturing techniques and personnel and industrial relations practice in Britain: evidence and implications', *British Journal of Industrial Relations*, vol. 27, no. 2, 1989.
103. P. Briggs, 'The Japanese at work: illusions of the ideal', *Industrial Relations Journal*, vol. 19, no. 1, 1988, p. 24.
104. *Ibid.*, p. 28.
105. T. Elger and C. Smith, 'Exit, voice and "mandate": management strategies and labour practices of Japanese firms in Britain', *British Journal of Industrial Relations*, vol. 36, no. 2, 1998, pp. 203–4.
106. M. A. Shadur and R. L. Tung, 'Introduction: new developments in HRM in the Asia Pacific region', *Employee Relations*, vol. 19, no. 4, 1997, p. 292.
107. R. Bean, *Comparative Industrial Relations: an introduction to cross-national perspectives*, Routledge, 1994, pp. 190–92.
108. H. V. Perlmutter, 'The tortuous evolution of the multinational corporation', *Columbia Journal of World Business*, vol. 4, no. 1, 1969, pp. 9–18.
109. Drumm, *op. cit.*, p. 38.
110. T. Turner, D. D'Art and P. Gunnigle, 'Pluralism in retreat? A comparison of Irish and multinational manufacturing companies', *The International Journal of Human Resource Management*, vol. 8, no. 6, 1997, pp. 825–40.
111. X. Coller and P. Marginson, 'Transnational management influence over changing employment practices: a case study from the food industry', *Industrial Relations Journal*, vol. 29, no. 1, 1998, pp. 4–17.
112. P. Marginson and K. Sisson, 'Transnational capital and European industrial relations', in Hyman and Ferner (eds), *op. cit.*, pp. 29–33.
113. Bean, *op. cit.*, pp. 52–3.
114. F. van Waarden, 'Employers and employers' associations', in J. van Ruysseveldt, R. Huiskamp and J. van Hoof (eds), *Comparative Industrial and Employment Relations*, Sage, 1995, p. 72.
115. P. B. Beaumont, *The Future of Employment Relations*, Sage, 1995, p. 28.
116. van Waarden, *op.cit.*, pp. 83 and 84.
117. K. Sisson, 'Employers' organisations', in *op. cit*, p. 134.
118. 'Changing role of employers' associations surveyed', *IRS Employment Trends*, no. 552, January 1994, pp. 4–13.
119. Bean, *op. cit.*, p. 54.
120. Sisson, *op. cit.*, p. 132.
121. Sisson, *op. cit.*, p. 133.
122. *IRS Employment Trends*, no. 552, *op. cit.*, p. 12.
123. Commission on Industrial Relations, Study 1, *Employers' Organisations and Industrial Relations*, HMSO, 1972, p. 28.
124. V. G. Munns, 'The functions and organisation of employers' associations in selected industries', in *Royal Commission Research Paper No. 7*, HMSO, 1967, p. 9.
125. E. Wigham, *The Power to Manage: A history of the Engineering Employers' Federation*, Macmillan, 1973, p. 216.
126. W. Grant and D. Marsh, *The Confederation of British Industry*, Hodder and Stoughton, 1977, p. 87.
127. 'Do employers want partnership?' *Labour Research*, March 1998, pp. 21–2.

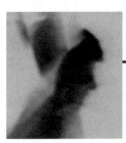

chapter eight

The government

Learning objectives

The government undoubtedly plays an important role in determining the nature of the employment relationship. By the end of this chapter, you should be able to:

■ identify different views about the representational role of government;

■ understand the underlying political ideologies and their impact on government approaches to industrial relations and labour market regulation;

■ appreciate differences in government strategies (intervention or deregulation) in three main areas: unemployment, incomes and low pay; individual protective legislation; and the regulation of the status, power and conduct of trade unions;

■ explain the European Union's role in labour affairs, the development of the 'social dialogue' process and the issue of 'social dumping'.

Definition

The government may be defined as the politically based body which directs and controls the institutions of regulation within an organised society and whose policies and actions are, in the UK and other democracies, legitimised through the electoral process.

Key issues

While you are reading this chapter, you should keep the following points in mind:

■ Democracy legitimises differences in political ideology within a society. We must accept that this inevitably means there will be different views about what constitutes 'social justice', the desirability (or otherwise) of 'social conflict' and the role of government in exercising 'social control' – all of which impact on the industrial relation system.

■ Labour flexibility has increasingly become the focal point for government strategies aimed at improving economic competitiveness and reducing unemployment. However, we must recognise that unconditional labour market deregulation could adversely affect socially desirable employment policies (social benefits, training, employee protection legislation and even incomes policy or a minimum wage).

■ The European Union provides a second tier of 'government' in the labour market and industrial relations system. We need to be aware that the EU level is becoming more dominant and its approach, based on the 'social partnership' and 'statutory regulation' models prevalent in most other EU countries, is at variance with the 'traditional' UK model (adversarial voluntarism).

8.1 Introduction

Most people would agree with Poole that 'despite considerable problems in identifying the personnel, locating its various segments and reaching an acceptable definition, the state is indisputably the "third force" in the industrial relations system'[1]. Indeed, the experience of the UK, and other countries, during the 1980s and 1990s might suggest that the government has become the primary force in determining the nature of industrial relations:

■ Government is, by virtue of its law-making role, 'the only actor in the situation which can change the rules of the system'[2].

■ Government strategies and policies exert a major influence in determining the economic and social contexts within which the other parties (management, employees and unions) conduct their relationship.

■ Government has responsibility (directly or indirectly) for guiding and influencing the activities of a varying combination of other institutions within society – such as 'public services' (like education and health), 'public enterprises' (like those concerned with energy, transport and communication) and local government authorities.

Consequently, van Waarden argues[3], the diversity in national industrial relations systems is significantly related to the differences in degree, method and content of government intervention not only into the industrial relations system itself but also the wider economic and social framework.

8.2 The role of government

In the past, UK industrial relations was often regarded as being founded on the principle of 'voluntarism'; to the extent that, in 1960, Kahn-Freund was able to say that there was 'no major country in the world in which the law has played a less significant role in the shaping of [industrial relations] than in Great Britain'[4]. However, the same cannot be said now. Since the early 1970s, both Conservative and Labour governments have, in different ways, taken a more active and interventionist role in the operation of the labour market and industrial relations system, thereby shaping the nature of the employment relationship (both individual and collective).

Objectives of government

Crouch argued that, like management's objective at the organisational level, the **government's prime overall objective is economic** in character: namely, 'to maintain and enhance the stability and productivity of the British economy' through the pursuit of 'four not easily compatible goals; full employment, price stability, a favourable balance of payments and protection of the exchange rate'[5]. Poole[6] has suggested that government strategies are directed towards the 'problem of control' in three fundamental areas: employment levels (including job creation and protection), work relationships (including union rights, the role of collective bargaining and industrial democracy) and the distribution of economic rewards (including low pay and rate of wage increases).

However, to regard the government's objectives and strategies in industrial relations as purely the result of economic influences disregards the influence of the **more fundamental social objectives** which provide the basis for political differentiation and consequently differential governmental action (see Box 8.1). The manner in which governments balance their various economic objectives and approach industrial relations matters is conditioned by their view of the nature of the society they wish to create or, at least, encourage: individualistic or corporatist.

It is important to recognise that the **representative position of the government**, and therefore the basis for its policies and legislation, may be viewed from three quite different assumptions.

1. Some may regard the government as the expression of an inherently distinct **national interest** which, in the area of industrial relations, occupies a neutral position between the conflicting interests of employers and management, on

---

Box 8.1	Three types of public policy intervention

■ *The volume of employment.* State action is based partly on an economic management imperative directed towards improving labour productivity and competitiveness and partly on a social order logic which recognises the need to minimise unemployment. Public policy in this area focuses on not only economic, fiscal and social welfare policies (particularly the level of public expenditure) but also employment policies within state controlled organisations (including publicly owned enterprises).

■ *A general framework of employment regulation.* State action is based primarily on a social order logic. The employment relationship is a social as well as economic relationship between the parties. Public policy is concerned with the social process by which the relationship is determined and regulated and the extent of protection, equalisation and control of labour flexibility within the contractual relationship.

■ *The employment flow.* State action is based on a social order logic which influences both economic and social variables. Public policy in this area centres on the role of social policies, training provisions, unemployment benefits and retirement policies in shaping the structure of the workforce (the flows in and out of different labour markets).

Source: S. Erbès-Seguin, 'Public policies and employment', *Warwick Papers in Industrial Relations*, no. 29, November 1989.

the one hand, and employees and trade unions on the other. From this standpoint, Farnham and Pimlott argued, the intervention of the government in industrial relations is justified 'to protect the employment interests of individuals when no other means are available, or to uphold the wider interests of society as a whole when these appear to be threatened by particular industrial pressure groups'[7]. However, 'national interest' is an abstract concept which cannot be determined or assessed in any realistic way. It is whatever the government, mass media or anyone else perceives it to be; indeed, it may often be used by the government or others as an apparently self-evident and acceptable justification for what are in reality ideologically based policies and decisions. The divisions within society over most major governmental policies and decisions suggest an absence of any consensus as to what constitutes the national interest.

2. Some may view the government's policies and legislation as no more than the expression of a **sectional interest** within society, which coalesces and expresses itself in a political party and which predominates by virtue of having been legitimised by the electorate. Certainly Lewis argued that 'legal policy cannot be divorced from the interests and ideology of the law makers and from the wider political and industrial conflict'[8]. It is the ideological base of the political party which provides the foundation for a government's legislation and other policies. However, the ideological affinity which appeared to exist in the UK between, on the one hand, the Labour Party and the trade union movement and, on the other, the Conservative Party and employers, has become weaker during the 1980s and 1990s (particularly the loosening of the relationship between the Labour Party and trade unions).

3. The government may be seen as little more than 'democratic icing' on the top of a political system which, irrespective of the political party in power, inherently supports the **maintenance of the capitalist interest**. Certainly, Blyton and Turnbull believe that 'state intervention in the economy in general, and the employment relationship in particular, is inseparable from the nature of the capital-labour relations ... capitalist economies have a capitalist state, wherein the capitalist class might not govern but it certainly rules'[9]. In the same vein, Hyman has argued that the possibility of any radical government initiative in economic policy or industrial relations is restricted by 'policy constraints which stem necessarily from the capitalist context of political life'[10] and which lead inevitably to a governmental preoccupation with the need to 'maintain economic stability', to maintain 'the confidence of industry' and to 'curb excessive wage increases'. Furthermore, much of the public and political debate on policy options is constrained by 'a notion of "national interest" which is closely bound up with the interests of employers; and a conception of labour organization, objectives and action (in so far as these conflict with employer interests) as necessarily sectional and probably selfish, irresponsible, disruptive and subversive'[11].

Hyman also points out that an **apparent policy of non-intervention** in economic and industrial relations matters 'did not mean state neutrality; in withdrawing from an active economic role, the state endorsed the propriety and legitimacy of economic relations in which unequal power prevailed ...

non-intervention of the state was non-intervention *in favour* of capital'[12]. From this standpoint, it is the capitalist economic system which, by inhibiting the ability of Labour governments to represent properly the 'non-capital' sectional interests within society, created the semblance of a governmental consensus of the 'national interest' in respect of economic and industrial relations matters for most of the postwar period. However, Beaumont argues that the government is neither 'a neutral representative of the public or social interest' nor 'a captive of class forces, economic forces or the capitalist mode of production'[13] but rather has some degree of relative autonomy – particularly, as in the case of Thatcherism in the early 1980s, at times of economic crisis.

Liberalism and corporatism

Both Crouch[14] and Strinati[15] have put forward an **analytical framework of government approaches to industrial relations** which relates the nature of the dominant political ideology to the relative power and autonomy of trade unions (see Figure 8.1). This framework can be useful in distinguishing not only different national approaches but also shifts in national approaches over time.

Market individualism is characterised by an apparent balancing of competitive interests through a 'market system' which legitimises the concepts of property rights and an objective basis to income inequalities. Labour is weak, unorganised and subordinate to the employer through the indirect control of the 'market' and the relationship between them is, at best, paternalism or, at worst, exploitation; labour is simply a commodity which only has a value in so

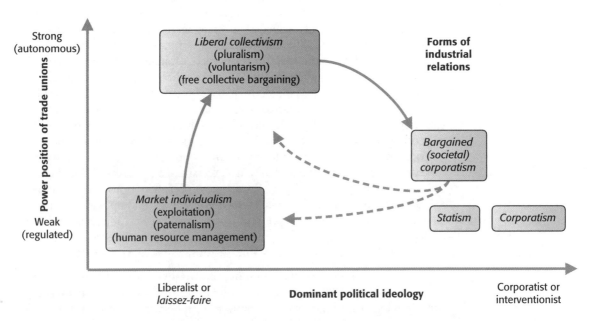

Figure 8.1 Governmental approaches to industrial relations

far as it is bought and sold. Although the role of government is largely passive, Crouch argued it is also 'highly coercive in so far as the law firmly upholds property rights against the countervailing power of subordinates'[16]. There is likely to be little legislation to protect employees and, even where the right to organise formally exists, the economic function of unions may in practice be restricted. This 'market individualism' model is deficient in so far as it assumes that the employment contract is primarily an economic relationship between two individuals, when it is usually between an individual and an organisation and involves a social relationship in which the individual is subordinated to the authority and control of the organisation. Certainly, the individual's dependence on capital for his or her livelihood is not reciprocated by capital's dependence on him or her (a single unit of its labour commodity). This form of industrial relations has been associated with the early stages of industrialisation in most western countries and may also be in evidence in newly industrialising countries. The organisation of labour into trade unions is a necessary element in redressing the imbalance and, consequently, its development requires the dominant liberalist or *laissez-faire* ideology to accommodate this growing subordinate ideology of collectivism.

The result of such an accommodation can be seen in the **liberal collectivism** form of industrial relations, which has dominated UK industrial relations and is closely bound up with the concepts of 'pluralism' and 'voluntarism'. This approach has been termed 'liberal pluralism' by van Waarden and defined as 'a passive state which upholds the principle of non-intervention' and in which 'state regulation ... is confined to creating a (modest) legal framework within which private individuals and businesses can conclude agreements'[17]. Within this model, Crouch argued, 'the identity of dominant and subordinate interests remains distinct, and a separation of political, economic and ideological dimensions continues to exist' but 'authority usually comes to accept a strategy of indulgence as a means of absorbing subordinate pressure'[18]. The indulgency accommodation is characterised by a limited acceptance of autonomous trade unions, which represent, negotiate and reconcile conflicting interests with management through the collective bargaining process. However, by the same process, the dominant interests of management continue to be protected through the maintenance of a boundary between issues for collective bargaining and issues for determination by managerial prerogative. Thus, Crouch argued, government 'action to enhance subordinates' rights will exist alongside the limited coercive measures which ensure the perpetuation of domination'[19]. It is not incompatible for government, through its legislative role, to support the extension of both individual and collective employee rights while at the same time constraining collective employee power (i.e. as expressed through the activities of trade unions) under the guise of maintaining a 'balance of power' between the parties in their operation of the industrial relations system. Indeed, such apparent impartial actions reinforce the image of the government acting in the national interest.

However, the existence or development of a **corporatist political ideology** is likely to result in a different model of industrial relations, a model which is more common among other European countries. The **bargained corporatism** form of industrial relations (also referred to as 'societal corporatism' or 'neo-corporatism) has been apparent in countries such as Sweden, Germany and The Netherlands where there is 'active state interference, but usually in consultation with the social partners' and based on 'active support for their organizations and their mutual relations'[20]. It is, as Poole points out, firmly founded on 'types of cultural and ideological philosophy (such as Catholicism, Conservatism and Social Democracy) which emphasize harmony and the identity of interests of interdependent functional groups'[21]. Crouch described the model as one in which 'the government interposes itself between the unions and their normal bargaining partner, the employer, but in so doing becomes itself their bargaining partner; and the government is able to offer several things which cannot be achieved in bargaining ... such as social policy reforms, workers' rights, changes in economic and fiscal policy'[22]. Within this model, Taylor[23] further distinguishes between those countries, such as Sweden, where trade unions are 'integrated' within a consensus approach to government policy formulation and have the status of quasi-governmental institutions (for example, the administration of unemployment funds) and those countries, such as Germany, where unions are 'included' in frequent consultations with government but are not an institutionalised part of government decision making.

Poole differentiates 'societal' or 'bargained' corporatism from the more extreme form of **'state corporatism'**, where the different functional interests, particularly labour, are suppressed, subordinated or incorporated into the political system (often based on a single political party or a dominant party which is able to marginalise any opposition). Such an approach has, in the past, been associated with the former Communist countries of eastern Europe and, at the opposite end of the political spectrum, Spain under the Franco regime. However, as Bean has pointed out, the subordination of the union movement to the needs of economic development has also been a central part of government strategy in some newly industrialised countries such as Malaysia, Singapore and Korea; to the extent that 'the primary actor in the industrial relations scene is the government itself'[24]. Similarly, van Waarden differentiates the **statism** of France, where the unions' weak industrial organisation has resulted not only in their marginalisation in the political processes but also a more active and direct state intervention in establishing terms and conditions of employment.

In a later variant of the model, which relates the extent of co-ordinating capacity of both labour *and* capital with the strength of organised labour, Crouch argues that a stable industrial relations system only exists at the extremes of either 'a pure labour market in which workers have no organizations at all ... [or] organization is very weak [and] workers cannot disrupt effectively', or where there is 'a highly organized system in which a central organization has authority on behalf of the mass of employed persons'[25]. It could be argued that the UK moved away from the 'pure labour market' in the latter half of the nineteenth century but has never really ever approached the alternative stable model. **UK industrial relations has developed through a number of distinct stages** (see Figure 8.1).

1. The *market individualism* of the nineteenth century, based on a dominant liberalist ideology and weak trade unions, gradually gave way to *collective liberalism* over the first half of the twentieth century, as the dominant liberalist

ideology sought to accommodate subordinate ideologies represented by the increasing power and autonomy of trade unionism (with perhaps some retrenchment during the depression of the late 1920s and early 1930s and some advances to a more corporatist approach during the two world wars as the government sought the co-operation of labour in maintaining the war effort). The strengthening of liberal collectivism after 1945 was supported by the existence of full employment for a significant part of the period, which precluded a direct confrontation between dominant and subordinate interests within society.

2. However, from the 1960s onwards there was an increasing need, irrespective of the political party in power, for more government 'management' of the economy if the twin objectives of economic policy (full employment and price stability) were to be achieved. This produced an apparent movement towards a more *bargained corporatism* model by both Conservative and Labour governments (although most evident under Labour governments, where the inherent party ideology favoured such an approach) characterised by tripartite discussions on economic and social issues and union acceptance of wage restraint through both voluntary and statutory incomes policies.

3. After 1979 there was a significant shift in the dominant political ideology away from corporatism and toward *neo-liberalism/laissez-faire* based on the removal, or at least significant reduction, of direct government economic planning and a reliance on 'free market forces', monetarism and acceptance of high unemployment as the means of maintaining international economic competitiveness and stability. At the same time, trade union power became weakened by economic conditions and management strategies and more regulated by legislation. However, while the government sought a return to 'market individualism', 'collectivism' remained, albeit in modified forms, in those areas where trade unions were able to maintain some presence and management was prepared to continue some form of collective relationship.

4. The election of 'new' Labour in 1997 has produced another shift in government approach to industrial relations. In order to become electable, the Labour Party felt it necessary to distance itself from the trade union movement (unions becoming simply 'one of many pressure groups seeking to influence the government'[26], rather than 'the senior partners as of old'[27]) and, like social democrat or labour parties in other countries, to move 'away from Keynesian based state intervention, full employment and welfarism, towards greater support for market competition, deregulation and privatization'[28]. It projected a 'third way' between the Conservative deregulated individualism of the free market and previous attempts at a more corporatist regulation. This 'third way' has included a number of themes – including 'stakeholder economy', 'welfare to work', 'social partnership' and 'fairness at work' – although, significantly, the government's approach to partnership is primarily one of 'partnership at work' at the level of the organisation, rather than 'social partnership' at the macro society level[29].

It is important to recognise that UK government strategy towards industrial relations is, to some extent, constrained by the different dominant political ideology and form of industrial relations which exists in most other European Union countries and which is expressed through the policies and Directives of the European Union. There are now, in effect, **two political ideology axes** to be considered in the context of UK industrial relations – one national and the other European – and the critical issue is the extent to which these support or conflict with each other.

Position of the judiciary and police

The **judiciary is largely independent** of the government. Although Strinati[30] argued that this autonomy arises from the judiciary having a 'mediatory role' in social relations, many others cite the apparent hostility of the judiciary towards the interests of employees and trade unionism as evidence of its autonomy being supportive of the dominant ideology within society. It is important to understand that the judiciary, in the UK, occupies a dual role within the state system:

- It interprets and applies statute law legitimised by Parliament.
- It determines and legitimises the common law (legal regulation of those areas not covered by statute).

There is little doubt that in the UK the common law approach to both individual and collective labour matters is based firmly on a liberal individualistic ideology. This in turn influences the judiciary's interpretation of statute law. Strinati described the **past conflict between the judiciary and the government** in terms of 'preserving the implications of laissez faire versus the provision of legal recognition of the functions of trade unionism'[31]. This can clearly be seen in the expression of statutory rights for trade unions as 'privileges' or 'immunities' which exempt them from the application of *laissez-faire* legal doctrines. Consequently, Crouch argued, wherever the courts are faced with a situation 'where the scope of the legal immunity is unclear, the judiciary, as guardian of the liberal tradition of Common Law, is likely to revert to a logic of reasoning hostile to combinations'[32].

Any notion of judicial impartiality is further weakened by the nature of **judges and the judgmental process**. The socioeconomic and ideological background of most judges, and the legal profession from which they come, is more compatible with those of the dominant managerial ideology within society than with those of the subordinate ideology of collectivism and trade unionism. Lord Justice Scrutton[33], as long ago as 1920, recognised the difficulty in industrial relations matters of understanding and relating to ideas and perceptions which were in essence alien to his own. At the same time, the judgmental process requires that the judiciary decide between the rights of contestants in any particular case rather than mediate a compromise. Consequently, Wedderburn argued, 'a court that intervenes in an industrial conflict cannot be "neutral"; it will take one side or the other'[34] and, generally, in so doing will add the weight of 'legal right' to management's side.

The **development of Industrial Tribunals** in the 1970s (now called Employment Tribunals), with their intended emphasis on a more practical and impartial approach through the inclusion of two 'lay assessors' (one employer and one trade union), was seen by some as a significant move towards overcoming the defects, for labour, of the traditional legal system. However, this has not been the case. Bootham and Denham[35] found, from an examination of Tribunal cases covering unfair dismissal connected with trade union membership, that not only did the decisions appear to be very supportive of the managerial prerogative but also the system itself still individualises the contractual relationship even where the issue has its roots in the collective act of seeking to organise and secure union recognition. Furthermore, despite the introduction of this form of special 'labour court', jurisdiction in respect of issues relating to the more important matter of employer and trade union rights in the conduct of industrial disputes remains with the traditional High Court.

The primary **role of the police**, in relation to industrial relations, has been to maintain 'peace' and 'public order' during picketing. In carrying out this function the police have to protect both the rights of those picketing, which the law defines as peacefully communicating and persuading, and the rights of non-strikers and employers to continue working. However, the reality of the purpose of picketing, namely to stop the supply of labour and materials to an establishment, means that these rights are incompatible. Thus, because the law recognises only a limited right of picketing and not the reality, police action to constrain picketing within the law will invariably be perceived as anti-union and supportive of management (see Box 8.2). This has been the case, particularly, in respect of enforcing the limit of six on the number of pickets introduced by the Code of Practice in 1980. There have also, in the past, been a number of newspaper reports in the UK of the use of the police apparatus (involving the Special Branch and possible telephone tapping) for surveillance of union 'militants' and during major disputes[36]. While, Kahn *et al.* believe that in the UK 'police forces do not ... maintain any regular, systematic intelligence gathering operation about industrial disputes'[37], the same certainly cannot be said for countries where governments regard unions as a focus for the expression of social unrest (such as South Africa during the *apartheid* regime and Indonesia).

Box 8.2	Police and picketing – NUM/NCB dispute, 1984

The police role in picketing has been particularly dramatised at times of mass picketing where the numbers of both pickets and police involved, and the associated tension, confrontation and sometimes violence, have brought the issue firmly into the area of 'law and order'. The NCB/NUM dispute in 1984 showed that any empathy between strikers and police (who, in most disputes, come from the same local community) is lost when police are drawn in from outside areas in large numbers to confront mass picketing – rather the reverse, an exacerbation of tension and possible violence. The police role, normally confined to the site of the picketing, was significantly extended during that dispute when police both stopped striking miners from leaving Kent and Yorkshire to picket in Nottinghamshire and ejected visiting pickets from private houses under the threat of arrest on the grounds of 'reasonable suspicion' that they would 'breach the peace'.

8.3 Government intervention and strategies

The past three decades have seen contrasting government strategies in the UK:

■ The Labour government's strategy during the late 1970s, based on a corporatist ideology, was to support trade unionism and collective bargaining; to promote the use of conciliation and arbitration processes to resolve disputes; to regulate incomes; and to promote employee participation and enhance employee protection during and at the end of the employment contract.

■ In marked contrast, the Conservative government's strategy during the 1980s, based on a liberalist/*laissez-faire* ideology, was to redress the perceived power imbalance in favour of trade unions and allow management to re-exert its prerogative; to promote 'responsible' trade unionism; to protect individual members against union 'tyranny'; and to promote employment opportunities and labour flexibility through deregulating employment.

■ Now, 'new' Labour's employment strategy emphasises 'inclusion', 'social partnership' and 'fairness at work' (but without any special favours towards trade unions). It has introduced a national minimum wage, re-introduced a statutory recognition procedure and has been more prepared to adopt the social dimension of the European Union. Certainly, Metcalf, a member of the Low Pay Commission, believes that the Commission's work was 'an exemplar of social partnership' which 'rehabilitated unions and employers into a process that contrasts sharply with the "there is no such thing as society" confrontational Thatcher era'[38]. Similarly, the TUC and CBI presented the government with a joint report, identifying both areas of agreement and disagreement, during the government's consultation process for the proposed statutory recognition procedure[39].

Market regulator

Governments influence the operation of the labour market in a variety of ways. Perhaps not surprisingly, given its persistently high levels in most industrialised countries, attention has been focused on government **strategies aimed at dealing with unemployment** (see Box 8.3). In this context, Schmid *et al.*[40] distinguish between a *passive labour market policy* (the replacement of at least part of the employee's lost wages through unemployment benefit) and *active labour market policies* (investment in measures intended to redirect the unemployed into new jobs through training and development, mobility allowances or temporary job creation). They point out that in most countries these policies are not integrated but managed through separate mechanisms (with active policies being associated with government institutions having responsibility for 'employment', 'trade' or 'education' and the passive policy being associated with government institutions of 'social welfare'). This institutional division is compounded at times of recession with its associated increase in unemployment and reduction in government revenue. The cost of maintaining active labour market policies may be under greater pressure, at the very time they are most needed, because of the increased demand on the passive unemployment benefit (which is often a legal entitlement) – the only real alternative being to reduce the level of the benefit entitlement. Furthermore, in so far as labour market policies (either passive or active) are financed directly by the contributions of employers and those in employment, any increased demands may result in increasing labour costs.

Hollinshead and Leat[41] point out that liberal individualist (*laissez-faire*) governments are likely to adopt strategies which seek to 'price people back into jobs' by reducing social security benefits and the organisation's social wage costs and, at the same time, place the responsibility on management for ensuring an adequately trained labour force. Certainly, the Thatcherite policies of the 1980s focused on reducing union power, on deregulation of the labour market and on individualisation of the employment relationship. However, corporatist governments are more likely to accept responsibility for developing training initiatives (particularly for the young and unemployed), support management's own training, encourage the sharing of the available work (through reduced overtime, job sharing and general reductions in working hours) and protect living standards by maintaining levels of social security support. As Visser argues[42], the turnround in economic performance and unemployment in The Netherlands during

---

Box 8.3	Worldwide unemployment

The ILO estimates that 1 billion people across the world (one third of the workforce) are either unemployed or under-employed – 150 million are formally unemployed and over 900 million want to work more or are not earning a living wage. Wages, as a proportion of total national income, have declined in most countries since the mid-1980s.

Two of the main challenges facing labour markets in industrialised countries are as follows:

■ High and persistent unemployment coupled with the emergence of the 'working poor';

■ Informalisation of economies accompanied by dualism in labour markets leading to increased 'insider–outsider' differentiation.

Three alternative approaches are emerging:

■ Distribute what jobs are available more evenly (by job sharing and reducing working time); this might allow something like full employment, albeit at a lower general level of income for everyone, but it could decrease labour productivity and further reduce international competitiveness.

■ Develop a competitive edge in hi-tech, high-skill production which might stimulate the economy (but not necessarily employment), and ensure that those not employed are able to be occupied in 'socially useful' activity.

■ Adopt a low labour cost strategy to try to regain some of the jobs which have been lost to the developing world (with a consequent effect on their employment levels), however, the current labour cost differentials are so great that this may be difficult if not impossible.

Sources: Address by the Director of Employment (ILO) at an Employment Department seminar in September 1994, reported in 'Labour markets in the world economy', *Employment Gazette*, November 1994, p. 383; S. Milne, 'Billion jobless worldwide', *Guardian*, 24 September 1998.

the 1980s and early 1990s was largely the result of 'responsive corporatism' involving the adoption of 'jobs-before-incomes' policies (particularly by unions) within co-ordinated collective bargaining based on bipartite central guidelines. Certainly, Sparrow and Marchington believe that the 'new' Labour government has sought to integrate the two policy strands through its ' "new deal" for the unemployed with changes in welfare provisions and recruitment subsidies as part of a welfare-to-work programme'[43]. Indeed, with the number of unemployed claiming benefit declining to about a million and it being claimed that there is a similar number of job vacancies, the government has started to talk about 'full-employment' – even though the statistics are open to a very wide range of interpretations[44].

Government is also always concerned about the **level of incomes**, and their potential effect on inflation, as part of its role in managing the economy. However, it is important to distinguish between an indirect role exercised through the government's fiscal and monetary policies (*incomes management*) and a more direct role in regulating the results of collective bargaining (*incomes policy*). Towers defined an incomes policy as 'a package of measures, applied simultaneously or sequentially, which seek to intervene directly in the processes of income determination and the working of labour markets for the purposes of moderating the rate of price inflation, and which also seeks to contribute towards greater equality in the distribution of pay and improvements in labour market efficiency'[45].

An active **incomes policy** role formed an important element of UK government strategy throughout the 1960s and 1970s. However, it was generally short term, negative and economic in character, involving a temporary restriction on the level of pay increases as an aid to achieving a reduction in inflation, price stability and international competitiveness. Davies[46] identified several key issues which affected the operation and acceptability of incomes policy:

- *Norm criteria*. The criteria needed to be simple, flexible and fair and was based on either the expected growth in the 'national product' or, more usually, the existing or anticipated range of inflation (with pay increases being restricted to a level lower than the rate of inflation). Although the incomes policy 'norm' was intended to be a maximum, it invariably represented the minimum which employees expected to receive and, on the whole, did little to change the existing pattern of wage differentials.

- *Exceptions to the norm*. Exceptions included both special emotive groups (nurses, police, firemen, etc.) and strong bargaining groups who might have otherwise openly challenged the incomes policy by seeking to secure higher wage increases through direct action (miners). Self-financing increases based on improvements in productivity were also allowed. Although such deals encouraged a shift in bargaining towards 'ability to pay' and 'productivity' criteria, nevertheless they created a major loophole by which trade unions and employers could collude in agreeing 'above-norm' increases under the pretext of productivity improvements.

- *Control and enforcement*. Only the Social Contract (1974–9) came close to the ideal of a voluntary policy administered by the parties themselves. More usually control was exercised by an 'independent' institution appointed by the government (National Incomes Commission, 1962–4; National Board for Prices and Incomes, 1965–70; Pay Board, 1973–4). However, the decentralised character of UK pay determination mitigated against effective control and most attention was directed towards major private sector national agreements (such as engineering) and the public sector, which was under the direct or indirect control of the government itself and 'set an example'. Furthermore, there was no real effective sanction against any breach of the incomes policy; indeed, who should be sanctioned – the employer for giving the increase, the employees for demanding or accepting it, or both?

■ *Co-operation*. Trade unions have been hesitant about becoming involved in the operation of an incomes policy because it could restrain their collective bargaining activities, undermine their credibility with their membership and, in effect, allow the government to determine the pay increase for their membership.

The **Conservative government's strategy after 1979** was to avoid any form of general 'incomes policy' (because of its corporatist connotation), while vigorously following a policy of 'incomes management' through its fiscal policies. However, McCarthy argues that there was 'a self-induced if invisible incomes policy' in respect of the public sector, based on cash-limits, which 'was justified by reference to the need to contain public expenditure, rather than because of the example it would set the private sector'[47]. He further argues that the pursuit of a decentralised, fragmented and individualised pay 'free-for-all' (by both government and management) has produced a new form of top-down inflationary wage drift which will require new methods of monitoring and regulation outside the traditional collective bargaining-related incomes policy system. At the same time, the government reduced or abandoned previous institutions of tripartitism: in particular, the role of NEDO (established in 1961 to provide a forum for examining problems within the economy and individual industries) was weakened during the 1980s and finally disbanded in 1992, and the MSC (set up in 1973 to develop and oversee a co-ordinated approach to training) was replaced by a government-controlled Training Agency in 1989, which very soon gave way to the development of unco-ordinated, locally based Training and Enterprise Councils run principally by employers. Crouch argues that Conservative governments 'felt confident that they could take risks with social stability'[48] – primarily because the Labour Party did not appear to offer an effective challenge to be an alternative government and because 'social alienation' was felt most by the generally unorganised unemployed or marginally employed.

See Country profiles 8.1 and 8.2

A number of countries have successfully operated incomes policies over long periods. However, this requires not only that the criteria for pay increases contain some notion of 'social justice' and address problems of pay anomalies but also that the government is prepared to include employers, unions and others in economic and social policy planning – a social contract. In 1990, the TUC Congress endorsed a proposal[49] to co-ordinate the timing of major collective bargaining arrangements with the government's annual Economic Review, a 'public discussion' between government, CBI and TUC on the UK's economic prospects (a similar arrangement to that which exists in Germany and Japan) and the setting of a rate for a national minimum wage. However, the trade unions were at pains to emphasise that this would not be an 'incomes policy'; nor would it involve statutory pay restraint.

In addition to influencing or regulating the rate of wage increase as part of its management of the economy, a government may also have a 'social justice' concern to ensure a **minimum level of wages**. Until 1993, the UK had a number of statutory **Wages Councils**. They originated in the Trade Boards Act (1909) because of a concern regarding the low level of wages in the 'sweated trades', and in 1988 there were 24 Councils plus two Agricultural Wages Boards covering a total of 2.5 million employees. The bulk of these employees were in four industries: retail, catering, clothing and agriculture – industries charac-

Country profile 8.1   Ireland's understandings

Ireland has a long history not only of a centralised approach to wage determination, the first *National Wages Policy* being in 1948, but also of its integration with a social dialogue between government, management and unions. The *First Programme for Economic Expansion* (1959) was directed towards the involvement of trade unions on consultative bodies established to plan the development of Ireland's industrial sector and promote employment rather than contain wage conflict.

During the late 1960s Ireland experienced increasing wage conflict and in 1970 an *Employer–Labour Conference* was established as an alternative to the introduction of a statutory incomes policy. Its objective was to rationalise pay bargaining by setting wage rates across the country. It concluded six National Wage Agreements during the 1970s; up to 1975 this was done on a bipartitite basis but from 1975 the government played a more active role (albeit as part of the employer representation). However, towards the latter part of the 1970s there was increasing pressure from both employers and trade unions to shift the focus of bargaining away from the centralised level. The government responded in 1979 by negotiating a *National Understanding for Economic and Social Development* directly with employers and trade unions containing sections on employment, taxation and social welfare issues as well as a pay agreement (this was followed by a second National Understanding in 1980).

The Understanding broke down largely because the government was unable to achieve its economic and social policy commitment and employers continued to pressure for decentralisation of pay bargaining. Consequently, there were no centralised agreements for much of the 1980s. However, in 1987 the government managed to gain acceptance, from not only

unions and employers but also other interested groups, for a *Programme for National Recovery* which set out agreed general guidelines for pay and a reduction in hours (to be implemented through local bargaining) and targets for government economic and social policy. At the same time, the government implemented measures aimed at cutting public sector costs and reducing inflation. This was followed, in 1991, by a further *Programme for Economic and Social Progress* which set out a ten-year strategy for both the economy and industrial relations. Like its predecessor, it continued the policy of seeking moderate pay increases (based on a three-year agreement) alongside developments in economic and social policy (including encouraging developments in employee involvement).

A new *Programme for Competitiveness and Work* was concluded in 1994, followed by *Partnership 2000 for Inclusion, Employment and Competitiveness* in 1996. The significance of this latter 'understanding' lies in the larger role for other interested groups in the discussions leading up to the agreement (particularly those representing the unemployed and voluntary organisations) and the inclusion of clauses not only allowing for limited locally agreed increases but also committing the parties to promoting industrial harmony (by referring disputes to the Labour Relations Commission, Labour Courts or other third-party mechanism) and developing a partnership approach at the organisation level.

Sources: F. von Prondzynski, 'Ireland: corporatism revived', in A. Ferner and R. Hyman (eds), *Changing Industrial Relations in Europe*, Blackwell, 1998; 'New national pay deal agreed', *European Industrial Relations Review*, no. 277, February 1997, pp. 24–5 and 30–31.

Country profile 8.2   The Australian 'Accord'

In Australia an 'Accord' was drawn up between the Australian Labour Party and the Australian Council for Trade Unions prior to the 1982 election and encompassed a broad range of issues including legislation, taxation, social security, investment policy and non-wage incomes as well as wages. After the election the Accord was endorsed by a National Economic Summit Conference which brought together not just government (both federal and state level), employers and unions but also representatives of welfare groups. The Accord moved into its Mark VIII version in 1995.

During the first half of the 1980s the wage part of the Accord provided for wage indexation (linked to increases in cost of living) within centralised awards. Most unions accepted this and those which tried to obtain pay increases outside the Accord were not only unsuccessful but unsupported by the rest of the union movement. However, the government withdrew its commitment to full wage indexation in 1985 (at a time of severe economic crisis) and the wage award increases during the second half of the 1980s became more dependent on unions agreeing to measures which enhanced productivity and performance and improved 'structural efficiency'. During the 1990s the emphasis moved towards the development of enterprise agreements, with the centralised award acting as a 'safety-net' minimum increase.

Whitfield believes that the Accord was more successful than the UK's 'social contract' of the 1970s because there was a stronger link between the political party and the union movement; the Australian unions were facing a worse economic situation and did not have the same confidence as the UK unions following their 'defeat' of the Heath government; and the Australian arbitration system not only provided for a more centralised collective bargaining system but also was able to implement the policy in a more flexible way than had been the case in the UK.

Sources: K. Whitfield, 'The Australian wage system and its labor market effects', *Industrial Relations*, vol. 27, no. 2, 1988, pp. 149–65; K. Hancock and J. E. Isaac, 'Australian experiments in wage policy', *British Journal of Industrial Relations*, vol. 30, no. 2, 1992, pp. 213–36; E. M. Davis and R. D. Lansbury, 'Employment relations in Australia', in G. J. Bamber and R. D. Lansbury (eds), *International and Comparative Employment Relations* (3rd edn), Sage, 1998, pp. 125–30.

See also Country profiles 9.2 and 12.1 and Box 5.3.

---

terised by a high proportion of small and scattered organisations, a high proportion of female and part-time labour and a low level of unionisation. The Councils were tripartite bodies composed of trade union and employer representatives plus independent members whose role was to conciliate between the two sides or, if necessary, to vote with one or other side in order to finalise an 'agreement'. This agreement was expressed in the form of a statutory regulation legally enforceable on the organisations in the industry.

The **function of Wages Councils** may be viewed in two ways:

- As a means of **dealing with the problem of low pay**. However, the four industries remained the lowest-paid and, even with statutory enforcement, the proportion of employers investigated who were found to be underpaying was 41 per cent in 1981, but there were only eight prosecutions among the 12,000 establishments where infringements of Wages Councils' orders were discovered[50].

See Chapter 9 –
Collective bargaining

- As a **precursor and aid to the development of voluntary collective bargaining arrangements**. It was argued that their existence allowed trade unions to demonstrate their ability to represent and bargain on behalf of the employees and, in so doing, be able to develop their organisation to a sufficient level to secure and maintain voluntary collective bargaining arrangements. However, in 1980 ACAS reported[51] that the lack of progress in developing collective bargaining necessitated the retention of Wages

Councils and that there might even be scope for their extension into other areas of low pay.

While for some, Wages Councils were an important safety net ('ambulances which pick up those who are too weak to survive without help'[52]), others saw them as 'interfering with market forces by keeping wages, prices and unemployment artificially high'[53]. Certainly, the Conservative government believed that Wages Councils[54] hindered the expansion of employment in the service industries by pricing people out of possible jobs and by creating a bureaucratic administrative burden for both the government (in monitoring and enforcing the orders) and the small companies which comprised the majority of employers. The fact that 30 per cent of employees in these industries were paid the statutory minimum rate was cited as evidence that pay rates were higher than necessary to recruit and retain staff. The government, consequently, first restricted the scope of Wages Councils by excluding those under 21 years of age (approximately half a million) and limiting their regulation to setting only a basic minimum hourly rate and overtime entitlement and no other terms and conditions of employment (Wages Act, 1986). Then, in 1993 (TUERA), they were completely abolished. Significantly, Ireland still retains its similar system of Joint Labour Committees with 15 JLCs covering 88,000 employees[55].

An alternative approach to tackling the problem of low pay is a statutory **national minimum wage** (NMW), which many countries have had for some time[56] but which has only recently been introduced in the UK (National Minimum Wage Act, 1998). The major arguments against a NMW, like those supporting the abolition of the Wages Councils, centre on a belief that it restricts the operation of a 'free market', tends to push up all wages as employees above the minimum level seek to restore their differentials and reduces employment levels by 'pricing people out of jobs'. However, as Blackburn pointed out, the introduction of a NMW 'is not necessarily a very revolutionary reform' and in other western European countries such schemes 'are not designed to promote equality, but merely to relieve the worst extremes of poverty'[57] (i.e. are 'safety nets'). Indeed, he noted that some observers see these minima as 'molehill levels' and that the real problem of low pay can only be tackled by having some form of 'maximum income limits' as well as 'minimum wages'. Nevertheless, the introduction of the NMW in the UK has been heralded as 'without doubt one of the most far-reaching ... commitments in the field of social policy and arguably the most significant government intervention in private sector pay-setting since the ill-fated prices and incomes policies of the 1970s'[58].

The first step in establishing a NMW was the setting up of a Low Pay Commission (LPC) to **recommend the level at which it should be set**. In its 1997 Business Manifesto, the Labour Party had stated that any NMW 'must be sensible' and 'not harm competitiveness'[59]. This was carried though into the terms of reference of the LPC where, in determining the level of the NMW, it was required to take into account 'wider economic and social implications; the likely effect on employment and inflation; the impact on competitiveness of business, particularly small firms; and the potential impact on costs to industry and the Exchequer'[60]. Metcalf points out that the LPC arrived at a pragmatic 'hybrid definition of pay' which included 'bonuses, profit-related pay, merit pay and productivity payments; piece rates; sales commission; tips and gratuities paid ... via the employer; and free accommodation (only up to £20 a week)', but which excluded 'overtime or shift premium and call-out pay; special allowances for working in dangerous or unpleasant working conditions ..., standby and on-call allowances; London weighting and other location allowances; pension and life assurance contributions paid by employers; subsidized or free meals; staff discounts; and cash tips paid direct to a worker by a customer'[61].

While some unions, in their evidence to the LPC, argued for the NMW to be set at £4.60 per hour, some employers believed that £3.20 per hour was the maximum that could be afforded and remain competitive. In the end, the LPC recommended £3.60 per hour for those aged 21 and above and £3.20 per hour for those aged 18–20 (with this rate also applying to those over 21 years of age undertaking training for up to six months). The government accepted the LPC's recommendation of a 'basic' rate of £3.60 per hour, but lowered the recommended 'young person' rate to £3.00 per hour and extended its coverage to those aged 18–21. The NMW came into effect in April 1999 and, despite earlier statements that the NMW was not to be subject to an automatic annual up-rating, the government announced (February 2000) an increase in the 'basic' rate of 10p per hour and in the 'young person' rate of 20p per hour (although it continued to reject pressure to include 21-year-olds in the 'basic' rather than 'young person' rate)[62]. In addition, the LPC is to be reconvened to make further recommendations for 2001.

It was estimated that the introduction of the NMW gave increases averaging 30 per cent to about 2 million workers – the majority employed in three industries: retail, health and hospitality (hotel and catering)[63]. Metcalf argues that the **individuals most likely to gain** are 'females, part-timers, youths, non-whites, those with short tenure, single parents and those with no other worker in the household' and those working in small firms or 'who work from home, whose jobs are not permanent and who work at weekends'[64]. In line with previous research[65], the evidence during the first year of the NMW shows 'the biggest narrowing in the hourly pay gap between men and women since 1991' and 'there does not appear to have been a damaging knock-on effect on differentials higher up the pay scale'[66]. Nevertheless, there were reports of some retail and catering firms dropping their pay rates for young workers down to the NMW level[67], and of 'illegal employment practices [and] a climate of fear' among some low-paid workers (particularly ethnic female workers with relatively poor English) when they raised problems about their pay with their employer[68].

Under the legislation, there are two main **avenues of enforcement**. First, any employee who believes that he or she is being underpaid has the right to inspect the employer's records and may take a case to either the Employment Tribunal or civil court where the onus of proof is on the employer. Second, the combined Inland Revenue and Contributions Agency has powers to issue enforcement notices and, if ignored, to impose a penalty of twice the hourly NMW rate per day for each employee being underpaid. Significantly, the legislation also provides for criminal offences, with a fine of up to £5,000 for each offence, in respect of wilful refusal to pay the NMW and failure to keep proper records.

Employer

A substantial proportion of the national workforce in most industrialised countries is employed, directly or indirectly, by the government in the **public sector** (see Table 8.1(a)). However, the importance of the public sector stems not only from the size of its employment but also from its potential to cover a wide range of organisations and industries. In addition to the departments of government at both national and local levels (including such public services as health, education, police, fire and prisons) it may include public utility industries (communications, transport, coal, electricity, gas and water) and commercial organisations (aircraft and car manufacture, steel production and banking). Consequently, the policies and actions of the government in the public sector are likely to have a significant impact on the industrial relations system as a whole.

The **level of employment** in the UK public sector grew by over a quarter during the 1960s and 1970s from 24 per cent to 30 per cent of the total national workforce (see Table 8.1(b)). Although it has declined since 1979, it remains a substantial employer with some 5.1 million people (20 per cent of the total national workforce) in 1996. The vast majority of this reduction has been in the 'corporations' group and reflects the Conservative government's privatisation programme over the 1980s. It undertook some 30 different privatisation programmes, which included whole service industries (telecommunications, gas, electricity and water); major organisations in the production and manufacturing sectors (British Aerospace, Britoil, Rolls-Royce, British Shipbuilders, British Steel, Rover Cars) and transport (National Freight Corporation, Associated British Ports, British Airports Authority, British Airways, bus companies); and parts of government departments (Ministry of Defence dockyards, Royal Ordnance Factories, Trustee Savings Bank, National Girobank).

Much of the public sector has, in the past, displayed managerial characteristics different from those in the private sector. The centralised nature of its policy and decision making, although facilitating governmental liaison and control, tended to relegate 'managers' to a primarily administrative role in implementing the

Table 8.1(a) Public sector employment* (as % of total employment)

	1979	1990	1996
Japan	8.8	8.1	5.9
Germany	14.7	15.6	15.3
Netherlands	14.7	15.1	13.5
Australia	16.2	15.6	14.8
United States	16.1	15.5	13.2
United Kingdom	21.2	19.6	14.1
Sweden	29.9	31.8	30.7

* Excluding employees in public enterprises.

Sources: 1979 and 1990 – 'Public sector industrial relations into the 1990s', *European Industrial Relations Review*, no. 233, June 1993, Table 1, p. 14; 1996 – *National Accounts*, OECD, 1999.

Table 8.1(b) UK
public sector
employment (1961,
1979 and 1996)

	1961 Number	1979 Number	%	1996 Number	%	Change 1979–96 (%)
Total public sector	5859	7449	–	5130	–	–31
Corporations	2200	2065	28	410[1]	8	–80
Central government	1790	2387	32	987[1]	19	–59
NHS	*–*	*1152*	*16*	*1192[1]*	*23*	*+4*
Local government	1869	2997	40	2637	51	–12
Education	*–*	*1539*	*21*	*1183[2]*	*23*	*–23*

[1] The shift to NHS trusts has meant that in 1996 1.1 million NHS employees should be included under 'corporations' not 'central government'.

[2] The education figure for 1996 does not include some 'grant funded' schools, universities and other institutions of further or higher education which were within local government in 1979 but are now regarded 'private' sector.

Sources: Economic Trends, Annual Supplement 1997; S. Kessler and F. Bayliss, *Contemporary British Industrial Relations* (3rd edn), Macmillan, 1998, Table 7.1, p. 133.

allocated tasks rather than determining them. Certainly, Pendleton believes that the distinctiveness of industrial relations in the nationalised industries came from 'the exercise of political influence on the determination of business strategy, organization structure and labour relations decisions'[69]. At the same time, the ideology projected for and within the public sector of their responsibility for providing a 'public service' to the community was often associated with an internal unitary ideology in respect of organisational relationships. The employees' commitment to the objectives and activities of the service tended to be taken for granted.

The distinctive position of the public sector was further accentuated by the absence of or relative difficulty in applying and reconciling market criteria such as price, competition and profitability with social need and benefit criteria. Winchester suggests that the **past model of a 'good' public sector employer** was one of 'stability ... based on implicit understanding that as long as government and senior management discharged their responsibility to be "good" employers, then employees and their union representatives would accept a reciprocal obligation to avoid industrial conflict'[70]. This was reflected in a number of elements which underpinned industrial relations in the public sector:

■ The government accepted, and even encouraged, unionisation and the establishment of formal collective bargaining machinery, although a distinction was generally maintained between the negotiation of terms and conditions of employment at the national level and joint consultation on other issues at the organisational level.

■ Collective bargaining, particularly within the central government and local authorities segments of the public sector, relied on 'comparisons' with the private sector for determining appropriate pay levels rather than the government's 'ability to pay' or 'productivity'. However, these latter issues formed an important part of negotiations within the public corporation segment.

■ 'Independent' pay review bodies and inquiries were used, together with normal arbitration, as important adjuncts to bipartite negotiations in order to resolve differences without the need for industrial action.

However, this model came under increasing pressure during the late 1970s as the public sector came to be perceived as the focal point of instability and conflict within the industrial relations system culminating in the 'winter of discontent' in 1978–9. Thomson and Beaumont[71] attribute this shift to three economic factors:

■ Pay increases within the public sector, particularly among manual groups such as miners and local authority workers, were perceived to be setting the level for the 'annual wage round' and therefore significantly contributing to general wage inflation.

■ There was an increasing belief in the need to reduce the growth of public sector expenditure in order to redirect resources to the private sector as a necessary precursor of economic growth.

■ These factors resulted in a tighter application of incomes policy within the public sector and a consequent increase in industrial conflict.

To these may be added a fourth factor: namely, that the disputes generated within the public sector as a result of these economic factors included emotive disputes (NHS, dustmen, firemen, etc.) as well as less emotive ones (miners, electrical workers, etc.), but all of them seriously affected the public.

The public sector remained 'the main area of conflict in industrial relations' after 1979 because, as Kessler and Bayliss point out, the Conservative government believed 'that the public sector was intrinsically inefficient; it was over-manned, bureaucratic, a drain on the public purse and the home of powerful unions which were unconstrained by market forces'[72]. Apart from simply shifting activities completely to the private sector through privatisation, Ferner[73] argues that the remaining public sector was, in many countries but to different degrees, involved in a **'reconstruction of the state'** which centred around increased management freedom (through devolution of authority and financial control, but within tight budgetary controls), more separation of policy making (government) from its execution (through semi-autonomous agencies) and the exposure of the public sector to market forces (through competitive tendering and market testing). In the UK, this was accompanied by a number of **industrial relations strategies** directed towards the following:

■ *Decentralisation and fragmentation*. The establishment of distinct executive agencies within the 'civil service' and the encouragement of schools, colleges and hospitals to 'opt out' of centralised systems (coupled with the freedom of these separately managed units to establish their own terms and conditions of employment) have tended to create organisational variations within the same industry. At the same time, the use of competitive tendering and market testing for certain activities (such as cleaning and catering) has resulted not only in competition between public and private sectors but also in the fragmentation of employees within public sector organisations as management sought (often jointly with the union) to develop new working arrangements specific to these areas which would, hopefully, allow the 'in-house' bid to compete successfully on cost terms. Significantly, Winchester and Bach[74] note that, while the use of competitive tendering has resulted in a decline in the number of ancillary employees in the public sector, the number (and pay) of managers has increased.

■ *Weakening comparability*. The Conservative government abolished the Comparability Commission (set up by the Labour government in 1979), removed the right of trade unions to refer disputes to arbitration unilaterally (i.e. without the agreement of the employer), and retained the right to amend the findings of pay review bodies. Pay bargaining in the public sector moved firmly into the areas of 'labour market forces', 'ability to pay', 'productivity' and 'performance'. The issue was projected, by the government, as one of pay versus jobs: pay increases above the cash limits would lead to a reduction in the number of employees.

■ *Pursuit of performance and flexibility*. The concept of a 'good public sector employer' has shifted from one based on setting an example of supportive employment and welfare practices to one of following the lead of the private sector by adopting its competitive, flexible, performance-related ideas in its own employment practices[75]. However, Sinclair[76] argues that there are significant obstacles to the linking of pay to performance appraisal, not least because of difficulties in relating 'private market' concepts to the social, non-profit-making objectives that are still an inherent part of the aims of the 'non-trading' parts of the public sector (such as health, education and police).

Despite the tightening labour market in the late 1990s and the election of a Labour government committed to 'social partnership', 'fairness at work' and the removal of the 'internal market' approach in areas like the NHS, there does not appear to be any dramatic change in the government's approach to the public sector. Certainly the Labour government is equally committed to efficiency and performance in the public sector and has no plans to reverse the process of privatisation, although it has made some moves to tackle long-standing pay problems among teachers and nurses. It is important to recognise that the reduction in the size and scope of the public sector (through the privatisation of industries, services and employers), the 'opting-out' arrangements introduced for schools, colleges and hospitals (allowing them to determine and manage their own affairs) and the internal fragmentation of organisations through the introduction of private sector organisations (competitive tendering) have all contributed to a decrease in the government's role as an employer, and to a consequent decrease in its potential ability to control or influence the industrial relations both within these sectors and across the national industrial relations system as a whole.

Legislator

Kahn-Freund argued, in the early 1980s, that 'the principal purpose of labour law ... is to regulate, to support, and to restrain the power of management and the power of organized labour'[77] – in effect, ensuring a broad balance of power between the two main actors in the industrial relations system. However, in the mid-1990s, Dickens and Hall suggest that the law has taken on a different role. They believe that the period since 1979 has seen the 'final death of voluntarism, under which law was essentially an adjunct to an autonomous, self-regulated system of industrial relations', and more emphasis on the law as a mechanism 'in pursuit of government economic and social objectives ... being seen as a key instrument facilitating labour-market restructuring'[78]. The government's activities in this respect may be subdivided into two main areas.

Legislation on individual legal rights

While some of this legislation may be seen as **selective** in that it seeks to provide protection for particular groups who traditionally have been weakly organised (particularly women, ethnic minorities and young people), other elements are **universal** in their application and apply to all employees irrespective of whether they are well unionised or not. However, this legislation can in no way be described as providing a 'right to work' or 'right to job security'. The introduction of statutory obligations on the employer has not changed the common law basis of the contract of employment: the employee remains obligated to provide honest and faithful service, to do nothing harmful to the employer's interests and to obey all reasonable instructions. 'Reasonableness' under statute law is judged in relation to this common law view of the contract of employment, and no Tribunal or court has the power to order (force) an employer to employ, or continue to employ, any particular individual.

Unlike countries which have placed emphasis on statutory employment rights, it may be argued that their development in the UK, particularly during the postwar period, has been the **result of, rather than replacement for, trade unions and collective bargaining**. They can be seen as a process of legal confirmation and extension of benefits which had already been achieved by trade unions in a significant number of organisations through collective bargaining – it represents a transfer of such benefits to other less well-organised or non-unionised groups and organisations. At the same time, the establishment of a legal 'floor of rights' provides a springboard from which well-organised trade unions can seek further improvements through collective bargaining. However, the development of such legislation can also weaken the position of trade unions, in that its protection applies to all employees and therefore there may be less perceived need to join a trade union. At the same time, it conditionally 'legitimises' management actions such as dismissal and redundancy and may make trade union resistance to such 'lawful' management action difficult and appear unreasonable.

Legislative regulation of employment in the UK is not new – for example, in the early nineteenth century, before trade unions had become permanently established, the Truck Act (1831) placed an obligation on employers to pay wages in cash not kind, while the Factory Act (1833) was the first in a line of legislation which restricted the hours of work of women and young people[79]. However, it was not until the 1960s and 1970s that the UK saw a major extension of legal regulation into areas outside 'health and safety': the issue of contract of employment notices, minimum periods of notice, unfair dismissal, redundancy payments, maternity leave and payments, time off for public duties, etc. In addition, there was other important legislation in the areas of equal pay, sex discrimination and race relations, as well as further developments in health and safety at work.

During the 1980s, as Dickens and Hall point out, the Conservative government regarded this legislation 'not as essential minimum standards but as "burdens on business" (particularly in respect of small employers) which deter the employment of more people'[80]. They point out that, although the government did not abolish the substantive legal protection, it sought to limit its application to 'atypical' workers by extending qualifying criteria or indirectly worsened the position (for example, removing the limitations on the hours of work of women in the Sex Discrimination Act, 1986). The government was more concerned to establish rights for the individual in their relationship with a trade union (and to provide them with assistance in pursuing such cases through the creation of a Commissioner for the Rights of Trade Union Members and a Commissioner for Protection against Unlawful Industrial Action). Most importantly, the government consistently opposed (or tried to weaken) the creation of new protection rights within EU Directives and opted out of the Social Chapter of the Maastricht Treaty. Nevertheless, during the 1990s EU Directives and European Court decisions required the Conservative government to make some changes: for example, bringing the qualifying periods for part-time employees claiming unfair dismissal or redundancy into line with those for full-time employees[81] and extending redundancy and health and safety consultation to non-unionised employees and organisations[82].

Since its election in 1997, the 'new' Labour government has introduced not only the national minimum wage but also two other important individual rights (Employment Relations Act, 1999) – the right to parental leave (alongside improvements in maternity rights) and the right to be accompanied by a fellow worker or union official during any 'serious' disciplinary or grievance hearing. In addition, it has implemented EU Directives relating to working time and European Works Councils[83].

An important development, in 1971, was the establishment of specialised **Employment Tribunals** (originally called Industrial Tribunals) intended to provide an easily accessible, quick, inexpensive and relatively informal forum in which individual employees could seek legal redress for any infringement of these statutory rights. The Tribunals, which are regionally based, comprise a chairman with legal experience and two lay assessors drawn from panels of management and union practitioners. It was intended that an aggrieved employee should not be inhibited from pursuing his or her case; hence, the relative informality of the proceedings, the intention that each side (employee and management) should present its own case and that costs would be awarded against the losing side only if the Tribunal considers that the employee's claim or management's defence has been frivolous or vexatious. However, the system has become increasingly legalistic with approximately one-third of employees and half the employers being represented by solicitors or barristers. In this respect the employee is more hampered than the employer by the inability to obtain legal aid to pursue cases before a Tribunal.

However, many employers believe that it is too easy for an employee to make an unfounded claim in order to express a grievance in public or in anticipation that the employer will offer an out-of-court payment to avoid the inconvenience of a Tribunal hearing, and in so doing, will cause the employer to expend considerable time and effort in preparing to defend the case. This can be mitigated, to a certain extent, in three ways:

See Chapter 12 – Conciliation and arbitration

■ Conciliation through ACAS prior to any formal Tribunal hearing.

■ Arbitration through ACAS, with legally enforceable awards, as a voluntary alternative to a Tribunal hearing (Employment Rights (Dispute Resolution) Act, 1998). ACAS believes that this process 'offers an opportunity to return to the principles of speedy, informal and user-friendly justice that tribunals were originally intended to provide'[84].

■ Either side (but more likely the employer) may request a pre-hearing by the Tribunal to determine whether there are sufficient grounds to justify the case proceeding to a full hearing. This pre-hearing cannot stop the employee from exercising his or her right to a full hearing, although if he or she does proceed the Tribunal may be more disposed towards awarding costs if the case is found in favour of the employer.

Employment Tribunals are supplemented by the **Employment Appeals Tribunal**, whose composition is similar to that of the lower-level Tribunals and which acts as the appellate body for their decisions. The EAT also deals with such matters as appeals against the decision of the Certification Officer in respect of the granting of a certificate of independence or the political activities of trade unions. Despite the creation of this system of specialised 'labour courts', it is important to remember, as Hepple pointed out, that they are not a form of industrial arbitration but a 'court substitute' 'with the function of adjudicating disputes by the application of legal rules'[85]. Inevitably their growth has had the effect of overlaying the management of industrial relations with decisions based on legalism and legal values.

Legislation on collective rights

The government is able to **determine the power and status of the participants** in the industrial relations system. Until the 1970s, governmental intervention in the UK, based on a liberal collectivism approach, was primarily one of providing immunities for trade unions from the application of the *laissez-faire* doctrine by the courts. The voluntarist nature of industrial relations was upheld by the absence of any positive legal support for trade unions seeking to organise and obtain recognition from management and by the refusal to regard collective agreements made between trade unions and management as legally binding and enforceable arrangements. Having safeguarded the industrial position of trade unions through the provision of legal immunities, the government did not seek to directly control the exercise of industrial power.

However, as Lewis pointed out, since 1970 'successive governments representing different interests and ideologies have turned the legal framework of industrial relations into a political football'[86]. In 1971 the Conservative government, through the **Industrial Relations Act**, attempted a comprehensive reform of collective labour law which, still within a basically corporatist ideology, sought to balance some positive gains for trade unions (such as a statutory recognition procedure and rights to disclosure of information) and the individual employee (unfair dismissal) against greater regulation of trade unions' activities (particularly the closed shop and industrial action). However, most of these provisions proved unworkable at the time because the majority of trade unions openly resisted the legislation by refusing to register and the majority of employers appeared to decline to exercise the rights they were given under the legislation. Nevertheless, it showed that the creation of statutory obligations could create situations where individuals, by exercising their legal rights, could upset the collective system of regulation.

The basis of collective labour law was changed by the Labour government during 1974–6 through the **Trade Union and Labour Relations Act (1974)** and the **Employment Protection Act (1975)**, which together repealed much of the Industrial Relations Act (but keeping the unfair dismissal legislation) and provided trade unions with legislative support in areas such as obtaining recognition, the granting of paid time off work to undertake trade union duties, the disclosure of information for the purposes of collective bargaining and consultation prior to redundancies. The legislation strengthened the collective bargaining role of trade unions and was complemented by the government's strengthening of the policy of involving unions in tripartite discussions over economic and social issues and incomes policy.

However, the Conservative Party felt that these measures tilted the balance of power in industrial relations in favour of trade unions and, in particular, in favour of shop stewards and unofficial groups at the organisation level. Consequently, the Conservative government, after 1979, sought to restrict the power of trade unions and strengthen the position of management through the **Employment Acts (1980, 1982, 1988 and 1990)**, the **Trade Union Act (1984)**, and the **Trade Union Reform and Employment Rights Act (1993)**. This legislation involved three main elements:

See Chapter 11 –
Industrial action

1. It restricted the power of trade unions to undertake industrial action by:

    (a) making secondary industrial action and picketing unlawful;
    (b) narrowing the definition of a trade dispute for which trade unions may claim immunity for their actions;
    (c) making trade unions financially liable for unlawful acts carried out by its officers or members;
    (d) requiring unions to inform employers in advance of both a strike ballot and any resultant industrial action and, perhaps more importantly, to supply details of those who will be balloted and called upon to undertake the industrial action; and
    (e) strengthening the employer's right to dismiss strikers.

See Chapter 6 –
Representation at the
workplace

2. It established what Lewis referred to as 'rights to disorganise' by:

    (a) removing the statutory recognition procedure and right to have a 'closed shop' (union membership agreement);
    (b) codifying the right not to belong to a trade union firmly alongside the right to belong and giving the individual the right to join the union of

their choice (where there is more than one union organising employees of a similar class);

(c) requiring the employee every three years to provide the employer with written consent to deduct union subscriptions; and

(d) allowing the employer to offer better terms to employees who accept personal contracts which exclude any union role in negotiating terms and conditions.

*See Chapter 5 –
Trade union
organisation and
structure*

3. It intervened in the internal affairs of trade unions to ensure greater democracy by:

(a) protecting the individual from unreasonable exclusion or expulsion from a trade union;

(b) requiring that the union's NEC and General Secretary be directly elected by the membership through a secret postal ballot with independent scrutiny;

(c) restricting trade union political activities;

(d) requiring the use of secret postal ballots (again with independent scrutiny) in respect of strike action; and

(e) establishing a Commissioner for the Rights of Trade Union Members (CRTUM) and a Commissioner for Protection against Unlawful Industrial Action (CPAUIA) to assist individuals taking legal action against unions.

Despite the fact that these legislative restrictions were resisted by trade unions in the early part of the 1980s and were closely associated with a number of major disputes where, through employer action to enforce these new rights, unions were fined for contempt of court and had their funds sequestrated, nevertheless trade unions now appear resigned to having to work within this legal regulation.

Certainly, the 'new' Labour government does not intend to repeal all this legislation. However, under the **Employment Relations Act (1999)** it has:

- Removed the requirement for unions to supply employers with details of those who will be balloted and called upon to undertake the industrial action and made it automatically unfair to dismiss striking employees during the first eight weeks of a strike.

- Prohibited the use of 'blacklists' of union members or activists and provided protection where an employee refuses to accept an individual contract on different terms to those that would apply under a collective agreement.

- Abolished both CRTUM and CPAUIA and given the Certification Officer the responsibility for adjudicating any dispute between individual union members and their union.

- Reintroduced a statutory union recognition procedure and given union officials the right to accompany members in any 'serious' disciplinary or grievance hearing.

See Chapter 12 –
Conciliation and
arbitration

Conciliator

Government support for the processes of conciliation and arbitration has existed, in the UK, since the Conciliation Act (1886) and Industrial Courts Act (1919). This has played an important part in the government's policy of seeking to **maintain industrial peace** within the industrial relations system by encouraging trade unions and management, wherever possible, to utilise these facilities, rather than industrial action, to resolve their disputes. However, during the 1960s and 1970s the government also sought to use arbitration as a means of **influencing the outcome of negotiations** by indirectly enlisting the conciliator or arbitrator as an agent for the maintenance of the government's incomes policy. During the 1980s, the government view of arbitration changed from it being seen as an independent third-party intervention to assist the two sides to find a compromise solution to their dispute, to seeing it as an unreasonable restriction on management's freedom and responsibility to make the right decision in the best interests of maintaining the profitability and competitiveness of the business.

8.4 The European Union

The original six-country European Economic Community was established by the Treaty of Rome (1957) primarily to support economic development through increased trade derived from the elimination of barriers to the free movement of goods, services, capital and labour. Weiss notes that at that time 'social policy constituted an alien body' but as the Community has developed it has reached the stage where 'there no longer remains any doubt about the legitimacy of social policy as an independent and essential element of Community policy'[87]. Indeed, the final establishment of the Single European Market in 1992, at a time of increasingly competitive world markets, heightened rather than diminished **the issue of social policy regulation** and the Treaty of Amsterdam (1997) subsequently inserted 'fundamental social rights' as one of the EU's underlying general principles. There is little doubt that Due *et al.* were right when they stated, in the early 1990s, that 'the growing political and economic importance of the EC and its institutions are likely to emerge as a new and highly significant factor, exerting substantial influence on the labour market's industrial relations' and that, in particular, 'the interesting feature of EC co-operation is the emergence of quite new actors in industrial relations, such as the EC Commission and the European Parliament – actors whose roles are essentially supra-national'[88]. Indeed, Jensen *et al.*[89] suggest, using Dunlop's systems model terminology, that there is now a distinct 'EU industrial relations system' with its own actors, institutions and rule-making processes.

The European Union involves, perhaps necessarily, a complex interrelationship of supranational governmental institutions – the European Commission, the European Parliament, European Council (heads of government), the Council of Ministers (specific subject matters) and the European Court of

Justice[90]. The **complexity of the relationship** reflects a number of factors. First, as Teague[91] notes, there is a fundamental difference between the 'negative' integration implicit in the removal of government regulations which inhibit the free movement of goods, capital, labour, etc. and the 'positive' integration required in the development of common policies and institutions to regulate the market as a whole. Second, there are tensions within the EU regarding the political processes of decision making, not only in relation to the relative powers of the central institutions of the Commission, Parliament and the Council of Ministers but, more importantly, in respect of the balance between the EU (as a single entity) and the member national states. Third, so far as industrial relations matters are concerned, there are significant variations in the way in which industrial relations are conducted in each country. Certainly, there was a **conflict of political ideology** between 'liberalist/*laissez-faire*' UK Conservative governments of the 1980s and 1990s and the 'social democratic' ideology of most other EU countries whose more corporatist social partnership between government, capital and labour was reflected in the nature and direction of EU labour policy. This clash of ideologies has been ameliorated to some extent with the election of 'new' Labour in 1997, however, like the preceding Conservative governments, it too is keen for the EU to adopt more 'flexible' employment strategies in the labour market.

The tensions within the EU came to the fore in 1989–91 with the development of the Social Charter, its incorporation as the Social Chapter of the Maastricht Treaty and the UK Conservative government's 'optout'. Due *et al.* describe the **European Social Charter** as 'a sort of "constitution" for the European labour market'[92]. The objective is to ensure that the organisational benefits gained from the 'single market' after 1992 are shared with employees. It aims not only to introduce employment standards but also to enhance the rights of employees (whether through unions or not) to be involved in organisational decision making. Its provisions include the following:

- Fair remuneration and decent rates of pay for all employment;
- An overall improvement in employees' conditions and more protection and harmonisation of working time, flexibility, non-standard employment practices, redundancies, etc.;
- The right of unions to organise, be recognised, negotiate and to undertake industrial action;
- The development of employees' rights to information, consultation and participation.

In 1994, the Commission set out four guiding principles for EU employment policy for the late 1990s[93]: the key to social and economic integration is creating employment, social progress requires economic prosperity and competitiveness, convergence within Europe must also respect diversity within European societies, and common minimum employment standards restrain unfair economic competition. The 1997 Treaty of Amsterdam (which involved the UK's 'new' Labour government signing up to the Social Chapter) went a step further by inserting a new **Employment Chapter**. This committed governments to the objective of promoting a 'high level of employment' and the co-ordination of their employment policies and strategies. Although there is provision for the development of annual employment guidelines (to be agreed by qualified majority voting) and annual review of the implementation of employment policies in member states, nevertheless individual member states are not under any 'binding obligations' in respect of employment policy. Consequently, the Chapter represents 'something of a compromise between the differing views of member states' and 'the need to assuage the fear that the Community would be given real powers to determine employment policy' across the EU[94].

Rhodes argues that the UK's 'optout' from the Social Charter and Social Chapter of the Maastricht Treaty was the result of 'conflict between the proponents of "solidarity" and "subsidiarity", and between the advocates of lesser rather than greater labour market regulation'[95]. Similarly, Towers[96] believes that the UK's 'opt out' was based both on opportunism (the UK gaining a competitive advantage over other European countries to attract inward investment) and belief (that employers should be free to manage their organisations rather than be subjected to extensive legal regulation). Certainly, the Conservative government's desire to retain the ability to promote labour flexibility, as part of its strategy to increase competitiveness and reduce unemployment, was demonstrated in its resistance to the EU Directives on atypical forms of employment and working time.

While the Maastricht Treaty reaffirmed the **principle of subsidiarity** in stating that action should only be taken at the European level if the objectives cannot be 'sufficiently' achieved by the individual member but would be 'better' achieved at European level (Article 3), nevertheless it did redefine the boundaries for the different **processes for determining social policy issues:**

- Matters relating to pay, the right of association and the right to strike or lockout remain *outside the scope of European regulation* and therefore are a matter to be determined by each country.

- Prior to Maastricht, the development and introduction of any regulation on any social policy issues (apart from those relating to the 'working environment') required the unanimous agreement of all countries – thus any country had the right of veto. The Maastricht Treaty extended *qualified majority voting* from just 'working environment' to include 'working conditions', 'information and consultation with workers' and 'equality in labour market opportunities and treatment at work'. The extension of qualified majority voting means, for example, that there will no longer be a need to stretch the interpretation of 'working environment' (generally regarded as being health and safety) as was done with the Working Time Directive in order to avoid the potential use of the veto.

- Significantly, *unanimous agreement* is still required for issues relating to 'social security and social protection of workers', 'protection of workers on termination of contract', 'representation and collective defence of worker interests (including co-determination)' and 'financial contributions for promotion of employment and job creation'. However, as Weiss[97] points out, it can be difficult to draw a boundary between informing and consulting workers (requiring only qualified majority voting) and collective representation and co-determination (requiring unanimous agreement).

| Box 8.4 | The developing European social dialogue |

Intersector level

The process of European-level 'social dialogue' between employers and unions was initiated in 1985 by Jacques Delors. He believed that collective bargaining had an important role to play in securing a more flexible and consensual approach to the development and implementation of social policy within the European Union.

The initial process involved the creation of *working parties* of representatives from the ETUC, UNICE and CEEP and chaired by a Commissioner which produced *joint opinions*. The process was strengthened in 1989 through the establishment of a small steering committee (three employer and three union representatives chaired by a Commissioner) to initiate and stimulate new areas for dialogue as well as assessing and evaluating any joint opinions reached by the working parties[1].

These 'joint opinions' were vague, generalised and of little direct impact. Certainly, UNICE sought to maintain a distinction between 'dialogue' and 'negotiation' and was not prepared, in the light of the trend towards decentralisation, to go as far as the ETUC wished in developing the process into European level 'collective agreements'. Significantly, in 1990 CEEP signed a so-called *European framework agreement* with the ETUC (relating to health and safety, vocational training and training for new technology), which 'invited' public sector organisations to implement its provisions within their normal negotiating arrangements.

In 1991 the ETUC, CEEP and UNICE put forward a joint proposal for a more proactive role in formulating and implementing social policy; subsequently adopted in the Maastricht Treaty (1992)[2]. This contained two major developments in the social dialogue process:

■ In promoting consultation with management and labour and facilitating dialogue between them, the Commission will consult both parties on the possible direction of Community action in the social policy field *before* submitting any formal proposals.

■ If the Commission considers action advisable after such consultations, it will consult management and labour to obtain their opinion or recommendation on its specific proposals. At this point, management and labour may indicate their desire to initiate the process of dialogue between them, which 'may lead to contractual relations, including agreements' (Article 4.1) to be implemented 'in accordance with the procedures and practices specific to management and labour and the Member States' (Article 4.2).

Despite some difficulties, there have been three 'negotiations' between the social partners leading to EU Directives – part-time working, parental leave and fixed-term contracts. However, concerns have been expressed about both the range and representativeness of organisations in the consultation and negotiation processes[3].

Sector level

During the 1960s, the Commission established *joint committees*, with an equal number of employer and worker representatives, in such sectors as agriculture, fishing and road, inland waterway and rail transport (all of which were significantly affected by the development of a common European policy for their sector). Subsequently, joint committees were established for civil aviation, sea transport and telecommunications.

The Commission hoped, initially, that such committees would 'contribute to the construction of a European system of industrial relations and foster free collective bargaining'[4]. The union side of these committees is usually linked to the European Industry Committees, which bring together ETUC-affiliated unions in a particular sector and which may also be the European sections of International Trade Secretariats. However, the development of these committees has been hampered by the lack of a sectoral structure among the employers' organisations at the European level (such as UNICE).

In the 1980s, the Commission sought to extend the process of dialogue to other sectors (such as brewing,

| **Box 8.4** | The developing European social dialogue *(continued)* |

construction, textiles, banking, retail, etc.) through supporting the development of *informal meetings* to exchange views between management and labour and *informal working parties* to undertake joint studies on employment issues within the sector and provide a body which the Commission could consult on any specific proposals. Such arrangements are not dissimilar to the industry Neddies that existed under the NEDO in the UK. The Commission has proposed replacing these bodies with a new common format (Sectoral Dialogue Committees) in any sector where there is a joint request from the social partners[3].

While sectoral dialogue most closely replicates the bargaining structure in most EU countries, its development into a European level of collective bargaining may be hindered by both the development of multi-industry, multinational organisations and the lack of clarity about the relationship between the sector- and intersector-level dialogues[5]. Significantly, both the rail and maritime sector bodies have negotiated agreements on working time to fill the gap left by their exclusion from the general Working Time Directive – unfortunately the road transport sector failed to reach a similar agreement[6].

1. 'The social dialogue – Euro-bargaining in the making', *European Industrial Relations Review*, no. 220, May 1992, pp. 25–9.
2. 'Treaty on European Union – social policy protocol and agreement', *European Industrial Relations Review*, no. 223, August 1992, pp. 34–5.
3. 'Commission sets out options for the future of the social dialogue', *European Industrial Relations Review*, no. 276, January 1997, pp. 24–9; 'Commission reviews future of the social dialogue', *European Industrial Relations Review*, no. 295, August 1998, pp. 13–17.
4. 'The sectoral social dialogue', *European Industrial Relations Review*, no. 224, September 1992, pp. 14–17.
5. 'Prospects for sectoral dialogue', *European Industrial Relations Review*, no. 302, March 1999, pp. 22–4.
6. 'The maritime accord – a pioneering step for the sectoral dialogue', *European Industrial Relations Review*, no. 298, November 1998, pp. 14–16.

A further significant development brought about by the Maastricht Treaty has been an increased role for the social partners (management and unions) in the formulation of policy through the **Social Dialogue** mechanism (see Box 8.4). There have been two major developments in this area. First, at the intersector level, provision has been made for the social partners to reach their own 'agreements' which can then be implemented by Council decision. Second, at the sector level, joint committees in both the rail and maritime sectors have negotiated a 'European agreement' on working time (their industries were not covered by the earlier general Working Time Directive). Certainly, Weiss believes that the 'balance of power between the Commission and the social partners has been shifted considerably to the advantage of the latter'[98], although he is cautious about the ability of the social partners at the European level (ETUC, UNICE and CEEP) to conclude any meaningful 'European collective agreements' because generally they lack a mandate from their respective national representative organisations. The process of social dialogue at the European level has been complemented at the organisational level by the European Works Council Directive, requiring organisations with over 1,000 employees (including at least 150 employees in each of two member states) to establish a European-level Works Council (or other information and consultation mechanism) to deal with transnational issues.

See Chapter 10 – Employee involvement and participation

There is little doubt that a central issue facing the EU is determining the balance between policies directed towards employee protection and those

Case study 8.1 ■ Hoover – business strategy or social dumping?

In 1993 Hoover concluded a new agreement with the Amalgamated Engineering and Electrical Union (AEEU) for its Cambuslang (Scotland) site which employed 975 employees. Three days later it announced the closure of its factory in Longvic (France) and the transfer of activities to Cambuslang; resulting in the loss of 600 jobs in Longvic and the creation of 400 jobs in Cambuslang.

The Cambuslang agreement included the following elements:

■ *Measures to reduce labour costs* – including a one-year pay freeze, no overtime payment for covering production during breaks and a reduction in the shift premium;

■ *Measures to increase labour efficiency and flexibility* – including bell-to-bell working, some multi-skilling, removal of 'restrictive practices' relating to use of contractors and a commitment from employees to co-operate in initiatives to improve quality;

■ *Recruitment of all new employees* to be on a two-year fixed contract at a 15 per cent lower wage and no entitlement to join the pension scheme until the end of the two-year period.

While French workers felt this was an 'appalling agreement' and that the union had negotiated it 'with a gun to their head', the AEEU official for Scotland felt the union had 'nothing to be ashamed of', was 'in the business of defending our members' and had got 'the best deal we could with the company'. Nevertheless, ten days after the closure announcement was made, the European Metalworkers' Federation (including the AEEU and the French affiliated unions) issued a statement condemning Hoover's strategy and announcing

moves to improve co-operation between its member unions. French workplace reaction involved local demonstrations against the relocation, a ten-day strike at Longvic followed by an action plan of refusing to use the plant's stock or trade with Hoover plants in the USA and the UK and, in accordance with French legislation, bringing in consultants to examine and report on the company accounts.

At the same time, the UK government was accused by the French press of being a 'Trojan horse' within Europe 'sacrificing social standards to welcome foreign companies'. However, the UK government felt the increased investment and jobs at Cambuslang were a vindication of its policies aimed at increased labour flexibility through labour market deregulation. The French government called on the European Commission to investigate whether the provision of UK government and EC regional aid to Hoover and its use of the pension fund to invest in Cambuslang was in conflict with EC Directives and law. At the same time, it requested the OECD to investigate whether there had been an infringement of their 1976 Declaration on International Investment and Multinational Enterprises (recommending organisations to provide reasonable notice of changes in their operations and not to threaten to transfer operations in order to influence negotiations).

An important element of Hoover's decision lay in the differences in labour costs between France and Britain. Although average direct labour costs in the UK and France were virtually the same, average total labour costs in France were 25 per cent higher than in Britain because of the much higher average indirect labour costs resulting, in particular, from higher social security payments by the employer.

Source: 'The Hoover affair and social dumping', *European Industrial Relations Review*, no. 230, March 1993, pp. 14–20.

directed towards employment creation (put another way, whether the two policies can be achieved together or whether they conflict). This is closely bound up with the **concept of 'social dumping'** which raises issues of how far labour variations between countries, particularly labour costs, are a legitimate source of competitive advantage. Trade unions, in particular, are concerned that without some regulation and harmonisation of employment protection, working arrangements, social security costs and co-ordination of employment promotion programmes between countries, employees will suffer from the transfer of unemployment as individual countries, organisations and sites compete with each other to attract new investment and jobs on the basis of lower labour costs and greater labour flexibility.

See Case study 8.1

This concern for 'social dumping' is not confined to dumping between countries within the EU, but extends beyond its boundaries and can be seen in calls for the insertion of 'social clauses' into trade agreements with other countries (such as those of south-east Asia) requiring their adherence to minimum labour standards. Basic international labour standards already exist in the form of Conventions and Recommendations made by the UN-based International Labour Organisation (ILO) – originally established in 1919 as part of the League of Nations. However, as Swepston points out, these standards only become 'binding obligations' when a country ratifies a Convention, ratification is 'an entirely voluntary act' and supervision is by government self-reporting of implementation[99]. Some unions have sought to obtain assurances from European companies that that they will not seek to take advantage of cheap labour or lower labour standards in countries outside the EU by obtaining agreements that overseas employment practices will at least conform to ILO Conventions and Recommendations.

See Case study 8.2

Case study 8.2 ■ Faber-Castell – Germany

Faber-Castell manufactures writing, drawing and painting products and employs 5500 people in 14 production and 18 sales companies around the world (including 750 in a re-afforestation project in Brazil). In March 2000 it signed an agreement with IG Metall and the International Federation of Building and Wood Workers committing itself to ensure that the employment and working conditions in its overseas operations respect ILO Conventions and Recommendations. It also established a joint committee of management and union representatives to monitor the implementation of the agreement across its operations.

Code of Conduct regarding the Rights of Workers

1. Employment is freely chosen
Forced labour must not be used (ILO Convention nos 29 and 105). Workers will not be required to lodge 'deposits' or their identity papers with their employers.

2. No discrimination in employment
Equal opportunities and equal treatment regardless of race, colour, gender, creed, political views, nationality, social background or any other special characteristics shall be provided (ILO Conventions nos 100 and 111).

3. Child labour is not used
Child labour must not be used. Only workers aged 15 and over, or over the age of compulsory education if higher, may be employed (ILO Convention no. 138).

4. Respect for the right to freedom of association and free collective bargaining
The right of all workers to form and join trade unions shall be recognised (ILO Conventions nos 87 and 98). Workers' representatives must not be discriminated against and must have access to

Case study 8.2 ■ Faber-Castell – Germany *(continued)*

all the work-places necessary to exercise their duties (ILO Convention no. 135 and recommendation no. 143). Employers shall adopt positive views of the activities of trade unions and an open attitude to their organising activities.

5. Decent wages are paid

Wages and benefits for a standard working week shall meet at least legal and industry minimum standards.

Unless wage deductions are permitted by national legislation, they may not be made without expressed permission of the workers concerned. All workers must be given written, understandable information in their own language about wages before taking up their work, and the details of their wages in writing on each occasion that wages are paid.

6. Hours of work are not excessive

Working time should follow the appropriate legislation or national agreement for each trade.

7. Occupational safety and decent working conditions

A safe and hygienic working environment shall be provided and best occupational health and safety working practices shall be promoted, bearing in mind the prevailing knowledge of the trade and of any specific hazards.

Physical abuse, the threat of physical abuse, unusual penalties or punishments, sexual or other forms of harassment and threats by the employer shall be strictly forbidden.

8. Conditions of employment must be established

Employers' obligations to workers according to national labour legislation and regulations on social protection based on permanent employment must be respected.

Source: www.ifbww.org, 9 March 2000.

■ Summary propositions

- The government has become the dominant party in determining the nature of industrial relations; however, its approach can vary dependent on its political ideology (*laissez-faire* or corporatist) and the relative power and autonomy of trade unions.

- In the current climate of increased global capitalism and international market competition, the government is seeking to balance policies directed towards protecting employees and policies directed towards creating employment.

- There is now a two-tier 'government' in the labour market and industrial relations system – the national government and the European Union – which may conflict with each other (convergent 'social partnership' protection at the centre, labour flexibility and competition at the fringe).

Activity See if you can get some 'primary' materials from the main political parties (and government) relating to industrial relations and employment issues (such as manifestos, consultative or discussion documents, press releases, etc.) as well as any press reports of their pronouncements. You could phone or write to them locally or nationally, or browse their web sites (they all have one). Once you've got some materials, try to identify their general approach to industrial realtions as well as any specific policies on such areas as unemployment, pay (including low pay), employment rights, etc.

In a similar way, try to obtain materials from the EU or ILO (by post or via their web sites) and identify how any regulations are made and implemented and what roles governments, management and unions play in the decision-making processes.

Further reading

- D. Strinati, *Capitalism, the State and Industrial Relations*, Croom Helm, 1982. This book examines the relationship between class structure, class conflict and state power and puts forward a sociological explanation of some of the determinants of state intervention in industrial relations.
- C. Crouch, *The Politics of Industrial Relations*, Fontana, 1982. A very readable examination of the development of government intervention in industrial relations through the postwar period up to the introduction of Thatcherism.
- P. B. Beaumont, *Public Sector Industrial Relations*, Routledge, 1992. This book provides a clear examination of the development of industrial relatons in the British public sector during the 1980s.
- S. Kessler and F. Bayliss, *Contemporary British Industrial Relations* (3rd edn), Macmillan, 1998. Chapter 4 (Government values and policies) examines both the Conservative 'Thatcherite' strategies and the likely impact of the 'new' Labour, while Chapter 7 (Government as employer and quasi-employer) provides more detailed information of developments in different parts of the public sector.

References

1. M. Poole, *Industrial Relations: Origins and patterns of national diversity*, Routledge & Kegan Paul, 1986, p. 99.
2. C. Crouch, *The Politics of Industrial Relations* (2nd edn), Fontana, 1982, p. 146.
3. F. van Waarden, 'Government intervention in industrial relations,' in J. van Ruysseveldt, R. Huiskamp and J. van Hoof (eds), *Comparative Industrial and Employment Relations*, Sage, 1995, p. 110.
4. O. Kahn-Freund, 'Legal Framework', in A. Flanders and H. A. Clegg (eds), *The System of Industrial Relations in Great Britain*, Blackwell, 1960, p. 44.
5. Crouch, *op. cit.*, pp. 141 and 147–8.
6. Poole, *op. cit.*, pp. 102–3.

7.   D. Farnham and J. Pimlott, *Understanding Industrial Relations* (5th edn), Cassell, 1995, p. 211.

8.   R. Lewis, 'Collective labour law', in G. S. Bain (ed.), *Industrial Relations in Britain*, Blackwell, 1983, p. 361.

9.   P. Blyton and P. Turnbull, *The Dynamics of Employee Relations* (2nd edn), Macmillan, 1998, p. 148.

10. R. Hyman, *Industrial Relations: A Marxist introduction*, Macmillan, 1975, p. 125.

11. *Ibid.*, p. 145.

12. *Ibid.*, p. 132.

13. P. B. Beaumont, *Public Sector Industrial Relations*, Routledge, 1992, pp. 15 and 17.

14. Crouch, *op. cit.*; C. Crouch, *Class Conflict and the Industrial Relations Crisis*, Heinemann, 1977.

15. D. Strinati, *Capitalism, the State and Industrial Relations*, Croom Helm, 1982.

16. Crouch (1977), *op. cit.*, p. 28.

17. van Waarden, *op. cit.*, p. 110.

18. Crouch (1977), *op. cit.*, p. 30.

19. *Ibid.*, p. 31.

20. van Waarden, *op. cit.*, p. 110.

21. Poole, *op. cit.*, p. 109.

22. Crouch (1982), *op. cit.*, p. 213.

23. A. J. Taylor, *Trade Unions and Politics*, Macmillan, 1989, p. 97.

24. R. Bean, *Comparative Industrial Relations* (2nd edn), Routledge, 1994, p. 219.

25. C. Crouch, 'The state: economic management and incomes policy', in P. Edwards (ed.), *Industrial Relations: Theory and practice in Britain*, Blackwell, 1995, p. 231.

26. J. W. Leopold, 'Trade unions, political fund ballots and the Labour Party', *British Journal of Industrial Relations*, vol. 35, no. 1, 1997, p. 35.

27. J. Monks, 'Government and trade unions', *British Journal of Industrial Relations*, vol. 36, no. 1, 1998, p. 126.

28. J. McIlroy, 'The enduring alliance? Trade unions and the making of New Labour, 1994–1997', *British Journal of Industrial Relations*, vol. 36, no. 4, 1998, p. 538.

29. P. Ackers and J. Payne, 'British trade unions and social partnership: rhetoric, reality and strategy', *The International Journal of Human Resource Management*, vol. 9, no. 3, 1998, pp. 529–50; S. Tailby and D. Winchester, 'Management and trade unions: towards social partnership', in S. Bach and K. Sisson (eds), *Personnel Management* (3rd edn), Blackwell, 2000, pp. 365–388.

30. Strinati, *op. cit.*, p. 41.

31. *Ibid.*, p. 42.

32. Crouch (1982), *op. cit.*, p. 159.

33. Quoted in K. Wedderburn, *The Worker and the Law* (2nd edn), Penguin, 1971, p. 26. © K. W. Wedderburn, 1965, 1971.

34. *Ibid.*, p. 25.

35. F. Boothman and D. Denham, 'Industrial tribunals: is there an ideological background?' *Industrial Relations Journal*, vol. 12, no. 3, 1981, pp. 6–14.

36. *Guardian*, 19 April 1984.

37. P. Kahn *et al.*, *Picketing: Industrial disputes, tactics and the law*, Routledge & Kegan Paul, 1983, p. 86.

38. D. Metcalf, 'The British National Minimum Wage', *British Journal of Industrial Relations*, vol. 37, no. 2, 1999, pp. 176 and 177.

39. 'Do employers want partnership?' *Labour Research*, March 1998, pp. 21–2.

40. G. Schmid, B. Reissert and G. Bruche, *Unemployment Insurance and Active Labour Market Policy*, Wayne State University Press, 1992.

41. G. Hollinshead and M. Leat, *Human Resource Management: an international and comparative perspective*, Pitman, 1995, p. 132.

42. J. Visser, 'Two cheers for corporatism, one for the market: industrial relations, wage moderation and job growth in The Netherlands', *British Journal of Industrial Relations*, vol. 36, no. 2, 1998, pp. 269–92.

43. P. Sparrow and M. Marchington, 'Re-engaging the HRM function', in P. Sparrow and M. Marchington (eds), *Human Resource Management: The new agenda*, FT Pitman, 1998, p. 296.

44. L. Elliott, 'Counting on confusion over the unemployed', *Guardian*, 6 March 2000.

45. B. Towers, 'A return to incomes policy?' *Industrial Relations Journal*, vol. 12, no. 2, 1981, p. 9.

46. R. J. Davies, 'Incomes and anti-inflation policy', in Bain (ed.), *op. cit.*, pp. 419–55.

47. W. McCarthy, 'From Donovan until now: Britain's twenty-five years of incomes policy', *Employee Relations*, vol. 15, no. 6, 1993, p. 7.

48. Crouch (1995), *op. cit.*, p. 238.

49. 'A new agenda: bargaining for prosperity in the 1990s', GMB/UCW, 1990.

50. C. Pond, 'Wages Councils, the unorganised and the low paid', in Bain (ed.), *op. cit.*, p. 197.

51. ACAS, *Annual Report*, 1980, HMSO.

52. F. J. Bayliss, *British Wages Councils*, Blackwell, 1962, p. 145.

53. C. Gabriel and S. Palmer, 'Wages councils: reformation or dissolution?' *Personnel Management*, February 1984, p. 26.

54. 'Wages Councils – striking a balance', *Employment Gazette*, April 1985, p. 136; *European Industrial Relations Review*, May 1985, p. 31.

55. P. Gunnigle, G. McMahon and G. Fitzgerald, *Industrial Relations in Ireland*, Gill & Macmillan (Dublin), 1995, p. 87.

56. 'Minimum pay in 18 countries', *European Industrial Relations Review*, no. 225, October 1992, pp. 14–21.

57. S. Blackburn, 'The problem of riches: from trade boards to a national minimum wage', *Industrial Relations Journal*, Summer 1988, p. 134.

58. 'A national minimum wage for the UK', *European Industrial Relations Review*, no. 290, March 1998, p. 14.

59. *Labour's Business Manifesto: Equipping Britain for the Future*, Labour Party, 1997.

60. Low Pay Commission terms of reference, quoted in Metcalf, *op. cit.*, p. 174.

61. *Ibid.*, pp. 177–8.

62. K. Maguire and L. Elliott, 'Labour to raise minimum wage', *Guardian*, 15 February 2000.

63. 'Minimum wage becomes a reality', *Labour Research*, April 1999, pp. 11–12.

64. Metcalf, *op. cit.*, p. 182.

65. S. Bazen and G. Benhayoun, 'Low pay and wage regulation in the European Community', *British Journal of Industrial Relations*, vol. 30, no. 4, 1992, pp. 623–38.

66. M. Atkinson, 'Minimum fuss', *Guardian*, 15 October 1999.

67. R. Smithers, 'Store chains "use minimum wage to slash rates"', *Guardian*, 3 May 1999.

68. P. Kelso, 'Workers still losing out on minimum wage', *Guardian*, 2 October 1999.

69. A. Pendleton, 'The evolution of industrial relations in UK nationalized industries', *British Journal of Industrial Relations*, vol. 35, no. 2, 1997, p. 166.

70. D. Winchester, 'Industrial relations in the public sector', in Bain (ed.), *op. cit.*, p. 176.

71. A. W. J. Thomson and P. B. Beaumont, *Public Sector Bargaining: A study of relative gain*, Saxon House, 1978.

72. S. Kessler and F. Bayliss, *Contemporary British Industrial Relations* (3rd edn), Macmillan, 1998, p. 159.

73. A. Ferner, 'The state as employer', in R. Hyman and A. Ferner, *New Frontiers in European Industrial Relations*, Blackwell, 1994, pp. 53–4.

74. D. Winchester and S. Bach, 'The state: the public sector' in Edwards (ed.), *op. cit.*, pp. 306–7.

75. S. Freeman and G. Morris, 'The state as employer: setting a new example', *Personnel Management*, August 1989, pp. 25–9.

76. J. Sinclair, 'Change and continuity in public sector employment relations', *Work and Employment*, Bristol Business School, University of the West of England, Spring 1996, pp. 2–4.

77. O. Kahn-Freund, *Labour and the Law* (3rd edn), Stevens, 1983, p. 4.

78. L. Dickens and M. Hall, 'The state: labour law and industrial relations', in Edwards (ed), *op. cit.*, p. 256.

79. See Chapter 5 (Statutory control of employment), Wedderburn, *op. cit.*, pp. 222–63.

80. Dickens and Hall, *op. cit.*, p. 257.

81. *Employment Protection (Part-time Employees) Regulations*, 1995.

82. *Collective Redundancies and Transfer of Undertakings (Protection of Employment (Amendment)) Regulations*, 1995; *Health and Safety (Consultation with Employees) Regulations*, 1996.

83. *Working Time Regulations*, 1998; *Transnational Information and Consultation Regulations*, 1999.

84. ACAS, *Annual Report*, 1998, p. 10.

85. B. Hepple, 'Individual labour law,' in Bain (ed.), *op. cit.*, p. 143.

86. Lewis, *op. cit.*, p. 392.

87. M. Weiss, 'The significance of Maastricht for European Community social policy', *The International Journal of Comparative Labour Law and Industrial Relations*, Spring 1992, p. 4.

88. J. Due, J. S. Madsen and C. S. Jenson, 'The social dimension: convergence or diversification of IR in the Single European Market?' *Industrial Relations Journal*, vol. 22, no. 2, 1991, p. 88.

89. C. S. Jensen, J. S. Madsen and J. Due, 'Phases and dynamics in the development of EU industrial relations regulation', *Industrial Relations Journal*, vol. 30, no. 2, 1999, pp. 118–34.

90. For a succinct explanation of the various institutions see Hollinshead and Leat, *op. cit.* (Chapter 19: The European Union) and M. Leat, 'The European Union', in G. Hollinshead, P. Nicholls and S. Tailby (eds), *Employee Relations*, FT Pitman, 1999, pp. 211–67.

91. P. Teague, 'Between convergence and divergence: possibilities for a European Community system of labour market regulation', *International Labour Review*, vol. 132, no. 3, 1993, p. 391.

92. Due *et al.*, *op. cit.*, p. 93.
93. 'Social policy White Paper', *European Industrial Relations Review*, no. 248, September 1994, pp. 27–32.
94. 'Social policy under the Treaty of Amsterdam', *European Industrial Relations Review*, no. 283, August 1997, p. 15.
95. M. Rhodes, 'The social dimension after Maastricht: setting a new agenda for the labour market', *International Journal of Comparative Labour Law and Industrial Relations*, Winter 1993, p. 298.
96. B. Towers, 'Two speed ahead: social Europe and the UK after Maastricht', *Industrial Relations Journal*, vol. 23, no. 2, 1992, pp. 83–9.
97. Weiss, *op. cit.*, p. 7.
98. *Ibid.*, p. 11.
99. L. Swepston, 'Supervision of ILO standards', *International Journal of Comparative Labour Law and Industrial Relations*, vol. 13, no. 4, 1997, pp. 327–44.

part three

Processes

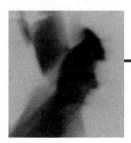

chapter nine

Collective bargaining

Learning objectives

It is principally through the process of collective bargaining that employees and trade unions seek to regulate the employment relationship jointly with management. By the end of this chapter you should be able to:

■ identify the content and relative importance of collective bargaining;

■ understand the nature of collective bargaining: its different functions, the different approaches to collective bargaining and its relationship to joint consultation;

■ distinguish the role and characteristics of national multi-employer bargaining from those of organisational single-employer bargaining;

■ explain the pressures for and effects of decentralisation of collective bargaining.

Definition

Collective bargaining is a method of determining terms of employment and regulating the employment relationship, which utilises the process of negotiation between representatives of management and employees and results in an agreement which may be applied uniformly across a group of employees.

Key issues

While you are reading this chapter, you should keep the following points in mind:

■ Collective bargaining is much more than just a mechanism for pay determination. It is important that we understand its significance also as a process for regulating the 'managerial authority' aspects of the employment relationship and for providing employees with a means to participate in workplace decision making – particularly if we are to consider alternatives to collective bargaining.

■ HRM strategies and the EU Directive on European Works Councils have resulted in the introduction or enhancement of a variety of mechanisms for 'employee' involvement and consultation at the workplace. We need to consider how the operation of these mechanisms (and, in particular, the role of employees representatives) may impinge on any existing collective bargaining process – whether they are to be separate from or integrated with collective bargaining.

■ Collective bargaining has become more decentralised, with less emphasis on national multi-employer agreements. We should be aware that, as a consequence, collective bargaining is likely to focus much more on micro-organisational factors and issues, rather than on wider macro-economic and social issues.

9.1 Introduction

Collective bargaining has been described by Dubin as 'the great social invention that has institutionalized industrial conflict'[1] and by the Donovan Commission as 'a right which is or should be the prerogative of every worker in a democratic society'[2]. Despite the changed economic circumstances, legal framework, management strategies and decreased union membership and power during the 1980s and 1990s, collective bargaining still occupies an important position in UK industrial relations. Certainly, Mathieson argues that 'the union/non-union wage differential, or "union mark-up", remains a feature of industrial relations'[3]; in other words, it still seems to 'pay' to be a member of a union and have them negotiate on your behalf. Similarly, Metcalf believes that trade unions have, by reducing some elements of pay differentials, been able to promote economic equality alongside sex and racial equality; they act as a 'sword of justice' in the labour market[4].

Undoubtedly, there has been a decline in **collective bargaining coverage** in the UK since the 1970s – with the proportion of employees whose pay is determined by collective bargaining dropping from about three-quarters in the mid-1970s to just over one-third in 1998[5]. However, the proportion remains substantial in the public sector and recently privatised sectors (79 per cent in public administration, 69 per cent in electricity, gas and water, 64 per cent in education and 50 per cent in health). It is also relatively high in some private sector areas (46 per cent in transport and communication, 44 per cent in financial services and 33 per cent in manufacturing), but low in others (14 per cent in retail and only 7 per cent in hotels and restaurants)[6]. It is important to recognise that collective bargaining is more likely to be a feature of larger, rather than smaller, establishments; in 1998, the proportion of private sector employees covered by collective bargaining was 31 per cent in establishments of 25 or more employees, compared to only 7 per cent in smaller establishments.

It is also important to remember that the **relationship between collective bargaining coverage and union density** is not a simple one of 'where union affiliation is high, coverage will be extensive, and where membership is low, coverage will be more limited'[7]. In some countries, even with very different industrial relations systems, the level of collective bargaining coverage is much higher than the level of unionisation – for example, union density in France, Germany and Australia is about 10 per cent, 32 per cent and 35 per cent respectively, while the levels of collective bargaining coverage are estimated to be 92 per cent, 90 per cent and 85 per cent respectively. This can be attributed not only to the greater use of multi-employer national- or sector-level agreements but also, and more importantly, to the existence of legal provisions giving trade unions the right to bargaining at industry level and/or for collective agreements to be extended to *all* organisations, whether unionised or not, within the particular industry or sector (see Box 9.1). However, while such legal provisions support and extend the process of joint regulation, they may also act to discourage employees from joining trade unions because they will receive the benefits whether or not they are members. The lower levels of collective bargaining coverage in countries such as the UK (35 per cent), Japan (20 per cent) and the USA (18 per cent) is, in part, a reflection of the predominance of organisational level bargaining within their systems.

Certainly, Milner[8] shows that UK collective bargaining coverage only lagged behind union density during the unions' formative period (late nineteenth and

---

Box 9.1   Extending collective bargaining by legislation – France

The structure and operation of collective bargaining in France has been determined by two major pieces of legislation.

The *1936 Act* was intended to encourage the development of collective bargaining even though the level of unionisation was low.

■ It defined multi-employer industry or sectoral bargaining as the primary bargaining level.

■ It enabled the Minister of Labour to extend a collective agreement to cover all organisations in a particular industry or sector.

■ It recognised the existence of a collective agreement even if signed by only one (minority) union.

The *1982 Act* sought to encourage the development of organisational level collective bargaining.

■ It required industry or sector negotiations to consider pay each year and job classifications every five years.

■ It required organisations which have union branches to seek negotiations each year on pay and hours, although there is no obligation to reach an agreement.

■ It allowed a non-signatory union to veto an organisational-level agreement if it is contrary to the terms of an industry or sector agreement (providing the union can win 50 per cent of the votes in employee representative elections).

French collective bargaining operates at three levels: multi-industry, industry or sector and organisation:

1. *Multi-industry*. These are centralised 'framework' agreements which are implemented through industry and organisation agreements. Since the late 1980s, agreements have covered technological change, unemployment insurance and supplementary pension funds, vocational training, early retirement and working time.

2. *Industry or sector*. In 1995 968 industry agreements were concluded, 75 per cent of which dealt with pay (setting pay rates above the national minimum wage level).

3. *Organisation*. In 1995 8,550 agreements were made covering 3 million employees (20 per cent of the workforce), 49 per cent of which related to pay and 42 per cent related to working time.

Sources J. Goetschy, 'France: the limits of reform', in A. Ferner and R. Hyman (eds), *Changing Industrial Relations in Europe*, Blackwell, 1998, pp. 357–94.

See also Country profiles 4.1 and 6.2.

early twentieth centuries) – unions had first to establish their membership in order to secure recognition from employers and, initially, collective bargaining was largely on an establishment basis. The subsequent development of national industry-wide collective bargaining institutions resulted in more employees being covered by collective bargaining than were union members, reaching a peak in the mid-1970s (80 per cent of employees covered by collective bargaining – including Wages Councils, against a union density of 50 per cent). However, since the mid-1980s the gap has narrowed, largely as a result of the dissolution of a range of multi-employer, industry-wide bargaining arrangements, until the two are about the same.

9.2   The nature of collective bargaining

The essential characteristic of collective bargaining is that 'employees do not negotiate individually, and on their own behalf, but do so collectively through representatives'[9]. It can only exist and function in the following circumstances:

- If employees identify a commonality of purpose, organise and act in concert;
- If management is prepared to recognise their organisation and accept a change in the employment relationship which removes, or at least constrains, its ability to deal with employees on an individual basis.

The legislative framework

See Chapter 6 – Representation at the workplace

Despite its central role in the industrial relations system, collective bargaining in the UK has frequently been noted for its **apparent voluntary nature and lack of legal regulation** (notwithstanding periods of national incomes policy during the 1960s and 1970s). In the USA, for example, legislation has provided some support for the right of representation through not only a statutory union recognition procedure but also a legal requirement for the employer to 'bargain in good faith' However, apart from a short period in the 1970s, the UK has not had any statutory support for union recognition (although the 'new' Labour government has reintroduced a statutory procedure – Employment Relations Act, 1999). It is also important to recognise that governments may use legislation to deny organisations the right to represent employees, to regulate the structure of collective bargaining or to restrict its scope (see Box 9.2).

In the UK, the legal view of the **individual contract of employment** is based on nineteenth-century *laissez-faire* concepts and, Aikin and Reid argued, makes two fundamental assumptions about the contract of employment:

- It 'has been arrived at by two parties of equal bargaining strength'.
- It is 'intended to bind only those two individuals'[10].

However, these assumptions are questionable for the majority of employees.

Box 9.2	Restricting collective bargaining by legislation – Malaysia

Trade union density and collective bargaining coverage are both about 10 per cent in Malaysia. Collective bargaining is constrained by legislation in several ways:

■ Limiting the definition of a collective agreement to one made between a single employer and single union – *excluding the possibility of multi-employer or multi-union bargaining*;

■ Excluding certain 'managerial prerogative' areas (such as recruitment, promotions, dismissals, redundancies and work allocation) from the scope of collective bargaining – *limiting the scope and terms of collective bargaining*;

■ Providing for the terms of a collective agreement (e.g. hours, holidays, overtime) in 'pioneer enterprises' (foreign investment) and 'export processing zones' to being no more favourable than the minimum statutory terms for a period of five years from establishment of the enterprise – *reducing the incentive for employees to organise or join unions to undertake collective bargaining*;

■ Giving the Minister of Labour wide powers to disallow trade unions in 'essential services', to suspend a union for six months if it is felt to be acting 'against the national interest' and to be the final determiner of union recognition claims – *making union representation and activity dependent on acceptance by the government.*

Sources: D. Ayadurai, 'Malaysia', in S. J. Deery and R. J. Mitchell (eds), *Labour Law and Industrial Relations in Asia*, Longman Cheshire (Melbourne), 1993, pp. 61–95; S. Kuruvilla and P. Arudsothy, 'Economic development strategy, government labour policy and firm-level industrial relations practices in Malaysia', in A. Verma, T. A. Kochan and R. D. Lansbury (eds), *Employment Relations in the Growing Asian Economies*, Routledge, 1995, pp. 158–93.

The contract of employment is not a simple personal contract between two individuals but is a contract between an individual and a corporate entity which has its own legal existence independent of the managers who are, at any point in time, its current controllers. An individual employee cannot, by any criteria, be regarded as having equal bargaining power to that of the employing organisation. Furthermore, for the vast majority of employees, the variable terms of the contract of employment (additional to any unwritten but universal terms implied by the common law) are not arrived at by individual agreement between the employee and his or her 'employer'. In practice, they are incorporated into the contract from either a collective agreement, negotiated and agreed between representatives of management and union, or unilateral management policies – both of which are intended to be applied to *all* employees who come within the designated group.

The **legal position of collective agreements** in the UK was clearly set out in 1969: 'The fact that the agreements *prima facie* deal with commercial relationships is outweighed by the other considerations, by the wording of the agreements, by the nature of the agreements, and by the climate of opinion ... Agreements such as these, composed largely of optimistic aspirations, presenting grave practical problems of enforcement and reached against a background of opinion adverse to enforceability, are ... not contracts in the legal sense and are not enforceable at law ... they remain in the realm of undertakings binding in honour'[11]. Even during the brief incursion of the Industrial Relations Act (1971–4), when collective agreements were presumed to be legally enforceable between the signatories, employers acquiesced to union demands for the inclusion of a specific clause stating 'this is not a legally enforceable agreement'. The subsequent Trade Union and Labour Relations Act (1974) reiterated the principle that a collective agreement cannot be legally enforced between the parties unless it is in writing and contains an express provision that the parties intend it to be legally enforceable. It is only, therefore, through the express or implied incorporation of the collective agreement into the individual contract of employment that there is any general legal basis for enforcing the terms of a collective agreement.

However, the issue of **whether collective agreements should be legally enforceable** was raised again in the early 1990s – particularly, whether the law should be amended to 'encourage' employers and unions to agree to legal enforceability[12]. It has been argued that legal enforcement of collective agreements would put pressure on union officials to ensure that members complied with the terms of the agreement (particularly any 'no-strike' clause), thereby inhibiting unconstitutional or unofficial strikes and providing management with greater 'managerial security' to plan and organise its activities.

However a number of **problems** exist:

- *What constitutes a collective agreement?* The vast majority of collective agreements are formalised in written documents. Nevertheless, many arrangements (agreements) in respect of operational situations at the departmental or workgroup level may lack formal written codification and rely on 'verbal understandings'. It would be extremely difficult to make these subject to determination through legal interpretation; they would tend to remain outside the scope of the law, resulting in a two-tier system of collective agreements.

- *What is the purpose of establishing the collective agreement itself as a legal contract directly enforceable between the signatory parties (union(s) and management or employers' association)?* The primary purpose is to make trade unions liable to an injunction and/or damages if they seek to change the terms of a collective agreement during its 'lifetime'. However, most collective agreements in the UK are not fixed term and collective bargaining is regarded as a dynamic process. The terms of a collective agreement need to be interpreted, clarified or redefined as circumstances change. A legal requirement to maintain the existing term could inhibit the trade union's ability to renegotiate, or require the courts to determine whether the situation had changed sufficiently to make the existing term inapplicable. Inherent in the notion of legal enforceability of collective agreements is the need to determine the boundary between maintaining an existing term and redefining the term (negotiation).

- *What effect will it have on strike activity?* Drawing on the American experience, it has been recognised that 'legally enforceable collective agreements do not necessarily mean that fewer days are lost because of strikes, but strikes tend to be concentrated in the period of renegotiation of the agreement'[13]. The legal enforcement of collective agreements may, at best, do little more than encourage more prolonged disputes.

See Chapter 11 –
Industrial action

In the UK, legislative changes during the 1980s have constrained trade unions in respect of unofficial industrial action *without* making collective agreements legally enforceable. Trade union immunity no longer applies if the union undertakes or supports industrial action which has not been approved by a properly conducted secret ballot or does not repudiate any unlawful action by its members. This effectively isolates any members who undertake unofficial industrial action from any union support. At the same time, the employer's position has been strengthened by placing unofficial strikers outside the protection of unfair dismissal legislation. However, this does not preclude unions from taking official 'unconstitutional' industrial action (i.e. in breach of the terms of any disputes procedure).

See Chapter 12 –
Conciliation and
arbitration

See Chapter 8 –
The government

Beaumont[14] notes that the **'public or social interest'** in collective bargaining has been expressed in several ways. Initially, the major concern of governments, acting in a so-called 'neutral' role between management and unions, was *procedural*: the establishment of some form of third-party intervention (conciliation or arbitration) to minimise or avoid the possible effects of a 'failure' of the collective bargaining process (use of industrial action). In some countries, such as the USA, this has been associated with a legal restriction being placed on the 'right to strike' among some groups of public sector employees (essential services). Second, governments may seek to regulate the *substantive* outcome of collective bargaining through formalised incomes policies. This produces a potential conflict between its macro-level responsibilities for economic management and its micro-level role as an employer. Third, government policy and legislation may be directed toward *the structure of collective bargaining* itself. In the UK, for example, the formal centralised bargaining model put forward by the Whitley Committee Report (1916) was not only adopted throughout most of the public sector but also influenced the development of collective bargaining structures in the newer private sector industries (such as chemicals). More recently, in the 1980s and 1990s, the Conservative government supported the decentralisation of collective bargaining through its privatisation programme and the abolition of Wages Councils and, at the same time, removed the duty to 'encourage collective bargaining' from ACAS's terms of reference.

It would be incorrect to regard collective bargaining in the UK as being totally without *any* legal support. Since the Employment Protection Act (1975) trade unions have had the right to request information from the employer without which they would be 'materially impeded' in carrying out their collective bargaining role or which would be 'in accordance with good industrial relations practice'. More recently, under pressure from the EU, the Trade Union Reform and Employment Rights Act (1993) required employers to *consult* recognised independent unions 'in good faith with a view to reaching agreement' in respect of transfer of undertaking and redundancy – however, this is much weaker than a requirement to *negotiate and agree*. In 1996, this consultation right was extended to 'employees' and the regulations amended to allow management to chose whether it consulted via union or employee representatives. Furthermore, but not strictly collective bargaining, many UK

See Chapter 10 –
Employee
involvement and
participation

organisations have established European Works Councils (or other consultative mechanism) in line with the EU Directive. Both of these developments reflect the difference in approach to collective bargaining between the UK and most of its European partners.

In the early 1970s, Wedderburn pointed out that 'the ordinary worker scarcely recognizes his individual contract of employment ... but he will frequently be sharply aware of an agreement between his union and the employer'[15]. However, there has been a shift in the UK during the 1980s and 1990s towards the **development of individual contracts**, particularly among managers, professional and technical groups in areas such as newspapers, the NHS, local government and the privatised corporations (telecommunications, gas, electricity and water). These 'personal' contracts 'bypass one or more elements of an existing union agreement, which are then expected to be settled on an individual basis between the employee and their manager'[16]. Such contracts may not completely replace collective agreement terms but only some terms (for example, placing performance-related pay on an individual basis). They have frequently been introduced first for senior managers (and then progressively lower in the organisation) and offered on a 'voluntary' basis with the incentive, for the employee, of obtaining higher pay or better benefits than if they remain with the collectively agreed conditions. Clearly, the development of such contracts is closely linked not only to other strategies to decentralise collective bargaining but also to the wider labour market deregulation.

However, while some believe that 'personal' contracts 'put ordinary workers on a par with directors and senior managers entitled to ... a stake in the success of their firms ... and the end of the "wage slave mentality"'[17], for others 'they provide employers with a license to arbitrarily alter pay levels and job content'[18]. The move towards individualisation of pay is not limited to the UK but can be seen also in France and Italy and, Ponzellini argues, 'is a sign of growing management discretion and of a crisis in traditional bargaining systems'[19]. Similarly, Bacon and Storey conclude that the individualisation of pay and contracts, when coupled with the individualisation of work organisation (greater functional flexibility, teamworking, etc.) and the decentralisation and marginalisation of collective bargaining, has meant that 'key areas which were subject to regulation by collective bargaining have been reintegrated into the sphere of management prerogative'[20]. Certainly, some managements have offered employees higher pay (or other improvements in terms of employment) to induce them to accept an individual contract. However, the new Labour government has introduced legislation to ensure that employees do not suffer any detriment (or even dismissal) because they refuse to accept an individual contract where the terms are different to those which would apply to them under a collective agreement (Employment Relations Act, 1999).

The functions of collective bargaining

The term 'collective bargaining' was originally used by the Webbs[21], who identified and differentiated three major categories of trade union activity:

- **Mutual insurance** – the provision of Friendly Society benefits in the event of sickness, unemployment, industrial action, etc.;
- **Collective bargaining** – the negotiation of terms and conditions of employment direct with employers on behalf of their members;
- **Legal enactment** – the lobbying for legislation supportive to their members' interests.

Mutual insurance could, even without any acceptance of collective bargaining by the employer, provide trade union members with a limited capacity to withstand impositions or pressures from the employer. However, the real power of trade unionism lay in collective bargaining where employees could achieve better terms because the employer could not treat labour as individual, isolated units. Nevertheless, collective bargaining was viewed only as a transient phenomenon. As trade union membership and power increased, and the working classes achieved a more influential position within society, so the emphasis would shift from collective bargaining to statutory regulation. Ultimately, the employees' terms and conditions of employment would depend not on their variable industrial power to force satisfactory terms from an employer but on a wider and more uniform social, political and legal acceptance and enforcement of these rights on their behalf.

More modern writers have concentrated on collective bargaining as a **process of interaction between management and union**. Flanders[22], in his critique of the Webbs, argued that the word 'bargaining' was misleading and that collective bargaining should more properly be regarded as a **method of job regulation, distinguished from others by the joint authorship of the rules it produced**. His objections to the Webbs' view, which in turn have been criticised by Fox[23], centred on the collective bargaining process being neither equivalent nor an alternative to individual bargaining.

First, in Flanders' view, collective bargaining does not involve the actual sale or hire of labour as an active part of the process; this remains a matter for determination on an individual basis between the employer and the potential employee. While Fox argued that 'individual bargaining' also need not result in an exchange if the proposed terms are considered to be unsatisfactory by either party, this does not detract from Flanders' central argument that the collective agreement is 'a body of rules intended to regulate ... the terms of employment contracts', that 'collective bargaining is itself essentially a rule-making process' and, therefore, it is 'more correct to refer to collective bargaining as regulating, rather than replacing, individual bargaining'[24]. Despite its regular renegotiation, the collective agreement has a permanent existence within the organisational system independent of the individuals who are its employees and any potential employee is, in practice, unable to vary its terms in respect of his or her individual contract of employment.

Second, negotiation is, in reality, a pressure group activity and the resultant collective agreements are, therefore, 'compromise settlements of power conflicts'[25]. The strike or other forms of industrial action should not be regarded as the collective equivalent of the individual's refusal to accept employment, or resignation from employment, when the terms of employment are not satisfactory.

See Chapter 11 –
Industrial action

Industrial action is only 'a temporary refusal to work in accordance with the prevailing employment contracts ... combined with the firm intent, at least on the part of the great majority of workers involved, of not terminating their contracts'[26]. However, Fox believed that the process of individual bargaining also utilised power in the determination of the terms of the contract but that the extent of the power disparity between the parties was obviously much greater than in collective bargaining and almost exclusively in favour of the employer.

Clearly, as Harbinson noted, the important difference between individual and collective bargaining lies in the fact that the latter 'is strictly a relationship between organisations'[27] and therefore an indirect regulation of the relationship between management and employee. It may, as both Fox and Flanders agree, be viewed as a political process encompassing more than just economic issues and may be contrasted with other rule-making processes which have different sources of authority: *unilateral regulation* (by management, employees or union) and *state regulation* (by legislation or government policy).

Chamberlain and Kuhn have suggested that collective bargaining serves a number of distinct functions, each emphasising a different concept of the process and a different stage in its development:

- **A market or economic function** wherein it 'determines on what terms labour will continue to be supplied to a company by its present employees or will be supplied in the future by newly hired workers'[28]. In this context the collective agreement may be regarded as a formal contract and the grievance procedure as a non-legal means for ensuring the employer's compliance with its terms. The process is primarily concerned with determining the substantive terms on which people are to be employed.

- **A governmental function** in which collective bargaining may be regarded as principally a political process based 'on the mutual dependency of the parties and ... the power of each to "veto" the acts of the other'[29]. The bargaining relationship may, using a political analogy, be viewed as a continuing 'constitution' in which the collective agreement is a body of law, determined by the management/union negotiators as the legislature, and executive authority is vested in management who must exercise it in accordance with the terms of the constitution. The grievance procedure is available both as a judicial process, to deal with any differences in respect of interpretation and application of the law or the exercise of executive authority, and as a supplementary legislative process, to agree on issues not covered by the collective agreement. The content of collective bargaining is concerned as much with procedural issues and the distribution of power and authority as it is with substantive issues and the distribution of money.

- **A decision-making function** which 'allows workers, through their union representatives, to participate in the determination of the policies which guide and rule their working lives'[30]. The collective agreement is, in effect, a formal memorandum of the decisions that have been reached and is a limitation on management's freedom and discretion to act unilaterally. The grievance procedure forms an integral part of the joint decision-making process and the distinction between matters of right and matters of interest is blurred. The concept of mutuality, which underlies this view of collective bargaining, recognises that 'authority over men requires consent' and 'involves defining areas of joint concern within which decisions must be sought by agreement'[31].

These differing views of collective bargaining are not mutually exclusive and most negotiations contain elements of all three. However, collective bargaining should not be viewed just as a process for employees exerting pressure on management but also, as Blyton and Turnbull argue, as a mechanism for 'managerial control' in so far as 'it institutionalises conflict by channelling the power of organised labour into a mechanism that, while acknowledging that power, at the same time circumscribes it and gives it greater predictability'[32]. While the broad function of collective bargaining is to establish a *common rule* for a defined group of employees on a jointly agreed basis, it must also allow for *diversity and variation* to cope with the uniqueness of each situation.

The content of collective bargaining

The content of collective bargaining may, for convenience, be divided into three broad areas: substantive terms and conditions of employment, procedural rules and working arrangements. There is little doubt that the way in which these areas have been addressed has changed over the twentieth century – particularly during the 1980s and 1990s (see Box 9.3). Certainly, Kessler and Bayliss believe that the 'scope of collective bargaining ... has diminished as a result of growing managerial power and assertiveness' and the 'subject matter has become much more focused on what workers do rather than on what they are paid'[33].

Box 9.3   Changing bargaining agenda

'The collective bargaining agenda [during the 1980s] was firmly set by management. This agenda for much of the period included, first, the reduction in the size of the labour force, changes in working methods and increased efficiency and flexibility; and second, revised pay structures (for example, fewer grades and more integrated structures, and revised payment systems, in particular the spread of PRP). Also, management set the agenda through the introduction of "something for something" bargaining.'

'In the mid-1990s there was a change in that the TUC ... launched its campaign for New Unionism and for Social Partnership' with the objective 'to leave behind adversarialism and stress the value of union cooperation with management to increase efficiency, and to achieve an economy which competes on the basis of high skills, high pay and high productivity ... Unless the union is in a position to bargain for what individuals want, the employer is likely to fail to do other than offer only what is in the company's immediate or preconceived interest.' Developments have included seeking 'greater security of employment in return for greater flexibility, moderation in pay claims and cooperation in achieving higher efficiency [and] wider choice of the mix of work and leisure, with time off being taken in more varied forms to match changing family circumstances.'

'Unions need to develop the bargaining agenda in ways which have an appeal to individuals.'

Source: S. Kessler and F. Bayliss, *Contemporary British Industrial Relations* (3rd edn), Macmillan, 1998, pp. 293–4.

Substantive terms and conditions

See Chapter 14 –
Pay and working
arrangements

Substantive terms and conditions of employment are concerned with the regulation of 'economic' relations (wages, hours, holidays, etc.), which is often regarded as the primary purpose of both trade unions and collective bargaining. Improvements in substantive terms of employment in the UK have been generally achieved by trade unions through the process of direct bargaining with employers rather than, as in some other countries, through statutory regulation of minimum terms.

- *Pay.* Pay may include not only basic rates and pay scales but also overtime rates, minimum earnings for PBR schemes, guaranteed payments when work is not available and allowances for special working conditions or arrangements such as shift working or working in abnormal conditions. Generally these items are renegotiated annually in the light of any change in the cost of living, comparisons with the level of wages in other occupations and organisations, and the productivity and profitability of the organisation or industry. Since the early 1980s management has sought to reduce pay standardisation and uniformity and increase pay flexibility and variability (through decentralisation of collective bargaining and relating pay to organisation, group and/or individual performance).

- *Hours of work.* Hours of work have tended to reduce in waves. Before 1914 many industries worked a 72-hour, six-day week and it was not until after the First World War that the eight-hour day (48-hour, six-day week) was generally achieved. This reduced to a 44-hour, $5\frac{1}{2}$-day week after the Second World War and a 40-hour, five-day week in the mid-1960s. Although the pressure for shortening the working week has been couched in terms of creating more leisure or job opportunities, past reductions have usually resulted not in fewer hours being worked but a transfer of hours to overtime working, thereby enhancing the employees' earnings. A real reduction in the actual hours worked requires either the employees to accept a reduction in their level of earnings or the employer to agree to a substantial increase in basic wage rates in order to maintain the employees' existing level of earnings. The reduction in hours for manual workers to 37 hours during the 1980s, bringing them in line with non-manual employees, was accompanied by management strategies to increase productive time through both time flexibility and time intensification (reduced breaks, bell-to-bell working, etc.).

- *Paid annual holidays.* Paid annual holidays have been a phenomenon primarily of the postwar period. It was not until 1928 that a government inquiry recommended that employees should receive a minimum of one week's paid holiday and even this was not generally achieved until the end of the Second World War. By the latter part of the 1970s this had become three or four weeks for most employees, and by the 1990s many groups received five or six weeks' holiday. The UK's adoption of the EU Working Time Directive includes the right to four weeks' paid holiday (including statutory holidays). This is in marked contrast to the USA, where the norm has remained at two weeks for most employees. Payment for holidays is usually made at normal basic pay or average earnings. However, in some European countries employees may receive extra payment for the period of their holidays – in some cases double payment. This may be regarded as simply 'deferred' wage payments or as recognition of the need for employees to make full use of their holiday if they are to remain effective as employees for the remainder of the year.

■ *Fringe benefits*. Fringe benefits include such items as pension, sick pay, company car, cheap loans and private medical facilities. Incomes policies in the 1970s provided a major impetus for the provision of such benefits as both employers and trade unions looked to alternative, and less obvious, methods of rewarding employees – particularly non-manual employees. It should be recognised that, where such benefits become subject to collective agreement, they can no longer be regarded as optional 'fringe' items for which employees should be grateful but become standard terms to which they have a right. The increasing costs of such benefits (particularly if applied to all employees whether they are relevant or useful to them) have led some managements to introduce a 'cafeteria' approach to benefits, where employees can select which benefit they want and to what level, subject to an overall cost ceiling.

Procedural rules

Procedural rules are concerned with the regulation of 'managerial' relations (the exercise of managerial authority and the participation of employees and their representatives in organisational decision making). They establish the regulatory framework for managing the tension between management's desire for control of its labour and the employees' desire for protection against arbitrary management decisions and actions. These rules introduce a degree of certainty into the organisational relationship by defining what issues are to be subject to joint regulation, how they are to be handled and the expected roles of the various parties. As such, they may be more important than substantive, economic rules: they share power and authority rather than money. Beyond the initial union recognition procedure, joint procedures may be established for virtually any area dependent on management's willingness to accept sharing of decision-making responsibility – grievances, discipline, redundancy, consultation, job evaluation, etc.

See Chapter 15 –
Grievance, discipline
and redundancy

In the past, many managers argued that the *status quo* principle contained in many agreements, that management should not implement any change until it had been agreed or the disputes procedure had been exhausted, allowed trade unions and employees to delay negotiations in order to put greater pressure on management in the hope of securing a greater concession for agreeing to the change. However, the reverse is equally true if there is no *status quo* clause: management is more able to resist making concessions once the change has been implemented and is being worked by the employees.

Working arrangements

Working arrangements refers to defining the nature of the work and the way it is to be carried out by employees and has been associated primarily with the

See Chapter 14 –
Pay and working
arrangements

development of organisational-level bargaining. It is an important feature of 'productivity', 'new technology' and 'flexibility' agreements, which deal with the introduction of new work arrangements and often contain provisions relating to manning levels, inter-job flexibility, time flexibility, use of contractors, etc. However, while the general aim of such agreements is often to increase work flexibility, the fact that working arrangements are codified within a collective agreement may itself create inflexibility. It provides an accepted definition of what is, and therefore what is not, part of the employee's job and may be used by employees as the justification for not carrying out other work which may be required of them by management. However, the defining of work arrangements is not confined to formal collective agreements but also takes place in other systems within the organisation – operating procedures, job descriptions, etc. Consequently, they are at the discretion of management except in so far as they are subject to a joint procedure (for example, job evaluation).

The collective bargaining relationship

While conflict of interest forms an inherent part of the management/employee relationship and provides the input into the collective bargaining process, the collective bargaining relationship itself is founded on their **mutual dependence** (the need to reach an agreement or solution to their differences). Freedom not to reach an agreement can exist only if both parties have a viable alternative. If only one party has such an alternative then the other, because of its necessity to reach an agreement, has no bargaining strength and must therefore settle on whatever terms are offered – *negotiation* becomes *imposition*. It could be argued that, in modern industrialised societies with increased emphasis on quality performance, employee commitment and investment in organisation-specific human capital, neither management nor employees have such viable alternatives – employees, as a collective body, are unable or unwilling to relinquish their employment and seek other work, and management cannot quickly and easily replace a part of its workforce. However, the perception of the degree of mutual dependence may and does vary: for example, management's perception of its dependence on securing employee acceptance of change may decrease at times of recession, competitive markets and high unemployment. Nevertheless, it is assumed that the initial intention of both parties at the commencement of any negotiation is to reach a satisfactory resolution of their differences and maintain the employment relationship.

It is possible to differentiate **two basic models** of collective bargaining relationship. The absolute requirement to achieve some form of agreement in order to maintain the employment relationship and the organisation's operations led Chamberlain and Kuhn to use the term **conjunctive bargaining** to refer to situations where 'the parties agree to terms as a result of mutual coercion and arrive at a truce only because they are indispensable to each other'[34]. The use, or threatened use, of coercion is a dominant feature of such bargaining and the terms of the resultant agreement are dependent on the relative bargaining power of the two parties. The relationship between the parties is such that the minimum co-operation needed to reach, and maintain, the agreement is generally regarded also as the maximum desired co-operation.

Collective bargaining cannot proceed beyond this level, to what Chamberlain and Kuhn referred to as **co-operative bargaining**, unless both parties accept that 'neither will gain additional advantages unless the other gains too'[35]. The dominant feature of this collective bargaining approach is the willingness of the parties to make concessions in order to achieve objectives which would not otherwise have been possible. This does not imply that the parties are pursuing a single common interest but that their different interests are more capable of achievement if each is prepared to allow the other to move towards its objective: for example, the linking of management's need to secure changes in working arrangements, thereby improving productivity and efficiency, with the employees' desire for better pay and benefits and greater job security. Walton and McKersie[36] make a similar distinction using different terms. *Distributive bargaining* reflects a basic conflict between the parties over the division of some limited resource (e.g. money to be distributed as pay or profits) and may be equated to a fixed-sum game wherein one side's gain is the other side's loss. *Integrative bargaining* reflects a greater commonality of perception and acceptance of the issue to be resolved and results in a problem-solving approach or varying-sum game wherein the parties, by co-operation, can increase the value of the resource to be distributed between them.

See Chapter 13 –
Negotiation

It would appear, on the surface, that conjunctive bargaining should be abandoned in favour of co-operative bargaining. However, the **transition from conjunctive bargaining to co-operative bargaining involves perceived dangers** for both sides:

■ It requires management to be willing to accept employee influence, whether through collective bargaining or other forms of participation, in areas previously regarded as matters of 'managerial prerogative'.

■ It requires unions to accept joint responsibility in areas where they have previously preferred to reserve their right to challenge management after the decision has been made.

■ It can lead to an increasing divorcement between employees and their representatives if union negotiators are perceived as apologists for, and an adjunct of, management.

■ Perhaps most importantly, the principle of co-operation can itself become an expected feature of all negotiations and the minimum basis on which one, or both, of the parties will be prepared to conclude an agreement. It may even reach the stage where coercion, the primary ingredient of conjunctive bargaining, is used in order to secure 'co-operation'.

It is therefore perhaps better to view the two approaches as being complementary aspects of any negotiation rather than as two distinct forms – one desirable and the other undesirable. Certainly, Beaumont believes that, during the 1970s and 1980s, the centralised negotiations in the public sector became more adversarial and distributive in their orientation and this may have ' "spilled over" adversely to influence the union-management processes involved in lower level negotiating and consultative arrangements'[37] which were of a more 'integrative bargaining' nature. The 'social partnership' approach advocated during the 1990s is clearly based on the development of a co-operative integrative relationship in any bargaining.

The desirability of a more co-operative approach to the bargaining relationship and an expansion of its joint decision-making function was forcibly argued by McCarthy and Ellis in the early 1970s[38]. In their view, management in every organisation is continually faced by two challenges:

■ From within the organisation, derived from increased employee expectations in both monetary and managerial terms;

■ From outside the organisation, derived principally from market competition and the need for technological change.

Management should not, in their opinion, respond to the latter by attempting to suppress the former through an authoritarian style of management. Rather it should pursue a policy of **management by agreement**, where decision-making authority would be 'shared with workers through an extension of the area of joint regulation' and 'unions would have the right to seek to influence management policy in any area'[39]. The principal effect would be to shift the emphasis of bargaining from recriminations over the past (claims, disputes and grievances arising from the actions or non-actions of either party, but principally management) to **predictive bargaining** concerning future problems likely to affect the employment relationship. However, McCarthy and Ellis accepted that it would not automatically result in an absence of conjunctive bargaining and its associated use of coercive power. They recognised that 'the right of ultimate recourse to unilateral action on the part of either party is derived from a frank admission that there are major and at times irreconcilable differences between management and workers', therefore, 'workers must have the right, in the end, to determine how far they are prepared to modify their demands as a result of taking into account what are essentially management problems' and 'similar rights must also be permitted to management'[40]. However, they believed that the atmosphere created by a changed relationship between the parties could induce a greater acceptance of the use of external conciliation or mediation to resolve their differences, rather than resorting to the use of industrial power.

It is clear that the bargaining relationship is regarded, even in its most co-operative form, as a **bipartite process** which, Flanders noted, makes no 'provision for bringing to light and safeguarding the public interest in the results of collective bargaining'[41]. The primacy of the parties to conclude any agreement which *they* believe to be to *their* joint benefit is implied in the acceptance of the voluntary nature of the collective bargaining process. The **public interest**, demonstrated through government policy or legislation, acts as an external constraint on the negotiating parties rather than as an active participation of a distinct and separate third party in the negotiating process. However, as Beaumont points out, 'public sector bargaining rarely involves a process in which only two separate, distinct and relatively homogeneous union and management parties are involved'[42]. Rather, the **public sector is characterised by multilateral bargaining**. Not only is there a division and differing priorities between paymaster (government) and employer (NHS, local authority, etc.) but, particularly in the case of local authorities, the employers' side of the bargaining institutions may involve differing political ideologies and policies resulting from the role of elected councillors. Even in the civil service, where the government is itself the management, and therefore nominally the bipartite nature of collective bargaining is maintained, nevertheless the objectives and strategy of the 'management' are influenced by government views of the wider public interest – the government, as an employer, must set an example which will influence and be followed by others.

Disclosure of information

The term 'disclosure of information' refers to the transfer, to union or employee representatives, of information generated as an integral part of the managerial function of planning, controlling and decision making, and which traditionally has been retained within the exclusive possession of management. As Dickens points out, any apparent unanimity regarding the desirability of 'disclosure' owes 'much to the fact that [it] can mean different things to different people and that different expectations are held as to its possible effects'[43]. Moore believes that the word 'disclosure' 'correctly acknowledges that unequal access to information prevails, and confirms the notion that such discriminatory access represents a real power resource to a company and its managers in their dealings with trade unions'[44].

The potential **relationship between disclosure of information and the nature of collective bargaining** is shown in Figure 9.1. It is clear that low disclosure of information by management is likely to result in either non-bargaining (imposition) where management has high bargaining power, or coercive action where there is a more equal balance of bargaining power because of the absence of any information from management to modify union expectations or to assess management's case. High disclosure of information coupled with high

Figure 9.1 Disclosure of information and collective bargaining

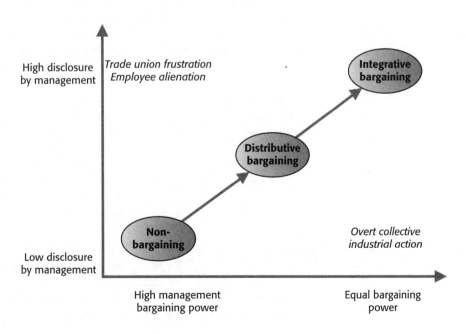

management bargaining power may result in trade union frustration and employee alienation as they perceive that they are powerless to affect or influence anything in the light of the information they receive. Perhaps, as Moore argues[45], a strong union may not need information to substantiate its bargaining position, while a weak union may not be able to benefit from greater disclosure of information. It is only possible to adopt a more integrative (joint problem-solving) approach to collective bargaining where there is both high disclosure and relatively equal bargaining power.

The **pressure for greater disclosure of information** has come from three sources. First, greater emphasis on linking pay with productivity, performance and working arrangements and adopting a more joint problem-solving approach widens the scope and complexity of collective bargaining requiring more detailed information regarding the organisation's present and planned operations. Second, the development of management strategies aimed at securing greater employee commitment and involvement all require employees to have better information about their organisation. Third, there has been external pressure for organisations to be more socially responsible and accountable for their decisions and activities.

A number of **arguments against the disclosure of information** have been put forward, principally by managers.

See Chapter 13 –
Negotiation

■ *Relative power relationship.* The possession of knowledge by one party to the exclusion of the other is an important determinant of relative bargaining power (particularly in conjunctive bargaining). Management's prior disclosure of operational, financial and other information may allow union negotiators to more easily identify management's negotiating limits. Significantly, Dickens[46] found that 48 per cent of managers believed disclosure of information could lead to 'better' collective bargaining – by which they meant more 'moderate', 'responsible' or 'realistic' (lower) union claims or expectations. Similarly, 59 per cent of managers believed the major disadvantage was the union's 'misinterpretation', 'misuse' or 'inability to understand' the information (in other words, they were concerned that the union would not interpret the information in the same way as management).

■ *Expansion of joint regulation.* There would appear to be little real purpose or advantage in disclosing managerial information on a formal and regular basis if its assumptions, logic and implications cannot, at the very least, be questioned and debated by the recipients. It is then a relatively small, but important, step from simply discussing the information to questioning the validity of the associated management decision and seeking to modify it or bring it under some more permanent mode of joint regulation. To many managers this would represent a substantial and serious erosion of their managerial prerogative and control within the organisation.

■ *Varying degrees of precision of information.* A great deal of management activity is concerned with gathering and analysing incomplete information relating to uncertain situations in order to plan for a range of contingencies. Managers, therefore, are reluctant to divulge this information because unnecessary time and effort may be spent discussing issues which never materialise – possibly creating unnecessary difficulties and conflict with their employees and unions.

▪ *Confidential information*. The more important, and from the unions' viewpoint most worthwhile, organisational information is often regarded as confidential and restricted to senior management. Senior management may consider it improper to disclose such information to employee representatives when it has not been made generally available to the majority of managers. From the employee representatives' position, it must also be recognised that access to such information, and in particular the need to maintain its confidentiality, may place a strain on relationships with constituents.

The Employment Protection Act (1975) established **a legal requirement for the disclosure of information**, on request, to the representatives of recognised independent trade unions. The request for disclosure has to be substantiated on the grounds that, without it, the trade union would be to a material extent impeded in carrying on such collective bargaining and that its disclosure would be in accordance with good industrial relations. However, the Act places two restrictions on the process of disclosure:

1. **Certain types of information are specifically excluded**; information which:

    (a) would be against the interests of national security to disclose;
    (b) could not be disclosed without contravening a prohibition imposed by or under an enactment;
    (c) has been communicated to the employer in confidence;
    (d) relates specifically to an individual unless he or she has consented to its being disclosed;
    (e) would cause substantial injury to the employer's undertaking by its disclosure for reasons other than its effect on collective bargaining;
    (f) has been obtained by the employer for the purpose of bringing, prosecuting or defending any legal proceedings.

2. Even when the information is regarded as being appropriate to collective bargaining and not of a precluded nature, there are **safeguards for the employer in respect of the manner of disclosure**; management cannot be required to:

    (a) produce, allow inspection of, or copy any document; or
    (b) compile or assemble any information which would involve an amount of work or expenditure out of reasonable proportion to the value of the information in the conduct of collective bargaining.

It is important to recognise two things:

▪ The onus is on the trade union representatives to ask for the information they require rather than on management to provide it automatically, and they must also know the manner in which management collects this information.

▪ The amount of information that might legally be requested depends on the extent to which issues within the organisation are subject to joint regulation through collective bargaining; management is under no legal obligation to disclose information in respect of those issues which are simply a matter of joint consultation (except redundancy). Consequently, as management withdraws elements from the scope of collective bargaining (for example, individualising pay) so it restricts the information a union may demand.

The legislation has been supported by an *ACAS Code of Practice*[47] outlining the range of information which is in line with 'good industrial relations practice'. While much of the *current* information about an organisation is already probably known to the union, it is the *future* information relating to planned changes and developments in investment, product development, work arrangements, etc., as well as performance or financial information on costs, productivity and profits, which is of more importance. However, it is these latter types of information which employers are more reluctant to disclose on the grounds that its public availability might cause substantial injury to the organisation.

The **enforcement procedure** for this piece of legislation has been described by Torrington and Chapman as 'bizarre'[48]. Initially, the union may present a complaint to the Central Arbitration Committee (CAC) that the employer has failed to comply with a request for information. If conciliation by ACAS is inappropriate, or fails to resolve the matter, the CAC (if it finds in favour of the union) will make a declaration specifying both the information to be disclosed and a period of time, of not less than one week, in which the employer must disclose the information to the union representatives. Then, if the employer fails to comply with the CAC's declaration, the union may present a further complaint regarding the employer's non-compliance *and* a claim for improvement or change in the employees' terms and conditions of employment. The CAC, in its normal arbitration capacity, will then hear both the union and management's case in respect of that claim and make an award which has legal effect as part of the employees' contract of employment. The procedure is intended to pressure, rather than compel, management to disclose the information – at least during the CAC arbitration hearing – or allow its case to be weakened by default.

Hussey and Marsh[49] found, in its first years of operation, that only 41 out of the 151 references resulted in a full hearing and that the annual rate of references had rapidly declined to about 20 per year (where it has since remained). They attributed this decline to a variety of possible factors: the use of detailed information being the antithesis of traditional collective bargaining, its potential 'undermining' effect on union claims or arguments in a worsening economic climate, the possible improvement of disclosure practices at the organisational level, and union disenchantment with the legal process. Certainly, they found that the CAC interpreted the phrase 'materially impeded' to exclude disclosure where it felt the union already had sufficient information or could obtain the information from other sources (e.g. its members), or where the information was unnecessary for the issue being negotiated. Significantly, they also found that the CAC, while supporting the general principle of a 'free flow' of information from management to union, nevertheless interpreted 'good industrial relations practice' to include restricting the disclosure of information where it might cause or extend the conflict between the parties. However, as the CAC itself pointed out, it is important to recognise that while 'a positive award may have given the union less than it was asking for, ... a nil award may disguise the fact that during the informal procedures ... a considerable release of information took place'[50]. Certainly, another review of early CAC awards[51] found that even where an award was made the union often found the information to be of little use in collective bargaining.

Relationship between collective bargaining and joint consultation

Joint consultation has a long history, within UK industrial relations, co-existing alongside collective bargaining. It has been described as 'the discussion between management and workers ... of matters of joint concern which are not the subject of negotiations with trade unions'[52], 'leading to advice to management but leaving free management's right and responsibility to make the final decision'[53] and seeking 'to enlist the co-operation of all employees in the efficient operation of the company ... and in the implementation of management's decisions'[54].

It is important to recognise that joint consultation is a process wherein management not only determines the issues on which it wishes to seek the views and opinions of its employees but also retains the discretion to decide the final outcome without subjecting it to joint agreement with employees or their representatives. Within this framework its content is directed towards operational needs and problems; the process is primarily one of discussing the implementation of decisions already made by management; and the criterion for success is the effect it has on improving employee commitment and the efficiency of the organisation. It is not intended as a means to extend employee influence in organisational decision making. The extent to which employees are able to influence the final decision or to have their wishes and interests taken into account is dependent exclusively on the 'goodwill' of the management making the decision. Indeed, many managers have favoured joint consultation rather than collective bargaining precisely because it involves less erosion of their prerogative.

The relationship between joint consultation and collective bargaining is often conceived as one of differentiation and separation – that **issues of common interest and conflict need to be handled in different ways**. With this in mind, Henderson suggested that 'negotiation is a means of reconciling divergent interests, consultation a means of promoting action where there are no obvious conflicts'[55]. However, McCarthy believed this contains an important and unacceptable paradox: namely, 'that management should only agree to share responsibility on controversial and conflicting subjects, [while] on non-controversial and common interest issues ... it cannot do more than consult' and 'that agreements are only possible when the two sides are basically opposed; when they are really united there cannot be any question of an agreement'[56]. The differentiation between joint consultation and collective bargaining has been seen in two areas:

■ **Subject matter** (excluding from joint consultation any item which normally is subject to negotiation). This inevitably means that if the scope of collective bargaining expands then the scope of joint consultation must reduce. The result can be the creation of what may be termed the 'car park, canteen and toilet syndrome'. In other words, joint consultation becomes relegated to the role of a grievance forum (a reversal of the intended process of management consulting employees on matters of concern to management) and a communication vehicle for management to provide general information about the state of the organisation.

See Chapter 6 –
Representation at the
workplace

■ **Employee representation**. Whereas it may be argued that any employee, whether a union member or not, may both participate in the election of employee representatives and offer him- or herself as a candidate for election, representation in the collective bargaining process and institution has traditionally been drawn exclusively from trade union members, who represent both their fellow members and their union as an organisation. However, Henderson pointed out that management should be aware of the potential 'limitations of a committee in which employee representatives do not have the independence and authority of responsible trade union backing'[57].

Such a separation means that there is always the danger that management might use, or be perceived by the union and employees to use, joint consultation as a method of avoiding having to negotiate with the union. Similarly, there may be pressure from the union to transfer items from the consultative institution to the collective bargaining institution to bring them under formal joint regulation.

However, it is important to bear in mind that the **process and institutions of joint consultation are not necessarily coterminous**. While it may be relatively easy to define any boundary between the *institutions* of joint consultation and collective bargaining (by reference to their constitution, composition and subject matter), the boundary between the *processes* of joint consultation and negotiation is more diffuse. If, when it 'consults', management says 'If we make this change to our original decision, will it now be acceptable?' and modifies its stance to take account of employee objections, how does this differ from negotiation? The real difference lies, first, in there being no requirement placed on management by the process itself to make such a modification, and second, in the result being expressed not as a formal joint agreement binding and enforceable on management but as a management action or decision which will not be opposed by employees in its execution.

Marchington and Armstrong[58] argue that the belief that there was, during the 1980s, either a 'revitalisation' or 'marginalisation' of joint consultation is too simplistic. The realities of the way joint consultation is operated suggests **four different models**:

■ **The non-union model**. Here the main objective of consultation is to avoid employee dissatisfaction from arising (and the need for union representation) and to create a closer identification with the organisation by informing employee representatives of the organisation's position (as seen by management) and persuading them that management's decisions are 'right' or 'necessary'. However, as Marchington points out, the establishment of such an employee forum 'may eventually lead to an increasing awareness of ambiguities and contradictions, and perhaps its ultimate demise'[59] – it may become the means by which employees identify and develop interests distinct from management's and provide the basis for the future development of unionism and collective bargaining.

- **The marginal model**. In this model, joint consultation consists of relatively trivial items presented in a bland way, with any consultative committee having little role in decision making or even making recommendations. Marchington and Armstrong believe that this marginalisation of joint consultation can arise where 'employers feel less need to consult with employees in any meaningful way since management control is enhanced in a recession'[60]. However, as Marchington points out, it may be difficult actually to abandon joint consultation because of the 'considerable symbolic value attached to the consultative committee, and its continuation is taken as a measure of management commitment to the workforce'[61] but, at the same time, the marginalisation of joint consultation reduces any need to abandon it. This model may be associated with either strong collective bargaining (where trade unionism is strong) or, equally, weak collective bargaining (where management has the power advantage).

- **The competitive model**. This involves the 'revitalisation' of joint consultation with more emphasis on high-level information and discussion of the organisation's current and future situation combined with the development of various direct forms of employee involvement (team briefings, etc.). Through this, Marchington argues, 'militant expressions of trade unionism can be constrained by a more knowledgeable workforce' and the consultative committee can be used 'to persuade stewards to adopt a more moderate and supportive perspective towards the company'[62]. Management will seek to keep consultation and collective bargaining distinct from each other while enhancing the content of consultation.

- **The adjunct model**. In this model, sometimes referred to as the 'advanced' form of consultation, informing, consulting and negotiating are integrally linked together in the process of handling industrial relations within the organisation, although it may still, perhaps, retain some distinction between negotiating focusing on distributive issues/approaches while consultation focuses on more integrative issues/approaches. Marchington believes that joint consultation is 'seen to be a key part of the representative institutions ... to play a part in company issues and to help lubricate relations in a more informal and less highly charged atmosphere than that of annual negotiations or dispute resolution'[63].

See Chapter 10 – Employee involvement and participation

The position of joint consultation has been strengthened by two additional developments within the broader framework of employee participation. First, Employee Councils have been introduced in a number of organisations not only to integrate the consultative and negotiating processes in one body but also to do so on the basis of 'employee' rather than 'union' representation. This development has been particularly associated with single-union agreements and some of the privatised corporations. Second, a number of organisations have established European Works Councils or other consultative mechanisms, in line with the EU Directive, to discuss issues which cross national boundaries.

9.3 The structure of collective bargaining

Collective bargaining 'structure' refers to the 'regularised patterns of union–management interaction, or the network of institutionalised bargained relationships'[64]. However, even within an individual country there is generally no single uniform structure of collective bargaining and there are certainly wide variations between countries; as Bridgford and Stirling note, collective bargaining 'displays the characteristics of a varied and multi-form mosaic'[65]. This variety arises from differences in three major aspects of collective bargaining[66]:

■ Collective bargaining may be **conducted at different levels** within the industrial relations system, ranging from the national or industry level, through the regional or district level to the organisational level and with different linkages between the various levels. For example, an industry-level agreement may specify only minimum substantive terms (to be supplemented at organisational level) or specifically exclude certain terms to be determined by organisational-level agreements. This results in the employee's terms and conditions of employment containing elements from more than one collective agreement.

■ There is **variation in the coverage of the bargaining units** (the group of employees to be covered by a particular collective agreement). In one organisation or industry all manual workers may be covered by the same collective agreement, while in another organisation or industry different categories of manual workers may have their own separate agreements. Similarly, there may be separate agreements covering manual and non-manual employees or, particularly at the organisational level where management strategy is directed towards harmonisation, they may be covered by the same agreement.

■ The **process of collective bargaining may vary** in respect of *form* (ranging from comprehensive written agreements to informal unwritten understandings), *scope* (ranging from a limited set of substantive terms – simply basic wage rates and hours – through a more comprehensive set of substantive terms to encompassing a wide range of procedural and managerial issues as well), and *depth* (the degree of influence union or employee representatives have on the outcome).

However, it is possible to identify three distinct categories or elements which may exist within collective bargaining structures. First, there are national multi-employer bargaining arrangements (a form of external regulation of the individual organisation or enterprise); these may be subdivided between (1) economy-wide arrangements and (2) industry- or sectoral-level bargaining institutions. Second, there is single-employer enterprise or organisational-level bargaining (internal regulation).

National multi-employer bargaining

National **economy-wide arrangements** have been a particularly feature of the bargained or state corporatist approaches to industrial relations (Scandinavian

See Chapter 8 –
The government

countries, The Netherlands and some of the 'tiger' economies of south-east Asia, such as Singapore (see Box 9.4)). Such arrangements often involve tripartite negotiations between central confederations of trade unions and employers and government, to make recommendations for improvements in wages and other terms of employment in the light of the country's economic performance. These provide the 'benchmark' for subsequent negotiations at industry and/or organisational levels. Such arrangements provide, in effect, an 'agreed' incomes policy which supports both government and management economic strategies by keeping down labour costs, reducing conflict and supporting industrial modernisation and economic growth, and, at the same time, they support the unions' objective of 'wage solidarity'. The countries which have successfully operated such arrangements have tended to be relatively small with an integrated internal labour market and a relatively restricted range of industries often exposed to international competition. As Bridgford and Stirling point out, the nearest the UK has come to such an arrangement was in 1974 when the Labour government negotiated a 'Social Contract' with the TUC in which 'the government agreed to introduce supportive employment legislation and to increase income tax for higher earners in exchange for a voluntary income policy'[67]. However, this was only a temporary accommodation between government and unions and did not include employers. In France there is a range of intersectoral bargaining; however, this is concerned not with wages but, rather, with agreeing a common approach to the implementation of such issues as job security, training, early retirement, pensions, single status and short-time working (see Box 9.1).

The terms **national, industry or sectoral agreement**, which have, as Bean points out 'been the prevailing practice in most West European countries'[68], generally refer to a multi-employer agreement, negotiated between national trade unions and employers' associations, which covers employees of a given description in a specified industry or sub-industry. It is important to remember, first, that an industry may have more than one 'national industry' agreement; the collective bargaining institutions, and resultant collective agreements, may be segmented on a sub-industry and/or occupational basis. Second, such 'national industry' agreements are intended to cover only those organisations within the industry which are members of the employers' association which has negotiated the agreement. Nevertheless, organisations which are not members of the employers' association may decide to apply the terms of the agreement as an alternative to negotiating their own collective agreements (voluntary extension), or the law may require the agreement to be applied by all organisations in the industry (legal extension). However, organisations which are not members of the employers' association do not have access to any disputes procedures negotiated with the unions for resolving differences relating to the interpretation and application of the national agreement.

Industry-wide bargaining has **advantages for both unions and management**:

- *Unions*. Industry-level agreements ensure that 'common rule' is applied across as wide an area as possible (possibly even outside federated organisations). In the wages sphere, it reinforces the concept of a 'rate for the job' based on the inherent nature of the job, rather than the financial or productive performance of the particular organisation or its local labour

Box 9.4	National Wages Council – Singapore

The National Wages Council (NWC) was set up in 1972 following legislation (1968) which restricted the substance of collective bargaining by protecting managerial prerogatives and specifying minimum working conditions for most workers and consequently resulted in declining union membership.

The NWC is a tripartite body comprising representatives from unions, employers' associations and government (with a 'neutral' economist chairperson). Its primary function is to set annual wage guidelines in the light of the performance of the economy, consistent with sustaining employment and growth, and to influence collective bargaining in line with 'public policy'. Its annual wages guidelines are submitted to the government and, although not mandatory (i.e. trade unions and employers are free to set their own wage rates), the Industrial Arbitration Court closely follows its guidelines in any dispute referred to it.

The NWC has adopted a policy of not differentiating between industrial sectors in its wages guidelines because all organisations compete for labour within the same limited labour market. However, it has made *recommendations* which apply wage increases differentially to tackle particular labour problems: in 1977 linking increases to merit rating (to promote individual performance) and being employed for more than one year (to restrict 'job-hopping') and in 1981 making a range of increases to reflect differences in both individual and organisational performance. After the 1985–6 recession and wage freeze, the NWC sought to encourage employers to introduce flexible wage systems using a yearly bonus, not consolidated into the basic wage, to reward for improved organisational performance. This had the effect of linking pay 'gains' to micro-organisational rather than macro-economic factors (although macro factors determine the level of yearly bonus for public sector employees), diminishing the role of an 'annual pay increase' and, therefore indirectly, reducing the wage-fixing role of the NWC.

Sources: C. Leggitt, 'Singapore', in S. J. Deery and R. J. Mitchell (eds), *Labour Law and Industrial Relations in Asia*, Longman Cheshire (Melbourne), 1993; Chew Soon Beng and R. Chew, 'The development of industrial relations strategy in Singapore', in A. Verma, T. A. Kochan and R. D. Lansbury (eds), *Employment Relations in the Growing Asian Economies*, Routledge, 1995.

See also Country profiles 4.3.

market, and prevents wage based competition between both workers and organisations (particularly at times of unemployment). It allows the union's bargaining strength to be equalised across organisations to establish a minimum which may not be reduced but may be enhanced at the organisational level where the union has sufficient strength or the organisation's financial or productivity position warrants such enhancement. Furthermore, as Bean points out[69], the socialist-oriented nature of many western European unions underpins their preference for bargaining structures which promote solidarity rather than segmentation of the workforce.

- *Management*. Industry-level bargaining has the advantage that it allows employers to present a unified collective response to trade union pressure (i.e. individual organisations cannot be 'played off' against each other). It also has the effect of standardising and stabilising wage costs for all organisations and prevents 'unfair' competition between organisations based on differing wage levels (particularly important in labour-intensive industries). However, the wage rate set at the national level in many private manufacturing industries has tended, in the past, to be that which could be afforded by the least productive and profitable organisations within the industry, consequently, the more profitable and productive organisations could, if they wished, pay higher rates. Industry-level bargaining may also have the advantage, dependent on the extent to which there is additional organisational level bargaining, of keeping trade union influence away from the workplace and the determination of working arrangements.

It is possible to distinguish between **three potential roles for industry-level pay bargaining**:

- It may **determine actual rates** to be paid – as has generally been the case in the UK public sector with detailed and comprehensive national agreements.

- It may **act as a floor**. Elliott describes this situation as one where 'when national wage rates rise all workers who currently enjoy rates in excess of the nationally agreed rate have their rates adjusted upwards either to re-establish some fixed relationship with the nationally agreed rate or because the change in the national rate provides the agreed signal for a change in workplace rates'[70].

- It may **act as a safety net**. Elliott points out that in this situation the industry level 'provides only some agreed minimum below which nobody will be allowed to fall'[71] and, therefore, any increase in the national rate will only affect those who were marginally above the old national rate but are now below the new national rate.

Clearly, the effect of industry-level bargaining on actual wages and earnings will depend on which role it is fulfilling. In the late 1970s, before the decline in multi-employer national bargaining, Brown and Terry argued that in much of the British private sector the national agreement provided little more than a 'safety net' and that in reality 'increases in ... nationally negotiated rates appear to be the result of belated and increasingly unsuccessful attempts to raise the rates into a more realistic relationship with actual standard earnings'[72]. In other words, industry-level wage rates followed, and were responsive to, organisational-level bargaining rather than vice versa. However, Elliott[73] found that while the national basic rate declined as a percentage of weekly earnings in some industries between 1968 and 1978, it increased in others. The increasing importance of the national rate in these industries may have been indicative of the worsening financial position of many organisations, a tougher management stand on wage increases and a weakening of the trade unions' ability to enhance national rates through organisational bargaining (more employees were coming closer to the 'safety net' role of the national rate rather than it providing a 'floor' to be built on).

Within the British structure of collective bargaining it is possible to identify three main categories of multi-employer bargaining institutions:

See Chapter 8 –
The government

1. *Statutory machinery*. Wages Councils (first established in 1909) were introduced to provide collective bargaining in situations where pay was low and trade unions were too weak to secure collective bargaining on a voluntary basis. They were intended as a temporary protection within which trade unionism and voluntary collective bargaining could develop but, in practice, they became a permanent form of collective bargaining institution (in 1988

there were 26 councils covering 2.5 million employees primarily in retail, catering, clothing and agriculture). They differed from other forms of collective bargaining arrangements in that, first, the government decided their establishment or abolition, decided which unions and employers' associations were to be represented and appointed the independent representatives, and second, any agreement was promulgated as a statutory order, applied to all employers in the industry and enforced by a Wages Inspectorate. However, the determination of the terms of any agreement remained principally a matter for direct negotiation between the two parties concerned but always bearing in mind the existence of the three independent members. The Wages Act (1986) restricted the scope of Wages Councils and they were finally abolished by the Trade Union Reform and Employment Rights Act (1993). Following their abolition there were indications that pay rates declined but with no increase in employment levels[74].

See Case study 9.1

2. *Formal voluntary machinery.* This form of institution involves a high degree of formality which, in some cases, extends to a permanent and separate secretariat, creating an impression that it is almost independent of the employers and trade unions which negotiate within it. These institutions (variously called Joint Industrial Council (JIC), National Joint Industrial Council (NJIC), National Joint Council or Committee (NJC)) have a common base in the Whitley Committee report (1916) which 'recommended the establishment of industry-wide collective machinery for all industries ... supported by joint committees at district and works levels'[75]. They were established on a voluntary basis between unions and employers in the 'newer' twentieth-century industries such as chemicals, civil engineering, local government, gas and electricity.

3. *Ad hoc machinery.* In many industries (like engineering, printing and textiles) which had established collective bargaining machinery prior to the Whitley Committee (1916), the collective bargaining arrangements did not have the high degree of formality associated with JICs, NJCs, etc. In these industries, multi-employer collective bargaining was conducted simply through the medium of a meeting between the various trade unions and employers' associations as and when necessary.

Single-employer organisational bargaining

Single-employer organisational (enterprise) bargaining may exist as the only or **predominant form** of collective bargaining structure in some industries (for example, car manufacture and oil refining in the UK) or countries, or may form part of a 'layered' collective bargaining system enhancing industry-level agreements. Both the USA and Japan are characterised by their emphasis on single-employer organisational bargaining. In the case of the USA this has arisen primarily because of the scale of the country: the difficulty of unions in organising on a nation-wide basis, the geographically segmented nature of the labour market and the self-sufficiency of the large organisations in most private sector

Case study 9.1 ■ Electrical contracting industry
Continuing multi-employer bargaining

In the mid-1990s, the electrical contracting industry, which deals with the installation of electrical systems in buildings, employed about 82,000 people (approximately half of whom were qualified electricians). The industry has a large number of self-employed workers and small sub-contractors (only a small number of organisations are large or medium-sized) and labour costs are a high proportion of total costs.

The Electrical Contractors' Association (ECA) has about 2,000 members, including all large and most medium-sized companies, whom, it claims, account for 80 per cent of the industry's work. The union side has been represented by the electricians' union (originally ETU, then EEPTU and now part of the AEEU) which, since its Communist ballot rigging scandal in the early 1960s, has tended to be a 'right-wing' union.

In 1966 the ECA and ETU established a Joint Industrial Board (JIB), with an equal number of representatives from each side and, more importantly, an independent chair and chief executive and its own secretariat. The objective of this 'unique' joint institution is not only to negotiate wages but also to regulate employment, productive capacity, skills and benefits.

■ It administers sick pay, accident, private medicine and pension schemes for the industry.

■ It oversees training in the industry, certificates the individual's competence (labourer, apprentice, electrician, approved electrician and technician).

■ It sets standard wages (for each category of worker), hours and holiday entitlements and approves any 'controlled incentive scheme' at organisational level.

■ It operates a disputes conciliation procedure (some 36 cases each year), which also encompasses unfair dismissal claims and is exempt from the statutory Tribunal system.

The agreement enhances labour market stability and predictability for management by assuring the quality of the labour (the accreditation process) and removing competition based on differences in wage costs (the wage regulation process). Indeed, throughout the 1980s and 1990s the national negotiated rate accounted for 80 to 90 per cent of the employee's total earnings. However, it is under some pressure from a growing level of self-employment (individual sub-contractors outside the ECA), workers being paid on a day-rate or 'job price' basis (contrary to national negotiated rates) and organisational diversification beyond electrical work.

Source: H. Gospel and J. Druker, 'The survival of national bargaining in the electrical contracting industry: a deviant case?' *British Journal of Industrial Relations*, vol. 36, no. 2, 1998, pp. 249–67.

See also Case study 11.1.

---

*See Country profiles
6.1 and 7.1*

industries. However, as Bean notes, multi-employer bargaining does exist in industries such as trucking, construction and retail, which are characterised by smaller, labour-intensive firms operating in competitive markets[76]. In Japan, enterprise bargaining (with its emphasis on the internal labour market characterised by permanent employment, seniority-based wage systems, promotion for core employees and 'house' unions) has predominated as a result of the 'carry-over to modern industry of patterns of social relationships and obligations which characterised feudal Japan'[77].

It is important to recognise that organisational bargaining may not be confined exclusively to one level but **may itself be 'layered'** at a combination of levels. For example, there could be *company-level bargaining* on general conditions (such as pensions, holidays and other conditions which are to apply to all employees), *plant- or site-level bargaining* on pay (which may then vary in relation to site performance or local labour markets) and *department-level bargaining* (determination of the employees' actual working arrangements). This may apply whether or not there is industry-level bargaining as well. Plant or site bargaining is particularly important in those organisations which are multi-industry as well as multisite and, therefore, the nature of the work and processes involved will vary between the sites and require different terms and conditions of employment. At the same time each site could, on an individual basis, be federated to different employers' associations and therefore operate under different national industry agreements.

It has been argued that there are **two important advantages** with single-employer organisational bargaining:

- It encourages management to develop a more positive approach to industrial relations within its organisation. Industry-level bargaining tends to weaken management's control of its wage costs, in that the determination of wage rates and other substantive terms is outside its direct control and may even be inappropriate to its circumstances. Management, by bargaining at the organisational level, is able to integrate pay within a comprehensive and organisationally related framework of industrial relations strategies and policies aimed at supporting business needs and developments to improve organisational performance. (See Box 9.5.)

- The terms of the collective agreements are no longer decided by people outside the organisation who are remote from its particular situation and problems and over whom the individual organisation's management and employee representatives have little direct control or even influence. The regulation becomes more direct and internalised, so that both management and employee representatives become responsible for, and committed to, the agreements they reach.

However, organisational-level bargaining may also present certain problems through the **greater fragmentation** of the collective bargaining structure. First, without a coherent policy and co-ordination, the existence of a series of bargaining units within the organisation, each with its own separate agreement and bargaining date, can lead to constant 'catching up' or 'leap-frogging' comparability claims between the various groups. This situation is accentuated, and co-ordination made more difficult, in those organisations where there are a variety of unions representing distinct groups of employees. Second, it may provide greater scope for 'comparability inflation' between organisations. A pay increase in one organisation, based on changes in work methods or improved profitability, can easily give rise to expectations of a similar increase in other organisations (competing in the same labour market) even where there is not the same willingness or opportunity for similar work changes. It provides an opportunity for unions to develop a 'key bargaining' strategy: that is, selecting one organisation which can afford the pay increase and then seeking to achieve the same level of pay settlement in other organisations. Third, because of the multiplicity of negotiations and agreements, organisational bargaining is less susceptible than industry bargaining to external verification and regulation during any period of incomes policy.

Box 9.5	National Power – short-circuiting old bargaining machinery

'We had inherited from the public sector a system of federated bargaining with negotiating machinery composed of three tiers: one across the industry as a whole, one at company level and one at local committee level. There were also separate agreements for each of three different groups of staff – manual employees, engineers and administrative staff. All the electricity boards negotiated with trade unions on an industry basis.

While this type of negotiation was appropriate to a public utility industry, to continue with this approach would have meant National Power, as a private company, sitting down with other generators who are our competitors in the market and with the distribution companies who are our customers. We would also be fixing wage rates with the unions which bore no relationship to local market rates or the profitability of the company. We decided, therefore, that we must negotiate on our own ...

We felt that the retention of three separate agreements for manual, administrative and engineering groups of staff would allow us to negotiate with each group separately about issues which specifically concerned that group.

This would speed up, rather than slow down, the process of negotiation on issues which remained to be discussed after the main points had been settled.

However, we have not closed our minds to single-table bargaining at some point in the future and ... the new grading structure and flexible working arrangements will make it easy to move to a single-table approach ...

Each of the three agreements has a two-tier negotiating structure. A company-level committee will discuss issues which it has been jointly agreed should be consistent across the whole company: for example, basic pay increases, length of the working week, sick pay, holidays, and overtime rates. Local negotiating committees will discuss issues which can vary between locations, such as shift rotas ...

In line with the policy of devolution, we have also introduced revised disputes and grievances procedures which keep any issues firmly in the control of the line manager, with discussions on issues which arise on site always taking place on site.

There can be no reference to anyone else. If there can be no agreement on site, this could result in a local union ballot for industrial action. However, the resulting dispute would remain a local one.'

Source: G. Bishop and R. Lewin, 'Short-circuiting old bargaining machinery', *Personnel Management*, February 1993, pp. 28–32.

Decentralisation of collective bargaining

It is important to recognise that some degree of organisational single-employer bargaining is inevitable even with strong industry-level agreements. Many of the non-substantive aspects of collective bargaining (i.e. those related to the regulation of 'job or work' and 'managerial authority' as opposed to 'pay') have always been, and indeed need to be, conducted at the immediate workplace or point of working rather than at the national level. At the same time, national multi-employer agreements often need to be interpreted and applied at the workplace level. The central issue in respect of decentralisation of collective bargaining, therefore, relates to what is the most appropriate level for the determination of pay and other substantive terms of employment.

Bean argues that 'the main elements of bargaining structures tend to persist and remain relatively stable. They do not usually break out suddenly from their traditional framework and veer off in some new direction' but, rather, gradually modify in response to 'shifts in market and technological factors, government policy and work aspirations'[78] – to which may be added management strategies.

Thus, at any point in time, collective bargaining structures contain elements of continuity (past needs) and change (future needs). Certainly, in the case of the UK, it is clear that **decentralisation of collective bargaining is not a new phenomenon** – in 1968 the Donovan Commission identified the existence of a 'two-tier' or 'layered' arrangement of collective bargaining in much of the UK manufacturing sector, in which the informality and fragmentation of organisational-level bargaining undermined the supposed regulatory effect of industry-level bargaining. This arose largely from the inability and inappropriateness of formal multi-employer industry agreements to regulate the increasing range of issues which were becoming subject to collective bargaining. Perhaps most importantly, changes in working methods and improvements in productivity could not, given the diversity of organisational requirements, be regulated effectively from the national level. The subsequent reform of collective bargaining during the 1970s in much of the private sector, based on greater formalisation of bargaining at the organisational level, was part of a conscious management strategy aimed at regaining managerial control and, it has been argued, further reduced the role of industry-level multi-employer bargaining and national agreements.

See Chapter 7 – Management

Bridgford and Stirling suggest that any discussion of the decentralisation of collective bargaining first 'begs the question: decentralization from what?'[79]. The answer will vary between different organisations, industries and countries depending on the nature of the existing bargaining structure. Thus, there are **different dimensions to decentralisation** (see Figure 9.2). For those countries, such as Sweden, which have operated strong corporatist economy-wide bargaining arrangements, decentralisation has meant shifting the focus of collective bargaining to the industry or sector level – which in the UK would be seen as a centralised bargaining level. In Germany, with its high levels of sectoral collective bargaining coverage, the process has focused on the insertion of 'a wide variety of clauses allowing deviations from collectively-agreed terms and conditions, including pay and working time'[80]. However, moves towards

See Country profile 9.1

Figure 9.2 Structure of collective bargaining

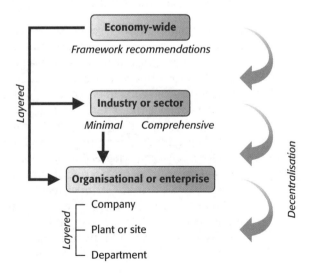

(See Country profile 9.2)

company negotiations raises the issue of who should negotiate such agreements on behalf of the employees – trade unions or the works councils (made up of employee representatives and, currently, with no right to initiate industrial action)[81]. Similarly, in Australia the decentralisation of 'collective bargaining' has meant not just a structural shift in the level at which pay is determined, but also a shift in the qualitative nature of the process – less emphasis on third-party arbitration awards and more on bipartite negotiated agreements.

In the UK, as Deaton and Beaumont pointed out, there are two distinct dimensions to decentralisation: 'the move away from multi-employer to single-employer structures, and secondly, within the single employer category, the decision to bargain at either the company or plant level'[82]. However, decentralisation need not be simply an 'either/or' situation (industry or organisation). A 'two-tier' arrangement may apply, with organisational bargaining 'topping up' national terms and conditions to a lesser or greater extent. Thus, decentralisation can also arise from a changing balance between the two levels (the industry agreement becoming less comprehensive and regulatory and more a framework of agreed common principles). Similarly, within single-employer bargaining (outside any national agreement) corporate- and site-level bargaining can co-exist, with some terms being uniform across the organisation while others vary between different sites of the organisation. Therefore, it is perhaps more useful to regard 'centralisation' and 'decentralisation' 'as constituting the two ends of a

Country profile 9.1   Sweden – Centralised co-ordination?

The 'Nordic' model of industrial relations has, in the past, been characterised by co-operation between capital and labour within a centralised system of collective bargaining. The pressure for a centralised approach in Sweden originated in a series of 'trials of strength' disputes in the early twentieth century. The employers responded to the development of strong workplace unionism and a politically active labour movement, based on close co-operation between the LO and the SAP (Swedish Social Democratic Party), by combining within employers' associations to present a collective unified front. This resulted in a shift in power and authority to the central level on both sides.

The advent of a Social Democratic government in 1932 (continuously in power until 1976) strengthened centralised economic and social co-operation between government and unions, while employers saw the development of centralised self-regulation as a means of avoiding direct governmental legal intervention. The 'golden age' of centralised bargaining in Sweden came during the 1950s–1970s and was associated with low levels of industrial action, sustained economic growth, high productivity and high wage levels. The structure involved three levels of collective bargaining:

■ A central framework of recommendations negotiated between the SAF (the Swedish Employers' Confederation) and the LO (the largest union confederation, which represents manual workers in the private sector). Over time this framework became increasingly detailed;
■ Industry or sectoral negotiations between individual employers' associations and trade unions on the implementation and adaptation of the central agreement to meet specific industrial conditions;
■ Organisational negotiations on issues specific to the organisation.

Generally, centralised bargaining provided employers with stable and moderate pay increases in line with economic development, while the LO achieved a means to pursue its 'wage solidarity' policy (compression of differentials and equality of pay irrespective of the productivity or profitability of the individual organisation). Indeed, Kjellberg argues that this 'solidaristic wage policy functioned as an extra-governmental form of incomes policy' (1:80).

Country profile 9.1   Sweden – Centralised co-ordination? *(continued)*

Two major factors began to undermine the centralised system:

- *Challenge to the dominance of the LO.* Collective bargaining was dominated by the SAF/LO agreement covering manual workers in the private industrial sector. The wage levels reflected the need to maintain Sweden's international competitiveness but were used also as the benchmark for other groups (private service and public sectors). However, increasing employment and unionisation in the white-collar, service and public sectors during the 1970s resulted in the establishment of separate 'bargaining cartels' to negotiate central agreements in these sectors. This replaced the dominance of the SAF/LO with 'a multi-polar bargaining structure characterised by increasing competition between groups over the distribution of income' (2:21).

- *Wage drift.* Some industrial manual groups were able to secure greater increases at the lower levels of bargaining than recommended within the central agreement. As a consequence the LO sought and achieved a system of 'wage development guarantees' (based on the average wage drift) to compensate those who were not so successful. The system was adopted in the other sectors as a way of keeping private service and public sector pay in line with private manual industrial pay. This had the effect of institutionalising wage inflation.

The drive during the 1980s towards decentralisation was led initially by transnational companies more exposed to international competition. Employers were concerned to reduce labour costs, increase flexibility and variability and integrate pay with other HRM strategies aimed at improving organisational performance. However, the 1980s was a period of both continuity (centralisation) and change (decentralisation). While the unions and the Social Democratic government (1982–91) continued to favour centralisation, employers were divided: many employers saw centralisation as a mechanism for maintaining pay restraint, while those in the international competitive markets sought change.

The 1980s was a period of swings between centralised and decentralised bargaining as each failed to contain rising wage costs. In 1983 the VF (engineering employers' federation) broke away from the centralised SAF/LO negotiations and concluded their own industry agreements with manual and white-collar unions which allowed for increased skill differentials and local increases based on productivity. In the 1990/91 bargaining round, following the SAF's refusal to negotiate a centralised agreement and protests at the government's subsequent proposal for a wage freeze and ban on strikes, the government established a national tripartite mediation commission (Rehnberg Commission). This produced a two-year 'stabilisation agreement' (including a ban on local negotiations during the first year) and a 'pre-established consensus on the desirability of both wage restraint and co-ordination' (1:90) within which industry or sectoral agreements could be negotiated. A similar process oversaw the 1993 bargaining round, but was less successful in co-ordinating the 1995 round. Consequently, the industry or sectoral level has become the most influential in terms of pay determination.

In 1997 a 'framework accord' was agreed by a number of unions and employers' associations in the private sector (covering about 20 per cent of the Swedish workforce) providing for mediation and arbitration in the event of a 'failure to agree' in industry negotiations. It is believed that this accord contributed to the general success of the 1998 bargaining round (3:30). In 1998, a government commission (Öberg Commission) recommended, in addition to restrictions on industrial action, the establishment of two new bodies: a tripartite body to promote 'understanding between the social partners' and a new national mediation body to promote co-ordination of collective bargaining (in particular, common expiry dates) and with the power to appoint mediators *without* the consent of the parties (although there would be no power to impose a settlement).

Trade unions opposed these recommendations, because of proposed restrictions on industrial action, and the LO sought to engage the SAF in an alternative strategy based on an 'alliance for economic growth'. However, the SAF rejected any move back towards a centralised pay bargaining arrangement.

Sources:
1. A. Kjellberg, 'Sweden: restoring the model?', in A. Ferner and R. Hyman (eds), *Changing Industrial Relations in Europe*, Blackwell, 1998, pp. 74–117.
2. 'The rise and fall of centralised bargaining', *European Industrial Relations Review*, no. 219, April 1992.
3. 'Pay determination under the spotlight', *European Industrial Relations Review*, no. 305, June 1999.

See also Country profile 5.3.

Country profile 9.2   Australia – Decentralisation and flexibility in collective bargaining

The Australian industrial relations system is a 'hybrid of arbitration and bargaining' (1:60). Compulsory arbitration, introduced in 1904 following bitter industrial conflict in the 1890s, was regarded as a 'bold social experiment' intended to restructure the collective bargaining relationship and promote greater justice and equality in wage determination.

This compulsory arbitration approach has resulted in a highly regulated complex statutory system of awards at both federal and state levels. The awards, which provide legally enforceable wages and employment conditions, are a mixture of Commission decisions (third-party conciliation or arbitration) and registration of voluntary agreements (consent awards). About 80 per cent of all employees, public and private sectors alike, are covered by these awards or agreements. In addition, there is legislation establishing minimum conditions for all employees (pay, hours, and holidays and other leave). At the apex, National Wage Case hearings take place every one or two years and involve submissions not only by employers and unions but also by the government. Since the early 1980s, the Commission decisions have formed an integral part of Australia's national 'Accord'.

Since the early 1990s, the Australian government has adopted a strategy of encouraging decentralisation of collective bargaining to the workplace with the aim of making 'direct bargaining the primary focus for fixing wages and conditions and for achieving greater productivity and flexibility in the workplace' (3:3). Organisations can now negotiate different types of organisational agreements:

- *Certified agreement* – made between employers and unions (the organisation must be covered by either a federal or state award).

- *Enterprise flexibility agreement* – made directly between employers and their employees subject to majority employee approval (the organisation must be covered by a federal award). A union which has members in the organisation and is a party to the relevant award has a right to take part in the negotiations but cannot veto an agreement approved by a majority of the employees. This is designed to extend bargaining to workplaces with little or no union presence.

- *Workplace agreements* – made between employers and their employees on an individual or collective basis without union involvement; in effect, the registration of non-union agreements or contracts.

These types of agreement are integrated into the award system:

- There must be procedures for preventing and settling disputes and processes for consultation about work changes and performance.

- The terms of any organisational agreement overrides the provisions of the relevant award for that condition, but if there is no provision in the organisational agreement for a particular condition provided for in an award then the award terms still apply.

- A 'no-disadvantage' test is applied to organisational agreements. Award conditions may be changed so long as employees are not disadvantaged in respect of the package as a whole – 'the test is intended to protect well-established and accepted standards across the community such as maternity and parental leave, hours of work, minimum wages, superannuation, and termination, change and redundancy provisions' (3:10).

Sources:
1. R. Lansbury and J. Niland, 'Managed decentralization? Recent trends in Australian industrial relations and human resource policies', in R. Locke, T. Kochan and M. Piore (eds), *Employment Relations in a Changing World Economy*, MIT Press, 1995, pp. 59–90.
2. E. M. Davis and R. D. Lansbury, 'Employment relations in Australia', in G. J. Bamber and R. D. Lansbury (eds), *International and Comparative Employment Relations* (3rd edn), Sage, 1998, pp. 110–43.
3. *Making Workplace Agreements*, Department of Industrial Relations (Federal Government, Canberra), May 1994.

See also Country profile 8.2 and 12.1.

spectrum encompassing greater or lesser degrees of centralisation rather than mutually exclusive alternatives'[83].

Surveys in the UK in the late 1970s identified a number of structural factors which might help explain the **differences between industries**. For example, Deaton and Beaumont[84] found that multi-employer bargaining was associated with a high regional concentration of organisations (i.e. operating within a similar labour market), high union density within the industry and multi-unionism, while single-employer bargaining was associated with larger establishments, multisite organisations, foreign ownership, organisations operating within non-competitive product markets and the existence of specialist industrial relations managers at a senior level.

However, by the early 1990s, there was a marked **decrease in the importance of multi-employer bargaining** in the UK private manufacturing and service sectors. Brown *et al.*[85] estimate that whereas in 1950 80 per cent of private sector employees had their pay fixed by collective bargaining (split 60/20 in favour of multi-employer bargaining), by 1970 the coverage of collective bargaining had reduced to 70 per cent (evenly split between multi- and single-employer bargaining) and in 1990 the overall coverage was 50 per cent (split 10/40 in favour of single-employer bargaining). Millward *et al.* believe that this decline in the relative importance of multi-employer bargaining 'came about from a move to other levels of bargaining (especially plant level) or, more commonly, to unilateral determination by management'[86]. As Huiskamp points out, 'the industry-wide agreement loses ground on two fronts: on the one hand, larger companies are turning more and more to company agreements, and on the other, the smaller firms are withdrawing from collective agreements altogether'[87].

The **main driving forces for decentralisation** of collective bargaining during the 1980s and 1990s have come from management and government rather than from trade union power at the workplace. Bean[88] suggests that these 'centrifugal tendencies' can be explained by reference to the 'crisis' in the advanced industrialised economies created by the growth of the new economies of south-east Asia (and elsewhere), periods of widespread recession and increased international competition coupled with the advancement of new technology. Organisations have had to adopt a twin strategy of reducing costs (particularly labour) and increasing flexibility, which inevitably focus on the organisation itself. The development of HRM (supporting the strategic needs of the business and securing a committed workforce) has focused on organisational restructuring, more flexible working arrangements, human resource development, linking pay to performance, etc. As Purcell points out, an integral part of corporate strategy and business policy has been the devolution of more authority and responsibility to managers of distinct profit centres or business within the organisation with a consequent need 'to make the structures of industrial relations fit the corporate need of profit centre and business unit decentralisation'[89]. The Conservative government[90] certainly believed that national pay bargaining based on the concepts of cost of living, comparability or some belief in a going-rate was 'outmoded' and inflationary, created unemployment and, consequently, should be replaced with local pay determination which emphasises ability to pay (profitability) and performance (both organisational and individual) and is likely to be more linked to local labour market conditions. Clearly, change in structure is inextricably bound up with shifting the argument bases which may be used to justify pay increases. As Fatchett pointed out, 'for a Government committed to the belief in the supremacy of the free market, national level collective bargaining is regarded as an inefficient interference with the operation of markets'[91]. However, Brown *et al.*[92] believe that the management desire to decentralise bargaining has not come so much from a perceived benefit in being able to secure lower wages but, rather, from the perceived benefits of creating an internal organisational labour market based on individualism, performance and constant adaptation.

In the late 1980s, Booth argued that 'the distinction between industry-level and organisation-level bargaining is largely irrelevant'[93] in respect of pay **determination in the public sector** because they were either single-employer industries or because the national agreements were comprehensive and automatically applied at the employer organisation level. However, this is no longer true. The Conservative government's programme of privatisation across a wide range of industries (ports, gas, electricity, water, telecommunications) provided an opportunity for the resultant private management to reassess the desired structure and approach to collective bargaining and, if not to abandon multi-employer bargaining completely, at least increase the scope for organisational bargaining. Furthermore, reforms in the remaining parts of the public sector encouraged the decentralisation of collective bargaining through, for example, the establishment of distinct executive agencies in the civil service[94], hospital trusts in the NHS[95], independent local management at all levels of the education sector (all with the right to determine their own terms and conditions of employment) and by encouraging local authorities to 'opt out' of national agreements. At the same time, national agreements or pay review body awards were expected to allow for an element of locally negotiated pay, to be related either to individual performance or to the recruitment and/or retention of staff with skills which were in short supply – a more 'two-tier' structure. However, as Thornley points out, the 1997 report of the Pay Review Body for Nursing Staff 'included a vigorous indictment of the conduct of the local pay experiment' although it 'remains wedded to the ideal'[96]. She found, from a survey of union negotiators, that local pay bargaining had increased the potential for conflict at the organisational level and led to a decline in morale and trust in management among employees.

Certainly, the 1980s and 1990s have seen the **abandonment or decreased influence of a significant number of multi-employer bargaining arrangements**. One survey[97] identified 16 private sector multi-employer bargaining arrangements which were abandoned between 1986 and 1989 (covering some 700,000 employees) and a further ten (covering 170,000 employees) where the influence of the national agreement was reduced. To this must be added the subsequent abolition of a further eight multi-employer bargaining arrangements between 1989 and 1993[98] (including the engineering industry – the largest of all covering some 900,000 employees) and the abandonment of national bargaining in areas such as the water and rail industries. A number of reasons can be identified for these developments:

■ Management's desire to **reform working practices**, particularly in relation to the introduction of new technology: for example, in national newspapers

See Case study 9.2

and independent television (where there were only a relatively small number of employers facing a competitive situation).

■ The **withdrawal of major organisations** in the industry from the national bargaining arrangements in order to conduct their own bargaining: for example, the NatWest Bank in the banking sector; Tesco and other major supermarket groups in the multiple food trade; Sealink, Cunard and P&O in shipping.

■ **Disputes and failures to reach agreement** at national level: for example, in the engineering industry, although pay had been negotiated on a two-tier system for many years, the national agreement on the working week, holidays, etc. was generally implemented throughout the industry and it was the unions' campaign for a shorter working week and the subsequent dispute which led to the ending of national bargaining on pay and all conditions. As Pickard notes, 'the sticking point was the employers' insistence that ... any national deal should be in the form of an enabling agreement, committing member companies to reduce hours only if they could negotiate productivity savings to pay for the change ... it was exacerbated unintentionally by the union decision, when talks broke down, to take local, rather than national, industrial action ... the unions were negotiating settlements at some of the targeted companies of precisely the type the employers had envisaged in trying to secure a national enabling agreement: a cut in the working week to 37 hours, with productivity clauses which lowered the cost to the company'[99].

See Case study 9.3

■ **Privatisation**. In some of the privatised industries (for example, ports, water and rail) multi-employer bargaining has been abandoned completely, while in others the role of organisational bargaining has been strengthened.

Case study 9.2 ■ Retail food
Decline in multi-employer bargaining

In 1991, the retail food sector employed 818,000 people: characterised by high proportions of women, part-time employees and young people. Although there are some 50,000 grocery outlets in the UK (a substantial decline from the 150,000 in 1960), the sector was dominated by five major supermarket chains (Tesco, Sainsbury, Gateway/Somerfield/Kwik Save, Argyll Group (Safeway, Presto and Lo-Cost) and Asda), which accounted for 41 per cent of employment in the sector (338,951 employees) and 61 per cent of the total grocery trade in Britain. In addition, there were several other medium- to large-sized regionally based supermarket chains. The level of unionisation among the big supermarkets varied – for example, Tesco (70 per cent), Gateway (23 per cent), Sainsbury and Safeway (10 per cent).

Until the late 1980s there were two national-level wage-setting mechanisms:

■ A statutory based Wages Council which set legally enforceable minimum pay rates (of primary importance in the 'small shop' segment);

■ Voluntary multi-employer collective bargaining (Multiple Food Trade Joint Committee) covering national and regional supermarket chains. However, three major supermarket chains were outside this arrangement – Marks & Spencer and Sainsbury (which do not recognise trade unions) and Asda which, through its then parent company (Allied Dairies), recognised and negotiated with GMB.

The break-up of national multi-employer bargaining was sparked-off, in early 1988, by Tesco's decision

Case study 9.2 ■ Retail food *(continued)*
Decline in multi-employer bargaining

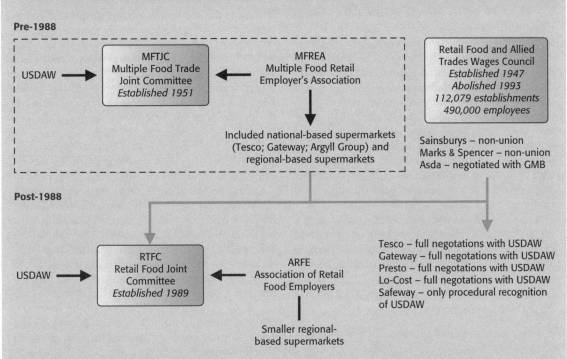

Pre-1988

USDAW →

MFTJC
Multiple Food Trade
Joint Committee
Established 1951

← MFREA
Multiple Food Retail
Employer's Association

↓

Included national-based supermarkets
(Tesco; Gateway; Argyll Group) and
regional-based supermarkets

Retail Food and Allied
Trades Wages Council
Established 1947
Abolished 1993
112,079 establishments
490,000 employees

Sainsburys – non-union
Marks & Spencer – non-union
Asda – negotiated with GMB

Post-1988

USDAW →

RTFC
Retail Food Joint
Committee
Established 1989

← ARFE
Association of Retail
Food Employers

|

Smaller regional-
based supermarkets

Tesco – full negotiations with USDAW
Gateway – full negotiations with USDAW
Presto – full negotiations with USDAW
Lo-Cost – full negotiations with USDAW
Safeway – only procedural recognition
of USDAW

to withdraw from the Multiple Food Trade Joint Committee (a decision which was linked to its withdrawal from multi-employer bargaining for its bakery workers). Tesco believed that multi-employer bargaining hindered the development of a more strategic and organisation-specific approach to human resource management and industrial relations as part of a 'repositioning' in the marketplace as a high-quality supermarket. At the same time it felt that greater involvement of shop stewards and line management in organisational-level negotiations would enhance employee involvement and commitment.

Following the dissolution of the MFTJC after the 1988 national wage negotiations, each of the major national supermarket chains (with the exception of Safeway, which had been non-union prior to its acquisition by Argyll in 1987) formally recognised USDAW and established company-level bargaining machinery. This reflected the centralised nature of their strategic and operational business decision making. Perhaps as

expected, USDAW sought to maintain some industry parity by submitting similar claims to each company. Significantly, the companies themselves formed a Liaison Committee within the British Retailers' Association to exchange information.

After the break-up of the MFTJC, the smaller regional supermarket chains established a new association (Association of Retail Food Employers) to negotiate national-level agreements with USDAW in order to avoid leap-frogging competition between themselves.

The Trade Union Reform and Employment Rights Act (1993) abolished all Wages Councils – thereby removing statutory collective bargaining machinery for the employees in small retail shops.

Sources: M. P. Jackson, J. W. Leopold and K. Tuck, *Decentralisation of Collective Bargaining*, Macmillan, 1993 (Chapter 5); 'Industrial relations in the food industry', *IRS Employment Trends*, no. 567, September 1994, pp. 12–16.

Case study 9.3 ■ Water industry
Privatisation and the abandonment of multi-employer bargaining

The water industry is concerned with the supply of clean water, sewerage treatment, flood protection and water recreation. Until 1973 these activities were carried out by a mixture of over 1,000 local authorities and a number of quasi-private Statutory Water Companies (SWCs) established by Acts of Parliament during the nineteenth century. The Water Act (1973) transferred local authority responsibility for water, sewerage, etc. to ten Regional Water Authorities (RWAs) and established a National Water Council (NWC) to regulate and co-ordinate the activities of both the RWAs and SWCs. In 1991/2 the RWAs employed 52,500 people compared with 7,000 employed by the SWCs.

In common with other parts of the public sector, the industry had relied (since 1919) on formalised national-level multi-employer collective bargaining machinery. There were four main negotiating bodies:

■ National Joint Industrial Committee for 27,000 manual production workers;

■ National Joint Craft Committee for 5,500 maintenance workers;

■ National Joint Staff Council for 32,500 non-manual staff;

■ Joint National Council for Chief and Senior Officers for 600 senior employees.

The privatisation of the water industry (in 1989) was preceded by two important organisational changes:

■ The Water Act (1983) replaced the single statutory NWC with two voluntary bodies – the Water Authorities Association (representing the RWAs) and Water Companies Association (representing the SWCs).

■ Activities relating to flood protection and regulating the water environment were transferred from the RWAs to a new separate non-departmental public body – the National Rivers Authority. This allowed the RWAs to focus on water supply and sewerage treatment and become public limited companies.

Despite the Water Act's removal of statutory underpinning, the increased opportunity for independence of individual water authorities or companies and, also in 1983, the first water industry national strike, two reports commissioned by the employers in that year recommended the maintenance of national multi-employer bargaining (on a voluntary basis) to avoid the problems of competitive leap-frogging. Not surprisingly, this was supported by the trade unions.

However, in the run-up to privatisation, there was mounting pressure in some RWAs to act like private companies. In particular, they felt there was a need to develop more strategic, flexible and organisationally focused approaches to human resource management which linked with and supported the individual organisation's business objectives. Consequently, first Thames Water (the largest RWA) gave notice of withdrawal from the national negotiating machinery in 1986, followed by Northumbrian Water (the smallest RWA) in 1988. In 1989 the other water authorities followed suit despite the preference of one or two (such as Welsh Water) to maintain a national framework of pay negotiations which had, in the past, provided industrial relations stability.

Privatisation and the move away from national multi-employer bargaining produced a variety of initiatives and changes amongst the different 'new' water companies:

■ *Diversification and decentralisation*. Some companies separated the core activities of water supply and sewerage from subsidiary activities (such as engineering, leisure, head-office, etc.) with different terms and conditions of employment.

■ *Recognition and representation*. Although union derecognition was rare, there was a shift in emphasis from union representation to employee representation. Perhaps the most significant development was Northumbrian Water's restriction of recognition to a 'confederation' of unions with only one seat on its new negotiating forum – a Company Council of employee representatives.

■ *Single-table bargaining, harmonisation and performance-related pay*: While only some companies introduced single-table bargaining for manual production, craft and staff, most intro-

Case study 9.3 ■ Water industry *(continued)*
Privatisation and the abandonment of multi-employer bargaining

duced new pay structures for both manual and staff employees which reflected changes in work arrangements (e.g. multi-craft) and were more flexible and linked to performance appraisal.

■ *Long-term agreements and changes in settlement dates.* The most significant development was in Welsh Water where, as part of its 'partnership approach', a pay formula was agreed which aimed to link future pay increases to changes in the cost of living, comparability with other pay movements in Wales (independently surveyed)

and the performance of the company. The spread in settlement dates across the companies has made it more difficult for the unions to maintain even a semblance of 'national' bargaining by presenting a common claim to all employers.

Sources: M. P. Jackson, J. W. Leopold and K. Tuck, *Decentralisation of Collective Bargaining*, Macmillan, 1993 (Chapter 7); 'Industrial relations developments in the water industry', *IRS Employment Trends*, no. 516, July 1992, pp. 8–15.

See also Case study 10.3.

Korczynski suggests that the establishment of multi-employer bargaining arrangements in the engineering construction industry in 1981 was perhaps the last 'comprehensive centralisation' in the UK and could not have happened in 1991 'because of the significant differences in state policy'[100]. However, it would be wrong to regard the movement as all one way: that is, towards the abandonment of multi-employer bargaining. In three cases (licensed clubs, lace finishing, and flax and hemp) new national multi-employer bargaining arrangements were set up following the restriction of the scope of the Wages Councils by the Wages Act (1986) in order 'to restore the influence of joint regulation'[101]. Similarly, in multiple food retailing a new multi-employer bargaining arrangement covering smaller firms was set up following the withdrawal of the big supermarket groups. It would seem that multi-employer bargaining may still be more attractive than single-employer bargaining for the smaller unionised organisation.

The greater emphasis on single-employer bargaining structure has presented a particular problem for **multisite organisations**: whether to centralise bargaining at the corporate level or decentralise it at the site level. While in part this choice may be influenced by both the size of the organisation as a whole and the relative sizes of the individual sites, it is more likely, as Brown suggested, to be 'strongly affected by the heterogeneity of a company's products and by the history of its evolution by merger, takeover, or internal growth'[102]. Clearly, the **choice of organisational bargaining structure** is a strategic one because it has implications not only for the number and types of 'bargaining units' (which employees will be grouped together under the same terms and conditions of employment) but also for the extent to which there is a common organisational culture. Ogden[103] noted that while the choice is primarily a management decision, it can result as much from a 'defensive response' to trade union pressure as an 'offensive initiative' by management. Management may seek corporate bargaining as a means to restrict the scope of site bargaining in response to powerful workgroups at the site level or the union's use of intersite comparisons.

However, Ogden pointed out that such a move might involve a cost to management. Corporate bargaining is not conducive to productivity bargaining and detailed work changes which need to be determined and negotiated at the point of production. Equally, unions may themselves welcome corporate bargaining as an opportunity to extend the scope of collective bargaining into areas of strategic corporate decision making – this could not be achieved so easily if bargaining was confined to the site level.

Kinnie argued strongly that, while accepting that management has three alternative organisational bargaining structures (centralised, decentralised or a 'half-way house'), management should reject the last alternative. In examining examples of centralised and decentralised bargaining structures, he noted that 'the structures of management and bargaining are closely matched, producing a consistent pattern of control'[104]. In the centralised organisation, the existence of an integrated production pattern and central control of finance and production matters meant that centralised bargaining facilitated the regulation of union intersite comparisons. In the decentralised organisation, diversified production and markets coupled with intersite competition for investment resources from the centre, accentuated the divisions between the sites and allowed management, in the absence of any effective intersite co-ordination, to justify decentralised bargaining and eliminate intersite union comparisons. However, in organisations which had adopted a half-way house structure (centralised control of finance but decentralised collective bargaining) management and bargaining structures were inconsistent. This led to union representatives questioning the autonomy and authority of site management, perceiving central guidelines to site management as interference with local autonomy and an attempt to impose central control and, therefore, concentrating on intersite comparisons as sites on lower wages sought to achieve the levels of the other sites and the latter, in turn, sought to maintain their differential.

However, it is perhaps inevitable that most multisite organisations will adopt some form of half-way house structure. Certainly, Kinnie suggests that decentralisation of management and bargaining structures 'do not necessarily lead to an increase in decision-making discretion for establishment managers'[105], while Purcell[106] believes that management can have the best of both worlds by corporate co-ordination and control of 'decentralised' bargaining through budgetary control mechanisms and monitoring personnel activities of individual sites, units, etc. The 1990 WIRS survey[107] reported that some 60 per cent of establishment-level managers 'consulted' with higher management *before* the start of manual pay negotiations – what is not known is how directive was the 'consultation'. The effect of this may be to create a two-tier system *within* the organisation, similar to that identified by the Donovan Commission in the 1960s, in respect of the relationship between industry and organisational bargaining and subject to similar tensions and conflicts. Furthermore, Arrowsmith and Sisson have identified that, in practice, decentralised bargaining is also 'co-ordinated' by information flows *between* organisations, including 'benchmarking' and identifying 'best practice'. They suggest that employers 'move like ships in a convoy' and that the 'extensive availability of information means that there is little or no need for a more formal co-ordination of approach to pay and working time'[108].

◾ Summary propositions

- ◾ The process of collective bargaining is concerned with regulating both economic and managerial relations on a joint 'rule-making' basis.

- ◾ Collective bargaining is a voluntary, bipartite process; its character is determined by management's and employees' perception of the nature of their mutual interdependence. There has been a trend away from an adversarial and towards a co-operative (partnership) relationship.

- ◾ The structure of collective bargaining is dynamic and varies between different countries, industries and organisations. The emphasis of collective bargaining in the UK has shifted away from common multi-employer agreements at the industry-level and towards more flexibility at the organisational level in order to respond more effectively to variations in organisational situations and needs.

Activity   Try to get some collective agreements from two or three organisations in different sectors (you could possibly combine with other students to get them from organisations you work for or other local or national organisations). See if you can obtain both substantive and procedural agreements. (Depending on the agreements you are able to obtain, they might also be useful in relation to Chapter 6 – Representation at the workplace, Chapter 14 – Pay and working arrangements and Chapter 15 – Grievance, discipline and redundancy.)

You can then examine this material and try to identify what evidence it provides in relation to:

1. The style of collective bargaining relationship (adversarial or co-operative);

2. The different functions of collective bargaining (content and subject matter covered by the collective agreements);

3. The structure of collective bargaining (national or organisational agreements) and its relationship to joint consultation or other forms of employee involvement or participation.

◾ Further reading

- ◾ M. P. Jackson, J. W. Leopold and K. Tuck, *Decentralization of Collective Bargaining*, Macmillan, 1993. This provides a useful range of case studies (both private and public sector) examining decentralisation of collective bargaining in the UK.
- ◾ R. Bean, *Comparative Industrial Relations* (2nd edn), Routledge, 1994. Chapter 2 provides a useful comparison of different national collective bargaining models.

■ P. Blyton and P. Turnbull, *The Dynamics of Employee Relations* (2nd edn), Macmillan, 1998. Chapter 7 provides a useful examination the development of collective bargaining in the UK together with a British Steel case study.

References

1. R. Dubin, 'Constructive aspects of industrial conflict', in A. Kornhauser, R. Dubin and A. M. Ross (eds), *Industrial Conflict*, McGraw-Hill, 1954, p. 44.
2. *Report of Royal Commission on Trade Unions and Employers' Associations* (Donovan Commission), HMSO, 1968, p. 54.
3. H. Mathieson, 'Trade unions and reward', in R. Thorpe and G. Homan (eds), *Strategic Reward Systems*, FT Prentice Hall, 2000, p. 185.
4. D. Metcalf, 'Industrial relations and economic performance', *British Journal of Industrial Relations*, vol. 31, no. 2, 1993, pp. 225–84; D. Metcalf, 'Fighting for equality', *Centrepiece*, vol. 5, no. 2, 2000.
5. P. Bland, 'Trade union membership and recognition, 1997–98', *Labour Market Trends*, July 1999, pp. 343–51 (table 6).
6. *Ibid*. (table 7).
7. 'Bargaining characterised by national diversity', *IDS European Report*, no. 395, November 1994, p. 24.
8. S. Milner, 'The coverage of collective pay-setting institutions in Britain, 1895–1990', *British Journal of Industrial Relations*, vol. 33, no. 1, 1995, pp. 69–91.
9. Donovan Commission, *op. cit.*, p. 8.
10. O. Aikin and J. Reid, *Employment, Welfare and Safety at Work*, Penguin, 1971, pp. 19–20. Reprinted by permission of Penguin Books Ltd. © Olga Aikin and Judith Reid, 1971.
11. *Fords v T&GWU and AUEW* (1969).
12. Green Paper on *Industrial Relations in the 1990s*, HMSO, 1991.
13. Green Paper on *Trade Union Immunities*, HMSO, 1981, p. 55.
14. P. B. Beaumont, *Public Sector Industrial Relations*, Routledge, 1992, pp. 98–9.
15. K.W. Wedderburn, *The Worker and the Law*, Penguin, 1971, p. 160. © K.W. Wedderburn, 1965, 1971.
16. J. Pickard, 'When pay gets personal', *Personnel Management*, July 1990, p. 42.
17. Graham Mather, Director General of the Institute of Economic Affairs quoted in Pickard, *Ibid.*, p. 41.
18. 'Contract to kill collective action', *Labour Research*, December 1989, p. 13.
19. A. M. Ponzellini, 'Innovation in pay policies between industrial relations and the management of human resources', *International Journal of Human Resource Management*, vol. 3, no. 2, 1992, p. 219.
20. N. Bacon and J. Storey, 'Individualization of the employment relationship and the implications for trade unions', *Employee Relations*, vol. 15, no. 1, 1993, p. 15.
21. S. and B. Webb, *Industrial Democracy*, Longman, 1902.
22. A. Flanders, 'Collective bargaining: a theoretical analysis', *British Journal of Industrial Relations*, vol. 6, no. 1, 1968, pp. 1–26.
23. A. Fox, 'Collective bargaining: Flanders and the Webbs', *British Journal of Industrial Relations*, vol. 12, no. 2, 1975, pp. 151–74.
24. Flanders, *op. cit.*, pp. 4–6.
25. *Ibid*.
26. *Ibid.*, p. 7.
27. F. H. Harbison, 'Collective bargaining and American capitalism', in Kornhauser *et al.* (eds), *op. cit.*, p. 270.
28. N. W. Chamberlain and J. W. Kuhn, *Collective Bargaining*, McGraw-Hill, 1965, p. 113.
29. *Ibid.*, p. 121.
30. *Ibid.*, p. 130.
31. *Ibid.*, p. 135.
32. P. Blyton and P. Turnbull, *The Dynamics of Employee Relations* (2nd edn), Macmillan, 1998, p. 193.
33. S. Kessler and F. Bayliss, *Contemporary British Industrial Relations* (3rd edn), Macmillan, 1998, pp. 212 and 213.
34. Chamberlain and Kuhn, *op. cit.*, p. 428.
35. *Ibid.*, p. 429.
36. R. E. Walton and R. B. McKersie, *A Behavioral Theory of Labor Negotiations*, McGraw-Hill, 1965.
37. Beaumont, *op. cit.*, p. 120.
38. W. E. J. McCarthy and N. D. Ellis, *Management by Agreement*, Hutchinson, 1973.
39. *Ibid.*, pp. 96–7.
40. *Ibid.*, p. 108.

41. A. Flanders, *Collective Bargaining: Prescription for change*, Faber & Faber, 1967, p. 19.
42. Beaumont, *op. cit.*, p. 117.
43. L. Dickens, 'What are companies disclosing for the 1980s?' *Personnel Management*, April 1980, p. 28.
44. R. Moore, 'Information to unions: use or abuse?' *Personnel Management*, May 1980, p. 34.
45. *Ibid.*, p. 37
46. Dickens, *op. cit.*, pp. 29–30.
47. 'Disclosure of information to trade unions for the purpose of collective bargaining', *ACAS Code of Practice*, HMSO, 1998.
48. D. Torrington and J. Chapman, *Personnel Management* (2nd edn), Prentice Hall, 1983, p. 442.
49. R. Hussey and A. Marsh, *Disclosure of Information and Employee Reporting*, Gower, 1982, pp. 17–33.
50. Central Arbitration Committee, *Annual Report 1979*.
51. 'CAC disclosure of information awards', *Industrial Relation Review and Report*, January 1980.
52. 'Written evidence of the Ministry of Labour', *Royal Commission on Trade Unions and Employers' Associations*, HMSO, 1965, p. 23.
53. N. Sear, 'Relationships at factory level', in B. C. Roberts (ed.), *Industrial Relations: Contemporary problems and perspectives*, Methuen, 1962, p. 163.
54. *Communications and Consultation*, CBI, 1966.
55. J. Henderson, *A Practical Guide to Joint Consultation*, Industrial Society, 1970, p. 4.
56. W. E. J. McCarthy, 'The Role of Shop Stewards in British Industrial Relations', Research Paper 1, *Royal Commission on Trade Unions and Employers' Associations*, HMSO, 1966, p. 36.
57. Henderson, *op. cit.*
58. M. Marchington and R. Armstrong, 'The nature of the new joint consultation', *Industrial Relations Journal*, vol. 17, no. 2, 1986, pp. 158–70.
59. M. Marchington, 'The four faces of employee consultation', *Personnel Management*, May 1988, p. 45.
60. Marchington and Armstrong, *op. cit.*, p. 160.
61. Marchington, *op. cit.*, p. 47
62. *Ibid.*, p. 46.
63. *Ibid.*, p. 47.
64. R. Bean, *Comparative Industrial Relations* (2nd edn), Routledge, 1994, p. 79.
65. J. Bridgford and J. Stirling, *Employee Relations in Europe*, Blackwell, 1994, p. 125.
66. W. E. I. McCarthy, P. A. L. Parker, W. R. Hawes, and A. L. Lumb, 'The reform of collective bargaining at plant and company level', *Department of Employment, Manpower Paper No. 5*, HMSO, 1971.
67. Bridgford and Stirling, *op. cit.*, pp. 126–7.
68. Bean, *op. cit.*, p. 80.
69. *Ibid.*, p. 83.
70. R. F. Elliott, 'Some further observations on the importance of national wage agreements', *British Journal of Industrial Relations*, vol. 19, 1981, p. 370.
71. *Ibid.*
72. W. Brown and M. Terry, 'The changing nature of national wage agreements', *Scottish Journal of Political Economy*, vol. 25, no. 2, 1978, p. 125.
73. Elliott, *op. cit.*, p. 375.
74. 'Wages Council abolition hits pay', *IDS European Report*, no. 394, October 1994, p. 17.
75. Blyton and Turnbull, *op. cit.*, pp. 196–7.
76. Bean, *op. cit.*, p. 54.
77. *Ibid.*, p. 85.
78. *Ibid.*, p. 89.
79. Bridgford and Stirling, *op. cit.*, p. 129.
80. 'Flexibility, change and the future of sectoral bargaining', *European Industrial Relations Review*, no. 285, 1997, p. 25.
81. 'German bargaining under attack', *Labour Research*, September 1998, pp. 25–6.
82. D. R. Deaton and P. B. Beaumont, 'The determinants of bargaining structure: some large scale survey evidence for Britain', *British Journal of Industrial Relations*, vol. 18, no. 2, 1980, p. 201.
83. 'Pay bargaining: to centralise or decentralise?' *Industrial Relations Review and Report*, No. 397, August 1987, p. 13.
84. Deaton and Beaumont, *op. cit.*, p. 210.
85. W. Brown, P. Marginson and J. Walsh, 'Management: pay determination and collective bargaining', in P. Edwards (ed.), *Industrial Relations: Theory and Practice in Britain*, Blackwell, 1995, p. 137.
86. N. Millward, M. Stevens, D. Smart and W. R. Hawes, *Workplace Industrial Relations in Transition*, Gower, 1992, p. 225.
87. R. Huiskamp, 'Collective bargaining in transition', in J. V. Ruysseveldt, R. Huiskamp and J. van Hoof, *Comparative Industrial and Employment Relations*, Sage, 1995, p. 152.
88. Bean, *op. cit.*, p. 90.
89. J. Purcell, 'How to manage decentralised bargaining', *Personnel Management*, May 1989, p. 53.
90. *Employment for the 1990s*, HMSO, 1989.
91. D. Fatchett, 'Workplace bargaining in

hospitals and schools: threat or opportunity for the unions?' *Industrial Relations Journal*, vol. 20, no. 4, 1989, p. 255.

92. Brown *et al.*, *op. cit.*, p. 138.
93. A. L. Booth, 'The bargaining structure of British establishments', *British Journal of Industrial Relations*, vol. 27, no. 2, 1989, p. 226.
94. R. F. Elliott and K. A. Bender, 'Decentralization and pay reform in central government: a study of three countries', *British Journal of Industrial Relations*, vol. 35, no. 3, 1997, pp. 447–75.
95. 'Local bargaining in the NHS: a survey of first and second wave trusts', *IRS Employment Trends*, no. 537, June 1993.
96. C. Thornley, 'Contesting local pay: the decentralization of collective bargaining in the NHS', *British Journal of Industrial Relations*, vol. 36, no. 3, 1998, pp. 428 and 429.
97. 'Developments in multi-employer bargaining: 1', *IRS Employment Trends*, no. 440, May 1989.
98. 'Decline in multi-employer bargaining charted', *IRS Employment Trends*, no. 544, September 1993.
99. J. Pickard, 'Engineering tools up for local bargaining', *Personnel Management*, March 1990, pp. 41–2.
100. M. Korczynski, 'Centralisation of collective bargaining in a decade of decentralisation: the case of the engineering construction industry', *Industrial Relations Journal*, vol. 28, no. 1, 1997, p. 25.
101. *IRS Employment Trends*, no. 440, *op. cit.*, p. 8.
102. W. Brown (ed.), *The Changing Contours of British Industrial Relations*, Blackwell, 1981, p. 13.
103. S. G. Ogden, 'Bargaining structure and the control of industrial relations', *British Journal of Industrial Relations*, vol. 20, no. 2, 1982.
104. Dr Kinnie, 'Local versus centralised bargaining: the dangers of a "halfway house"', *Personnel Management*, January 1982, p. 33.
105. N. Kinnie, 'The decentralisation of industrial relations? – recent research considered', *Personnel Review*, vol. 19, no. 3, 1990, p. 33.
106. Purcell, *op. cit.*, p. 55.
107. Millward *et al.*, *op. cit.*, p. 234.
108. J. Arrowsmith and K. Sisson, 'Pay and working time: towards organization-based systems?' *British Journal of Industrial Relations*, vol. 37, no. 1, 1999, p. 68.

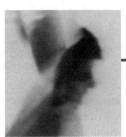

chapter ten

Employee involvement and participation

Learning objectives

By the end of this chapter, you should be able to:

- understand the differences in concept, strategy and form between employee 'involvement' and employee 'participation';

- explain the different forms of direct employee involvement based on dissemination of information, delegation of decision making and 'financial' participation;

- appreciate the role of works councils and worker directors and their relationship to trade unions, collective bargaining and joint consultation.

Definition

The terms involvement and participation are often used in a generalised and interchangeable way to cover all processes and institutions of employee influence within the organisation (including joint consultation and collective bargaining). However, it is perhaps better to see involvement as enhancing the support and commitment of employees to the objectives and values of the organisation and participation as providing employees with the opportunity to influence and take part in organisational decision making.

Key issues

While you are reading this chapter, you should keep the following points in mind:

- If we believe that employees are not simply economic factors of production hired to carry out the instructions of management, then we must consider what role (and rights) they should have in determining the organisational decisions which, after all, affect not just their 'working life' but their whole life, and that of their family.

- While it may be desirable to enhance the status, opportunity and work satisfaction of the individual through direct employee 'involvement' mechanisms, we need to be aware that it may reduce the capacity of employees to challenge and influence managerial decisions by undermining collectivism and the representational role and power of trade unions.

■ In the past, employee interests and influence in the UK have been represented primarily through trade unions and collective bargaining. We should be conscious that the introduction of the European model – statutory support for employee rights to information, consultation and joint decision making (the principle of 'co-determination') through works councils and possibly worker directors – is likely to present a major challenge.

10.1 Introduction

While Bean argues that 'it is generally conceded in the liberal democratic world that working people should have a *right* to participate in the making of decisions which critically affect their working lives'[1] (my italics), Hyman and Mason point out that it is 'one of the most complex, dynamic and controversial aspects of organizational structure and employment relationships in advanced industrialized countries'[2]. At its heart lies the issue of what should be (*a value judgement*) the objective, extent and form of employee access to and influence on decision making within the organisation. It is, as Brannen argued, concerned with 'the control of workers, in the sense both of control by them and control exerted on them within the system of production'[3]. However, it is important to distinguish between three distinct approaches, with very different objectives and underlying rationales.

Industrial democracy (or workers' control)

This is a sociopolitical concept or philosophy of industrial organisation which focuses on the introduction of democratic procedures to restructure the industrial power and authority relationship within organisations, thereby creating a system which, Hyman argued, involves 'the determination by the whole labour force of the nature, methods and indeed purpose of production'[4]. Its central objective is the establishment of employee self-management within an organisation, whose ownership is vested in either the employees or the state and whose managerial function is exercised ultimately through a group, elected by the employees themselves, which has the authority over all decisions of the organisation including the allocation of 'profits' between extra wages and re-investment[5]. However, according to Hyman and Mason, industrial democracy has 'little currency in contemporary market-driven economies where any worker or activist concern for industrial control has been fragmented and displaced by defensive struggles to retain individual employment and to protect employment rights'[6]. While some institutional arrangements contain an element of a 'democratic control' (for example, co-determination through workers directors in Germany and the Swedish collective wage-earner funds), this represents only a limited modification of the capitalist managerial authority system rather than a fundamental restructuring. Nevertheless, Mitchell argues that the 'potential [of global capitalist organisations] to weaken democracy at the state level demands a corresponding increase in democratic principles within the firm' and this 'signals a recognition of the modern firm as a social entity and not merely as an embodiment of private rights to capital'[7].

Employee participation

Hyman and Mason use the term 'participation' to refer to those initiatives by the state, unions or employees 'which promote the *collective* rights of employees to be represented in organizational decision-making'[8] (my italics). The emphasis is on employees as a collective body in some form of partnership with capital in organisational decision making. Wall and Lischeron differentiated 'participation' from 'collective bargaining' by emphasising 'the involvement of [employees] in the decision making processes which *traditionally* have been the responsibility and prerogative of [management]'[9] (my italics). In countries such as the UK and USA, collective bargaining has, in the past, been the primary, or even exclusive, method for exerting employee influence within the organisation and has, in general, been limited to joint decision making about pay and terms of employment (including an element of operational work regulation). Thus, 'participation' represents a distinct evolutionary development directed towards extending collective employee influence beyond this relatively narrow distributive 'wage/work bargain' into much wider areas of organisational planning and decision making at both the operational and, more importantly, strategic level. However, in countries such as Germany and The Netherlands, these 'traditional' areas of organisational decision making have been subject to employee influence (generally through Works Councils) for nearly 50 years. Whatever the mechanism, Patemen argued that 'real' participation ideally requires both sides to have 'equal power to determine the outcome of decisions'[10]. In the absence of such power equality, employees can only rely on management goodwill (i.e. its acceptance of and commitment to a participative philosophy or style of organisational management). There must be more than just the provision of information to employees or their representatives; there must be a genuine opportunity for employees to influence major strategic organisational decisions. Elliott, perhaps pre-empting the 'partnership' approach of the 1990s, suggested that any development from distributive collective bargaining towards co-operative 'participation' would require changes on both sides: 'unions should be shouldering new responsibilities in what should involve at least a lessening, though probably not a rejection, of the adversary system, and managements should be sharing some of their decision-making powers'[11].

Employee involvement

From the 1980s there has been a change in direction and emphasis (closely associated with the human resource management concept) which is indicated by the adoption of the term employee 'involvement' rather than 'participation'. Employee involvement has been variously described as 'the means used to harness the talents and co-operation of the workforce in the common interests they share with management'[12], 'any activity which helps to release the full potential of people at work'[13] and 'a range of processes designed to engage the support, understanding, optimum contribution of all employees in an organisation and their commitment to its objectives'[14]. The mechanisms introduced under the heading of 'involvement' include 'empowerment', teamworking, briefing groups and quality circles. These measures have been introduced by management in order to optimise the utilisation of labour (in particular, improve organisational quality and flexibility) and at the same time secure the employee's identification with and commitment to the aims and needs of the organisation. Such measures may allow employees greater influence and control over decision making, but only in relation to their immediate work operations, hence the phrase sometimes used of 'task participation'. Certainly, Marchington and Wilkinson believe that employee involvement has been 'management sponsored', reflects a 'management agenda' and 'has excluded the opportunity for workers to have an input into high-level decision making'[15].

It is clear that while 'involvement' is intended to enhance the support and commitment of employees to the objectives and values of the organisation (as determined by management), 'participation' is designed to provide the employees with the opportunity to influence and take part in organisational decision making. As Hyman and Mason point out, 'the paradigm of employee involvement (EI), employee participation (EP) and industrial democracy (ID) is essentially one of ascending levels of control by employees over their work and organizations'[16]. Similarly, Marchington and Wilkinson refer to the 'escalator of participation' from information, through communication, consultation and co-determination to control[17].

10.2 Approaches to involvement and participation

The traditional functional view of industrial organisations contrasts the managerial role of directing and co-ordinating the activities of the organisation (through the functions of planning, organising, motivating and controlling) with the employees' role of being recruited and trained to perform certain defined tasks (the function of doing). Walker believed that the central issue was how to 'bridge the gap' between these functional roles by establishing forms of interaction through which 'workers', while remaining in workers' positions, may take part (directly or through representatives) in certain functions defined as 'managerial'[18].

Typology of forms

Clearly, there are a variety of ways in which to 'bridge the gap', not least through joint consultation and collective bargaining, and these may be differentiated by reference to three constituent elements (see Figure 10.1):

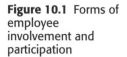

Figure 10.1 Forms of employee involvement and participation

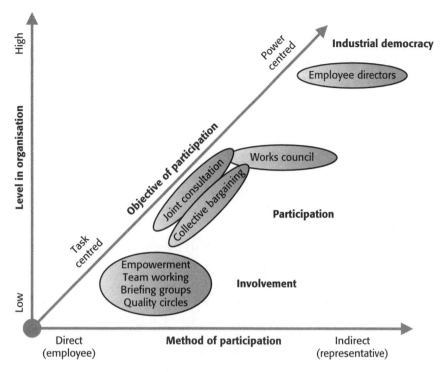

■ **Method or extent. Direct forms** allow employees to be personally and actively involved in the decision-making process; **indirect forms** restrict the mass of employees to a relatively passive role and rely on employee representatives to carry out the active role of discussing and deliberating with management on their behalf.

■ **Level within the organisational hierarchy**. The process can take place at any level, from that of the employee's immediate work situation to the board level.

■ **Objective or scope**. The managerial functions and decisions which provide the content of the participatory processes may be **task centred** (concerned primarily with the structure and performance of the operational work situation) or **power centred** (concerned with the more fundamental managerial authority and decisions which determine the framework or environment within which operational decisions have to be made).

There is also a fourth element which needs to be borne in mind – namely, the *quality* of the process of interaction between employee(s) and management (see Box 10.1). However, by using the three structural elements, it is possible to contrast **two strategies**.

Direct forms of involvement

Direct forms, such as the development of formal and regular briefing groups or consultative meetings between the employees and their supervisor (more open style of management) and/or the creation of new work organisation arrangements (work redesign), focus attention on the individual employee or workgroup and the immediate operational situation (task centred). This strategy may be referred to as **descending involvement**, in so far as management invariably initiates the development for its own purposes (involvement is offered) and, as part of the change, may transfer authority and responsibility from itself to the employees for a limited range of work-related decisions (methods of working, allocation of tasks, maintenance of quality, etc.). However, the content of the process is confined largely to the implementation phase of operational decisions already made by management. This approach is intended to motivate the individual employee directly, to increase job satisfaction and to enhance the employee's sense of identification with the aims, objectives and decisions of the organisation (all of which have been determined by management).

Indirect forms of participation

Indirect forms, such as widening the content of collective bargaining, the creation of Works Councils and the appointment of worker directors, focus attention on the exercise of the managerial prerogative and the balance of power between management and employees in the organisation's decision-making process (power centred). This strategy can be referred to as **ascending participation** because it seeks to protect the interests of the employees by extending their collective influence into a wider range of decisions at the higher levels of the organisation and because, in relation to the extension of collective bargaining and the appointment of worker directors, the initiative for the development may come from the employees and their unions (participation is demanded) or the state. Thus, it is primarily concerned with extending employee influence, through the process of joint regulation, into areas of policy and major organisational planning which previously have been the sole prerogative of management.

The central issue is the extent to which these two strategies conflict with or are complementary to each other.

Box 10.1	Particpation – the fourth dimension

It is the *nature and quality of the process of interaction* which determines the extent or depth to which employees (individually, in groups or through their representatives) are allowed and able to contribute to and influence organisational decisions (whether operational or strategic). This may range from only *informing* by management, through *consultation* to *negotiation* and finally *co-determination* (equal influence in both setting the agenda as well as deciding the outcome of organisational decision making). Participation is primarily a philosophy, not a particular institutional form – whether of the direct, descending kind or the indirect, ascending kind. Therefore, it can take place at any time and in any organisational framework so long as management is genuinely and unreservedly prepared to share responsibility for the decision-making process with employees and/or their representatives.

Pressures for participation

There have been two pressures for the development and extension of employee participation or involvement – sociopolitical and industrial. Certainly, the concept of 'industrial democracy' was often an integral ideological element of the industrial and political development of labour movements throughout Europe during the late nineteenth and early twentieth centuries. However, such mechanisms as the factory 'productivity committees' introduced in the UK during the Second World War were primarily a pragmatic and temporary organisational arrangement aimed at increasing production. In the years immediately following the war, a number of European countries (such as Denmark, Belgium, France, Germany and The Netherlands) legislated for the establishment of Works Councils as a means of reducing disputes and securing a co-operative effort between management and employees in economic reconstruction[19]. The UK, in contrast, continued to rely on traditional collective bargaining mechanisms and did not really start to consider 'participation' until the 1970s.

The 1960s and early 1970s was a period of significant **social development** centred around the culmination of the movement away from postwar austerity and the 'coming of age', in terms of working and voting, of the first generations whose formative years had been ones of relative peace rather than war. The period can be characterised as one of relative economic prosperity with stable and secure employment (including periods of labour scarcity), increased knowledge and awareness derived from education and the mass media, and greater preparedness to question established values, attitudes and institutions. Most importantly, it produced a change in attitudes towards formally constituted authority in many spheres of society (family, schools and universities, the Church, political parties and even government and the state) and a focusing of attention on the concept of 'government by consent'. The period saw the demise of the 'deferential society' and the rise of the 'democratic imperative': that is, 'those who will be substantially affected by decisions made by social and political institutions must be involved in the making of those decisions'[20].

In the industrial sphere these developments resulted in **increased aspirations among employees** – in terms of not only material rewards (wages) but also the management of the organisation (authority). At the same time, the increased size and complexity of industrial organisations contributed to the **alienation of employees** from their work. At one extreme of the organisation, industrial power and major decision making was concentrated in the hands of a limited number of senior managers (usually remote from the mass of the organisation's employees), while at the other extreme the emphasis on the division and specialisation of labour in order to improve efficiency and productivity tended to reduce employee identification with both the end product of the organisation and the organisation itself. This led to attention shifting away from the purely legal and economic aspects of the contractual relationship between employer and employee and towards the psychological and sociological aspects of the relationship between the individual and his or her work situation. There was a greater acceptance of the notion that industrial organisations have both an economic function (the provision of goods or services in the most efficient way) and a social function (the provision of a satisfactory and meaningful work environment for the people who produce those goods or services).

At the same time, management recognised that **technological, industrial and economic change**, at the organisational level, could be carried out more smoothly, quickly and effectively with the active and full support of the employees concerned than if it made the decision alone and then sought to implement it against the negative reaction of employees. The process of involving employees in decisions which affect their working lives could lead not only to direct improvements in production and working arrangements (by drawing on the knowledge and experience of employees) but also to greater employee commitment to organisational strategies and change. The development of employee 'participation' can be viewed as a management strategy aimed at retaining and formalising control over the labour process at times when its legitimacy is threatened or labour power is high.

These social and industrial pressures during the 1970s were reflected and reinforced in the **political sphere** where the debate centred on two main issues:

- The apparent contradiction between the notional democratic basis of society outside the organisation and the absence of meaningful employee participation within the organisation;
- The need to obtain the understanding, co-operation and consent of employees in the process of industrial and economic change (at both the macro economy level and micro organisational level).

The **Labour governments** in the UK during the 1960s and 1970s, in particular, not only supported national-level tripartite discussions through NEDO but also favoured direct legislative intervention to obtain the adoption of more formalised and representative forms of employee participation at the organisational level (including worker-directors). For example, they appointed worker-directors as part of the reorganisation of the British Steel Corporation (1967) and Post Office (1977), established the Bullock Committee of Inquiry on Industrial Democracy (1975) and, in the subsequent White Paper (1978), advocated a ballot of the employees to secure one-third employee representation on the board in organisations of over 2,000 employees.

However, the shift in the political and industrial contexts since 1979 has been reflected in a **shift away from 'participation' and towards 'involvement'**. Ramsay[21] believes that the 1980s witnessed a combination of a change in government policy (which, in line with reducing trade union power and deregulating the labour market, did not support power-centred forms of indirect participation), the development of a 'more confident' management approach to organisational employee relations (emphasising strategic business needs, managerial objectives and individualism) and a change in trade union priorities (concentrating on defending employment rather than extending industrial democracy). **Conservative government policy** favoured the voluntary evolution of direct 'involvement' rather than 'indirect' participation through legislated compulsion. Indeed, as Townley[22] points out, it was a Liberal amendment to the **Employment Act (1982)** which introduced the requirement for companies with more than 250 employees to include a statement in their annual report:

> 'describing the action that has been taken during the financial year to introduce, maintain, or develop arrangements aimed at –
>
> (i)   providing employees systematically with information on matters of concern to them as employees;
> (ii) consulting employees or their representatives on a regular basis so that the views of the employees can be taken into account in making decisions which are likely to affect their interests;
> (iii) encouraging the involvement of employees in the company's performance through an employees' share scheme or by some other means;
> (iv) achieving a common awareness on the part of all employees of the financial and economic factors affecting the performance of the company' (S.1).

Marchington and Wilding believed that the practical impact of this requirement was 'likely to be marginal not only because there are no sanctions which can be used against employers who file a nil return but also because most of the larger companies will have no trouble in putting together a catalogue of involvement practices from somewhere within the organisation'[23]. However, some personnel managers and directors believe that stronger legislation is inevitable and that employers should be obliged to disclose information and financial performance to all employees[24].

Certainly, the increasing globalisation and liberalisation of world trade (both goods and services) has focused the attention of many organisations on the **need to be internationally competitive**. The consequent drive to improve organisational performance has meant, Hyman and Mason argue, that 'an increase in productivity, or more specifically in labour productivity, assumes mythic proportions for both managers and government policy-makers'[25]. They identify two management approaches to securing increased productivity and performance. While the 'coercive' confrontational approach relies on threatening employment security to secure acceptance of change, the 'integrative' approach relies on adopting techniques and practices which 'encourage improved employee performance through establishing or reinforcing a sense of common purpose between employer and employees'[26] – direct task-centred employee involvement.

However, since the early 1970s, there has been **continued political pressure from within the European Union** for the strengthening, codification and institutionalisation of 'representative' employee participation. Three major strands can be identified. First, some proposals have been based on the principle of uniformity across the EU (subject only to the size of the organisation) – such as the early proposal for worker-directors within a two-tier board structure (*Fifth Directive*, 1972), which did not come to fruition, and the 1998 proposal for Company Works Councils (*Directive on National-level Information and Consultation*). Second, in 1994 the EU finally adopted the *European Works Councils Directive* which applies to pan-European organisations with more than 1,000 employees operating in two or more member states and requires them to establish a European-level Works Council. Third, since 1976, the EU has been seeking to ensure that any *European Company Statute*, under which organisations could opt to be regulated by European rather than national laws, would include a requirement for employee participation – including possibly worker directors. However, it is clear that the principle of 'uniformity' has given way to allow national subsidiarity and variation subject only to any alternative system of participation being 'equivalent in effect' – EU Directives establish the principle, but organisations and nations are left some scope for variations in the form.

Management and union perceptions of 'involvement' and 'participation'

It is important to recognise that there are **diverse expectations** regarding both the purpose and form of employee 'participation' or 'involvement'. Marchington argued that there is an inherent danger that management 'may assume that *their* definitions and *their* solutions are acceptable to the different interest groups'[27]. While management may, initially, seek to limit the process to the provision of information, consultation and/or the establishment of direct forms of involvement, nevertheless 'what managements appear to regard as the maximum acceptable to them ... [union representatives] seem to regard as the minimum basis upon which to build up their influence over a wider range of issues and with more joint decision making'[28]. Furthermore, it is an **organic process** with its own potential momentum. Participation or involvement at one level or on one type of issue may lead to expectations and demand for its adoption at other levels and on other issues. It is difficult, if not impossible, for management to call a halt at any particular point and, in effect, say 'employees may participate so far, but no further'. McCarthy and Ellis believed that management should accept from the start that 'within a system of management by agreement there would no longer exist any area of management decision-taking where management itself could claim an absolute and unilateral right to resist union influence in any form'[29].

The **management view** appears to be based on a **perception of a unitary 'community of interest'** between employees and management in the goals of the organisation (its survival, well-being and development). Buckingham suggested that 'the differences between the two sides of industry are dwarfed by our overriding national need to compete successfully with the rest of the world'[30] and this was reflected in the IPM's (now IPD) approach to employee participation; for example,

■ 'employee participation and involvement plans and strategies should take as their starting point the high degree of common interest and mutual interdependence which must exist in any successful organisation'; and

■ 'the fundamental emphasis of any participation and involvement programme should be on increasing the profitability and success of the organisation ... and increasing the sense of common purpose and motivating employees to maximise their contribution by endeavouring to gain their understanding of, and commitment and contribution to, the organisation's success'[31].

Through the adoption of such a strategy, which acknowledges and utilises the employees' aspirations to be more involved, management believes it will improve the technical quality of decisions, increase the acceptability of those decisions, encourage employee identification with the success of the organisation and improve job satisfaction. The emphasis of management's approach is, therefore, one of improving organisational harmony, efficiency and productivity (employee 'involvement').

The **trade union view**, on the other hand, appears to be founded on the assumption that the enterprise is a **pluralistic organisation**, with sectional and competing interests, which needs to be formally regulated on a joint basis. Their emphasis, therefore, is on participation as a means of extending employee influence in the organisation's decision making; particularly through the enhancement and strengthening of representational systems. Certainly, many writers have challenged the managerial notion of organisational consensus as a basis for developing employee participation. For example, Marchington suggested that the high degree of common interest or mutual interdependence assumed by the IPM 'may not be present in all that many organisations'[32] and Ramsay argued that 'participation schemes are subject to an ongoing context of conflicting interests between management and labour' and therefore 'management proposals are an exercise in pseudo-democracy insofar as they attempt to impose an instrumental and integrative framework'[33]. Indeed, ACAS has pointed out that the TUC and many trade unions are likely to be 'cautious of forms of participation which seem to bypass established management-union arrangements'[34].

These differences can be seen in the findings of a number of surveys carried out during the 1980s:

- Warner[35] found that management's perception of the degree of employee influence on decision making remained relatively constant as between direct and indirect forms of participation (at 'little' and 'moderate'). However, while union representatives felt that employee influence through direct forms of participation was generally 'little', they rated employee influence through indirect participation higher than management at between 'moderate' and 'much'.

- Dickson found that while union representatives were often 'suspicious of direct participation unaccompanied by indirect participation' because it 'might be an attempt by managers to gain greater productivity from employees without a commensurate increase in employee benefits', managers 'favoured the introduction of direct participation prior to indirect participation in the hope that some of the perceived positive effects could be transferred to indirect participation'[36].

- Bartlett found little disagreement between managers and subordinates regarding the *potential value* of forms of 'co-determination' or 'negotiation' but increasing discrepancy in respect of forms of 'consultation' and 'reporting' (managers ascribing higher 'potential value' than subordinates). Significantly, in respect of the *perceived success* of the various forms, he found that 'the only method that both groups rate as highly successful in practice is that in which their interests most clearly coincide – the joint safety committee', while 'conversely maximum disagreement emerges over collective bargaining over company strategic plans'[37].

■ Wilson *et al.* found that out of 150 strategic decisions surveyed only 29 (19 per cent) involved trade unions and in only three of the 19 private sector organisations, as opposed to nine out of the ten public sector organisations, did the management rate the union influence as 'quite a lot' or higher. However, they note that even in these cases the union is 'wholly reactive to managerially defined topics' and 'if the unions are in any degree negative towards the decision, their influence achieves little or nothing'[38].

■ Neumann identified a number of constraints on workers' propensity to participate; these include personal apathy, mistrust of management motives, deeply held values and beliefs, and fear caused by lack of knowledge and confidence[39].

Poole argued that 'the higher the level of decision-making the less likely it has been for workers to have any major influence on the outcomes of events, and the more vigorously managerial "prerogatives" have been defended'[40]. In his view, 'the bulk of schemes for employee participation initiated by management have been restricted in terms of the scope, level and range of issues involved'[41] and, while many of these schemes 'may have had important effects in so far as industrial "efficiency" is concerned, it is doubtful whether they imply any significant erosion of managerial "prerogatives"'[42]. Indeed, Hyman and Mason suggest that 'management might direct certain issues into lower-level involvement forums, to discuss and negotiate these issues through a non-strategic mechanism, in order to limit the potential of these issues being discussed in a more meaningful strategic context'[43] – 'involvement' being used to avoid 'participation'. The situation is compounded when participation is related to the stages of decision making. Thus, Huiskamp notes the **'participation paradox'** identified by one major European survey[44] whereby 'participation is limited in the planning stage, when the possibility of having an impact is greatest, and increases in the implementation stage, when this possibility is much smaller'[45]. Participation becomes limited only to influencing and improving operational implementation of strategic change rather than helping to determine the change agenda and make strategic choices.

10.3 Employee involvement

See Chapter 7 – Management

There is little doubt that employee 'involvement', as opposed to 'participation', is a management initiative. Slomp argues that it is 'part of a one-sided managerial policy, the approach being to grant privileges rather than endow the enterprise workforce with enforceable rights'[46], while Marchington points out that 'the decision about whether or not to "involve" employees rests with management, who are able to define and limit the terms under which EI can take place'[47]. Ramsay[48] identifies a **complex set of potential management objectives** for employee involvement: changing employees' attitudes and awareness of the business (increasing their sense of loyalty, commitment and support for management); providing means of incentive and motivation (leading to acceptance of work change (*passive*), direct improvement in productivity and quality (*active*) and/or increase in job satisfaction and development (*personal*)); extending employee influence or ownership (increased employee influence or control of the work situation); changing the relationship with trade unions (either negating their role or incorporating them within a co-operative organisational framework). Significantly, one survey of 62 organisations in 1993 showed that while absenteeism, industrial disputes and labour turnover neither increased nor decreased as a result of employee involvement in 70 per cent of the organisations, two-thirds reported increased effective decision making, employee job satisfaction and productivity[49].

Certainly, it would appear that almost any activity could be regarded as a form of 'employee involvement'. For example, Tillsley found that '85 per cent of employees reported the use of at least one method of employee involvement at their workplace'[50], perhaps not too surprising when the methods included memos and notice board, house magazine, staff appraisals, suggestion schemes, employee attitude surveys and informal conversations with managers and colleagues. It is important to note, as Marchington *et al.* found, that 'multiple techniques led to potentially conflicting pressures and confusion or communications overload for the staff' and that, in some organisations, 'the enduring picture was one of fads and fashions, stimulated in part by a regular turnover of managers who each introduced their own version of employee involvement to replace that of their predecessor'[51]. They identified four common problems associated with the development of employee involvement: lack of continuity, lack of middle management support and commitment, adoption of inappropriate systems and employee scepticism. Significantly, employees and trade unions are often less of a hindrance to the successful operation of employee involvement initiatives than senior or middle management[52].

There has been a tendency for employee involvement and participation to be viewed simply within an **organisational communication** framework. Holden, for example, regards employee involvement as 'but one aspect of organisational communication'[53], Storey[54] includes participation and involvement under the heading of 'leadership and motivation' alongside communication and goal-setting, appraisal and pay, while Hyman and Mason[55] put forward a matrix framework for examining the different forms of employee involvement based on communication flow (upward or downward) and employee focus (individual or group). However, a significant aspect of employee involvement also centres on **decision making**. Thus, although they differ in their direction of the communication flow, Ackers *et al.* differentiate direct communications (which 'transmit information downwards to the individual employee'[56]) from problem solving groups, while Geary distinguishes between *consultative* participation, where 'employees are encouraged, and enabled, to make their views known' (emphasising upward communication), and *delegative* participation, where 'responsibility for what has traditionally been an area of management decision making is placed largely in employees' hands: participation is designed into peoples' jobs'[57]. Similarly, Marchington and Wilkinson introduce 'centrality to the work process'[58] as an important element in categorising different forms of 'involvement'.

It is useful to divide the various forms of employee involvement into three basic categories: communication, delegated decision making and financial participation.

Communication

One of the **popular myths** of industrial relations has been to ascribe any problem, or failure to resolve a problem, to 'misunderstandings' or 'inadequate communication' between management, employees and/or unions. However, as the CIR noted in the 1970s, it would be entirely wrong to 'overrate the significance of communications both as a cause of the problems facing managements and employees and as a means of solving problems ... Communications cannot in themselves remove conflict of interest and values'[59]. Most often the source of conflict lies in the differences of objectives, interests, perceptions and attitudes, which significantly affect the way in which information and situations are interpreted (see Box 10.2). Communication between management, employees and unions, on both the interpersonal and inter-organisational levels, provides no more than *a means* to identify differences, develop a better understanding and seek accommodation within a mutually acceptable solution.

Since the early 1980s there has been a **shift in the emphasis of organisational communication** away from 'disclosure' of information to *trade unions* in support of the collective bargaining process and towards 'dissemination' of information to *employees* in order to secure their greater involvement in and identification with the organisation's interests and objectives. A Department of Employment survey in 1988[60] showed that 42 per cent of the practices referred to in company reports related to some form of direct communication or meetings with employees (e.g. company magazines or newsletters, employee reports, circulars, notice boards, line management communication/meetings (both formal and informal), briefing groups, quality circles, etc.). Significantly, most of these practices relate primarily to communicating *to* employees. Townley[61] points out that the continued emphasis, during the 1980s and 1990s, on

Box 10.2	Three basic rules about communication

- The reactions of employees to any event will be favourable only if it matches or exceeds their expectations.

- Where an announcement will fall short of expectations, there are only two alternatives to avoid trouble: improve the content of the announcement until it does match expectations, or take time to reduce expectations to the level of the subsequent announcement.

- Preparing employees for unwelcome news (i.e. moving expectations in a negative direction) requires time and sensitive handling.

Source: D. Drennan, 'How to make the bad news less bad and the good news great', *Personnel Management*, August 1988, pp. 40–3.

communication with employees is underpinned by two rationales: first, as a process of education to inform employees about the business and market realities of the 'enterprise culture' associated with highly competitive international markets; and second, as a strategy of securing organisation commitment and giving employees a sense of 'ownership' and 'empowerment'. Perhaps not surprisingly, trade unions may feel that such communication strategies are directed toward 'attitudinal restructuring' (making employees more favourably disposed towards management) and subverting the union's collective representational role.

Employee reports

In examining the **objectives** of employee reporting Hussey and Marsh pointed out that Reeves'[62] distinction between company-centred aims and employee-centred aims 'has the advantage of identifying, and indeed polarising, immediate management interests on the one hand and the social and moral responsibilities of management on the other'[63]. *Company-centred aims* are based on a desire to reinforce management's influence and control within the organisation through increasing employee identification with the interests of the organisation, promoting a greater awareness and understanding of management's position, improving productivity and reducing disputes. *Employee-centred aims*, on the other hand, are based on more 'ethical' considerations such as the organisation's 'responsibility' to inform its employees and the desirability of employee representatives having information to support their role in joint consultation and other forms of participation in decision making. Hussey and Marsh found that most managers saw the main objectives of employee reporting as being 'greater involvement of employees in the affairs of the company', 'encouraging a sense of responsibility' and 'discharging the proper responsibilities of the company', while only a handful included 'motivating employees towards high productivity' and 'moderating high wage demand'[64]. It would appear that management does not see the provision of general company financial information to employees in the same light as disclosure of information to trade unions within the collective bargaining framework. Such employee reporting would appear not to be intended as a direct threat to the collective bargaining role of trade unions but rather, perhaps, as an indirect conditioning of their members' expectations.

The general picture of **employee attitudes** towards such dissemination of information appears to be 'satisfaction' within scepticism about the process. Hussey and Marsh found that although a substantial majority of the employees in each occupational category felt employee reports were 'very' or 'quite' interesting, the proportion declines (perhaps not surprisingly) from the managerial to the unskilled level[65]. Significantly more of those aged 50+ believed reports to be very or quite interesting than those aged 16–20[66]. However, a substantial majority of employees agreed with the statement that 'by the time management tells us anything we have heard from other channels' (the 'grapevine') and 'the information the company gives is often biased to show only the managers' side.' Only a minority agreed that 'management is very frank and honest about giving information'[67].

Team briefings

These arrangements normally involve a **downward cascade** of information from the top to the bottom of the organisation through regular, formal, direct meetings between a group of employees and their immediate supervisor or manager. The information communicated relates to the organisation as a whole (for example, organisational performance, new developments, strategic decisions and their rationale) to which more immediate local workgroup information is added (it is often suggested that the wider organisational information should account for only some 30 per cent of the information in a team briefing meeting). Such team briefings are intended to provide information not only to enhance the employees' identification with the organisation and support their participation in more active decision-making involvement mechanisms but also, Torrington and Hall suggest, to provide 'authoritative information ... delivered face to face to provide scope for questions and clarifications, and ... emphasises the role of supervisors and line managers as the source of information'[68]. However, their credibility rests to a large extent on their regularity and continuing significant content. It is all too easy for meetings to be cancelled because of time pressures to do other things or because of the absence of any significant information to be communicated. Furthermore, the increased use of 'peripheral' employees (part-timers, those on short-term contracts, etc.) may militate against the effectiveness of team briefings. Marchington noted in one retail organisation that employees, even when they were paid for attending such meetings outside their normal times, 'had other commitments outside of working hours, while others were unwilling to come in on their day off'[69].

Perhaps the most crucial aspect of team briefings is whether they are intended to be simply a one-way downward communication of information or an opportunity for **two-way discussion**. As Hyman and Mason note, management may be reluctant to allow 'two-way communication flows, for fears that it could develop into a consultation forum. Indeed even general discussion of the information communicated (rather than specific questions) may well be discouraged'[70]. However, it is only through questioning and discussing (two-way dialogue) that management is really able to *explain* its problems and solutions and gain employee acceptance and commitment, or employees are able to have any influence on management decision making. Team briefings may also be used as 'a regular mechanism via which to pick up concerns and grievances at the earliest opportunity'[71], thereby marginalising the role of the union. Indeed, they can be used as an integral block on which to build an organisation-wide information, consultation and representation system.

See Case study 10.1

Other HRM mechanisms

It would seem that any mechanism in which employees have an opportunity to express their views could be regarded as 'involvement' (including attitude surveys, suggestion schemes, employee appraisal and 'speak-out' programmes). While these mechanisms are often put under a heading of 'two-way communication', most are, in reality, single directional communication from employee to management and do not involve 'dialogue'. Indeed, Townley describes them as

Case study 10.1 ■ Heathrow Express

Heathrow Express was set up in 1994 by BAA to run the rail link from Heathrow to central London. Its development of a customer service style has included the introduction of flexible, multifunctional 'customer service representatives' (including the train drivers).

The company introduced an 'information and consultation process' in 1999. This aims to integrate consultation and representation based on employee representatives (or 'facilitators'), selected by each work team, who are expected to 'represent different views among their membership, enter into *debate* with management and then *feedback* to their teams' (Edward Hussey, Head of HR) (my italics). There are four levels:

■ **Team meetings** – held monthly within a 'business brief' to allow employees the opportunity to 'feedback and comment' and to resolve any local issues;

■ **Focus groups** – six cross-functional groups of 6–8 people, held every two months, to discuss improvements in 'business processes and employment practices'; organised and run by the 'facilitators' and report directly to the relevant manager;

■ **Review group** – held every three months, involving the 'facilitators' and managers and chaired by the Managing Director, to review the activities of the focus groups and discuss general business performance. Once a year it deals with terms and conditions of employment (including pay and benefits);

■ **Business review meeting** – held once a year (at the same time as one of the Review group meetings), involving the 'facilitators' and a group of managers chaired by BAA's Managing Director for Rail, to receive briefing on financial performance, consider business plans and review performance impact of changes brought about by the Focus groups.

If an issue cannot be resolved within these meetings, there is provision for a final-stage *'problem-solving mechanism'* – a meeting involving BAA's Managing Director for Rail, the Managing Director for Heathrow Express, the chair of 'facilitators' and the 'facilitator' dealing with the issue.

Source: 'Heathrow Express takes off', *IRS Employment Trends*, no. 688, September 1999, pp. 12–16.

'methods used to ascertain the views of employees' (employee feedback)[72], while Hyman and Mason categorise them as 'upward communication for individual employees'[73]. Certainly, Hyman and Mason suggest that, for such mechanisms as attitude surveys and 'speak-out' programmes to be regarded as forms of employee involvement, management must do more than simply gather information but must be seen to be responding to the views, opinions and ideas they receive. Similarly, with suggestion schemes, they point out that the traditional UK view of them as primarily a vehicle to achieve cost-savings (with some payment for the idea being given to the employee) can be contrasted with the Japanese view of them as being mechanisms for 'self-motivation'. Perhaps only employee appraisal involves a two-way dialogue between manager and employee, but even here, as Townley argues, the process must be seen as 'a more open developmental approach, with discussion of achievements, aspirations, values and, in addition, grievances'[74], rather than a simple performance-reward assessment. Indeed, perhaps appraisal only starts to become 'involvement' when it includes self-review and subordinate assessment as well.

Delegated decision making

Emphasis on the **sociotechnical system and job design** has come about through a concern both to improve the quality of working life and to adapt organisations and working arrangements to significant market and technological changes. It has been recognised that previous approaches to work organisation based on 'scientific management' principles (rationalisation, specialisation and centralisation) have not always secured the expected improvements in productivity, have often resulted in frustration and alienation among employees and are an inappropriate basis for providing labour flexibility. White suggested that the development of forms of work organisation based on increased employee involvement should be seen as 'a procedure not for dealing with a unique situation but starting a process of planning, implementation and appraisal which is open ended'[75]. It may be viewed both as a *means* (process of management through which operational organisational changes may be more easily achieved) and as an *end* in its own right (that individuals gain 'some control over how their work is done, how it is developed and organised, and changes that are made to it'[76]).

Much of the activity associated with work design has centred on the concept that jobs should, as far as possible, entail the use of employee discretion in carrying out the work, provide opportunities for learning, carry attributable responsibility for control of work and outcomes and enable people to contribute to decisions affecting their jobs and the goals of the organisation[77]. At its basic level this has involved the following:

- **Job rotation** – allowing the individual a degree of variety of work by rotating between different, but generally related, tasks on the horizontal plane;
- **Job enlargement** – creating more complete and satisfying jobs by combining previously separate, specialised tasks on the horizontal plane within one single job;
- **Job enrichment** – increasing the individual's responsibility by devolving, on the vertical plane, additional functions (record keeping, quality control, etc.) previously carried out by management.

All these forms of restructuring allow the individual a greater degree of control over his or her work situation, although it is only the last which really provides for involvement in areas of decision making that have been traditionally the prerogative of management. It is this element which has provided the basis for the development of the concept of **employee empowerment** during the 1980s. The idea is that employees should take 'ownership' of the tasks they perform (and any associated problems), be accountable for output results (including quality) and, consequently, be 'empowered' with enhanced authority to act to resolve problems and achieve the required output. This has been associated with the development of looser, less task-specific job descriptions and the development of more teamworking (see Box 10.3).

Quality circles

Quality circles comprise small groups of employees 'who voluntarily meet on a regular basis to identify, investigate, analyse and solve their own work related

| Box 10.3 | Employee empowerment |

'While the boundaries surrounding empowerment seem rather fluid at present, its main feature appears to involve individual job ownership by employees ... [However,] empowerment tends to be introduced in companies which have removed layers of supervisory management and is used to cover existing tasks with fewer staff, with any "reward" being intrinsic to the added responsibilities associated with "empowered" jobs. This makes individual employees vulnerable in at least two ways: first, added responsibility invariably increases stress levels; and second, "empowered" employees are held responsible for the efficiency of their work, but job boundary protection in the form of job descriptions and employee specifications becomes less evident. Any performance failures can then be attributed to the "empowered" employees rather than the poverty of managerial or organizational support. Basically and critically, empowerment becomes a euphemism for work intensification.'

Source: J. Hyman and B. Mason, *Managing Employee Involvement and Participation*, Sage, 1995, p. 191, reprinted by permission of Sage Publications Ltd.

problems'[78]. However, while it is the members themselves who determine the issues to be considered, collect and analyse data and make recommendations, this is generally done under the leadership of their supervisor and the group can only recommend solutions, with management retaining the right to accept or reject their ideas. The voluntary basis of such activity is in marked contrast to Japan, where quality circles are 'part of an all-embracing total quality management programme, involving all workers from top management to the shopfloor'[79]. Collard and Dale note that, while the volunteers involved in quality circles believe that they provide 'an opportunity to have some influence, however marginal, on the immediate work situation'[80], other employees often feel themselves to be 'outsiders'.

Although quality circles achieved some prominence in the UK in the 1980s, there has been a subsequent decline. First, poor implementation and lack of proper management support resulted in the collapse of some schemes. In particular, Collard and Dale note that 'many a quality circle has come to grief'[81] because management has not implemented its recommendations or adequately explained why recommendations cannot be implemented, thus employees no longer feel the effort is worth while. Second, quality circles are relatively limited in scope but provided a first transitional step to be subsequently replaced by broader TQM and customer care programmes. Certainly, Beaumont argued that they 'suffered in general from being introduced as a stand-alone, self-contained innovation in a larger, unchanged organizational setting and culture'[82].

The subsequent development of TQM and customer care programmes involve all employees and a shift in organisational culture; they emphasise continuous problem solving and performance-improvement activity organised around the empowerment of employees, teamworking and greater decentralised and cross-functional management decision making.

Semi-autonomous workgroups or teamworking

Bailey suggested that 'the degree of autonomy and facility for self-organisation'

See Case study 10.2

inherent in group working provides the employees with 'the opportunity to influence and exercise leadership' through 'delegating complete task responsibility to the group'[83]. The **delegation of authority to the workgroup** may encompass team responsibility in two main areas:

- Setting goals, objectives or targets to be achieved; quality and performance; budgetary or cost control; co-ordination with other groups (both within and outside the department);

- Determining the division and allocation of tasks and responsibilities between individuals; training and development of individuals; scheduling individual time off; selecting new members of the team.

However, as Bailey pointed out, for many managers 'the idea of *autonomous* groups has all sorts of connotations of loss of control, threat to their position and authority and anarchy on the shop floor'[84] (my italics). Marchington and Wilkinson certainly regard teamworking and self-management as 'significantly more far reaching ... in terms of centrality to work processes and the level and scope of subject matter which are within the control of employees'[85] than other forms of direct employee 'involvement'. Bell argued that a critical question to be decided is 'whether the leader should come from within the group itself and remain part of it, a peer among peers, or should he [or she] be appointed from outside, a manager with the managed?'[86] In this context, he argues that the continuation of an emphasis on external managerial supervision will result in the process of decision making becoming 'one of consultation or at most joint decision making, not delegated authority'[87]. If the status of the workgroup is to be enhanced to its full potential for employee involvement, the supervision role must change from one of directing and controlling the work of individuals to one of co-ordinating and providing a resource, when required, to aid workgroups in achieving their agreed tasks and goals.

Similarly, Huiskamp believes that it is important to consider the extent to which 'such types of work-related participation are dominated and restricted by

Case study 10.2 ■ GM Saturn Corporation (USA)

'We believe that all people want to be involved in decisions that affect them, care about their jobs, take pride in themselves and in their contributions, and want to share in the success of their efforts. By creating an atmosphere of mutual trust and respect, recognizing and utilizing individual expertise and knowledge in innovative ways, providing the technologies and education for each individual, we will enjoy a successful relationship and a sense of belonging to an integrated business system capable of achieving our common goals which ensures security for our people and success for our business and communities.' (*Agreement between GM Saturn and United Auto Workers*).

GM Saturn's strategy is based on 'people-first values' which regards 'committed' employees as the organisation's most important asset: to be developed and empowered, treated with trust and respect, and involved in decision making. The strategy was developed and implemented with the agreement of the trade union.

The process of securing 'committed' employees

Case study 10.2 ■ GM Saturn Corporation (USA) *(continued)*

starts at the *recruitment* stage, where the company places as much emphasis on assessing the applicant's personal qualities and values as well as his or her job-related skills or experience. Half of the *new-employee orientation course* is devoted to explaining the company's values. This includes not only providing new employees with a mission card setting out the company values (which they are expected to carry at all times) but also discussions and exercises aimed at immediately getting the new employee to think about how these values can be translated into his or her actual work behaviour. Much of the employees' subsequent *training* focuses on interpersonal skills such as teamworking, decision making and problem solving rather than 'technical' training. The training programme for supervisors also emphasises the need for constant consideration of whether their actions and behaviour towards employees are consistent with the stated company values. The company also has a *career development programme* involving workshops where both the individual and his or her team assess each employee's development needs.

All production work is based on *self-directed teams* who have formal responsibility for 30 'work functions'. These include not only widened 'production' functions (such as responsibility for equipment maintenance, controlling their own material and inventory, quality inspection and self-correction of substandard work) but also traditional 'supervisory' functions (such as planning their own work, designing their own jobs, determining their own work methods, covering absences and, significantly, selecting new team members from the company's 'candidate pool').

Perhaps most importantly, the first stated function for all teams is to 'use *consensus decision making*', within which no formal leader should be apparent and all members of the team should be at least 70 per cent 'comfortable' with the group decision and 100 per cent 'committed' to its implementation. This is supported by a structured system (designated RASI: Responsibility, Approval, Support and Inform) which requires the groups clearly to identify the type or purpose of any meeting (presentation, problem solving, decision making, etc.), which member of the group has Responsibility (owns the task, initiates action, involves other team members, etc.) and the roles of other team members (Approval – ensures

resources are available for implementation, approves or vetoes the decision/action; Support – input information, questions, offers options; Inform – listens, expresses opinions, uses information). The conclusion of each meeting centres on assessing the effectiveness of the meeting itself.

So far as *terms and conditions* are concerned, the company has adopted the principle of 'lifetime employment without guarantees', all employees are salaried (clocking in and out has been replaced by self-reporting of working hours) and there are few job classifications (all assembly workers and non-skilled maintenance workers are classified as 'operating technicians'). A central feature is a *performance-related pay* system where a proportion of the employees' salary is 'at risk'. During the start-up phase only 5 per cent was 'at risk', which was 'earned back' on a skill-based approach by employees attending the appropriate training and developing their skills. However, when fully up and running, employees would receive a guaranteed base pay equal to 80 per cent of the average time-rate paid by other US car manufacturers, with the remaining 20 per cent being 'earned back' by reference to factors such as meeting productivity targets, individual and work unit performance, quality bonus and company profits above a specified level of return. Performance above the targeted level would result in additional profit sharing.

Significantly, the *relationship between management and union* has also been strengthened. Every supervisory employee (from first-line supervisor, through Head of Personnel to the Company President) is 'paired' with a union partner and they jointly make virtually all work-related decisions.

'Saturn's commitment really comes down to how you feel about people – your attitudes – more than anything, because all the other Saturn programs – the work teams, the extensive training, the way people are paid – all flow from these people's [management] attitudes.' (UAW's 'partner' to Saturn's Head of Personnel).

Source: G. Dessler, *Human Resource Management* (6th edn.), Prentice Hall (Englewood Cliffs), 1994.

See also Country profile 2.1.

management'[88]. Certainly, some argue that the development of 'responsible autonomy' through 'delegated authority' is, in reality, little more than expanding or enhancing the employee's job or work situation so that it appears to allow the employee some degree of 'self-control' (but only in areas and in a direction which supports the achievement of management objectives and increases organisational effectiveness and efficiency). In so doing, it requires employees to adopt and pursue management ideals and values as an integral part of their working situation. The process also involves management's expectations being 'clearly defined in job descriptions and enforced at appraisal time'[89]. As Hawkins pointed out, it would be wrong to assume that 'desire for intrinsic satisfaction with, or "self-actualisation" in, the job is an overriding priority of most workers for most of the time'[90]. Most employees are also concerned with their extrinsic rewards (money) and may well expect an improvement in the level of these extrinsic rewards as an integral and justified part of any proposal to restructure their work and increase their job flexibility or responsibility.

See Chapter 14 – Pay and working arrangements

Financial participation

There have been significant developments in the UK since the early 1980s in linking pay to performance or profits. However, the development of *individual*-based profit- or performance-related pay is more suitably considered within the context of increased individualisation and flexibility in payment systems. Financial participation schemes, on the other hand, are more focused towards employees (as a group) sharing in the organisation's financial gains and may be implemented for two reasons:

- It is inherently right that employees should receive a share of the profits, added value, etc. that they have helped to create.
- Unlike individual schemes, these schemes focus on the performance of the organisation as a whole and encourage employee co-operation with management strategies to improve organisational performance.

There is a wide range of financial participation schemes[91] but they can be divided into two main types. First, **supplementary 'pay' schemes** involve payments to employees based on improvements in the organisation's financial position. Some assess the organisation's performance in terms of productivity or value added (gain-sharing plans) while others are based on profit sharing (and therefore are not applicable to non-profit organisations). The payments are supplementary to the employee's normal remuneration, are often paid out once or twice a year and may be constant between employees (each receives the same amount) or may vary depending on such factors as the individual's length of service and level of normal remuneration (senior employees and those with longer service receive the most). Such schemes should not be confused with individual or workgroup PBR or bonus schemes or with any payment made under collective agreement for changes in working arrangements.

Second, there are **employee share-ownership schemes** which have existed in a number of different forms and received tax advantages under UK legislation since the late 1970s. There are three basic types of scheme:

■ *Approved profit-sharing schemes* where the employees' portion of any 'profit-sharing' is used to purchase shares which are then held in a trust before being distributed to employees (or they may elect to receive their profit-share as cash);

■ *Save as you earn schemes* where employees save out of their earnings specifically with the intention to exercise an option (several years in the future) to buy shares at the current price. SAYE schemes have to be open to all employees in the organisation with five years service;

■ *Discretionary share option schemes* where management offers selected employees (generally senior managers) the opportunity to exercise a future option to purchase shares at the current price. Under the 1984 legislation the limit was set at four times salary or £100,000, but in 1995 this was reduced to £30,000.

It is argued that such schemes not only develop a sense of 'property ownership' among employees by giving them a 'stake in their firm' but also integrate them into the 'market economy'. However, it is only the first and second types of scheme which really apply to 'average' employees and in the SAYE schemes it is their own savings out of normal earnings which buys the shares, albeit at a discount. Indeed, Pendleton notes that while there are some 900 'approved profit-sharing' schemes in the UK covering about 900,000 employees with an average 'shareout' of £400–500 per annum and a further 1,200 SAYE schemes, there are over 6,500 'discretionary' schemes and some 500 new schemes being added each year. Perhaps not surprisingly, Pendleton suggests this could indicate that 'many companies have attached rather more importance to executive reward packages than developing broad-based employee share ownership schemes'[92].

An attempt was made in Sweden during the 1980s to introduce 'economic democracy' through compulsory contributions from companies (based on a percentage of their profits above a specified level) into **'wage-earner funds'** which reinvested the money in company shares. This was intended to lead to the collective ownership of organisations. The original Meidner Plan adopted by the LO (Swedish Trade Union Confederation) in 1976 envisaged a single national union-administered wage-earner fund but the system introduced by the government in 1983 was based on five regional funds administered by boards appointed by the government after consultation with the unions. Although union representatives were in the majority, the boards also had politicians, academics and leaders of public organisations but private sector business leaders boycotted the scheme. In practice these funds 'operated in the same manner as insurance companies and pension funds'[93] and were abolished in 1991 by the new Conservative – Liberal coalition government. In Ireland, the establishment of an employee share ownership plan in Telecom Eirann in 1998 (which would give employees a 15 per cent stake in the newly privatised company) was linked to union and employee acceptance of a 'partnership' plan, which included changes in work practices and increased labour flexibility, abandonment of a profit-sharing scheme, 2,500 voluntary redundancies and introduction of employee contributions to pensions[94].

It should be remembered, first, that most of these financial participation schemes are inapplicable to the public sector and, second, even in private sector organisations they merely share money (not power, authority or decision making within the organisation). They are, at best, supplements to the process of involvement or participation.

Trade union response

Trade union resistance to the introduction of employee involvement, particularly forms of 'delegated participation', may stem from a number of factors:

■ Management's apparent emphasis on the intrinsic rewards of increased job satisfaction resulting from such changes may be seen as an attempt to play down the importance of extrinsic rewards.

■ Trade unions may regard management's primary intention in introducing such work changes as being the improvement of productivity and costs rather than increasing the employees' role in decision making. These may conflict with trade union objectives such as maintaining existing levels of employment.

■ The development of 'direct' forms of participation may be regarded as an attempt to undermine the existing representative arrangements with a consequent diminution in the role of the union and its representatives.

Certainly, Bailey argued that trade unions may be suspicious and perceive these developments as 'no more than a subtle way of exploiting the worker to achieve greater production without rewarding him for his efforts'[95]. In approaching this issue, trade unions may adopt either of **two strategies**:

■ Avoid discussing any changes until management announces its proposals and then seek to negotiate any changes in terms and conditions of employment (including pay) – assuming that management is prepared to enter into such negotiations.

■ Accept the development of employee 'involvement' but seek to open a dia-logue with management in order to influence the nature and form of any changes.

For example, the TGWU's guidelines[96] for its negotiators on the introduction of employee 'involvement' or 'participation' arrangements suggest:

■ All aspects of employee involvement or participation should be subject to negotiation by the union.

■ Employee representatives should be chosen in line with the union represen-tative machinery.

■ Working groups should be accompanied by the presence of a shop steward.

■ In no case should schemes be allowed to undermine union structures or collective bargaining.

However, Geary notes that there is a paradox in union co-operation and agreement to the work changes necessary to achieve 'delegative participation' in that such agreements 'often contain clauses which prohibit further negotiations over subsequent changes in working practices'[97] thereby increasing, rather than restricting, management freedom to determine the work situation. It is important to recognise that, as Marchington and Wilkinson argue, neither management nor employees expect direct employee involvement 'to produce radical changes ... or ... to resolve contradictions within the employment relationship'[98].

10.4 Employee participation

See Country profile 10.1

See Chapter 9 – Collective bargaining

The main focus of attention in employee 'participation' (as opposed to 'involvement') has been on worker directors and Works Councils. In Germany, these mechanisms have played an important part in giving substance to the postwar principle of 'social partnership'. Indeed, Wächter points out that the principle of 'co-determination, a building block of German economic stability and social welfare, is also deeply rooted in the German collective consciousness and in German traditions'[99]. However, such forms of employee participation cannot be considered in isolation from collective bargaining through trade union representation (see Figure 10.2). It is important to bear several factors in mind:

■ For many trade unionists their very independence, and that of their trade union, depends on their right and ability to oppose management. Forms of employee participation which incorporate them into management decision making may reduce their independence.

■ Any delineation between employee participation and collective bargaining must, in practice, be flexible and reflect the complementary, rather than competitive, nature of the two processes. Issues that arise in one may have implications which require consideration and decisions within the other.

■ Management may believe that employee participation should focus on individuals as 'employees' rather than 'trade union members', but unions may well view the full involvement of non-unionised employees on equal terms as a management attempt to weaken their role and power within the organisation.

Worker directors

Employee representation on the board (worker directors) has been established, by law, in many European countries – although in Greece and Ireland it has been restricted to the 'state' sector and in The Netherlands the employees have only a right to 'veto' the appointment of board members[100]. Only a few organ-

Figure 10.2 Channels
of representation

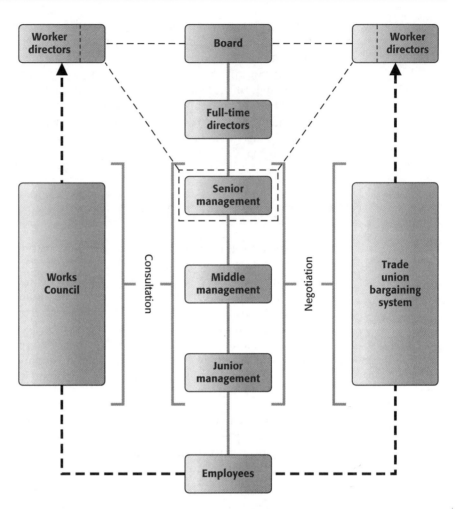

isations in the UK have introduced such arrangements – the most notable examples being the experiments in the British Steel Corporation (1967) and the Post
Office (1977). However, the issue has come to the fore again as the adoption of
an EU Company Statute becomes more likely. The proposals[101] would require
the management of companies wishing to be regulated under EU rather than
national laws to reach an agreement with employee and union representatives
on mechanisms for informing and consulting employees and, 'where applicable',
the board-level participation of employees. The 'standard rules', to be applied if
no agreement is reached, include provision for both a 'representative body'
(similar to a European Works Council) and for this body to elect or appoint
'worker directors' if employees in any of the 'participating' companies of the
'European' company would have such a right. Earlier proposals had included a
definite right, in all 'European' companies, for employees to elect or appoint 20
per cent of the board members.

Much of the debate in the UK about worker directors centred around the
report of the Bullock Committee of Inquiry on Industrial Democracy (1977)[102]
and the subsequent Labour government's White Paper on Industrial Democracy

Country profile 10.1   Germany – *Mitbestimmung* (co-determination)

Germany's industrial relations system involves two interrelated elements:

■ *Collective bargaining* between unions and employers' associations at the sector or industry level (economic regulation);

■ *Employee participation* in organisational decision making through Works Councils and worker directors (work regulation).

Works Councils and worker directors first appeared after the First World War to counter the development of 'workers' soviets' (worker control). Although abolished during the Nazi period, they reappeared as part of the postwar 'social partnership' between labour and capital not only to aid economic reconstruction but also to provide a distinct ideological break with fascism (and, at least for employers in the steel industry, as an alternative to nationalisation). The initial 1950s legislation was expanded by the Social Democratic government in the 1970s.

Worker directors

Germany's two-tier board structure, introduced in the 1870s, comprises an *executive board* (which manages the organisation and initiates policy and strategy) appointed by and reporting to a *supervisory board* (which oversees its work and approves strategic decisions). Worker directors are part of the supervisory board, nominated by the Works Council and/or trade unions and elected by the employees.

The original Co-Determination Act (1951) provides for 'parity' in the iron, steel and coal industries (about 50 organisations). Half the supervisory board are worker directors who, jointly with the shareholder directors, co-opt a 'neutral' chairperson. In addition, the worker directors have to approve the appointment of the Labour Director on the management board (who is often an experienced union member).

The Works Constitution Act (1952) provides for one-third worker directors on the supervisory board of all private sector enterprises of more than 500 employees. The Co-Determination Act (1976) extended this to parity in enterprises with over 2,000 employees (about 750 organisations). However, unlike the iron, steel and coal industries, the chairperson (who has a casting vote) is elected by shareholders, one worker director seat is reserved for the 'senior executive' group of employees and the worker direc-

tors have no right of veto over the appointment of the Labour Director.

Works Council

The Works Constitution Acts (1952 and 1972) provide for Works Council in all private sector enterprises with more than five employees and company-level councils in multiplant organisations. The Personnel Representation Act (1974) extended this to public sector organisations in the form of 'staff councils'. Councils range in size from one member (enterprises with 6–20 employees) to 31 members (enterprises with 7,001–9,000 employees). There are more than 40,000 Works Councils, with over 220,000 elected councillors and, although only 10 per cent of enterprises with 6–10 employees have one, the proportion is 80 per cent of enterprises with over 100 employees.

The Works Council is exclusively an employee body (not joint); both employees and trade unions may nominate candidates (although senior management and supervisors are excluded from standing); manual and non-manual employees are proportionately represented; and it is open to all employees over 18 years (including part-time and temporary workers) – there is a separately elected Youth and Trainee Delegation. All Works Council members have legal protection from dismissal and, in the larger councils, some members must be allowed to undertake Works Council duties 'full-time'. Although the Works Council has to report on its activities every three months to a general meeting of employees, the employees cannot mandate it to take a particular course of action.

Works Councils are legally required to co-operate with management in good faith, observing the terms of any external collective agreements in force, with a view to the welfare of the workers and the firm. It has the right to:

■ *Co-determination* (management has to secure its agreement) on workplace rules, hours of work and holidays (including overtime and short-time working), payment systems, health and safety, policies on recruitment, regradings, transfers and dismissals, plans to deal with restructuring or redundancy and vocational training.

■ *Receive information and be consulted*, through a special Economic Committee, on the economic and financial situation of the company, trends in production and sales, investment plans and planned rationalisation measures (in particular

Country profile 10.1 Germany – *Mitbestimmung* (co-determination) *(continued)*

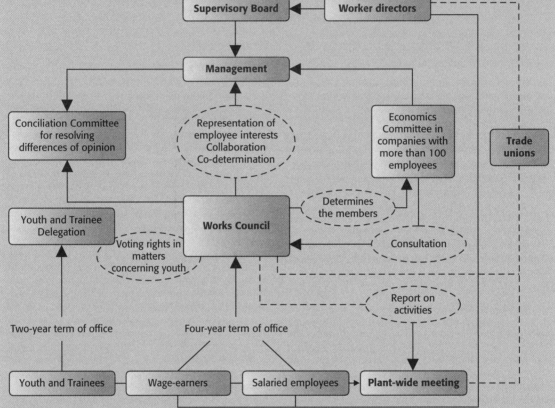

Source: Adapted from 'German works councils – paper tigers?' *Die Mitbestimmung* (Special English Edition), 1992, p.54

any reduction in operations or closure of establishments).

Generally, there is co-operation between Works Councils and not only worker directors but also trade unions. Nearly 80 per cent of Works Council members are trade union members. Trade union officials have the right to attend both Works Council meetings and the quarterly meeting with employees and, in addition, are the main providers of training, information and advice for the Works Councils. On a reciprocal basis, members of Works Councils have an important role in recruiting new union members, the formulation of union claims and organising strike action where necessary.

However, the decentralisation of industrial relations has increased the role of the Works Councils in negotiating works agreements with management to 'interpret and apply' the sector- or industry-level agreements negotiated by the trade unions. Thus, Works Councils are 'taking on the character of company unions', giving 'union representatives in the company more autonomy from the trade union "outside"' (3 : 146).

Sources:
1. O. Jacobi, B. Keller and W. Müller-Jentsch, 'Germany: facing new challenges', in A. Ferner and R. Hyman (eds), *Changing Industrial Relations in Europe*, Blackwell, 1998.
2. H. Slomp, 'National variations in worker participation', in A.-W. Harzing and J. van Ruysseveldt (eds), *International Human Resource Management*, Sage, 1995.
3. R. Huiskamp, 'Collective bargaining in transition', in J. van Ruysseveldt, R. Huiskamp and J. van Hoof, *Comparative Industrial and Employment Relations*, Sage, 1995.
4. 'Workers on the Board – doing what they can with no illusions' (pp. 40–43) and 'German works councils – paper tigers?' (pp. 52–54), *Die Mitbestimmung* (Special English Edition), 1992.

See also Country profiles 5.2 and 7.2.

(1978). It is evident from this debate that UK management and trade unions have **differing perceptions of the worker directors' role:**

- **Management** expects, as the European experience suggests, worker directors to 'encourage a climate of mutual confidence and cooperation throughout the enterprise'[103] and help develop a 'coalition' between employees and management. Worker directors can reduce conflict, by making employees more aware of the problems and constraints which face management, and improve the quality of board room discussions and decisions, by contributing their views and experience.

- **Trade unions** have been split over the relevance and importance of worker directors. Some believe that worker directors would detract from the union's role as a countervailing power to management and inhibit their ability to challenge management decisions. Others, like the TUC, believe that 'in the absence of board-level representation, trade unionists find it very difficult to influence ... key decisions'[104]. The function of worker directors is to do more than simply give their views to management – it is to represent and jointly make decisions on behalf of the employees.

Unitary or two-tier board structure?

The UK debate about worker directors has been significantly influenced by the differences between the UK's single (unitary) board and, for example, Germany's two-tier (Supervisory and Management) board structure. The central issue revolves around whether the worker director should be an integral part of the normal management of the organisation or concerned only with broad policy issues and the general overseeing of management.

The employer members of the Bullock Committee argued that the UK's unitary board was 'in effect the apex of a Company's management team' and therefore they were 'completely opposed to the introduction ... of special interests ... which might provoke a confrontation or extend the scope of collective bargaining into top level management decision-making'[105]. Further, they argued that, if any supervisory board was created as part of a two-tier system, it 'should not involve itself with the detailed decision making of existing boards of directors, not even with determining policy; but should be primarily concerned with the quality of the management of the company and its capacity to run the company profitably and competitively'[106]. In the BSC experiment, worker directors were appointed only to the lower divisional boards, whose responsibility was simply to advise the divisional managing director, rather than to the main board which was the only body which had authority to make major policy decisions.

However, the Main Report of the Bullock Committee favoured the retention of the unitary board structure. It argued that a two-tier structure could negate the very thing that the introduction of worker directors was intended to achieve – namely, employee participation in organisational decision making – because it 'would, in its desire to preserve the freedom of management, so delimit the powers of the [supervisory] board on which employees are represented that employee participation in decision-making would be very restricted'[107].

Certainly, Costello's examination of the Irish experience of worker directors in seven state enterprises found that, because the board's responsibilities were confined to the establishment of broad corporate objectives, 'this precluded worker directors from raising many of the issues which were of concern to the employees who had elected them. Most of these issues were seen to fall within management's responsibility and attempts to raise them in the boardroom were invariably ruled out of order'[108].

It is important to recognise that, whatever the board *structure*, the introduction of worker directors is unlikely to affect significantly the **power and decision making of senior management**. Many organisations 'have developed a *de facto* two-tier system, delegating responsibility for the formulation and implementation of policy from the main board perhaps to a management committee'[109]. Brannen *et al.* found that in the BSC experiment formal and informal meetings of management and full-time directors were more significant in organisational decision making than formal board meetings[110]. Furthermore, Batstone *et al.* found that in the Post Office the worker directors 'did not act as a caucus' and 'tended to accept the notion of the full-timers as *primi inter pares*'[111]. The ability of worker directors to exert an effective influence on management decision making is likely to be inhibited by several factors:

- The infrequency of formal board meetings;
- Their exclusion from other directorial and senior management meetings;
- The predominant role of the board being the formal endorsement of proposals or decisions offered by senior management;
- Their reliance, in the absence of any alternative source from their union or outside experts, on these same senior management for information and advice on which to base their decisions or challenges to the proposals laid before them.

Minority or parity on the board?

In the BSC experiment, the worker directors were in a minority, while in the Post Office there was equal representation. Even in Germany, where since 1976 parity of representation has been required in companies with more than 2,000 employees, the chairman of the board (elected by the shareholders) has the casting vote in board decisions. The Bullock Committee reported that even minority representation gives 'employees a valuable insight into the process of development and determination of company policy at the top level and access to management information' which is then 'useful to employees and their trade unions in discussions and negotiations with management at other levels of the enterprise'[112]. In addition to allowing some influence on management decision making, minority representation means that worker directors do not have to accept collective responsibility for any board decisions with which they disagree. However, the TUC has been very clear that without parity of representation worker directors can have no real effective share in decision making; so far as they have been concerned, equality of responsibility requires equality of representation. Significantly, the Bullock Committee Main Report avoided the minority/parity issue somewhat when they recommended a $2X + Y$ formula for representation – where $2X$ denoted equal numbers of shareholder and worker directors and Y denoted co-opted independent members.

Accountability?

In both the BSC and Post Office, the worker directors were not elected but appointed by the Chairman from a list of trade union nominees. They were, as Brannen *et al*. point out, regarded as 'experts in their own right ... people who could bring to the board the authentic view of the average man on the shop floor'[113]. Clearly, if worker directors are to be 'representatives', there has to be some formalised link with employees. Two alternative mechanisms have been discussed – either linked to recognised trade unions (the so-called 'single-channel' mechanism) or linked to employees (possibly through some form of consultative committee).

Elliot noted that in BSC, worker directors were in reality a 'third channel' 'divorced not only from the main union bargaining procedure but also from the union consultative process'[114]. Consequently, it was argued that the **single-channel union-based** approach provided a ready-made mechanism for representing the employees' interests, ensuring the worker director's accountability to the employees and providing 'the expertise and independent strength necessary to support employee representatives and to enable them to play an effective role in decision-making on the board'[115]. The Bullock Main Report, strongly influenced by government support at the time for encouraging and strengthening the role of trade unions and collective bargaining, proposed that worker directors should be selected by a Joint Representation Committee (JRC) made up of independent recognised unions within the organisation. The JRC would also, on a continuing basis, provide the necessary support for the worker directors and act as the interface between them and the collective bargaining process. The proposals did not envisage that individual worker directors would be subject to direct election by the employees.

While most employers argued strongly that any worker director should be an employee of the organisation, the Bullock Committee did not preclude the possibility that, as in Germany, a **union full-time officer** (who was not an employee of the organisation) might appropriately be selected as a worker director. Certainly they did not feel that a worker director who was a shop steward or branch official should be required to relinquish his or her trade union office – as had been the case in the early days of the BSC experiment. In their opinion the retention of the union position aided the integration of the worker director role with the collective bargaining process and facilitated the maintenance of links with other employees. However, Marchington and Armstrong[116] found that some shop stewards were concerned about potential 'role conflict' and 'loss of contact with membership/development of élites' should they become a worker director. Similarly, concerns were expressed regarding the **position of managers** and other professional groups of employees. However, the Bullock Main Report rejected any notion of reserving one worker director's seat for this group. Clearly, if any such provision were to be made, it could provide, or at least create the impression of providing, management with an in-built majority on the board.

Linking worker directors exclusively to recognised trade unions has been criticised because it strengthens the role of the trade union within the organisation and ignores the rights and interests of non-union employees. Indeed, the Bullock Committee Minority Report advocated using a **Works Council consultative structure** as the basis for the selection and reporting back of worker directors because it could encompass all employees irrespective of whether or not they were union members. Since then, the decline in management support for trade unions, the development of strategies to enhance employee 'involvement' and EU pressure towards Works Councils (allowing employee as well as union representation), all make it unlikely that worker directors would be introduced into UK-based companies on a single-channel union-based basis. However, it should be recognised that linking worker directors to a Works Council will require a clear and accepted understanding between the parties of its integration with, or delineation from, any system of collective bargaining based on trade union representation.

Works Councils

Works Councils were introduced in most European countries as an integral statutory part of the postwar industrial relations system to aid co-operative efforts for economic recovery. However, despite a legislative requirement for their establishment in organisations above a certain size (ranging from six employees in Germany to 100 employees in Belgium), Slomp notes that the compliance rate in Belgium is only 60 per cent, while in Germany it ranges from 80 per cent of organisations with over 100 employees down to only 10 per cent of organisations with fewer than ten employees[117]. In contrast, the UK's voluntary industrial relations approach has favoured looser and less formalised 'joint consultative committees'[118]. However, some organisations have introduced company, employee or advisory councils as part of their strategy towards union derecognition, single unionism and new relationships with trade unions (often associated with the introduction of 'Japanese' management practices).

See Case study 10.3

The legislation in most European countries provides **certain rights to Works Councils**: the *right to receive regular information* on the general position and prospects of the enterprise; the *right to offer advice or be consulted* on economic matters (including rationalisation and collective redundancies); and the *right to joint decision making* in a range of social and personnel matters (such as working hours, payment systems, health and safety, staff assessment and vocational training, etc.). Works Councils are intended to be an organisational-level consultative body of employee representatives, running in parallel with, but separate from, union/management negotiations about terms and conditions of employment at the industry or sectoral level. This division allowed the development of a more co-operative (integrative) relationship between management and employees within the organisation, with the more conflictual (distributive) wage bargaining being conducted between unions and employers associations outside the organisation (see Box 10.4). However, the trend towards

Case study 10.3 ■ Northumbrian Water Ltd – *Company Council*

Northumbrian Water was privatised in 1989 (with most employees becoming shareholders) and, with the abandonment of national-level multi-employer bargaining in the industry, it introduced radical changes in its industrial relations. The objective was 'to move towards an "us" rather than "us and them" approach to employee relations, with one "big team" pulling together' and to model employee representation on the 'democratic parliamentary system' (Company Personnel Adviser) (1 : 14).

Before 1989, the company recognised eight unions (NALGO and NUPE (now merged), AEU and EETPU (now merged), GMB, TGWU, APEX and UCATT) and negotiated within three bargaining units (manual, craft and non-manual staff). The initial aim was to replace this with a single union in order to support the development of harmonisation and single-status. However, following union protests, the company agreed to recognise the unions jointly as a Confederation of Northumbrian Water Trade Unions (CNWTU). At the same time, a Northumbrian Water Ltd Employee Association (NWEA) was formed to represent the 17 per cent of the workforce who were not union members.

Management introduced a 'council' system of employee representation to deal directly with employees (rather than through unions) and to integrate negotiation and consultation.

Employee Councils were set up in each operating area for 'constructive discussion' of local issues and to act as an information and discussion channel between the Company Council and employees. The employee 'councillors' were elected by secret ballot in functional 'constituencies' of about 20 employees regardless of job or status.

A *Company Council* was introduced comprising seven 'company councillors' (one from each Employee Council) and four management representatives (including the Managing Director – who chairs the Council, and the Human Resource Director – who acts as secretary). CNWTU and NWEA each had only an 'advisory' seat, although the Council quorum required that one had to be present. The functions of the council are as follows:

■ To 'discuss, negotiate, amend and agree' terms and conditions of employment, procedures for grievances and discipline, health and safety and other company-wide issues;

■ To consult and advise on 'company-wide issues concerning employee relations';

■ To do this within a framework which recognises that 'the development and maintenance of harmonious employee relations is vital to ensure the prosperity of all employees and the company' and which promotes 'trust, care and cooperation in the development and improvement of employee communications, recognition and reward'; and

■ All company councillors are expected to 'conduct themselves in such a way as to promote harmony and progress of employee relations'.

The role of the Company Council includes receiving communication of decisions already made by management (information), discussions to provide information prior to a management decision (consultation) as well as discussions to secure Council agreement (negotiation) – the management 'aims for as many items as possible to fall into this category' (2 : 15). A sub-committee of the Company Council also acts as the final stage of the Grievance Procedure. Minutes of the Council meetings are put up on notice boards but it is up to the employee councillors to decide whether there should be any further feedback discussion with their constituents.

It is perhaps significant that, in 1991, the first pay negotiations under this new process resulted in backing for management's 'final' offer by the 11 members of the Company Council but rejection by the employees in a ballot. Management then brought in an academic consultant to review whether the offer was 'reasonable', following which an improved offer was made and accepted by a majority of the employees.

Sources:
1. 'Industrial relations developments in the water industry', *IRS Employment Trends*, no. 516, July 1992, pp. 13 and 14.
2. 'A question of involvement', *IDS Study*, no. 561, September 1994, pp. 13–15.

See also Case study 9.3.

decentralisation in collective bargaining has blurred this distinction, with the inevitable potential for change in the relationship between management and the Works Council. It is their **relationship to union workplace activity** which provides the basis for Slomp's[119] division of Works Councils into two types:

■ *Joint employee-management councils* (Belgium and Denmark). In both countries there is high union density and organisation at the workplace and to have a Works Council of only employees would, in effect, duplicate the existing union role. The legislation recognises this by giving the unions a monopoly in nominating candidates for the Works Councils. Thus, the Works Council is secondary to the union and serves primarily as a statutory-based forum for union delegates, as workforce representatives, to meet and negotiate with management.

■ *Autonomous employee councils* (Germany and Netherlands). The level of union density and workplace union organisation is lower and the Works Council is autonomous from the trade union within the dual system of unions negotiating at sectoral level and Works Councils dealing with organisation-level issues. Thus, it is in the unions' interests to limit the activities of Works Councils. Although non-union employees can nominate candidates, in Germany, for example, over 80 per cent of Works Council representatives are union members.

Significantly, Works Councils in Sweden have become largely redundant since the 1976 Co-determination Act extended union bargaining rights to all social and personnel matters (union representation has become virtually the only institution of employee representation within the organisation).

Two **main advantages** have been put forward for Works Councils (apart from any potential to develop a more co-operative relationship within the organisation):

■ They can represent the whole of the workforce (not just those who are unionised) and are just as appropriate in non-union firms.

Box 10.4	Works councils and trade unions

'In countries where works councils operate, they cannot be considered in isolation from trade union representation in the enterprise. The two are twin institutions, acting almost as communicating vessels. When we consider them in combination, we see that the nature and extent of worker participation is determined not by the existence of a "dual system", but by the level at which the major terms and conditions are negotiated. Where formal sector agreements predominate, both the employers and the unions create a sheltered niche for worker participation, while at the same time limiting its scope and forcing it into a role of cooperation. [Where] enterprise-level regulation of the terms and conditions of employment predominates, both trade union representatives and works councils may be agents of conflict (and bargaining) with management. This means that the main line of division in worker participation is determined by the national system of industrial relations, rather than by legal rules or union strength in itself.'

Source: H. Slomp, 'National variations in worker participation', in A.-W. Harzing and J. van Ruysseveldt (eds), *International Human Resource Management*, Sage, 1995, pp. 316–17. Reprinted by permission of Sage Publications Ltd.

■ They can be concerned with major strategic policy decisions as well as more operational implementation matters.

However, Beaumont notes that in Germany while 'employees attach more priority to works councils than to unions in representing their views and interests in the workplace'[120], many managers believe that 'works councils will in the final run support the company ... take into account the pressing needs of the company more than a trade union ... [and] explain and defend certain decisions of the company toward the employees'[121]. Certainly, Ramsay argues that while Works Councils can 'be a genuine step towards democracy', they can also 'be used by management to foment an enterprise consciousness, and perhaps to divert workers from supporting unions and/or facilitate the exclusion of proper bargaining relations'[122].

As James[123] points out, **pressure from Europe** for management to consult employee representatives already existed under Directives relating to collective redundancies (1975), transfer of undertakings (1976) and the health and safety of workers (1989). However, until the European Court of Justice decision in 1994 that these rights applied to all employees (whether unionised or not), UK legislation had confined these consultation rights to situations where trade unions were recognised. The pressure for the general introduction of some form of Works Council has been strengthened by Commission proposals[124] for a Directive 'to establish a general framework for informing and consulting employees' in organisations with more than 50 employees. Employee representatives would have a right to be informed about 'company activities and its economic and financial situation' and to be informed *and* consulted about employment matters and 'decisions likely to lead to substantial changes in work organisation or in contractual relations'. It has been suggested that the proposals would require 'substantial changes to the existing systems of employee representation'[125] in both the UK and Ireland (the only two EU countries without such a statutory guaranteed mechanism) – not least because the proposals refer to the right to 'independent, permanent and stable representation' and to 'annul the legal effects' of any decisions made without the proper consultation.

Importantly, a **European Works Councils Directive** was adopted in 1994 which represented 'the first successful attempt by the Community to create a trans-national industrial relations/employee participation structure or procedure, and is thus a major milestone in the 37-year history of EC social policy'[126]. The Directive[127] provides for a European Works Council (EWC) (or other information and consulting procedure) to be established in any multinational organisation with at least 1,000 employees (including at least 150 employees in each of two member states). It allowed 'voluntary' agreements to be established prior to the formal implementation date (September 1996). The process for the introduction of a EWC may be initiated by management or by 100 employees or their representatives from establishments in two member states and requires the establishment of a 'special negotiating body' (comprising employee representatives) to negotiate an agreement with management within three years. It is up to the parties to agree the precise composition, functions and procedures of any EWC or other arrangement. However, if management is not prepared to negotiate or an agreement is not reached, then an EWC will have to be set up in line with certain **minimum standards** laid down in the Directive:

- A minimum of three and maximum of 30 members with membership proportional to the number of employees in each state (subject to a minimum of one member per state);

- A meeting with central management once a year to consider in particular 'the structure, economic and financial situation, the probable development of the business and of production and sales, the situation and probable trend of employment, investments and substantial changes concerning organisation, introduction of new working methods or production processes, transfers of production, mergers, cut-backs or closures of undertakings, establishments or important parts thereof, and collective redundancies' (Section 2 of the Annexe to the Directive);

- Special meetings where 'there are exceptional circumstances affecting the employees' interests to a considerable extent, particularly in the event of relocations, the closure of establishments or undertakings or collective redundancies' (Section 3 of the Annexe to the Directive);

- Entitlement to hold their own meeting prior to meeting management;

- Right to be assisted by experts of their own choice.

Despite the UK's 'optout' of the Social Chapter (and consequently the Directive on EWCs), many UK companies with operations across Europe nevertheless did establish some form of European-wide Company Council or did not seek to exclude their UK employees. Following the election of 'new' Labour in 1997, regulations were introduced in 1999 to give effect to the EWC Directive.

There is wide diversity in the EWCs established – not least in their titles (see Table 10.1). Some organisations (like International Service System and United Biscuits) negotiated their agreements with recognised trade unions (either national unions or through international union federations), linked the selection of EWC members to established negotiating or employee representation machinery in each country, allowed for the involvement of union officers and, in the case of ISS, provided for feedback via established joint machinery. Clearly, the EWC is not seen as competing with existing industrial relations machinery. Others (like BP Oil) based the EWC on 'employee' representatives without direct union involvement, despite the fact that they recognise trade unions for collective bargaining purposes (it thereby provides an alternative forum). The Honda EWC was established as a result of a management initiative and excludes any union role in its operation.

Of the 400 'voluntary' EWC agreements reached before 1996, two-thirds established a joint management–employee body (rather than the employee-only body provided for in the Directive), despite the fact that national or international unions were signatories to almost half the agreements[128]. In contrast, of the 100 agreements negotiated after the 'voluntary' deadline, the vast majority have been signed by the 'special negotiating body' on behalf of the employees (although unions were involved alongside the SNB in about 30 per cent of cases) and about 50 per cent of the EWCs are employee-only bodies[129]. It is

	International Service System (Denmark)	United Biscuits (UK)	BP Oil (UK)	Honda Europe NV (Netherlands)
Title:	Council for European Social Dialogue	European Consultative Council	Europe Employee Forum	Communication & Consultation Group
Employee signatories:	FIET (International Federation of Commercial, Clerical, Professional & Technical Employees)	GMB (on behalf of ECF-IUF: the European food industry committee affiliated to ETUC)	Elected employee representatives from 11 BP oil companies	Representatives 'on behalf of' Honda employees in Europe
Aim:	Information and consultation on matters relating to ISS Group: ▪ structure, economic and financial situation; ▪ probable trends in employment and investment; ▪ changes in organisation, work methods, training and safety; ▪ mergers, closures, cut-backs or collective redundancies Committee: 3 employee representatives to be informed and consulted on any plans relating to acquisitions, mergers, relocations or collective redundancies which affect the interests of employees beyond the boundaries of one country	▪ Joint understanding of the performance of the business, of its operating environment and the marketplaces, and of other matters of genuine mutual concern; ▪ Exchange of information and views between management and employees with the aim of establishing a transnational dialogue	Information and consultation on: ▪ performance and strategy of group; ▪ transnational matters which may have serious implications for interests of employees Link Committee: 5 employee representatives to maintain communication between central management and Employee Forum and to agree Forum agenda (may initiate items)	▪ The presentation, clarification and understanding of information regarding issues of European activity and/or influence; ▪ The exchange of views and establishment of dialogue over European business subjects which shall be taken into consideration within the company decision-making process.
Frequency of meetings:	Annual plus extra-ordinary meetings	Annual half-day (within one month of announcement of annual results)	Annual 1 day	Annual 2 days (first day communication, second day consultation)
Selection of employee representatives:	(a) elected worker directors (b) elected by enterprise committees or works councils (c) appointed by management in consultation with local unions	Nominated by national trade unions or works councils	In line with national law and practice with the proviso that they must be elected by employees or by members of forums elected by employees	Nominated and elected according to local law and custom and practice
Qualification of employee representatives:	Permanent employees for 1 year	3 years' service	*No information*	Full-time permanent employees
Trade union involvement:	Up to 2 representatives of FIET or any associated union	▪ 1 UK GMB full time officer (also representing the ECF-IUF) ▪ 2 other UK union full-time officers (USDAW and TGWU) ▪ 1 non-UK union full-time officer	No direct union involvement	No direct union involvement
Employee side pre-meeting:	Half-day	Half-day	Allowed for	No provision
Dissemination:	(a) Via enterprise committees or works councils or similar body; or (b) To be jointly decided by local subsidiary management and Council employee representative	Joint statement of key points circulated to all sites for briefing to all employees	Report prepared by secretary (Director of Human Resources) and Link Committee chair to be circulated to participants and business managers (to be conveyed to as many employees as possible)	Relevant manager and employee representative report back together to all employees in their unit

Sources: 'EWC agreement at ISS', *European Works Council Bulletin*, Winter 1995, pp. 13–15; 'The first UK European Works Councils', *European Industrial Relations Review*, no. 251, December 1994, pp. 20–22; 'European Works Councils update – trends and issues', *European Industrial Relations Review*, no. 256, May 1995, pp. 14–22.

Table 10.1 European Works Councils

estimated that only some 40 per cent of potential organisations have an EWC, leaving 700 organisations still to act. Significantly, in 12 out of 17 UK organisations with EWCs, management was the sole initiator although European union federations were involved in subsequent discussions or negotiations[130]. The main advantages were seen to be 'exchanging information with employee representatives' and 'getting management views over to employees', while the main disadvantage was 'raising employee expectations'.

It has been suggested that EWCs provide an opportunity not only to open a dialogue 'between employee representatives and the most senior level of management' but also 'to foster a pan-European culture and understanding' and 'encourage the transfer of best practice from one country to another'[131]. However, as Ramsay points out, the EWC Directive 'excludes reference to "participation" (normally read as joint regulation in Europe)' and this 'lack of codetermination powers leads to a fear of marginality' or even 'management control by selling their own message convincingly'[132]. Nevertheless, in 1997, the Renault EWC helped mobilise European opposition to the company's closure of a Belgium plant, including strike action, and won its case in the French court for breach of the EWC agreement – unfortunately, neither action stopped the closure of the plant.

▪ Summary propositions

- ▪ Management favours task centred, direct forms of 'involvement' centred on securing the support and commitment of the individual employee to the objectives and values of the organisation.
- ▪ Trade unions favour power-centred, indirect forms of 'participation' based on the established representational role of trade unions to extend employee influence on management decision making.
- ▪ Pressure from the EU for the introduction of Works Councils in organisations at both European and national level may lead to significant changes in UK approaches to both employee participation/involvement and union representation

Activity   The material you collected on the management of industrial relations (Chapter 7 activity) may well include some useful information on the organisation's approach to employee involvement or participation (particularly relating to briefing groups, employee reports, semi-autonomous team working, employee councils). Examine this material and try to identify, for example, what forms of employee involvement and/or participation exist, how they are intended to operate, what role is played by trade unions and how they relate to any collective bargaining arrangements in the organisation.

Further reading

- J. Hyman and B. Mason, *Managing Employee Involvement and Participation*, Sage, 1995. A comprehensive and useful discussion of a range of perspectives and debates relating to both 'involvement' and 'participation'.
- IDE International Research Group, *Industrial Democracy in Europe Revisited*, Oxford University Press, 1993. This study reviews the changes and developments in employee participation in a range of organisations in different countries between the mid-1970s and mid-1980s.
- M. Poole, *Towards a New Democracy: Workers' participation in industry*, Routledge and Kegan Paul, 1986. A very useful examination of a range of issues and factors affecting employee participation.
- M. Marchington and A. Wilkinson, 'Direct participation', in S. Bach and K. Sisson (eds), *Personnel Management* (3rd edn), Blackwell, 2000. A concise but extensive examination of direct forms of employee involvement.
- *Bullock Committee of Inquiry on Industrial Democracy*, HMSO, 1977. An important text on worker directors.

References

1. R. Bean, *Comparative Industrial Relations* (2nd edn), Routledge, 1994, p. 160.
2. J. Hyman and B. Mason, *Managing Employee Involvement and Participation*, Sage, 1995, p. 1.
3. P. Brannen, *Authority and Participation in Industry*, Batsford, 1985. p. 36.
4. R. Hyman, *Industrial Relations: A Marxist introduction*, Macmillan, 1975, p. 180.
5. International Labour Office, 'Participation of workers in decisions within undertakings', *Labour–Management Relations Series*, no. 33, 1969, pp. 30–42.
6. Hyman and Mason, *op. cit.*, p. 8.
7. A. Mitchell, 'Industrial democracy: reconciling theories of the firm and state', *The International Journal of Comparative Labour Law and Industrial Relations*, vol. 14, no. 1, 1998, p. 40.
8. *Ibid.*, p. 21.
9. T. D. Wall and J. A. Lischeron, *Worker Participation*, McGraw-Hill, 1977, p. 36.
10. C. Pateman, *Participation and Democratic Theory*, Cambridge University Press, 1970, p. 67.
11. J. Elliot, *Conflict or Cooperation: the growth of industrial democracy* (2nd edn), Kogan Page, 1984, pp. 124–5.
12. D. Farnham and J. Pimlott, *Understanding Industrial Relations* (5th edn), Cassell, 1995, p. 83.
13. Involvement and Participation Association, *Industrial Participation*, autumn 1989, p. 2.
14. *IPM Code of Professional Conduct and Codes of Practice*, 1990. p. 26.
15. M. Marchington and A. Wilkinson, 'Direct participation', in S. Bach and K. Sisson (eds), *Personnel Management* (3rd edn), Blackwell, 2000, p. 340.
16. Hyman and Mason, *op. cit.*, 1995, p. 18.
17. Marchington and Wilkinson, *op. cit.*, pp. 342–3.
18. K. F. Walker, 'Workers' participation in management: concepts and reality', in B. Barrett, E. Rhodes and J. Beishon (eds), *Industrial Relations and the Wider Society*, Open University, 1975, p. 435.
19. H. Slomp, 'National variations in worker participation', in A.-W. Harzing and J. van Ruysseveldt (eds), *International Human Resource Management*, Sage, 1995, table 14.1, p. 294.
20. Commission of the European Communities, 'Employee participation and company structure', *Bulletin of the European Communities*, Supplement 8/75, p. 9.

21. H. Ramsay, 'Commitment and involvement', in B. Towers (ed.), *The Handbook of Human Resource Management*, Blackwell, 1992, p. 208.

22. B. Townley, 'Communicating with employees', in K. Sisson (ed.), *Personnel Management* (2nd edn), Blackwell, 1994, p. 608.

23. M. Marchington and P. Wilding, 'Employee involvement inaction?' *Personnel Management*, December 1983, p. 35.

24. 'Personnel directors at odds with Government policy on participation', *Personnel Management*, December 1990, p. 5; P. Crofts, 'IPM comes out in favour of new statutory right to information', *Personnel Management Plus*, November 1990, p. 1.

25. Hyman and Mason, *op. cit.*, p. 24.

26. *Ibid.*, p. 26.

27. M. Marchington, *Managing Industrial Relations*, McGraw-Hill, 1982, p. 155.

28. *Ibid.*, p. 154.

29. W. E. J. McCarthy and N. D. Ellis, *Management by Agreement*, Hutchinson, 1973, p. 96.

30. G. Buckingham, 'Participation in practice: the emerging consensus and what to do about it', *Personnel Management*, October 1980, p. 38.

31. *Ibid.*, p. 38.

32. M. Marchington, 'Employee participation – consensus or confusion?' *Personnel Management*, April 1981, p. 38.

33. H. Ramsay, 'Phantom participation: patterns of power and conflict', *Industrial Relations Journal*, vol. 11, no. 3, 1980, p. 47.

34. ACAS, *Employee Participation – A Look at the Current Scene*, undated, p. 4.

35. M. Warner, 'Workplace participation and employee influence: a study of managers and shop stewards', *Industrial Relations Journal*, vol. 13, no. 4, 1982, tables 3 and 4, p. 20.

36. J. Dickson, 'The relation of direct and indirect participation', *Industrial Relations Journal*, vol. 12, no. 4, 1981, p. 32.

37. B. Bartlett, 'Auditing to progress participation', *Personnel Management*, February 1982, pp. 34–5.

38. D. C. Wilson *et al.*, 'The limits of trade union power in organisational decision making', *British Journal of Industrial Relations*, vol. 20, 1982, p. 333.

39. J. Neumann, 'Why people don't participate when given the chance', *Industrial Participation*, Spring, 1989.

40. M. Poole, *Towards a New Industrial Democracy: Workers participation in Industry*, Routledge & Kegan Paul, 1986, p. 17.

41. *Ibid.*, p. 44.

42. *Ibid.*, pp. 47–8.

43. Hyman and Mason, *op. cit.*, p. 151.

44. P. Cressey and P. Williams, *Participation and New Technology*, European Foundation for Improvement of Working Conditions (Dublin), 1990.

45. R. Huiskamp, 'Industrial democracy, employee participation and operational autonomy', in J. van Ruysseveldt, T. Huiskamp and J. van Hoof (eds), *Comparative Industrial and Employment Relations*, Sage, 1995, p. 163.

46. Slomp, *op. cit.*, p. 292.

47. M. Marchington, 'Involvement and participation', in J. Storey (ed.), *Human Resource Management: A critical text*, Routledge, 1995, p. 282.

48. Ramsay, in Towers (1992), *op. cit.*, pp. 211–12.

49. 'Employee involvement – the current state of play', *IRS Employment Trends*, no. 545, October 1993, table 3, p. 7.

50. C. Tillsley, 'Employee involvement: employees' views', *Employment Gazette*, June 1994, p. 211.

51. M. Marchington, A. Wilkinson and P. Ackers, 'Waving or drowning in participation?' *Personnel Management*, March 1993, pp. 47 and 48.

52. *IRS Employment Trends*, no. 545, *op. cit.*, table 2, p. 6.

53. L. Holden, 'Employee involvement', in I. Beardwell and L. Holden, *Human Resource Management: A contemporary perspective*, Pitman, 1994, p. 560.

54. J. Storey, *Developments in the Management of Human Resources*, Blackwell, 1992, pp. 100–11.

55. Hyman and Mason, *op. cit.*, pp. 76–7.

56. P. Ackers, M. Marchington, A. Wilkinson and J. Goodman, 'The use of cycles? Explaining employee involvement in the 1990s', *Industrial Relations Journal*, vol. 23, no. 4, 1992, p. 272.

57. J. F. Geary, 'Task participation: employees' participation enabled or constrained?', in Sisson (ed.) (1994), *op. cit.*, p. 638.

58. Marchington and Wilkinson, *op. cit.*, p. 345.

59. 'Communications and Collective Bargaining', *CIR Report*, no. 39, HMSO, 1973, p. 2.

60. 'Employee involvement', *Employment Gazette*, October 1988.

61. Townley, *op. cit.*, pp. 611–18.

62. T. K. Reeves, 'Information disclosure in employee relations', *Employee Relations*, vol. 2, no. 3, 1980.

63. R. Hussey and A. Marsh, *Disclosure of Information and Employee Reporting*, Gower, 1982, p. 62.
64. *Ibid.*, table 7.2, p. 62.
65. *Ibid.*, table 12.2, p. 117.
66. *Ibid.*, table 12.3, p. 117.
67. *Ibid.*, table 10.4, p. 90.
68. D. Torrington and L. Hall, *Human Resource Management* (4th edn), Prentice Hall, 1998, p. 500.
69. M. Marchington, 'Employee involvement schemes', *BIM Employment Bulletin & IR Digest*, March 1989, p. 2.
70. Hyman and Mason, *op. cit.*, p. 80.
71. Marchington (1989), *op. cit.*
72. Townley, *op. cit.*, p. 603.
73. Hyman and Mason, *op. cit.*, pp. 82–8.
74. Townley, *op. cit.*, p. 605.
75. G. C. White, 'Technological change and employment', *DE Work Research Unit, Occasional Paper 22*, July 1982, p. 11.
76. O. Tynan, 'Improving the quality of working life in the 1980s', *DE Work Research Unit, Occasional Paper 16*, November 1980, p. 4.
77. *Ibid.*, p. 3.
78. Department of Trade and Industry, *Quality Circles*, 1985.
79. Hyman and Mason, *op. cit.*, p. 91.
80. R. Collard and B. Dale, 'Quality circles' in K. Sisson (ed.), *Personnel Management in Britain*, Blackwell, 1989, p. 370.
81. *Ibid.*, p. 363.
82. P. B. Beaumont, *Human Resource Management: key concepts and skills*, Sage, 1993, p. 181.
83. J. Bailey, *Job Design and Work Organization*, Prentice Hall, 1983, p. 79.
84. *Ibid.*, p. 106.
85. Marchington and Wilkinson, *op. cit.*, p. 349.
86. D. W. Bell, *Industrial Participation*, Pitman, 1979, p. 209.
87. *Ibid.*
88. Huiskamp, *op. cit.*, p. 166.
89. Geary, *op. cit.*, p. 649.
90. K. Hawkins, *The Management of Industrial Relations*, Penguin, 1978, p. 121.
91. See M. Armstrong and H. Murlis, *Reward Management* (3rd edn), Kogan Page, 1994 (chapters 21, 23 and 24) and R. Thorpe and G. Homan, *Strategic Reward Systems*, FT Prentice Hall, 2000 (chapters 19 and 20) for information on gainsharing, profit-sharing and share-ownership schemes.
92. A. Pendleton, 'Profit sharing and employee share ownership', in Thorpe and Homan, *op. cit.*, p. 344.
93. O. Hammarström and T. Nilsson, 'Employment relations in Sweden', in G. J. Bamber and R. D. Lansbury (eds), *International and Comparative Employment Relations* (3rd edn), Routledge, 1998, p. 241.
94. 'Telecom Eireann ESOP is seen as a watershed in the industry', *European Industrial Relations Review*, no. 298, November 1998, pp. 17–20.
95. Bailey, *op. cit.*, p. 177.
96. 'Employee involvement and the trade unions', *IRS Employment Trends*, no. 459, March 1990, p. 3.
97. Geary, *op. cit.*, p. 646.
98. Marchington and Wilkinson, *op. cit.*, p. 354.
99. H. Wächter, 'German co-determination – Quo vadis? A study of the implementation of new management concepts in a German steel company', *Employee Relations*, vol. 19, no. 1, 1997, p. 28.
100. 'Survey of board-level employee representation' *European Industrial Relations Review*, no. 205, February 1991.
101. 'European Company Statute nearing adoption?' *European Industrial Relations Review*, no. 293, June 1998, p. 26.
102. *Report of the Committee of Inquiry on Industrial Democracy* (Bullock Committee), HMSO, 1977.
103. Hawkins, *op. cit.*, p. 137.
104. TUC, *Industrial Democracy*, 1977, p. 45.
105. Bullock Committee, *op. cit.*, p. 176.
106. *Ibid.*, p. 178.
107. *Ibid.*, p. 77.
108. M. Costello, 'Ireland's experiment with worker directors', *Personnel Management*, October 1983, p. 57.
109. Bullock Committee, *op. cit.*, p. 72.
110. P. Brannen, E. Batstone, D. Fatchett and P. White, *The Worker Directors*, Hutchinson, 1976.
111. E. Batstone, A. Ferner and M. Terry, *Unions on the Board*, Blackwell, 1983, p. 165.
112. Bullock Committee, *op. cit.*, p. 93.
113. Brannen *et. al., op. cit.*
114. Elliott, *op. cit.*, p. 172.
115. Bullock Committee, *op. cit.*, p. 111.
116. M. Marchington and R. Armstrong, 'Employee participation: problems for the shop steward', *Industrial Relations Journal*, vol. 12, no. 1, 1981, p. 50.
117. Slomp, *op. cit.*, table 14.1, p. 294.
118. See M. Marchington, 'Joint consultation in practice' in Sisson (ed.) (1989), *op. cit.*, pp. 378–399.
119. Slomp, *op. cit.*
120. P. B. Beaumont, *The Future of Employment Relations*, Sage, 1995, p. 165.

121. Manager's comment quoted in Beaumont, *ibid*.

122. H. Ramsay, 'Fool's gold? European works councils and workplace democracy', *Industrial Relations Journal*, vol. 28, no. 4, 1997, pp. 315 and 316.

123. P. James, 'Worker representation and consultation: the impact of European requirements', *Employee Relations*, vol. 16, no. 7, 1994, pp. 33–42.

124. 'Commission issues national-level information and consultation proposal', *European Industrial Relations Review*, no. 299, December 1998, pp. 13–15.

125. 'UK workers to get a look-in', *Labour Research*, February 1998, pp. 19–20.

126. 'European Works Councils – the action begins', *European Industrial Relations Review*, no. 250, November 1994, p. 14.

127. See 'European Works Councils Directive', *European Industrial Relations Review*, no. 251, December 1994, pp. 27–32.

128. 'An analysis of Article 13 EWC agreements', *European Industrial Relations Review*, no. 296, September 1998, pp. 16–8.

129. 'Article 6 agreements in focus', *European Industrial Relations Review*, no. 305, June 1999, pp. 25–8.

130. 'A survey of UK companies and EWCs', *European Industrial Relations Review*, no. 291, April 1998, pp. 14–9.

131. 'European Works Councils', *Incomes Data Services Study*, no. 637, November 1997, p. 1.

132. Ramsay (1997), *op. cit.*, pp. 318–9.

chapter eleven

Industrial action

Learning objectives

Employees are able to exert collective power through disrupting management's use of their labour. By the end of this chapter, you should be able to:

- identify the different views of the role of conflict in social systems and the various forms conflict might take in industrial relations;

- understand the economic, organisational and social factors which may influence the use of industrial action and the changing pattern of strikes in the UK;

- explain the changes in the UK's legal regulation and their effect on trade unions and the conduct of industrial action.

Definition

Industrial action includes any temporary suspension of normal working arrangements initiated unilaterally by employees (whether through their union or not), or management, with the aim of exerting pressure within the collective bargaining process.

Key issues

While you are reading this chapter, you should keep the following points in mind:

- Although the strike (withdrawal of labour) is certainly the most visible and frequently discussed form of industrial action, we should not discount the role and importance of the other forms of 'expressions of conflict' or 'industrial action'. The level of strike activity may not, therefore, be an indication of 'good' or 'bad' industrial relations.

- While the strike can be viewed primarily as part of the collective bargaining process within industrial relations, it may also play an important demonstrative role in the sociopolitical processes within society. We need to be aware that strike activity can involve a strong sociopolitical, as well as economic, element.

- All human actions are subject to some form and degree of social control. However, if we support the employees' right to organise and to have their organisation recognised by employers, then shouldn't we also support their right to 'withdraw labour' if they cannot reach agreement with management on the terms and conditions of their continuing employment? How should we balance 'rights' and 'protection' with 'constraints' when we draw the boundary of 'lawful' industrial action?

11.1 Introduction

While the use, or threat, of industrial action is, as Hyman pointed out, 'an inherent accompaniment to trade unionism and collective bargaining'[1], it has also been perhaps the most controversial issue in industrial relations:

■ Those who emphasise the potentially harmful consequences of a system which accepts and even encourages the use of such power have argued, like Hutt, that it 'is an intolerable abuse of economic freedom ... a type of warfare under which privileged groups can gain at the expense of the unprivileged' and embodies the unacceptable principle that 'power to disrupt may be properly relied upon by those who are in a position to organize disruption (to secure whatever objectives they believe are good, or for their own advantage)'[2].

■ Those who emphasise the critical role played by the display of power in both shaping the employment relationship and influencing the outcome of any specific negotiation have argued, like Grunfeld, that 'it is only the ultimate power of trade union officials and their rank and file members to disrupt production, services or the conduct of an enterprise by the withdrawal of labour which prevents even the most enlightened managerial regime from becoming mere paternalism'[3] or, like Kornhauser *et al.*, that 'collective bargaining would have little meaning were it not for the possibility of a strike, with attendant losses on both sides, since there would be little pressure on the parties to modify their positions and reach agreements'[4].

Despite the general reduction in the level of strike action in most countries over the past two decades, its use is still an important aspect of industrial relations (see Box 11.1). In examining the role of industrial action, it is important to bear three points in mind:

■ While the strike is only one of a range of activities which may be classified as 'industrial action', so 'industrial action' is not the exclusive province of employees and unions but may also be instigated by management.

■ The potential for industrial action is a constant, integral but generally quiescent element in the negotiating process and its use confirms the relative bargaining advantage between the parties and acts as an inducement to make concessions which will lead to an acceptable solution.

■ The strike may be part of the sociopolitical processes within society as well as the industrial and organisational processes of collective bargaining.

Box 11.1	Industrial action – alive and kicking

Strikers vent fury in Seoul

'... The strike by more than 120,000 South Korean industrial workers once again turned the spotlight on the harsh social cost of International Monetary Fund enforced austerity. ...

Two thousand workers gathered at Seoul's railway station singing protest songs as tens of thousands more walked off production lines throughout the country to vent their fury at lay-offs by corporate giants such as Hyundai. ...

The militant Korean Confederation of Trade Unions, representing more than 500,000 workers, ignored government warnings that the strike risks damaging efforts to woo back investor confidence. It is threatening to mobilise even more workers ... if the government fails to meet its demands. These include an end to mass lay-offs, better unemployment benefits, reform of the conglomerates and a renegotiation of the IMF bail-out. ...'

Source: Nick Cumming-Bruce, *Guardian*, 28 May 1998.

Tube walk-out kicks off series of stoppages

'The first direct industrial challenge to Labour Government policy kicked off ... when thousands of London Underground workers began a two-day strike over the effects of plans to privatise part of the Tube network.

London Underground admitted that the walk-out by the Rail, Maritime & Transport union members – which coincides today with the third stoppage by Essex firefighters over job cuts and safety – was bound to bring chaos to Tube services, even though the majority of drivers belong to another union, Aslef.

The mainline rail network also faces disruption this week when 9,000 RMT maintenance workers start a four-day strike from Friday against Railtrack contractors over changes to pay and conditions.

Meanwhile, the broadcasting unions are on the point of calling more industrial action at the BBC, if the corporation's "final offer" at the conciliation service Acas today does not meet their concerns about jobs, salaries and conditions under the latest planned management reorganisation. ...'

Source: Seumas Milne, *Guardian*, 15 June 1998.

Rail strikes against EU policy bring traffic chaos

'Rail traffic ground to a halt across the continent yesterday as rail workers began strikes against the European Union plans to open the freight market to competition.

Strikes stranded passengers and goods in Belgium and severely disrupted rail traffic in France, Greece and Luxembourg.

In Britain, Austria, Germany and The Netherlands rail workers expressed opposition to the EU plans, but through leaflets, news conferences and letters to transport ministers rather than industrial action, unions said. ...

Six French rail unions joined yesterday's action over EU deregulation plans and have called out workers for at least 48 hours from Friday to back shorter hours and better conditions in France. Protests are planned by hospital, post office, telecommunications and job centre workers. ...'

Source: Paul Webster, *Guardian*, 24 November 1998.

Biggest ever pay strike hits South Africa

'South Africa was hit by the largest strike in its history yesterday as hundreds of thousands of public sector workers stayed away to protest at the government's unilateral imposition of a below-inflation pay rise.

| Box 11.1 | Industrial action – alive and kicking *(continued)* |

White teachers joined black prison warders in a stoppage that shut the bulk of schools, forced the government to bus in emergency staff to run Pretoria central prison and ground many government departments to a halt.

Surgeons were unable to perform routine operations at Johannesburg's main hospital after many nurses stayed away. But emergency medical and police services were largely unaffected after the unions told essential workers to report for duty. ...

The protest is ... the stiffest test yet of the alliance between the ruling African National Congress, the trade union confederation Cosatu, and the Communist party which has become increasingly strained by the government's conservative economic strategy. ...'

Source: Chris McGreal, *Guardian*, 25 August 1999.

Irish hospitals in chaos as nurses begin strike over pay

'The biggest strike in the history of the Irish Republic began yesterday when 27,500 nurses began an indefinite stoppage over pay and working conditions, throwing hospital services into chaos. ...

They were picketing more than 1,000 hospitals and medical centres, and seemed to be winning the fight for public support. ...

All except emergency cover was withdrawn in the first national strike by nurses ... A thousand operations and 7,000 out-patient appointments were cancelled within the first hour. ...'

Source: John Mullin, *Guardian*, 20 October 1999.

11.2 Function and forms of industrial action

The expression and resolution of conflict of interest through negotiation, within established procedures and institutions of collective bargaining, generally does not involve recourse to industrial action by either party. The existence of a conflict of interest should not, therefore, be seen as synonymous with the use of overt collective industrial action. In examining the role of industrial action within the industrial relations system it is necessary to consider not only its function in the conduct of the collective bargaining relationship and the various forms it might take but also the factors which may influence its use (see Figure 11.1).

Function of industrial action

Conflict within social structures, such as the industrial relations system, may be viewed from **three perspectives**:

■ The expression of conflicting ideas and interests represents a **direct challenge to the internal order and stability of the social system**. It is feared that, without such order and stability, the social system may degenerate into

Figure 11.1 Role and forms of industrial action

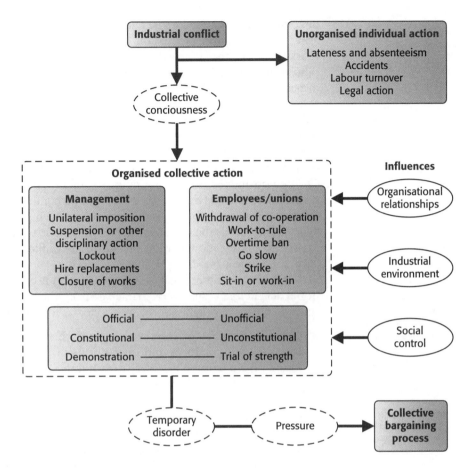

a state of anarchy and lawlessness. Therefore, it is the expression of conflict which is perceived as being the problem to be controlled or even removed.

■ Conflict is a **necessary prelude to the development of a new social order**. A social system can only move from one state of order to another if the existing *status quo* is overtly challenged and defeated. Therefore, it is the *status quo* that is perceived as the issue to be resolved.

■ The open expression of conflict is an **important element in the maintenance of stability within the social system**. It provides the means for identifying and balancing different interests within a dynamic and constantly developing social system.

This last functional perspective underlies the **institutionalisation of conflict** within industrial relations. The growth of organised labour, and its consequent recognition by both employers and the state through the development of collective bargaining arrangements, results in trade unions becoming an accepted part of 'the establishment' at both organisational and national levels. Thus, Dubin argued that trade unions and management became 'joint managers of discontent' within an industrial relations system which has 'self-limiting boundaries that distinguish permissible from subversive industrial disorder'[5], while Clarke regarded the strike as 'the price paid for industrial self-regulation of conditions of employment' and the means to 'bring into the open, and serve to dispel, long-festering grievances, or achieve socially and/or economically desirable improvements'[6]. However, it is important to distinguish between **communal and non-communal conflict**[7]. It is only the former, where despite conflict there remains a basic community of interest between the parties concerned, which can be regarded as having a functional role in maintaining the stability of the industrial relations system. While the survival of the firm may provide a basis of common interest for most employees, union and managers in most situations, nevertheless Hyman argued that 'not all conflicts are capable of containment and absorption by the social structures which give rise to them' and that 'unless and until the basic structure of industry and society is radically recast ... the institutionalisation of industrial conflict will of necessity remain partial and precarious'[8].

A strike or any other form of industrial action is often **perceived as an irrational act**. Hyman[9] suggested that, apart from those who reject the basic principle of conflict in organisations, such a view is founded on two main beliefs:

See Chapter 9 –
Collective bargaining

■ That **any conflict of interest can, and should, be resolved within the recognised procedures and institutions** of the industrial relations system including reference, if necessary, to arbitration as an alternative to the use of industrial action. This view appears to emphasise the third party's identification of a 'content' compromise, which the two parties themselves have failed to find, and plays down the role of 'perceived relative power' in determining the outcome of any negotiation. Certainly, it appears to ignore:

  ▮ the difficulty of identifying and assessing power;
  ▮ the fact that it may have to be demonstrated periodically in order for it to be assessable; and
  ▮ the need within a negotiation for both parties to be able to demonstrate the importance they attach to an issue and their resolve to stand firm.

■ That the **costs to employees of undertaking industrial action far exceeds any gain that may result from its use**. Certainly Gennard's research[10] in the 1970s and early 1980s showed that strikes, although not necessarily other forms of industrial action, could involve the employees in significant financial loss, and possible hardship, with only minimal relief through strike benefit from their union or Social Security payments for their dependants. However:

  ▮ the initial expectation of most strikers is that their dispute will be of a short duration and therefore any potential financial loss is unlikely to be a significant factor in deciding to strike, but it may become more important in a 'return to work' decision as the strike lengthens;
  ▮ the assessment by either party of their position at the beginning or during a strike cannot be judged purely in economic terms or as a single, isolated incident. Its significance lies as much in the fact that it represents the expression of a resistance point and an unwillingness to compromise and, as such, conditions the future management/employee relationship.

Hyman, however, suggested that industrial action can also be regarded as a **rational social action**: 'a calculative attempt to obtain alterations in the work situation or the employment relationship'[11]. While the ultimate function of industrial action is to support and strengthen the process of establishing new and more favourable terms under which the employment relationship may continue, its immediate purpose is to **create temporary industrial disorder** within the existing employment relationship. All forms of industrial action, whether they seek to stop or merely interrupt the production processes, are in Dubin's view 'weapons for maximising industrial disorder'[12] within one or both of the economic and authority relationships of the organisation. The pressure created by such actions stems from not only the economic consequences for the organisation but also management's general concern to maintain an ordered labour environment within which to plan and execute its operational decisions. It is important to realise that the disorder is intended to be only temporary – it is an intervention strategy within the negotiating interaction. As such, it is an integral and necessary element of the industrial relations system and its use is not necessarily indicative of some breakdown in the regulatory system as a whole, but merely a recognition that the 'logic' of argument and verbal persuasion is inadequate for resolving the conflicting interests which are present on that issue at that point in time.

Forms of industrial action

Bean suggests that 'the conflict universe encompasses both collective and individual responses, including not only strikes (concerted, temporary cessations of work) but sabotage, work slowdowns and boycotts as well as individual actions such as absenteeism and quitting'[13]. It is possible, therefore, to distinguish between **unorganised individual forms of action** (such as absenteeism and turnover) and **organised collective forms of action** (such as strikes, work to rule and go slow). While both categories of behaviour express discontent, their difference lies primarily in the intention behind them. Hyman argued that with 'unorganised conflict workers typically respond to the oppressive situation in the only way open to them as *individuals*: by withdrawing from the source of the discontent', while 'organised conflict ... is far more likely to form part of a conscious strategy to change the situation which is identified as the source of the discontent'[14].

However, it is not clear whether these different categories of expressing discontent are **interchangeable and alternative**. Knowles' early study[15] suggested that there is an inverse relationship between the two patterns of behaviour (i.e. where the level of organised collective action is high, the level of unorganised individual action is low), from which it is possible to infer that in weakly organised groups, or groups which have little industrial power, conflict may be more likely to be manifest through unorganised individual action. Conversely, there is evidence from Bean[16], Kelly and Nicholson[17] and Edwards[18] to suggest that the two behaviour patterns are complementary (i.e. groups displaying high levels of organised collective action are also likely to display high levels of unorganised individual action). Nevertheless, it is important to recognise, as Turner *et al.*

pointed out, that 'if the collective expressions of specific discontent are suppressed or inhibited in some forceful way, they may find an outlet in a more dispersed and individual fashion'[19]. Certainly, increased legal restrictions on collective industrial action can result in employees and unions turning to the courts and Employment Tribunals to both express grievances and seek legal redress.

All too often, industrial action has been attributed simply to the presence of agitators on the union side who encourage the expression of conflict for their own power aggrandisement or as part of a deliberate design for social, economic and political revolution. Clearly, the conversion of discontent into organised collective action requires the **existence or creation of a collective consciousness** among the employees if there is to be the necessary solidarity to commence and sustain the action, which, as Hyman notes, involves 'the articulation of trade union activists whose commitment to unionism often stems partly from their political awareness'[20]. Batstone *et al.* suggest that the 'mobilisation of strike action', and by implication the mobilisation of any collective action, should be seen as 'a social process involving systems of influence and power'[21]. The mobilisation of the collective consciousness requires dissemination of information, consultation and eventually 'negotiation and agreement' among the employees involved and the outcome of this process is determined primarily by the quality of the leadership's (shop stewards' and/or full-time officers') network of influence among the membership. Batstone *et al.* believe that the mobilisation of the collective consciousness requires a balance to be struck between the union's requirement for unionateness among its membership and the membership's instrumental requirements of the union. Thus, they argue that it is only through 'political notions such as fairness and justice ... that workers can easily justify challenging the status quo' but that these 'notions of conflict and union principles ... must be related to the experience and perceptions of the workers concerned'[22]. At the same time, the leadership must balance the creating of a collective consciousness with the need to maintain direction and control of its expression within the negotiating process.

Employee discontent may be expressed through a **variety of organised collective action** (see Box 11.2):

- **Withdrawal of co-operation** – withdrawal of representatives from joint institutions, particularly those associated with consultation and productivity; excessive use of the formal procedures; strict interpretation of any *status quo* provision; absence of flexibility on the part of employees and their representatives in the resolution of work problems;
- **Work to rule** – strictly interpreting the duties specified in the contract of employment, collective agreement, job description or other rules (e.g. safety procedures) and requiring precise instructions from management regarding the execution of work;
- **Overtime ban** – collective refusal to work outside normal contractual hours of work, thereby affecting the rate of production;
- **Go-slow** – working without enthusiasm and at a lower level of performance/ output than normal;

Box 11.2	Action short of a strike

'Blue flu' strikes the Irish police

' ... Support for the one-day action among 6,500 gardai was said to be close to 100 per cent. Because the law forbids police to strike, officers rang in sick. Their condition was dubbed blue flu ... The Garda Representative Association ... also plan to refuse to issue speeding or parking tickets.'

Source: John Mullin, *Guardian*, 2 May 1998.

German bank unions threaten euro launch

In a dispute over pay and conditions, German banking unions warned 'that the smooth introduction of the euro could be seriously disrupted as the 470,000 banking staff refuse to do extra work ... '

A union spokesperson said 'preparations for the smooth entry of the euro [and to ensure information systems are millennium-bug free] require an enormous amount of extra work, and we could simply refuse to do this.'

Source: David Gow, Mark Milner and Jill Treanor, *Guardian*, 14 December 1998.

Sabotage their systems and steal their stationery ...

' ... By a variety of means – some responsible, some deviant – [employees] are still able to assert their rights, their disapproval, or hit employers where they feel it most – in the pocket ...

In the service industries, where the essence of the job is to give that little bit extra, employees (more often than not, poorly paid) can exert considerable power by giving that little bit less. A curled lip from a check-out girl or the telephone manner of a Neanderthal can adversely effect the image of companies desperate to hang on to customers. Factory floor workers commonly bite back by playing dumb, or withholding knowledge from management ...

But increasingly the pattern of dispute in the Nineties has moved from the collective to the individual. If you can't beat them, sue them, seems to be the idea. ... '

Source: Alex Spillius, *Independent on Sunday*, 10 March 1996.

■ **Strike** – temporary withdrawal of labour and stoppage of work;

■ **Work-in/sit-in** – occupying the workplace and, possibly, continuing to work but denying management access to or control of the output thus 'demonstrating that the plant is a viable concern' or 'preventing the transfer of plant and machinery to other factories'[23]. Thomas argued that 'occupation demonstrates publicly in a most vivid manner that management is no longer in control'[24].

The strike is often depicted as the ultimate and most favoured form of collective action in that, by stopping work and leaving the workplace, the employees clearly demonstrate both the importance of the issue in dispute and their solidarity. Certainly it is easier for the union to ensure that there is collective solidarity (all members are complying with the required action) in a strike than in other forms of industrial action. Other forms (except the work-in or sit-in) may be seen as preliminary action intended to develop collective consciousness and to be abandoned in favour of strike action if they do not achieve the required concession from management. Alternatively, they may be regarded as of equal importance, or even preferred, to strike action for two reasons:

- They involve the employees and union in less financial loss than a strike while still exerting a significant cost on the management in terms of lost production (although, a ban on overtime may, in practice, be beneficial to management by reducing its labour costs).

- They may not be perceived, at least by employees if not by the law, as breach of contract but simply the carrying out of those duties which they are contractually obliged to do. Certainly, if management takes disciplinary action in such situations, it is likely to reinforce the employees' collective consciousness and solidarity.

Flanders noted that in the UK during the 1960s there was an 'increasing use of "cut price" industrial action such as overtime bans, working to rule and going slow'[25]. Hyman[26] attributed this to, first, the increasing affluence of employees and an associated increase in their financial commitments, which reduced their willingness to lose pay through strike action, and, second and most important, the effectiveness of these other forms of industrial action in securing concessions from management. However, later survey findings[27] suggest a decline during the 1970s and 1980s in the use of these other forms of industrial action. Brown suggested that this was due to management being 'more prepared to hold out against limited actions when they are operating at a low level of capacity (and thus when overtime bans and the like are relatively painless) than when they want to maximize production'[28]. Significantly, these surveys show the following:

- The overtime ban was the most frequently used form of alternative action for both manual and non-manual employees.

- The work to rule accounted for a larger proportion of the industrial action among non-manual employees than among manual employees. This may result from not only their preference for a 'constitutional' form of industrial action but also their greater facility to utilise a formal job description as the legitimate source for defining the limits of their work requirement.

However, Edwards[29] notes that the weakening of workplace union organisation during the 1980s has made it more difficult to maintain the necessary co-ordination and discipline required to maintain non-strike sanctions.

Official and unofficial

In the past, the term **official** was primarily intended to designate, within the union organisation, that it would financially support its members and had the effect of designating the existence of a dispute to other trade unionists, thereby enlisting their support by, for example, not crossing picket lines. However, the appropriate person or body within the union's rules who could authorise or approve industrial action varied between unions dependent on their constitution. It was this constitutional variation which led Turner *et al.* to comment that 'it is not at all unusual for a strike to be official for some of the workers involved

See Chapter 5 –
Trade union
organisation and
structure

and unofficial for others' or that 'under some union constitutions, where the power to authorize strikes is shared between local and national bodies ... a dispute may be declared, even for the same group of workers, official and unofficial at the same time'[30].

It is unfortunate that the term **unofficial** has often been used loosely not only to refer to any industrial action initiated by employees or shop stewards but also to imply that such action is irresponsible and should be subject to greater control by the union organisation. It may be argued that the development and strengthening of collective bargaining at the organisational level, primarily in the hands of shop stewards, required that control of industrial power should be vested and exercised at that level. Yet, in most unions, the formal organisational authority for sanctioning the use of industrial action remained at a higher level remote from the negotiations. Consequently, there was a range of situations which could be classified as **'quasi-official' industrial action:**

See Chapter 9 – Collective bargaining

- Action initiated by shop stewards as an integral part of their collective bargaining role (a role recognised by both management and union);

- Action supported by the union but not formally approved because:
  - it was felt to be impolitic to be seen supporting such action; or
  - there was insufficient time, before the industrial action was over, for it to be considered by the appropriate authority within the union; or
  - the union simply did not wish to pay strike benefit to its members.

See Case study 11.1

The term 'unofficial', therefore, really applied only to industrial action initiated by employees or shop stewards outside the union's negotiating strategy and which was often intended to express dissatisfaction with the course of negotiations (perhaps, directed as much against the union negotiators as against management). Nevertheless, the distinction between 'official' and 'unofficial' (or 'quasi-official') was important in respect of the potential role of the union in the conduct of negotiations. By not making the action official, the union was not tied to those demands and could adopt, what was to the union hierarchy, a more realistic approach to the negotiations. In many situations the union full-time officer was able to adopt, or be invited by management to adopt, a 'quasi-conciliation' role between management and the shop stewards or employees undertaking the unofficial or quasi-official industrial action While management would usually insist that the full-time officer exert his or her authority as the formal representative of the union and secure a return to normal working before any further negotiations took place, this may have involved prior informal acceptance by management that there were areas in which they were prepared to negotiate and through which a satisfactory conclusion was possible.

However, the **legislative changes introduced during the 1980s** have made trade unions legally accountable for the actions of their officers and committees. Consequently, 'lawful' and 'official' have become almost synonymous terms; a union is unlikely to authorise or endorse any industrial action which is not lawful because it will lose its immunity from legal action. At the same time, management has been given greater freedom to dismiss employees involved in unofficial industrial action (i.e. not authorised or endorsed by the appropriate person or committee within the union), in that such employees are precluded

Case study 11.1 ■ Electricians to walk out in pay deal revolt

'An unofficial strike by thousands of electricians ... is expected to shut down some of the biggest construction sites in the country, including the Millennium Dome in Greenwich, Royal Opera House and Jubilee Line extension on the London Underground.

The illegal walkout, over a pay deal negotiated by the Amalgamated Engineering and Electrical Union, will embarrass Sir Ken Jackson, AEEU general secretary and self-proclaimed union moderniser, who told the TUC conference on Tuesday that union–employer partnerships heralded the prospect of a 'strike-free Britain'. Within 24 hours, 430 AEEU toolmakers at Ford's Dagenham plant in Essex staged a one-day strike in a dispute over bonuses.

Now Sir Ken is faced with a far bigger revolt by members working in the electrical contracting industry, who believe AEEU officials have given too much away in their annual pay negotiations.

Shop stewards co-ordinating the planned walk-out – agreed at a meeting of hundreds of electricians in London – ... expected up to 8,000 electricians to take part in London, Dover, Newcastle, Hull, Liverpool, Edinburgh and Grangemouth, near Edinburgh. The dome and the Jubilee Line, where work is well behind schedule, are particularly vulnerable to stoppages ...

A network of well organised AEEU stewards, representing a skilled workforce which now has the whip hand in a tight labour market, has seen off several attempts by contracting employers in recent years to undermine the electricians' position or target union activists. Two years ago mass unofficial walkouts at big construction sites laid the ground for a national

vote against an AEEU-negotiated deal to introduce semi-skilled workers into electrical contracting jobs. Last year, stoppages on the Jubilee Line extension lead to improved pay rates and the reinstatement of site organisers.

Setting out his vision of a world without strikes, Sir Ken said there would be "no return to the bad old days. Workers want to work, they don't want to strike. I want to see a strike-free future for British industry". An AEEU spokesman explained later that this was "only an aspiration".

Yesterday leaflets circulating on the big London construction sites accused union leaders of making spineless concessions to the electrical contracting employers.

"They never consult their members", one Jubilee line steward – who asked not to be named – said of the AEEU leadership.

"Ken Jackson is a prima donna sitting in an ivory tower who never speaks to shop floor workers. He should start talking to his shop stewards or resign".

But Paul Corby, the AEEU national organiser of construction, said the workers were "jumping the gun". The pay deal was not set in stone and the stewards should not be attacking the union.

When the offer was finalised, it would be put to a ballot and if electricians rejected it the union would consider national industrial action ... '

Source: Seumas Milne, *Guardian*, 17 September 1999.

See also Case study 9.1.

from taking any claim for unfair dismissal before an Employment Tribunal and the union is precluded from subsequently taking official industrial action in support of their reinstatement (Employment Act, 1990).

Constitutional and unconstitutional

In the USA and many European countries, it is normal for there to be a requirement not to undertake industrial action **during the period of the collective agreement**. However, such requirements 'are generally *relative* insofar as they only relate to the provisions of an existing agreement'[31] (i.e. matters of right) and unions are free to undertake industrial action on any matter not covered by a collective agreement (for example, management proposals for work changes, rationalisation, etc.). The effect of such a provision is to provide relative certainty and 'peace' during the currency of the collective agreement (particularly if the agreement is for a period of two or three years), although it may result in larger-scale strikes or other industrial action when the collective agreement is due for renegotiation.

See Chapter 15 –
Grievance, discipline
and redundancy

In the UK, **unconstitutional action** refers to industrial action which is initiated in contravention of a clause, generally in the grievance/disputes procedures, stating that industrial action, by either party, should not be undertaken until all the stages of the procedure have been exhausted. This clause, in effect, defines the circumstances in which industrial power may legitimately be exercised. It has been often argued that unconstitutional action is unacceptable because it breaches such jointly agreed and established procedures for resolving differences between management and employees. However, this is valid only if both the procedure is adequate and management does not abuse its inherent bargaining advantage by delaying negotiations within the procedure.

A number of the 'new-style' agreements in the 1980s, often based on single-union recognition, included a **specific 'no-strike'** clause (i.e. an undertaking by the union that, in return for referring any dispute to binding arbitration, it will not instigate industrial action). This is distinct from simply agreeing to use the process of binding arbitration to resolve any outstanding disputes – that is, establishing an arrangement which will substantially reduce, if not remove, the need to undertake industrial action. Certainly, as Hillage points out, many trade unions were 'deeply suspicious of agreements limiting what they see as a fundamental right to withdraw labour'[32] and, as Hall notes, the TUC's guidelines on no-strike clauses recommended that unions should 'not make recognition agreements which remove the right to take industrial action ... this is not meant to deter unions from agreeing to procedures for arbitration'[33]. It can be argued that a union will be reluctant to authorise or endorse industrial action where it has accepted a 'no-strike' clause and therefore any action by its members or employees is likely to be 'unofficial' (rendering them vulnerable to selective dismissal).

Demonstrative action and trials of strength

The principal intention of **demonstrative action** is to highlight the importance employees attach to the issue in dispute or to express their dissatisfaction with the progress of a negotiation. It is particularly appropriate in what are often termed 'perishable disputes' – those situations where dissatisfaction needs to be displayed immediately while the issue is fresh or where 'power' exists only at that point in time. Delay in the use of industrial action until the recognised procedure is exhausted may allow management to implement their decision and thereby make it more difficult for the employees to secure a favourable decision (for example, the dismissal of an employee or redundancies). In the past such action has been generally unconstitutional, unofficial and of short duration. However, the requirement for unions formally to ballot members before undertaking industrial action (Trade Union Act, 1984), as opposed to having a 'show of hands' at a meeting, has reduced, if not negated, the union's or members' ability to undertake immediate demonstrative action. **Trials of strength**, on the other hand, involve a more protracted use of industrial action as an integral

See Chapter 13 –
Negotiation

element of the negotiating process and with the intention of confirming or modifying the perceived relative bargaining advantage between the parties. It is, therefore, likely to be constitutional, official and of longer duration.

Management and industrial action

It is perhaps inevitable that industrial action should be **perceived as exclusively an employee or union phenomenon**. Where employees or union are seeking change, management can, if it wishes to maintain the *status quo*, adopt a passive approach by simply saying 'no' within the negotiations and thereby place the onus on employees or union to take the initiative and responsibility for utilising direct industrial action in pursuit of their claim. Equally, where management initiates change, it can, if the employees or union refuse to accept its proposals, adopt a strategy of imposing new arrangements unilaterally and thereby, again, place the onus on the employees or union to take direct industrial action as a means of resisting the change. Ghilarducci notes that 'since labor is the moving party, management, no matter how aggressive, seems passive and innocent during a strike' and, indeed, may benefit from a strike (both in the specific strike and in general) if it 'causes internal union dissension, weakens interunion solidarity, makes union negotiating conduct seem obdurate and violent and union goals seem anti-productivity growth and greedy'[34].

Management does have at its disposal a number of specific actions which may be regarded as involving the unilateral use of industrial power. Certainly, it may **dispense with the services of employees** either on a **temporary basis** (lockout) or on a **permanent basis** (dismiss employees and hire replacements). While the lock-out and the hire of replacements were relatively common in the early days of trade unionism, they have become less so. However, the increased freedom given to management under the Employment Acts (1980, 1982 and 1990) to dismiss strikers has led to a greater preparedness on the part of some management (e.g. British Rail in 1985) to dismiss striking employees as a prelude to re-engaging a chastened workforce, excluding militants or hiring replacements, or even as part of reducing its workforce.

Management may also utilise its ultimate sanction of **closing or threatening to close the organisation**. The use of this sanction, because of its implied permanency, may be considered a much more powerful sanction than the employees' temporary stoppage of work through strike action. The credibility of such a threat, and therefore its effect in exerting pressure on employees and union, will be greatest where either the organisation's continued economic viability is clearly in question and/or the organisation has the capacity to move production elsewhere. Such threats may provoke retaliatory action on the part of employees or unions in the form of a work-in or sit-in.

Similarly it may be argued that management has the ability, and the right, to **impose unilaterally** new working arrangements (including withdrawing overtime or speeding up work) and to take **disciplinary action** against employees who refuse to accept a change or as a response to a work to rule, overtime ban or go-slow. Such actions may be seen as management forms of industrial action (intended to exert pressure on employees to change their position). However,

Hyman argues that these 'routine practices of employers do not *count* as "industrial conflict"; they are part of the normal, repressive reality of work'[35].

Strike patterns

There are **three main indices** which are used to assess strike activity:

■ **Number of stoppages**. Generally no distinction is made between strikes and lock-outs, however, certainly in the UK during the postwar period, the number of lock-outs has been very small.

■ **Number of workers involved**. In the UK this includes both those directly and indirectly involved (laid off or on short time) at the establishment where the stoppage occurs but excludes workers indirectly involved at other establishments; it tends to overstate the number of strikers but, perhaps more importantly, understate the number of people not working as a consequence of strike action.

■ **Number of working days lost**. This is the number of workers involved multiplied by the length of the stoppage and, when expressed as a figure per 1,000 employees, is the most commonly used index for comparison purposes.

However, the statistics **measure the extent rather than the effect of strike activity**. For example, the Donovan Commission argued that Britain's high incidence of short unofficial and unconstitutional strikes during the 1960s had a disproportionate effect by undermining management's confidence and initiative to make changes within the organisation. Turner[36], on the other hand, argued that the effect of these strikes was confined largely to the organisation within which they occurred and it is the longer strikes which have the greatest effects because, after a certain period, they will indirectly affect the working of other organisations not involved in the original dispute. Certainly, it is extremely difficult to 'cost' the effects of any strike – in social as well as financial terms, and to the wider economy and society as well as the individual people and organisation(s) involved.

An examination of **Britain's strike figures** shows a number of trends (see Figure 11.2).

■ *Number of stoppages*. Before the Second World War there were only four years in which the number of stoppages exceeded 1,000. After 1941 there was a steady increase in the number of stoppages, and between 1955 and 1979 the number was consistently above 2,000 with a peak of 3,906 in 1970. From the late 1970s there has been a steady and significant decline to a low of only 159 strikes in 1998.

■ *Number of working days lost*. In the three years immediately after the First World War (1919–21), 147 million working days were lost through strike action – exceeded only by the 161 million working days lost in 1926 (the year of the General Strike). During the 1950s and 1960s, however, the number of working days lost averaged 3.4 million per year and in only four years did it exceed 5 million. In marked contrast, the 1970s had an annual

Figure 11.2 UK
industrial action
1915–98

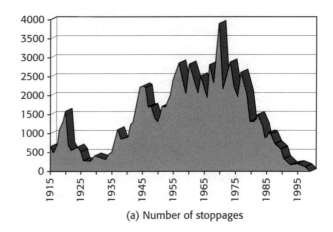

(a) Number of stoppages

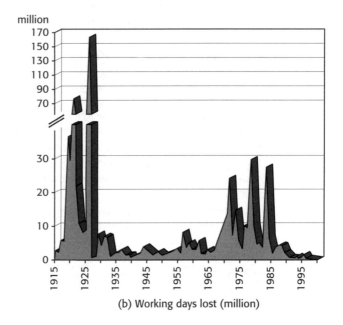

(b) Working days lost (million)

average of 12.7 million working days lost (exceeding 10 million in seven of
these years and below 5 million in only one year). During the 1980s,
although the number of strikes was only 30–50 per cent of the 1960s level,
the number of working days lost per year returned broadly to the 1960s level
of 3–6 million working days per year (apart from the 27 million working
days in 1984 as a result of the NUM strike). The 1990s have seen a marked
decrease in the level of working days lost – in most years below 0.5 million.

- *Size and duration of strikes.* While in the early 1960s over three-quarters of
strikes lasted less than three days, by the late 1970s the proportion had
dropped to less than half. In eight years, during the 1970s and 1980s, a
substantial proportion of the total working days lost were accounted for by
a single major dispute (for example, the NUM dispute in 1985 accounted for

Table 11.1 UK
duration of stoppages
(1998)

	Working days lost		Number of stoppages	
	000s	%	No.	%
1–5 days	55.2	25.2	130	78.3
6–10 days	158.6	56.2	21	12.7
11–30 days	3.3	1.1	7	4.2
30+ days	49.3	17.5	8	4.8
Total	*266.4*		*166*	

Source: J Davies, 'Labour disputes in 1998' *Labour Market Trends*, June 1999, Table 9, p.308.

83 per cent of working days lost that year). The distribution pattern of strikes remains broadly similar in the 1990s, but at a much lower level – 80 per cent of strikes lasting less than five days and accounting for only 25 per cent of the working days lost (see Table 11.1). It is important to remember that the decline in multi-employer collective bargaining has the effect of turning any union national campaign (as, for example, the engineering unions' campaign for a shorter working week during 1990) into a possible series of small strikes rather than one big one.

The UK's postwar strike pattern can be divided into **three broad periods**:

- *1950s and 1960s*. This period was associated with increasing economic growth and aspirations among employees (following the depression of the 1920s and 1930s and the Second World War) coupled with increasing assertiveness in workplace bargaining. The latter part of this period, in particular, is often referred to as one of **shopfloor revolt** and was characterised by an increasing strike frequency but at the organisation, rather than industry, level and of relatively short duration.

- *1970s*. This period was associated with a declining economic situation and increased government intervention (the Industrial Relations Act (1971) and almost continuous incomes policies – although this had started in the mid-1960s). It was a period of more **formal challenge** within the industry and national levels of the industrial relations system, characterised by more widespread and protracted disputes; often with a 'political' element demonstrating opposition to legislation or incomes policy and involving strike activity in the public sector (most affected by the incomes policies).

- *1980s and 1990s*. The 1980s were associated with significant changes in the economic and political environments: not least a substantial decline in the manufacturing sector, privatisation and commercialisation of the public sector and sustained high levels of unemployment, coupled with declining union membership, restrictive trade union legislation and managerial initiatives to re-exert their prerogative. Hyman termed this period **coercive pacification** wherein 'sustained mass unemployment and a governmental offensive have systematically undermined most workers' collective strength and confidence'[37]. The 1990s have seen an increased emphasis on organisational competitiveness, labour flexibility, changes in working patterns and employment structures, coupled with the development of HRM strategies to secure employee commitment within a more individual employment relationship. This has been characterised by a shift towards the concept of **partnership** between management, employees and, where recognised, union. The past two decades have seen a substantial reduction in all three indices of strike activity, but with a blip in 1984/5.

See Case study 11.2

Knowles[38] divided the **causes of strikes** into three main groups: basic issues (wages and hours of work), solidarity issues (recognition, closed shop, inter-union disputes) and frictional issues (working arrangements, discipline, redundancy, etc.). Since the early 1980s, the balance appears to have shifted away from 'basic' or 'solidarity' issues and more towards 'frictional' issues. Similarly, there has been some shift in the **spread of industrial action across sectors**. Since the late 1960s strike activity has spread from manual workers in the traditionally strike-prone industries (mining, manufacturing, transport) and become a significant feature in other industries (in particular the public sector) and among non-manual employees. Indeed, the sharp decline in strike activity in manufacturing in the early 1980s was 'balanced by sharp increases in public administration and education'[39]. Beaumont notes that the public sector contribution to total working days lost rose from less than 20 per cent during most of the 1960s to over 80 per cent in some years during the 1980s[40]. The importance of this shift, he argues, stems not just from the involvement of employees who in the past have not been regarded as strike-prone (civil servants, teachers, etc.) but also from the high 'cost' of such strikes which affect wide parts of the general public and the possible 'constitutional overtones' of strikes which are, at least in part, directed against government policies (whether incomes policies of the 1970s or the flexibility and deregulation policies of the 1980s and 1990s).

During the 1960s and 1970s, much was made of **international comparisons** which showed that the UK was more strike-prone than other countries – particularly its industrial competitors such as Sweden, Germany and Japan. However, as Screpanti points out, there was a general international strike wave in 1968–74 (similar to ones in 1869–75 and 1910–20), correlating with the upper turning point (boom to recession) of the long-term economic cycle of the western capitalist economic system. This comprises 20–30 years of rapid economic growth followed by an equally long period of stagnation and recession, during which strike activity is severely reduced as a result of the effect on 'levels of employment, wage rate and other elements of workers' welfare and self-confidence'[41]. However, while most countries experienced a decline in their level of strike activity from the early 1980s onwards, the UK's position altered significantly *relative* to other countries – from well above average to below average (see Figure 11.3). Indeed, the UK now rates 'consistently below both the EU and OECD average'[42].

However, any international comparison is complicated by differences in national industrial relations systems and, in particular, the function performed by the **strike may have different meanings and significance**. For example, Aligisakis contrasts the very high strike propensity in Spain or Italy, where the 'act of striking is considered a means of political protest', with the low strike propensity in Germany, The Netherlands and Scandinavia, which 'can be

Case study 11.2 ■ Ford and BT

Ford votes for strike ballot

'Thousands of workers at the huge Ford plant at Dagenham yesterday voted for a ballot on industrial action over allegations that managers at the Essex site are tolerating or even practising shopfloor bullying and racial discrimination. Unions want to arm themselves with a strike mandate in case talks with the company fail to resolve the problems.

Jacques Nasser, president of Ford worldwide, will be meeting British union leaders, possibly next week, to discuss unrest at Dagenham triggered by two incidents involving workers from ethnic minorities. On Tuesday, the plant was hit by a wildcat strike that cost the production of 1,200 vehicles, with a second, more limited, walkout on Thursday.

Mass meetings began at 6.30 am yesterday, and by 10 am 2,000 workers had taken part. By the end of the day, informal voting had given Dagenham's two main unions – the Transport & General Workers and the Amalgamated Engineering and Electrical Union – a clear call to press ahead with formal strike ballots. These could take four weeks to organise ...

Transport union spokeswoman Karen Livingstone said a strike mandate would allow the union "to move quickly if things don't work out" in talks with Mr Master and other senior Ford chiefs. Duncan Simpson, national motor-industry officer for the engineering union, said: "The workforce is frustrated that Ford is unwilling to deal effectively with racism at Dagenham".

Mr McAllister said Ford operated a "zero tolerance" policy towards all types of abuse, bullying and victimisation at its plants. Were Ford able to improve this policy, he said, then it would do so, but warned that unofficial strikes could do nothing but harm to the future of Dagenham.

As if to underline the fragility of Dagenham's position in a glutted world motor market, yesterday's mass meetings cost the company no production at all, because the plant is currently on short-time working and Friday is a "down day". ... '

Source: Dan Atkinson, *Guardian*, 9 October 1999.

National strike pulls plug on BT

'Thousands of BT customer service workers ... staged the first-ever national strike at call-centres – the mushrooming new factories of the 1990s service economy – in protest against what they say are bullying managers, unrealistic targets, understaffing and casualisation. ...

Up to 4,000 BT staff at about 40 call centres – which deal with queries about sales, bills and repairs – are estimated to have taken part in the 24-hour stoppage, which follows an 81% yes vote on a 50% turnout.

But the company has been able to rely on a minority of non-union and agency workers – who could not be balloted because of laws against "secondary action" – to fill part of the gap. ...

Jeannie Drake, CWU deputy general secretary, said the strike had been solidly supported and represented "years of mounting frustration" at BT call centres. One of the flash-points had been threats of disciplinary action if calls were not completed within 285 seconds.

But discontent is also focussed on what the union describes as a management culture of harassment and bullying, increased use of short-term contract agency workers and inadequate staffing.

BT says it recognises there are staffing problems and has stepped up recruitment to deal with the complaint. The company wants to maintain a dialogue with the CWU to resolve the dispute. ...

Call centres are Britain's fastest-growing industry and now employ more than 400,000 people'.

Source: Seumas Milne, *Guardian*, 23 November 1999.

See also Case studies 1.1, 6.3 and 7.2.

Figure 11.3
International strike
comparison (all
industries and
services)
(*Working days lost
per 1000 employees
as a percentage of
average for the seven
countries; five year
moving averages*)

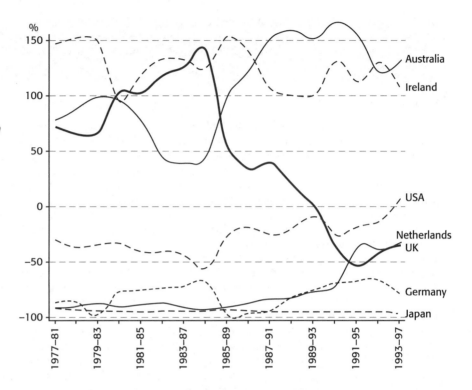

explained by the social democrat tradition of participation, by neo-corporatist measures and by consensus theory ... a labour relations model tending towards negotiation and compromise'[43]. Furthermore, Germany's low level of industrial action may, in part, be due to the separation of the regulation of workplace issues (through Works Councils) from collective bargaining over terms and conditions through trade unions and employers' associations at the industry or sector level. However, in the absence of such institutionalisation, it is important to recognise that strike action, because of its high visibility, may have 'an important role in broader societal struggles for power'[44]. Edwards and Hyman note that in France and Italy there is little provision for the inclusion of trade unions in policy making institutions, despite significant support for left-wing parties, and consequently 'unions typically used short though massive strikes as demonstrations of protest'[45]. Indeed, Aligisakis believes that the role of the strike is generally shifting from being a warning or pressure within the 'industrial' negotiation process to being a more general 'political' protest against the capitalist system.

Influences on industrial action

Edwards argued that 'the strike-proneness of industries or plants cannot be seen as the result of the operation of a few distinct "independent variables"'[46], but rather that structural factors interact with 'the day-to-day decisions of managers, shop stewards and others' and, therefore, 'it is no good blaming a "poor" strike

See Case study 11.3

record on [structural variables] ... the greater part of the responsibility lies in the handling of industrial relations'[47]. Certainly, studies of individual strikes, such as Pilkingtons in 1970[48], air traffic controllers in the USA in 1981[49] and the UK NCB/NUM dispute in 1984/5[50], show that no strike can be explained purely in terms of 'structural' factors but that these must be related to the motives, attitudes and perceptions of the participants. Therefore, there is no single or straightforward causal explanation for the extent or distribution of industrial action in different industries, different countries or over time.

Economic environment

It is frequently argued that aggregate strike activity can be correlated with the **business cycle of expansion and recession**. However, there is an apparent contradiction in the relationship. Hunter argued that the general expectation is of 'strike frequency falling in recession and rising in boom periods'[51] as the union's relative bargaining power is weakened or enhanced by economic conditions. Edwards, on the other hand, pointed out that 'workers may have more reason to strike in a recession than in a boom if they have to defend themselves against an employer's attack, and, in a boom, employers may be willing to grant workers' demands without a strike'[52]. This apparent contradiction may be reconciled if strike frequency (number of strikes) is related to strike duration (length of strike). The UK evidence suggests that during periods of economic boom, although strike frequency may increase, most strikes are of short duration. Equally, although strike frequency may reduce during periods of recession, any strike may be more severe (of longer duration) as the employees' desire to protect their living standards is met by increased management resistance resulting from declining profits of the organisation.

Certainly, the relationship between **unemployment and strike activity** operates at two levels:

- At the **micro level** of specific disputes or negotiations, management may seek to link low profits, spare capacity and high unemployment directly with the threat of redundancy if unions do not moderate their stance – thus weakening the employees' resolve to utilise industrial action.

- At the **macro level**, it may be argued that as the economy changes from expansion or stability to recession, there is likely to be a maintenance, or even an increase, in the frequency and duration of strike activity as employees and unions seek, in the light of their experience in the previous period of boom when they were strong, to utilise strike action to protect themselves from a decline in their living standards. Only after the recession conditions have existed for some time, and therefore affect the perceptions of the participants, will unemployment exert any general influence on strike propensity and lead to a decline in strike activity.

Industrial/organisational environment

The strike is an action within social systems and, therefore, Kerr and Siegel argued that strike propensity could be linked to differences in relationship between work, people and society. They identified two groups of factors:

■ The **employees' industrial location relative to society**. Industries will be strike-prone where 'the workers form a relatively homogeneous group which is usually isolated from the general community and which is capable of cohesion' and comparatively strike-free where 'workers are individually integrated into the larger society, are members of trade groups which are coerced by government or the market to avoid strikes, or are so individually isolated that strike action is impossible'[53].

■ The **nature of the work and people employed**. Where the work is 'physically difficult and unpleasant, unskilled or semiskilled, and casual or seasonal, and fosters an independent spirit ... it will draw tough, inconstant, combative and virile workers, and they will be inclined to strike', whereas where the work is 'physically easy and performed in pleasant surroundings, skilled and responsible, steady, and subject to set rules and close supervision, it will attract women or the more submissive type of man who will abhor strikes'[54].

Subsequently, Kerr[55] also suggested a number of **organisationally related factors** which may affect strike propensity:

■ *Size of organisation*. Large organisations tend to have higher levels of unionisation, greater emphasis on formalised relationships, and greater divorcement of employees from management than small organisations.

■ *Production patterns and technological change*. Intermittent production patterns, frequent changes or crises, or rapid technological changes reduce organisational stability and may create feelings of insecurity and stress, increasing the potential for industrial action.

■ *Nature of the work*. Assembly-line type of work, with its associated 'deskilling' of work, close supervision, boredom and frustration, tends to produce greater employee dissatisfaction than other work systems.

■ *Cost and market factors*. Pressure on prices, profits and costs is likely to bring management into conflict with employees over achieving 'labour savings'.

Certainly, those industries which in the past have been relatively strike-prone (such as coal mining, docks, iron and steel, shipbuilding and car manufacture) display many of the above characteristics. However, the **changes in the industrial and labour force structure** during the 1980s and 1990s have seen a decline in manufacturing (and, in particular, a move away from assembly-line mass production forms of technology and work arrangements), an increase in the service sector (involving, particularly, female and part-time employment) and a decline in the size of organisations (through both rationalisation and decentralisation). Consequently, Edwards argues, 'since the strike-prone sectors have lost jobs, there are simply fewer workers subject to whatever special forces operate within them'[56]. However, strike activity within the service industries (both private and public) is accounting for an increased proportion of the, albeit reduced, overall level of strike activity.

Case study 11.3 ■ Dock strikes (UK and Australia)

In September 1995, 320 Liverpool dockers employed by the Mersey Docks and Harbour Company (MDHC) refused to cross a picket line set up by 80 other dockers dismissed by a sub-contract firm (Torside). The dispute took place against a background of declining jobs in the port (down from 6,000 in the mid-1980s to under 500), the fear of increasing labour casualisation (with the spectre of the pre-National Dock Labour Scheme (1946–89) situation of men queuing at the dock gates each day waiting to be offered work) and an unemployment level in Liverpool of nearly 13 per cent.

The MDHC (in which the government had a minority shareholding and which had made £34 million profit in the previous year) deemed the dockers to have dismissed themselves and refused to allow them to return to work. The management immediately advertised the dockers' jobs and used contract firms to provide replacement casual workers. The dispute provided the MDHC with the opportunity to change working methods and arrangements radically and to reduce the power of the union. They claimed that productivity increased by 50 per cent – a claim challenged by the dockers themselves.

The dispute produced tension between the two sides. The dockers claimed that police used aggressive tactics against their pickets; they also called in health and safety officials to stop the MDHC from housing the new casual labour in portakabins on the site. For its part, the MDHC alleged the dockers molested and intimidated those they regarded as 'scab labour' or 'strike-breakers'. However, the dockers were not 'young firebrands' but rather had 'grey hair, pension rights and children at university'[1]. In pursuing their dispute, the dockers' income dropped from around £19,000 p.a. to a few pounds each week provided from collecting buckets and other donations – from both the UK and abroad.

In the early weeks, the MDHC did offer to re-employ 200 of the dockers, but on individual contracts without collective bargaining rights and with a reduction in pay. At another time, the dockers were offered £10,000 each for the loss of their job. These offers were rejected because they did not meet the dockers basic demand – reinstatement for all, although some leaders felt that reinstatement for younger dockers and a good early retirement package for those in their 50s might have been accepted.

Dockers went around the UK addressing meetings (some 950 meetings in the first two months) and collecting donations for their hardship fund. They enlisted the support not only of a wide range of union branches and political groups but also of churches and 'a starry array of play-wrights, rock stars, and comedians'[3] – including Liverpool footballers who wore supportive T-shirts at a European Cup match.

Perhaps their greatest achievement was to obtain 'a show of international labour solidarity believed to be without precedent this century'[4]. They also gave 'new meaning to the term "flying picket"'[2] when a small group went to the USA and picketed Atlantic Container Line ships in Newark, New Jersey, where state law allowed workers (in this case US longshoremen) to refuse to cross an actual picket line (secondary boycott). By sending representatives abroad, they persuaded dockers in other countries to demonstrate their support by going slow or refusing to handle ships from Liverpool – Japan, the western US seaboard ports, Canada (where the use of strike-breaking labour is illegal), Australia and South Africa (where dockers reciprocated the support they had received against apartheid). The action certainly affected MDHC's share price early on but the company claimed that, within 3–4 months, shipping services disrupted at the beginning of the dispute had returned to normal.

The strike continued for over two years and remained, throughout, an unofficial one. The dockers' union (T&GWU) felt constrained in what it could do if it was to avoid legal action and the possible sequestration of its funds. However, it is estimated that the union contributed some £700,000 to the dockers' hardship fund. The eventual 'settlement' negotiated by the T&GWU in January 1998, and accepted by the dockers, was a £28,000 'pay-off' for each docker. During a House of Commons employment committee hearing in July 1996 the Managing Director of Torside said that the company had informed a regional official of the T&GWU that it was prepared to reinstate its 80 dockers almost immediately after the dispute had begun. However, this offer appears not to have been passed onto the strikers.

Case study 11.3 ■ Dock strike (UK and Australia) *(continued)*

Sources:
1. Martyn Halsall, 'Dockers make last stand', *Guardian Weekly*, 10 December 1995.
2. Seamus Milne, 'Flying pickets chase ship by plane', *Guardian*, 20 December 1995.
3. Fiachra Gibbons, 'Union leader is traitor in strikers' film', *Guardian*, 2 July 1999.
4. John Pilger, 'What did you do during the dock strike?' *Guardian*, 13 July 1999.

Patrick Stevedores (Australia)

Overnight, in April 1998, Patrick Stevedores (PS) – one of the two main companies operating Australia's docks – deployed hundreds of security guards with dogs at its 14 terminals around Australia to shut-out and then dismiss its 1,400 dockers – all members of the Maritime Union of Australia (MUA). The background to the dispute lay in a desire by the employers and government to reform dock labour, in particular to remove the MUA closed shop, which they regarded as a labour monopoly resulting in high wages, low productivity and excessive strike action.

The action of PS certainly had the support of the government (which was potentially facing an early election and looking for vote-winning issues) and other groups which wanted more economic and competitive docks. There had already been reports that Australian workers were being trained as stevedores outside the country and the National Farmers' Federation (whose members had an interest in 60 per cent of the country's exports) had leased facilities from PS to establish their own non-union stevedoring organisation. Furthermore, within hours of the dock-

ers' dismissal, the government announced it would finance a relatively generous redundancy package.

The leasing of facilities to the NFF had led, in March, to MUA picketing and industrial action at PS facilities around Australia. PS carried out the final dismissal of the 1,400 dockers by declaring four subsidiary companies (which were the direct employers of the dockers) to be insolvent – following a 'reshuffle' of company assets which left them with no assets and operating losses. While these companies were placed in administration by the company bankers, PS used another subsidiary to recruit 400 new contract employees from the NFF company to continue its docks operations.

The MUA responded to the dismissals by mounting a campaign of picketing PS facilities, organising demonstrations and rallies in major cities and seeking support from the International Transport Federation. Most importantly, within two weeks, the MUA had obtained a court order for the reinstatement of the 1,400 dockers. The MUA argued that the dismissals had resulted from an unlawful conspiracy between the company, the NFF and the government. This decision was confirmed by the High Court two weeks later, although the MUA demanded that PS remove the security guards before its members would return to work.

It was estimated that it would take two months to deal with the backlog of 12,000 containers and for freight shipping to return to normal.

Sources: C. Zinn, 'trade unions go to battle on the waterfront', *Guardian*, 9 April 1998; *Financial Times*, various news stories during April and May 1998.

Industrial relations environment

While union density may provide some evidence of collective consciousness among employees, it does not provide an indication of their preparedness to strike. For example, high union density in the public sector has not, in the past, been associated with high strike-proneness. Other factors in the public sector (such as its centralised national bargaining structure, the use of comparability as the basis for determining pay and the emphasis on 'good employer') tended to mitigate against the use of strike action.

The Donovan Commission attributed the rise in strike activity during the early 1960s (excluding coal mining) to the breakdown in the regulatory role of the 'formal' industry-level bargaining and its replacement by fragmented bargaining at the organisational level in response to the enhanced power of trade unions. Thus, it anticipated that greater formalisation and centralisation of organisational bargaining would reduce the incidence of strike activity. Similarly, although the reduction in strike activity in the UK during the mid-1970s may have been linked to the development of the Social Contract between government and the TUC, Davies[57] suggests that the operation of incomes policy generally had little effect in reducing strikes. Strike activity tended to increase at the point of return to 'normal' collective bargaining as unions sought to make up for any losses sustained during the period of restraint. Certainly, government action to control wages within the public sector (whether through formal incomes policy or not) has, to a large extent, been responsible for the increase in propensity for industrial action among groups such as civil servants, nurses, firemen and teachers.

At the organisational level, if the union has to fight to achieve or maintain recognition from a hostile management, or feels insecure in its position, then the resultant relationship is more likely to be characterised by aggression, a reluctance to co-operate and the overt use of power. Similarly, union officials may become more aggressive bargainers in the period prior to their re-election, as they seek to demonstrate both their ability and preparedness to protect the interests of members. Since the early 1980s, UK trade unions have faced increased insecurity resulting from changes in the past collective arrangements and even possible derecognition. It could be argued that, without the surrounding changes in the economic and political environments, such challenges to the established role of unions within the organisation would have provoked a more openly hostile response. However, 'new' Labour's introduction of a statutory recognition procedure and limited protection for employees undertaking lawful industrial action (Employment Relations Act, 1999) may make the political environment more supportive of the union's role in the organisation and less hostile towards the use of industrial action.

Social control

The propensity to strike will, obviously, be affected by the **attitude of society towards the use of industrial action**. The ambivalent attitude displayed by society on this issue has been summed up by Frayn: 'public opinion ... unquestioningly concedes the right of men in a free society to withdraw their labour. It just draws the line at strikes'[58]. At the individual level, one's own strike may be seen as legitimate while the other person's strike is often regarded as unreasonable and unnecessary. Strikes which affect or threaten to affect the daily life of 'the person in the street', through the immediate absence of goods or services, may be regarded as less reasonable than those which appear to affect only the employer through lost production. Wolfson[59] contrasted the essentially private interest of management, union and employees in the issue and result of a dispute with the public interest in the means used to resolve the dispute.

However, it is important to realise that the **public interest is not a single, homogeneous entity**. At the **immediate level of the striker** it can act to either reinforce or undermine the cohesiveness of strike action. The normally close community relationship displayed in the mining industry, which in the past had provided community support based on an acceptance of the legitimacy and necessity for industrial action, was seriously divided in the 1984–5 dispute between working and non-working miners. In contrast, electricity workers, who have a similar if not greater industrial power to that of miners, tend to be dispersed within a wider multi-interest community and therefore were subject to undermining pressures from friends and neighbours when their industrial action led to 'blackouts' and inconvenience within the community.

At the wider level, the 'public interest' is often perceived as being expressed by government and the mass media. The **mass media** tend to emphasise the harm and losses generated by the use of industrial action. During the ambulance work-to-rule in 1989, the mass media dramatised the effect on patients in terms of possible deaths (despite the fact that emergency services were being maintained). Such coverage not only exerts pressure on strikers to return to work but also acts as a socialisation process implying that all industrial action is in some way morally reprehensible and to be discouraged.

Government translates the 'public interest' into **formal social control** through the creation or modification of the legal framework surrounding industrial action. From 1980 onwards the Conservative government strengthened this formal social control through **legislation** which has not only narrowed the area of lawful industrial action but also made it easier for management, union members and even private citizens to take legal action against trade unions which act unlawfully. It is important to recognise that defining something as unlawful implies that it is morally 'wrong' and thereby forms part of the general socialisation process – 'the law, as part of a complex of other [*wider political and social*] changes, has indirectly shaped assumptions about the desirability and efficacy of action'[60].

In addition the government reduced what many believe is a **state subsidy of strike activity** – namely, the payment of social security benefits for the striker's dependants. Gennard[61] argued that this state subsidy theory is based on a belief that the availability of such state benefits has several effects:

- It increases the employee's preparedness to strike or continue a strike by mitigating his or her potential financial loss.
- It reduces the union's responsibility to provide financial support to its members and thereby removes any incentive for it to moderate its claim or seek a settlement.
- It reduces the employer's resistance.

However, his research showed that the availability of social security benefits has little influence on the decision to strike or continue a strike, while Durcan and McCarthy[62] found that despite these benefits most households lost some 60 per cent of their disposable income during a strike. Nevertheless, as Gennard pointed out, many believe that state support should be confined to those 'who, through no fault of their own, are unable rather than unwilling to help themselves' and 'strikers are in a condition of need through their own voluntary actions'[63]. Consequently, the Conservative government amended the benefit provisions so that, in addition to only receiving benefits for dependants and not him- or herself, the striker is assumed to receive some payment from the union and this is deducted from his or her entitlement.

11.3 The legal framework

Perhaps surprisingly, the 'right to strike' is not explicitly set out in any International Labour Organisation Convention or Recommendation; although its Committee on Freedom of Association declared in 1952 that strike action is 'one of the principal means by which workers and their associations may legitimately promote and defend their economic and social interests ... [it] is a right and not simply a social action'[64]. Certainly, the UK, unlike other European countries, has **no positive right to strike**. At common law a strike is both a breach of the individual's contract of employment and a collective restraint of trade, but because it can be regarded as socially necessary, industrial action has been given a degree of protection by statute law (**immunity from a claim for damages**). Thus, trade unions are not, and never have been, outside the law, but rather it is the law which has delineated the extent of their freedom to act. The Conservative government's Green Paper on Trade Union Immunities (1981) recognised that these immunities 'do not abolish the offences and wrongs against which they provide protection. Rather they remove liability in the circumstances of a trade dispute' and 'if they were repealed altogether, then trade unions and individuals would be at risk of legal action every time they organised a strike'[65]. However, after its election in 1979, the Conservative government progressively reduced the boundary of lawful industrial action (these changes were consolidated in the Trade Union and Labour Relations (Consolidation) Act (1992) – TULR(C)A). Significantly, the 'new' Labour government elected in 1997 has retained most of this legislation, although the Employment Relations Act (1999) has amended some of the ballot provisions and, perhaps most importantly, provided some protection for strikers against dismissal.

It is useful to consider, first, the twin concepts of 'a trade dispute' and 'trade union immunities', which are central to the legal status of industrial action, and then the legal regulation of picketing and dismissal of strikers.

Trade dispute

The immunities which individuals or trade unions enjoy are confined to actions undertaken 'in contemplation or furtherance of a trade dispute'. The original **definition** of a trade dispute was contained in the Trade Disputes Act (1906): 'any dispute between employers and workmen, or between workmen and workmen, which is connected with the employment or non-employment, or the terms of employment, or with the conditions of labour, of any person' (S. 5.5(3)). However, the definition was changed during the 1970s and 1980s and is now:

A dispute between workers and their employer which relates wholly or mainly to one or more of the following –
(i)   terms and conditions of employment or the physical conditions in which any workers are required to work;

(ii)   engagement or non-engagement, or termination or suspension of employment or the duties of employment, of one or more workers;

(iii) allocation of work or the duties of employment as between workers or groups of workers;

(iv)   matters of discipline;

(v)   the membership or non-membership of a trade union on the part of workers;

(vi)   facilities for officials of trade unions;

(vii) machinery for negotiation or consultation, and other procedures, relating to any of the foregoing matters, including the recognition by employers or employers' associations of the right of a trade union to represent workers in any such negotiation or consultation or in the carrying out of such procedures. (S.218, TULR(C)A)

Three important points emerge in respect of the changes made by the Employment Act (1982):

1. The **phrase 'between employers and workmen' was replaced by 'between workers and their employer'**. As a result it removes any dispute between workers and employers other than their own, or between a trade union and an employer where the workforce itself has no dispute with management. Consequently, trade unions and their members do not have immunity when undertaking industrial action in furtherance of a general policy: for example, the International Transport Workers' Federation 'blacking' of certain ships as part of its general campaign against flags of convenience[66] or the POEU's instruction to its members not to connect Mercury Communications to British Telecom's system following the government decision to privatise BT and end its monopoly[67]. This change could also affect the position of trade unions in respect of 'political strikes' in response to government legislation or policy, in that the dispute is not directly and specifically between employees and their employer but with the government. Furthermore, because worker is defined as a person 'employed by that employer', the House of Lords held that a dispute regarding allocation of work between workers is limited to employees or groups employed by the same employer and does not encompass the 'farming out' of work to contractors – this is a business decision[68].

2. The **phrase 'between workmen and workmen' was deleted**. This change has the effect of removing immunity from any dispute between groups of workers or trade unions where the employer is not involved. However, this does not mean that all inter-union disputes are outside the definition of a trade dispute and therefore have no protection of immunity. Indeed, the government recognised that 'in most cases, disputes between workers or trade unions automatically involve the employer of the workers concerned'[69]. Disputes over work arrangements or union representation invariably involve the employer both in the causation and resolution of the dispute.

3. The **phrase 'is connected with' was replaced by 'relates wholly or mainly to'**. The effect of this change is to require that the predominant

purpose of the trade dispute is industrial and to ensure that immunity does not apply to actions which are intended primarily to further the wider fraternalistic or political aspects of trade unionism. Instead of claiming that there was some, albeit slight, connection between their actions and one of the items listed, trade unions have to show that it is the major element in pursuing their action. While this provides for legal action against trade unions and their members on the grounds that their intention is 'political' rather than 'industrial', it requires the courts not only to separate the differing elements present in many disputes but also to determine criteria for assessing the relative importance of the various elements before deciding which predominates: a matter largely of subjective perception rather than objective fact.

Clearly, the objective of the legislation has been to narrow the definition of a trade dispute and thereby exclude from immunity any industrial action which is not directed primarily towards the industrial situation or the immediate employer/ employee relationship.

Trade union immunities

The basic immunities for both trade unions and their members in respect of **civil liability** in tort (damages) was established by the Trade Disputes Act (1906). This gave trade union members protection against civil liability for conspiracy and gave organisers of industrial action protection against liability for inducing another person to breach a contract of employment (subject, in both cases, to their actions being 'in contemplation or furtherance of a trade dispute'). Such protection was necessary for all actions, not just strikes. Although, unions might argue that a work-to-rule or overtime ban was simply employees adhering strictly to the terms of their contract of employment, the courts held that it was the 'combined wilful disruption' of such action that amounted to 'industrial action' (see Box 11.3). Furthermore, in 1964 the House of Lords[70] held that *threatening* a strike amounted to the **tort of intimidation** and was, therefore, unlawful. The situation was immediately rectified by the Trade Disputes Act (1965). Similarly, the 1906 Act provided no immunity for directly inducing a **breach of commercial contract**. The general thinking of the courts[71] appeared to be that while inducement to breach a contract of employment was protected by the 1906 Act, nevertheless the use of an unlawful act (breach of contract of employment) as a means to induce a breach of commercial contract rendered the whole process unlawful and therefore not protected by the civil immunities of the 1906 Act. This uncertainty was only finally resolved by the Trade Union and Labour Relations (Amendment) Act (1976).

The extent of trade union immunities was highlighted in 1979 when the House of Lords[72] reversed a Court of Appeal decision and held that the immunities provided protection to any industrial action so long as the people carrying out the action genuinely believed that it might further a trade dispute. The Court of Appeal had argued that industrial action which was either too remote from the original dispute to be considered as action 'in contemplation or furtherance of a

Box 11.3	Work to rule

In 1972 the three rail unions (ASLEF, NUR and TSSA) undertook a strict work-to-rule (plus a ban on overtime and rest-day working) in pursuit of their pay claim. The Secretary of State sought to order a ballot of members under the emergency procedures provided in the Industrial Relations Act (1971). The unions argued that, in 'working to rule', their members were simply carrying out the terms of their contract.

Lord Denning: 'The rules are in no way terms of the contract of employment ... they are only instructions to a man as to how he is to do his work. If some of these rules are construed unreasonably, as, for instance, the driver takes too long examining his engine or seeing that all is in order, the system may be in danger of being disrupted. It is only when they are construed unreasonably that the railway system grinds to a halt. It is clearly a breach of contract first to construe the rules unreasonably, and then to put that unreasonable construction into practice ... The [union] instruction was intended to mean, and it was understood to mean, "Keep the rules of your employment to the very letter, but, whilst doing so, do your very utmost to disrupt the undertaking" ... If [the employee], with the others, takes steps wilfully to disrupt the undertaking, to produce chaos so that it will not run as it should, then each one who is a party to those steps is guilty of a breach of his contract ... what makes it wrong is the object with which it is done'.

Lord Justice Buckley: ' ... in the case of a contract of a commercial character the wilful act of one party which, although not, maybe, departing from the literal letter of the agreement, nevertheless defeats the commercial intention of the parties in entering into the contract, constitutes a breach of an implied term of the contract to perform the contract in such a way as not to frustrate that commercial objective ... within the terms of the contract the employee must serve the employer faithfully with a view to promoting those commercial interests for which he is employed.'

Lord Justice Roskill: 'The fact that under normal conditions railways operate satisfactorily when the rule book is interpreted as it clearly is normally interpreted suggests ... that over the years a course of dealing and common understanding in the performance of the instructions has arisen, from which an employee is not free arbitrarily to depart.'

Source: *Secretary of State v ASLEF (No. 2)*, Court of Appeal, 1972 (in G. Pitt, *Cases and Materials in Employment Law*, Pitman, 1994, pp. 432–6).

trade dispute', or was incapable of furthering a trade dispute, could not be construed as being protected by the immunities. In the view of the Conservative government, the 1974 and 1976 legislation 'licensed all industrial action even if it were directed against those far removed from the original dispute'[73].

Consequently, **secondary industrial action** (i.e. sympathetic or supportive industrial action by employees at organisations not involved in the primary dispute) was one of the first areas to be tackled by the Conservative government. The intention was to stop industrial action spreading to organisations which had no connection with or influence over the primary dispute, or at least provide legal redress for breach of commercial contract to organisations so affected. The Employment Act (1980) limited lawful secondary action to the prevention or disruption of supplies between the primary dispute and a customer or supplier, or between a customer or supplier and an associated employer (where there was an attempt to substitute for the original supply). The Employment Act (1990) removed immunity completely from calling or threatening to call secondary action.

As a result, any industrial action taken by employees (who are not party to the primary dispute), whether to exert industrial pressure by interrupting production or services or simply to show support or solidarity for other workers in dispute, is unlawful. This applies as much to one group of employees seeking to support another group of employees within the same organisation as it does to employees of a different organisation. It is important to note that the trend in some organisations during the 1980s for management to 'break up' the organisation into a series of distinct legal entities, as part of their strategy of devolution and decentralisation, makes the potential impact of removing immunity from secondary industrial action more serious. The practical effect of the legislative change is to further segment and isolate trade unionists and make it impossible, lawfully, for them to express their fraternalism one with another.

Furthermore, as part of the government's legislative strategy to make the operation of **union membership agreements** (closed shop) unlawful, the Employment Act (1988) removed immunity from any action intended to pressure an employer to dismiss (post-entry) or not employ (pre-entry) a person who was not a member of a union.

At the same time as removing immunities from certain types of industrial action, the legislation has clearly established **trade union liability for unlawful actions**. The Employment Act (1982) provided that trade unions can be held liable for any unlawful act which is authorised or endorsed by a responsible person within the union (i.e. its executive committee, President, General Secretary or any employed official, committee or other person). However, the union is absolved from liability if the official or committee, in authorising or endorsing industrial action, exceeds their authority as specified in the union's rules and their action is repudiated by the executive committee, President or General Secretary of the union. To provide an effective **defence**, such repudiation must satisfy the following criteria:

- It must be carried out as soon as is reasonably practicable.
- It must be notified in writing to the person or committee which authorised or endorsed the action.
- The executive committee, President or General Secretary must not subsequently behave in a manner which could be construed as being inconsistent with their repudiation of the action.

However, the court accepted that a union was not liable as an organisation when its members, in conjunction with other groups of employees, followed the strike recommendation of a joint negotiating committee against the expressed advice of its union official[74]. The Employment Act (1990) subsequently extended the union's liability to 'any officer elected or appointed in accordance with the rules of the union to be a representative of its members' or 'any committee comprising a group of people constituted in accordance with the rules of the union'. Furthermore, to absolve itself from any liability for an unlawful act the union must, in addition to the requirements placed on it by the 1982 Act, take reasonable steps to provide individual written notice of its repudiation to all members involved in the action and their employers and the written notice must contain a statement informing the members that the union will give no support to unofficial industrial action and that if they are dismissed they will have no right to claim unfair dismissal.

In addition to seeking an injunction (against either individuals or a trade union) to stop the continuation of any unlawful act, the employer may claim damages. However, the level of damages that may be awarded against a trade union is limited dependent on its size:

Up to 4,999 members	£10,000
5,000–24,999 members	£ 50,000
25,000–99,999 members	£100,000
100,000 or more members	£250,000

Such damages may not be enforced against the political or provident funds of a trade union. While at first sight the maximum level of damages appears relatively small, it must be realised that they apply to each individual legal action brought against a trade union and not each individual dispute. For example, in 1983 the members of the Newspaper Publishers' Association collectively sued the NGA for some £3 million in respect of its secondary action in support of the *Stockport Messenger* dispute. In addition, as was seen repeatedly in 1983–4, trade unions can also face unlimited fines for contempt of court when they fail to abide by injunctions awarded by the court and high administrative costs of sequestration when they refuse to pay such fines. The combined effect of these measures could be to bankrupt a union.

As part of the government's strategy to make the union leadership more accountable to the membership, the Trade Union Act (1984) **removed immunity from industrial action which is not supported by a ballot**. This has been further amended by the Employment Act (1990), the Trade Union Reform and Employment Rights Act (1993) and the Employment Relations Act (1999). To retain immunity the ballot must fulfil the following requirements:

- It must be by individual secret voting, conducted by post and subject to independent scrutiny.

- The ballot paper must indicate that the proposed industrial action is in breach of contract.

- A majority of those voting must be in favour of industrial action. In 1996, the Conservative government's Green Paper proposed raising the threshold to a majority of those eligible to vote[75].

- The union's authorisation and instigation of industrial action must take place within four weeks of the ballot (although the 1999 Act allows the validity of a ballot to be extended by up to a further four weeks if both parties agree) and the ballot must specify which official(s) has authority to call the industrial action. The 1996 Green Paper proposed requiring a union to re-ballot its members very two or three months during protracted industrial action (including, for example, a series of one-day strikes).

- Unions must not only give employers seven days' notice of any industrial action but must also inform employers seven days in advance of a ballot, supply them with a copy of the ballot paper and 'describe' the employees who will be entitled to vote. This latter requirement was interpreted by the Court of Appeal[76] to mean providing the names of the union members being balloted and, subsequently, being called upon to undertake industrial action. However, the 1999 Act removes any requirement for unions to disclose the names of their members to management.

The Donovan Commission argued in 1968, in response to similar proposals, that they were founded on 'a belief that workers are likely to be less militant than their leaders and that, given the opportunity of such a ballot, they would often be likely to vote against strike action'[77]. Certainly it reflects a distrust of a 'show of hands' at a mass meeting where individuals may feel pressured into 'going along with their fellows'. The requirement to include a reference to 'breach of contract' on the ballot paper suggests a hope that it will weaken the individual's inclination to use industrial action. Nevertheless, ACAS reports that in 1997 the two main independent balloting organisations conducted 1,052 strike ballots (69 per cent of which resulted in a favourable vote) and 664 ballots for action 'short of a strike' (93 per cent of which resulted in a favourable vote)[78]; although a number of the ballots encompassed votes on both forms of action. However, only a small proportion of these ballots actually resulted in industrial action; indeed, in 1997 there were only 206 recorded strikes. It may be argued that the formalisation of the process to sanction industrial action in practice strengthens, rather than weakens, the union's position by more than simply providing legal protection to any subsequent strike. Kessler and Bayliss[79] certainly believe that the conduct of the ballot has now become an integral element in the negotiating process designed to place additional 'legitimised' pressure on management to make concessions.

However, the strength which a union may draw from a positive majority vote in favour of industrial action can, to some extent, be undermined by both legal challenges by management regarding the conduct of the ballot and the **protection of the individual** afforded under the Employment Act (1988). The individual union member has the right to seek, through the courts, to restrain the union from continuing with industrial action if the individual member believes the ballot was not a 'properly conducted secret ballot'. TURERA (1993) has given a similar right to *any* person who believes that an 'unlawful act' has had the effect of preventing, delaying or reducing the quality of goods or services to him or her. The Act also established a Commissioner for Protection against Unlawful Industrial Action, who could assist individuals in taking such legal actions but only if it was against a union as an organisation (not individual officials or members). The Commissioner received only six applications, four of which it did not support, before the role was abolished under the Employment Relations Act (1999). Perhaps more importantly, the Employment Act (1988) specified that for a union to expel, discipline or otherwise discriminate against a member who does not take part in industrial action would be 'unjustifiable discipline'– even when the industrial action is official and lawful and has been supported by a majority of the membership in a ballot. This strikes at the very heart of both the fraternalist solidarity expected by unions and the democratic principal of majority rule/decision making[80].

Picketing

While the act of striking provides the initial withdrawal of labour from the employer, the act of picketing has one or more of the following objectives:

- To persuade other employees to join or otherwise support the strike;
- To withhold supplies or alternative labour from the employer;
- To ensure that the strikers do not return to work before the dispute is settled.

However, the law recognises the only purpose of picketing as being to peacefully obtain or communicate information or peacefully persuade any person to work or not work. Under the 1906 Act it was lawful for one or more persons, in contemplation of furtherance of a trade dispute, to attend at or near any place (other than a person's place of residence) for the purpose of picketing. Thus, the only real restrictions on picketing were that it should be peaceful and that it should not take place outside a person's home. However, during the 1970s a minority of situations became associated with 'mass picketing' (involving hundreds, and in some cases thousands, of people and sometimes involving violence against those who sought to cross the picket line) and 'flying pickets' (groups of strikers going or being sent to picket organisations in an attempt to spread the strike or secure the blacking of goods). Despite the infrequency of such occurrences the Conservative government felt that the right to picket should be restricted.

Consequently, the Employment Act (1980) provided that it is **only lawful for a person to attend at or near his or her own place of work** or, in the case of union officials, at or near the place of work of a member whom they are accompanying and whom they represent. Thus, the law introduced a distinction between primary and secondary picketing similar to that made in respect of industrial action: primary picketing (at one's own place of work) is lawful but secondary picketing (at a place other than one's own place of work) is unlawful. Furthermore, the phrase 'his own place of work' restricts the employee to the actual site, depot, etc. where he or she normally works and, therefore, it would be unlawful secondary picketing to picket even another site of the organisation or its head office. At the same time the Code of Practice on Picketing[81] has sought to reduce the size of pickets by advising that in normal circumstances there should not be need for more than six people at any one entrance. Although the Code is not itself directly enforceable, any contravention of its guidance may be taken into account by a court in hearing a claim in respect of unlawful picketing[82]. The fact that seeking, through picketing, to persuade employees of other employers not to deliver goods is tantamount to inducing a person to breach his or her own contract of employment (secondary industrial action) was recognised in the Employment Act (1990) and pickets undertaking such activity still retain immunity even though the general immunity for secondary industrial action was removed.

Picketing is perhaps the one remaining area where the **criminal law** can intrude into the conduct of industrial relations. In so far as picketing is conducted outside the employer's premises in a public place then the conduct of the individuals on the picket line is subject to action by the police and criminal law in respect of 'obstruction of the highway', 'breach of the peace', 'abusive behaviour' or even 'assault'. In the past, the police exercised discretion in carrying out their duties and generally sought not to exacerbate a situation by arresting pickets. However, the 1984 NCB/NUM dispute once again focused attention on the role of the police and the 'law and order' issue. The widespread mass picketing, mass policing and increasing violence highlighted the inherent incompatibility of the practical intention of picketing, the legal rights relating to picketing and the rights of others to continue or return to work. The use of large numbers of police to ensure that handfuls of working miners got past pickets and the large number of pickets arrested led, as Kahn *et al.*[83] predicted, to the loss of any 'cultural resonance' or 'empathy' between strikers and police and its replacement by a perception, at least among the strikers, of the police undertaking a 'political' or 'partisan' role in supporting management and the government and weakening the strike[84].

Dismissal of strikers

While one or two judges have attempted to suggest that a strike should be regarded as a unilateral suspension of the contract of employment, the traditional basis of the **common law** has maintained it to be a breach of the contract of employment sufficient to justify the employee's dismissal. A lawful withdrawal of labour can only be achieved if the employees give notice equivalent to that required to terminate their contract: that is, resign.

This common law principle was carried through into the **unfair dismissal legislation** in 1971, although it was mitigated by the basic intention of the legislation to ensure that all dismissals were treated in an equitable manner. Thus, the legislation provided that **for the dismissal of a striker to be fair, management could not be selective** but had to dismiss all employees who had gone on strike or none and, if it wanted subsequently to offer re-employment, it must re-engage all strikers or none. However, a court decision in 1978 highlighted that, as the wording of the law stood, equity had to be demonstrated among the group which had taken part in the industrial action and, therefore, if only one of the original strikers had returned to work then the employer could not fairly dismiss those who remained on strike. At the same time it was argued that, because there was no time limit set for judging equity in respect of the re-engagement of strikers, management could be guilty of an unfair dismissal if it offered re-engagement to some, but not all, dismissed strikers, even though it did so months or even possibly years after the dispute was over.

The Employment Act (1982) clarified and strengthened the provisions relating to the **dismissal of strikers** in two ways:

■ By delineating the group of employees within which equity must be judged as being the group on strike at the time of the individual's dismissal. Although the Bill proposed that the employer should be able to dismiss strikers only after they had received a written warning of their impending dismissal at least five days before it was to become effective, this was not carried through into the Act;

■ By introducing a time limit of three months after which a dismissed striker may be re-engaged without the employer becoming liable for a claim for unfair dismissal because other strikers who were dismissed at the same time have not been re-engaged.

The dismissal of strikers is perhaps the **most fundamental part of the law relating to industrial action**. The establishment of immunities from claims for damages for trade unions and their members, when acting in contemplation or furtherance of a trade dispute, would appear to be of questionable value while the employees who undertake such lawful action risk being dismissed – irrespective of the cause of a strike or whether it was official or unofficial, constitutional or unconstitutional. Certainly, the dismissal of strikers by British Rail in 1985 appeared to be a significant factor in the subsequent 'no' vote on industrial action by NUR guards and British Rail's unilateral introduction of one-man-operated trains. The dismissed men were, the union argued, hostages for the union's agreement to this change in working practices. It is this aspect of legislation which, in most European countries, gives the basis of the 'right to strike' – a lawful strike (if not all strikes) is regarded as a suspension, not a breach, of the contract of employment and therefore does not give rise to any right to dismiss[85].

The 'new' Labour government has gone some way to addressing this issue. The Employment Relations Act (1999) makes it automatically unfair to dismiss employees during the first eight weeks of 'lawfully organised industrial action'. However, this may have the effect of inducing management to challenge the legality of the industrial action more, including the union's ballot arrangements, in order to remove this restriction. It will also be unfair, under this legislation, to dismiss employees after this eight-week period if a Tribunal finds that management has not taken 'all reasonable procedural steps' to resolve the dispute. Wood and Godard argue that the legislation creates a situation similar to that in the USA, where the National Labor Relations Act (1935) made it illegal to dismiss employees on strike but within three years the Supreme Court held that an employer could hire permanent replacements (with the strikers only having priority for any 'new' jobs)[86]. In their view, not restricting management's ability to take on temporary or permanent replacements is 'opening the door for employers to attempt to "break" the union'[87].

Furthermore, management has been given **complete freedom to dismiss unofficial strikers** (Employment Act, 1990) by the removal of any right for an employee to take a claim before an Employment Tribunal if he or she is undertaking unofficial industrial action at the time of the dismissal. The only limitation placed on management by the legislation is that, if the union repudiates the industrial action, irrespective of whether or not the union has informed the individual members of the repudiation, then the employee is not deemed to be undertaking unofficial industrial action until a full working day later. In addition, trade union immunity has been removed for calling, threatening to call or organising industrial action in support of anyone dismissed while taking part in unofficial industrial action. The consequence is that management may selectively dismiss among those employees engaged in unofficial industrial action (shop stewards, 'ringleaders', 'troublemakers', or any other reason).

Other possible measures

*See Country
profile 11.1*

The political and legal constraints on the operation of industrial action may reflect social, cultural and political differences – hence the difficulties in transferring legal regulations from one country to another. Two specific measures have been considered in the UK to restrict the incidence or effect of strike action. First, the Industrial Relations Act (1971) contained a provision for a **cooling-off period** before the implementation of a strike, based on the Taft Hartley Act in the USA. This allowed the government to apply to the court for an order delaying strike action for up to 60 days in those situations where it felt that the strike would seriously affect the national economy, national security or public order, or would endanger life. It provided an opportunity for the government to intervene in a major dispute by requiring the parties to reconsider their respective positions. However, while the purpose of a cooling-off period is to provide an opportunity for further negotiations, the time can equally be used to 'hot up' the dispute as both sides play 'brinkmanship' in delaying concessions during the designated period or make their preparations for the strike which might ensue.

Second, many would argue that there should be some **restriction of the right to strike among essential workers**. In this context, 'essential' refers to the workers' position within the general community rather than within any individual organisation and is generally felt to include such groups as police, gas, electricity, water and sewerage workers, health service employees and refuse collectors. It is argued that a strike by these employees exerts pressure on their employer only through the effect it has on a wide range of other organisations or, in particular, the general public and that such disruption of the general community is unacceptable. Differential treatment of such employees existed in the UK under the Conspiracy and Protection of Property Act (1875), in that gas, water and (later) electricity employees were liable to criminal prosecution if, by breaching their contract of employment, they deprived inhabitants of their supply of gas, water or electricity (repealed only in 1971).

As Kessler and Bayliss point out, the issue of restricting the right to strike for such groups 'is bound to reappear whenever a strike is in prospect in an essential service which could inconvenience the public'[88]. Indeed, in 1996 the Conservative government proposed to pass the responsibility to *management* by giving it the right to seek an injunction on the basis that it was providing an 'essential service' and the industrial action would have 'disproportionate and excessive effects'[89]. On the other hand, the 'new' Labour government has been prepared to restore the right of prison officers to undertake industrial action (withdrawn by the Criminal Justice and Public Order Act, 1994)[90] but, according to one news report, planned 'to ban strikes in a public service for the first time' in response to proposed industrial action by the Fired Brigades Union in 1999[91]. Any move to restrict the 'right to strike' in essential services must consider the following points:

■ The **power to disrupt the community** has, in the main, been exercised with some degree of restraint and strikers have often offered to maintain essential services or supplies during the dispute. The removal of the 'right to strike' may itself provoke strong resistance and the withdrawal of such concessions.

■ It is always difficult to establish accepted criteria for determining **which groups of employees should be covered** by this restriction. Indeed, it can be argued that because of the interdependent nature of industry and society there are many groups whose strike action can seriously affect all or a wide section of the community (e.g. oil-delivery drivers). The ILO has defined essential services as those 'the interruption of which would endanger the life, personal safety or health of the whole or part of the population'[92], although it recognises that this may depend as much on the length or scope of the industrial action as it does on the particular industry or service within which it takes place. Certainly, it does not include radio and television, postal services, education or even the supply and distribution of foodstuffs.

■ The complete removal of the 'right to strike' from such groups would need to be accompanied by the introduction of some **acceptable system of automatic arbitration** if the employees are not to be left powerless in relation to their employer and the determination of their terms and conditions of employment. Certainly, the ILO believes that such groups 'should enjoy sufficient guarantees to protect their interests' and that where this includes arbitration it should ensure that 'decisions are binding on both parties and are fully and promptly applied'[93]. However, it may be argued that the introduction of such an acceptable system of arbitration would itself make the use of industrial action by employees unnecessary.

See Country profile 11.1

Many countries do, in fact, restrict strike action in different essential services. For example, Beaumont notes that in Canada there have been 'experiments in the public sector with the notion of a "controlled" strike, in which strikes are permitted but a designated proportion of employees ... must remain at work to provide essential services'[94]. Similarly, Bridgford and Stirling note[95] that in 1990 Italy introduced legislation requiring ten days' notice of strike action and the maintenance of a minimum level of service in a range of public sector areas (including not only hospitals, refuse collection, energy, postal services and public transport but also courts, customs, museums, banks, schools and radio and television). However, the **privatisation of public services** means that 'essential services' are no longer primarily the responsibility of government and private employers in these sectors may be reluctant to have a system imposed on them which is fundamentally different to that of other private sector employers, in that it restricts their right to determine their own industrial relations outcomes (i.e. restricts their managerial prerogative). Certainly, attempts by a number of states in the USA in 1947 to establish legislation to restrict strikes and provide for compulsory arbitration in a range of essential, but private sector, services such as electricity, gas, water and fuel were successfully challenged under the Taft–Hartley Act (1947), which applied to all employees (other than government employees) and which permitted strikes.

Enforcement of the law

Although it is government, through Parliament, which establishes the limits of trade union rights to undertake industrial action, it is **management which has**

Country profile 11.1   Industrial action in south-east Asia

The pattern of industrial action in south-east Asian countries appears to be affected by a variety of factors:

■ The adversarial conflictual nature of industrial relations (as demonstrated by the use of industrial action) is, it is often argued, alien to the cultural values of deference to authority, teamworking and consensual decision making, hence, there is a preference for resolving any disputes through conciliation, mediation and arbitration rather than industrial action.

■ Trade union density is relatively low, collective bargaining less developed and management style often autocratic or paternalistic (with a consequent reluctance to share power with employees and a frequent strategy of obstructing the activities of trade unions).

■ Government policy and legislation is driven by concerns to maintain 'industrial peace' and limit wage costs in order to secure economic development and, in particular, inward foreign investment. Furthermore, the political environment in some countries has been non-democratic and/or involved periods of martial law.

The extent of industrial action appears to be relatively low (see table). However, a distinction is often drawn between *disputes* and *strikes*. The figures for both Taiwan and South Korea refer to the number of registered disputes rather than strikes. Similarly, during 1985–9, there was an annual average of 1,490 strike or lock-out notices filed in the Philippines but only an average of 357 strikes actually took place each year, while in Malaysia there was an annual average of 985 recorded disputes but only 17 strikes per year.

It appears that there is a fairly extensive use of *other forms of industrial action*, rather than the strike: sit-ins, hunger strikes, demonstrations, union meetings during working time or, as in the case of service industries in Thailand such as banks and hotels, the wearing of black mourning dress while at work. The use of forms of industrial action which do not involve actual withdrawal of labour may be due, in part, to the legal restrictions placed on strike action and, in part, to the employees' insecurity derived from low wages, the absence of strike benefit from their union and the surrounding high level of unemployment. The use of 'hidden conflict' forms of action such as group resignation from the organisation may, also, be a reflection of both the employees' unwillingness to be seen to confront management directly, through the threat of collective industrial action, and the relative undeveloped and restricted nature of collective bargaining.

In most of the countries, strikes are illegal in many parts of the *essential services and public sector* and any dispute is subject to compulsory arbitration. While in Singapore the restriction is limited to gas, electricity and water (with other defined essential services required to give 14 days' notice of strike action), in other countries the restriction is broader and may include transport, petrol-refining, hospitals and medical services, banking and telecommunications, or even tourism (Thailand) and export-oriented industries (Philippines) – industries which form a significant proportion of waged employment in these countries. In Malaysia, the only restriction on strikes in essential services is that 21 days' notice of such action has to be given. Furthermore, in both Singapore and Malaysia political strikes (intended to coerce the government) and sympathetic strikes are illegal.

In other industries, legislation often restricts the use of strike in favour of a requirement to use *conciliation and/or arbitration*. In most countries, strikes are illegal if the dispute is referred to arbitration (although in Taiwan a strike may take place before arbitration has commenced). In Thailand strikes (but not other forms of industrial action) are prohibited during the period of a collective agreement, during negotiations and during the five days allowed for conciliation (all disputes must be referred to conciliation). Perhaps most significantly, in Singapore, Malaysia and South Korea important areas of *managerial prerogative* (hiring, promotions, transfers, dismissals, etc.) are excluded from collective bargaining and, consequently, cannot be a matter for 'dispute' and therefore any industrial action is illegal.

Even in the apparently more stable democratic countries (Singapore and Malaysia) *penalties for illegal industrial action* can include fines and imprisonment and unions may be deregistered if they undertake illegal acts. For example, the last two significant cases of industrial action in Singapore resulted in action against the unions involved: a strike at Metal Box in 1977 by the non-NTUC Metal Workers' Union resulted in its deregistration and replacement by an NTUC-affiliated union and the 1980 work to rule by SIA Pilots' Association resulted in its deregistration and the prosecution of both union officers and members.

The impact of the political environment can be clearly seen in some countries:

Country profile 11.1   Industrial action in south-east Asia *(continued)*

■ *Philippines*: Martial law was introduced in 1972, following increased social and industrial disturbances, and for a short period all strikes were, in effect, banned. The lifting of martial law in 1981 was followed in 1986 by a change in government and the introduction of a constitutional guarantee of the right to organise, collective bargain and undertake strike action. Later legislation, in 1989, has sought to encourage the use of voluntary (as opposed to compulsory) arbitration.

■ *South Korea*: The South Korean constitution, introduced in 1948 and influenced by US occupation, guaranteed basic trade union rights of association, collective bargaining and collective action. However, until 1987 it was generally 'ignored, suspended or abused by government and management actions' and dispute settlement involved 'overt government intervention, often with total disregard for workers' civil rights and personal safety' (Rauenhorst (1990) quoted in 1:141–2).

The change to a more democratic government in 1987 resulted in a sharp increase in disputes primarily concerned with wage increases (from 276 in 1986 to 3,749 in 1987, although they declined in subsequent years).

■ *Taiwan (ROC)*: The abandonment of martial law in 1987 (after 40 years during which strikes were illegal) came at a time of the emergence of a more assertive, independent and confrontational union movement and consequent increasing industrial disputes (over 1,400 per year in 1985 and 1986 compared to under 500 per year throughout the 1970s). The change also saw a substantial increase in the number of employees involved in such disputes.

Sources:
1. S. J. Deery and R. J. Mitchell, *Labour Law and Industrial Relations in Asia*, Longman (Melbourne), 1993.
2. A. Verma, T. A. Kochan and R. D. Lansbury (eds), *Employment Relations in the Growing Asian Economies*, Routledge, 1995.

Industrial action statistics (annual average)

	Singapore		Malaysia		Philippines[1]		Thailand		Taiwan (ROC)[2]		South Korea[3]
	No	WDL[4]	No	WDL	No	WDL	No	WDL	No	WDL	No
1960–4	67	230 429	n/a	n/a	n/a	n/a	n/a	n/a	30	n/a	n/a
1965–9	12	30 369	n/a	n/a	110	783 000	n/a	n/a	29	n/a	n/a
1970–4	6	6774	n/a	n/a	110	1 142 510	190	168 609	244	n/a	n/a
1975–9	2	1811	48	57 588	55	144 500	93	254 679	444	n/a	109
1980–4	0	0	24	11 619	183	678 402	28	87 521	900	n/a	178
1985–9	0	0	17	17 760	357	1 957 646	5	52 162	1558	11 913	1556

1. Philippines: Strikes were banned under martial law between October 1972 and November 1975, therefore, figures for 1970–4 are averaged over three years (1970, 1971 and 1972) and figures for 1975–9 are averaged over four years (not including 1975).
2. Taiwan (ROC): Figures relate to the number of 'disputes'; strikes only became legal with the lifting of martial law in July 1987, therefore, figure for working days lost in period 1985–9 is annual average for three years (1987, 1988 and 1989).
3. South Korea: Figures relate to the number of 'disputes'.
4. WDL = Working days lost.

to enforce these limits. The nature of the civil law is such that it is the aggrieved party, not the state, which has to take action to protect its legal rights. In the past it had been argued that management was reluctant to take legal action against either the trade unions with which it had to deal or its employees and that the use of law was incompatible with its primary objective to resolve the dispute and secure its production. Reliance on and frequent use of the law, it was argued, was likely to sour rather than improve industrial relations within the organisation.

However, the period since 1980 has seen an **apparent increased preparedness**

by some managements to resort to the law as part of their strategy for handling industrial disputes. Clearly this development can be related not only to changes in the law, particularly the removal of trade union organisational immunity, but also the general development of a 'tougher' legalistic management approach to industrial relations in the 1980s. Younson's survey of some 20 cases between September 1980 and April 1984 showed that nine cases related to picketing (seven secondary picketing and two 'nuisance' or 'intimidatory' picketing), six related to 'blacking' and three related to secondary industrial action and that contempt fines were awarded in four cases (most notably, £675,000 levied against the NGA in the *Stockport Messenger* dispute). He concluded that the 'cases have not generally been initiated by employers involved in the 'primary' dispute'[96]. However, this was before the introduction of the ballot requirement of the 1984 Act.

A later survey by Evans covering the period May 1984 to April 1987 found a substantial increase in the number of injunctions. Of the 80 cases surveyed, 11 cases related to picketing, 16 to secondary industrial action and 47 to pre-strike ballots. In 67 of the cases, the injunction was sought against the union, as an organisation, rather than members, shop stewards or individual union officers, which led Evans to comment that 'the availability of injunctions and damages against unions and the loss of immunities for union funds have clearly proven attractive to employers'[97]. The trade union immediately withdrew the industrial action in 31 out of the 73 cases where an injunction was awarded. Significantly, 14 cases related to the public service sector, which Evans attributed to their obvious high-profile, immediate effect on the public creating political pressures to respond and 'the introduction of "commercialism" into managerial strategies and culture which has in turn undermined traditional trust and bargaining relations with unions'[98].

A further survey in 1994[99] showed a sharp increase in cases in 1994 following a decline in 1992 and 1993, with 12 out of the 13 cases in 1994 relating to balloting arrangements following the changes introduced in the 1993 Act. The survey also noted an increasing trend for injunctions to be sought against individuals (rather than the union organisation), particularly where the union had repudiated the industrial action in order to avoid costly legal claims. Furthermore, unions also reported the increasing use of the threat of legal action by employers to induce them to change their approach to the use of industrial action.

Initially, the **trade union response** to this plethora of court actions by employers was to ignore court decisions, contempt of court fines and sequestration even to the extent, as in the NUM case, of moving their funds outside the UK. However, it became clear that prolonged resistance of this kind could easily result in a substantial loss of funds and an almost permanent state of union funds being tied up under the control of sequestrators. In this context, the News International and miners' disputes of the mid-1980s and their associated court cases may have acted as a watershed in determining the trade union movement's response to this legislative change. If they were to protect their funds, already threatened by declining membership, the unions had to adopt a stance of disassociating the formal union organisation from unlawful industrial action.

■ Summary propositions

- ■ The primary function of industrial action is to allow employees and unions to exert power within the collective bargaining process by introducing temporary disorder into the economic and authority relationships of the organisation.

- ■ There is no simple or single causal explanation for variations in the pattern of strike activity over time or between countries, industries or organisations; rather various structural influences interact with the economic, social and political environments to affect the aspirations and perceptions of the participants.

- ■ The UK legal framework surrounding industrial action has been significantly tightened since 1980; however, the introduction of some protection from unfair dismissal for lawful strikers is perhaps the first step towards the codification of a 'right to strike'.

Activity   It would be useful if you looked through current newspapers (national or local) to find any news reports relating to industrial action in either the UK or other countries. Try to identify the type of employees involved, the issue(s) in the dispute, the type of industrial action, how it is managed by unions and management, what effect the industrial action has on the employees, organisation and community and was any legal action involved.

■ Further reading

- ■ R. Hyman, *Strikes* (4th edn), Macmillan, 1989. An extremely readable and comprehensive examination of strikes and industrial conflict from a sociological perspective.
- ■ M. P. Jackson, *Strikes: industrial conflict in Britain, USA and Australia*, Wheatsheaf Books, 1987. This book reviews strike activity and trends in three distinctly different industrial relations systems.
- ■ E. Batstone, I. Boraston and S. Frenkel, *The Social Organization of Strikes*, Blackwell, 1978. This study examines the social processes involved in the mobilisation of strike action within an organisation.
- ■ P. Kahn, N. Lewis, R. Livock and P. Wiles, *Picketing: Industrial disputes, tactics and the law*, Routledge & Kegan Paul, 1983. This examines the effect of the Employment Act (1980) on the conduct of industrial disputes.

References

1. R. Hyman, *Strikes* (4th edn), Macmillan, 1989, p. 231.
2. W. H. Hutt, *The Strike Threat System*, Arlington House, 1973, pp. 282–3.
3. C. Grunfeld, *Modern Trade Union Law*, Sweet & Maxwell, 1966, p. 367.
4. A. Kornhauser, R. Dubin and A. M. Ross (eds), *Industrial Conflict*, McGraw-Hill, 1954, p. 12.
5. R. Dubin, 'Constructive aspects of industrial conflict', in Kornhauser *et al.*, *ibid.*, p. 45.
6. R. O. Clarke, 'Labour–management disputes: a perspective', *British Journal of Industrial Relations*, vol. 18, 1980, p. 23.
7. L. A. Cosser, *The Functions of Social Conflict*, Routledge & Kegan Paul, 1956.
8. R. Hyman, *Strikes* (3rd edn), Fontana, 1984, pp. 108–9.
9. *Ibid.*, p. 110–44.
10. J. Gennard and R. Lasko, 'The individual and the strike', *British Journal of Industrial Relations*, vol. 13, no. 3, 1975; J. Gennard, 'The effects of strike activity on households', *British Journal of Industrial Relations*, vol. 19, 1981, pp. 327–44; J. Gennard, 'The financial costs and returns of strikes', *British Journal of Industrial Relations*, vol. 20, 1982, pp. 247–56.
11. Hyman (1984), *op. cit.*, p. 136.
12. Dubin, *op. cit.*, 1954, p. 44.
13. R. Bean, *Comparative Industrial Relations* (2nd edn), Routledge, 1994, p. 130.
14. Hyman (1984), *op. cit.*, p. 56.
15. K. G. J. Knowles, *Strikes*, Oxford University Press, 1962.
16. R. Bean, 'The relationship between strikes and "unorganised" conflict in manufacturing industry', *British Journal of Industrial Relations*, vol. 13, no. 1, 1975, pp. 98–101.
17. J. Kelly and N. Nicholson, 'Strikes and other forms of industrial action', *Industrial Relations Journal*, vol. 11, no. 5, 1980, pp. 20–31.
18. P. K. Edwards, 'Strikes and unorganised conflict; some further considerations', *British Journal of Industrial Relations*, vol. 17, no. 1, 1979.
19. H. A. Turner, G. Clack and G. Roberts, *Labour Relations in the Motor Industry*, Allen & Unwin, 1967, p. 190.
20. Hyman (1989) *op. cit.*, p. 187.
21. E. Batstone, I. Boraston and S. Frenkel, *The Social Organization of Strikes*, Blackwell, 1978, p. 1.
22. *Ibid.*, p. 218–19.
23. *Sit-ins and Work-ins*, Institute of Personnel Management, 1976, p. 2.
24. C. Thomas, 'Strategy for a sit-in', *Personnel Management*, January 1976, p. 33.
25. A. Flanders, *Management and Unions*, Faber, 1970, p. 112.
26. Hyman (1984), *op. cit.*, pp. 58–9.
27. W. W. Daniel and N. Millward, *Workplace Industrial Relations in Britain*, Heinemann, (PSI/SSRC), 1983; N. Millward and M. Stevens, *British Workplace Industrial Relations 1980–1984*, Gower, 1986; N. Millward, M. Stevens, D. Smart and W. Hawes, *Workplace Industrial Relations in Transition*, Dartmouth, 1992.
28. W. Brown (ed.), *The Changing Contours of British Industrial Relations*, Blackwell, 1981, p. 85.
29. P. Edwards, 'Strikes and industrial conflict', in P. Edwards (ed.), *Industrial Relations: Theory and practice in Britain*, Blackwell, 1995, p. 443.
30. Turner *et al.*, *op. cit.*, p. 223.
31. 'The regulation of industrial conflict in Europe', *European Industrial Relations Review*, report no. 2, 1989, p. 2.
32. J. Hillage, 'No strike deals – can they really work?' *Manpower Policy and Practice 1*, autumn, 1985, p. 15.
33. M. Hall, 'An uncertain future for the unions', *Personnel Management*, September, 1985, p. 35.
34. T. Ghilarducci, 'When management strikes: PATCO and the British miners', *Industrial Relations Journal*, vol. 17, no. 2, 1986, p. 116.
35. Hyman (1989) *op. cit.*, p. 184.
36. H. A. Turner, *Is Britain Really Strike Prone?*, Cambridge University Press, 1969.
37. Hyman (1989) *op. cit.*, p. 226.
38. Knowles, *op. cit.*
39. P. K. Edwards, 'Industrial action 1980–1984', *British Journal of Industrial Relations*, vol. 25, no. 2, 1987, p. 287.
40. P. B. Beaumont, *Public Sector Industrial Relations*, Routledge, 1992, table 6.1, p. 125.
41. E. Screpanti, 'Long cycles in strike activity: an empirical investigation', *British Journal of Industrial Relations*, vol. 25, no. 1, 1987, p. 110.
42. J. Davies, 'International comparisons of labour disputes in 1998', *Labour Market Trends*, April 2000, p. 149.

43. M. Aligisakis, 'Labour disputes in western Europe: typology and tendencies', *International Labour Review*, vol. 136, no. 1, 1997, pp. 91–2.

44. Bean (1994) *op. cit.*, p. 132.

45. P. K. Edwards and R. Hyman, 'Strikes and industrial conflict: peace in Europe', in R. Hyman and A. Ferner (eds), *New Frontiers in European Industrial Relations*, Blackwell, 1994, p. 255.

46. P. K. Edwards, 'The pattern of collective industrial action', in G. S. Bain (ed.), *Industrial Relations in Britain*, Blackwell, 1983, p. 228.

47. P. K. Edwards, 'The strike-proneness of British manufacturing establishments', *British Journal of Industrial Relations*, vol. 19, 1981, p. 146.

48. T. Lane and K. Roberts, *Strike at Pilkingtons*, Fontana, 1971.

49. Ghilarducci, *op.cit.*

50. 'Industrial relations in the coal industry', *Employee Relations*, vol. 9, no. 2, 1987, pp. 9–15.

51. L. Hunter (1980) 'Dispute trends and the shape of strikes to come', *Personnel Management*, October 1980, p. 48.

52. Edwards (1983) *op. cit.*, p. 215.

53. C. Kerr and A. Siegel, 'The inter-industry propensity to strike – an international comparison', in Kornhauser *et al.* (eds), *op. cit.*, p. 195.

54. *Ibid.*

55. C. Kerr, 'Industrial peace and the collective bargaining environment', in G. S. Golden and V. D. Parker (eds), *Causes of Industrial Peace under Collective Bargaining*, Harper & Row, 1955.

56. Edwards (1995) *op. cit.*, p. 446.

57. R. J. Davies, 'Economic activity, incomes policy and strikes: a quantitative analysis', *British Journal of Industrial Relations*, vol. 17, no. 2, 1979, pp. 205–23.

58. M. Frayn, 'A perfect strike' in R. Blackburn and A. Cockburn (eds), *The Incompatibles*, Penguin, 1967, p. 160.

59. T. Wolfson, 'Social control of industrial conflict', in Kornhauser *et al.* (eds), *op. cit.*

60. Edwards (1995), *op. cit.*, p. 447.

61. J. Gennard, *Financing Strikers*, Macmillan, 1977, pp. 123–4.

62. J. W. Durcan and W. E. J. McCarthy, 'The state subsidy theory of strikes: an examination of statistical data for the period 1956–70', *British Journal of Industrial Relations*, vol 12, no. 1, 1974.

63. Gennard, *op. cit.*, p. 137.

64. B. Gernigon, A. Odero and H. Guido, 'ILO principles concerning the right to strike', *International Labour Review*, vol. 137, no. 4, 1998, p. 443.

65. *Trade Union Immunities*, HMSO, 1981, p. 24.

66. *Ibid.*

67. *Mercury Communications* v. *POEU* (1983).

68. *Dimbelby & Sons* v *NUJ* (1984).

69. *Trade Union Immunities*, *op. cit.*, p. 52.

70. *Rookes* v *Barnard* (1964).

71. *Thomson* v *Deakin* (1952); *Stratford* v *Lindley* (1965).

72. *Express Newspapers* v *MacShane* (1979).

73. *Trade Union Immunities*, *op. cit.*, p. 22.

74. *Austin Rover* v *T&GWU, AUEW and Others* (1984).

75. *Industrial Action and Trade Unions* HMSO, 1996.

76. *Blackpool & Fylde College* v *NATFHE* (1994).

77. *Report of Royal Commission on Trade Unions and Employers' Associations* (Donovan Commission), HMSO, 1968, p. 114.

78. ACAS, *Annual Report*, 1997, p. 43.

79. S. Kessler and F. Bayliss, *Contemporary British Industrial Relations* (3rd edn), Macmillan, 1998, p. 255.

80. J. Gennard, M. Steele and K. Miller, 'Trends and developments in industrial relations and industrial relations law: trade union discipline and non-strikers', *Industrial Relations Journal*, vol. 20, no. 1, 1989, pp. 5–15.

81. *Code of Practice: Picketing*, HMSO, 1980.

82. *Thomas and Others* v *NUM (South Wales)* (1985).

83. P. Kahn, N. Lewis, R. Livock and P. Wiles, *Picketing: Industrial Disputes, Tactics and the Law*, Routledge & Kegan Paul, 1983.

84. P. Wallington, 'Industrial relations, the police and public order – some lessons of the miners' strike', *Employee Relations*, vol. 10, no. 1, 1988, pp. 3–12.

85. 'The regulation of industrial conflict in Europe', *European Industrial Relations Review*, report no. 2, 1989.

86. S. Wood and J. Godard, 'The statutory union recognition procedure in the Employment Relations Bill: a comparative analysis', *British Journal of Industrial Relations*, vol. 37, no. 2, 1999, p. 215.

87. *Ibid.*, p. 234.

88. Kessler and Bayliss, *op. cit.*, p. 254.

89. *Industrial Action and Trade Unions* (1996) HMSO.

90. M. Thatcher, 'Prison officers turn screw on industrial action ban', *People Management*, February 1998, pp. 12–13; A. Perkins, 'Straw

deal for prison officers', *Guardian*, 19 May 1998.

91. S. Milne, 'Labour ready to ban fire service strikes', *Guardian*, 7 August 1999.
92. Gernigon *et al.*, *op.cit.*, p. 450.
93. *Ibid*, p. 448.
94. Beaumont, *op. cit.*, p. 130.
95. J. Bridgford and J. Stirling, *Employee Relations in Europe*, Blackwell, 1994, p. 150.
96. F. Younson, 'Who's been using the law in industrial disputes?', *Personnel Management*, June 1984, p. 32.
97. S. Evans, 'The use of injunctions in industrial disputes May 1984–April 1987', *British Journal of Industrial Relations*, vol. 25, no. 3, 1987, p. 420.
98. *Ibid.*, p. 425.
99. 'Employers step up legal challenges', *Labour Research*, September 1994, pp. 7–9.

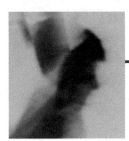

chapter twelve

Conciliation and arbitration

Learning objectives

It is important that management, unions and employees should be able, if necessary, to call on an independent third party for help in resolving their differences. By the end of this chapter, you should be able to:

- identify the differences between conciliation and arbitration;

- understand the role of each in relation to the collective bargaining process, their potential impact on the participants' relative bargaining power and government policy towards conciliation and arbitration;

- compare and contrast the concepts of 'pendulum' arbitration and conventional 'open' arbitration;

- explain the role and work of ACAS in respect of both collective and individual issues.

Definition

Conciliation and arbitration are means of intervening into the negotiating process which may assist the two parties to resolve a dispute or failure to agree, but while conciliation is an assisted continuation of negotiation, arbitration involves the imposition of a binding award.

Key issues

While you are reading this chapter, you should keep the following points in mind:

- We must be careful not to assume that all differences, disputes or 'failures to agree' can, with enough time and goodwill, be resolved by discussion or logical argument and that, therefore, conciliation or arbitration are inherently the 'right and only' way to tackle such impasses.

- If there are some groups within society whose work is so essential or integral to its day-to-day life that we must consider constraining their use of industrial action, then shouldn't we also constrain their employer from taking advantage of this situation by ensuring that any differences can, if necessary, be referred to binding, independent and impartial arbitration?

- If a third party is to be involved, then to what extent and in what way should they be able (or indeed encouraged) to introduce their own ideas, suggestions or solutions? After all, they don't have to live with the consequences.

12.1 Introduction

The establishment of formal systems and institutions of conciliation and arbitration within the industrial relations system reflects the fact that 'most systems of labour relations ... presuppose the possibility of disagreement and disputes'[1] between the parties involved. While some disputes of right (contract interpretation) may be handled by the normal law courts or specialised labour courts, conciliation and arbitration are intended primarily as adjuncts to the collective bargaining process. They are available where the parties to a negotiation fail to determine a solution on their own: that is, when they have reached an impasse with no further prospect of movement by either side and, where applicable, with no further levels of joint negotiating machinery to which the issue may be referred. Therefore, they should be viewed principally as **intervention strategies which utilise the involvement of an independent third party in the conduct of the collective bargaining process**. The intervention may be initiated by the parties themselves (unilaterally or jointly) or by the state, through its delegated agency, as the representative of external interests.

However, the two **strategies of conciliation and arbitration are fundamentally different** in their method of operation and, in particular, in the relationship between the 'third party' and the other two parties (see Figure 12.1):

■ In **conciliation** the 'third party' supports the direct bipartite negotiating process by assisting the parties to identify the cause and extent of their differences, to establish alternative solutions and their various implications and to develop and agree a mutually acceptable settlement. The responsibility for making decisions and reaching a solution still remains a joint one between management and union – as it would if there was no intervention. The conciliator acts as a medium for the continuation of the dialogue. Wood described the role as 'a catalyst, aiming to lead the parties to an agreement without ... interfering in the actual decision making'[2], while ACAS has described it as 'a creative force in dispute resolution, assisting the parties to identify and explore ways of settling their differences'[3]. ACAS makes it clear that it 'has only the powers of persuasion and reason, and cannot impose or even recommend a settlement – agreements reached in conciliation being the property of the parties'[4].

■ In **arbitration**, on the other hand, the direct negotiation between management and union is replaced with a process of adjudication which involves the third party in making a decision (award) between the two conflicting positions. The arbitrator 'is empowered to take a decision which disposes of the dispute'[5] and, therefore, is not required to seek a direct reconciliation between the two parties; as Wood noted, 'the parties lose their power over the settlement entirely'[6]. It is the arbitrator's decision, rather than a joint decision of the two parties, which determines the settlement and he or she may accept one or other of the positions put to him or her or, as is perhaps more often the case, determine a point somewhere between the two positions.

Figure 12.1
Conciliation and
arbitration
processes

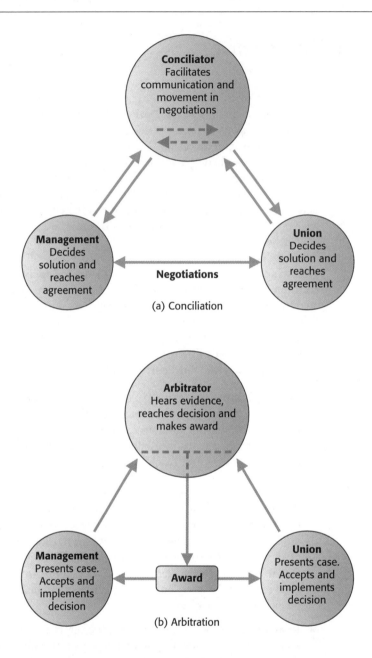

(a) Conciliation

(b) Arbitration

Margerison and Leary suggested that conciliation (and, by implication, arbitration) is little more than 'short term crisis intervention to aid the resolution of a dispute'[7] and that there is a third, and perhaps more useful, intervention strategy which may be adopted – mediation.

■ The term **mediation** may be used in two different ways. First, in the short-term resolution of a particular dispute, it may be used to indicate that the third party is 'more active in assisting the parties going so far as to submit his own proposals for settlement'[8]. Although the third party takes a greater degree of initiative, it is still a fundamental requirement of the process that any settlement must be determined and agreed by the parties themselves. Second, it may be viewed as a more long-term intervention strategy, which Margerison and Leary believe is concerned 'not only to resolve existing conflict, but to plan for the prevention of similar conflict' and involves 'help with the implementation of decisions at both the interpersonal and organisational levels'[9]. Certainly, ACAS sees the development of an 'advisory mediation' strategy based on the use of workshops and joint working parties as the focus of its work in 'preventing', as opposed to resolving, disputes.

12.2 The nature of conciliation and arbitration

The precise nature and role of conciliation and arbitration within the industrial relations system depend primarily on two factors:

- ■ The perceived relationship of these processes to the 'normal' bipartite process of direct negotiations between management and union (including the possible use of industrial action);
- ■ Whether these processes are to be used by the parties on a voluntary or compulsory basis.

Relationship to the collective bargaining process

It is perhaps inevitable that conciliation and arbitration are contrasted, as processes, with the direct bipartite process of management/union negotiations or, as intervention strategies into the negotiating process, with the parties' own use of industrial action. However, it is important not to lose sight of the fact that they are an **integral part of the total collective bargaining system** and not simply some form of external appendage to the system (see Figure 12.2). This is most evident in the case of conciliation. The process of direct negotiation is continued – with its reliance on achieving compromise between the parties and the necessity for the parties themselves to determine and agree the final settlement – but in a different form and under a different title. Although arbitration involves a significantly different and less direct process, it is nevertheless generally preceded by some form of direct negotiation between the parties, during which they have sought, through offers and compromise, to resolve their differences. The parties will continue to seek to influence, although not directly determine, the final outcome through the presentation and argument of their case to the arbitrator.

Conciliation and arbitration may be used simply to bridge the final gap between the parties or solve outstanding issues within an otherwise successful negotiation. Therefore, the use of these intervention strategies, like the use of industrial action by the parties themselves, cannot be regarded as automatic evidence of the failure or breakdown of collective bargaining because they are themselves part of that system. Their use is indicative only of an inability of the

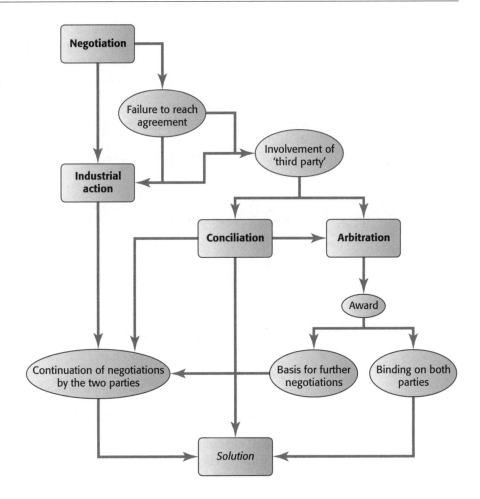

direct negotiation process, in a specific set of circumstances, to resolve the differences between the parties and the desire of the parties to pursue alternative strategies to secure a settlement. Certainly, Goodman and Krislov found that 66 per cent of the trade union officers and 81 per cent of the managers surveyed did not feel that the use of conciliation should be regarded as an indication of an immature approach to industrial relations[10].

The merits of third-party intervention strategies of conciliation and arbitration, as compared with the participants' own intervention strategy of industrial action, may be viewed from three different perspectives:

- From an **ends perspective** (which emphasises the inherent requirement for the collective bargaining system to achieve a resolution to disputes), they may be viewed as parallel, equal and alternative strategies – each available in the event of a breakdown in negotiations and each capable of securing a settlement and the continuation of the contractual relationship.

- From a **quality of means perspective** (which places emphasis on the achievement of a settlement through processes based on a joint and direct agreement and regulation), arbitration may be regarded as subordinate and inferior to either conciliation or the participants' own use of industrial power to resolve their differences.

■ From an **effect of means perspective** (which places greatest emphasis on the maintenance of industrial peace and the avoidance of disruption within the industrial relations system), the intervention strategies of conciliation and arbitration may be perceived as preferable and superior strategies to the use of industrial action.

The attitude, in the UK, towards the role of conciliation and arbitration reflects elements of both these last two perspectives. The **primacy of voluntary and direct negotiations** is reflected in a number of ways:

■ There is a general belief among all the parties that conciliation or arbitration should not be used until the normal, jointly agreed negotiating and disputes procedures in the organisation or industry have been exhausted. However, Kessler noted that the existence of unofficial and unconstitutional strikes led, in practice, 'to some undermining of this rule, otherwise conciliators would have stood on the touchlines while serious disputes took place'[11].

■ Where third-party intervention is invoked there is a clear preference among management and unions for conciliation rather than arbitration and there is no automatic resort to arbitration if conciliation fails. As Lowry notes, with arbitration both sides 'effectively lose control of events'[12] and for many employers, in particular, it means that 'key business decisions are handed over to well-meaning but ill-informed outsiders'[13].

■ Generally, arbitration takes place as the result of a joint request and with both sides agreeing to accept the resulting 'award'. Sometimes the award may not provide the final settlement but, rather, provide a fresh basis for further bipartite negotiations.

■ Conciliation may be invoked to circumvent an impasse in the negotiating process created by the use of industrial action and thereby allow the negotiations to continue, albeit in a slightly different form.

Clearly, it can be important for the continuation of negotiations and achieving a settlement that these third-party intervention strategies are available. Goodman and Krislov[14] found that both managers and trade union officers felt that conciliation could play a **positive role in supporting the negotiating process** (see Box 12.1):

*See Chapter 13 –
Negotiation*

■ It can provide an avenue for the maintenance of the negotiating dialogue at a time when it would otherwise break down. Indeed, there may be occasions, such as outright refusal by either side to negotiate on a particular issue, where conciliation provides perhaps the only possible means for establishing or maintaining contact between the parties.

■ The introduction of a third party, who must be informed of the issues and viewpoints involved in the dispute, requires both parties to set out their position in a reasoned and orderly manner. The act of having to prepare a 'statement of case' for the conciliator or arbitrator may itself provoke a re-examination of the situation and movement in position by either or both parties.

■ The conciliator or arbitrator, because he or she is independent and has not been involved in the development of the dispute, is able to approach the issues with a fresh and unprejudiced mind. He or she is able, having identified the common ground as well as the points of difference between the parties, to indicate approaches which may not have been seen by the parties to the dispute. Lowry notes that a survey in 1985 showed that 94 per cent of managers and 89 per cent of union officials felt that conciliators should not hesitate to make suggestions[15].

■ Lowry notes that 'sometimes a union will accept an invitation to a conciliation meeting, not because it is expecting the employer to improve upon his last offer, but because such a meeting provides confirmation that the last offer has in fact been made'[16]. Certainly, the use of conciliation or arbitration may allow the proposal of a solution which has been precluded by the mandates within which either or both of the negotiators have been required to negotiate by their principals. Thus, the 'blame' for a solution outside the original mandate can be shifted from the negotiator to the third party. It would appear, however, that this role for conciliation and arbitration is generally perceived as being of value to the *other side* – Goodman and Krislov found that only some 17 per cent of trade union officers and 22 per cent of managers felt that conciliation 'had helped *them* to withdraw from a difficult position'[17] (my italics).

See Chapter 9 –
Collective bargaining

While conciliation or arbitration may be necessary to ensure the maintenance of the collective bargaining relationship, it is important to realise that their use, particularly on a frequent basis, **may distort the relative bargaining power** between the parties concerned. Machinery for conciliation and arbitration, within an industrial relations system which retains the right to strike, is offering 'employers and workers the choice of seeking a settlement of disputes between them through such procedures or by a trial of strength'[18]. Conciliation and arbitration do not replace industrial action but complement it: industrial action remains part of the process of exerting pressure for change in decisions (it may be threatened or used during negotiations before an impasse is identified or it may be used if the results of conciliation or arbitration are unacceptable). In this context the use of conciliation or arbitration can be regarded as no more than a voluntary postponement of industrial action rather than precluding its use. Alternatively, Loewenberg *et al.* argue that 'arbitration, if effective, neutralizes bargaining power'[19], in that the issue is decided by argument before an independent assessor rather than by industrial muscle. However, as Hyman points out, this ignores the fact that 'the power relationship of the parties – shaped ultimately by an assessment of the damage that each can inflict in open conflict – provides the background to any resort to arbitration'[20]. In practice, the conciliator or arbitrator seeks to secure a settlement which is not only 'right' in relation to the facts of the case as presented, but also acceptable to the two parties in terms of their assessment of the likely gains/costs associated with the use of industrial action.

It is significant that **both management and trade unions may perceive the intervention of conciliation or arbitration to be a weakening of their bargaining power**. From the management perspective, while a specific union

| **Box 12.1** | The role of the conciliator |

'... the only power available to conciliators are reason and persuasion; the only assumption they can make is that both parties come to conciliation because they desire agreement or understanding, and that either one or perhaps both of them is prepared to modify its previous position in order to bring that about ... it is a major task of the conciliator to identify "signals", to pick up hints and develop ideas, however tentatively and vaguely they may be floated. By listening, communicating, asking intelligent questions and injecting new ideas of his own, a conciliator can often manage to identify or suggest a possibly new approach by one side or the other'. (pp. 24–5)

'The reason why the conciliation process is preferred lies in the single word, control. The trade union and the employer who agree to conciliation remain very much in control of events. Either can pull out at any time – the union can decline to vary its claim and the employer can decline to improve his offer. Continued disagreement may be preferred to an agreed settlement on unsatisfactory terms. But when both sides agree to arbitration and to be bound by the outcome, they effectively lose control of events. Win, lose or draw, they are stuck with the award'. (pp. 84–5)

Source: P. Lowry, *Employment Disputes and the Third Party*, Macmillan, 1990.

'ACAS conciliation staff will:

■ remain impartial and independent at all times;

■ seek to understand both the dispute and the attitude of the parties to it;

■ gain the trust and confidence of both parties so that a sound working relationship can be developed;

■ make constructive suggestions to facilitate negotiations where appropriate;

■ provide information (eg about legislation) at the request of the parties'.

Source: ACAS, *Preventing and Resolving Collective Disputes*, p. 3.

request for conciliation or arbitration may be perceived as indicative of the union's lack of bargaining power (i.e. its membership is not prepared to resort to the use of industrial action), the use of either strategy may be seen as potentially detrimental to management's bargaining position and, in particular, its decision-making authority and responsibility. Decisions which can have a profound effect on the operation and success of the organisation now involve an 'outsider' who has no long-term commitment or responsibility to the organisation. Goodman and Krislov point out that, despite having reached the limits of their concessions in direct negotiations, management often feels that its last offer is regarded during conciliation or arbitration as an 'irreducible minimum above which a compromise would be made'[21]. It believes that trade unions can, through conciliation or arbitration, obtain a settlement which is beyond the level warranted by their case and/or beyond the limit to which management is able or prepared to go. As a result, management may, if it believes conciliation or arbitration to be likely, either keep offers in reserve for this phase (thereby reducing the prospects of a solution through direct negotiations and so creating a self-fulfilling prophecy) or make informal 'without prejudice' offers during the negotiation which may be withdrawn in the event that the issue does go to conciliation or arbitration[22]. In response to this latter strategy, the union must decide whether the possible gains from conciliation or arbitration are likely to be substantial and certain enough to justify rejecting, and therefore losing, the last offer on the table.

From the trade union perspective, the processes of conciliation and arbitration may be seen as potentially supportive of management's bargaining power, in that their use involves a restriction on the union's capacity to mobilise its industrial power and exert the maximum pressure on management. Management's pursuit of conciliation or arbitration may be perceived by unions as little more than a strategy to weaken, or at best postpone, their use of industrial power and thereby secure a more favourable settlement for management. Consequently, rather than relinquish or postpone the use of industrial action, the union or its members may regard it as both legitimate and necessary for there to be a demonstration of industrial power and employee feeling to accompany or precede the intervention of conciliation or arbitration. The use of industrial action in such circumstances is intended to influence the conciliator or arbitrator as much as, if not more than, management.

Goodman and Krislov suggest that there may be a belief among managers and trade union officials that 'the stronger party in a dispute would not permit conciliation'[23]. This suggests not only that the participants regard any call for conciliation or arbitration as a sign of weakness, but also that conciliation or arbitration can and will take place only in those situations where the relative bargaining power between the parties is reasonably evenly balanced. However, a suggestion of 'going' to conciliation or arbitration may, at one level, be no more than a strategy within the negotiating process to induce further concessions and a settlement, and as such may be initiated by either party irrespective of their relative bargaining advantage. A 'real' demand for conciliation or arbitration, on the other hand, is likely to arise where the initiating party believes its case to be strong, on logic or equity grounds, but it lacks the necessary industrial power to achieve an acceptable settlement. The demand for conciliation or arbitration is, in effect, a challenge to the stronger party to forgo its bargaining advantage and allow an opportunity for the weaker party to achieve a better settlement than would have been obtained through a continuation of direct negotiations.

See Chapter 8 – The government

An examination of **government policy towards conciliation and arbitration** reveals three distinct objectives.

1. *To maintain industrial peace.* Ever since the late nineteenth century, conciliation and arbitration have played an important role in the government's policy of seeking to maintain industrial peace within the industrial relations system. The government has sought to minimise the use of industrial action not only by establishing and maintaining the facilities for conciliation and arbitration (at public expense) but also by encouraging management and unions to avail themselves of these facilities. In addition, the government has had the facility to take a more direct role by itself initiating the processes of conciliation or arbitration in those disputes which it considers to be serious because of their effect on the economy or the community. The ultimate success of conciliation or arbitration in this area depends on their being

perceived by management and unions as, in some way, more fair and equitable processes for the resolving of differences than the use of industrial power.

2. *To influence the operation of the industrial relations system.* Most governments have tried to constrain the development of unofficial or unconstitutional strikes by resisting the use of conciliation or arbitration outside the normal recognised negotiating procedures or until they have been exhausted. Governments have also written-in a role for conciliation or arbitration where employers resist union recognition or the disclosure of information. During the 1980s, the government changed the balance of bargaining power within the public sector by restricting the unions' access to arbitration (e.g. teachers and the civil service). The right to invoke arbitration unilaterally was withdrawn and replaced by the requirement for a joint request. This has significantly reduced trade union power and increased management's power. Arbitration can only take place if both parties agree and, as already pointed out, the stronger party may well resist the intervention of conciliation or arbitration.

3. *To influence the outcome of negotiations.* Some governments have sought to use the processes of conciliation and arbitration to influence directly the outcome of negotiations, particularly wage negotiations. They have sought, in some cases by exhortation and in others by direct instruction, to enlist the conciliator or arbitrator as an agent for the implementation of their incomes policy. Clearly, such an approach has immense implications for the continued acceptability of conciliation and arbitration to management and unions. While it might appear that management would welcome support from conciliators or arbitrators in keeping down wage increases, nevertheless the long-term acceptability of conciliation and arbitration depends on their impartiality and their freedom from external influence or control. The government's desire to maintain industrial peace (i.e. minimise the use of industrial action) appears to be in conflict with its desire to contain or influence the level of wage increases. Many would agree with McCarthy and Ellis that governmental 'policies designed to influence income movements and incomes criteria must be separated from those policies designed to reform collective bargaining and contain industrial conflict; both in their day-to-day application and in their form of organisation'[24]. Government attempts in this area led, in the early 1970s, to increasing criticism of the Department of Employment's conciliation service – to such an extent that the CBI and TUC jointly established their own independent conciliation panel. It was this indication of management and union joint concern regarding the official institution for conciliation which was largely responsible for the creation of ACAS, in 1974, as an autonomous body outside direct day-to-day governmental control.

The relationship between direct negotiations and the processes of conciliation and arbitration is complex, varied and dynamic. However, there appears to be a **fundamental and inherent dilemma** in that relationship. All parties in the industrial relations system would agree that there is a clear need for conciliation and arbitration to be readily available in order to provide channels for the

See Chapter 13 –
Negotiation

resolution of differences which cannot be settled in the negotiating dialogue. Nevertheless, excessive reliance on these processes may well undermine the process of direct negotiations, in that one or both parties become reluctant to make concessions in the negotiating dialogue for fear of prejudicing their position, and the final outcome, should conciliation or arbitration be used. In particular, arbitration is generally perceived as involving some element of 'splitting the difference' between the two sides and, therefore, if the parties believe there is a high probability of the issue going to arbitration, there is little incentive for either side to move towards the centre by making concessions in the negotiating dialogue.

Voluntary or compulsory

The term **voluntary** generally implies that management and union have complete discretion to make, or not make, such *ad hoc* or permanent arrangements as they consider necessary and appropriate for resolving any impasse that may arise during their negotiations. The facilities established and maintained by the state at public expense are available should the parties wish to make use of them rather than establish their own individual arrangements. The term **compulsory**, on the other hand, implies a removal of management's and union's freedom to determine their own affairs and involves the imposition, through legislation, of an external requirement that their disputes must, if they cannot be resolved through the direct negotiating dialogue, be referred to conciliation and/or arbitration. Such an approach is generally associated with a legal restriction on the employees' right to strike and may be applied to all employees or only those in certain specified industries or situations.

See Chapter 11 –
Industrial action

However, it is important to recognise that any system of conciliation or arbitration need not be wholly voluntary or compulsory but **may contain elements of both approaches**. The voluntary or compulsory nature of the processes can apply at any or all of three distinct phases of their operation – the establishment of the institutions, the use of processes and the implementation of the outcome. Compulsion by the government, therefore, need not encompass all three phases but may be directed towards only one of them. For example, the government may apply compulsion in the implementation of any outcome from conciliation or arbitration, while leaving the parties free to decide, in the first place, whether to make use of these processes, or it may establish a compulsory requirement that these intervention processes be used in certain or all disputes, while leaving the issue of whether the outcome is implemented to the discretion and agreement of management and union. Equally, within an essentially voluntary approach, management and union may determine whether to establish machinery and what form it will take and then, as part of their joint agreement, accept a self-imposed compulsion in its use and the implementation of its outcome (a form of 'voluntarily compulsory' system).

Conciliation and arbitration in the UK has been characterised by its voluntary nature. Only during two important, but abnormal, periods (1915–18 and 1940–51) has the UK sought to graft a comprehensive system of compulsory arbitration onto its normal collective bargaining arrangements. The pressure to introduce compulsory arbitration resulted from the existence of a state of war and the emphasis placed on the need to minimise any loss of production resulting from strikes and to regulate wage levels at a time of inflationary pressures within the economy. It was, therefore, the product of special external pressures and a temporary measure to be removed once, or soon after, the emergency was over. Even then, however, the UK's approach to compulsory arbitration was based on government support for **unilateral arbitration**. Hepple points out that, rather than impose arbitration against the wishes of both parties, the underlying principle of the British system was that 'at the request of either party to a dispute, the matter could be referred by the appropriate government minister for arbitration without the consent of the other party'[25] and the resulting arbitration award was legally binding. This largely voluntary approach is in marked contrast to other countries, such as the USA and Australia, who have maintained differing but more permanent systems of arbitration.

See Country profiles 12.1 and 12.2

Hepple[26] believes that the most significant feature of the UK's experience of unilateral arbitration is not so much that it was superimposed, as a wartime emergency, on an already relatively well-established system of voluntary collective bargaining, but rather that it continued until 1959, despite the prohibition and sanctions on industrial action being withdrawn in 1951. He argues that unions supported the system for three main reasons:

1. There was an 'almost total absence of enforcement of the penal sanctions against stoppages'[27] – even during the war.
2. The system was useful to trade unions in situations where they were weakly organised or where the strike weapon was ineffective.
3. In situations where the unions were well organised or had industrial power, the processes of arbitration and negotiation with industrial action could be used in tandem.

The removal of sanctions, however ineffective or little used, increased employers' concern that the system was too one-sided. Consequently, the general legal right to invoke unilateral arbitration was abandoned in 1959. All that remained was S.8 of the Terms and Conditions of Employment Act (1959) (later incorporated within Schedule 11 of the Employment Protection Act, 1975), which allowed trade unions to use the process of unilateral arbitration against an employer whose terms and conditions of employment were less favourable than the established or recognised ones in that industry. It supported trade union efforts in seeking to secure 'common rules' across an industry or trade. It was rescinded by the Employment Act (1980).

Experience of the operation of compulsory arbitration in its different forms highlights four main issues.

1. *Is it to be unilateral or compulsory arbitration?* Under the former, the initiative to invoke the process, and thereby secure statutory support for the implementation of any award, is at the discretion of one or other of the negotiating parties; under the latter, it is the government which prescribes the circumstances in which arbitration must take place. While in theory, under unilateral arbitration, both management and unions have an equal right and opportunity to make use of the process, in practice it will be perceived by

Country profile 12.1   Australia – compulsory arbitration

The Australian system of compulsory arbitration was developed in the 1890s at a time of extensive and often bitter industrial conflict. It was regarded as a 'bold social experiment' intended to promote greater justice and equality in wage determination. Subsequently, it has become an integral and dominant part of the collective bargaining arrangements with some 80 per cent of employees, public and private sectors alike, being covered by awards or agreements made under the system.

The federal Australian Industrial Relations Commission (AIRC) has power to intervene in 'disputes' which cover more than one state. However, the term 'dispute' does not require the existence, or threat, of industrial action before the AIRC may act but simply the existence of a difference between a union and employer. The parties are under an obligation to refer a 'dispute' to the Commission or the AIRC may take the initiative to intervene in the 'public interest'. Although the public proceedings of the Commission are relatively formal, the Commissioner may break the proceedings to 'come down from the bench' for informal private discussions with the parties to conciliate a settlement.

In the late 1980s the AIRC was handling some 4,000–5,000 cases a year which can be divided into four categories (3 : 102):

- *One-off disputes* about a particular issue;
- *Industry cases* relating to varying a sectoral award;
- *National test cases* concerned with innovations in particular conditions of employment (such as shorter working week or maternity leave);
- *National Wage Cases* which seek a general improvement in wage levels.

It is the *National Wage Cases* (generally an annual event) which have tended to standardise and centralise the Australian wage system and which are important in relation to the government's incomes policy. The government's active participation in such cases (presenting its own evidence of the 'national interest') creates a tripartite rather than bipartite arbitration process. The AIRC's approach to determining National Wage Awards has changed over the years (2 : 111–116). In the beginning, in 1907, a 'basic wage' was fixed based on 'the normal needs of an average employee ... living in a civilised community'. In the 1920s 'margins' were introduce to provide for skill differentials. In 1967, the two elements were amalgamated into a 'total' award.

In the 1970s and early 1980s the primary focus was on restricting 'over-award' payments (increases above the award level negotiated directly between unions and employers) while introducing indexation in federal awards (automatic cost-of living adjustments). The concept of 'comparative wage justice' appears to have been the major guiding factor in AIRC decisions rather than 'capacity to pay' (3 : 104).

However, decisions in the late 1980s became conditional on unions and employers discussing measures to improve 'structural efficiency'. In the 1991 decision the AIRC, having previously 'expressed reservations about the ability and maturity of the parties to effectively engage in enterprise bargaining', nevertheless declared itself 'prepared, on balance, to determine an enterprise bargaining principle' (4 : 65).

However, the system does not simply replace negotiations between management and unions; rather, such negotiations are carried out within the procedures of statutory tribunals and the framework of their awards. Indeed, the system allows for 'consent' awards (agreements which are registered with the tribunal or commission to confirm and give legal effect to the result of voluntary negotiations).

Sources:
1. K. F. Walker, 'Compulsory arbitration in Australia', in J. J. Loewenberg *et al.*, *Compulsory Arbitration*, Lexington Books, 1976.
2. E. M. Davis and R. D. Lansbury, 'Employment relations in Australia', in G. J. Bamber and R. D. Lansbury (eds), *International and Comparative Employment Relations* (3rd edn), Sage, 1998.
3. K. J. Mackie, 'Lessons from Down-Under: conciliation and arbitration in Australia', *Industrial Relations Journal*, vol. 18. no. 2, 1987, pp. 100–16.
   R. Lansbury and J. Niland, 'Managed decentralization? Recent trends in Australian industrial relations and human resource policies', in R. Locke, T. Kochan and M. Piore (eds), *Employment Relations in a Changing World Economy*, MIT Press, 1995, pp. 59–90.

See also Country profiles 8.2 and 9.2.

most employers as being biased in favour of the trade union. At the same time, management often argues that while it invariably complies with any arbitration award, whether or not it likes the terms, trade unions have greater freedom to ignore the findings of an unacceptable award and seek to improve on it by direct pressure on the employer. However, as Walker pointed out, compulsory arbitration is more likely to remove from the negotiating parties their 'responsibility for reaching agreement, and for the terms of agreement' and encourages them 'to stand firm and emphasises points of difference rather than common ground'[28].

2. *The extent to which industrial action should, and can, be prohibited.* Concern about the level and effect of strike activity has been the principal reason behind the introduction of compulsory arbitration – Loewenberg *et al.* argue 'arbitration becomes a quid pro quo for denying the right to strike'[29]. However, experience of the operation of compulsory arbitration, in the UK during wartime and in Australia, demonstrates that it has not led to a reduction in strike activity. Loewenberg *et al.* believe the fundamental dilemma is that 'unwillingness to prosecute recognized violations serves to encourage further violations' and 'token prosecutions promote resistance'[30]. It would seem, therefore, that a reduction in strike activity relies on imposing sanctions against all and every breach of the prohibition. Yet realistically, compliance on a wide scale cannot be imposed by state force (certainly not without provoking resentment and possible confrontation between government and trade unions) but has to be voluntarily accepted by the parties – in particular, the trade unions. McCarthy argued that it is somewhat ironic that access to unilateral arbitration may be most important for those 'many groups who are unable to use industrial action'[31] – groups with a low level of unionisation; groups where the use of the strike weapon lacks support because of social considerations; or groups where the strike weapon is ineffective, in the short term, in exerting pressure on the employer. Many white collar and/or public sector employees fall into the latter two categories.

3. *Assuming that compulsory arbitration is not applied to all employees in all situations, which industries and/or situations should be covered by the system?* Discussion in the UK has centred on the special position of 'essential services'. However, given the complex and interrelated nature of modern economies, it can be argued that many industries could fall within the definition of essential services. It could include a much wider range of industries than simply fire, police and health services: for example, electricity, gas, petroleum production and distribution, all forms of transport, agriculture, and significant parts of government and local authority services. Furthermore, if an industry is designated as essential, and therefore subject to compulsory arbitration, is the process to be applied in all disputes irrespective of the number of employees involved, the actual effect of any possible strike or even whether the issue is really suitable for resolution through arbitration? The alternative, as practised in some states in the USA, is to leave the government or courts to determine, on an *ad hoc* basis, which disputes are serious enough to be subjected to an arbitration award. Such an approach is less likely to undermine the voluntary collective bargaining process.

See Country profile 12.2

Country profile 12.2   USA – compulsory arbitration in essential services

After the comprehensive approach of World War II (during which some 20,000 disputes were handled in five years), the emphasis of compulsory arbitration shifted towards the maintenance of essential services.

In 1947 (following a high level of strike activity) a number of states sought to establish legislation to restrict strikes and provide for compulsory arbitration in a range of essential services such as electricity, gas, water, fuel, etc. However, these industries were in the *private sector* and became the subject of a series of successful legal challenges based on the Taft–Hartley Act (1947) which applied to all employees other than government employees and which permitted strikes. Consequently, most of these laws failed.

In the *public sector* it was not until the 1960s that federal and state government employees were permitted to organise and bargain on a collective basis. However, many state legislatures were, at the same time, anxious to maintain a restriction on the employee's right to strike – particularly those employees involved in public safety – and consequently provided

for compulsory arbitration in respect of specific groups such as police, firemen, prison guards or, more generally in some states, any essential service or where there was a danger to public health or safety. Thus, effective compulsory arbitration only applies to a very limited range of government employees and, perhaps more importantly, was introduced at a time when trade union recognition and collective bargaining was still in its initial stages of development.

Most agreements in both the private and public sectors provide, ultimately, for arbitration to resolve 'rights disputes'. These decisions have become built up into a quasi-'body of law' which many organisations refer to – whether unionised or not.

Sources: J. J. Loewenberg, 'Compulsory arbitration in the United States', in J. J. Loewenberg, W. J. Gershenfeld, H. J. Glasbeek, B. A. Hepple and K. F. Walker, *Compulsory Arbitration*, Lexington Books, 1976; H. N. Wheeler and J. A. McClendon, 'Employment relations in the United States', in G. J. Bamber and R. D. Lansbury (eds), *International and Comparative Employment Relations* (3rd edn), Sage, 1998, pp. 63–88.

4. *Whether or not the public interest should be taken into account in the determination of arbitration awards.* As Lowry notes, 'any arbitrator who is asked to be mindful of the national interest is in truth being asked to comply with a political requirement' and 'an arbitrator may take a different view from the politicians as to the national interest but he ought not, for that reason, be branded as unpatriotic, irresponsible or deaf'[32]. In the USA, state interest in the outcome of arbitration has been achieved by specifying, within the legislation establishing the arbitration system, the criteria on which arbitrators should base their decision, while in Australia the government is able to present its case direct to the arbitrator as a third interested party to the dispute. Clearly, the involvement of the government in the arbitration process shifts the focus of the process towards the promotion of public policy on wages and other issues and, consequently, may become less attractive to management and unions alike.

Pendulum arbitration

In pendulum arbitration (alternatively referred to as 'straight choice', 'final (or last) offer' or 'flip–flop' arbitration) **the role of the arbitrator is restricted to choosing between the final positions of the two parties**, unlike conventional or 'open' arbitration where the arbitrator can exercise judgement as to what is fair and equitable in the circumstances and propose a 'compromise' award. It first came to prominence in the UK in the mid-1980s as part of the 'new-style' single-union agreements. However, by no means all these agreements included provision for pendulum arbitration: one survey in 1989 showed that only 24 out of 52 such agreements (46 per cent) contained a pendulum arbitration clause[33]. Equally, a number of writers[34] have noted that pendulum arbitration is not necessarily an innovation in UK industrial relations; it was used by the Coal Industry Conciliation Boards at the turn of the twentieth century and, similarly, the independent members on Wages Councils provided a form of 'pendulum' through having to vote with one or other side if the unions and employers were unable to reach a satisfactory jointly agreed solution. One examination of references to arbitration showed that 25 per cent related to disputes of right which 'require the arbitrator to make a straight choice between one position or the other'[35], while another[36] found that 31 per cent of cases dealing with annual pay claims had been of a straight choice type, that arbitrators had not always made a 'compromise' award in the other cases even though they had this option and that where a 'compromise' award was made it was rarely pitched half-way between the union's claim and management's offer but rather a larger proportion came closer to the management's position than that of the union.

The concept of pendulum arbitration **originated in the USA** where, as ACAS noted in relation to the UK, the 'pendulum' nature of grievance arbitration in *matters of right* had been a well-established part of the process of contract interpretation. However, the development of pendulum arbitration in the USA in *matters of interest* was closely associated with the extension of collective bargaining rights to public sector employees in the 1950s and 1960s, some of whom were, at the same time, legally restricted in their right to strike. If groups of 'essential' employees were to forgo or be denied the right to strike, then it was felt necessary to have some form of compulsory third-party intervention to resolve disputes. However, conventional or 'open' arbitration was perceived to have two potential drawbacks: the 'chilling' effect (a reluctance by either or both sides to move to their real final position because of a perceived need to keep something in hand if the issue went to arbitration and the arbitrator 'split down the middle') and, stemming from this, the 'narcotic' effect (the reliance on third-party arbitration to resolve disputes becoming habit forming).

The essential issue, therefore, was **to make compulsory arbitration compatible with encouraging the parties to 'negotiate in good faith'**. Stevens[37] argued that the role of industrial action within collective bargaining is to introduce a 'cost' to either or both sides if a settlement is not achieved through the negotiation process. Therefore, if the use of industrial action is to be precluded, it is necessary to introduce a similar 'cost' element within the arbitration process which would induce full movement during negotiations and so overcome the 'chilling' and 'narcotic' effects. Certainly, Bruce and Carby-Hall believe that any arbitration involves a 'cost' element, in so far as there is 'the loss of either utility or profit which is experienced if the arbitrator's decision differs from the outcome which the respective parties would have preferred'[38]. The inclusion of a clear 'win/lose' situation through the pendulum concept strengthens this 'cost' element. On the face of it, this contradicts the central philosophy of negotiation based on the achievement of a mutually acceptable compromise. Certainly, Kessler argues that 'for one side to defeat totally the other is not a basis for continuing stable and orderly relations ... the essence of collective bargaining is compromise and flexibility'[39] and Yeandle and Clarke have noted that in one organisation 'the option of pendulum arbitration was consciously rejected ... since it was felt likely to promote a potentially divisive approach which would not be compatible with the overall personnel philosophy'[40].

However, pendulum arbitration only introduces a 'winner takes all' situation if it is used and, arguably, it is the threat of this which induces the two parties to bargain more reasonably to find their own mutually acceptable solution. As Singh has noted, pendulum arbitration is primarily 'a final deterrent – instead of industrial action – to ensure that the parties genuinely engage in realistic collective bargaining ... [and] are induced to make reasonable offers' and its success 'could be judged by the number of times it is not used'[41]. If the potential resort to pendulum arbitration does act as a deterrent and increase reasonableness in the preceding negotiations, then the 'win/lose' element it introduces into the collective bargaining process is likely to be small and, arguably, no more of a threat to the integrity of the collective bargaining process than the potential use of power through industrial action to force a change in position on one or other party. In what are, after all, subjective issues it could be argued that it is better to lose through argument in front of an independent third party who will be exercising some degree of fairness and equity in their judgement than be coerced to concede through force.

Although there was some discussion[42] in the UK about following the US example and introducing pendulum arbitration alongside restricting the right to strike among essential public sector employees, the government, during the 1980s, moved in the opposite direction and sought to maintain its prerogative to determine public sector pay by revoking the right of a number of public sector groups to 'unilateral arbitration' and refusing to use arbitration in some major disputes (e.g. the ambulance dispute in 1989–90). Pendulum arbitration in the UK is to be found, therefore, primarily in the private sector as part of the 1980s 'new-style' agreements aimed at reforming organisational industrial relations.

Arbitration has to deal with complex situations which the parties themselves have failed to resolve (see Box 12.2). Certainly, experience of pendulum arbitration has highlighted a **number of issues**:

See Chapter 14 – Pay and working arrangements

1. *Recession-proof.* As Bassett notes, it has been argued by some union supporters that pendulum arbitration is 'recession-proof', in that 'the decision is not based on purely economic factors, but on the soundness of the argument presented' and 'the case that seems most just should carry the day, no matter how industrially weak in traditional union muscle terms the employees might be'[43]. However, in a dispute of interest regarding an annual pay increase, the arbitrator has, in effect, to choose between the arguments used by management and union to justify and substantiate their case (not just simply the actual figures being offered and claimed) and these arguments may centre on very different concepts of 'equity': for example, a management case based on 'ability to pay' (internal organisation factors) and a union case based on 'cost of living' or 'comparability' (external factors). While under conventional or 'open' arbitration the arbitrator is absolved from having to make an apparent choice between the 'rightness' of either set of

Box 12.2	Arbitration

'Arbitrators are rarely presented with a simple choice between an employer's offer and a trade union's claim. The two parties often present complex packages with conflicting views on their consequential effects and divergent evaluations of detailed financial data. In such circumstances, developing a solution that resolves the industrial relations problem (and that is the arbitrator's ultimate objective) will rarely be straightforward'.

Source: ACAS, *Annual Report 1995*, p. 48.

' ... arbitration is an outcome of a "failure to agree". This means that an independent person will make a decision that in all probability will satisfy neither party to the dispute. What the parties are agreeing to is to abide by the decision of the arbitrator'.

Source: J. A. Kennerley, *Arbitration: Cases in industrial relations*, Pitman, 1994, p. 4.

arguments, within pendulum arbitration the award can appear to approve one or other of these bases for determining pay increases. Therefore, the extent to which pendulum arbitration is 'recession-proof' is questionable: in periods of recession, financial constraints or competitive pressures, the arbitrator may well feel that the management's argument based on 'ability to pay' is the more reasonable and the deterrent effect argued for pendulum arbitration may well lead the union to come closer to the management's offer in order to demonstrate its reasonableness to the arbitrator.

2. *Lack of flexibility and fairness.* The theory of pendulum arbitration assumes that one or both of the positions put to the arbitrator will be equitable – the deterrent effect assumes both sides will have negotiated in good faith to their final positions and any inequitable aspects will, therefore, have been ironed out. However, this may not always be the case and, as Kessler points out, 'if the two parties do not converge in bargaining, the arbitrator could be left in a very difficult position'[44] and may be required to choose between two positions, neither of which he or she regards as totally reasonable. Lewis notes that this can be overcome, albeit only on a selective basis, by the use of *obiter dicta* within the award and that 'the formulation of a preferred compromise by the arbitrator, even while making a pendulum award, can assist industrial relations in the longer term'[45]. Such an approach accords with the notion that at least part of the role of the 'third party' is to bring some independent scrutiny and fresh ideas to bear in trying to find a solution to a dispute.

3. *Difficulty in defining the final claim/offer.* Clearly, under pendulum arbitration the arbitrator needs to know the final positions of the two parties between which he or she has to decide. However, as Singh points out, this is not always as easy as it seems: 'is it at the point of the breakdown in negotiations or at the point of submitting the reference to the arbitrator or some other point?'[46]. This raises the issue of whether the parties are entitled to change their position between the final stage of the negotiation and putting their case to the arbitrator. Arguably, such a shift, presumably to present a more

reasonable case to the arbitrator, is tantamount to the 'chilling' effect (holding something back for the arbitration award); certainly, the management at Sanyo, faced with a revised union position immediately prior to the arbitration hearing, believed that 'the integrity of pendulum arbitration entirely depends upon both parties declaring their final position for consideration at the final negotiating discussions ... The concept behind pendulum arbitration is to make negotiators carefully consider the content and direction of their final negotiating position in the knowledge that, without agreement, these positions would be tested by arbitration ... Changes made at the arbitration stage are not in keeping with the concept behind the pendulum arbitration process'[47]. Yet, to disallow such movement right up to the last minute appears to be contrary to the flexibility advocated within dispute resolution. The position at Sanyo was further complicated because the parties differed in their interpretation of the term 'mediation' prior to arbitration: the management felt it was to be simply a clarification of the two side's final positions, while the union envisaged that it 'would involve a full-blown attempt by the parties to arrive at a settlement with the assistance of a mediator'[48].

4. *Difficulty in handling multi-issue disputes.* In a complex multi-issue dispute, the arbitrator would be required, under simple pendulum arbitration, to choose between the 'total packages' put forward by the two parties, without taking account of the merits of the parties' positions on each individual issue. Consequently, it could be argued that it would be preferable to require the arbitrator to exercise his or her pendulum choice on each item rather than on the package as a whole. Certainly, ACAS felt that 'where several issues are under discussion at the same time, it may be unhelpful for an arbitrator to be compelled to endorse the full position of one side or the other if long-term stability and equity are the aim'[49]. However, Kessler points out that the adoption of 'issue by issue' arbitration would mean 'moving away from the concept of pendulum arbitration to a situation where the arbitrator is in effect producing his or her own package'[50]. It is important to recognise that if the preceding negotiations have been conducted on a reasonable basis (which is likely to have involved trading off between the various items of the package before the two sides reach their final positions) then, if the arbitrator starts to mix up the two packages by choosing bits from each, this may well take the final award package beyond the intended final positions of one or both parties. This may result in the parties deciding, in future, to hold back a bit in their negotiations for such an eventuality, thereby reintroducing the 'chilling' effect into their negotiations.

One state in the USA (Iowa) has sought to overcome some of these problems by adopting a **'tri-offer' approach** involving mediation, fact finding by an independent third party and finally issue-by-issue pendulum arbitration. If the dispute does go to the final stage of arbitration, the arbitrator may select either the union, management or fact-finder's recommendation as the award for each issue. Certainly, the inclusion of a requirement for mediation prior to arbitration allows third-party intervention to facilitate the two parties resolving their own problem before being called on to adjudicate between the two positions and the inclusion of a fact-finding 'inquiry'-type process allows flexibility for the third party to introduce new ideas and possible solutions for consideration by the two parties. Research in the USA[51] has shown that over a five-year period, 70 per cent of all cases presented at fact-finding were found to have been settled without going to pendulum arbitration and, when a dispute did go to arbitration, the arbitrator often confirmed the fact-finder's recommendations. However, it may be argued that the introduction of a third independent set of proposals (the fact-finder's), which may differ from those of either the union or management, means that there is little practical difference between this approach to 'pendulum' arbitration and the more traditional 'open' arbitration.

Voluntary conciliation/arbitration procedures

See Country profile 12.3

The establishment and maintenance of voluntary procedures within the normal collective bargaining arrangements can play an important role in securing 'industrial peace'. In the past, the most common form of conciliation or arbitration in the UK was that contained within the disputes procedures negotiated between employers and trade unions. In 1981 Brown[52] found that over half of the establishments surveyed had made use of such an external disputes procedure operated by their employers' association during the previous two years. However, 37 per cent of the establishments surveyed had made provision for the involvement of some other third party, such as ACAS, for disputes which arose in connection with pay and conditions of employment. The inclusion of such a provision was more likely to occur where trade union density within the organisation was high, the organisation was foreign rather than UK owned and/or conducted its own wage bargaining rather than through an employers' association. The decline in multi-employer bargaining has reduced the role of employers' association and industry disputes procedures in providing what Lowry described as a 'breathing space' for 'fresh minds to be brought to bear on unresolved domestic issues'[53]. Significantly, Millward and Stevens' survey[54] found the proportion of establishments specifying the 'third-party' intervention as 'higher-level management' had almost doubled from 27 per cent to 51 per cent and the proportion specifying 'union official' had increased from 7 per cent to 24 per cent. This perhaps reflects the decentralisation of responsibility for collective bargaining to the establishment level in many organisations and apparently therefore the corporate-level management and national- or regional-level union officials being the 'third-party' intervention.

The decline in industry disputes procedures has meant that management and union must negotiate such agreement at the organisation level. In drawing-up an agreement on the use of arbitration in future disputes or 'failures to agree', it is important that the both parties should give consideration to the following issues:

■ **Scope of arbitration**. It is often argued, and indeed is the practice in the USA, that disputes of right (the interpretation and application of an existing agreement) are more suited to arbitration than disputes of interest (the determination of new terms and conditions of employment). However, the

Country profile 12.3   Switzerland – peace obligation in collective agreements

Switzerland has the lowest incidence of industrial action of any western industrialised country (generally less than one working day lost per year per 1,000 employees). This may be attributed to three factors:

1. *Industrial structure*: 60 per cent of the working population are employed in the service sector, its manufacturing is primarily high-quality specialised products and it is dominated by small and medium sized organisations (all factors associated *with lower strike-proneness*).

2. *Political system*: a broad consensual approach involves acceptance that all major political groups should be represented in government and both employers' and workers' organisations are closely involved in the lawmaking process. This is underpinned by the system of direct democracy which allows any group, on presentation of a petition with 50,000 signatures, to challenge legislation through a nation-wide referendum.

3. *Industrial relations*: most collective agreements contain 'peace obligations'.

Collective bargaining is restricted to the private sector and, unlike other European countries, there is a virtual absence of statutory collective labour law relating to trade unions, Works Councils, industrial action or collective agreements. However, under the Code of Obligations (the general law relating to contract and tort), collective agreements are regarded as legally binding contracts and therefore the use of coercion (industrial action) to settle any *dispute of right* relating to matters covered by the agreement is precluded. More importantly, as a consequence of management insistence, two-thirds of collective agreements go

further and contain an 'absolute' or 'unlimited' peace obligation which precludes the use of industrial action on any matter during the term of the agreement (i.e. including *disputes of interest* relating to matters not covered by the existing agreement). The peace obligation ceases when the collective agreement expires.

The system of voluntary absolute peace obligations was first introduced in 1937 in the watchmaking and metalworking industries (with government support) as an alternative to the government's measures in the previous year to introduce compulsory arbitration to prevent wage increases following the devaluing of the Swiss franc. The system became more prevalent from the 1950s as part of the general expansion of trade union recognition and collective bargaining following a period of high strike activity during the late 1940s.

The arbitration tribunals are relatively legalistic in that they are chaired by a judge (accompanied by one union and one employer nominee) and take place in a courtroom. The tribunal may, before making a formal arbitration award, put forward a mediation proposal for the parties to consider and hopefully form the basis of their own settlement. Any breach of the peace obligation may result in a fine (not as a form of compensatory damages but rather to maintain the integrity of the agreement).

Sources: G. Aubert, 'Collective agreements and industrial peace in Switzerland', *International Labour Review*, vol. 128, no. 3, 1989, pp. 373–88; 'Switzerland: the role of arbitration tribunals', *European Industrial Relations Review*, no. 224, September 1992, pp. 22–3; 'Switzerland: industrial relations background', *European Industrial Relations Review*, no. 240, January 1994, pp. 30–3; R. Fluder and B. Hotz-Hart, 'Switzerland: still as smooth as clockwork?', in A. Ferner and R. Hyman, *Changing Industrial Relations in Europe*, Blackwell, 1998, pp. 262–82.

majority of agreements in the UK do not exclude disputes of interest from the possibility of arbitration, subject only to the fact that they are normally matters for negotiation.

■ **Method of referral**. There are three possible methods of referral:
  ▎ *unilateral*, where either party has the right to invoke arbitration without the consent of the other;
  ▎ *joint*, where both parties have to agree to refer the matter to arbitration;
  ▎ *automatic*, where the issue goes to arbitration if it remains unresolved after a certain stage in the negotiating or disputes procedure.

The last method is, in effect, a joint referral because it involves a prior joint acceptance of the use of arbitration for unresolved differences. The majority of agreements in the UK provide for a joint or automatic method of referral. However, it is important to ensure that any referral is preceded by conciliation.

- **Arbitration body**. The agreement should specify how the arbitration is to be conducted – by a single arbitrator or a board of arbitration, on a permanent or an *ad hoc* basis. The majority of arbitration in the UK is conducted by a single arbitrator who must, of course, be acceptable to both parties. Where a board of arbitration is used it is quite common for the employer and trade union to select one member each and either jointly, or through ACAS, agree on an independent chairperson. Clearly, whether the arbitrator is to be permanent will depend largely on the extent to which the parties believe that such services will be needed.

- **Standing of the arbitration award**. The parties must agree, either when drawing up the procedure or prior to each arbitration, whether the arbitration award is to be binding on them. The alternative is to accept that the award will be used only as a basis for further negotiation between the parties. Normally, arbitrators do not give, and are not asked to give, the reasons for their decision because this is more likely to provoke further argument and disagreement between the parties.

12.3 Advisory, conciliation and arbitration service (ACAS)

Conciliation and arbitration, on both a voluntary and statutory basis, have a long history in the UK. Legislation can be traced back to the Statute of Apprentices (1562) and during the nineteenth century there were attempts to legislate for conciliation and arbitration in both specific industries, such as the Cotton Arbitration Act (1800) which dealt with some 1,500 cases in three years, and on a more general basis, such as the Arbitration Act (1824)[55].

The framework of modern state support for conciliation and arbitration was established at the turn of the twentieth century:

- **Conciliation Act (1896)** gave the minister general powers to investigate the cause and circumstances of any dispute and to appoint a conciliator (on an application from either party) or an arbitrator (on a joint application from both parties).

- **Industrial Courts Acts (1919)** established a permanent arbitration body (tripartite in character, involving employer and union nominees as well as independent persons) to which the minister could refer a dispute provided that both parties consented to arbitration, and that any arrangements for conciliation or arbitration within the industry had been exhausted.

The Industrial Court was retitled the Industrial Arbitration Committee in 1971 and then the **Central Arbitration Committee** (CAC) in 1975. CAC arbitration panels, comprising an independent chairman and two 'side' members drawn from employer and trade union panels, normally sit in public and receive both written and oral evidence from the parties concerned. The CAC inherited a unilateral arbitration function under the Fair Wages Resolution of the House of Commons (this required organisations in receipt of government contracts to provide terms and conditions of employment comparable to those usually applied within the industry). Its unilateral arbitration role was expanded to cover pay structures or collective agreements which were discriminatory (Equal Pay Act, 1970) and union recognition claims, disclosure of information to trade unions and Schedule 11 claims that an employer was not observing recognised or general terms and conditions of employment (Employment Protection Act, 1975). However, the Employment Act (1980) repealed the statutory union recognition procedure and Schedule 11 and, in 1983, the Conservative government abolished the Fair Wages Resolution. Consequently, the CAC's role has been confined to voluntary arbitration requests and unilateral arbitration in respect of equal pay claims and disclosure of information claims, however, its role in arbitrating on union recognition claims has been restored under the new statutory union recognition procedure (Employment Relations Act, 1999).

See Chapter 6 – Representation at the workplace

The 1919 Act also gave the minister power to set up *ad hoc* **Courts of Inquiry**. These have been used on a limited number of occasions in the past, when a particular dispute involved matters of major importance affecting the public interest. Their function is to investigate a dispute and then report and make recommendations to the minister who, in turn, is required to present the report to Parliament. A Court of Inquiry, Sharp argued, differs from the operation of the CAC in that its objective is 'not so much to settle the case by direct contact with the parties as to elucidate the facts for the benefit of the parties and public'[56] and 'serves a need where an airing of issues in the glare of deep publicity is a useful safety valve in an intractable dispute of general importance'[57]. In so doing, of course, its report has often provided the basis for a resolution of the dispute.

The responsibility for providing conciliation and arbitration mechanisms rests with the government, and the conciliation service of the Department of Employment achieved a high degree of respect and acceptance from both management and unions. However, by the early 1970s the independence of the service was under great pressure from two directions. First, many people began to perceive, within a government-administered conciliation and arbitration service, a conflict between its role in resolving disputes and the maintenance of the government's incomes policy. Second, with the advent of the Industrial Relations Act (1971), the industrial relations system became subject to greater legislative regulation, involving new bodies such as the National Industrial Relations Court and the Commission on Industrial Relations (CIR) and new roles for the conciliation and arbitration service. Consequently, as Farnham and Pimlott note, in the early 1970s 'the long-established voluntary system of state conciliation and arbitration almost ceased to exist' and 'a body of opinion emerged, representative of both trade unions and employers, which called for the establishment of a conciliation and arbitration service independent of government control and civil service influence'[58].

This led, in 1974, to the establishment of the Advisory, Conciliation and Arbitration Service (ACAS). Its Council consists of a full-time chairperson and 11 part-time members (including senior national union officers, directors of HRM and senior academics). Although they are appointed by the Secretary of State, **ACAS's independence** derives from it not being 'subject to directions of any kind from any Minister ... as to the manner in which it is to exercise any of its functions' (Para 11(1), Schedule 1, Employment Protection Act, 1975). Jim Mortimer, former Chairman of ACAS, notes that under the Labour government ACAS 'decided that [it] should not act as the interpreter, monitor and, least of all, as enforcement agent for the incomes policy' and under the Conservative government it 'decided not to be involved in drawing up the codes of practice on picketing and the closed shop'[59] because in both situations it could be seen as instrumental in carrying out government policy. However, while it has been government policy not to interfere in the day-to-day activities or decisions of ACAS, this has not precluded the government from determining ACAS's broad policy. Thus, the Conservative government removed the duty to 'encourage collective bargaining' in 1993 and, in 1999, the 'new' Labour government has removed the requirement to give priority to dispute resolution (so that it can focus on dispute prevention).

In 1998 ACAS handled some 508,000 calls for information and advice through its Public Enquiry Points (more than half from individual employees) and organised 466 conferences, seminars and workshops. The other areas of ACAS work may be divided between collective conciliation, arbitration, advisory mediation and individual conciliation.

Collective conciliation

See Case study 12.1

ACAS is available to provide conciliation at the request of either or both parties involved in a collective dispute or may offer to conciliate on its own initiative. It maintains the tradition of not seeking to conciliate where existing organisational or industry procedures have not been exhausted or where one party is opposed to the intervention of conciliation. Indeed, in 1997 and 1998 industrial action was avoided in over 90 per cent of the cases it handled.

It is important to note that the number of requests for collective conciliation not only rose substantially when ACAS was created, but has remained consistently above the number of stoppages in the UK (see Figure 12.3). Although the number of collective conciliation cases declined during the 1980s, in line with the decline in the number of stoppages, it remained relatively constant at about 1,200 cases per year through the 1990s while the number of stoppages declined further. ACAS believes that this confirms its acceptability as a conciliator and its ability to help secure a settlement before industrial action takes place.

An analysis of the issues and sources of requests for collective conciliation (see Table 12.1) shows that pay and conditions of employment remain the most frequent issue (although they have declined from 61 per cent of all cases in 1978 to 48 per cent in 1998). Trade union recognition, the second largest group in 1978 (17 per cent) has dropped to third place (11 per cent) in 1998, attributable to a general decline in new instances of trade union recognition

Case study 12.1 ■ Rail transport and shipping

Case 1 – Rail transport

'Talks between Merseyrail Electrics Ltd and the Associated Society of Locomotive Engineers and Firemen (ASLEF) had failed to find agreement over the restructuring of working practices and terms and conditions of employment of train drivers. Twelve one-day strikes had taken place between November 1997 and February 1998. ACAS had provided concili-ation, but no solution emerged. With further action due to commence on 20 February, the parties responded to an invitation by ACAS to attend further talks ...

The conciliation was held over four days and covered a list of items including pay, leave, sick arrangements, overtime and a raft of flexibilities. The talks produced a basis for settlement which included an agreement to allow the status quo to prevail on the long-term sick arrangements whilst ACAS facilitated a joint attempt to reduce absence levels. Otherwise the agreement, through consolidation of allowances and productivity and efficiency improvements, proposed a total restructuring of the working practices and condi-tion of employment of drivers. The union negotiators agreed to recommend acceptance to their National Executive Committee (NEC). The NEC accepted this recommendation ... , suspended the strikes ... and rec-ommended acceptance of the offer by the drivers'. In the subsequent ballot, 84 per cent voted to accept the offer (on a 90 per cent turnout).

Case 2 – Shipping

'A dispute broke out between Cory Ship Towage, Milford Haven and its tug crews, represented by the Transport and General Workers Union (TGWU), over the amount of salvage award paid to the workforce following the *Sea Empress* disaster ...

Every salvage vessel involved in the operation is entitled to a share of the salvage award. Cory Ship Towage was awarded a gross amount of money from which the Company was entitled to deduct any costs incurred during the course of the salvage. By the time all the deductions had been made, the crewmen were set to receive an award somewhere in the region of £1,000 each.

During the course of conciliation in April 1998 the focus of attention was on the deductions claimed by the company as its legitimate costs incurred during the operation. The appropriate records were scruti-nised and some items were identified as "normal running costs" and others as expenses not necessarily directly incurred as part of the salvage operation. By this means, and by dint of persuading the company to make a goodwill gesture, the award per crewman was increased by £1000. In this particular case the role of the conciliator was to bring the parties from a con-frontational mode to a more collaborative, joint problem solving approach'.

Source: ACAS, *Annual Report*, 1998.

since the peak in the early 1970s, the demise of the statutory recognition proce-dure (Employment Act, 1980) and less preparedness by management to accept conciliation on this issue. Significantly, the proportion of cases relating to dis-missal, discipline and redundancy has increased from 11 per cent in 1978 to 25 per cent in 1998. It is also important to note that the proportion of requests for collective conciliation coming solely from the trade union side has declined from 56 per cent in 1978 to 32 per cent in 1998 while joint requests, although a slight decline in absolute numbers, increased in proportional terms from 22 per cent in 1978 to 41 per cent in 1998. ACAS-initiated conciliation, on the other hand, has risen from 3 per cent of the total in 1978 to 17 per cent in 1998.

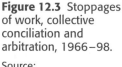

Figure 12.3 Stoppages of work, collective conciliation and arbitration, 1966–98.

Source:
ACAS, *Annual Report*, 1982, pp. 20, 30 (for period 1966–82); ACAS, *Annual Reports*, 1994–98

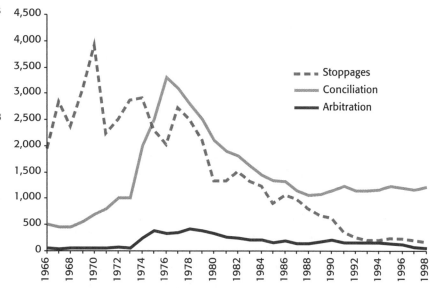

Table 12.1 Analysis of collective conciliation

(a) By cause of dispute	1978	1998
Pay and conditions of employment	1652	581
Trade union recognition	451	131
Demarcation and changes in working practices	26	77
Other trade union matters	130	80
Redundancy	91	144
Dismissal and discipline	218	157
Others	138	44
Total	2706	1214

(a) By source of request	1978	1998
Union	1507	384
Employer	504	126
Joint	607	502
ACAS	88	202
Total	2706	1214

Arbitration

ACAS officials do not, themselves, arbitrate. To do so would be detrimental to the confidentiality and impartiality of their conciliation role. It is felt that it would seriously affect the relationship between the conciliator and the two parties in dispute if the same people or organisation might be called upon to decide the issue by arbitration. However, ACAS does make provision, if both parties wish, for the appointment of a single arbitrator or board of arbitration or the referral of the dispute to the CAC – ACAS also has responsibility for maintaining the CAC and Police Arbitration Panel. Neither ACAS arbitrators nor the CAC give reasons for their award decisions: as the CAC stated in the late 1970s, 'what [the parties] want above all is settlement. To give reasons is to invite yet another reconsideration of the various issues – with a good chance of renewed strife. The nuances of the words chosen to express the reasons may rekindle old disputes'[60].

It is important to note that, like collective conciliation, the number of requests for arbitration rose after the creation of ACAS, although since 1978 the number has steadily declined in line with the decline in the number of stoppages. Significantly, ACAS noted in 1996 that the majority of arbitration cases followed on from ACAS's prior, unsuccessful, involvement with the parties through conciliation, rather than a direct reference to arbitration in accordance with the terms of a collective agreement[61]. In 1997, it noted an 'unusual development' in that all but one of the cases dealt with that year involved interpretation of an existing agreement rather than determining a 'new' claim[62]. However, the number of arbitration cases dropped sharply in 1997 and 1998 because of a significant fall in two groups of cases – grading cases and dismissal cases from collective procedures in the electricity supply industry. The number of arbitrations relating to pay and conditions of employment has dropped from 360 in 1978 to only 34 in 1998 (although these still account for 67 per cent of the total) (see Table 12.2).

The second largest group of cases relate to 'dismissal and discipline' (25 per cent). Perhaps the most significant feature is the fact that issues such as 'trade union recognition', 'demarcation', 'other trade union matters and 'redundancy' are no longer designated as specific categories in the ACAS statistics (perhaps reflecting the change in industrial relations climate, the perceived diminution in the role of unions in the 1980s or the inappropriateness of arbitration for resolving such disputes).

Advisory mediation

ACAS has sought to promote advisory mediation as a 'co-operative and joint problem solving approach' which 'can help prevent disputes occurring, tackle

Table 12.2 Analysis of issues for collective arbitration and mediation

1978			1998		
Pay and conditions of employment	360	86%	Annual pay	11	22%
			Other pay and conditions of employment	22	43%
			Grading	1	2%
			Sub-total	34	67%
Trade union recognition	-				
Demarcation	9				
Other trade union matters	4				
Redundancy	1				
Sub-total	14	3%			
Dismissal and discipline	39	9%	Dismissal and discipline	13	25%
Others	8	2%	Others	4	8%
Total	421		*Total*	51	

Source: ACAS, *Annual Reports*.

underlying issues and problems, develop better solutions, encourage an acceptance of changes and can result in more constructive long-term working relationships'[63]. It utilises two mechanisms, both of which are regarded as non-negotiating situations. First, it helps organise a *workshop* of employer and employee representatives to discuss and identify the potential barriers and problems which may be hindering the organisation's performance. This is followed by a *joint working party* to tackle the issues identified through a structured problem-solving approach of definition, analysis, evaluation, selection and implementation. ACAS staff may chair these meetings to support the discussions between management and employees.

Individual conciliation

ACAS also has an important role to perform in relation to legislation on individual rights (see Box 12.3). It has a duty, after the individual has made a complaint to an Employment Tribunal, to seek a conciliated settlement if either party requests it or if ACAS considers there is a reasonable prospect of success. To this end, ACAS receives copies of all originating applications (IT1) and respondent replies received by the Employment Tribunals. In addition, the individual can take a claim to ACAS that action has been taken in respect of which a complaint *could* be made to a Tribunal. These are generally referred to as 'non-IT1 cases' and in 1998 only some 1,700 (1.5 per cent) of the cases received by ACAS came into this category – compared with 17,724 (36 per cent) in 1989. In 1990 ACAS noted that 'almost all of these cases were in the unfair dismissal jurisdiction and virtually all were brought to the Service's attention by employers rather than employees'[64]. This confirmed a problem which ACAS had identified in 1984 when they criticised some managements for seeking, through ACAS conciliation, 'our assistance in "rubber stamping" agreements already made to "ease out" employees specifically in order to prevent any subsequent claim being determined by a tribunal'[65] – an agreement reached during ACAS conciliation debars an employee from making a claim to the Employment Tribunal. The principal role of the conciliation officer is to offer assistance to the parties involved to help them establish the facts and clarify their views and to seek where possible, a conciliated settlement. In ACAS's view this should not 'in any way affect or limit the rights of individuals to pursue complaints to industrial tribunals'[66] nor 'seek to persuade complainants to withdraw'[67]. Importantly, the Employment Rights (Dispute Resolution) Act (1998) has given ACAS the power to offer the option of arbitration in individual as well as collective disputes. This will be an alternative to the legal Tribunal system and should be 'relatively informal, confidential, certain, consistently prompt, free from legal constraints of case law and avoids the adversarial nature of tribunal proceedings'[68].

In 1998 ACAS received over 113,000 individual conciliation cases: more than double the number of cases in 1980 (see Table 12.3). The increase is largely accounted for by the advent of new jurisdictions: the Wages Act (1986) relating to non-payment of wages due, wages in lieu of notice, etc. and breach of contract cases under the Trade Union Reform and Employment Rights Act

---

Box 12.3   The benefits of individual conciliation

'... an ACAS Public Enquiry Point received an emotional call from the wife of a man who had just been summarily dismissed, having reported late for work. The matter was passed immediately to an ACAS conciliator who talked to the man and found out that although he had not made a claim to an employment tribunal, he felt he had been unfairly dismissed because of his race. The employee said he had telephoned his workplace earlier that day to say that he had a medical problem with his eyes and would be in late. However, when he arrived at work his employer summarily dismissed him. The conciliator contacted the employer later the same day when he received a different slant to events. He was told that the man had a history of lateness and although he had admonished him, the employer emphasised that he had not dismissed the man. After some discussion with both parties about the issues, the conciliator was told by the employer that he did not want to lose the employee and the employee said he wanted to retain his job. It was therefore agreed through ACAS that the employee would report for work the following day'.

Source: ACAS, *Annual Report*, 1998, p. 78.

Table 12.3 Individual conciliation

	Unfair dismissal		All discrimination[1]		Protection of wages		Breach of contract		Other		Total	
	1980	1998	1980	1998	1980	1998	1980	1998	1980	1998	1980	1998
Received	41 925	40 153	1063	16 260	n/a	24 981	n/a	23 576	3457	8664	46 445	113 636
Settled	18 072	17 888	144	5 670	n/a	8 765	n/a	8 395	1028	3345	19 244	44 063
Withdrawn	8 637	10 423	354	5 289	n/a	8 108	n/a	6 389	1311	2477	10 302	32 686
To Tribunal	11 445	10 975	376	3 162	n/a	6 899	n/a	5 976	1108	2051	12 929	29 063
Completed	38 154	39 286	874	14 121	n/a	23 772	n/a	20 760	3447	7873	42 475	105 812

[1] This includes cases under Equal Pay Act (1970), Sex Discrimination Act (1975), Race Relations Act (1976) and Disability Discrimination Act (1996).
Source: ACAS, *Annual Reports*.

(1993), the majority relating to claims for notice and holiday pay. The number of unfair dismissal cases remain relatively constant at about 40,000 but have declined as a proportion of the total cases from 90 per cent in 1980 to 35 per cent in 1998. ACAS notes that 'cases are becoming more complex, with many applicants claiming under several jurisdictions' and this 'placed additional responsibilities upon conciliation officers, who had to ensure that all issues were discussed, clarified and understood by the parties and that all outstanding matters were covered in any resulting settlement'[69]. Overall, ACAS appears to have a large measure of success in its individual conciliation role with some 42 per cent of cases being settled by conciliation. Furthermore, ACAS believes that, unlike a Tribunal hearing, its involvement in individual conciliation allows it to identify underlying problems in an organisation and propose strategies which might help resolve them.

■ Summary propositions

- ■ Conciliation and arbitration provide channels through which management and unions may, if they wish, seek to resolve their differences by introducing a third party; the availability or use of such processes does not automatically mean an avoidance or reduction in the use of industrial action.
- ■ Conciliation is supportive of the joint regulatory collective bargaining process, while arbitration, on any extensive scale, may undermine that process.
- ■ The 'winner takes all' concept underlying pendulum arbitration is incompatible with the principles of compromise and flexibility underlying the negotiation process and organisational experience in the UK suggests that it requires modification to bring it closer to conventional 'open' arbitration.

Activity   Try to think of a past situation in which you had a 'dispute' with another person or with an organisation which was difficult to resolve (it could have been with a neighbour, or a complaint to a shop or supplier about poor goods or service). You might have been able to refer it to a 'third party' for conciliation or arbitration and, if you did, what was your experience (were you satisfied)? If there wasn't one but you would have liked there to be one, would you have expected it to 'represent' you rather than 'conciliate' or 'arbitrate' between you and the other person?

■ Further reading

- ■ ILO, *Conciliation and Arbitration Procedures in Labour Disputes*, 1980. This provides an extensive comparative study of both conciliation and arbitration, in particular, the government's role.
- ■ P. Lowry, *Employment Disputes and the Third Party*, Macmillan, 1990. This is a useful examination of the work of ACAS by a former Chairman of ACAS.
- ■ C. J. Bruce and J. Carby-Hall, *Rethinking Labour–Management Relations: The case for arbitration*, Routledge, 1991. This contrasts the use of a compulsory arbitration system for resolving disputes with the more traditional strike-threat system.
- ■ ACAS, *Annual Reports*.

References

1. ILO, *Conciliation and Arbitration Procedures in Labour Disputes*, 1980, p. v.
2. Professor Sir J. Wood, 'The case for arbitration', *Personnel Management*, October 1980, p. 52.
3. ACAS, *Annual Report*, 1998, p. 39.
4. ACAS, *Annual Report*, 1997, p. 33.
5. ILO, *op. cit.*
6. Wood, *op. cit.*
7. C. Margerison and M. Leary, *Managing Industrial Conflict: The Mediator's Role*, MCB Books, 1975, p. 3.
8. ILO, *op. cit.*, p. 15.
9. Margerison and Leary, *op. cit.*
10. J. F. B. Goodman and J. Krislov, 'Conciliation in industrial disputes in Great Britain: a survey of the attitudes of the parties', *British Journal of Industrial Relations*, November 1974, p. 336.
11. S. Kessler, 'The prevention and settlement of collective labour disputes in the UK', *Industrial Relations Journal*, vol. 11, no. 1, 1980, p. 17.
12. P. Lowry, *Employment Disputes and the Third Party*, Macmillan, 1990, p. 85.
13. *Ibid.*, pp. 38–9.
14. Goodman and Krislov, *op. cit.*, pp. 341–8.
15. Lowry, *op. cit.*, p. 31.
16. *Ibid.*, p. 22.
17. Goodman and Krislov, *op. cit.*, p. 340.
18. ILO, *op. cit.*, p. 31.
19. J. J. Loewenberg, W. J. Gershenfeld, H. J. Glasbeek, B. A. Hepple and K. F. Walker, *Compulsory Arbitration*, Lexington Books, 1976, p. 210.
20. R. Hyman, *Strikes* (3rd edn), Fontana, 1984, p. 114.
21. Goodman and Krislov, *op. cit.*, p. 347.
22. W. E. J. McCarthy and N. D. Ellis, *Management by Agreement*, Hutchinson, 1973, p. 125.
23. Goodman and Krislov, *op. cit.*, p. 349.
24. McCarthy and Ellis, *op. cit.*, p. 124.
25. B. Hepple, 'Compulsory arbitration in Britain', in J. J. Loewenberg *et al.*, *op. cit.*, p. 88.
26. *Ibid.*
27. *Ibid.*
28. K. F. Walker, *Industrial Relations in Australia*, Harvard University Press, 1956, p. 365.
29. Loewenberg *et al.*, *op. cit.*, p. 185.
30. *Ibid.*
31. W. E. J. McCarthy, 'Three studies in collective bargaining', Research Paper No. 8, *Royal Commission on Trade Unions and Employers' Associations*, HMSO, 1968, p. 42.
32. Lowry, *op. cit.*, p. 83.
33. 'Single union deals', *IRS Employment Trends*, no. 442, June 1989.
34. Sir J. Wood, 'Last offer arbitration', *British Journal of Industrial Relations*, vol. 20, no. 3, 1985, pp. 414–24; J. G. Treble, 'How new is final offer arbitration?' *Industrial Relations*, vol. 25, no. 1, 1986; A. Brown, 'Research findings show that criticisms of the arbitration process are mostly without foundation', *Personnel Management*, May 1990.
35. ACAS, *Annual Report*, 1984, p. 39.
36. Brown, *op. cit.*, p. 2.
37. C. Stevens, 'Is compulsory arbitration compatible with bargaining?' *Industrial Relations*, vol. 5, no. 2, 1966.
38. C. J. Bruce and J. Carby-Hall, *Rethinking Labour–Management relations: The case for arbitration*, Routledge, 1991, p. 91.
39. S. Kessler, 'The swings and roundabouts of pendulum arbitration', *Personnel Management*, December 1987, pp. 40, 42.
40. D. Yeandle and J. Clark, 'Growing a compatible IR setup', *Personnel Management*, July 1989.
41. R. Singh, 'Final offer arbitration in theory and practice', *Industrial Relations Journal*, winter 1986, pp. 329–30.
42. Institute of Directors, *Settling Disputes Peacefully*, 1984.
43. P. Bassett, *Strike Free: New industrial relations in Britain*, Macmillan, 1987, p. 116.
44. Kessler (1987), *op. cit.*, p. 40.
45. R. Lewis, 'Strike-free deals and pendulum arbitration', *British Journal of Industrial Relations*, vol. 28, no. 1, 1990, p. 49.
46. Singh, *op. cit.*, p. 334.
47. Sanyo management quoted in Kessler (1987), *op. cit.*, p. 41.
48. *Ibid.*
49. ACAS, *Annual Report*, 1987, p. 22.
50. Kessler (1987), *op. cit.*, p. 40.
51. D. G. Gallaher and M. D. Chaubey, 'Impasse behaviour and tri-offer arbitration in Iowa', *Industrial Relations*, vol. 21, no. 2, 1982, pp. 129–47; R. Hoh, 'The effectiveness of mediation in public sector mediation systems: the Iowa experience', *The Arbitrator's Journal*, vol. 39, no. 2, 1984, pp. 20–40.
52. W. Brown, *The Changing Contours of British*

Industrial Relations, Blackwell, 1981, pp. 47–50.

53. Lowry, *op. cit.*, p. 15.
54. N. Millward and M. Stevens, *British Workplace Industrial Relations 1980–84*, Gower, 1986, table 7.6, p. 181.
55. See I. G. Sharp, *Industrial Conciliation and Arbitration in Great Britain*, Allen & Unwin, 1950.
56. *Ibid.*, p. 362.
57. Wood (1980), *op. cit.*, pp. 52–3.
58. D. Farnham and J. Pimlott, *Understanding Industrial Relations* (5th edn), Cassell, 1995, p. 225.
59. J. Mortimer, 'ACAS in a changing climate: a force for good IR?' *Personnel Management*, February 1981, p. 24.
60. CAC, *Annual Report*, 1977, p. 21.
61. ACAS, *Annual Report*, 1996, p. 57.
62. ACAS (1997), *op. cit.*, p. 59.
63. *Ibid.*, p. 43.
64. ACAS, *Annual Report*, 1990, p. 26.
65. ACAS (1984), *op. cit.*, p. 63.
66. ACAS (1990), *op. cit.*, p. 28.
67. ACAS, *Annual Report*, 1978, p. 79.
68. ACAS (1997), *op.cit.*, p. 75.
69. ACAS, *Annual Report*, 1995, p. 51.

part four

Practices

chapter thirteen

Negotiation

Learning objectives

Without negotiation, the determination of the employment relationship would simply be a matter of management imposition. By the end of this chapter, you should be able to:

■ explain the role of the negotiator, in particular, the task and skills required and the importance of the relationship with the people he or she represents;

■ understand the phases of a negotiation and the strategies used within the encounter, in particular, preparation and the identification of bargaining limits and the use of information, argument and persuasion to modify expectations and secure movement;

■ appreciate the importance of securing and maintaining a relationship of trust between negotiators.

Definition

The term negotiation applies to a particular process of dialogue between people to resolve their differences and reach an agreement. In industrial relations this is conducted primarily through representatives of management and employees.

Key issues

While you are reading this chapter, you should keep the following points in mind:

■ We all negotiate at some time or other in our normal lives – buying or selling a house, car, etc. or complaining about poor goods or service. We feel we have a 'good case', we want something better than we are being offered and so we try to persuade another person to shift their position and offer something which is more acceptable. Industrial relations 'negotiations' are just the same.

■ Negotiation takes place between *people* and we need to have confidence in each other, be able to respect each other and have trust in each other. In other words, negotiation is not about winning by threats or subterfuge.

13.1   Introduction

Unfortunately, and confusingly, the terms 'collective bargaining' and 'negotiation' often appear to be used synonymously. It is perhaps more useful to regard negotiations as part of collective bargaining. The term 'collective bargaining' emphasises the structural or institutional arrangements of industrial relations and encompasses the parties, goals, environments and content as well as the processes utilised in resolving the conflict of interest between management and employees. The process of negotiating has been described by Walton and McKersie as 'the deliberate interaction of two or more complex social units which are attempting to define or redefine the terms of their interdependence'[1]; by Gottschalk as 'an occasion where one or more representatives of two or more parties interact in an explicit attempt to reach a jointly acceptable position on one or more divisive issues'[2]; by Brown as 'an intentional activity carried out between representatives whose role is legitimized by those whom they represent'[3].

The essential characteristics of a negotiation are as follows:

- It is an explicit and deliberate event.
- It is conducted by representatives on behalf of their principals.
- The process is intended to reconcile differences between the parties involved.
- The outcome is dependent, at least in part, on the perceived relative power relationship between the participants.

It is important to recognise, however, first that the process of negotiation involves both intra- as well as inter-organisational aspects (it takes place both within the management and employee or union groupings as well as between them) and, second, that it is just as likely to occur between an individual employee representative and management at the department or section level in the context of handling grievances, discipline, etc. as it is to be utilised by senior management, personnel specialists or union full-time officers at the organisational level in the context of the wage negotiations or other major issues.

13.2   The negotiator

The negotiator, whether as an individual or as part of a negotiating team, is carrying out a task on behalf of an interest group. It is only by interacting with negotiators representing other interest groups that a reconciliation of the groups' differing interests can be achieved. A negotiator must, through the process of negotiation, seek to become as aware of the goals, aspirations and strategies of the other interest groups as his or her own.

The psychological basis of negotiation

It may be argued that the **relative real power advantage** between management and employees is a more important determinant of the final outcome of any negotiations than the skills and abilities of the individual negotiators[4]. Indeed, some would say that, because management's ability to withhold employment permanently by closing the organisation is seen as a far more powerful sanction than the employees' limited ability to withhold their labour on a temporary basis, management has an inherent power advantage in negotiations and is able to determine both the issues and limits of any negotiation. Negotiations may be regarded as merely a facade of marginal issues and gains. However, if the underlying assumption (that management is prepared at *all* times and for *any* reason to close its organisation permanently) is untrue, then the power relationship between the two parties must be regarded as being both more balanced (but not necessarily equally balanced) and more variable from one negotiation to another, with both management and employees being prepared to accept the short-term, temporary closure of the organisation as a means of exerting pressure on each other.

Torrington and Hall note that while the 'power of the two parties may not actually be equal ... they are both willing to behave as if it were'[5]. However, this apparent 'power equalisation' within the negotiation process will only exist if there is the desire, on both sides, to take account of the needs of the opposing interest group and seek an agreement which is mutually acceptable. It is the **perceived relative bargaining advantage** which is important in conditioning both the behaviour of the negotiators and the outcome of their negotiations. Bargaining advantage may be expressed in terms of each side's perception of the relative costs to the other side of agreeing or not agreeing (see Figure 13.1). For example, management will perceive itself to have a bargaining advantage if it believes the costs, to the union and employees, of not agreeing to its offer outweigh the costs of agreeing. Generally these costs are difficult to quantify. In addition to assessing the potential financial cost to union and employees of undertaking industrial action to secure an improved offer, management must also 'cost' such items as the failure of the union negotiators to meet their members' expectations and their desire to maintain credibility with their members. It is possible, on this basis, for both sides to enter a negotiation with a *perceived* bargaining advantage over the other. These initial perceptions of bargaining advantage, and therefore the perceived relative bargaining power, will be refined during the course of the negotiations as more information regarding the objectives and strategies of both parties becomes available.

Magenau and Pruitt[6] put forward **a model of negotiating behaviour** based on three variables: the motivation of the negotiator to maintain a demand (MD) or to reach an agreement (MA) and the level of trust between the negotiators (see Figure 13.2). They argue that the strength of the motivation to maintain a demand (MD) is determined by the perception of relative bargaining power and the level of aspiration underlying the demand, while the strength of the motivation to reach an agreement (MA) is determined by the perceived value of the agreement and the urgency with which it is sought. It is the balance between these two motivations, related to the level of trust between the negotiators, which produces different negotiating behaviour. Thus, even where there is high trust, if the motivation to maintain a demand significantly exceeds the motivation to reach an agreement (MD > MA), the likely outcome is the adoption of distributive bargaining behaviour based on coercion of the other party. If, on

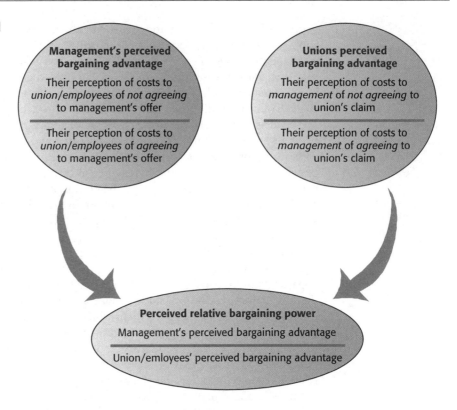

Figure 13.1 Perceived bargaining advantage

the other hand, the motivation to reach an agreement significantly exceeds the motivation to maintain the demand (MA >MD), the behaviour pattern adopted is likely to be concessionary. However, it is in the middle area, where motivation to maintain the demand and motivation to reach an agreement are approximately equal, that 'neither distributive behaviour nor simple concession making seems appropriate, and the bargainer takes co-ordinative initiatives to the extent that he trusts the other'[7]. In a similar way, Walton *et al*. distinguish between *forcing strategies* which centre around 'distributive bargaining, structuring attitudes to emphasize hostility toward the other side, and managing internal differences to promote solidarity on one's own side while exploiting divisions on the other side', and *fostering strategies*, which centre on 'integrative bargaining, structuring attitudes to emphasize trust, and managing for consensus in both parties'[8]. It is this latter negotiation strategy which, arguably, should predominate within any 'partnership' approach to the employment relationship. However, most negotiations take place in, or move towards, the centre area of the Magenau and Pruitt model, involve a range of issues on which the parties may have different levels of motivation, and are based on constrained, not unreserved, trust relationships. Consequently, it is not unusual to find a variety of negotiating behaviour being displayed within a single negotiation.

The existence of a desire on the part of both parties to reach a mutually satisfactory conclusion to their negotiations does not preclude the **threat, or use, of industrial sanctions** by either party. Indeed, Hawkins argued that 'the ability of each side to apply sanctions is a fundamental aspect of their bargaining power'[9],

See Chapter 9 –
Collective bargaining

See Chapter 11 –
Industrial action

as is, therefore, the accompanying feeling of duress it may create in the other side. The use of threats during negotiations, whether implicit or explicit, may be regarded as part of the necessary flow of information between negotiators in order to arrive at a common view of their relative bargaining advantage. If the threat is unsuccessful in achieving this common view, because the recipient implicitly rejects its validity or strength, the party making the threat must then decide whether to demonstrate its validity and strength by carrying out the threat. The perceived relative bargaining advantage will then be confirmed or modified by whether or not the sanction is imposed and, if it is, the effect it has. The use of threats and their implementation are intended as a demonstration and confirmation by one party that their perception of the relative bargaining advantage is correct, and also to produce a changed perception in the other party and therefore a more favourable settlement. They are not, generally, used as an attempt to impose one party's initial position on the other.

The successful conclusion of a negotiation is largely dependent on the negotiators' assessment or judgement of the other party's position and intention. This will be derived from the negotiators' **perception of what is said and how it is said**. In this context it is important to remember that 'perception is reality' and therefore, as Warr pointed out, 'habits, expectations, attitudes and prejudices ... affect what we see and the conclusions we draw'[10]. Not only will negotiators for different interest groups interpret data and arguments in different ways during the course of the negotiations, but different members of the same negotiating team may interpret the course and outcome of the negotiations differently dependent on their perceptions, recall and emphasis. Furthermore, negotiations involve an interpersonal process between the negotiators which overlays the inter-organisational aspect inherent in their representational role. Certainly Warr emphasised that the perception of the negotiators comprises a mixture of 'emotional, feeling reactions with conclusions drawn from factual information'[11]. The manner of the negotiators and their personal relationships, therefore, may be as influential as facts and arguments in determining the outcome of a negotiation.

All negotiations involve some degree of **pressure or stress for the negotiators**. Such pressures may arise not only from the difficulties inherent in seeking

Figure 13.2
A model of negotiating behaviour

Source: J. M. Magenau and D. G. Pruitt, 'The social psychology of bargaining', in G. M. Stephenson and C. J. Brotherton (eds), *Industrial Relations: A social psychological approach*, John Wiley, 1979, p. 204.

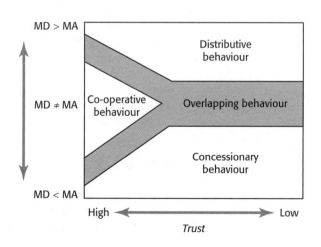

to identify how a compromise may be achieved but also from such additional pressures as extremely long or complex negotiating sessions, the imposition of 'unreasonable' time constraints within which a settlement has to be reached, the perceived high cost of a 'wrong' decision, perceived 'unreasonable' demands being exerted on the negotiator by either his or her principals or the other negotiator, or even a desire on the part of the negotiator to be seen to 'succeed'. Warr believed that on such 'occasions when balanced, complex judgement is required, psychologically we close up under tension and fall back on simpler all-or-nothing reactions'[12]. The hardening of attitudes and positions resulting from such pressures is counter to the flexibility generally required from negotiators in order to establish areas of compromise. If negotiators perceive themselves to be under such pressure, it is likely to be communicated to the other negotiator by subjecting them in turn to demands which may begin to be perceived as being 'unreasonable' and may result in a 'take it or leave it' conclusion to the negotiation.

Warr argued that, in order to achieve a mutually satisfactory compromise, negotiators must 'persuade, cajole and coerce each other to move their positions closer together'[13]. Most negotiators, while recognising the **necessity of making concessions** by moving away from their initial position, are nevertheless often hesitant to make such moves and may even regard them as tantamount to a loss on their part. This perception of concessions equating to loss may arise in two ways:

- Once a concession is offered (unless offered on a conditional basis), it cannot easily be withdrawn and, therefore, tactically it represents a reduction in the bargaining zone and limits the negotiator's scope for any further concessions on that issue.

- It may be regarded as conveying a loss of image and prestige in the eyes of the other negotiator, who may be encouraged to stand firm in anticipation of further concessions to come.

This latter loss may be felt most when the negotiator has maintained a position for some time during the negotiations, has developed a range of arguments to substantiate that position and has resisted any suggestions from the other negotiator that the stance should be modified. To overcome the apparent losses engendered by making concessions, the negotiator may seek to make the concession offer conditional upon a successful conclusion being reached on all issues within the negotiations, or conditional upon an 'equal' concession coming from the other party on the same or another issue, or may minimise the extent of the concession, and therefore minimise any potential loss, and regard it as the prelude to a process of mutual concessions wherein more significant concessions (losses) may be made but only on a reciprocated basis.

Task of the negotiator

Negotiators are acting, in a representative capacity, as the link between principals who themselves never meet. The **objective of the negotiator** is, therefore, to reach an agreement which is mutually acceptable not only to the negotiators

Box 13.1	Why are people afraid of negotiating?

'Many people believe successful negotiating requires skills and abilities they do not possess, or do not want to be seen as possessing. They believe that people get what they want in negotiations through being tough, aggressive, dishonest, forceful and so on ... Whilst there are people who get what they want through being dishonest, misleading, and so on, this does not mean that these behaviours make successful negotiators. On the contrary ... successful negotiators are often understanding and conciliatory. They are quiet and listen to the other side, explain their point of view without bullying, often concede when the other side has a valid point and even change their positions and preferred solutions. This suggests that to be successful, many people need to have a somewhat different view of what negotiation involves and what skills are needed to be effective.'

Source: J.-M. Hiltrop and S. Udall, *The Essence of Negotiation*, Prentice Hall, 1995 p. 2.

involved but also to the principals they represent and which, in the light of the circumstances prevailing at the time, secures the maximum possible advantage to their interest group.

The **elements of the negotiator's task** may be set out as follows:

- To provide advice to his or her principals on, and subsequently prepare, the initial bargaining objectives and strategy for the interest group;
- To arrange and conduct negotiating meetings;
- To state, explain and defend the interest group's case;
- To listen to, investigate and seek to understand the other party's case;
- To assess, within the predefined strategy and in the light of information gained during the negotiation, when to adjust or confirm positions and/or when to exert pressure on the other party's negotiator to modify positions;
- To inform, advise and consult with his or her principals on the progress of the negotiations and, if necessary, revise the objectives and strategy of the interest group;
- To seek to influence the other party's negotiator, and through this the other party's principals, to modify their position;
- To maintain an effective and continuing personal relationship with the other party's negotiator.

Kniveron has classified the skills **required by a negotiator**, in seeking to carry out these tasks, under three headings[14]:

- **Social interpersonal skills**. Negotiating is not about 'thumping the table' to get what you want (see Box 13.1). The negotiator has to be able to recognise, interpret and utilise both the verbal and non-verbal communications which are an essential part of any negotiation. The negotiator must pay close attention not only to what is said but also to the manner in which it is said, and equally to what is not said. It is these 'clues' which aid the negotiator to interpret and assess the attitudes and strength of feeling of the other party and, from this, make judgements as to what is, and is not, important within the context of that negotiation. Facial expressions, the words and phrases used and, if the negotiation comprises more than one person on each side, 'who says what' all provide important information for determining real, as opposed to stated, positions and for indicating areas of possible concession and compromise.

- **Information handling skills**. The negotiator must be fully conversant with the issues under negotiation and the context within which they are to be negotiated. In the initial preparation phase, the negotiator must decide what information will be required, how it is to be presented and within what framework of argument and justification. During the negotiating encounter, the negotiator must have sufficient knowledge and flexibility in its use to be able to respond readily to points or counter-arguments raised by the other party.

- **Discretionary judgement skills**. The negotiator must, as the representative of an interest group, make judgements regarding the implementation of the predetermined strategy and, in particular, determine when and how changes in arguments and position should take place. Kniveron argued that ultimately it is the negotiator's responsibility 'to assess all aspects of the information content and social skills experience, and estimate whether the solution is the best that could be reached in the circumstances, and to assess whether it will be acceptable to the parties represented'[15].

It may be argued that the varied nature of both the task and skill of the negotiator is made easier if there is more than one representative present at the negotiating encounter. It affords the opportunity for role and skill specialisation, particularly between the information-handling and analysis skills and the social and presentation skills (see Box 13.2). It is important that each member of the **negotiation team** is aware both of his or her own role and that of the other members right from the preparation stage. For example, the recorder and analyst roles may play less part in the actual interchange within the negotiation encounter, but are crucial in supplying information for use by the negotiator role and analysing the negotiation in any adjournment.

While the involvement of more than one person may strengthen the negotiations, it is also a potential source of weakness. The existence of differing

---

Box 13.2   Team roles

- *Negotiator* – main spokesperson and controller of the team.
- *Recorder* – notes what is said and the reactions of the opposing team.
- *Analyst* – prepares information, considers strengths and weaknesses in both cases, examines implications and effects of concessions.
- *Specialist* – provides detailed knowledge and experience of the issue under negotiation.

personalities and perceptions within the negotiating team may increase the opportunity for the opposition to identify, and then utilise, any factional conflict which exists. It is vital, therefore, that control is exercised by a main negotiator role over all members of the team to ensure that the roles are supportive of one another and combine to present an integrated stance. The individual members of the team should only enter the formal and informal interchanges within the negotiating encounter with the prior knowledge and consent of the co-ordinating negotiator role. Any disagreements within the team should not be expressed in the presence of the opposition but reserved for debate during any adjournment.

Relations between negotiator and principals

The activities of the negotiator result from a **system of interaction between negotiator and principals** who, while they are not direct participants in the negotiating encounter, nevertheless establish the boundaries of the negotiation and the negotiator's authority and ultimately approve and control the negotiating activities. Walton and McKersie noted that the negotiator occupies a key role which 'makes decisions about strategy and tactics and ... exercises influence regarding the objectives pursued but ... ultimately must account to his principals'[16] – the employees or union members on one side and senior management on the other. Walton and McKersie used the phrase **intra-organisational bargaining** to describe the relationship between negotiator and principals. This relationship involves reconciling not only differing views within the interest group (factional conflict) but also differences between the negotiator and the interest group (role boundary conflict).

Factional conflict arises because of the heterogeneous nature of both the management and employee or union groups on whose behalf the negotiation is conducted. There may be differences not only over the **objectives** to be pursued and the **priorities** to be attached to them but also over the **means** to be adopted to achieve them. While this form of intra-organisational bargaining is perhaps most clearly evident within the employees or union interest group – particularly within a multi-union Joint Shop Stewards Committee, where each shop steward represents a potentially different interest subgroup and to whom the union negotiating team is accountable for the final agreement that is reached – it is also an integral part of the development of a corporate bargaining strategy on the management side. Factional conflict may involve, in wage bargaining for example, issues such as whether the same pay increase should be applied to all grades or whether certain grades, such as skilled workers, should receive a higher increase; whether a pay increase should be pursued at the expense, if necessary, of a reduction in the length of the working week; whether a pay increase should be linked to improvements in productivity; whether industrial action should be undertaken or resisted in order to secure what is perceived to be a reasonable level of settlement. Negotiators cannot isolate themselves from this area of conflict because they are bound 'to prefer (or see a necessity for) a position which differs from that of some elements'[17] of the interest group they represent.

Walton and McKersie argued that **role boundary conflict** arises primarily because the 'negotiators for the two parties have a relationship with each other not shared or valued by their respective principals'[18] and that, as a consequence, the negotiator may conflict with his or her principals when he or she 'cannot, or prefers not to, ignore the demands and expectations of his opponent'[19]. Negotiators therefore experience role conflict because they are unable to satisfy the other negotiator's expectations of their role while at the same time satisfying the expectations of their own principals. In essence, negotiators may be confronted by a difference between the expectations of their principals and what they believe, in the light of their past knowledge and experience of the other party and their assessment of the current negotiation, to be realistically obtainable within a mutually acceptable solution. Walton and McKersie divide the principals' expectations of the negotiator between **substantive expectations**, relating to the issues and content of the negotiation, and **behavioural expectations**, concerned with the attitude and approach to be adopted by the negotiator during the course of the negotiation. They suggest that the negotiator may respond to the perceived role conflict by conforming to, ignoring or seeking to modify either or both of these sets of expectations (see Figure 13.3).

They argue that certain **response strategies** are not available to the negotiator:

■ Any strategy involving modifying the principals' behavioural expectations of the negotiator is not feasible in the short time scale of most negotiations.

■ A strategy involving conformity with the principals' substantive expectations will not allow the necessary latitude to the negotiator to resolve the inter-organisational conflict with the other interest group's negotiator.

■ A strategy which involves ignoring both the principals' substantive and behavioural expectations may lead to the negotiator's complete loss of credibility and possible rejection and replacement by another negotiator.

Thus, the negotiator has, in effect, only three viable alternatives:

■ Ignore the principals' behavioural expectations, which are an integral support to their substantive expectations, and directly confront them in order to argue for a modification and reduction in their substantive

Figure 13.3
Negotiator's response to role conflict

Source:
R. E. Walton and R. B. McKersie, *A Behavioural Theory of Labour Negotiations*, McGraw-Hill, 1965, p. 304.

		Response to principals' substantive expectations		
		Modify	*Ignore*	*Conform*
Response to principals' behavioural expectations	*Modify*	*Not feasible*	*Not feasible*	*Not feasible and not acceptable*
	Ignore	Direct pressure for change from the negotiator	Negotiator likely to be rejected by principals	*Not acceptable*
	Conform	Indirect pressure for change from negotiation process	Change sought after negotiation completed	*Not acceptable*

expectations to a level which the negotiator believes will allow a mutually acceptable solution to be reached in the inter-organisational negotiations.

- Continue to give the appearance of conforming to the principals' behavioural expectations and allow the indirect pressure of the apparent intransigence of the other interest group to change the principals' substantive expectations of what is achievable.

- Ignore the principals' substantive expectations during the negotiation and, after its conclusion, minimise the apparent losses sustained in the principals' substantive expectations by justifying the settlement on the grounds that it was the best that could be achieved in the circumstances.

It is on the basis that 'the negotiator usually gains a realistic view of the situation considerably in advance'[20] of the principals, that Walton and McKersie maintain that the **purpose of intra-organisational bargaining** is to bring 'the expectations of principals into alignment with those of the chief negotiator'[21]. The formal **mandate** within which negotiators are required to carry out their task, and which therefore defines their degree of autonomy by identifying when they should refer matters back to the principals for further consideration, is the result of such intra-organisational bargaining.

13.3 The negotiating encounter

The negotiating encounter usually involves a number of distinct phases – preparation, opening the encounter, the negotiating dialogue, and termination (see Figure 13.4). However, in smaller negotiations the divisions are often less clear, while in some other negotiations the timing of Phases I and II may not be the same for both parties. For example, the side taking the initiative in seeking the negotiation (A) may undertake its preparation, state its case and have its position clarified by the other side (B) before B is able to undertake its own preparation, state its own case on the issue involved and have its position clarified by A.

Phase I – preparation

Preparation is invariably the key to successful negotiating. It allows negotiators to develop a clear understanding of their task and increases their confidence in their ability to carry it out. Few negotiations are either concerned with single, simple issues or unconnected with other issues within the organisation. Preparation must take into account the **wider context of environmental constraints and pressures** which surround both the organisation and the parties involved as well as the issue itself. In addition, consideration must be given to what is likely to be the **opposition's position**, and justifying arguments, and what will be their reaction to any planned arguments and offers to be made during the course of the encounter – as Torrington pointed out 'negotiators have to prepare counter-attack as well as attack, defence as well as initiative'[22].

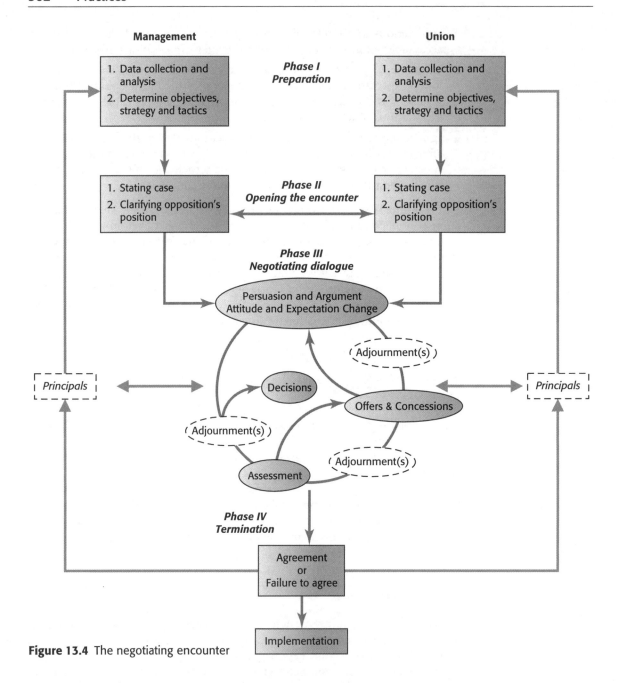

Figure 13.4 The negotiating encounter

Part of the preparation may involve **agreeing an agenda** between the two parties. The meeting to agree an agenda may be the only formal link between the parties during this phase of the encounter. It provides an opportunity, although not the only opportunity, for each party to gauge informally the other's position on the various issues prior to the formal opening of the encounter. Each party may well have different perceptions of the strategic or relative importance of the various issues and, therefore, determining the

sequence in which issues are to be considered may itself be the first area of negotiation between the parties. Obviously any 'technical' linkage between issues may predetermine the sequence (one issue cannot be considered until the outcome of another is known). Outside this particular constraint, Torrington argued, 'both sides may welcome a sequence of topics which starts with something easy on which they can quickly agree'[23], thereby establishing the right atmosphere for the rest of the meeting. However, others argue that it is better to start with those items over which there is likely to be the most difficulty and on which a 'satisfactory conclusion' to the whole negotiation is dependent. Holding out the prospect of concessions on the 'easier' issues may be more useful in aiding an agreement on the difficult issues than referring back to them, once they have already been made, as evidence of 'good faith'.

The negotiator and principals, as well as gathering and analysing such quantitative and qualitative data as is available or considered necessary, must also determine their **bargaining limits** on the issues to be negotiated. These limits comprise the **target they wish to achieve** and the **limit (or resistance point) beyond which they are not prepared to make any further concessions**. Figure 13.5 sets out management and union bargaining limits in respect of three issues – pay, hours and holidays. It can be seen that on the issue of a pay increase management's bargaining limits range from a target of 2 per cent (based perhaps on the financial state of the company) to a limit of 4 per cent (based perhaps on *their* assessment of other settlements) while the union's bargaining limits range from a target of 6 per cent (based perhaps on *their* assessment of other settlements) to a limit of 3 per cent (based perhaps on their assessment of the minimum their members will accept). This would give an overall **bargaining zone** of between 2 and 6 per cent and, with an overlap between the two resistance points, a **likely settlement zone** of between 3 and 4 per cent – thus an agreement should be possible. However, on the issue of the shorter working week, the resistance point of both sides is a one hour reduction without loss of pay – there is no overlap and the settlement is to be found only at the limits of both parties. Thus, it will be difficult, but not impossible, to identify and achieve a settlement because the closer they come to their resistance points, the more reluctant they may become to make further movements. On the issue of an increase in holidays, there is a clear gap between the bargaining limits of the two parties. While both sides are prepared to settle for an increase of two days, management is only prepared to accept this as an alternative to a shorter working week. Consequently, the two items are inter-linked, at least by one side, and a successful negotiation will probably depend on the three items (pay, hours and holidays) being treated as a package – with moves in one area being 'traded-off' against moves in one of the others.

Once the bargaining limits have been determined, it is then necessary to prepare the **information and arguments to be used** during the encounter. While Torrington argued that 'only the simplest details can be attempted, and that these need projection for maximum impact and penetration'[24] during Phase II of the encounter, nevertheless these main points and arguments need to be supported by more detailed information and subsidiary arguments during Phase III. It is important to remember, when preparing this package of information

Figure 13.5
Negotiating limits

1. General pay increase (% *increase in basic rate*)

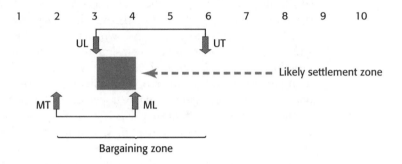

2. Shorter working week

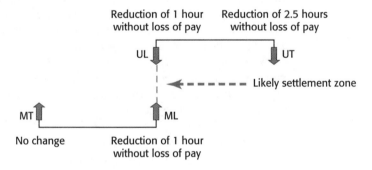

3. Increase in annual holidays

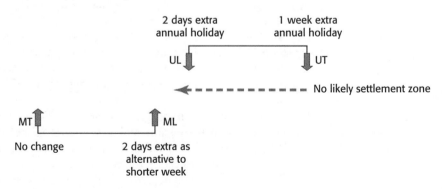

and argument, that it will need to justify not only the initial case being put forward on each issue but also each successive 'fallback' position as concessions are made and there is movement away from the target point and towards a settlement or the limit point. Each position should be capable of being sustained by some apparent 'logical' information and argument. This, perhaps, is the crucial difference between negotiations and simple bargaining.

Phase II – Opening the encounter

This phase of the negotiation is often referred to as 'the dialogue of the deaf' or 'challenge and defiance' because, as Torrington noted, 'the negotiators appear to be ignoring the arguments presented by the others and concentrating their whole efforts on the presentation and consolidation of their own case'[25]. However, for both parties, the real **objective** of this phase is to reveal only the broad outline of its own position while gathering as much information as possible concerning the opposition's case (to confirm or modify prior conceptions regarding the opposition's bargaining limits). This phase is generally characterised by a higher degree of **formality** than the subsequent phase of the encounter, in that each side initially seeks to confine itself to presenting a previously prepared statement of its position. Each side is, nevertheless, listening very carefully to the opposition's case, noting the opposition's reaction to its own case and preparing to seek 'clarification' of the other's position.

The issue of **who should open the encounter** is generally determined by which party is seeking the negotiation. Thus, in a negotiation relating to a wage claim, it would be the union which opens by stating its justification for an increase and the level of increase it expects, while management will open the encounter if it is seeking the agreement of the union to work changes, redundancy, etc. It may be argued that whichever side opens the encounter, while it has the initiative to set the tone and boundaries of the negotiation, is also at an initial disadvantage in respect of gathering information because it is first to start disclosing its position. Therefore, the negotiator must decide the **nature of the initial opening statement**. The negotiator may adopt either a stance of only stating the problem and then requesting the opposition to reply by setting out what they intend to do about it, or go further and also set out the desired solution and then invite a response from the opposition. The negotiator must decide how specific the opening statement is to be and how much information it is to contain.

Although both parties realise that this opening phase is only the prelude to a real dialogue and compromise, the opening statements will tend to emphasise the justice of their respective target positions and the impossibility, or at least the difficulty, of making any concessions. Therefore, in order to obtain additional information, it is necessary for each negotiator to persuade the opposing negotiator to expand their formal opening statement. This may be achieved by using such **tactics** as expressing disbelief that the opposition really means what it is saying, apparently misunderstanding the opposition's position, or asking direct questions and making requests for further clarification. These are all designed to get the opposition to restate its position using different words, which may, as a result, convey more information regarding their attitude to the issues under negotiation.

It is important to remember that the **style and tone** adopted by the negotiators during this opening phase will set the scene for the subsequent dialogue in Phase III. If either negotiator adopts, or is perceived to adopt, an unduly aggressive attitude it may prejudice the movements, based on concessions and compromise, necessary in the next phase. The keynote throughout the opening phase should, therefore, be 'firm and clear' but not 'belligerent'.

Phase III – The negotiating dialogue

This phase is often referred to as 'thrust and parry' because, as Hawkins noted, each side is seeking, at least initially, 'to develop its own case and undermine the arguments put forward by the other'[26]. The movement from Phase II to Phase III of the encounter may occur either as a conscious decision of both negotiators, possibly involving an adjournment to consider the information gained during the opening phase, or as a more instinctive movement generated by the process of clarifying each other's position during the opening phase. The more formal the negotiating situation, the more likely it is to be the former.

The **objective** of the negotiator during this phase should be to use information, arguments and counter-arguments in order to achieve the following:

■ To modify the perceptions and attitudes of the opposing negotiator thereby reducing expectations;

■ To identify and secure a mutually acceptable agreement which involves the greatest possible movement in the opponent's position for the least necessary movement in his or her own position.

See Chapter 3 – Concepts and values in industrial relations

This phase of the encounter is perhaps more characterised by a **problem-solving orientation** – the problem to be resolved being the identification of a point of mutual acceptability. Both parties need to trust each other sufficiently to be prepared to move away from their target points and towards the likely area of settlement, if one exists, or the identification that no settlement is likely within the existing bargaining limits of the two sides (see Box 13.3). This phase therefore involves a less formalised, more flowing approach to the negotiations, with much greater interplay between the negotiators and the generation of ideas, suggestions, offers and counter-offers. It consists of a cycle of activity moving from persuasion to offers and concessions, which results, if acceptable, in a decision or, if unacceptable, a return to the persuasion stage and further offers and concessions. The negotiators may, where there is more than one item to be dealt with and there is a 'perceived' impasse on one of them, agree to put it aside for further consideration at a later stage in the dialogue and concentrate their attention on an alternative item.

This phase is also characterised by the development of a **more interpersonal, and less representative, role relationship between the negotiators**, even, as previously noted, to the extent that the expectations of their respective principals may be perceived, individually or jointly, as an impediment to their achieving a

| **Box 13.3** | Trust: a process context |

'The opening phase of a negotiation consists of each party establishing its own position and exploring the position and commitment of the other side. Trust in the limited sense of integrity can be established – by not acting outside the normal conventions of behaviour – but trust in the sense of being willing to take unilateral action will not exist. The reason for this is that in the early stages both parties will be convinced of their own position and expect unilateral action (in the form of making concessions) to come from the other side.

Having established their own positions and fully understanding the other side's position, the point will come in the negotiations when both sides realize that they need to move into an exploratory phase in order to seek ways of reconciling their incompatible positions. However, the transition from the differentiation to the exploration phase is one of the most difficult periods in the negotiation; it is unlikely to be sudden but will involve a change in emphasis and in the dominant behaviours of the negotiators. The former phase is concerned primarily with information exchange about the parties' positions and is quite likely to be defensive and conflictual as each side tries to find out the other's true position. The exploration phase involves looking for solutions which might resolve the issue; it is much more tentative and involves a greater degree of risk.

... In the absence of mutual trust it is difficult to generate alternative outcomes to the dispute, leaving pressure tactics as the only remaining option. Therefore it is at this point that the negotiators need to focus on the establishment of trust rather than concentrate on the issue itself ... A willingness to engage in the risky business of exploring options does not automatically evolve; it has to be established'.

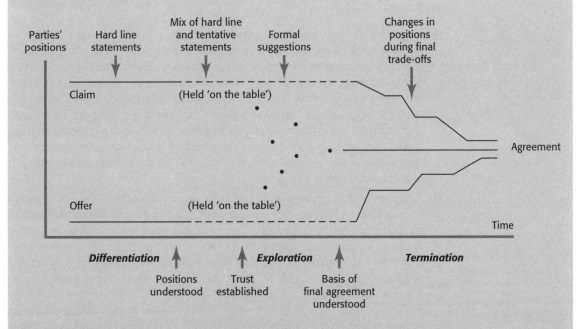

Source: R. E. Fells, 'Developing trust in negotiations, *Employee Relations*, vol. 15, no. 1, 1993, pp. 33–45.

solution. Where the negotiators are part of a negotiating team, they may, particularly when the negotiation continues over a number of meetings, make use of 'off-the-record' **informal meetings** to explore their respective positions and possible reactions to offers that might subsequently be made in the formal meeting. The danger of this approach is that it may easily be regarded as 'behind the scenes collusion' by the other members of the negotiating teams (or principals) and therefore treated with a degree of suspicion.

Another feature of this phase is the relative frequent use made of **adjournments**. At the **tactical** level, an adjournment may be required because a negotiator wants 'time out' to consider the arguments and/or offers put by the other party, or for the opposition to consider arguments and/or offers and reconsider its position, or, if part of a negotiating team, because the opposition has succeeded in dividing the team and the negotiator needs an opportunity to re-establish control. At the **strategic** level, the negotiator may require an adjournment in order to confer with principals and, in the light of the progress of the negotiations, seek to modify their expectations and thereby revise the mandate and bargaining limits. Whoever calls for an adjournment should ensure that it is not perceived as a sign of weakness or hesitancy by leaving the opposition with something to think about during the period of the adjournment.

The negotiator must always be aware of the need to pursue a strategy of movement if the negotiation is to reach a successful conclusion (see Box 13.4). A number of **tactics** may be employed in order to secure some movement in the opposition's position. These may be divided between those of a negative (aggressive) character and those of a more positive (conciliatory) nature:

- **Negative**. A negotiator may direct questions at those among the opposition's team who appear the weakest, least experienced or most conciliatory, in an attempt to split the opposition and create factional conflict within their team; challenge the competence or representatives of the opposing negotiator; threaten to withdraw any concessions already made or even withdraw from the negotiations completely unless the opposition adopts a more 'realistic' attitude or position; impose a deadline by which the opposition must agree; and imply or threaten that there will be serious consequences for the opposition if no agreement is reached. All of these are intended to put pressure on the opposition.

- **Positive**. The negotiator may highlight the weaknesses in the opposition's information and arguments – in particular, those aspects of the issue which it is not aware of, has failed to give due weight to or wishes to ignore – while at the same time emphasising his or her areas of strength; pre-empt movement from the other side by, as it were, reading the opposition's mind and suggesting a concession it might make without significantly damaging its position; offer a *quid pro quo* by linking hypothetical concessions – preferably a smaller concession than the one the opposition is expected to make in response; and refer to the nature and extent of concessions and agreements already made by both parties. These tactics are intended to emphasise the mutuality of the negotiation and are based on the inherent desire of both parties to make concessions and compromises in order to reach a satisfactory agreement.

Box 13.4	The strategy of movement

This requires creating an awareness in the other side that the elements are present which both require and allow movement to take place:

■ The other side has to be made aware that his or her original position is untenable.

■ The other side has to feel that the gain from movement is greater than not moving.

■ You have to indicate that there is a possibility of movement in your position.

■ The means of moving has to ensure a maintenance of credibility for the other side.

You can never *assume* that the other side will take the initiative or responsibility for commencing the process of movement. No negotiation should flounder simply because both sides were adopting an 'after you' approach.

It must be remembered that both parties should benefit from the negotiation and the negotiators need to be seen to be representing and protecting their principals' interests. Thus, it may become necessary for one negotiator to offer the opposition face-saving reasons for why they have been unable to secure a settlement within their bargaining limits.

Phase IV – Termination

The termination phase is just as important to a successful negotiation as either the preparation or encounter phases. During the final stage of the negotiating dialogue, once an overall agreement is in sight, it is very easy for the negotiator to experience a psychological uplift at the apparent success of the negotiations and to suffer a lapse of concentration. It is at this point that a negotiator may, without fully realising it, commit him or herself to a course of action which may have been resisted earlier in the negotiation, or even agree to something new, perhaps of only a relatively minor nature, which is 'thrown in' by the opposition at the last moment, without sufficiently considering its implications. Therefore, the negotiator should not regard the dialogue phase as completed until all issues have been satisfactorily resolved and both negotiators agree there are no further issues to be considered.

The **objective** of the termination phase is to ensure that the two negotiators have a common perception of the content and terms of their agreement. This may be achieved by reiterating the decisions reached and putting them in a **formal written agreement** to be signed by the two negotiators. Indeed, the attempt to put the agreement into writing may highlight differences in perception with regard to the outcome of the negotiation and may require further 're-fining' negotiation to establish the precise terms of the written agreement. However, the negotiators may not be in a position to sign the written agreement until it has been formally approved by their principals. Perhaps all too often the less formal negotiation suffers because its outcomes are not codified in a written agreement and is therefore liable to differential interpretation by the two sides.

During this termination phase, neither negotiator should exhibit **undue signs of elation** with the result; this will only suggest to the opposition that in some way it has been unsuccessful in the negotiation, that there was more that it could have achieved, or that it has missed some important implication of the agreement. This may lead to a desire on its part to seek immediately to reopen the dialogue and reconsider the concessions it has made, or to resist the implementation of the agreement. The mutual acceptability of any agreement rests, to a large extent, on the personal trust between the negotiators concerned that neither has tried deliberately to 'hoodwink' the other. Indeed, if a negotiator believes that the opposition has missed some important point which, when it becomes known, may jeopardise the successful implementation of the agreement, he or she must give serious consideration to drawing the matter to the opposition's attention.

Both parties should ensure that the negotiations are followed by, preferably, **a joint communication** of its terms to all their principals: employees, members and management. The agreement reached is for their use and therefore they should be aware of its details.

Finally, perhaps the most difficult termination arises when there is an evident **failure to agree** between the two parties. Negotiators must be prepared to recognise when they have exhausted all possibilities of concession and compromise and that further negotiation on the issue is more likely to lead to entrenched and antagonistic attitudes than a resolution of the problem. In such situations, the termination involves identifying the negotiators' respective final positions and therefore the exact extent of their disagreement. The negotiators are, in effect, defining the issue which must be presented to their principals for further examination and possible renegotiation (perhaps at a higher level involving fresh negotiators).

Conventions of negotiation

It is generally important to observe certain conventions in conducting negotiations.

- **Role of negotiator**. Each negotiator has the right and authority to state and argue his or her side's case and reach an agreement on their behalf. Thus, subject to their approval, the negotiator has the authority to commit his or her principals and neither negotiator should seek to appeal over the head of the opposing negotiator and undertake 'negotiations' direct with his or her principals. However, management does not, generally, accept that this restricts its right to communicate direct with its employees, particularly, to inform them of the details of its final offer when it has been rejected.

- **Approval of principals**. The negotiator may, if necessary, make an agreement conditional upon its acceptance by his or her principals. On the management side, this will arise when the negotiator has, on his or her own authority, gone beyond the bargaining limits established as part of the mandate, which is only likely to happen if the negotiator feels that the principals will accept his or her judgement in this matter. On the union side, shop stewards and full-time officers are, because of their elective accountability to the membership, more often likely to want to refer any settlement to their members for approval before formally agreeing it with management. This does not mean, however, that they do not have the confidence of their membership or that the membership is likely to reject the solution they have negotiated. Rather it is an acknowledgement of the fact that they are the servants of the membership and cannot impose solutions on them.

- **Setting for the negotiation**. Generally it is management which provides the room, etc. to be used during the negotiation and while it may be possible to create an environment which puts the union representatives at a disadvantage – for example, facing a window or sitting in low chairs – this is not conducive to establishing an atmosphere of mutual trust between the two parties. Therefore, management should, as far as possible, ensure that the union negotiators have the same facilities as themselves and that refreshments, etc. are provided as appropriate.

- **Team negotiation**. If the negotiation is to be conducted by a team, it is important to ensure that there is only one main spokesperson on each side, and that the two sit opposite each other so that they may communicate directly to each other rather than across other members of the teams.

- **Personal conduct**. At no time should a negotiator lose his or her temper during the encounter: to do so is to lose the initiative and control of the negotiation. Neither should he or she indulge in a personal attack on the opposing negotiator: the other negotiator is carrying out a role and the two negotiators are likely to meet again on future occasions.

Summary propositions

- Negotiation is not simply a 'ritual' but a process which allows the representatives of different interest groups to reach a mutually acceptable settlement of an issue while, at the same time, seeking to maximise the advantage to be gained for their interest group.

- A successful negotiator is one who has command of the facts and is able, through argument and persuasion, to encourage movement away from prearranged positions.

Activity   We all negotiate at some time or other in our normal lives – buying or selling something, complaining about poor goods or services, trying to 'get our way' with children, partners or work colleagues. So, take a few minutes to think about one of these 'domestic negotiations' you might have been involved in recently, and then try to identify what was the issue, what was your objective, how did you try to persuade the other person (did you threaten or cajole), what was their reaction and, importantly, were you successful?

■ Further reading

- ■ J.-M. Hiltrop and S. Udall, *The Essence of Negotiation*, Prentice Hall, 1995. A very useful examination of the negotiating process: sequence, strategy and tactics.
- ■ P. Warr, *Psychology and Collective Bargaining*, Hutchinson, 1973. Examines the psychological elements of negotiation drawing on the experience of one particular negotiation.
- ■ R. E. Walton and R. B. McKersie, *A Behavioral Theory of Labor Negotiations*, McGraw-Hill, 1965. A standard work on the strategies and tactics which may occur in various bargaining models.

■ References

1. R. E. Walton and R. B. McKersie, *A Behavioral Theory of Labor Negotiations*, McGraw-Hill, 1965, p. 3.
2. A. W. Gottschalk, 'The background to the negotiating process', in D. Torrington (ed.), *Code of Personnel Administration*, Gower Press, 1973.
3. W. Brown, *Piecework Bargaining*, Heinemann, 1973, p. 25.
4. A. Flanders, 'Collective bargaining: a theoretical analysis', *British Journal of Industrial Relations*, vol. 6, no. 1, 1968, p. 6.
5. D. Torrington and L. Hall, *Human Resource Management* (4th edn), Prentice Hall, 1998, p. 659.
6. J. M. Magenau and D. G. Pruitt, 'The social psychology of bargaining', in G. M. Stephenson and C. J. Brotherton (eds), *Industrial Relations: A Social Psychological Approach*, John Wiley, 1979.
7. *Ibid.*, p. 205.
8. R. E. Walton, J. E. Cutcher-Gershenfeld and R. B. McKersie, *Strategic Negotiations: A theory of change in labor–management relations*, Harvard Business School Press, 1994, pp. xiv–xv.
9. K. Hawkins, *A Handbook of industrial Relations Practice*, Kogan Page, 1979, pp. 206–7.
10. P. Warr, *Psychology and Collective Bargaining*, Hutchinson, 1973, p. 5.
11. *Ibid.*, p. 8.
12. *Ibid.*, p. 10.
13. *Ibid.*, p. 30.
14. B. H. Kniveron, 'Industrial negotiating: some training implications', *Industrial Relations Journal*, vol. 5, no. 3, 1974, pp. 27–37.
15. *Ibid.*, p. 32.
16. Walton and McKersie, *op. cit.*, p. 282.
17. *Ibid.*, p. 293.
18. *Ibid.*, p. 284.
19. *Ibid.*, p. 299.
20. *Ibid.*, p. 295.
21. *Ibid.*, p. 5.
22. D. Torrington, *Face to Face*, Gower Press, 1972, p. 35.
23. *Ibid.*, p. 34.
24. *Ibid.*, p. 34.
25. *Ibid.*, p. 39.
26. Hawkins, *op. cit.*, p. 201.

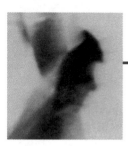

chapter fourteen

Pay and working arrangements

Learning objectives

The pay people receive and the way they are expected to work are at the heart of the employment relationship. By the end of this chapter, you should be able to:

■ identify various equity criteria which may be used to judge the 'fairness' of pay and how these are reflected in the arguments used in pay bargaining;

■ explain the nature and development of profit- or performance-related pay arrangements;

■ understand management strategies directed towards changing working arrangements; in particular, the 'flexible firm' model and numerical, time and functional flexibility.

Definition

The term pay can, in a restricted sense, refer only to direct monetary payments (including allowances, premia payments and bonuses) or, in a wider sense, it can also encompass a range of financial welfare benefits (including pension, company cars, cheap loans, etc.). The term working arrangements can be applied to the way jobs are constructed and labour used (their activities and how these relate to organisational needs).

Key issues

While you are reading this chapter, you should keep the following points in mind:

■ Determining pay is not a simple technical mechanism or automatic motivator. It is primarily a subjective process, revolving around our perceptions of 'equity' and the 'felt-fair' factor. If we feel 'satisfied', or better still if we feel 'good', about our pay then it will *help* us to be motivated and committed, but if we don't … !

■ The central issue about working arrangements is 'control' – who controls them and for what purpose? We need to consider whether labour flexibility is for the employees' benefit or the organisation's need, and how we maintain an acceptable balance between any work demands and the need for (and requirements of) outside 'family' life.

14.1   Introduction

The wage/work exchange is at the heart of both the individual's contract of employment and the process of collective bargaining between management and union. The formal manner in which the wage/work exchange is expressed through the organisation's wage and salary system is perhaps one of the clearest indications of the organisation's basic philosophy, values and attitudes towards its employees. In return for payments and benefits, employees are expected to carry out their allotted role/task efficiently and to the best of their capabilities; while the terms efficiency, productivity and performance are frequently heard when assessing labour utilisation within the organisation.

14.2   Pay determination

It is not the intention in this chapter to examine the operation and problems of different forms of wage/salary systems[1] but rather to consider the principles and perceptions which underlie the determination of pay and working arrangements and recent developments in both areas.

Pay determination must be seen in both economic and sociopolitical contexts (see Box 14.1). In the former it may be regarded as the determination of the price at which a commodity (labour) will be bought and sold – reminiscent of the old annual hiring of servants and farm labourers. As such, it centres on the individual's desire to maximise income and through this living standards, and management's desire to minimise the organisation's wage costs which are a neg-

Box 14.1	The role of wages

'Labour differs from other commodities exchanged within the economic system because it cannot be separated from the workers supplying it, and they take their social values and norms with them into the workplace. In our societies, wages fulfil a large number of different functions which may often not all be compatible one with another. For firms, wages are, in the first instance, a cost of production, and the more competitive their product markets become, the greater the need to minimize wage costs. But they are also a source of motivation, a means by which managers can persuade workers to carry out the tasks they want, and increasingly, to the level of quality they require. For workers, wages are primarily a source of income, but they can also be a source of social prestige, and may be judged according to their fairness. For economists, they are seen additionally as the chief mechanism in a decentralized market economy whereby labour is allocated to the jobs in which it will be most productive. There are doubtless many other social functions that are fulfilled by wages. These are just a few principal ones, and it is clear that they may often conflict, making wages an easy target of conflict and social struggle'.

Source: D. Marsden, 'Wages from a European perspective', in J. van Ruysseveldt, R. Huiskamp and J. van Hoof (eds), *Comparative Industrial and Employment Relations*, Sage, 1995, pp. 173–4, reprinted by permission of Sage Publications Ltd.

ative element in the financial balance sheet. In the latter context, it centres on the determination of a 'fair and reasonable' payment for the contribution made by one of the organisation's assets. As Evans notes, pay is both 'a mechanism for control and motivation' and 'a visible manifestation of the "psychological contract"'[2] between management and employee.

Equity in pay

The axiom of 'a fair day's wage for a fair day's work' is often put forward as if there were a universal, absolute and self-evident criterion by which it is possible to judge the merits (or otherwise) of the outcome of pay determination. However, notions of what constitutes 'a fair day's wage' and 'a fair day's work', and therefore what is a fair and equitable equation between the two, are matters of **individual perception**, and the criteria by which individual employees, management and unions make such judgements are many and varied (see Figure 14.1). 'Equity' is, therefore, not an absolute but a relative concept requiring comparisons to be drawn with other factors, individuals or situations and, as Jaques noted, often involves 'the nature of differential treatment rather than equal treatment of individuals'[3].

Economic comparisons

Income from employment provides the means for satisfying both economic and social needs. Therefore, a **living wage** implies something more than simply a 'subsistence wage' which provides only for the basic necessities of food, clothing and shelter. Jaques suggested that there are three distinct types of income expenditure:

- Constrained expenditure, equating to a subsistence level of income, which is characterised by 'excessive concern over each item of expenditure'[4];
- Discriminatory expenditure, wherein the individual's income is sufficient to allow choice in satisfying needs and requirements;
- Indiscriminate expenditure, equating to the existence of surplus income, which is characterised by 'spur-of-the-moment spending, driven by whims and fancies'[5].

On this basis, the 'living wage' sought by most employees is that which will be sufficient to meet, in full, their discriminatory expenditure needs plus allowing them to indulge in occasional indiscriminate expenditure; the actual amount will, of course, depend on domestic circumstances. In the past, it was all too common to view the male's income as providing for the family's constrained and discriminatory expenditure, while the female's income was seen as secondary supplementary income to provide for indiscriminate expenditure. Hence, the perception that married females sought employment primarily for social, inter-personal reasons, viewed their income as simply 'pin money' and were, there-fore, less concerned about an equitable wage or salary. Yet, in reality the female may be the major or sole source of income or a combination of two incomes may be necessary in order just to satisfy the family's constrained expenditure

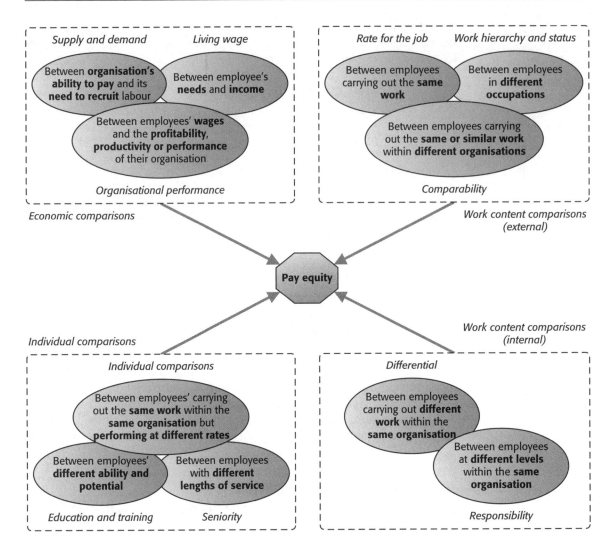

Figure 14.1 Equity in pay

needs. Therefore both males and females are likely to display an equal concern in ensuring that the level of their incomes is sufficient, and remains sufficient, to meet living needs.

The concept of a living wage tends to be perceived and expressed in terms of the individual's **standard of living relative to the rate of inflation and changes in the cost of living**. Pay increases equal to, higher than or lower than the past rate of inflation are generally regarded as maintaining, increasing or reducing the individual's standard of living, irrespective of the level of income or pattern of expenditure. Most employees expect management to ensure, through regular pay increases, that their standard of living is not eroded and, if possible, improved. The distribution of income on the basis of need is generally regarded as a matter of social and political policy (taxation and social benefits), rather than workplace negotiations.

Some people believe that pay levels should reflect a balance between **supply**

and demand in the labour market. Certainly, many managers would argue that the level of wages should not be beyond their ability to pay and does not need to be above a level which allows them to recruit labour of the right type, skill and experience. However, if the market rate is higher than the organisation's ability to pay, and management determine its pay level on the basis of the latter, it is likely to experience a movement of employees away from its organisation and difficulties in recruiting new employees to replace them. Equally, if the organisation's ability to pay exceeds the market rate, and management uses the latter to determine its pay level, it may have less difficulty in recruiting employees and its existing employees are unlikely to leave, but there may be feelings of resentment among the employees at not receiving what they perceive to be an equitable wage. Thus, management must strike a balance between these two approaches if the organisation is both to retain the commitment of its existing employees and to be able to recruit new ones.

Clearly, there is a need for some **equitable relationship between the returns to labour and the returns to capital** – each is an essential part of the overall productive and financial performance of the organisation. However, while management may perceive a greater need than employees for the organisation to make sufficient provisions for dividends and reinvestment, employees will wish to ensure that such provisions are not at the expense of recognising their contribution to the achievement of profits. Indeed, it may be argued that labour, as an asset and investment in the business, has a right to receive a share of *any* improvement in organisational performance (not just that resulting from labour changes), in the same way as capital receives a share when the improvement results from labour. Organisational performance may be reflected in normal pay increases or through **profit sharing, share ownership or other schemes** which seek to distribute the value added by the organisation. However, as with incentive payment schemes, these should not be used to 'top up' unequitable wages and salaries.

Individual comparisons

Many organisations have operated pay systems based on grade scales with progression by annual increments related to service (**seniority**), or have provided accelerated increments or other forms of additional payments for qualifications or skills acquired by the individual (**education and training**). At the same time, many people would argue that an equitable payment system should recognise the employees' differing capacities for **effort and performance** and reward them differentially. Such schemes are intended not simply to reward employees when they periodically exert extra effort in their work but to motivate employees to work permanently at a higher level of effort and performance. In the past such reward systems were largely confined to individual or group payment by results (output bonus) schemes among manual workers. The NBPI noted in the late 1960s[6] that for such schemes to be successful there must be an effective system of measurement, the work should be primarily employee controlled and the employee must be able to identify the extent to which his or her effort makes a direct contribution to pay. The same broad principles can be applied to the more recent performance-related pay arrangements. At the same time, the proportion of the individual's pay derived from an incentive scheme should be such that it is large enough to be worth striving for, but not so large or fluctuating that failure to achieve the payment will prejudice the employee's ability to budget expenditure. It should not, therefore, be used as an alternative to establishing equitable basic pay rates.

Work content comparisons (external)

The **rate for the job** principle of equity is based on a belief that employees who carry out the same work, or utilise the same skills, should receive the same level of payment. It is the type of work performed by the employee (tasks), rather than individual attributes or abilities, quantity or quality of their work or the organisation for which they work, which should be the prime determinant of pay. This belief underlines the fraternalist characteristic of trade unionism by reinforcing the group identity and loyalty of the employees concerned and emphasising its indivisible nature. In effect, the weaker, less able member is protected, in financial terms, at the expense of the freedom of the stronger, more able member to maximise income potential, whether it is derived from physical strength, skill or intellectual ability. Indeed, manual workers often have been resistant to any form of 'merit' payment system which seeks, generally at management's discretion, to reward individual attributes and which, in their view, suggests favouritism. The concept of applying a single rate for a given job across organisations underpins multi-employer collective bargaining and the determination of 'national' rates.

Comparisons with the level of wages being paid in other organisations implies the existence of a common labour market and that the employer should be prepared to pay the apparent 'going rate' for labour. Indeed, it is perhaps the closest an individual employee may come to identifying the 'market rate' for his or her particular type of labour without actually seeking alternative employment with another organisation. For the employer to offer wages below the rate for similar jobs in other organisations may be perceived as indicative of a lack of concern for the welfare of employees, or a desire to obtain labour at the cheapest price possible by taking advantage of their relative inertia and immobility, while for the employee to accept less than this rate may be perceived as almost an admission that he or she is not worthy of a higher rate.

Sometimes people will look at the apparent **relative value placed on a job or occupation by society**. A job or occupation is generally considered to be 'underrated' by its incumbents, and possibly outsiders, when the rewards to *all* employees in that group are perceived to be significantly lower than appear to be warranted by the job's responsibility or the tasks they have to perform. Status comparison is perhaps the most important concept of equity, and at the same time the most difficult to determine, for those specialist and often unique jobs such as civil servants, police, nurses and teachers. In many cases they work for a 'single employer' (the state) and therefore cannot realistically seek the same work at a higher rate of pay with an alternative employer. It is because of their peculiar position that both permanent pay review bodies (doctors, nurses, senior civil servants) and *ad hoc* inquiries have utilised comparisons with 'benchmark jobs' in the private sector as a basis for determining a 'fair' increase.

Work content comparisons (internal)

While it is possible for equity to be applied to some work in terms of the individual's 'physical' output, the contribution made by many other jobs to the overall performance of the organisation can only be assessed in the **less tangible forms of judgement and decision making** (particularly those involving technical, professional, supervisory and managerial work). There appears to be a general acceptance of the view that the individual's pay should correspond in some way to the complexity of the job or its level of authority and accountability (responsibility). While it is possible to compare jobs on the basis of their 'time span of discretion' – that is, the elapsed time before an error of judgement may be identified and rectified[7] – the more usual method is by a formal system of job evaluation which compares jobs in relation to a number of predetermined factors. Within job evaluation it is the job, not the person, which is being assessed. However, it is not an objective, scientific or impartial method of assessment. Whatever the precise system, it is necessary first to decide what factors are to be included and, most importantly, what weighting is to be given to each of these factors. The relative size of these weightings indicates those job attributes which should be rewarded more than others.

It may be argued that there should be **differentials in pay** between different kinds of work within the organisation because of their respective value and importance to the achievement of the organisation's objectives. However, the individual's perception of the value of his or her work relative to the work of others in the organisation is often distorted by a lack of detailed knowledge concerning the content of the other work and an exaggerated view of the conditions, constraints and pressures of his or her own. Indeed, very often the jobs with which direct comparisons are most likely to be made are the ones which are perceived as a constraint on the individual's own work and which he or she feels should be done better or done away with. Differential comparisons are likely to be made not only in respect of the level of pay but also in respect of working hours, holidays, pension and other fringe benefits.

Clearly these differing concepts of equity interrelate and, therefore, a successful wage or salary system, or pay negotiation, is one which recognises and seeks to reconcile them. North and Buckingham argued, 30 years ago, in favour of a 'three tier wage system based upon agreed job worth, performance-based variability, and a share in prosperity element'[8].

Arguments used in pay bargaining

See Chapter 13 – Negotiation

The wage negotiation may be regarded as a **review of the equity of the wage or salary level**. The various concepts of equity have, therefore, to be translated into specific and quantified claims and offers. Most pay negotiations focus on defining a percentage increase on the basic rate, which has the effect of maintaining differentials between grades. Negotiators may confine their primary negotiation to a benchmark job or grade from which the increase for other jobs or grades may subsequently be agreed. This job or grade may be the one with the greatest number of employees, the one considered to be the basic job or grade for the particular bargaining unit concerned, or the one most directly comparable with outside groups or organisations. It is also necessary to determine the past time-scale over which comparisons are to be made and an equitable relationship judged.

Cost of living

Arguments based on changes in the **Retail Price Index** (RPI) – an indication of the individual's 'purchasing power' (after tax and other deductions from income) – are appeals to the equity of maintaining a 'living wage'. It is the minimum which most employees and unions will consider to be a reasonable increase even in periods of economic recession. However, the RPI is only representative of 'average' expenditure and may not, therefore, provide a true reflection of the effect of inflation on a particular individual's or group's cost of living. In the early 1980s, the government tried to introduce a Prices and Taxation Index which reflected the effect on disposable incomes of changes in the level of taxation. The hope was that, when a reduction in taxation resulted in employees retaining more of their gross income, this would have the effect of offsetting, at least in part, their demands for wage increases based on rises in the cost of living. In the late 1980s, the government encouraged the use of another index which, this time, distinguished between 'headline inflation' and 'underlying inflation', with the 'underlying inflation' figure excluding changes in mortgage interest rate and VAT taxation (essential elements of the government's monetarist strategy). Again, this distinction was not accepted by negotiators, particularly on the trade union side, because the elements excluded by the underlying inflation figure are significant contributors to the individual's expenditure and cost of living.

Generally, cost of living is negotiated from a **historical viewpoint**, over the period since the previous settlement, rather than in respect of the future. This is largely because the rate of increase in the past is known, while the future rate is a matter of personal judgement and prediction which may be affected, subsequently, by a wide range of factors. However, with this historical perspective employees are, in fact, always disadvantaged in that the value of their wages is being eroded from the moment it is agreed and will not be restored until the next negotiation.

There appears to have been some resurgence of interest in **long-term agreements** (i.e. agreements lasting two or more years). It has been estimated that only some 6–8 per cent of agreements in the UK are of more than 12 months' duration, whereas some 65 per cent of agreements in the USA are of three or more years' duration[9]. The initiative for long-term agreements has come from management, who believe that they can provide a period of relative pay stability and help cost planning and the implementation of major organisational changes. However, it is important to recognise that 'the duration of settlements and the interval between pay increases should not ... be confused ... while many agreements have been concluded which run, for two or three years – so moving away from an "annual round" of negotiations – in relatively few instances have negotiators opted for pay rises at intervals other than 12 months'[10]. Indeed, most of these agreements provide for some form of indexation, threshold or re-opening clause should future inflation or external pay levels exceed the levels expected when the agreement was concluded. While it may be argued that such **threshold** clauses (**indexation**) remove the need for unnecessary conflict and pseudo-negotiations around the cost of living, and therefore allow negotiators to concentrate on the issue of a 'real' wage increase, in practice the amount of room left for negotiating 'real' wage increases is very limited.

Comparability

Arguments derived from the equity concepts of responsibility, differentials, comparability and status may be loosely referred to as comparability arguments because they all centre on the relationship in pay between different groups of employees. Comparisons may be made in respect of both internal and external relativities, although internal relativities provide the most important basis for 'leap-frogging' bargaining, as one group seeks to close a differential and the other seeks to restore it. In the past, comparability was an important aspect of pay determination in the public sector (to the extent that there was a permanent Civil Service Pay Research Unit which conducted surveys), and, indeed, remains so for certain unique and perhaps emotive groups (pay review bodies for nurses, teachers, police and armed services).

It would be wrong to assume that only employees and trade unions are interested in using comparability. Many organisations conduct **pay surveys**, which are, after all, comparability studies, to try to identify the relationship between their own wages and salaries and those of their competitors. However, in making any external comparisons, it is important first of all to ensure that 'like' jobs are being compared. The increasingly organisation-specific nature of jobs, and variations in the nature and degree of flexibility expected within each, makes this more difficult. Second, it is important to compare not only basic rates of pay but also earnings, hours, holidays and other fringe benefits. It is necessary at some stage to evaluate the worth of, for example, holidays, index-linked pension or a company car, for it may be argued that in the absence of such benefits an employee should receive a higher level of pay.

The argument is often put forward that the employer should offer a pay increase in line with that offered by other employers – the **going rate of settlement**. This is another form of comparability but, rather than comparing the actual rate of wages paid to different groups, the comparison is made with the level of increase being achieved. The implication is that there is some kind of norm level of increase during a given 'pay round'. In reality there is normally a spread in any given period and therefore it is possible to select those figures which best support the argument to be put forward. However, the use of this argument does avoid the need to identify direct comparator groups of equivalent employees and, at the same time, provides the opportunity for unions to seek to transfer a level of settlement achieved by one group, perhaps because of their industrial power, productivity or other reasons, to other, less fortunately placed groups. The concept of a 'going rate of settlement' seeks to bypass the reasons for variations between different situations and superimpose some form of commonality.

Profitability

The profitability of an organisation is the most usual method of determining the organisation's **ability to pay** in the private sector. The essential problem in this area is how to **define profits and assess whether the organisation is profitable** – pre-tax, in the same way that wages are negotiated, or post-tax, the amount left for the organisation to distribute between labour, shareholder and reinvestment. However, it is not just the absolute level of profits, which may appear excessively large when expressed in millions or billions of pounds, that establishes the profitability of an organisation but the relationship of that level of profits to assets, sales, return on capital employed, wage costs, etc., on both a current basis and over a period of time. The lack of a 'reasonable' level of profits in the current pay period does not, automatically, signify an inability to pay. It may be possible for the organisation to meet a current wage increase out of reserves or through an expected return to profitability in the future – although management is always likely to argue that a high wage increase may result in higher costs and prices with a resultant loss of competitiveness.

The problem, for employees and unions, in assessing profits and profitability is that their **information** is limited to that supplied by management. Although unions may request further detailed information, the onus is on them to identify precisely what information they require for their purposes. Daniel noted, from an examination of one annual pay round in manufacturing in the 1970s, that it is 'a little difficult to see how managers could expect effectively to deploy arguments about the financial position of the establishment in periodic negotiations over rates of pay when they denied union negotiators the basic information on which they could assess such arguments'[11]. The situation is further complicated in respect of **group companies** through such practices as the consolidation of accounts and the existence of transfer-pricing policies, possibly on an international scale. In this situation it is important to establish whether the company or site in negotiation is to be treated as an autonomous, self-financing organisation which must justify its own levels of pay, or whether it is to be regarded as part of a group, backed by the combined resources of the whole group and able to draw on the profits or funds of the whole to meet any shortfall in its own ability to pay.

Productivity

Even though the organisation's profitability has not improved, unions may seek to justify a wage increase on the grounds of an improvement in the **overall productivity of the organisation**. It is therefore not necessary, as with direct productivity bargaining, to identify a precise linkage between some change in the utilisation of labour and the change in the level of output. The assumption is simply that, if overall productivity has improved, the labour element must have made some contribution and therefore should be suitably rewarded. Whether the contribution has come from using new machinery or simply working harder does not matter and does not have to be proved. The two most common criteria used to establish an improvement in overall productivity are some measure of quantity or value of output per employee. Comparisons between the changes in either or both of these may also be made with the changes in the employees' earnings in order to demonstrate that the former have been greater than the latter and thereby justify a pay increase.

Developments during the 1980s

Kessler identifies three groups of factors which have contributed to the pay-related developments of the 1980s and 1990s:

See Chapter 9 –
Collective bargaining

■ Organisational restructuring has substantially changed many people's jobs (task flexibility), while 'flatter' organisational structures have reduced the opportunity for reward through promotion.

■ Institutional changes in collective bargaining (decentralisation) and the de-regulation of the labour market has 'unsettled some of the established pay moorings'[12].

■ Managerial desire and ability to use pay 'to deal with new objectives, especially in circumstances characterized by the intensification of competition and the need for organizational efficiency and effectiveness'[13].

There is little doubt that management has sought to link pay levels and systems more closely to the achievement of business objectives, organisational performance and ability to pay, while at the same time introducing greater variability and flexibility in pay.

Profit-related pay

In 1987 the government introduced tax concessions to encourage payment schemes in which part of the individual's pay is directly and formally linked to the organisation's profits. Initially, income tax relief was given on half this pay element, up to 20 per cent of the employee's pay or £4,000. Duncan pointed out that the presumption underlying the government's strategy was that 'the profit-linked element of pay should replace some portion of previously fixed earnings so that "normal" pay will vary with profitability'[14]. In 1990 the Inland Revenue reported that there were 1,179 schemes covering some 230,000 employees; however, many of them were not new schemes but simply conversions of previous profit-sharing arrangements[15]. In 1991, the government increased the tax concession to the entire profit-related pay element and, according to Pendleton, the "salary sacrifice" [scheme] became the most popular'[16]. Certainly, by 1994 the Inland Revenue reported the existence of 7,486 schemes covering almost 2 million employees[17]. However, a survey in 1994[18] showed not only that in 43 per cent of the respondent organisations the profit-related element amounted to less than 5 per cent of total pay but that only 35 per cent of organisations paid the money with regular pay – indications that the schemes were primarily used as a bonus on top of normal pay rather than some degree of 'salary sacrifice'. Significantly, over 50 per cent of the organisations surveyed had no service qualification period before employees were eligible to participate in the scheme. In 1996 the government announced that the tax concession was to be phased out.

See Chapter 10 –
Employee
involvement and
participation

 The main arguments in favour of such pay arrangements centre on providing the employee with a sense of identification with, and a share of, the success of the business, while providing management with a 'wage cost buffer' in periods of reduced profitability (i.e. their wage bill should reduce by the extent of the profit payment element). However, while such schemes appear to have been relatively popular in the private sector, they are inapplicable to the public sector –

even those segments which have been reorganised to be self-financing or market oriented to compete with private sector organisations on an equal basis. Furthermore, Duncan argued that 'despite the much-vaunted flexibility of the provisions, they promote but one kind of scheme and method of relating pay to performance which is unlikely to be suited to the pay objectives, pay priorities and individual circumstances of a majority of firms'[19]. The effect of the introduction of profit-related pay schemes on the negotiating process is certainly debatable: on the one hand, it may be argued that 'if workers are to have a significant part of their pay linked to profit, it is likely that they would wish to have a greater say in the management decisions which may affect that profit'[20], while on the other hand, as the profit element grows 'the role of trade unions as pay negotiators will diminish, since an increasing part of pay depends on profits'[21].

Performance-related pay (PRP)

Fowler noted that 'paying more to employees who work well than to those who work less well is a practice as old as employment itself'[22]. Nevertheless, there has been an **increased management emphasis on linking pay more closely to 'performance' concepts of pay equity**. However, as Kessler points out, 'pay for performance is a concept laiden [*sic*] with interpretative complexities and giving rise to a range of different structures and systems'[23]. At the broadest level it may encompass any pay arrangement which *explicitly* links at least some part of the employee's pay to the performance (however defined and assessed) of the individual, group or organisation. It could include, therefore, the traditional forms of merit pay, individual and group output-related bonuses and organisation-level gain-sharing plans. However, the distinctiveness of the more recent development of 'performance-related pay' lies in its integration with formal performance appraisal and the individualisation of pay across an increasing range of employees – hence, ACAS's use of the term 'appraisal-related pay'[24].

Initially, PRP was very much a feature of pay determination for managers. However, Cannell and Long's survey[25] conducted for the IPM and NEDO provides an interesting insight into the **developing extent of PRP** in both the private and public sectors. Their survey showed that 47 per cent of private sector organisations had schemes covering all non-manual grades (not just managers) and 21 per cent had schemes for some non-manual employees; significantly, 56 per cent included some clerical and secretarial grades in their PRP scheme. In contrast, only 37 per cent of public sector organisations had some non-manual grades covered by PRP (and non-management grades were clearly less likely to be included) and only 10 per cent included some clerical, secretarial or administrative grades within PRP. A later IPD survey[26], covering 1,100 organisations with 1.5 million employees, found that 40 per cent of management and 25 per cent of non-management employees in the organisations surveyed were covered by an individual PRP scheme. It would appear that PRP is much less prevalent among manual employees, perhaps, as Brough points out, because 'the degree of discretion accorded to individual employees to accomplish their goals is typically very limited'[27]. This suggests that PRP may only be appropriate alongside a significant work redesign involving greater 'empowerment' of manual employees.

See Case study 14.1   The introduction of PRP has formed an integral element of the industrial relations strategy of many organisations as they have sought to **change the culture of the organisation** towards a more quality or **performance orientation**, or, in the case of the public sector, sought to introduce a more commercial or managerial attitude. Indeed, Armstrong suggests that it was seen in the 1980s as '*the* answer to motivating people ... developing performance-orientated cultures ... [and] as a major lever of change'[28]. Kessler believes that two distinct sets of goals underpinned the introduction of PRP in most organisations – first, 'the "holy trinity" of traditional pay goals, i.e. recruitment, retention and motivation', and second, its ability 'to influence a variety of behaviours, attitudes and relationships given the procedures and systems needed to operate it', including 'forcing managers to meet and communicate with staff'[29]. While PRP may help to attract and retain the 'right' kind of employees, it must motivate all employees (not just the *excellent* performers) if it is to improve employee commitment generally within the organisation. In this context, Harries notes that the 'felt-fair' principle, which is essential for any successful reward system, may be lost in PRP schemes because managers experience 'discomfort about its use essentially to punish the poor performer'[30].

If money does act as a motivator, then the size of the performance-related payment is important – estimates of the required size of pay increase needed to affect performance range from 10 to 25 per cent. Similarly, if PRP is the individual's only source of annual pay increase (i.e. there is no general annual scale increase) and he or she receives a payment for 'satisfactory' performance which is approximately equal to general pay increases in other organisations, then any motivational effect is likely to be zero. It must also be recognised that the level of PRP may not be constant year to year; the amount available for pay increases will be dependent on the organisation's 'ability to pay' at any given point in time. Consequently, the same level of performance assessment this year as last year may not attract the same level of payment as the previous year – if it is less, then employees may become disillusioned with the system and demotivated.

The other main cultural improvement brought about by PRP relates to the nature of the **new employment relationship** it engenders. There is little doubt that for some organisations the individualisation of pay through PRP represents a deliberate attempt to reduce the role of the trade union not just in pay determination but also more broadly. As Kessler and Purcell pointed out, PRP is 'unique amongst payments systems in stripping away those collective procedures and institutions which have obscured the essentially individualistic nature of the employment relationship'[31]. It certainly can enhance managerial control and the role of the line manager in monitoring and assessing (and hopefully supporting) the individual's performance – including determining the individual's pay increase. However, as Lawson points out[32], performance assessment is subjective and may easily be distorted by the manager assessing too harshly or too softly. In so far as this reduces the 'felt-fair' factor, it may act as a catalyst for grievances, union representation and a return to collectivism. Furthermore, the individualisation of performance assessment and pay may run counter to other HRM strategies in the organisation – in particular, the development of integrated teamworking.

The **trade union response** to PRP may be to resist it on principle and not

Case study 14.1 ■ Contrasting approaches to PRP

These two cases contrast the introduction and operation of PRP in organisations with very different styles of industrial relations management.

Journalists at a national newspaper

The past industrial relations history of Fleet Street had been characterised by powerful shopfloor union organisation among the production workers, able to inflict considerable immediate damage through industrial action. The introduction of new technology in the early 1980s, coupled with new legislative restrictions on trade unions and industrial action, provided the impetus for change. The focus of the changes was the re-establishment of managerial authority, the marginalisation of unions and greater emphasis on the manager/individual relationship.

The newspaper already had a merit pay system in which 1–2 per cent of the paybill was distributed on an informal 'custom and practice' basis by the editor. Although collective bargaining over pay increases was retained, in 1988 management introduced a 4 per cent 'non-negotiable' element of the paybill for merit pay increases. Management were concerned to introduce the scheme quickly, without union involvement and with scope for managerial discretion in determining individuals' pay. Consequently, there were no consistent or accepted performance criteria, no formal appraisal process and no appeals mechanism.

Although one of management's objectives was to establish a two-way dialogue between individual journalists and their managers about pay and career development (the latter supported by the journalists themselves), nevertheless the journalists were critical of the competence of assistant editors to undertake a proper evaluation, resented being labelled as simply 'satisfactory' and were suspicious of information gained from discussions about career development being used in determining their merit pay increase.

A privatised pharmaceutical organisation

This organisation was privatised in the early 1980s.

The catalyst for the introduction of PRP came from the introduction of new senior managers from outside and the need to develop a performance-driven culture to improve competitiveness in the private sector. However, the organisation still retained a culture characterised not only by the strong scientific professional and technical base of its employees, but also by a civil service relationship involving an integrated graded pay structure, uniform terms and condition of employment and strong involvement of trade union representatives.

PRP was seen, by management, as an important element in changing management style and providing managers with a mechanism to help them manage more effectively. The unions, for their part, opted not to oppose PRP on principle but rather to seek to influence its design and operation. The PRP arrangements were integrated into a new salary structure and system developed by a joint working party of management and union over a two-year period. Across-the-board uprating of the new incremental pay grades remained an annual negotiating item. Progression through the grade was to be by formal performance appraisal; each grade had a 'determined rate'; progression up to this level was by accelerated increments (for those in the top two performance rating categories), normal increments (for those in the third and fourth performance rating categories) and half a normal increment (for those in the bottom category); progression beyond the 'determined rate' was non-incrementally based and for performance which was 'beyond the norm' or 'sustained satisfactory' performance.

Source: I. Kessler, 'Performance related pay: contrasting approaches', *Industrial Relations Journal*, vol. 25, no. 2, 1994, pp. 122–35.

co-operate with management in its introduction. Such an approach is likely to leave the union further isolated from any possible representational role. The alternative is to seek to retain a degree of influence over the procedural elements of the system, to ensure fairness and consistency in its application. Certainly, Heery suggests that 'there is nothing intrinsic in [PRP] which prevents it mixing with the old industrial relations'[33] and that it 'is not detaching employees from membership, but rather is stimulating demand for union protection'[34]. On the pay-determination side, unions may still have a role in negotiating basic annual grade increases and/or negotiating the global sum available for PRP (with its allocation to individuals being at the discretion of management). A number of organisations have sought to remove the distinction between an annual pay award (based on general factors such as cost of living changes) and individual performance payments and merge the two, making all salary progression dependent on individual performance. This raises serious questions in respect of the trade union's negotiating role. As the CAC pointed out in a decision regarding the trade union's claim for disclosure of information in respect of a performance-related pay scheme: 'It is clear to us that the new payment system will severely restrict the role of the trade unions in negotiations. It will not, however, reduce the importance of the task of the trade unions to monitor what is happening to ensure there is fairness. Indeed the downgrading of the negotiating function in its simple sense adds added importance to the more sophisticated monitoring and checking that the individual managers will need from their trade unions to ensure that distortions are not growing unchecked'[35].

In Fowler's view it would be misleading to regard this emphasis on 'performance' as implying that other factors are no longer important, in that 'if staff are to be recruited and retained, salary levels have to keep up with the market, and market rates are probably the biggest single determinant of the overall scale of annual increases'. Therefore performance-related pay schemes 'have to provide the majority of staff with at least some pay increase annually, and their operation would be prejudiced by any significant increase in pay or price inflation'[36]. There are also those who believe that it is not the monetary aspect of PRP which stimulates improvements in performance (at either an individual or organisation level) but, rather, the involvement of individuals, with each other and with their line manager, in an continuous programme of performance dialogue and evaluation[37].

Flexible or cafeteria benefits

See Case study 14.2   A number of organisations[38] have introduced a more flexible approach to the provision of benefits by allowing individual employees to determine, from a menu and within an overall budget, what package of specific benefits they would like to meet their own particular needs and circumstances. The system generally involves a 'core' of 'basic' benefits which all employees receive and a 'ceiling' on the extent to which the employee may add to, or include, a particular benefit. Significantly, the Royal Bank of Scotland scheme 'offers the whole of each person's "value account" – basic salary and benefits, plus regional allowances – as a fund to use flexibly, with no limit on the amount that can be spent on any benefit'[39]. In any system, it is necessary to consider how frequently the employee may choose to amend his or her package of benefits and how the individual benefits are to be 'valued' (in either absolute or relative terms). However, such an approach does provide trade unions (and management) with the opportunity to divorce the issue of seeking to increase the range and extent of such benefits (based on desirability of the benefit) from the cost of providing them (which has to be offset against wages). The two issues can be determined or negotiated separately.

14.3 Working arrangements

Ever since the early 1960s, UK management has sought to introduce new working arrangements which would replace the division of labour characterised by assembly-line production (Taylorism) and, thereby, improve labour utilisation and efficiency. However, the way in which they have sought to do this has changed over the period primarily as a result of changes in the economic, industrial and technological environments and changes in the power of trade unions.

Productivity bargaining

McKersie and Hunter defined the essential characteristic of productivity bargaining, which differentiates it from other forms of bargaining or payment systems, as being management and union formally '*negotiating* a package of changes in working method or organisation, *agreeing* on the precise contents of the package, their worth to the parties and the distribution of the cost savings'[40] (my italics). Productivity bargaining **emphasises formal changes in a series of often interrelated working arrangements which may hinder the efficient utilisation of labour**. The productivity payment to employees is fixed at the time of negotiating the agreement and paid on the employees' acceptance of the new working arrangements without being linked to the achievement of any specified level of extra production. Management, therefore, controls the achievement of increased productivity through their implementation and utilisation of the new working arrangements. Stettner described productivity bargaining as 'bargaining to make change acceptable'[41] and in this context it requires a greater degree of trust and co-operation than conventional wage bargaining.

The first major 'classical' productivity agreement negotiated in the UK was at the Esso Refinery, Fawley (1960), and, in the view of Flanders, was 'without precedent or even proximate parallel in the history of collective bargaining in Great Britain'[42]. McKersie and Hunter noted that from the mid-1960s 'the influence of a prolonged period of strongly administered prices and incomes policy served to generate a virtual explosion of productivity bargaining'[43] (by allowing pay increases above the norm if financed from improvements in productivity) and contrasted the 73 agreements made between 1960 and 1966 with the 4,091 agreements made between the beginning of 1967 and the end of

Case study 14.2 ■ **National & Provincial Building Society**
Flexibile pay and benefits

Flexible Pay and Benefits

N&P employed 4200 people – 25 per cent at its head office and the remainder in some 300 branch offices across the UK. In the early 1990s N&P introduced a package of changes in pay and benefits aimed at providing greater flexibility and rewarding competence and performance.

1. *Pay*. Individual performance-related annual pay reviews were introduced in 1988 within the existing sixteen-grade pay system. In 1991 the pay structure was simplified and reduced to five categories and 'development of competence' was introduced alongside 'individual contribution' for the annual pay reviews. In 1993, the pay structure was further simplified to three broad 'role types' – *players* (administrative and clerical staff), *team-leaders* (supervisors and junior managers) and *managers* – each with a wide salary range. At the same time part of the pay for employees in the branches was linked to their team performance.

2. *Benefits*. Prior to the changes, N&P provided a standard package of benefits:

   ■ Contributory pension (with normal pension age of 60 and provision for early retirement through ill-health).
   ■ Annual holidays (varying from 21 to 30 days, depending on status and length of service).
   ■ Sick pay (three months' full pay and three months' half pay for administrative and clerical employees, and six months' full pay and six months' half pay for supervisors and managers).
   ■ Life insurance.
   ■ Mortgage subsidy (varying according to status).
   ■ Private health insurance (for supervisors and managers).

The aim of the changes was to provide a non-hierarchical structure of benefits which accommodated individual need. In 1992 the pension arrangements were changed to allow employees to vary their contributions between 2 per cent and 15 per cent of salary (the employer's contribution being limited to a maximum of 10 per cent) thus allowing employees, if they wished, to accrue pension rights more quickly and over a shorter period or to reduce contributions in periods of high family expenditure. At the same time, sick-pay provisions were harmonised upwards for all employees to six months' full pay and six months' half pay.

In 1993 N&P introduced greater benefits flexibility under the title 'Choices'. The new system provided all employees with the following *fixed benefits*:

■ Contributory pension (but variable);

■ 20 days' annual holiday;

■ Personal accident insurance;

■ Minimum level of life insurance (for those not in the pension schemes).

Each employee was then allocated a *flex-fund*, all or part of which could be used to purchase extra benefits or taken as taxable cash. Employees could also contribute extra from their salary to purchase more benefits than provided by their flex-fund. The amount of the flex-fund varied between the three 'role-type' categories but was the same for each employee within the category. It was initially based on the notional value of the original mortgage concession, five days' holiday and the private medical insurance provided for supervisors and managers. The value of the flex-fund automatically increased in line with general pay increases (through the value of the five days' holiday) but, importantly, could also be increased as part of the annual general 'pay' increase – in 1994, the value of the flex-funds was increased by 30 per cent for players and 25 per cent for team-leaders and managers. (A system of protection was provided for existing employees who had acquired benefit rights which were more than the value of the flex-fund.)

The flex-fund could then be used to purchase a number of benefits:

■ Life assurance (up to four times salary for those not covered by the pension fund);

■ Holiday entitlement (up to a maximum of ten additional days);

Case study 14.2 ■ National & Provincial Building Society *Continued*

■ Mortgage discount (varying levels of discount) – as an encouragement, £1 of the flex-fund was worth £1.30 of discount;

■ Private medical insurance for employees and family;

■ Dental insurance;

■ Permanent health insurance (75 per cent of normal salary during long-term illness or disability without the need to end employment by taking ill-health early retirement.

Employee decisions about the allocations of their flex-fund were made in April each year, although there was provision to allow changes to be made at other times if there was a 'significant change in personal circumstances' (marriage, birth, death, house purchase, etc.) or change in flex-fund entitlement through change in working hours or role-type. In 1994 the breakdown of employee choices was:

■ Mortgage discounts: 71 per cent;

■ Extra holiday: 62.5 per cent;

■ All or part cash: 36 per cent;

■ Private health insurance: 23 per cent;

■ Dental insurance: 13 per cent;

■ Permanent health insurance: 1.4 per cent;

■ Life insurance: 0.3 per cent (high number of employees receive maximum benefit under the pension scheme).

Source: 'Flexible benefits at the N&P', *Pay and Benefits Bulletin*, no. 358, August 1994, pp. 7–10.

1969. However, many of these later so-called productivity agreements were not of the comprehensive type, rather they were little more than output-related bonus schemes designed and introduced to circumvent the constraints of incomes policy.

Two factors in particular induced management to look more closely at productivity and labour utilisation in the 1960s:

■ **Full employment coupled with expanding demand** meant not only that increased output had to be met from within the existing level of manpower but also that employees and unions had the power to claim, and receive, wage increases at the organisational level significantly above those negotiated at the national level. Formal joint bargaining was the only realistic way to try to link pay increases with improvements in productivity.

■ **Restrictive demarcation labour practices** hindered the effective use of labour – particularly skilled labour. The effect on the organisational climate of the existence of restrictive practices was identified as early as 1951 when Zweig noted that 'the restrictive spirit harms more than restrictive rules' and that 'every legitimate and commonly agreed practice can become restrictive if the restrictive spirit is infused into it'[44]. Confronting these problems through productivity bargaining was an attempt by management to regain a measure of control.

It is possible to identify a number of areas which formed part of productivity agreements (and, indeed, which have been important elements of subsequent strategies to change working arrangements).

- ◼ *Job flexibility*. This widened the potential scope of the employee's work through:
    - ▮ **horizontal flexibility**, where an employee is required to carry out a wider range of tasks within a similar skill level (for example, intercraft flexibility or an operator being able to operate more than one kind of machine or part of the process);
    - ▮ **vertical flexibility**, where an employee is required to undertake work which is normally of a lower grade or level of skill; and
    - ▮ **geographical flexibility**, where an employee is required to move temporarily in order to cover an absence or excess workload in another work area.

- ◼ *Time flexibility*. This enabled work to be covered, as far as possible, by employees working normal but changed hours and thereby minimised the use of overtime. Perhaps the most significant item of time flexibility related to the compensation for working overtime: many productivity agreements not only reduced the use of overtime but also removed payment for overtime – overtime working being compensated by time off.

- ◼ *Manning levels*. This involved a reduction in the number of people required arising from other changes in the agreement (particularly job and time flexibility), the identification of specific overmanning practices associated with existing production or service methods, or the introduction of new methods or technology which required less people. However, unions were anxious to secure a guarantee that no immediate or direct redundancies should result from the introduction of such work changes.

- ◼ *Payment structures*. Emphasis on output, productivity and working arrangements provided an opportunity to introduce work measurement and/or job evaluation, if these were not already in use, as the basis for a more systematic examination of the content and relative worth of different jobs, and to simplify the payment system by reducing the number of pay grades and consolidating previous variable or supplementary payments into the basic rate.

- ◼ *Sociotechnical improvements*. Many productivity agreements incorporated the notion of workgroups – perhaps as the boundary of expected job flexibility (job rotation) or, more importantly, in the context of the devolution of decision making.

See Chapter 9 –
Collective bargaining

North and Buckingham argued that productivity bargaining was 'much more than a short-term wage-work bargain or "buy out" of restrictive practices' because it allowed for 'a radical restructuring of the industrial relations situation'[45]. By its very nature, it emphasised a **co-operative rather than conjunctive approach** to the negotiating situation and Hawkins believed that 'the development of a new style of management appears to have been an essential prelude to the initiation of productivity bargaining'[46]. Generally, the process of productivity bargaining **differentiated between determining the new working arrangements and negotiating new wage levels**. The responsibility for the determination of the working arrangements and their operation was usually delegated to a small working party of representatives of both sides (possibly 'seconded' on a full-time basis). While the working party had authority to reach agreement on the working arrangements, nevertheless it often also involved lengthy discussions and consultation between the members of the working party and their respective principals (intra-organisational bargaining). The advantage of using a working party approach is that discussion may be conducted on a freer basis and with less formal negotiating constraint. In addition, its members become the 'experts' on the agreement at the subsequent negotiation and implementation stages.

New technology agreements

It can be argued that, since the start of the Industrial Revolution, technological and industrial development have been a continuous integrated process involving the elimination of some types of work and the creation of others. However, the nature and rate of that change has increased through the 1980s and 1990s – to the extent that it has been called the **Technological Revolution**. It is the combination of the nature and pace of the change, interlinked with an environment of recession and weakened trade union power, that perhaps made the 'new technology agreements' of the 1980s different from earlier 'productivity bargaining'. While productivity bargaining was primarily associated with changing the working practices of *people* (the people continued to carry out the same or similar work but working more flexibly and hence more effectively), the emphasis of new technology in the 1980s was on introducing new and significantly different *technical systems* based principally on computerisation.

The development and introduction of such systems has a double **effect on employment levels**: as Manwaring noted, it results 'in goods which are both less labour intensive to produce and use'[47]. However, it also has an **effect on the nature of work** for those who continue to be employed within the new systems. Certainly, Benson and Lloyd argued that computerisation introduces 'logic and memory into production, displacing those previously uniquely human qualities'[48] and Manwaring felt that such systems enhance management's potential control of production because 'the bargaining strength of unions, established in relation to present or past technologies ... derives from the need of employers to use workers in the process of production'[49]. James adopted a similar view when he argued that not only does the introduction of new technology 'transform jobs in ways which make them inherently less amenable to worker control' but also the pace of such change 'threatens the ability of work groups and unions to maintain a degree of control over the jobs affected'[50] through the gradual modification of custom and practice within the organisation.

It is within this context that the **trade unions' response to new technology** must be seen. In 1979 the TUC prepared a report on the introduction of new technology[51] which set out guidelines for union negotiators covering the following points:

- ◼ Full trade union involvement and agreement before new technology is introduced;
- ◼ Inter-union collaboration where appropriate;

- Access to all relevant information and regular consultation on company plans;
- Commitment to expand output/services and no redundancies or, if not possible, planned redeployment and/or improved redundancy payments;
- Training, at full earnings, for those affected by the new technology;
- Reduce basic working hours and systematic overtime;
- Avoid disruption to existing pay structures/relativities, maintain or improve income levels, move towards single status (harmonisation);
- Ensure computer-based information not used for work performance measurement;
- Maintain stringent standards of health and safety;
- Establish joint management/union arrangements to monitor and review progress.

Clearly, trade unions tried to ensure that the introduction of new technology was subject to collective agreement and that its benefits were reflected both in the terms and conditions of the employees and in expanding employment. However, James[52] noted that only one of the four **types of agreement** he identified had a substantive element defining the terms and arrangements under which changes were to be introduced. It is the other three categories of varying degrees of procedural agreements which he believes should be termed 'New Technology Agreements'. He argued that the importance of such agreements lies not in their detail but in their guiding principles reflecting a management/union acceptance of the joint control of work. While for management the agreement represented 'some degree of freedom from union opposition and probably a measure of union co-operation', for the union and employees it signified that 'the introduction and ongoing monitoring of the new technology is brought into the area of joint regulation'[53]. However, it would appear to be a somewhat **imbalanced interdependence**. Certainly, Benson and Lloyd concluded from their survey of new technology agreements that 'health and safety is the most strikingly precise of the issues agreed: the others, such as job security, consultation and disclosure, and sharing benefits – are usually either tentative or vague, and all depend heavily on the maintenance of considerable strength and vigilance on the part of the unions'[54].

It appears that trade unions were **unable to secure a direct share of any economic benefits** for their members, either monetary improvements or a reduction in working hours. So far as increases in wages are concerned, Manwaring noted that 'though unions have often ... secured agreements that there will be no reduction in earnings and no downgrading for those offered redeployment, they have seldom secured an increase in earnings for operating new technology'[55], which is, at best, a somewhat negative achievement. James was less pessimistic in that he believed 'changes in financial rewards subsequent to technical change are frequently dealt with in the normal run of substantive bargaining', although 'the proportion of a pay increase due to the acceptance of technical change may not be specified'[56]. In view of the general paucity of financial information provided to unions by management, either when discussing the introduction of new technology or during a normal pay negotiation, this represents a less than satisfactory process for determining the distribution of the benefits which may result from new technology.

Finally, it may be argued that it was the reduction in trade union power through recession and their consequent inability to secure substantive negotiations and agreement over the introduction of new technology, rather than any inherent difference in new technology as opposed to productivity changes, which resulted in the primarily procedural nature of many new technology agreements. Certainly, Benson and Lloyd believed that 'the limitation of technology agreements ... stand alongside the low wage settlements, the abortive industrial actions, the often-hopeless factory occupations and mass redundancies as evidence of trade union weaknesses'[57].

Labour flexibility

During the later part of the 1980s, the twin concepts of 'flexibility' and 'core/periphery' employees achieved prominence as possible elements of management's strategy to become more competitive while, at the same time, being reluctant to recruit more full-time permanent employees These concepts have been integrated within the **'flexible firm' model**[58]. It is the model's underlying *concept* of 'labour flexibility' which has permeated much of current human resource management thinking and provides the justification for the developments in more flexible and variable working patterns. The 'flexible firm' model contains several important features (see Figure 14.2):

1. The need for modern organisations to be responsive, adaptive and competitive in cost, performance, quality and service terms (*economies of scope rather than economies of scale*).

2. The requirement for *numerical flexibility* and *time flexibility* (ability easily to adjust labour inputs to meet changes in requirements); *functional flexibility* (employee interchangeability between different tasks); and *pay flexibility* (greater individualisation and variability in pay to reflect individual and/ or organisation performance and changing labour market conditions – considered in previous section).

3. The differential application of flexibility to the organisation's workforce to produce the following groups:

    ▌ *A 'core' group* of employees 'with full-time, permanent status ... central to the longer term future of the organization'[59], characterised by relatively stable and secure employment; organisational investment in their training, development and involvement; and through whom management may seek functional, time and pay flexibility.

    ▌ *'Peripheral' groups*, who may provide an employment 'buffer' for the organisation and which may be either:
    (a) full-time employees who have 'skills that are more readily available in the labour market ... have less access to career opportunities, little investment in their training ... and tend to be characterised by high

labour turnover which makes workforce reductions relatively easy by natural wastage'[60]; or

(b) employees working under a variety of casual, temporary and/or part-time contracts to meet short-term labour needs and, consequently, with very little job security or, indeed, job interest. As Towers points out, it is this group of employees whom trade unions are 'strongly campaigning to recruit ... into membership and to negotiate rights equal to those of permanent workers'[61].

▌ *People who are not direct employees* of the organisation but who, nevertheless, may be considered a part of its 'human resource'. This group may include ex-employees whom the organisation has assisted to become self-employed in the same area of work as when they were employees (possibly as part of a reorganisation and/or redundancy package with a guarantee of a certain level of work for a period of time from their ex-employer) or those involved in contracted-out non-core activities (such as catering). The organisation is no longer constrained by an employer relationship in its dealings with these people.

There has been considerable debate about whether the 'flexible firm' concept is being applied as a conscious, coherent and integrated human resource management strategy. There are those, like Pollert[62], who believe there is a lack of clear empirical evidence to show that the developments in labour flexibility are part of a spreading deliberate management strategy rather than a continuation of the more traditional, *ad hoc*, piecemeal, contingency responses. Certainly, IDS surveys have questioned the **extent to which organisations have adopted a truly integrated approach** and believe that 'the so-called "Flexible Firm", employing the whole gamut of flexible working practices, sub-contracting, and

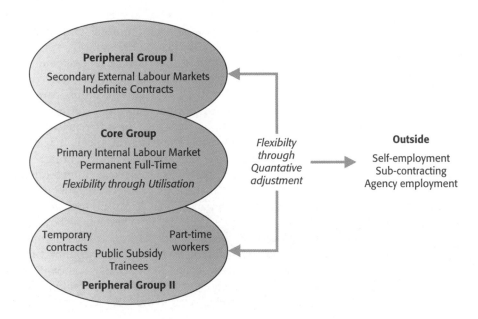

Figure 14.2
The flexible firm model

short-term contracts is very much a paper concept'[63]. They show that 'for the vast majority of companies flexible working consists of slow change over a number of years', which 'may take the form of an initial "enabling" clause or agreement, which is subsequently built on and enlarged'[64] and that perhaps 'agreements on flexibility are less important than the climate in which change is made'[65].

However, Proctor *et al.* believe that the strategic nature of these developments may lie in their being the result of consistent *patterns* of decision making within organisations, rather than a single deliberate decision being made at the highest level of the organisation. Certainly, they believe that the importance of the model is that it 'offers a framework within which changes in a certain area of firms' operations, in a certain country, at a certain time, can be analysed'[66]. Indeed, it could be argued that the fundamental element of the model (the division between core and peripheral groups) rests on an assumption that there is an easily available external labour supply to provide numerical flexibility through the 'hire and fire' of peripheral workers (i.e. relatively high levels of continuing unemployment). Therefore, where unemployment is low and it may not be possible easily to vary labour supply through changing the number of people employed (*numerical flexibility*), greater emphasis on changing the pattern of working time (*time flexibility)* might be expected.

Numerical flexibility

Numerical flexibility is at the heart of the 'flexible firm' model; differing levels of job security and attachment to the organisation provide the fundamental division between 'core' and 'peripheral' workers. The central issue is the extent to which management should (or should not) have freedom to determine the nature of employment contracts and to change the size of its workforce as and when necessary to meet its work requirements.

There are still many who regard 'normal' employment as (or at least should be) full-time, daytime (Monday to Friday), on a permanent (open-ended) contract. Indeed, this concept underlies the long-standing practice of premia payments to people who work shifts (often referred to as 'unsocial' hours payments). However, the past relatively simple common division of working arrangements between normal daywork, shiftwork and part-time work no longer properly reflects the range of different working patterns which have developed in recent years. The terms **'atypical'**, **'peripheral'** or **'non-standard'** (or the less emotive terms 'irregular' and 'contingent') are generally used to cover, in particular, part-time and fixed, limited-duration contract working. There is little doubt that such working arrangements are extensive and increasing (to the extent, perhaps, that it can no longer be regarded as atypical but rather standard) (see Table 14.1). The figures show that the level of *part-time working* varies considerably between countries in Europe but that it is a predominant feature of female employment in every country (up to a high of 66 per cent of female employment in The Netherlands). Although a much lower proportion of the workforce is employed under *fixed, limited-duration contracts* (and, perhaps surprisingly, the level is lower in the UK than in other countries), Hunter *et al.*[67]

Table 14.1 Part-time and temporary working, 1994

	Part-time employees (% of total employment)			Employees on limited duration contracts (% of total employment)		
	All	Female	Male	All	Female	Male
UK	23.8	44.3	7.1	6.3	7.4	5.3
Sweden	25.3	43.4	8.1	13.5	14.6	12.3
Netherlands	36.4	66.0	16.1	10.9	15.0	7.9
Germany	15.8	33.1	3.2	10.2	10.9	9.7
France	14.9	27.8	4.6	10.9	12.3	9.7

Source: 'Atypical work in the EU', *European Industrial Relations Review*, no. 262, November 1995, p. 33.

note that the 2.5 percentage point growth in non-standard employment in the UK between 1983 and 1987 was mostly through greater use of temporary, agency and self-employed labour. Treu[68] states that relaxation of regulations about the use of fixed, limited-duration contracts in both Germany and Italy has been directed towards 'first-time job seekers' – almost a form of 'employment training contract' for young people. At the same time, the concept of a 'weekday, daytime' working pattern norm is no longer true. It appears that across the EU[69] some 31 per cent of employees 'normally or sometimes' undertake shifts, evening or night-work (the proportion of men working such patterns being generally slightly higher than women). The figures for the UK are significantly higher than for other EU countries (52 per cent overall; 60 per cent of men and 43 per cent of women).

As the figures indicate, the **effect of differentiation between 'core' and 'periphery'** not only segments the workforce, both within the organisation and the wider labour market, between those in relatively secure employment and those with little, if any, job security, but is likely to have a disproportionate effect on women. Certainly, Atkinson recognised that an implicit element of the model and strategy was that 'an individual's pay, security and career opportunities will increasingly be secured at the expense of the employment conditions of others, often women'[70]. Similarly, Harley concluded from his examination of the development of atypical work in Australia that because 'the majority of workers in peripheral employment ... are women ... the negative effects of the growth of peripheral employment are unequally distributed across society, reinforcing existing patterns of social inequality'[71]. However, Hunter *et al.*[72] express some caution about viewing the development of atypical work patterns in purely negative terms. They argue as follows:

- *The peripheral group is heterogeneous*. While many peripheral workers may be clearly identified with secondary labour market characteristics (low pay, low skill and low individual industrial power), there are other important high skill elements within the peripheral group with greater individual industrial power (professional, technical and managerial people). This may be particularly true for those in the self-employed groups.

■ *Atypical work patterns may be wanted as much as imposed*. People themselves may not wish to work full-time or may wish to have breaks from work. Certainly, governments have sought to pursue positive social objectives by adopting policies and legislation (through establishing various degrees of maternity and paternity rights) which support and protect individuals who wish to maintain a work role but in a way which is limited and compatible with having young children. The pursuit of such social welfare objectives (whether in the area of maternity or in areas such as physical disability of the individual or care of elderly or sick relatives) will inevitably increase the proportion of employees with atypical work patterns. However, Arrowsmith and Sisson report that 40 per cent of male, and 30 per cent of female, employees who took temporary contracts in 1998, 'took such a job only because they could not find a permanent contract'[73].

■ *Atypical workers may not be lower paid*. The desire to maintain internally consistent pay structures may mean that people are not paid at a lower rate of pay (in hourly rate terms) simply because they are part-time or working on a limited duration contract. However, Hunter *et al*. quote examples where organisations subcontract work out where the price advantage derives from the subcontractors' lower pay, or increase part-time work because their pay rates are too low to attract full-time employees (which implies that people seeking part-time work have either a lower expectation or perception of likely pay). Furthermore, atypical workers are likely to lose out in many organisations from their exclusion from many fringe benefits (in particular, their ineligibility to join the organisation's pension scheme)[74].

See Chapter 15 –
Grievance discipline
and redundancy
procedures

It has been argued that the **development of protective law** on the recruitment and, particularly, dismissal of employees has not only hampered management's ability to adjust the size of its labour force quickly to the level of work requirements but also substantially increased the costs of 'downsizing' (the requirement to **pay compensation for the individual's loss of job**). This, it is argued, has made management reluctant to recruit new full-time permanent employees, particularly at times of high market uncertainty, preferring instead to recruit part-time or full-time workers on fixed, limited-duration contracts who, in the past, have not been as protected by employment legislation. While the Employment Protection (Part-time Employees) Regulation (1995), introduced under pressure to conform fully with EU Directives, removed the differential qualifying period between full- and part-time employees, part-time employees may still be cheaper to employ by virtue of their weekly earnings being below the threshold for employer National Insurance contributions. However, de Grip *et al*. believe that 'the increase in various forms of atypical employment has become a central issue for labour market policy in the European Union'[75].

Significantly, the process of 'social dialogue' within the EU has produced two agreements between the ETUC, UNICE and CEEP (to be made binding through EU Directives). First, in 1997, an agreement was concluded[76] which provided that part-time employees should not be treated less favourably than full-time employees in respect of terms and conditions of employment (albeit on a pro-rata basis). This was given effect in the UK under the Employment Relations Act (1999). Second, the social partners concluded a further agreement in 1999 covering fixed-term contracts[77]. In addition to requiring 'no less favourable treatment' to that of employees on permanent contracts, it also requires member states to constrain any 'abuse' of fixed-term contracts by requiring objective justification for any renewal of a contract, or by limiting the number of renewals or the total number of years a person may be employed under fixed-term contracts.

Time flexibility

As Arrowsmith and Sisson note, 'working time, along with pay, is the defining feature of the employment relationship'[78]. Indeed, Blyton points out that working time arrangements and flexibility affect not only 'the way management pursues a more productive organization of the working period' but also 'have a direct and forceful impact on many aspects of employees' lives, including their job satisfaction, family responsibility, social life and physical and mental well-being'[79]. He suggests that working time patterns involve three elements – duration, organisation (arrangement) and intensity.

The initial focus, as industrialisation progresses, is generally on reductions in the *duration of working time* (basic hours per week, the number of working days per week and the amount of annual holidays) as one of the benefits (along with better pay and fringe benefits) associated with increasing organisational and national prosperity. In the UK hours of work have reduced in periodic waves from 72 hours a week in the nineteenth century (12 hours a day, six days a week with only limited, often unpaid, public holidays) to the current norm of 35–9 hours per week over a $4\frac{1}{2}$–5-day week with 4–6 weeks' annual holiday plus eight public holidays – all paid. However, there is a **wide variation in working hours** among EU countries. For example, not only does The Netherlands have a much higher level of part-time working (see Table 14.1) but, perhaps more significant, all other EU countries have a large concentration of employees (65–75 per cent) working within a narrow 'standard' band of hours around 35–40 hours per week, while in the UK some 40 per cent of employees work 41–70+ hours per week (some resulting from a longer 'basic' working week, but most from working overtime). Until recently the UK was the only country which had no legal restrictions on working hours[80], however, this has changed with the implementation of the EU Directive through the Working Time Regulations (1998) and, in particular, its limit of an average 48-hour working week (including overtime)[81].

Since the 1970s **attention has focused more on the organisation or arrangement of working time** in order to provide *flexibility or variability* in the individual's working time, which Bosch defines as 'deviation from an even breakdown of a certain agreed number of hours of work over an equally agreed number of weekdays'[82]. Traditionally, time flexibility has been provided by overtime, shiftworking and part-time working: all patterns of working which have existed from the start of industrialisation and which encompass substantial numbers of employees – for example, 3.9 million or 18 per cent of employees in the UK are involved in shiftworking (see Table 14.2).

Table 14.2   UK employee patterns of working hours, 1993 (by sex and status, 000s)

	Total employees	Flexitime	Annualised hours	Compressed working week	Shiftwork	Total	%
Full-time							
Males	10 597	1114	914	475	2310	4813	45.4
Females	5746	948	593	232	865	2638	45.9
Part-time							
Males	687	63	46	*	108	217	31.6
Females	4655	457	397	38	635	1527	32.8
Total	**21 685**	**2582**	**1950**	**745**	**3918**	**9195**	**42.4**

Source: G. Watson, 'The flexible workforce and patterns of working hours in the UK, *Employment Gazette*, July 1994, p. 242.

The original 'flexible firm' model did not include time flexibility as a separate and distinct form of flexibility and, as Blyton points out[83], the significance of developments in the pattern of working time has perhaps been obscured because of the tendency for 'time flexibility' to be subsumed under the broad heading of numerical flexibility, which concentrates on developments in part-time and short-term contract work primarily as a means of overcoming any rigidity or constraints on management's ability to 'hire and fire' labour (i.e. quickly change the size of its workforce).

Initially, the stimulus for greater time flexibility was 'employee needs' centred: to ease commuting problems, facilitate greater female participation in employment in order to overcome the perceived shortage in labour supply deriving from the 'demographic timebomb', and to support other organisation design changes (such as group working) associated with greater employee involvement. Since the early 1980s, the emphasis has shifted towards satisfying 'organisation needs': to improve labour and/or organisational efficiency and the quality of customer service and thereby enhance organisational competitiveness. Table 14.2 shows that 45 per cent of all UK full-time employees are involved in some form of time flexibility working (including shiftworking, which accounts for nearly a half of male full-time flexibility), while almost one-third of part-time employees work some form of time flexibility in addition to any flexibility they provide by virtue of being 'part-time' (25 per cent of all employees are part-time).

Visser believes that, increasingly, the individual employee's working time is becoming distinct from organisational operating time[84]. Certainly, the current emphasis is on moving away from standardisation and towards new forms of greater flexibility and variation in working time.

See Case study 14.3

1. *Flexitime*. This is an arrangement where 'employees may, within prescribed limits, choose their starting and finishing times'[85]. It involves defining a 'core time' period of the day when all employees must be in attendance but allows them individual flexibility in their starting and finishing times within an overall working-day 'bandwidth'. At the end of each 'accounting period' (usually four weeks), the employees may carry forward a credit or debit within set limits. Flexitime was introduced into the UK (from Germany) in

the 1970s to ease commuting problems, facilitate wider female employment and enhance employee autonomy ('employee needs' centred). In the 1980s and 1990s management has given greater priority to its potential to extend the working day of the organisation to provide better customer service, to reduce or eliminate the cost of overtime (employees being recompensed in time off rather than enhanced overtime rates) and to reduce absenteeism and 'lax time' (i.e. employees taking extra time at lunch breaks or other time off to go shopping, to go to the doctor, etc.). However, some trade unions 'fear that it may dilute claims for a shorter working week and that it may in fact lead to more employer control over the working lives of staff'[86]. Certainly, flexitime requires some form of time recording and, therefore, for many non-manual employees it has been associated with the introduction of formal time-recording systems – some computerised with plastic cards, others using more traditional time clocks. Flexitime is most common among managerial, professional, technical and clerical occupations and in the service industries such as banking and finance.

2. *Annualised hours or flexi-year*. An employee's working time is expressed in annual hours (for example, a basic 38-hour week will become 1,770 hours per year, after allowing for holidays), which may then be allocated differentially over the year. This is not a new concept – the construction industry in the UK traditionally had a longer basic working week in the summer and a shorter one in the winter. The real time flexibility comes from pre-scheduling the majority of the hours variably over the year (to accommodate identified peaks and troughs in demand) but keeping some in reserve as 'un-committed' hours, which the employee 'owes' the organisation, to deal with unforeseen circumstances. An alternative approach adopted by some organisations has been to pre-schedule all the basic yearly hours but, in addition, employees may contract to work (if necessary) a specific level of additional time (overtime) for which they receive an additional payment, as an integral part of their weekly or monthly salary, whether or not they work the full amount. The annualised hours approach also has the advantage that it can allow a 'finer tuning' of future reductions in working-time duration (ten hours reduction in the annual rate equals 12 minutes per week!). However, it is important to recognise that its success, like so many other aspects of flexibility, depends on 'co-operation between employees and management, and amongst employees themselves … with systems likely to work better if employees are able to make their own informal rostering arrangements when cover is likely to be required at short notice'[87]. Furthermore, if the planned distribution of working time proves to be wrong, then 'there is a danger of running out of hours, particularly towards the year end, which then means the employer has once again to resort to overtime working at premium rates'[88] – if the employee(s) will do the extra hours. Annualised hours are most common among 'associate professional and technical' and 'plant and machine operatives' occupations and relatively evenly spread across production, manufacturing and service industries.

3. *Compressed week*. This involves compressing the basic working week into longer but fewer days: a four- or $4\frac{1}{2}$-day week, nine-day fortnight or 12-hour

working over a three-day week. It is still a standardised, albeit shortened, week. The compressed week is most common among manual occupational groups ('craft and related trades' and 'plant and machine operatives') and, therefore, also more common in the production and manufacturing industries.

4. *Undefined hours*. Two forms of time flexibility involve not stating working hours at all. The first has become known as the 'professional contract', where, it is argued, there is no *need* to state hours of work because the employee is a 'professional' whose time is regulated by his or her recognition of the needs of the job – a concept much discussed in recent years in relation to teachers and lecturers. The second is referred to as the 'zero-hours' contract, where the employee, if indeed the person is an 'employee', is not contracted for any specific hours but is simply called upon as and when needed – adopted in a number of retail organisations. This is, in effect, a continuation of the previous 'casual work' under a new name, with little (if any) legal protection and potentially open to managerial abuse. However, the organisations which have adopted it argue that its difference lies in the intention to maintain an on-going relationship between the individual and organisation.

Changes in the arrangement of working time also involve **changes in the control of working time**. For the individual employee, work is not (as the basic labour economics model assumes) simply a trading off of leisure for pay; it is also a forsaking of independence for control. Lee[89] has suggested a 'control continuum' (ranging from employee control concerned with the idea of 'freely allowed choice' to management control concerned with 'specifying, altering and extra' hours). Primary hours (basic contractual hours) have traditionally been regulated and controlled by management, while supplementary hours (overtime) are beyond contract and, therefore, voluntary (employee regulated and controlled) and receive additional recompense (at enhanced levels of payment) or 'time off in lieu'. However, recent developments in flexible working time patterns at least blur, if not eradicate, this distinction. For example, the initial emphasis in flexitime on meeting employee needs was accompanied by an apparent shift in control of primary contractual hours away from management and towards employees – the employee could choose and vary his or her starting and finishing times. The reality, however, was often somewhat different. As Lee[90] pointed out, prior to the introduction of 'flexitime' many of these managerial, professional, technical and clerical workers worked within a 'laxtime', or more accurately 're-laxed time', system – i.e. within formally fixed hours there was 'reasonable' latitude given by superiors (informal norms) which allowed individuals to arrive late or leave early or extend their lunch break in order to undertake personal business. With the introduction of flexitime this was replaced by formal time recording systems (often electronic) in order to facilitate the accounting of hours which, it can be argued, represented a re-establishment of management control. More significantly, the emphasis on management's need to extend the organisation's working day, thus *requiring* employees to be in early or stay late, has limited the extent of employee choice and control to, at most, deciding who does which and when rather than whether they do it all.

Case study 14.3 ■ Bremer Landesbank (Germany)

The Bremer Landesbank is a small regional commercial bank in northern Germany, employing 1,000 people in two locations, which had operated a traditional flexitime system for some years. However, in the late 1980s the management recognised the need to develop more flexible time patterns in order to maintain, and hopefully improve, customer access while accommodating a reduction in the employees' basic working week. Discussions with employees showed that they also felt the traditional system was too restrictive and wanted more opportunity to organise their own working time: the core time period (09:00 to 18:30) accounted for 30 out of the 39 hours' standard working week; the credit/debit carry-over limit at the end of each monthly accounting period was only 12 hours; recouping extra time worked through taking complete days off (flexidays) was limited to only one day every three months.

Any change in the pattern of working hours had to be agreed to by the staff council which, under the German system of industrial relations, has a statutory right of 'co-determination' on matters relating to starting and finishing times and the distribution of working hours. The new system, introduced in 1991, involved four main elements:

1. *Time bandwidth*. The normal time bandwidth of 07:30 (earliest start time) to 18:30 (latest finish time) can be varied for certain groups of staff to reflect the particular nature of their work (for example, the bandwidth for dispatch staff is much wider – 04:45 to 24:00).

2. *Function time*. The common 'core time' for all employees in the previous traditional system was replaced by the concept of 'function time': the period within the 'time bandwidth' during which a minimum level of staffing (both quantitative and qualitative) has to be maintained to provide an effective service. This 'function time' varies between groups of employees in the organisation according to the nature of their work and their relationship to, and the demands of, customers (external and internal).

3. *Time-autonomous groups*. Each group of employees submits its proposed 'function times' for consideration by management and then approval by the staff council. It is the group which then deter-

mines which staff need to be present at any particular time to ensure maintenance of operational effectiveness. Time off is a matter for consultation and agreement within the group.

4. *Continuous 'traffic-light' accounting*. The credit/debit limits are applied on a continuous basis and are divided into three zones:

   ■ *Green* (up to ±20 hours). This is regarded as normal activity.

   ■ *Amber* (±20 hours to ±30 hours). Initially, it is the employees' responsibility to undertake the necessary corrective action to bring his or her hours back within the 'green zone'. If this is impracticable because of organisational operational reasons, then management is required to take responsibility by re-allocating work or staff.

   ■ *Red* (±30 hours to ±40 hours). This is to be regarded as exceptional and temporary, and requires prior management approval. No employees may exceed ±40 hours.

Management also took the opportunity to tighten up *time allowed for breaks*. Employees are legally entitled to 30 minutes' break per day (for a working day of six to 8.5 hours) which does not count as working time, but, as a result of custom and practice under the previous system, this had expanded to a 15-minute morning break and a 45-minute lunch break with the additional 30 minutes being included within working time. Under the new system, one-third of break times (up to a maximum of 15 minutes) is counted as working time (i.e. any time in excess of 45 minutes per day will be the employees' own time).

The system maintains the concepts of a *standard day* (basic weekly hours divided by five) and *standard day working hours* (08:00 to 16:18) for calculating hours to be credited for various specified authorised absences (for example, urgent medical and public duties); other absences are to be accommodated through the employees' use of his or her flexitime.

It is perhaps significant that most employees appear to try to maintain a positive time balance (i.e. the organisation owing them time) rather than taking time off before they have worked extra hours.

Source: 'Variable working time at Bremer Landesbank', *European Industrial Relations Review*, no. 230, March 1993, pp. 20–23.

Similarly, annualised hours establishes a clearer contract to be available for 'extra unscheduled' work when required – whether it is through holding back part of the basic annual hours or by contracting for a specific extra level of over-time. It requires employees to commit themselves, in advance, to variability in their hours at the discretion of management and so limits or removes their ability to exercise choice at the time the variation in their normal working hours is required. Consequently, supplementary hours are becoming an integral part of the contract subject to managerial control. The underlying assumption in not specifying any hours in the 'professional contract' is that it is reasonable to expect the individual to put work first – above other commitments. Thus, time flexibility systems appear to enhance management's control of the employee's time rather than enhance the employee's choices.

One impetus for seeking increased time flexibility among employees has been the demand for the introduction of a **shorter working week**. Significantly, the agreement establishing the 35-hour week in the German engineering industry at the end of the 1980s stated that, in those years coinciding with a pay review, 'the material effects of the reduction in working time are to be taken into considera-tion ... [the] hours cut will be offset to some degree against pay increases'[91]. While pay restraint has been a similar feature in the introduction of the 35-hour week in France, it has also resulted in management initiatives which focus on 'real working time' rather than 'attendance time'[92] and greater time flexibility through annualised hours and extra rest days[93]. There has been a similar empha-sis on the *intensity of working time* in the UK. Management has generally insisted that the introduction of a shorter working week should be self-financing. In approaching the issue of time flexibility, whether or not in the context of reduc-ing the basic working week, management has placed increased **emphasis on the productive use of working time** by a variety of different methods[94]:

- **Eliminating or reducing breaks**. Reducing the length of paid breaks (tea, lunch or other breaks which are unproductive parts of the paid basic working week) can achieve a reduction in the basic week without reducing the 'pro-ductive' part of the working week. Similarly, removing fixed 'unpaid' breaks and requiring that they be taken as and when operational conditions allow again reduces unproductive time when 'machines' have to stop.

- **'Bell-to-bell' working**. This means being at the place of work (and, in 'Japanese-style' companies, having the workstation prepared and ready to start) at the official start-time, rather than clocking-on at the start-time and then taking time getting to the workstation and starting to actually work. However, it is important to recognise, in the context of reducing breaks, washing-up time, etc., that 'given time, they tend to reappear unoffi-cially ... there is a natural tendency to "unwind" towards the end of the working day'[95].

Functional or task flexibility

Treu suggests that the legal restrictions placed on the 'hiring and firing' of labour may had the effect of inducing management to look more closely at adopt-ing 'innovative forms of work organization in order to achieve optimal use of the various factors of production'[96]. Job, task or functional flexibility involves broadening (vertically or horizontally) the range of tasks, duties or responsibilities the employee may be required to undertake with, consequently, less role specialisation. It enhances, Tailby argues, 'a firm's ability to allocate and relocate employees ... [by the] relaxation and reorganisation of job boundaries'[97]. For many **non-manual employees** this has not taken the form of simply increasing the range of specific tasks identified within their job description (content), but rather by making the description of the role and duties less restrictive and more focused on the responsibilities and performance of the individual (output). This has frequently been related to the de-layering of organisations, implementation of the concept of 'empowerment' and use of performance appraisal (whether accompanied by performance-related pay or not). In effect, functional flexibility has been achieved by blurring the boundaries of the individual's job and expecting the employee to utilise their initiative in undertaking any work or activity which is necessary for the achievement of their objectives (and those of the organisation).

See Case study 14.4

So far as **craft/production flexibility** in production is concerned, Cross identified that in only some 10 per cent of the organisations surveyed in 1989 had any significant degree of interchangeability between maintenance and production employees been achieved[98]. Although the purpose of this inter-craft and craft/production flexibility is intended to reduce 'downtime' and maximise the use of capital machinery, management appear to regard the training of craft employees to do process work as 'uneconomic' – except for providing a further source for emergency cover. One IDS survey noted that 'the danger of "multi-skilling" becoming trade-less semi-skilling was a real one' but that there was 'no evidence to suggest that craft identity is being eroded in these agreements'[99]. Rather, the introduction of functional flexibility in this area has led to 'craft' employees acquiring additional closely related skills rather than becoming multi-skilled (i.e. being able to do a complete small job rather than divide its distinct tasks between different trades) and process employees becoming responsible for first-line maintenance. More significantly, Ackroyd and Proctor argue that rather than 'enskilling of "core" employees ... [profitable UK manufacture has been secured] ... by a combination of a heavy dependency on the flexible use of relatively unskilled labour and a willingness to utilize external sources of production'[100]. Similarly, Tailby points out that managers in organisations which originally had sought 'full flexibility' had 'come to question the extent to which the total interchangeability of labour "is desirable or viable in practical terms"'[101].

A further aspect of functional flexibility has been the introduction of **teamworking or groupworking** based on the concept that each person in the 'team' is capable of doing most, if not all, tasks. This form of flexibility raises two important issues:

■ **Relationship between the supervisor and the work group**. It is clear, according to one survey, that there are 'sharp differences between companies in what they really mean by teamworking, and in particular over the function of the team leader'[102]. Some organisations regard the 'team leader' as little more than a 'senior operator' (responsible for optimising plant operations and undertaking general administrative duties); others regard it as an

Case study 14.4 ■ **British Airways Engineering**
Functional restructuring

BA Engineering employed 9,500 people at seven locations in the UK carrying out maintenance and repair of BA's own aircraft and those of other airlines. It was strongly unionised with three bargaining units: non-craft (represented by TGWU), craft (represented by AEEU) and engineering and supervisory staffs (represented by MSF).

In 1992 it embarked on a major restructuring of its working arrangements centred on the abolition of supervisors and the development of multiskilling among the craft workers. These changes were aimed at supporting the continuing development of the company's Total Quality Management (TQM) approach by removing direct supervision, improving accountability and communication, and encouraging the development of greater personal responsibility and problem solving. The changes would also cut labour costs and focus attention on the working of the new 'business units' created within BA Engineering. At the same time, new EU legislation on aircraft safety and maintenance was likely to affect the company's training and certification procedures. The changes had to be negotiated with the respective unions and MSF, in particular, was concerned to maintain job security for its 'supervisor' members.

1. *Supervisors.* In 1986 the supervisors' 'management' role had already been reduced by requiring 50 per cent of their time to be spent carrying out 'hands-on' work. The 1992 change abolished the supervisor role completely and, consequently, the engineering and supervisory staffs bargaining unit. The 900 supervisors were to be assimilated into the new structure in one of three ways:

   ■ Promotion into the Technical & Management Group (TMG) as direct line managers or part of the new technical support groups;
   ■ Transfer into the new team-leader roles – Leading Aircraft Engineer (LAE) for craft teams or Co-ordinator for non-craft teams;
   ■ 'Demotion' to the new Technician grade.

   In addition to protecting the individual's salary where it was higher than the new grade, the company also introduced the title 'senior technician' to maintain some status for those supervisors assimilated into the technician grade. Initially all

supervisors were assimilated into LAE, Co-ordinator or Technician grade (in the maintenance area most supervisors became LAEs, while most supervisors in the material management and component overhaul area became technicians). Subsequently, all the ex-supervisors were able to apply for TMG jobs and nearly 40 per cent were promoted.

2. *Multiskilling.* Previously, employees in the 'tradesman' grade were apprenticed in a single trade and therefore there was an element of demarcation in the work they could undertake between mechanical, avionics and refurbishing. The new structure created two main grades:

   ■ *Technician.* This was the entry grade for apprenticed employees who initially carry out work related to their single trade. After five years there was a 'qualification bar' which could be passed only if the employee satisfactorily completed BA's multiskilling course (approved by the Civil Aviation Authority) and after which the employee was expected to use skills across mechanical, avionics and refurbishing work.
   ■ *Aircraft Mechanic.* This grade brought in skilled employees from non-craft group (without apprenticeships). BA Engineering developed a training package which, together with three years' on-the-job experience, was considered to be equivalent to an apprenticeship, thereby providing access to promotion to Technician grade.

All previous Aircraft Engineers and Tradesmen were transferred to the new Technician grade. Aircraft Engineers, like Supervisors, were assimilated into the new grade above the qualification bar with the title 'senior technician' and were, therefore, the first to undertake the new multiskilling course.

BA Engineering also abolished the system of extra payments for obtaining 'licences'. (Employees have to be licensed by the CAA, after successful completion of approved courses and examinations, to undertake maintenance work on different aircraft types.) In the

Case study 14.4 ■ British Airways Engineering *(continued)*
Functional restructuring

past BA had paid employees a minimum of £1,500 for each licence they obtained – the average was three licences per employee but some had as many as ten. BA believed that obtaining these licences should be regarded as a normal part of an employee's job in order to improve performance and not linked to monetary reward. Consequently, it was agreed that no new payments would be made and that existing 'licence pay' would be partly consolidated into basic pay where an individual moved to a higher-paid job

(i.e. it would fund increase in basic pay) and the remainder would be retained as a personal pay element.

BA estimated that these changes would increase productivity by 5–10 per cent through reduced 'downtime' of aircraft, better service to customers and reduced inventory.

Source: 'Restructuring for flexibility at British Airways Engineering'. *IRS Employment Trends*, no. 527, January 1993, pp. 12–15.

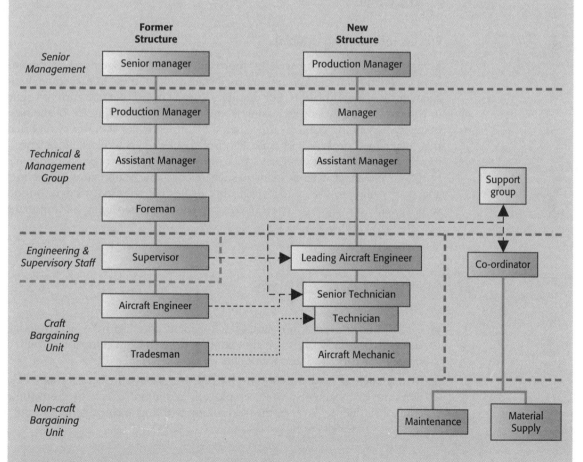

See also Case study 7.1.

'assistant' to the supervisor (dealing with work allocation, operational problem diagnosis, etc. but not such matters as discipline), while others give it an enhanced role in 'people management' (including, for example, assessing members of the team in relation to performance-related pay increases). Clearly the introduction of teams with their own 'leaders' has repercussions for the role of the supervisor: for example, in one organisation the introduction of teamworking led to the 'virtual abolition of the supervisor's role, with manufacturing cells operating as "autonomous work groups" under a system of joint union/management supervision'[103].

■ **Team stability**. Teamworking, to be successful, requires the individuals to identify with and be committed to *their* team. Therefore, while it may provide for greater functional flexibility as between the members of each team, it may introduce a degree of 'employee' inflexibility or resistance in respect of temporary or permanent moves between teams (particularly if teamworking is associated with any form of group based performance-related pay).

Process for achieving flexibility

Management's strategy in seeking improved working arrangements appears to have changed from the 'macho' imposed stance adopted by at least some managements in the early 1980s. For example, Towers noted that 'the current vogue in companies for ways of increasing labour flexibility is reminiscent of the productivity bargaining fashion of the sixties'[104]. Similarly, an IDS survey reported that 'negotiated deals ... with a trade-off of money for new working practices, remain the norm ... but where the price is not right, there has been considerable shopfloor resistance even in industries where competitive pressures are intense' and that 'while job-loss remains a feature of flexible working, pledges on job security and "no compulsory redundancy" clauses are becoming an important pre-condition of many deals'[105].

■ Summary propositions

■ There is no universal, absolute or self-evident criterion by which to judge equity in pay; rather it is a relative concept derived from comparisons with a range of factors (both economic and sociopolitical).

■ Management is constantly seeking to improve labour efficiency through new working arrangements, while employees and unions seek to exert some control (influence) over both the resulting working arrangements and their method of introduction.

Activity	Take some time to think about how you would like to be treated. Consider what factors or criteria you would use to judge 'equity' or the 'felt-fair' factor in relation to your own pay. Similarly, consider your own position in relation to time – the flexibility and control you would want (or expect to have) over managing your working time. How far do you think your feelings in respect of pay and time could (or will) be accommodated by an employer?

■ Further reading

■ M. Armstrong, *Employee Reward*, Institute of Personnel and Development, 1996; R. Thorpe and G. Homan (eds), *Strategic Reward Systems*, FT Prentice Hall, 2000. These books provide useful information on a wide variety of payment systems and the issues associated with developing remuneration strategies.

■ R. B. McKersie and L. C. Hunter, *Pay, Productivity and Collective Bargaining*, Macmillan, 1973. This covers the development of productivity bargaining up to the beginning of the 1970s and the content and implementation of productivity agreements.

■ I. Benson and J. Lloyd, *New Technology and Industrial Change*, Kogan Page, 1983. This provides a useful examination of the development of technical change and management/union responses.

■ A. Pollert (ed.), *Farewell to Flexibility*, Blackwell, 1991; P. Blyton and J. Morris (eds), *A Flexible Future? Prospects for Employment and Organisation*, de Gruyter, 1991. These two collections of papers provide a wide ranging discussion of various issues and aspects of the current developments in labour flexibility.

■ References

1. See M. Armstrong, *Employee Reward*, Institute of Personnel and Development, 1996 and R. Thorpe and G. Homan, *Strategic Reward Systems*, FT Prentice Hall, 2000.
2. J. Evans, 'Pay', in G. Hollinshead, P. Nicholls and S. Tailby (eds), *Employee Relations*, FT Pitman, 1999, pp. 342–4.
3. E. Jaques, *Equitable Payment*, Heinemann Educational Books, 1967, p. 146.
4. *Ibid.*, p. 182.
5. *Ibid.*, p. 181.
6. NBPI, *Report No. 65: Payment by Results Systems*, HMSO, 1968.
7. Jaques, *op. cit.*, p. 181.
8. D. T. B. North and G. L. Buckingham, *Productivity Agreements and Wage Systems*, Gower, 1969, p. 95.

9. CBI Pay Databank (UK) and Bureau of National Affairs (USA), quoted in 'Long-Term Agreements', *Incomes Data Services Study 450*, January 1990, pp. 3, 10.
10. *Ibid.*, p. 1.
11. W. W. Daniel, 'Influences on the level of wage settlements in manufacturing industry', in F. Blackaby (ed.), *The Future of Pay Bargaining*, Heinmann, 1980, p. 156.
12. I. Keesler, 'Remuneration systems', in S. Bach and K. Sisson (eds), *Personnel Management* (3rd edn), Blackwell, 2000, p. 269.
13. *Ibid.*, p. 270.
14. C. Duncan, 'Why profit related pay will fail' *Industrial Relations Journal*, vol. 19, no. 3, 1988, p. 186.

15. 'Profit Related Pay', *Incomes Data Services Study*, no. 471, December 1990, p. 1.
16. A. Pendleton, 'Profit sharing and employee share ownership', in Thorp and Homan, *op. cit.*, p. 346.
17. 'PRP in the 1990s: a survey of 333 employers', *IRS Pay and Benefits Bulletin*, no. 360, September 1994, p. 2.
18. *IRS Pay and Benefits Bulletin*, no. 360, *op. cit.*, tables 1 and 2.
19. Duncan, *op. cit.* p. 197.
20. *Incomes Data Services Study 471*, *op. cit.*, p. 3.
21. *Ibid.*, p. 5.
22. A. Fowler, 'New directions in performance pay', *Personnel Management*, November 1988, p. 30.
23. I. Kessler, 'Performance pay', in K. Sisson (ed.), *Personnel Management* (2nd edn), Blackwell, 1994, p. 465.
24. *Appraisal Related Pay*, Advisory Booklet no. 14, ACAS, 1990.
25. M. Cannell and P. Long, 'What's changed about incentive pay?' *Personnel Management*, October 1991, pp. 58–63.
26. 'Performance pay survey', Institute of Personnel and Development, 1998.
27. I. Brough, 'PRP for manual workers: issues and experiences', *Employee Relations*, vol. 16, no. 7, 1994, p. 28.
28. Armstrong, *op. cit.*, p. 239.
29. Kessler (2000), *op. cit.*, pp. 281–2.
30. L. Harris, 'Performance pay and performing for pay', in J. Leopold, L. Harris and T. Watson (eds), *Strategic Human Resourcing: Principles, perspectives and practices*, FT Pitman, 1999, p. 199.
31. I. Kessler and J. Purcell, 'Performance related pay: objectives and applications', *Human Resource Management Journal*, vol. 2, no. 3, 1992.
32. P. Lawson, 'Performance-related pay', in Thorpe and Homan, *op. cit.*, p. 313.
33. E. Heery, 'Performance-related pay and trade union de-recognition', *Employee Relations*, vol. 19, no. 3, 1997, p. 219.
34. E. Heery, 'Performance-related pay and trade union membership', *Employee Relations*, vol.19, no. 5, 1997, p. 440.
35. CAC decision in respect of British Airways, quoted in *Incomes Data Services Report*, no. 570, June 1990, p. 27.
36. Fowler, *op. cit.*, p. 30.
37. 'Performance pay gives ground to performance management', *IRS Employment Trends*, no. 560, May 1994, pp. 6–10.
38. 'Flexible Benefits', *Incomes Data Services Study*, no. 481, May 1991.
39. T. Blackman, 'Trading in options', *People Management*, May 1999, p. 43.
40. R.B. McKersie and L.C. Hunter, *Pay, Productivity and Collective Bargaining*, Macmillan, 1973, p. 5.
41. N. Stettner, *Productivity Bargaining and Industrial Change*, Pergamon, 1969.
42. A. Flanders, *The Fawley Productivity Agreements*, Faber & Faber, 1964, p. 13.
43. McKersie and Hunter, *op. cit.*, p. 24.
44. F. Zweig, *Productivity and Trade Unions*, Blackwell, 1951, p. 19.
45. North and Buckingham, *op. cit.*, p. 21.
46. K. Hawkins, 'Productivity bargaining: a reassessment', *Industrial Relations Journal*, spring 1971, p. 20.
47. T. Manwaring, 'The trade union response to new technology', *Industrial Relations Journal*, vol. 12, no. 4, 1981, p. 20.
48. I. Benson and J. Lloyd, *New Technology and Industrial Change*, Kogan Page, 1983, p. 182.
49. Manwaring, *op. cit.*, p. 22.
50. B. James, 'The trade union response to new technology', *Internal Papers in Economics (No. 5)*, Middlesex Polytechnic, 1980, p. 2.
51. TUC, *Employment and Technology*, 1979.
52. James, *op. cit.*, p. 8.
53. *Ibid.*, p. 11.
54. Benson and Lloyd, *op. cit.*, p. 176.
55. Manwaring, *op. cit.*, p. 8.
56. James, *op. cit.*, p. 10.
57. Benson and Lloyd, *op. cit.*, p. 182.
58. J. Atkinson, *Flexible Manning: The way ahead*, Institute of Manpower Studies, 1984; J. Atkinson and N. Meager, *Changing Working Patterns: how companies achieve flexibility to meet their needs*, National Economic Development Office, 1986.
59. A. Evans and J. Bell, 'Emerging themes in flexible work patterns', in C. Curson (ed.), *Flexible Patterns of Work*, IPM, 1986, p. 11.
60. *Ibid.*
61. B. Towers, 'Managing labour flexibility', *Industrial Relations Journal*, vol. 18, no. 2, 1987, p. 83.
62. A. Pollert, 'The flexible firm: a model in search of reality or a policy in search of practice?' *Warwick Papers in Industrial Relations*, no. 19, 1988; A. Pollert, *Farewell to Flexibility?* Blackwell, 1991.
63. 'Flexible Working', *Incomes Data Services Study*, no. 407, April 1988, p. 1.
64. *Ibid.*
65. 'Flexibility at Work', *Incomes Data Services Study*, no. 454, March 1990, p. 5.
66. S. J. Proctor, M. Rowlinson, L. McArdlke, J. Hassard and P. Forrester, 'Flexibility, politics

and strategy: in defence of the model of the flexible firm', *Work, Employment and Society*, vol. 8, no. 2, 1994, p. 226.

67. L. Hunter, A. McGregor, J. NacInnes and A. Sproull, 'The 'flexible firm': strategy and segmentation', *British Journal of Industrial Relations*, vol. 31, no. 3, 1993, p. 389.
68. T. Treu, 'Labour flexibility in Europe', *International Labour Review*, vol. 131, no. 4–5, 1992, pp. 502–3.
69. 'Atypical work in the EU', *European Industrial Relations Review*, no. 262, November 1995, pp. 33–4.
70. J. Atkinson, 'Manpower strategies for flexible organizations', *Personnel Management*, August 1984, p. 31.
71. B. Harley, 'The conditions associated with peripheral employment in Australia: an empirical analysis', *Employee Relations*, vol. 16, no. 8, 1994, p. 27.
72. Hunter *et al.*, op. cit., p. 402.
73. J. Arrowsmith and K. Sisson, 'Managing working time', in Bach and Sisson (eds), *op. cit.*, p. 297.
74. A. Balchin, 'Part-time workers in the multiple retail sector: small change from employment protection legislation?' *Employee Relations*, vol. 16, no. 7, 1994, pp. 43–57.
75. A. de Grip, J. Hoevenberg and E. Willems, 'Atypical employment in the European Union', *International Labour Review*, vol. 136, no. 1, 1997, p. 49.
76. 'Atypical working in Europe: part one', *European Industrial Relations Review*, no. 282, 1997, pp. 16–23.
77. 'Social partners succeed in regulating foxed-term contracts', *European Industrial Relations Review*, no. 304, 1999, pp. 14–17.
78. Arrowsmith and Sisson, *op. cit.*, p. 287.
79. Blyton, 'Working hours', in K. Sisson (ed.), *Personnel Management* (2nd edn), Blackwell, 1994, pp. 496–7.
80. 'Working time in Europe: part two', *European Industrial Relations Review*, no. 280, 1997, table, p. 18.
81. 'New working-time legislation', *European Industrial Relations Review*, no. 297, 1998, pp. 24–7.
82. G. Bosch, 'Reducing annual working time and improving schedule flexibility – causes, effects, controversies', in A. Gladstone *et al.* (eds), *Current Issues in Labour Relations: an international perspective*, de Gruyter, 1989, p. 193.

83. P. Blyton, 'Flexible times? Recent developments in temporal flexibility', *Industrial Relations Journal*, vol. 23, no. 11, 1992, p. 27.
84. J. Visser, 'New working time arrangements in The Netherlands', in Gladstone *et al.* (eds), *op. cit.*
85. 'Flexitime', *Incomes Data Services Study*, no. 477, March 1991, p. 1.
86. *Ibid.*, p. 4.
87. 'Annualised hours 2: manufacturing flexibility', *IRS Employment Trends*, no. 489, June 1991, p. 12.
88. 'Annual hours', *Incomes Data Services Study*, no 674, 1999, p. 2.
89. R. A. Lee, 'Controlling hours of work', *Personnel Review*, vol. 14, no. 3, 1985.
90. R. A. Lee, 'Recent trends in the managerial use of flexible working hours', *Personnel Review*, vol. 9, no. 3, 1980.
91. 'The shorter working week', *Incomes Data Services Study*, no. 461, July 1990, p. 9.
92. Y. Altman and F. Bournois, 'Temps perdu', *People Management*, June 1999, pp. 54–5.
93. 'The 35-hour week: one year on', *European Industrial Relations Review*, no. 307, 1999, pp. 14–9.
94. 'Reorganising working time', *Incomes Data Services Study*, no. 417, September 1988.
95. *Incomes Data Services Study*, no. 461, *op. cit.*, p. 7.
96. Treu, *op. cit.*, p. 506.
97. S. Tailby, 'Flexible labour markets, firms and workers', in Hollinshead *et al.*, *op. cit.*, p. 468.
98. M. Cross, 'Total productive maintenance', paper presented to North East Maintenance Association Conference (1989), quoted in 'Flexibility at work', *Incomes Data Services Study*, no. 454, March 1990, p. 3.
99. *Incomes Data Services Study*, no. 407, *op. cit.*, pp. 4, 6.
100. S. Ackroyd and S. Proctor, 'British manufacturing organization and workplace industrial relations: some attributes of the new flexible firm', *British Journal of Industrial Relations*, vol. 36, no. 2, 1998, p. 171.
101. Tailby, *op. cit.*, p. 471.
102. *Incomes Data Services Study*, no. 407, *op. cit.*, p. 7.
103. *Incomes Data Services Study*, no. 454, *op. cit.*, p. 4.
104. Towers, *op. cit.*, p. 79.
105. *Incomes Data Services Study*, no. 407, *op. cit.*, p. 1.

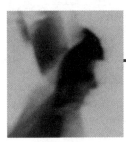

chapter fifteen

Grievance, discipline and redundancy procedures

Learning objectives Organisations need to define mechanisms and standards by which differences between management and employees are to be resolved. By the end of this chapter, you should be able to:

- explain the process for resolving grievances and disputes: the causes of employee dissatisfaction, its forms of expression and its relationship to collective bargaining;

- understand the nature of the formal disciplinary process: the basis of the rules and norms underlying employee behaviour, the aims and elements of the process and the law relating to unfair dismissal;

- appreciate the different perspectives of and objectives in a redundancy situation: the difficulties in determining selection criteria, the importance of communication and consultation and the legal framework around redundancy;

- understand the issues associated with the operation of procedures in each area.

Definition **The term procedure refers to those organisational mechanisms which provide a formal regulatory framework for handling specified issues and, in so doing, define and limit the exercise of managerial authority and power.**

Key issues While you are reading this chapter, you should keep the following points in mind:

- If management does not deal with its employees fairly and to their satisfaction within these organisational mechanisms, the employees may look outside the organisation to the increasing legal definition of employment rights and use the external legal processes to seek financial compensation.

- Perhaps the only way in which we can judge the effectiveness of these procedures is not by how little they are used but rather by how effective they are in constraining managerial prerogative and arbitrary management decisions and actions.

15.1   Introduction

The inherent desire on the part of both management and employees to exert control over the work situation implies, Thomson and Murray suggest, that joint procedures 'are the best, possibly the only, way of bringing the two separate control systems to terms with each other'[1]. Where such procedures are negotiated between management and unions, and involve employee or union representatives in their operation, they represent an important part of the organisational system of joint regulation: the formal interface between, at an organisational level, management and union and, at a more individual level, managers and employees. It is the decisions and practices implemented through such procedures which determine the nature of the management/employee relationship, provide the clearest evidence of management's intention and by which management is judged as an employer. While procedures can provide a degree of consistency in the way people are treated, management generally seeks to retain a degree of flexibility to treat issues on their merits.

15.2   Grievances and disputes

All organisations, whether trade unions are recognised or not, require some process which allows employees to express, and seek to resolve, dissatisfaction about their work situation (whether related to their terms and conditions of employment, working arrangements or managerial decisions). Although management has an obvious interest in ensuring that employees are not dissatisfied, the grievance and dispute process is **primarily an employee mechanism**:

- It is initiated by employees to express and resolve *their* dissatisfaction.
- It is a process which allows employees to challenge 'absolute' management power (in the absence of trade unions, it is often the only process).
- Its effectiveness should be judged, therefore, by employee (rather than management) satisfaction with its operation (process as well as outcome).

Significantly, it appears that employees are increasingly turning to the law to redress their grievances rather than relying on organisational processes. In 1998, ACAS received some 113,000 claims across a broad range of employment issues[2]. It has been suggested[3] that the increase has resulted from employees being more aware of and prepared to pursue their legal rights, the ability to obtain significant financial compensation and the expansion of union legal services to members coupled with law firms working on a 'no win, no fee' basis. Effective grievance procedures may go some way to relieving this pressure.

Typology of employee dissatisfaction

The variety of issues, their significance to both employee(s) and management and the different ways they may be presented make it difficult to define the

Figure 15.1 Typology of employee dissatisfaction

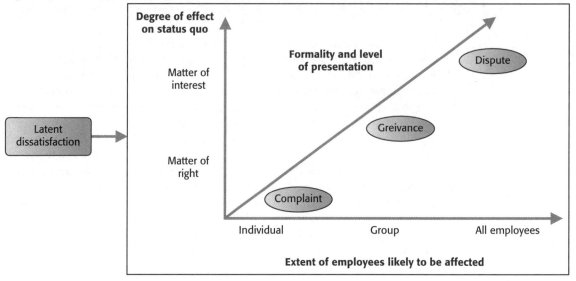

terms 'grievance' and 'dispute' in a precise and universal way. This variety stems from a number of factors (see Figure 15.1):

■ The **nature of the issues** to be resolved includes matters of right, which are concerned with the 'interpretation and application of existing rules', and matters of interest, which 'involve differences relating to the determination of new terms and conditions of employment'[4].

■ The **extent of the dissatisfaction** may be confined to an individual employee or be experienced collectively by a group or even all employees.

■ The **manner of presentation** to management may range from informal presentation to the immediate supervisor by either an individual, a group of employees or the employees' representative, through formal presentation within the grievance procedure, to a trade union claim being initiated within the recognised negotiating process.

Thomson and Murray argued that the essential difference between grievance and dispute 'lies in the way they are initiated and in the degree of proposed change in the status quo'[5]. Similarly, Torrington and Chapman differentiated a *complaint*, where 'dissatisfaction is being expressed, but not in a procedural way', from a *grievance*, where 'the complaint is presented formally and triggers the procedural machinery'[6]. Significantly, Torrington and Hall note that presenting a grievance is a 'formal, relatively drastic step, compared with commonplace grumbling' and hence 'rare since few employees will question their superior's judgement ... and fewer still will risk being stigmatised as a trouble-maker'[7]. Singleton pointed out that the term *dispute* is variously applied to grievances as soon 'as a shop steward is involved, when a full-time official of the union is called in' or if it 'is not solved at domestic level and is referred to an external procedure'[8]. Thus, the use of the term 'dispute' appears to be linked to the existence of unions and implies that the issue is to be handled on an inter-organisation basis (between management and union) and may, if necessary, involve the use of industrial action on the union's part if there is a continuing failure to agree.

It is perhaps useful to regard complaints, grievances and disputes as overlapping segments of a continuum based primarily on the manner and formality of the presentation of employee dissatisfaction. Whether a specific situation is likely to be regarded as a dispute rather than a grievance depends on the degree of formality of its presentation, the organisational level at which it is initially raised and the extent to which both parties regard the outcome as establishing new terms and conditions of employment.

Relationship to collective bargaining

See Chapter 9 –
Collective bargaining

The grievance/dispute process (see Figure 15.2) is complementary to the collective bargaining process (where it exists), in that it provides employees with a measure of continuing influence and control over decisions which affect them. A collective agreement is unable on its own, nor is it intended, to provide the means for joint regulation of the full range and variety of situations encountered in a work situation. The wording of most collective agreements is often imprecise, or even deliberately ambiguous, and involves the use of 'may', 'reasonable', 'where practical', etc. – all of which require clarification as to the precise circumstances in which they will or will not operate. Certainly, Hawkins believed that 'where a grievance procedure either formally or informally includes collective issues within its scope the dividing line between grievance settlement and collective bargaining becomes increasingly blurred'[9]. The grievance/dispute process is as much concerned with the determination of rules as it is with their interpretation and application.

It is possible to identify four distinct, but overlapping, ways in which the grievance/dispute process is integral to the collective bargaining system.

■ *Industrial jurisprudence*. Simply, this means that it may be used by employees or union to ensure that management complies with the terms of any collective agreement or its own policies and decisions. Many employee complaints may come under this heading and the employee's immediate superior (or the union representative) may be able to provide an immediate answer to, and resolution of, the complaint. However, it would be wrong to assume that the resolution of all complaints or grievances is simply a matter of referring to the appropriate document to find the answer.

■ *Continuing administration of collective agreements*. As Kuhn pointed out, the imprecise wording of most collective agreements means that 'few of its provisions apply automatically or without some person in authority making decisions about the nature of a given situation and the meaning of the agreement'[10]. If employees and union are to maintain the joint regulation established by the initial collective agreement, they must continue to negotiate its interpretation and application with management as specific situations arise within the workplace. This is achieved by the joint clarification or redefinition of the meaning and intention, if not the wording, of the collective agreement either through additional formal written agreements or the decisions

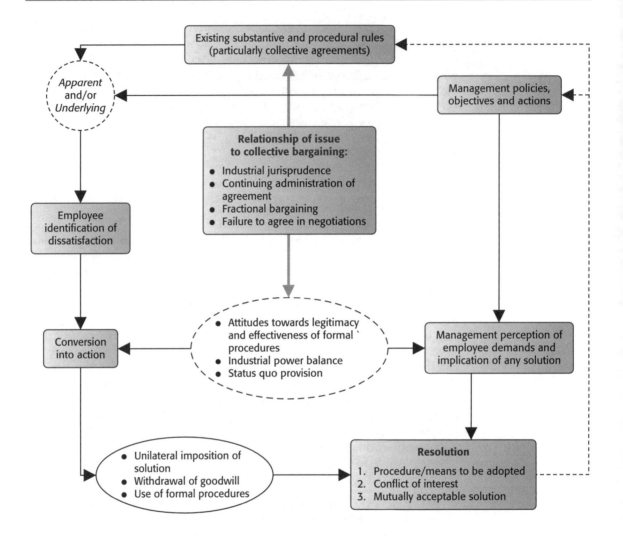

Figure 15.2 Grievance
/dispute process

becoming part of the regulatory framework through precedent and 'custom
and practice'. This aspect of the process is of increased importance in the
early stages of a new agreement when either side may be seeking to extend
the scope of its application and the other side seeking to restrict it.

■ *Fractional bargaining*. The grievance/dispute process may be used to reach
agreement on issues not covered by the terms of existing collective agreements. This, as Kuhn noted, 'can arise from any management activity with
which the workers become dissatisfied and feel they have the power to negotiate'[11]. The use of the grievance/dispute process to formulate new 'agreements' allows employees and union to extend the areas over which they have
a measure of joint regulation on an *ad hoc* basis. It provides an opportunity
for continuing pressure on, and erosion of, managerial prerogative. The
formal effect of such agreements is confined to the workgroup immediately
affected at the time. However, in so far as the agreement is considered by
both parties to be satisfactory for the specific situation in which the problem

arose, it also creates (through precedent) an expectation that its terms may be applied to other groups or in the future should the need arise. Thus, the gains made by one group through the grievance/dispute process may become regarded as terms which should apply to all.

■ *Resolution of any failure to agree which arises during negotiations.* It is to this aspect of its function, as a formal part of the main collective bargaining system, that the term 'dispute' may be most appropriately applied. The process may require both parties to submit their case to some external examination by referring the issue to an industry-level disputes procedure, if the organisation is a member of an employers' association, or by the involvement of a third party such as ACAS. Whatever method is used, any resolution becomes part of the final collective agreement in the same way as the other terms on which there was no failure to agree.

Thomson and Murray[12] found that most formal grievances, as opposed to complaints or disputes, related to either monetary issues (ranging from simple errors of payment calculation to losses of pay or changes in pay associated with payment by results systems, or appeals on job grading and evaluation) or work issues (including allocation of work, transfer of employees from one type of work to another or the physical conditions under which the work had to be carried out). Significantly, they found virtually no grievances arose in respect of major technical changes because 'conflict would have been resolved at the planning stage and hence not emerge as grievances'[13] or because such issues were considered to be negotiated items or disputes, rather than strictly grievances, by the organisations concerned.

However, the apparent concern expressed by employees through the grievance/dispute process may, in reality, be only the symptom of some more fundamental, but less tangible, **underlying concern** which may influence the operation of the process:

■ *Work satisfaction.* The satisfaction which employees seek from work, both extrinsic (financial reward or status) and intrinsic (the nature of their work), will vary both between employees and within each employee over time. The loss of 'work satisfaction', whether deliberate or inadvertent, often cannot easily be articulated as a specific grievance. This may result in the frustrated employee seeking to enforce 'due entitlements' which previously may not have been a matter of concern. A series of what appear to be minor grievances may be a reflection of a more general dissatisfaction with the work situation, which will remain unaltered even after the specific grievances have been resolved.

■ *Sociotechnical system.* Increased formal use of the grievance/dispute process may arise from structural factors associated with the relationship of the employees to their work and management. Where employees feel they have little direct control over their work processes, they may seek to gain more formal control over the managerial decisions which determine their day-to-day work situation by challenging management decisions through the grievance/dispute process. Alternatively, the system may create a perceived separation between employees and their immediate management, resulting in the formal presentation of issues which, in other circumstances, might have been raised as informal complaints. This may also arise where employees perceive the decision-making process to be centralised away from their own immediate management.

■ *Change and adaptation*. The instability and uncertainty created by frequent work changes, particularly with little notice, can result in the need for continual reassurance that management is taking account of employee anxieties and aspirations during its decision making. The grievance/dispute process allows employees to challenge change, obtain assurance that it is necessary and influence the change so that it causes the least disruption to them.

■ *Power and authority*. Any formal grievance or dispute which arises within an organisation challenges both management's right to make the decision unilaterally (process) as well as the actual decision (content). In so far as management wishes to satisfy employees by finding a mutually acceptable solution, the grievance process is part of joint regulation within the organisation.

Salipante and Bouwen[14] point out that most grievances contain a complex interrelationship of the different types and sources of conflict (see Box 15.1) and, as a consequence, the *public* formulation of a grievance to management may differ from, its *private* formulation among employees – it is more likely to be presented as a substantive issue.

The **conversion of latent employee dissatisfaction into manifest forms of action** is influenced by the extent to which the employees accept the **legitimacy and effectiveness of the formal procedures** for resolving such issues and the perceived power relationship between the employees and management. The

---

Box 15.1	Primary categories of sources of conflict

■ *Environmental* (nature of work and working conditions):
  ▮ economic terms and conditions of employment;
  ▮ physical job conditions;
  ▮ job demands being either too great or too little for the individual's skills and abilities.

■ *Sociosubstantive* (goals, means and inequities in treatment):
  ▮ ideological differences of interests, goals and means;
  ▮ differences over appropriate means to agree upon goals;
  ▮ perception of inequity stemming from organisational policy, procedure or decisions of an individual;
  ▮ divergence from work expectations.

■ *Sociorelational* (relationships between individuals, groups or organisations):
  ▮ institutional (employee/management, union/management and/or inter-union);
  ▮ prejudice (sexism, racism, etc.);
  ▮ competition among peers or cliques;
  ▮ personality conflict and personal problems.

Source: P. F. Salipante and R. Bouwen, 'Behavioural analysis of grievances: conflict sources, complexity and transformation', *Employee Relations*, vol. 12, no. 3, 1990. pp. 17–22.

acceptance and continued use of the formal recognised procedures depends not only on the fact that they are the constitutional means for resolving any differences or dissatisfaction but also on employee and union satisfaction with their manner of operation and the solutions reached within them. If employees or union feel that the formal procedures do not provide an adequate means for, or even hinder, the effective representation and protection of their interests, they may express their dissatisfaction in other ways. They may, for example, seek to impose their own solution by refusing to carry out the work which has caused the dissatisfaction or, if they lack the power to unilaterally impose a solution, withdraw their goodwill from the management and the organisation, resulting in increased absenteeism, labour turnover and a reduction in morale.

At the same time, the possession of **industrial power** may not only enhance the confidence of the individual and group to express dissatisfaction but also strengthen their ability both to ensure that management considers their problems and to influence management's decision in their favour. It may also increase the level of expectation among the members of the group as to what can, or should, be achieved if they use, or threaten to use, their industrial power. It is such 'strategic' groups which have the greatest capacity to indulge in 'fractional bargaining' through the formal grievance/dispute process, or, where they feel the formal procedures to be inadequate, to press for their reform or, if necessary, to impose solutions.

The **resolution phase** of the process requires some form of dialogue between employees and management. Management's response will be determined by its perception of the employees' dissatisfaction and its assessment of the likely implications of any solution for the maintenance of its policies and strategies. Any **conflict of interest** between employee aspirations and management objectives may only be resolved through 'negotiation' and the outcome, whether it relates to matters of right or of interest, or concerns a single employee or the whole group, will reinforce or modify the existing pattern of rules. Indeed, the continued use of the process to resolve such conflicts is a constant reaffirmation of the procedural rules. However, management will need to balance compromise against the benefit of pursuing the strategies and decisions it has formulated in the light of perceived business needs – even in the face of strong employee or union objection. Marsh pointed out that 'there is a sense in which procedure can be too successful ... for the effect of procedure is to achieve acceptable compromise and it may be that such compromise is not always in the economic or social interest'[15].

It can be argued that both parties have an interest in ensuring the **maintenance of the formal procedures** themselves. This concern for the grievance/dispute process is founded on two main arguments:

■ Because any collective agreement is itself a product of an agreed joint negotiating procedure and made in 'good faith' by both sides, it is reasonable to assume that both will wish to discuss, and if necessary negotiate, any differences between them regarding its further interpretation and application.

■ These procedures provide a constitutional forum within which both sides may argue their case and seek to persuade the other on a more or less equal basis, and neither, Marsh pointed out, should 'attempt to obtain settlements more favourable to itself by unconstitutional action'[16] involving the use of industrial power as a pressure.

Management will try to ensure that it does not encourage, and indeed actively discourages, **unconstitutional action on the part of employees or union**. Most procedures include a specific clause which precludes industrial action by either side until all the stages of the procedure have been exhausted, and normally management will refuse to negotiate under such duress – whether actual or only threatened. Management's position has been strengthened by legislation requiring unions to disassociate themselves from unofficial industrial action.

The procedure may also contain a **status quo** clause, under which the situation prior to management's intended decision or action prevails until either an agreement is reached or the grievance/dispute process is exhausted. This places the pressure for settlement more on management than on union or employees. Unlike wage bargaining, where delay in reaching an agreement is to the advantage of management, any delay in reaching a settlement over work changes is to the advantage of union and employees, by allowing them to continue to work a system with which they are satisfied and increasing the pressure on management to make concessions in order to secure their agreement to the proposed change as soon as possible. Without such a provision, management is able to implement its changes and *then* negotiate with employees and union afterwards. Certainly, many managements removed such status quo provisions during the 1980s as part of the drive for greater organisational flexibility.

The grievance/dispute procedure

The purpose of a **grievance/dispute policy** is to establish the organisational climate, objectives and manner in which managers (individually or collectively) will be expected to respond to any grievance or dispute presented by employees. The policy may contain statements like the following:

- Management *accepts the right* of employees, individually or collectively through a recognised union, to present complaints to management.
- Any differences which may arise between management and employees or union should, wherever possible, be *resolved quickly* and without recourse to the use of industrial action.
- Management is concerned to ensure that, in responding to any grievance or dispute, it *does not create an unacceptable precedent* which may subsequently be claimed to apply throughout the organisation.

All employers are required to **inform employees**, as part of their contract of employment notice, of both the person to whom they should go initially to seek redress of any grievances relating to their employment and, where applicable, any consequent steps. Certain **issues may be specifically excluded** from the grievance procedure because of their special needs. For example, health and safety matters may require to be referred to the Safety Officer for judgement, while those regarding the grading of a post may be dealt with through a special job evaluation appeals procedure involving judgement by a panel. Where the procedure is intended to encompass both individual and **collective matters** (particularly where the issue relates to the interpretation and application of existing collective agreements), it is important that it should clearly identify the appropriate stage, or stages, at which collective issues may initially be presented.

Stages and system of appeals

The adoption of a staged approach within the grievance procedure reflects organisational reality – namely, a hierarchy of roles based on increasing responsibility and authority. Thomson and Murray noted that the purpose of such an approach, in operational terms, is 'to ensure that those with effective authority ... can be reached in an orderly way and also to provide for a review of decisions by a new level of authority at each succeeding stage'[17]. However, the operation of the procedure should not become cumbersome and time consuming as a result of too many stages. It is essential, therefore, to incorporate only those definable and distinct levels of management authority which can, and should, play an effective role in resolving employee grievances. There are **three broad levels** at which the procedure operates:

- **Within a department**. This allows the departmental manager, who has responsibility for ensuring that the department fulfils its productive targets and complies with the organisation's policies and collective agreements, the opportunity to check, and if necessary correct, his or her own decisions or those of a subordinate line manager.

- **Outside the department but still within the organisation**. This allows more senior management to assess the issue within the wider context of the organisation's industrial relations position and strategy and, in particular, assess any implications it may have for other parts of the organisation or the future.

- **External to the organisation**. This allows for an unresolved issue to be subjected to some form of 'third party' scrutiny to judge whether management's decision is 'fair' and, if applicable, in accordance with the provisions of any collective agreement. This may involve using a nationally agreed industry disputes procedure (if the organisation is a member of an employers' association) or conciliation/arbitration through ACAS.

The apparent 'staged appeals' nature of the grievance procedure raises several issues:

- **Management is the sole judge**. The internal stages of the procedure generally require employees or their representatives to present their grievance to managers; management is, in effect, judging its own actions which are the cause of the employees' dissatisfaction. However, some procedures may provide for the final internal stage to be a joint employee/management body which seeks a consensus (negotiated) decision. Any external stage will, inevitably, involve management and employee(s) (or union) presenting their case for adjudication by either an arbitrator or, if through an external industry disputes procedure, a committee drawn from organisations and unions not involved in the dispute.

■ **Nature of the appeal system**. The procedure ceases if employee(s) or union receive an answer or decision which is acceptable to them; at that point they are satisfied and no longer have a grievance. Any failure to reach a solution at the lower stages of the procedure may result not just from the unwillingness of the manager concerned to make a concession, but from a perception that it involves a decision which is outside his or her authority and requires the approval of a more senior manager. Marsh draws a distinction between grievances involving essentially 'appeals to equity', where the procedure is used to decide 'what is fair, and there can be no logical stop to the process', and grievances involving the 'interpretation and application' of collective agreements, where 'only the parties at the level at which the agreement was made can logically say how it should be applied or interpreted'[18].

■ **Independence of each stage**. The appeal system, and formal wording of most grievance procedures, appears to rest on the assumption that each level of management dealing with the grievance is independent in both its decision-making role and its relationship to any previous level of the procedure. This assumption is incorrect. In reality the manager at each stage of the procedure is likely to contact other managers who have dealt with similar problems, or his or her superior to whom the grievance may go if it is unresolved or an industrial relations specialist manager. The manager may simply be seeking information, ideas or opinions on which he or she may base a decision or, as is more often the case, seeking some form of 'group decision' among the roles as to the best course of action. Thus, the senior management stage of the procedure is more one of providing the focus for a reassessment of the corporate decision than one of independent judgement on the quality and fairness of a lower-level manager's decision.

■ **Role of supervisors**. Most procedures seek to ensure that employees initially present their grievance to their immediate supervisor to try to ensure that it is resolved as quickly as possible and without the unnecessary use of the higher stages. However, it is significant that many supervisors do not regard the daily complaints or grumbles from employees as being the first stage of the formal grievance procedure; to them, a 'grievance' only exists when they *cannot* deal with the employee's problem. Therefore, in some procedures this first step is clearly limited to being only an informal stage of the grievance procedure. Recent developments in 'de-layering' and, in particular, the creation of teamworking require consideration about the role of team-leaders: are they to replace the traditional 'supervisor' stage and have a formal 'managerial' decision-making role in handling grievances, or should they be seen as the informal 'managers of dissatisfaction', with the grievance procedure only applying to issues they cannot resolve and starting at the departmental manager level?

■ **Role of union or employee representative**. As Singleton noted, for many supervisors the 'premature involvement of the union may create in him the feeling that the problem is already outside his sphere of responsibility'[19] and thus induce the supervisor to refer the matter to the next stage of the procedure. Equally, the exclusion of a union representative from the first stage of the procedure may inhibit some employees from presenting their grievances to management. Significantly, the Employment Relations Act (1999) has given all employees the right to be accompanied by either a union representative or a fellow employee during any grievance hearing – which is defined by the Act as 'concerning the performance of a statutory, contractual or other duty by the employer'; that is, it only covers 'a breach of existing terms of contracts or legal duties and not the pursuit of improvements'[20]. The Act further specifies that the representative is permitted to 'address' the hearing and 'confer' with the employee, but not 'answer questions' on his or her behalf. Thus, the legislation not only gives all employees, particularly non-union employees, the legal right to be accompanied but it also legally defines the role, which may be used by some management to restrict the current activities of union representatives in 'representing' their members. The legislation could also increase the formality of the first stage of the grievance process.

Formality of the procedure

- **Time limits**. Procedures often specify time limits within which management has to make a response – ranging from a few days at the earlier stages to one or two weeks at the later stages. While this is intended to protect employees and union from undue delay by management in considering a grievance, many managers would argue that such time constraints may be insufficient for an adequate consideration of the problem, particularly complex ones, resulting in the issue simply moving to a higher level of the procedure. However, management can, of course, seek to extend the stated time limits by agreement with the employees or union concerned. It should be remembered that even with time limits it may take three to four weeks before the internal procedure is exhausted.

- **Presentation of grievance in written form**. Management is often concerned that, without the grievance being formally presented in writing right from the outset, the content of a grievance is likely to change as it progresses through the various stages of the procedure. This is often regarded by management as a deliberate tactic on the part of union representatives either to cloud the real issue or to strengthen their case by moving it away from the specific situation which generated the grievance and into arguments based on more general principles. In fact, both union and management perceptions of the character of, and issues involved in, a particular grievance or dispute will inevitably change as it progresses through the procedure. It will be viewed in successively wider organisational and industrial relations contexts. Certainly, any argument that employees 'must' present their grievance in a written form, particularly in respect of the first stage, ignores the general informality of this stage and may well prejudice the position of those employees who either cannot write or have difficulty in expressing themselves in a written medium. However, it is good industrial relations practice for management at all levels of the procedure to keep a formal written record of any meetings or discussions.

- **Integrity of the formal procedure**. Finally, the integrity of the formal grievance/disputes procedures can only be maintained if senior managers, having allocated responsibility for dealing with grievances to certain defined levels of management, do not subvert it by offering employees, union representatives or union officials an 'open door' policy. Some senior managers believe that they can demonstrate their goodwill on industrial relations matters, and improve trust and understanding within the organisation, by allowing employees and/or their representatives free access to them with their problems. Such an approach, like the senior manager or director who deals with employees' grievances while touring the workplace, simply encourages the bypassing of the formal procedural arrangements. Breaches of procedure by employees and union representatives cannot be condemned if management itself is aiding and encouraging such breaches.

The grievance 'interview'

The formal interface between management and employees or union within the grievance procedure is often referred to as a 'grievance interview'. However, it would be wrong to assume that the process of negotiating is not relevant to these meetings. They are an integral part of the organisation's collective bargaining system (interpreting and applying collective agreements and subjecting management decisions to some degree of employee influence and joint regulation) and, therefore, are just as likely to involve the need to achieve a compromise between the parties as any formal negotiation.

See Chapter 13 – Negotiation

By the very nature of the grievance process, in that it is initiated by employee dissatisfaction, there is little that a manager can do in preparation for a particular grievance. However, all managers should be aware that any action or decision on their part is a potential source of employee dissatisfaction and, therefore, should always be in a position, if called upon, to explain and justify them. There are three distinct stages to handling the grievance interview:

1. **Establish the nature of the grievance**. The manager should be certain that all the relevant information has been obtained from the employee(s) or union representative and that he or she understands the character and extent of the grievance, especially any underlying causes. The manager has to listen, question and clarify. The manager must then decide whether the matter is within his or her sphere of responsibility and, if it is, whether he or she is in a position to make an immediate response, or whether time is required to gather more information or consult other members of management.

2. **State and explain the organisation's position**. The manager must be prepared to explain and, in response to questions or arguments from the employee(s) or their representative, defend the reasons for the response to the grievance. The manager, acting as a spokesperson for management, is seeking to convince or persuade the employee(s) or their representative of the correctness of management's decision.

3. **Identify mutually acceptable compromise**. Many grievances are not resolved simply by either the employee's or management's position prevailing but rather involve a moderation of management's intended position to meet, as far as possible, the employee(s) dissatisfaction – mutually acceptable

compromise through negotiation. Thus, management has to assess the importance of the issue to both employees and themselves and consider the likely implications of any possible alternative solutions, particularly outside the immediate situation in which the grievance has arisen and for the future.

Once the grievance or dispute has been settled, it is important that both parties are clear about the details of the decision. This should be recorded in writing to the employee(s) and representative. It should also be disseminated to the rest of management in order to help ensure an integrated, co-ordinated and equitable handling of industrial relations throughout the organisation.

15.3   Discipline and dismissal

Disciplinary action can often be an emotive and contentious issue, particularly when it results in the ultimate sanction of dismissal. It not only involves subjective concepts of 'fair' and 'reasonable', 'right' and 'wrong', but also concerns the power, authority and status of management. However, there is an absence of reliable data in the UK on the extent of formal disciplinary action. In 1990, Millward et al.[21] reported an annual average rate of dismissals of 1.5 per cent (equivalent to 350,000 of the working population), while a survey in 1991[22] gave a figure of 3 per cent of employees being involved in disciplinary action (equivalent to 750,000 of the total working population). Whatever the precise figures, Edwards points out that 'it remains true that the use of disciplinary sanctions is widespread'[23]. Significantly, the number of claims in respect of unfair dismissals is only some 45,000 per annum.

The formal disciplinary process

Human behaviour in organisations is regulated through a pervasive system of both formal and informal 'rewards' and 'punishment', intended to ensure that employees conform to the behavioural and performance standards necessary for the achievement of the organisation's business objectives. Torrington and Hall define 'discipline' as the 'regulation of human activity to produce a controlled performance'[24] and identify three types or levels of discipline:

Managerial – imposed by the formal authority leadership;
Team – need for mutual dependence and commitment;
Self – internalised self-control.

The formal disciplinary process is that element of the system concerned with **formal action taken by management against an individual who fails to conform to the rules established by management within the organisation**[25].

It is a **control process** in which management has 'the possession of authority, the utterance of commands and the operation of restrictions or sanctions to ensure compliance with those commands'[26]. Few companies have adopted a truly joint approach to the whole process. While the procedures for applying the

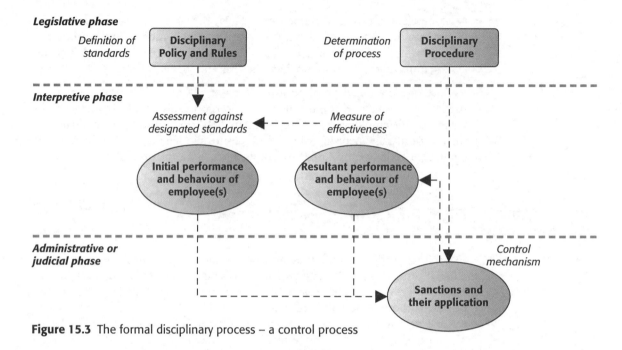

Figure 15.3 The formal disciplinary process – a control process

disciplinary rules have become more subject to joint regulation, there has been little, if any, compromise in the determination of the rules. In the 1970s, Mellish and Collis-Squires pointed out that official publications 'seem much "softer" on the question of joint control over the drawing up of substantive rules than they do about the administration of such rules'[27]. They argued that this is almost inevitable given that any legislative incursion into the area of discipline can only apply to dismissals and therefore has little jurisdiction or concern with the bulk of the formal disciplinary process and it perceives issues largely in individual terms and separate from the collective bargaining process.

The formal disciplinary process comprises a **number of elements** (see Figure 15.3):

1. Definition of desired standards of performance or behaviour. These may be codified in a specific set of disciplinary rules or, more likely, in some form of general organisational rules or, indeed, may be unwritten and assumed by management to be understood by employees.

2. Assessment of the employee's performance or behaviour against these standards. This assessment is not a formalised, periodic one, as in staff appraisal systems, but takes place only when management believes *prima facie* that the action of the employee is at variance with the designated standards.

3. The control mechanism itself (the disciplinary procedure) to implement corrective action by means of sanctions when the assessed initial performance or behaviour is found to be at variance with the designated standards.

4. Feedback on the effectiveness of the corrective action by assessing whether the resultant performance or behaviour of the employee now conforms to the designated standards.

Thus, it has a *legislative phase* (the determination of the rules and the procedure for enforcement), an *administrative or judicial phase* (the application of the control mechanism through the disciplinary procedure), and *interpretative phases* (the assessment by management of initial and resultant performance or behaviour of the employee). It is a formalised process, generally codified in written documents and embodying a quasi-judicial sequence of identification of offence, a 'trial' involving submission of evidence by both the prosecution and defence and pleas in mitigation, followed by the passing and execution of sentence.

As with society's penal system, there are potentially three aims for the formal disciplinary process (retribution, deterrence or rehabilitation) and it can be viewed primarily as either a punishment or training process. The **negative (punitive) approach** is directed towards retribution or deterrence based on the principle that 'few people would deny that those who deviate from accepted behaviour ought to experience some sort of unpleasant consequence'[28], however, it may achieve only the minimum standards of compliance to avoid punishment. The **positive (corrective) approach**, on the other hand, is directed toward rehabilitation based on a process of educative socialisation to create an attitude in which the individual not only conforms but also supports and is committed to the performance and behavioural standards. However, as Rollinson points out, 'discipline is more often used to teach people the rules *after* they have been broken' and management's behavioural expectations 'can be highly subjective, and include vaguely held expectations of the right attitudes or spirit of co-operation'[29]. Three important points should be kept in mind:

- The positive (corrective) approach is only applicable to less severe offences and sanctions; the *ultimate sanction of dismissal is retributive* or a deterrent to others. In practice, management is admitting that the differences between the individual's behaviour and the organisation's expectations cannot be reconciled and, therefore, the only solution is to remove the problem individual from the system.

- Whether any sanction constitutes *'punishment' depends on the perception of the recipient* and not the intention of the instigator. While some employees (such as those whose rewards or career progression is linked to formal performance or appraisal reviews) might not like to receive a formal reprimand because of the possible effect on their career, this does not mean that other employees will place as much emphasis on such warnings – particularly those in manual or lower clerical groups, for whom there may be little, if any, career prospects.

- The development of *responsible autonomy* forms of management control over labour, through teamworking, empowerment and performance appraisal, would appear to decrease the need for management to use *ad hoc* direct formal disciplinary action and replace it with more general and regular performance or appraisal review approaches – a more positive corrective approach. However, Edwards points out that the development of 'new' forms of self-discipline do not indicate necessarily an increased positive commitment on the part of employees but rather a greater managerial ability to control the employee's day-to-day personal conduct. He notes that, in the context of teamworking, groups may be 'reluctant to apply their own disciplines and managers were left relying on formal penalties because problems were not identified early enough'[30]. Furthermore, he argues that there is little if any evidence that the introduction of HRM strategies has resulted in a reduced use of formal disciplinary control or traditional sanctions; in his view 'any idea of a progressive trend from punishment through correction to self-discipline is thus too simple'[31].

The actions which warrant formal disciplinary action are commonly categorised as follows:

■ **Gross or serious misconduct** – offences warranting summary dismissal or at least severe disciplinary action for a single incident.

■ **Minor misconduct** – offences warranting only a verbal or written warning for a single incident, but progressing to more severe disciplinary action and eventual dismissal for a persistent offender.

However, as Mellish and Collis-Squires pointed out, such a distinction is only useful in relation to the procedural mechanism and the 'procedures in themselves tell us little about the disciplinary process'[32]. To understand the nature of the process, it is necessary to examine the **basis of the rules** themselves (see Box 15.2). The rules enforced through the formal disciplinary process comprise only one part of the norms, both formal and informal, which regulate the relationships within the organisation. Both Fox[33] and Hill[34] identified two derivations for organisational norms:

■ The industrial organisation is a microcosm of its external society, wherein the individuals who coalesce to form the organisation adhere to common, or dominant, norms and, therefore, carry over these norms and their adherence to them into the industrial setting.

■ The norms of the industrial organisation are not externally derived and common to all members but internally derived and sectionally based with management norms predominating as a result of either socialisation or management power.

As Edwards points out, 'it is not possible to break behaviour down into the normal, which falls within the rules, and the abnormal breaches of rules'[35]. An act of individual indiscipline considered actionable by management's norms may, in practice, be derived from the **individual's adherence to other sets of norms**. Mellish and Collis-Squires pointed out that 'the union – or fellow workers – may be a greater disciplining force upon the individual worker than the employer, and the norms they enforce may be significantly at variance with the norms of discipline preferred by the employer'[36]. For example, pilfering in docks and hotels[37] was found to be so common and 'accepted' that an individual case of disciplinary action by management for theft or fraud would, in reality, be a conflict between workgroup norms and management norms as opposed to a situation of individual aberration. The fact, therefore, that the application of a sanction does not lead to the suppression of the undesired behaviour may result from the undesired behaviour pattern being reinforced by pressures which are stronger than the pressure of the 'punishment'.

Box 15.2	Norms and behaviour

The rules that employees are expected to comply with may be divided into three categories:

- *General society rules relating to personal behaviour* (fighting, swearing, stealing, drunkenness, etc.). Individuals may choose the organisation for which they work but have little, if any, choice regarding the people with whom they must relate. Therefore, the organisation's disciplinary rules will, in part, reflect society's code of conduct concerning individual behaviour and relationships. However, both the individual's group norm and managerial attitudes may allow greater tolerance within the work situation; for example, swearing, which might be considered a breach of the peace in the external society, may be tolerated within the workplace. These rules are enforced not simply because management believes (morally) that they should be the agent for enforcing society's norms in the workplace, but because these acts also affect the achievement of the organisation's objectives (interrupting production and involving loss) and the inclusion of these rules more easily legitimises the whole disciplinary process.

- *Rules derived from external legislation* (health, safety and hygiene; sexual and racial discrimination). The existence, nature and legitimacy of these rules is dependent primarily on the political and legal systems (external objectives and policies) and their importance within the organisation (particularly health, safety and hygiene rules) will vary according to the organisation's product or technology. Their importance to management lies in the fact that failure of an individual or group of employees to comply with these external regulations can result in management being legally liable (including financial compensation).

- *Managerially determined general work control rules* (timekeeping and work performance) or *rules underpinning managerial authority and prerogative* (failure to obey instructions and insubordination). These rules are specific to the work environment, depend on the legitimacy of management's position within the organisation and have few, if any, direct equivalents within the general society's code of conduct. Management limits the freedom of the individual to undertake actions which might prejudice the smooth operation of the organisation (output) or disregard the instructions of the formal authority (management).

The employee's behavioural relationship to these rules may be divided into:

- *Aberrant*: Although the employee has broken the rule, he or she is not questioning its legitimacy, therefore, the application of formal disciplinary control will appear fair, providing the sanction is perceived to be reasonable in relation to the offence.

- *Non-conformist*: The breach of the rule results from the employee's non-acceptance of the legitimacy of the rule; therefore, any disciplinary action will always appear unreasonable.

Most managers, because of their own acceptance of the legitimacy of the rules, will tend not to differentiate between *aberrant* and *non-conformist* employee behaviour, or will see the non-conformist as, at best, irrational or, at worst, subversive. Consequently, a non-conformist may present the appearance of an aberrant to management (because he or she feels it will be more acceptable and may indeed mitigate the severity of the punishment), while continuing to challenge the rule in his or her peer group. It is possible to argue:

- Those rules deriving their legitimacy from society's general code of conduct or involving a direct challenge to managerial authority are likely to be contravened by only a small minority of employees because they involve breaches of fundamental socialised norms.

■ But those rules which rely almost exclusively on the managerial perceived need for control over the human part of the production process – for example, lateness and poor performance – may well be contravened by a more substantial proportion of the workforce at one time or another because they involve a lesser degree of socialisation on the part of the employee.

There is also a link between the formal disciplinary process and the **collective bargaining process**. Certainly, Ashdown and Baker separated individual acts from group 'indiscipline', which results from 'a widespread rejection of a working arrangement or rule and the resolution of any conflict lies in the negotiation of new work standards'[38]. Furthermore, management may issue formal warnings, suspension or even dismissals for 'failure to obey legitimate work instructions' against employees undertaking collective action in the form of 'working to rule'. If these sanctions are withdrawn as part of any settlement securing a 'return to normal working', and if management's intention from the start was to withdraw them, they can be seen as an exercise of power within the collective bargaining process. However, if management did not intend to withdraw them or the employees are not sufficiently strong to secure their withdrawal, they are likely to remain on the individual's record and may be taken into account if the individual is involved in any subsequent disciplinary action.

Not all behaviour which deviates from management's norms and expectations is necessarily subject to sanctions within the formal disciplinary process. A variety of situations have been identified in which there may be **reluctance to use the formal disciplinary process**. Boise found that 'second-line supervisors would often not impose penalties on employees for misconduct during peak workloads of the department, and they would hesitate to impose a penalty on an employee when replacements with his particular skills are in short supply'[39]. Maier[40] argued that the supervisor is faced with a dilemma: too much use of the formal disciplinary process to enforce compliance with the rules may lose co-operation in meeting production objectives, but if violations are not dealt with through the accepted formal process the supervisor may discriminate between employees and be inconsistent. Therefore, to resolve the dilemma, he or she may turn a blind-eye and ignore the existence of a violation.

Thus, individual managers may have differing **degrees of tolerance** in respect of the point at which the contravention of the rule is considered to be a matter for discipline, the point which divides informal from formal disciplinary action, and the points dividing the severity of sanctions to be applied within the formal process. In order to achieve consistency and comply with external constraints such as legislation and trade union pressure, the organisation establishes its own tolerance limits by means of the disciplinary policy and procedure – particularly the classification of offences into those of a major or minor nature. Once the contravention of a rule has been delineated as a major offence, the individual manager, faced with such a contravention, has less freedom to ignore it or treat it other than as a major offence requiring severe formal disciplinary action. The organisational tolerance limits contained in the formal policy and rules restrict the individual manager's degree of tolerance. However, the two tolerance 'limits' are interactive, in that the attitudes of managers largely determine the nature of the organisation's tolerance limits which, in turn, reinforce the individual manager's attitudes.

The legal framework

The employer's right to discipline is founded on the failure of the employee to fulfil his or her obligations under the contract of employment, which the common law defines as giving honest and faithful service, using reasonable skill and care in work, obeying all reasonable orders and not committing misconduct. It is only since the Industrial Relations Act (1971) that a dismissed employee has been able to claim compensation for 'unfair dismissal' or seek reinstatement or re-engagement (as opposed to the previous common law 'wrongful' dismissal, with maximum compensation equal to the wages for the normal contractual notice period). However, **certain groups are excluded**:

- Employees with less than one year's service. (The length of service qualification has moved over the lifetime of the unfair dismissal legislation – it started at two years in 1971, was reduced to one year, then six months and then back to one year in the 1970s, went back to two years in 1986 and has now been reduced to one year in 1999.)
- Employees over 65 or their normal retirement age (if less).
- Where there is a designated contracted-out dismissals procedure approved by the Secretary of State.

Until 1995 part-time employees working between eight and 16 hours a week had to have had five years' service before they could claim unfair dismissal and those working less than eight hours per week were not covered at all. However, this differential treatment was determined[41] to be indirect discrimination in breach of European law. The subsequent Employment Protection (Part-Time Employees) Regulations (1995) brought it in line with the qualifying period for full-time employees (at that time two years). However, the two-year period was challenged as being indirect discrimination because proportionally fewer women could comply with the requirement[42], but the Employment Relations Act (1999) has reduced the qualifying period to one year. It has also ensured that employees on fixed-term contracts can no longer be asked to waive their rights to claim unfair dismissal simply because their dismissal results from the non-renewal of the contract. This is particularly important with the use of fixed-term contracts as part of increased labour flexibility.

The term 'dismissal' applies to any situation where the employer terminates the contract of employment. This may take different forms:

- **Dismissal with notice** or payment in lieu of notice for disciplinary or other reasons;
- **Summary dismissal** without notice or payment in lieu of notice (generally for disciplinary reasons resulting from a formal investigation within the disciplinary process);
- **Instant dismissal** without notice (with or without payment in lieu of notice) for disciplinary reasons, but without any formal investigation into

the employee's conduct (this is contrary to the rules of natural justice and almost certainly an unfair dismissal).

In all these situations the employee has the right to present a claim to an Employment Tribunal. However, in the legal context, the term 'dismissal' also includes **constructive dismissal**. This arises where 'the employee terminates the contract, with or without notice, in circumstances such that he is entitled to terminate it without notice by reason of the employer's conduct'. Over the years, two approaches have been developed on this issue:

- The first, and perhaps strongest, line has been that for a constructive dismissal to be upheld the employee must show that 'the employer is guilty of conduct which is a significant breach going to the root of the contract of employment, or which shows that the employer no longer intends to be bound by one or more of the essential terms of the contract'[43]. In other words, the employee has to show that a single act on the part of the employer was a sufficient breach of the contract to amount to repudiation.

- The second, more diffuse, line has held that a constructive dismissal could be justified on the basis of a series of minor breaches, none of them individually amounting to repudiation of the contract, providing that taken together they amount to unreasonable action on the part of the employer. It has been held that 'an employer who persistently attempts to vary an employee's conditions of service (whether contractual or not) with a view to getting rid of an employee or varying the employee's terms of service, does act in a manner calculated or likely to destroy the relationship of confidence and trust between employer and employee'[44].

The Tribunals have held that constructive dismissal may arise just as much from the individual actions of managers (such as victimisation) as it can from organisational decisions (such as reorganisation involving demotion, loss of status or responsibilities for the employee).

The legislation sets out certain **'fair' grounds for dismissal** (any other reason is automatically unfair):

- The capability or qualification of the employee;
- The conduct of the employee;
- The employee was redundant;
- The continued employment of the employee would contravene a statutory duty or restriction;
- Some other substantial reason such as to justify dismissal.

In addition, the legislation sets out specific criteria for dismissals relating to pregnancy and trade union membership or activity. However, it is the interpretation placed on these statutory provisions by Tribunals which is most important in relation to the handling of discipline and dismissal in organisations. It is therefore useful to examine briefly certain types of dismissal.

1. *Capability*: The two most common reasons for dismissing an employee under this heading are ill health and poor work performance. To justify

dismissal on the grounds of **ill health**, the employer must demonstrate the following:

- Sickness or ill health was the cause of dismissal.
- Reasonable efforts were made to ascertain the employee's state of health, including consulting a doctor, and that the employee had been informed that further absence or ill health could result in dismissal.
- The dismissal was reasonable because of the nature of the employee's work and the effect the absence or ill health had on the organisation and other employees.
- Reasonable efforts had been made to find suitable alternative work within the organisation bearing in mind the employee's state of health.

It has been suggested that 'in cases of ill health the basic question that has to be determined ... is whether in all the circumstances the employer can be expected to wait any longer and, if so, how much longer'[45]. The answer is a balance between, on the one hand, operational efficiency and the success of the undertaking and, on the other, reasonable job security for employees absent through sickness or other causes beyond their control. The existence of a sick-pay scheme within the organisation does not, in itself, determine the time an employee is entitled to be absent before dismissal is justified.

In dealing with dismissal because of **poor work performance**, three aspects need to be considered:

- Is the employee incapable or inefficient in the performance of the work? The employer only has to demonstrate reasonable grounds for believing the employee to be inefficient and that this is the reason for the dismissal. In judging inefficiency, 'management must still require and impose its own standards, at least within certain limits: that is to say, any standard required or imposed must be a reasonable standard'[46].
- Has the employee been warned previously regarding poor work performance? Normally, failure to give any warning that performance is unsatisfactory, and that continued unsatisfactory performance could lead to dismissal, will result in the dismissal being regarded as unfair. The employee should, therefore, be informed as to the nature of the poor work performance, the acceptable standard that is required and the period of time within which to reach that standard.
- Has the employer provided the employee with the necessary reasonable support to improve the work performance? The employer should identify the cause of the poor work performance and, if it results from lack of training or other factors within the employer's control, provide the employee with reasonable assistance to overcome these problems.

2. *Conduct*: Apart from unauthorised absence and poor timekeeping, which generally require previous warning(s), most of the offences which come under this heading may justify summary dismissal for one occurrence. However, when dealing with these situations management must carefully examine the circumstances to establish whether they justify dismissal:

   - *Fighting*. The employee should be a willing participant to the fight and not simply defending him or herself against an assault by another employee. If the policy of the organisation is only to dismiss the aggressor, management will need to consider what constitutes aggression (is it the first blow or does it include verbal or other forms of non-violent aggression?).

▌ *Drinking*. Generally, the fairness of such a dismissal is based on its effect on the employee's work performance, safety or other aspects of the individual's behaviour, such as violence. Management needs to be clear in its mind whether its disciplinary rule relates to the act of drinking or the state of being drunk.

▌ *Swearing*. It is important to differentiate between swearing as part of the employee's everyday language and swearing at another person which is intended to be aggressive, abusive or insulting. It is also important to take account of tension or bad relationships which might be the cause of the outburst, the past record of the employee and whether the employee is prepared to apologise.

▌ *Failure to obey instructions*. To justify dismissal 'disobedience must have the quality of wilfulness'[47], the instruction must be one that management is entitled to give under the contract of employment and management must ensure that the employee is aware both that a formal instruction has been given and of the possible consequences which may result from continued refusal. Where the employee genuinely questions the 'legality' of the instruction under the contract of employment, management should be prepared to explain the basis and reason for the instruction.

▌ *Criminal acts*. Whether a criminal act justifies dismissal depends on its seriousness and, particularly in respect of an offence committed outside the workplace, potential effect on the continued suitability of the employee to perform his or her job. The criminal law and unfair dismissal law are separate areas of law with different degrees of proof. Therefore, being guilty of a criminal offence does not automatically justify dismissal and, equally, being found not guilty at criminal law does not automatically make a dismissal unfair. The question that has to be answered is: does the action of the employee amount to a serious breach of the contract of employment? Furthermore, management does not have to await the outcome of any criminal proceedings before making a decision to dismiss the employee.

3. *'Some other substantial reason'*. This is a potential 'catch-all'. However, the most significant line of cases has related to employees refusing to agree to changes in their terms and conditions of employment. Despite the fact that the employer's unilateral change in the contract is potentially a constructive dismissal, nevertheless the employee's refusal to accept such a change may be deemed to constitute 'some other substantial reason' justifying dismissal. Dickens believed that this 'has been so widely interpreted by tribunals as to provide something of an "employers' charter"'[48]. In order for management to substantiate such a defence, there must be a proven need for the change and the change must be reasonable in the light of the need; as Aikin pointed out, 'the reasonableness ... is to be considered from the employer's and not

from the employee's point of view and is based on his business needs'[49]. The issue which the Tribunal must decide is whether the employer was reasonable in dismissing the employee, not whether the employee was reasonable in refusing the change. Aikin stated that the Tribunal will usually expect the employer to have consulted with employees and/or unions before introducing the change and 'then follow the proper procedure in relation to those who refuse the new terms. They must have the new conditions explained, their own position made clear and given time to come to terms with it. They must understand that they risk dismissal if they cannot comply'[50].

The **determination of the fairness of a dismissal** is dependent on whether 'in the circumstances (including the size and administrative resources of the employer's undertaking) the employer acted reasonably or unreasonably in treating [the stated reason] as a sufficient reason for dismissing the employee; and that question shall be determined in accordance with equity and the substantial merits of the case' (S.6, Employment Act, 1980). Prior to 1980 the employer had 'to satisfy the tribunal that ... he acted reasonably' (S.57(3), Employment Protection (Consolidation) Act, 1978). The effect of this change was to neutralise the onus of proof and formalise the requirement that the Tribunal should judge the case not by their standards but by those of a 'reasonable employer'. Dickens argued that 'this managerial perspective reduces the applicant's chance of winning a case of unfair dismissal'[51].

In arriving at its decision, the Tribunal will take into account a number of factors:

- Was the dismissal for an admissible reason?
- Was the dismissal fair in the sense of equity of treatment between employees (did the employer condone similar behaviour in the past or with other employees)?
- Was the dismissal fair in the sense of did the offence or the employee's record justify dismissal as a suitable sanction?
- Did the employer follow a proper and adequate procedure before arriving at the decision to dismiss?

If the answer is 'yes' on all the above counts then the dismissal will be fair, but if the answer to any one is 'no' then the dismissal *may* be unfair. For example, even though the employee's action might justify dismissal, if the employer has not dealt with it in a proper and adequate procedural manner, the resultant dismissal may be judged to be unfair. In such a situation the tribunal has to determine the seriousness of the employer's procedural error and what effect it has had on the decision to dismiss.

The Tribunal has two broad **remedies for an unfair dismissal**: reinstatement/re-engagement and compensation.

1. *Reinstatement or re-engagement.* With reinstatement the employee returns to his or her former position and is treated as if he or she had never been dismissed; re-engagement, on the other hand, is more flexible in that the job may be comparable or otherwise suitable work or with an associated employer. The employer may object to reinstatement or re-engagement on

the grounds that it is impracticable. The Tribunal will then judge not only whether the employer has work for the employee but also the effect the return of the employee might have on the organisation and other employees. In some circumstances the nature of the offence, the attitude of other employees and possible friction between the employee and supervision may make this remedy impracticable. The Tribunal cannot compel an employer to re-employ a dismissed individual, but, if the employer refuses to abide by an order for reinstatement or re-engagement, the Tribunal may award additional compensation.

Lewis argues that 'it was made absolutely clear in the statute that "re-employment" was to be the primary remedy' but that the operation of the system 'still fails to offer job security'[52]. He found that, although 72 per cent of applicants initially requested reinstatement or re-engagement, this dropped to only 20 per cent by the time of a Tribunal hearing. The overwhelming majority of those who changed did so because they perceived there to have been a breakdown in the employment relationship. Thus, it is possible to argue that the failure of the Tribunals to use this remedy has been due to the wishes of the claimants themselves. However, of those that continued to claim 're-employment', only 57 per cent obtained an order from the Tribunal to that effect and in nearly two-thirds of these the employer refused to abide by the order. Of the 43 per cent who were unsuccessful in obtaining an order, half failed because the Tribunal considered it impracticable because of lack of job availability and half failed because the Tribunal felt it would be 'unjust' because of the individual's high contributory fault in the dismissal. Thus, Lewis concluded that 'only a minority of those seeking "re-employment" actually obtained it'[53]. In 1998, ACAS reported that only 583 out of the 17,888 cases of unfair dismissal it settled involved re-employment – just over 3 per cent[54].

2. *Compensation*. This is the most frequent remedy. The compensation is in two main parts:

   ▮ **Basic award**. This is equivalent to the amount that the employee would have received if made redundant and is, therefore, based on age and length of service.
   ▮ **Compensatory award**. This aims to recompense the employee for loss of earnings and benefits as a result of the dismissal. It may include full pay for the contractual notice period if the employee was dismissed without notice or payment in lieu of notice; loss of pay since the dismissal and in the future; and loss of benefits such as pension rights and company car.

The employee is under a **duty to mitigate the loss** by seeking alternative work. If he or she has found alternative work at a lower wage by the time of the hearing, the compensatory award will be based on the difference between the two amounts. However, if the Tribunal believes that the employee has not sought work or not been prepared to accept lower-paid work, it may reduce the award accordingly. In addition, any unemployment benefit the employee has received may be deducted from the compensation and the employee is not entitled to claim unemployment benefit for any period over which future loss of earnings has been calculated. Furthermore, the amount of the compensation may be reduced in respect of the extent to which the Tribunal feels the employee's actions contributed to the dismissal. Thus it is possible for the employee to be judged unfairly dismissed but the level of compensation reduced by as much as 80 per cent. On the other hand, an additional award may be made in those very few cases where the Tribunal makes an order for re-instatement or re-engagement but the employer refuses to comply. The Employment Relations Act (1999) has increased the maximum compensatory award to £50,000 and provided for the future indexation of award limits; but only 15 per cent of awards in 1993–4 were over £9,000[55] and the average award in 1996 was only £2,499[56] – reflecting the relative short service of most complainants.

The individual must present a claim for unfair dismissal within three months of the dismissal taking place – although the Tribunal may, in exceptional cases, decide to hear the case 'out of time'. There is facility within the procedure for a **pre-hearing** to assess the merits of the case and its prospects for success. This latter arrangement was introduced in 1980 because of a perceived reluctance of the Tribunals to award costs against 'frivolous' or 'vexatious' claims and so, as Capstick notes, 'an applicant who pursued a hopeless case out of ignorance ... or out of a desire simply to see what came out in the wash, was not therefore likely to have to pay his employer's costs even if he lost'[57]. The pre-hearing allows the Tribunal to 'advise' on the prospects of success of either the claimant's or respondent's case and such advice may be taken into account in deciding whether to award costs if the case proceeds and fails. Capstick found that in the first eight months of its operation only ten out of 932 pre-hearings were at the request of the applicant and the remainder were virtually evenly divided between requests from the respondents and requests from the Tribunal chairperson. In 50 per cent of the pre-hearings a warning was given against the applicant but in only seven cases was a warning given against the respondent. Out of 170 cases which went to a full Tribunal hearing, 136 were dismissed, 34 succeeded and in only ten cases were costs awarded in line with the earlier warning. Similarly, Wallace and Clifton found a high percentage of withdrawals following a pre-hearing warning about costs. Perhaps more importantly they found that pre-hearings also delayed the early stages of ACAS conciliation[58].

There is also a facility for **conciliation via ACAS** prior to a tribunal hearing. In 1998, 46 per cent of unfair dismissal claims were settled by ACAS conciliation, 27 per cent were withdrawn and 28 per cent went to a Tribunal[59]. However, Dickens has criticised these conciliated settlements as a cheaper alternative, for the employer, than going to the Tribunal and argued that 'despite ACAS' statutory duty to pursue settlements on [the basis of re-employment] ACAS officers do not generally attempt to reconcile the parties to the idea of re-establishing the employment relationship ... but merely help arrange the severance terms'[60]. Significantly perhaps, Concannon has identified that re-employment, usually with conditions, was obtained in the majority of the albeit limited number of cases which were referred **to arbitration via ACAS** (i.e. where 'the union had exercised its organisation and power to remove the

See Chapter 12 –
Conciliation and
arbitration

dismissal decision from being merely a matter of individual rights to one of col-lective interest'[61]). Importantly, the Employment Rights (Dispute Resolution) Act (1998) has given ACAS the power to offer the option of arbitration in unfair dismissals as well as conciliation or taking the case to a Tribunal.

This complements Dickens' description of the **typical tribunal applicant** as being 'male, non-union, manual worker dismissed by a small employer in the private services sector', which is 'characterised by small employment units and below average levels of unionisation' and where 'employees in such companies are at a greater risk from dismissal than those employed in large companies'[62]. It would appear that the legislation and Tribunal system only provide a minimal remedy, and little job protection, for non-unionised employees in smaller com-panies; employees in larger, well-unionised companies appear to achieve their protection through their union's representation in the collective bargaining process and dismissal procedure within the organisation.

The discipline and dismissal procedure

Most organisations approach discipline within a **policy framework** which recognises the following:

- It is the employee's responsibility to follow the organisation's rules and working procedures.

- Management will seek initially to correct an employee's poor performance or behaviour through informal counselling by the employee's immediate superior.

- Management will apply the formal disciplinary process only when informal counselling has been unsuccessful or the actions of the employee are such that informal counselling is inappropriate.

- Management accepts that no employee will be formally disciplined without a fair hearing and an opportunity to put his or her case.

- Management will seek to act fairly and consistently when administering discipline.

The purpose of **the disciplinary procedure** is to provide an acceptable mech-anism within which management may exercise its control over employees when their performance or behaviour does not reach the required standards. It con-strains management's freedom of action by specifying the manner in which such control is to be exercised. The *ACAS Code of Practice*[63] recommends that, irrespective of whether the organisation is large or small, unionised or non-unionised, the procedure should satisfy the following criteria:

- It should be a formal, written procedure.

- It should indicate to whom it applies and the appropriate employees should be provided with a copy.

- It should specify what disciplinary actions may be taken and which level of management has the authority to take such action.

■ It should ensure that the employee is notified of the complaint, given the opportunity to state his or her case and to be represented either by a union representative or fellow employee.

■ It should ensure that no disciplinary action is taken without a full investigation and that an employee is not dismissed for a single incident of misconduct unless it is gross misconduct.

■ It should provide the employee with the right of appeal against any disciplinary sanction.

However, not all disciplinary offences need to be dealt with under the same procedure. Some organisations, because of the particular nature of the offence and the way in which they wish to handle it, have established separate procedures to deal with absence through sickness and poor work performance. If this course is adopted it is imperative that the main disciplinary procedure states that such offences are outside its jurisdiction and which procedure will apply in such situations.

A number of **sanctions** may be applied under the disciplinary procedure.

■ *Verbal warnings*. This is the most frequent and least severe penalty. However, it is necessary to distinguish between informal verbal warnings, which are not part of the formal disciplinary procedure and which are frequently administered by a supervisor or manager as part of the day-to-day control of their subordinates, and any formal verbal warning which forms the first stage of the formal disciplinary procedure. These formal verbal warnings should be recorded and the employee provided with written confirmation that a verbal warning has been given. Some organisations, because of these problems, have abandoned verbal warnings as part of the formal process, leaving them entirely as part of the informal process.

■ *Written warnings*. Written warnings should clearly state the offence for which the employee is being disciplined, refer to any previous verbal or written warnings and indicate what future performance or conduct is expected and the likely consequences if there is no improvement. Many organisations have two levels of written warnings – a first and final written warning. Only in very exceptional situations should a final written warning not be followed by some more severe sanction for a future act of indiscipline.

■ *Suspension*. It is important to distinguish between a *precautionary suspension* pending a disciplinary investigation and a *disciplinary suspension* without pay as a sanction within the formal disciplinary procedure. Many people argue that a suspension without pay is useful because it involves a clear penalty (loss of money on the part of the employee) and, without it, there is no satisfactory intermediate action between a final written warning and dismissal. However, a suspension without pay can only be effected if the terms of the contract (either express or implied) allow for it. Moreover, any suspension, with or without pay, means that the work normally performed by the suspended employee is either not done or has to be done by other employees – perhaps involving the use of overtime.

■ *Transfer or demotion*. These may be used as a sanction in their own right or as an alternative to dismissal. However, they may involve a breach of the contract of employment unless they are clearly allowed within the contract or management secures the employee's consent to any transfer or demotion.

- *Fines and deductions from pay*. In the nineteenth century it was common for the employer to fine the employee for breaches of the rules, but today this has virtually ceased. The problem has always been that if the amount of the fine was small then it had little effect, but if it was large it could involve the employee in financial hardship and lead to resentment. Initially, the right to fine employees was constrained by the Truck Act (1896) but this only applied to manual workers. The Wages Act (1986) simplified the legal requirements in respect of fines and extended the scope to include all employees. Consequently, a fine may only be imposed if it is expressly provided for in the employee's contract of employment or the employee indicates agreement in writing. Furthermore, a deduction in respect of retail workers for any cash shortage or stock deficiency is limited to a maximum of 10 per cent of the employee's gross daily wage.

- *Dismissal*. A dismissal should only take place when there is no other alternative available. In this event the employer should ensure that the dismissal is fair and reasonable and in accordance with both the disciplinary procedure and legal framework.

A number of further aspects need to be considered in the operation of the disciplinary procedure:

- *Employee representation*. Most procedures allow for the employee to be accompanied by a union representative or fellow employee. Generally, the role of the union representative is clear: to present the employee's case and to ensure that management conducts the interview and disciplinary process in a fair and reasonable manner. However, the role of the 'fellow employee' is less clear. Some organisations believe that it is simply to observe and be a witness for the employee at any subsequent appeal as to what happened during the interview; other organisations regard it as a representational role. Significantly, as with grievances, the Employment Relations Act (1999) has given all employees the right to be accompanied by either a union representative or a fellow employee during any disciplinary hearing which 'could result in a formal warning or some other action against the worker'. However, the existing role of union representatives may be restricted by the references to being permitted to 'address' the hearing and 'confer' with the employee, but not 'answer questions' on his or her behalf.

- *Appeals*. Provision must be made for the employee to be able, within a specified time limit, to appeal against any disciplinary action to a higher level of management (either via the normal grievance procedure or through a special disciplinary appeal mechanism). Some organisations have established a joint appeals body (involving union or employee representatives as well as management) as a form of quasi-independent internal tribunal.

- *'Totting up' offences and 'wiping the slate clean'*. To move from one level of sanction to the next does not require the employee to commit a further act of indiscipline of a similar nature. An employee may receive a formal verbal warning for one offence, a written warning for another offence and be suspended without pay, demoted or even dismissed for yet another offence, even though the third offence, on its own, might not justify dismissal. The procedure should specify that any record of disciplinary action will be removed from the employee's record after a specified time (ranging from three months to two years depending on the severity of the offence and sanction) if the employee's conduct is satisfactory over that period. This may be coupled with the employee's right to examine his or her personnel file to ensure that it has been done.

■ *Disciplinary action against a union representative.* No disciplinary action beyond a verbal warning should be taken against a union representative, whether as a result of his or her actions as a representative or as an employee, before the case has been discussed with the senior union representative or full-time official. This does not mean that the disciplinary action has to be agreed but simply that the senior representative or full-time official is aware of the circumstances and planned management action.

The disciplinary interview

This is the **point at which the formal control mechanism is actually applied**. The supervisor or manager must remember, throughout, that he or she is prosecutor, judge and jury (presenting the evidence against the employee and then weighing up the evidence from both sides and making a decision as to whether the employee's actions justify disciplinary action). In **preparing for the interview**, the manager must:

■ Be satisfied that there is a *prima facie* case that the employee's performance is inadequate or his or her behaviour has contravened a rule;

■ Decide whether or not it is a matter for formal disciplinary action;

■ Determine, in the light of the employee's past record, what stage of the disciplinary procedure has been reached and what range of penalties are available should the facts of the case be proved;

■ Ensure that the employee is advised that it is a disciplinary interview in order to prepare his or her case and, if necessary, arrange for the attendance of representative and/or witnesses.

There are **two distinct stages** to the disciplinary interview:

1. *Establishing the facts of the case.* A disciplinary interview will, in practice, only take place when management already believes, *prima facie*, that there has been a breach of the organisation's rules by the employee. Thus, from management's side, the facts are generally established prior to the actual interview either by the collection of data (time-keeping, absence, poor work performance, etc.) or by interviewing witnesses in cases relating to the personal conduct of the employee. However, this information has to be reviewed with the employee present and having the opportunity to question it, including the cross-examination of any witnesses. The employee must also be afforded the opportunity to present his or her side of the case and, if necessary, call his or her own evidence and witnesses.

2. *Administering the disciplinary sanction*. There should be a break between the two stages, however short, to allow the manager to consider his or her decision and determine the appropriate course of action. The purpose of this second stage is to ensure that the employee is fully aware of why disciplinary action is being taken, the nature of the sanction being applied and its effect, and the standard of behaviour or performance expected in the future.

An inherent danger in the disciplinary interview is that the manager prejudges the situation because he or she has, as part of the preparation for the interview, already investigated management's case and examined the employee's previous record. This can result in the two stages becoming blurred and the manager reprimanding the employee before all the evidence has been heard and considered. The interview should never commence with the manager reprimanding the employee for the alleged offence.

15.4 Redundancy

White[64] differentiated 'job redundancy' (where a particular job ceases to exist but the incumbent employees are found alternative work within the organisation) from 'worker redundancy' (where the employees lose their employment), which could imply that real redundancy only exists in the latter circumstance. Furthermore, some organisations use the apparently less emotive terms 'deselection', 'outplacement' or 'rightsizing' as an indication that redundancy is a normal and natural part of operational and labour planning. However, the term 'redundancy' should be applied to **any situation where changes in the organisation's economic, operational or technological position results in a reduced labour level** (irrespective of how the reduction is achieved, or whether it involves the loss of only a single job or a more significant reduction in part, or all, of the workforce).

The nature of redundancy

The essential qualities of a redundancy situation are that it arises primarily from **causes external to the performance and capabilities of the individual employees** affected and, most importantly, it involves a potential conflict of interest between management's immediate objectives of maintaining an efficient and profitable organisation and the employees' immediate objectives of protecting their jobs and income. This conflict will arise despite any management arguments that the long-term viability of the organisation is essential if employees are to have any 'job security'. Sutherland argued that redundancy has 'assumed a growing importance, most especially so in a political economy apparently dominated by themes such as de-industrialisation and unemployment'[65]. Despite the fall in the number of redundancies from over 500,000 per year in the 1980s to about 200,000 per year in the late 1990s, only just over one-third of people find work within three months[66]. Every reduction in an organisation's labour establishment must be viewed not only as possible unemployment for the person who filled it, dependent on how the reduction is achieved, but also a loss of a potential job for those who are already unemployed and for future generations. Potentially, it can also have a traumatic effect on the individual (see Box 15.3).

Sutherland suggested that there are three perspectives which may be adopted in analysing redundancy:

■ The perspective of the **labour planner**, which focuses attention on 'that period of time in the organisation prior to the implementation of a pro-gramme involving involuntary quits'[67] and which views redundancy as an element in balancing the organisation's labour requirement. Certainly, Mumford noted that 'for the manpower planner, redundancy is generally seen as synonymous with failure'[68].

■ The perspective of the **labour economist**, which focuses attention on 'the oper-ation of, and adjustment processes in, the external labour market'[69] and which views redundancy as a means of redistributing labour within the economy.

Both of these perspectives incorporate a managerial ideology which emphasises the goal of operational efficiency at either the micro or macro level and accepts the legitimacy of redundancy as a means of achieving that efficiency.

■ The perspective of the **industrial sociologist**, which focuses attention on the differing value systems which exist within society and the organisation and

---

Box 15.3   Redundancy and the individual

It is important to realise that 'the feeling of self-worth which we derive from work arises because our society decrees that men [and women] are expected to work'[1]. This 'work ethic' often regards unemployment as, at best, a cause for sympathy but a necessary fact of economic life or, at worst, a reflection of the individual's inad-equacies or simply scrounging. The individual, in coming to terms with being redundant, is likely to pass through four psychological stages:

1. *Shock*. The initial reaction of most employees is to regard themselves as 'superfluous, no longer needed, obsolescent, useless'[2]. They may feel immobilised and lack any sense of purpose (undertaking any activity, however pointless, to fill time), or may even seek to 'keep up appearances' by leaving home and returning at normal times and fill in the time wandering around, reading in public libraries, etc. They may even not tell family and friends that they are redundant.

2. *Defensive retreat*. Many people may underestimate the potential seriousness of the situation (regarding it perhaps as only a temporary situation, under their control, which can be alleviated, at any time, by simply applying for a few jobs). Alternatively, they may emphasise the positive aspects of being redundant (more time with their family or an opportunity to do things which possibly previously they lacked either the time or money to do).

3. *Acknowledgement*. This begins 'with a feeling of bitterness and depression, as the positive factors in the situation disappear and the negative aspects come to the fore'[2] – it may be associated with exhausting redundancy compensation or failing to secure new employment as easily as anticipated.

4. *Adaptation*. It is only through a full realisation and assessment of the situation that the individual can proceed to seek either employment or other constructive activities which maintain a purpose and status in life.

Sources:
1. Institute of Employment Consultants and Federation of Personnel Services, *Unemployment: A new approach for the 80s*, 1979.
2. Newport and Gwent Industrial Mission, *Redundant? A Personal Survival Kit*, 1975.

which, therefore, regards the legitimacy of both the goal (operational efficiency) and the means (redundancy) as neither unquestionable nor agreed among the participants.

See Chapter 8 –
The government

Sutherland further argued that **shifts in government policy towards redundancy** can be explained in terms of changes in the influence of these perspectives. UK government policy in the 1960s, as epitomised in the Redundancy Payments Act (1965), was that 'although redundancy may involve the private individual in short run adjustment costs, in the long run the resulting redeployment of labour would prove socially beneficial'[70]. In the 1970s, however, government policy shifted more towards one of 'recognition that the cheapest mode of job creation in the short run was job preservation'[71]. Consequently, government actions, such as the Temporary Employment Subsidy (1975), were directed at avoiding redundancies. The change in policy was closely associated with a change in the level of unemployment. In the 1960s, with an unemployment level of only 1–2 per cent (i.e. full or over-full employment), redundancy could be justified as a means of 'freeing' a scarce resource, while the individuals who were made redundant were not likely to be unemployed for long. By the mid to late 1970s, unemployment was 5 per cent and rising, and therefore redundancy could be seen as directly adding to that level and creating a social and political problem for any government which was committed to a policy of maintaining full employment. In the 1980s and 1990s, the focus of attention shifted back to a labour economics perspective. Redundancy and its associated unemployment have been seen as a natural result of wage inflation and a necessary consequence of organisational attempts to create greater operational efficiency and competitiveness.

The **structure of industry is dynamic and constantly changing** in response to many pressures and, therefore, it is perhaps inevitable that some redundancies will always be occurring. While redundancies most often form an integral part of an organisation's attempt to reduce costs and improve its competitive base, they can also arise in dynamic and financially sound organisations. It is possible to identify **four main causes of redundancy**:

- *Structural decline* of older, and generally less efficient or technologically developed, manufacturing industries;

- *Decrease in the level of economic activity* of an organisation, a single industry or the economy as a whole;

- *Technological change* requiring less labour to provide a given level of output or service;

- *Reorganisation* of the work situation to obtain a more efficient use of existing plant and machinery and to reduce costs.

These factors may interrelate on a cumulative basis. In reacting to a structural decline of an industry or a decrease in the level of economic activity, the management of an organisation may seek to maintain its competitiveness and economic viability by reorganising work methods and/or introducing new technology.

Trade unions are reluctant to 'agree' to a redundancy (although inevitably they may have to 'accept' it) because it represents a negation of the concepts of 'job

See Chapter 4 –
Trade union
development and
function

security' and 'the right to work'. The **trade union's primary objective** is to resist, or at the very least, minimise the extent of any reduction in the organisation's labour force. They may well propose alternative strategies to cut costs, improve efficiency or develop business. Only in a small number of situations in the past has the union's or work-group's resistance to redundancy gone to the extent of a work-in or sit-in, although token strikes to demonstrate the employees' feelings have not been uncommon. It is only when redundancy is considered to be unavoidable that the union's **secondary objective** becomes one of seeking to secure the best possible terms for those employees likely to be made redundant.

At a broader level, union strategies have centred on seeking to reduce the level of unemployment by increasing job opportunities through shortening the working week and lowering the normal retirement age. A **reduction in the working week** appears to have immense potential for creating job opportunities. However, management responded to such changes during the 1980s not by increasing the number of employees, but by reducing or eliminating paid breaks or by reducing labour levels in order to avoid increasing their per unit costs. At the same time, employees themselves often preclude the translation of a shorter working week into more job opportunities by a reluctance to reduce their actual hours worked and to forsake the opportunity to enhance their earnings by working the time at premium overtime rates. In 1983 the TUC reported that 'there was little indication of hours reductions being tailored explicitly to avoiding redundancy'[72]. Significantly, the 1998 French legislation to reduce the working week to 35 hours, and thereby create more employment opportunities, included provision for financial incentives for employers (in the form of reduced social security provisions)[73] and the agreements negotiated for its implementation appear largely to be maintaining weekly pay, although some have agreed to forgo some future pay increases[74].

Proposals to **reduce the normal retirement age** have encountered resistance from both management and the government. While management is often prepared to utilise voluntary early retirement as part of a redundancy package, generally with some enhancement of the individual's pension entitlement, it is reluctant to accept a permanent and comprehensive reduction in the normal retirement age within the organisation. Any reduction has important implications, at both organisational and national levels, in respect of the funding of pension arrangements and, in particular, the rate of contribution by the individual, the organisation and the state.

The legal framework

The legal framework surrounding redundancy may be divided into three main parts:

- Payment of monetary compensation to redundant employees;
- Protection for the individual employee against unfair selection for redundancy and the provision for time off to seek work or training;
- Management consultation with employees and/or recognised independent trade unions prior to redundancies taking place.

Redundancy payments

The **intention** of the Redundancy Payments Act (1965) was 'to compensate a redundant employee for loss of his job, in the same way as he would be compensated for loss of a property right; to foster mobility of labour; and to help employers who were overstaffed to "shake out" excess labour, thus freeing them for more productive work elsewhere'[75]. The legislation was, and is, intended not to provide employees with job security but, rather, to relieve the financial hardship associated with the employee's job loss; the amount of compensation varies according to length of service rather than the length of time the employee may be unemployed or the difficulties in finding another job. Until 1986, when it was abolished, the organisation's financial burden of redundancy payments was reduced through a partial reimbursement from the state-administered Redundancy Fund financed by contributions levied from all employers.

Certain **groups of employees are excluded**:

- Employees with less than two years' service after the age of 18.
- Employees on a fixed-term contract of two or more years' duration, if the redundancy results only from the non-renewal of the contract and provided the employee has agreed, in writing, to waive rights to make such a claim. (This is particularly important with the use of fixed-term contracts as part of increased labour flexibility.)
- Employees over 65 or their normal retirement age (if less).

As with 'unfair dismissal', until 1995 part-time employees working between eight and 16 hours a week had to have had five years' service before they could claim redundancy payments and those working less than eight hours per week were not covered at all. However, the Employment Protection (Part-Time Employees) Regulations 1995 extended the two-year qualifying period to all employees.

The **legal definition of redundancy** is where a person's dismissal is attributable wholly or mainly to:

1. the fact that his employer has ceased or intends to cease, to carry on the business for the purposes of which the employee was employed by him, or has ceased, or intends to cease, to carry on that business in the place where the employee was so employed, or

2. the fact that the requirements of that business for employees to carry out work of a particular kind, or for employees to carry out work of a particular kind in the place where he was so employed, have ceased or diminished or are expected to cease or diminish.

The **level of statutory compensation** is based on the employee's length of continuous service as follows:

Service at age	Amount per year of service
18–21	$\frac{1}{2}$ week's pay
22–40	1 week's pay
41 and over	$1\frac{1}{2}$ weeks' pay

However, the entitlement is subject to a maximum of 20 years' service and a statutory maximum amount of a 'week's pay' (which currently amounts to a total payment of about £6,600). Where the employee's weekly pay varies (because of no fixed hours, overtime or bonus payments, etc.), a 'week's pay' is determined by averaging over a twelve-week period prior to the redundancy. In the final year preceding retirement age, the redundancy entitlement will be reduced by 1/12 for each month.

A number **of situations may affect the individual's right to claim redundancy payment**:

1. *Changes in work content*. The general legal principle underlying the determination of the existence of redundancy, and therefore the statutory right to redundancy payment, is that redundancy only exists if there is a reduction in the requirements of the business as a whole for employees to carry out a particular type of work. Therefore, changes in the type of employee or the skills required to carry out that work, or changes in the content of an individual's job consequent upon any reorganisation, may not, by themselves, constitute redundancy. The same may also apply to geographical relocation of the employee or changes from full-time to part-time or vice versa. Aikin and Reid point out that Tribunals have taken the view that an employee is expected to adapt to new methods and techniques and therefore, in order 'to decide whether a new job has been created or the old one continues, though with varied duties, ... it is necessary to look at the type of work that the employer required before reorganization and compare it with the work required after reorganization. The more different the work is, the more likely there is to be a finding of redundancy'[76]. The tests to be applied centre on the employer's contractual rights to require change and whether without such change the employee would have been made redundant.

2. *Assistance to redundant employees*. If management assists a potentially redundant employee by securing fresh employment with another organisation and then mutually agrees with the employee to terminate the contract of employment so that the employee may commence employment with the new organisation, this will not, in legal terms, amount to dismissal. Therefore, the employee will have no statutory right to redundancy payment, although this does not preclude an organisational policy or agreement to make such a payment.

3. *Advance warning of redundancy*. If management gives employees advance warning of possible redundancy and an employee resigns, having found alternative work, he or she will have no statutory right to redundancy payments. Such a management warning, if it does not specify when the redundancy is to take place, merely allows the employee to choose either to stay, receive redundancy payment and then look for other work, or to secure alternative work thereby avoiding being unemployed but without the benefit of receiving any compensation for the probable loss of his or her job. However, once management has given the employee specific notice to terminate the contract of employment, the employee may seek to terminate the contract at an earlier date by giving written notice to that effect. Management may respond, again in writing, by stating that it requires the employee to continue until the date on which the notice expires and that it will contest the employee's right to redundancy payment if he or she fails to do so.

4. *Disciplinary dismissal.* An employee is not entitled to redundancy payment if management can show that the dismissal resulted from misconduct or poor work performance: even though there were at that time redundancies in the organisation among the group of workers to which the complainant belonged. This may apply even if the dismissal results from the employee's refusal to agree to or undertake new duties as part of a reorganisation within the workplace. The onus is on the employer to show that the dismissal resulted from the employee's own conduct, performance or capabilities.

5. *Short-time working and layoff.* The legislation defines 'layoff' as being a situation in which an employee receives no pay at all from the employer and 'short time' as being a situation in which an employee receives less than half a week's pay for that week. If either situation continues for four consecutive weeks, or for any six weeks out of 13, the employee may terminate the contract with due notice and notify the employer that he or she intends to claim redundancy payment. The employer may serve a counter-notice, within seven days of receiving the employee's notification of intent to claim, to contest the claim on the grounds that it is reasonable to expect the work situation to return to normal within four weeks and remain so for at least thirteen weeks.

6. *Offer of alternative employment.* An employee will not be entitled to redundancy payment if, before the expiry of the notice period, he or she 'unreasonably' refuses the employer's offer of 'suitable alternative' employment. The *suitability* of the alternative employment may be assessed on an objective basis by comparing the terms and conditions of the alternative employment with those of the original employment (wages, hours, status, conditions, etc.). The *reasonableness* of any refusal to accept the alternative employment has to be judged on more subjective criteria relating to the personal circumstances of the individual employee (excessive personal or domestic difficulties derived from extra travelling time, working shifts, having to move house, etc.). The burden of proof in respect of both suitability and reasonableness lies with the employee and clearly the two issues cannot be divorced completely from each other. An offer of alternative employment may be made in respect of the same employer or an associated employer. When the alternative employment entails differences in the terms and conditions of employment, the offer should be made in writing so that the employee may assess the difference. In addition, there is a right to a trial period of four weeks under the new employment, at any time during which either the employee or the employer may terminate the contract and the employee will retain the right to claim redundancy payment as if he or she had been made redundant at the original date.

Other individual rights

While the law did not specify the selection criteria to be used by an employer in a redundancy, it did provide the employee with a degree of protection against an **unfair selection for redundancy**. It was potentially an unfair dismissal, with higher compensation than under redundancy legislation, if the employer selected the employee for redundancy in contravention of a 'customary arrangement or agreed procedure relating to redundancy'. This could be any policy, arrangement or agreement which had been applied in the past or agreed with the unions, or was a commonly applied practice or agreement within the industry. This protection was removed by the Deregulation and Contracting Out Act (1994).

An employee who has been given notice of dismissal by reason of redundancy is entitled, before the expiration of the period of notice, to be allowed **reasonable time off, with pay, during normal working hours to seek new employment or make arrangements for training**. This right is, however, available only to those employees who have two or more years' service. If the employer refuses to allow the time off or to make the payment in lieu, the employee may take a claim before a tribunal, which may then make an award against the employer not exceeding two-fifths of a week's pay. Thus, while the legislation does not define what constitutes 'reasonable time off', by implication the employee is only entitled to two days' paid absence.

Consultation with trade unions

See Chapter 6 – Representation at the workplace

Since the Employment Protection Act (1975), management has been required, when it is proposing to dismiss employees, to consult with **independent recognised trade** union(s) representing the group of workers from among which redundancies are to be made. However, in 1994 the European Court of Justice held that UK legislation did not comply with the EU Directives because it restricted consultation rights, on both redundancies and the transfer of the undertaking, to representatives of 'recognised unions' rather than representatives of the 'workforce' – thus, the right of employees to be *collectively* consulted should apply to all (whether unionised or not). This, as Aikin *et al*. note, runs 'counter to the use of unions alone for any "collective" giving of information or consultation, and would also run counter to the current move in the UK towards individual rights'[77]. The subsequent regulations[78] introduced by the government gave management the opportunity to choose between consulting recognised unions or 'elected representatives of the affected employees' (even where unions are recognised).

The 1995 regulations excluded redundancies of less than 20 people from the requirement to consult. The **minimum statutory periods** for consultation, which may run concurrently with any notice period given to the individual employees, are as follows:

- If 100 or more employees are to be made redundant in one establishment within a period of 90 days or less, the employer is required to consult at least 90 days before the first dismissal becomes effective.

- In other situations, the employer is required to consult at least 30 days before the first dismissal becomes effective.

Management is required to disclose, in writing, to union employee representatives the following information:

- Reasons for the proposed redundancy;

- Numbers and types of employees it is proposed to make redundant;

- Total number of employees of these types employed within the establishment;
- Proposed method of selecting those employees who are to be made redundant;
- Proposed method of implementing the redundancy, having regard to both any agreed procedure and the period over which the redundancy is to take place;
- Proposed method of calculating the amount of any redundancy payments.

Initially, the law only required management to give consideration to any representations made by union representatives in respect of these proposals and, when replying to them, to state any reasons it may have for rejecting any of their representations. However, as Aikin *et al.* note, the Trade Union and Labour Relations Act (1992) and Trade Union Reform and Employment Rights Act (1993) have amended the consultation requirements to conform with EU directives. First, the definition of redundancy (for consultation purposes) has been extended to include any dismissal which is 'not related to the individual concerned' (i.e. a disciplinary dismissal) and therefore now encompasses 'dismissals made to achieve a change in contract terms'[79]. Second, the consultation must include avoiding the dismissals, reducing the number and mitigating the consequences and must be undertaken 'with a view to reaching agreement' (or, as Aikin *et al.* state, 'negotiation without any need to actually come to a conclusion'[80]).

If a trade union believes that management has not complied with the statutory requirement to consult, it may make an application to a Tribunal for a **protective award**. This would require the employer to continue to pay the employees their normal remuneration for a specified period commencing from the date of the award or the date of the first dismissal (see Box 15.4). The protective award does not reduce the extent of the redundancy, protect the employees indefinitely or ensure that consultation with the trade union is carried out, but simply guarantees that the employees will receive payment of their wages for a further relatively short period. A protective award will not be made if

Box 15.4	Redundancy consultation

'Campbell's soup company has been fined £400,000 for failing to consult trade unions over the planned closure of a Homepride factory in a ground-breaking victory for sacked workers.

An industrial tribunal awarded 123 former employees of the Maryport factory in West Cumbria three months' salary after deciding the firm had failed to comply with an EU Trades Union and Labour Relations directive which was incorporated into UK law as long ago as 1993 ...

The law requires employees, or their representatives, to be consulted about whether closure of the business is an appropriate option. Furthermore, employees must be consulted before any irrevocable decision is taken about the future of their jobs. The unions successfully argued that at Maryport they were only consulted after a decision to shut the factory had been taken. Their input as to how the workers should be sacked and how much compensation paid was restricted.'

Source: T. Hunter, *Guardian*, 6 June 1998.

management can show, in its defence, that there were special reasons which meant that it was not reasonably practicable to comply with the statutory minimum and that it took all reasonably practicable steps to comply with the requirements. For example, Tribunals have held that the secrecy required in attempting to sell a company, or the fact that the redundancies had been caused or hastened by the cancellation of a contract, constitute special reasons precluding the necessity to comply with the statutory minimum periods for consultation with trade unions. However, the EU's proposal on national Works Councils contains a provision which would void a management decision (i.e. it would have no legal effect) where management failed to consult properly[81].

Handling redundancy

One recent survey states that, compared perhaps to the 1980s, management is adopting 'a more sensitive and compassionate approach to those who are being made redundant and measures to reassure and motivate the remaining work-

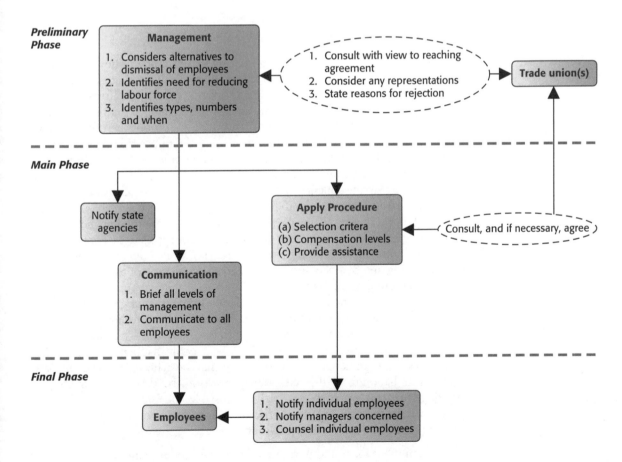

Figure 15.4 Steps in handling redundancy

force'[82]. There are three main phases in the handling of a redundancy situation (see Figure 15.4):

1. The **preliminary discussion phase** requires management, in consultation or negotiation with appropriate union or employee representatives, to:

   (a) establish the need for a redundancy, having considered alternative approaches to alleviating the need to dismiss employees; and
   (b) determine the numbers and types of employees to be dismissed and the period of time over which the reduction in the labour force is to be achieved.

2. The **main procedural application phase** is concerned with:

   (a) the selection of employees to be made redundant;
   (b) the level of compensation to be paid; and
   (c) the provision of assistance to redundant employees.

3. The **individual employee phase** involves the notification and counselling of the individual employees to be made redundant.

Redundancy policy and procedure

Mumford argued that without a **pre-existing redundancy policy and procedure** 'there is greater risk of a redundancy situation's being destructive, anomalous and a cause of contention and bad relations for a long time ahead'[83]. However, trade unions may regard an 'advance' agreement as an indication that management is planning a redundancy and, by implication, the union accepts the need for such a redundancy (thus weakening any opposition they may wish to make when the redundancy arises). At the same time, management may feel that they will be equally constrained if they agree to levels of compensation which may prove subsequently to be greater than they can realistically afford. A compromise between the desirability of having an advance agreement and the need to respond flexibly to any particular redundancy situation may be achieved by reaching an advance agreement on the general principles to be applied in any redundancy situation (including selection criteria), while leaving specific details, such as timing and compensation, to be agreed at the time of the redundancy.

Management's objectives are not only to reduce its labour force and costs but also to maintain the morale and goodwill of the remaining employees. The existence of redundancies within an organisation creates a feeling of insecurity even among those employees who are not to lose their jobs – if redundancy can happen once to some employees, then it can easily happen again to other employees. Management's second objective may be achieved, at least in part, through its handling of the redundancy situation, by demonstrating its preparedness to treat employees as fairly as possible consistent with its financial position at the time. A policy and procedure should also consider the more positive concept of **security of employment**:

- Commitment to, and importance of, effective labour planning;
- Regular review discussions between management and trade unions;

■ Retraining and transfers to balance labour needs within the organisation;

■ Use of alternative methods – stop on recruitment, the reduction or removal of overtime, a stop on subcontracting work out of the organisation and possibly an increase in subcontracting work in, and the introduction of layoffs, short-time working or other methods of work sharing.

Management should be certain, before seeking to establish the need for redundancy with union or employee representatives, that the use of such measures will, on its own, be insufficient to generate the required labour cost reductions. However, even at times of redundancy it may not be possible, or even desirable, for the organisation to stop all recruitment or overtime working. It may still be necessary to maintain the recruitment of certain categories of employees, among which it is not intended to have redundancies and for which it is not possible to retrain other redundant employees, and to continue limited essential overtime working in order to ensure that work is completed on time.

The **trade union's objectives** are primarily to resist, or minimise, the reduction in the organisation's labour force, while at the same time securing the best possible terms for those employees likely to be made redundant. Trade unions are generally as concerned to ensure that all alternatives are considered before employees are made redundant as they are to ensure that redundant employees receive the best possible financial compensation for the loss of their jobs. However, within the employees' ranks there is, if the financial compensation is attractive enough, often a divergence in attitudes between the union's desire to resist redundancies and the desire of at least some employees actually to be made redundant.

Selection criteria

The indiscriminate application of any selection criterion can 'result in a workforce incapable of producing anything'[84]. It is important, therefore, to focus selection decisions towards **future workforce needs** (in terms of the quality of human skills, abilities and potential needed for future business operations) rather than simple quantity reductions in current numbers or costs. It is also important to determine **the boundary within which the selection criteria are to be applied**: is it to be applied across the organisation as a whole or within departments, sections or units on a segmented basis? The varying effect can be demonstrated with the relatively straightforward 'last in, first out' criterion. Applied across the organisation as a whole, it could result in an unacceptable level of redundancy in some departments with a high proportion of short-service employees. Applied on the basis of each department separately, it could result in longer-service employees being made redundant in one department while shorter-service employees are retained in other departments. The boundary issue is, at least in part, related to the extent to which knowledge and skills are similar across departments and, therefore, how quickly employees can adapt to new work if transferred to fill gaps left by redundant employees. However, as Mumford noted, redundancies in most organisations are 'carried out on a departmental basis geared to the actual reduction in output of that department or section'[85].

One, or a combination, of the following approaches may be applied in selecting the particular employees to be made redundant:

1. *Voluntary severance*. The principle underlying this approach is that the employee, rather than management, should decide who is redundant; arguably, this is less traumatic for the organisation and employees. However, it may be the better employees, those likely to find alternative work, who are most likely to volunteer. Management may avoid this, and the random impact implicit in this approach, by reserving the right to refuse redundancy to employees whom it considers to be essential to future operations by virtue of their skill, work performance or experience. To encourage volunteers, it is usual for management to offer enhanced redundancy compensation above the minimum required under the redundancy payments legislation (including early retirement, without loss of pension rights, for older employees), thereby increasing the costs of the redundancy. Trade unions will normally seek to ensure that no employees, such as the long-term sick or those with poor work records, are pressurised into 'volunteering' to be made redundant. In the past it was believed that voluntary severance would be successful only on a 'one-off' basis and if the level of required redundancy was 10–20 per cent. If lower than 10 per cent, there may be too many volunteers (requiring further selection criteria to be applied and the possibility that some volunteers may feel aggrieved because their expectation of leaving with enhanced compensation has not been met). If higher than 20 per cent, there may be insufficient volunteers (requiring additional compulsory redundancies). However, the experience of the 1980s and 1990s has shown that organisations can repeatedly operate a voluntary severance programme and still obtain volunteers. Such apparent 'success' raises important questions about the 'success' of other HRM strategies in developing employee commitment to the organisation. Indeed, it can lead to a 'severance culture' in which 'employees will be planning for their exit opportunity rather than looking to enhance their long-term prospects with the company'[86].

2. *Last in, first out (LIFO)*. The principle underlying this approach is that the longer an employee's service with an organisation, the greater his or her implied right to a job. It has traditionally been favoured by many trade unions because it is a simple quantitative criterion which appears to avoid favouritism or discrimination. It also has the advantage for management that it is relatively 'cheap' (less compensation for short-service employees). However, the selection criterion is completely unrelated to ensuring the right balance of employee skills, abilities and potential needed for the future and is very likely, because of the link between age and length of service, to result in a skewed age profile for the employees remaining in the organisation and to create a labour planning problem for the future. Furthermore, it can lead to a divided workforce by creating a relatively protected group of longer-service employees alongside an 'at-risk' group of shorter-service employees. Indeed, its continual general use by many employers can easily create a group of employees who are made redundant, or are at risk of being made redundant, more than once because they are

unable to build up sufficient service with an employer to move into the more protected group.

3. *Efficiency*. Most managements would prefer to select their redundant employees from among those employees they consider to be least efficient by reason of their work performance, absence and timekeeping or disciplinary record. However, trade unions generally resist this approach, because they feel it is open to abuse by management, or, when they are prepared to accept its adoption, insist on being provided with the information used by management in its selection decisions and having the right to appeal on their members' behalf if they feel that they have been unfairly included. Obviously the use of this approach is dependent on management having adequate information relating to individual employee performance and conduct.

4. *Social need*. It is uncommon for employees' domestic circumstances to be taken into account in the selection criterion, although this may be used in determining additional special compensation or assistance to redundant employees. However, Mumford[87] cited one example where domestic circumstances (such as marital status, number of children and whether the employee was the sole family income) were combined with efficiency and length of service criteria on a weighted points basis. Under this scheme domestic circumstances could amount to a maximum of 100 points as against a maximum of only 50 points for length of service.

Level of compensation

It has been suggested that 'many companies announce redundancies to cut costs and remain competitive but are still largely profitable, and therefore can afford to be relatively generous'[88]. In addition to any general enhancement of the legal minimum, to make the redundancy easier to implement, the organisation may also make provision for **extra financial compensation not catered for within the statutory scheme**. These may include the following:

■ Payment to employees specifically excluded by the statutory scheme, such as those with less than two years' service or those under 18 years of age;

■ Assessment of compensation at the employee's full rate of pay rather than the maximum limit specified in the legislation;

■ Compensation based on the employee's total service rather than the 20-year maximum specified in the legislation;

■ Extra payments to those employees above a particular age or length of service;

■ Additional retention payments for employees required to remain beyond the date they wish to leave, or beyond the date at which the bulk of employees are to be made redundant;

■ Payment in lieu of notice even though the employee has been given prior notification of dismissal;

■ Continuing hardship payments to employees who, after a specified period, have been unable to secure alternative employment or who have had to accept employment at a significantly lower rate of pay.

Assistance to redundant employees

As a **statutory minimum**, the employer is required to notify the Department for Education and Employment of any redundancy in excess of ten employees and allow redundant employees reasonable time off to seek work or retraining. However, the employer may be able to provide **additional assistance** in a number of ways:

■ Providing on-site facilities for the state agencies to attend to advise employees on job opportunities, retraining schemes and facilities, unemployment and other state benefits;

■ Establishing their own 'employment agency' to contact associated companies or other employers in the locality or elsewhere to try to secure alternative work for their redundant employees;

■ Maintaining a list of redundant employees who will be given preference for employment should circumstances improve or a vacancy arise.

The employer may also go beyond simply helping the employee to secure new employment and may, through either the HRM department or consultants, provide wider individual employee counselling. This may include the following:

■ Discussing with the employee not only possible future careers and retraining but also the question of the individual starting a business;

■ Financial guidance on coping with unemployment and making the best use of the redundancy payment;

■ Self-appraisal and presentation skills (many employees may not have had to apply and be interviewed for a job for many years);

■ The psychological aspects of redundancy for both the individual and family.

Indeed, management may go so far as to provide or pay for redundant employees to attend special courses on any of these topics.

Communication, consultation and negotiation

It may be argued that there is never a 'right' time to tell employees of a potential redundancy in the organisation because this is likely to result in a lowering of employee morale by creating a feeling of insecurity. Some would argue that such information should be delayed for as long as possible and only provided when management believes that an effect on employment is likely. However, it may equally be argued that any unnecessary delay in informing employees and unions can easily lead to distrust and misunderstandings as a result of rumours. Regular communication to and discussion with employees and unions on the state of the organisation help avoid this problem. It is possible to identify three distinct groups to whom senior management needs to communicate if a redundancy is to be handled with the minimum of rumours and suspicion:

■ *Recognised trade unions.* Obviously trade unions will be involved in discussions about the need for a redundancy, any alternative strategies and identifying the types and numbers of employees to be made redundant. It would be unrealistic to expect union representatives to enter into such discussions in secrecy; they must be able to discuss the issues with their members if they are both to represent their members' interests and make a realistic contribution in any discussions with management. In some situations union representatives may be involved, jointly with management, in applying the agreed selection criterion. More normally, they will be notified by management of the employees selected for redundancy and may subsequently be involved in processing grievances on behalf of their members in respect of their selection for redundancy or the level of compensation they are to receive.

■ *Employees* (both as a group and the individuals selected for redundancy). It is important that all employees should receive regular communications regarding the progress of discussions with the trade unions and the subsequent implementation of the redundancy programme. Similarly, those to be made redundant should be informed individually by their manager and have the opportunity to discuss their position. It is also important for management not to forget that 'the needs of the "survivors" may also have to be addressed'[89] – they need to be 'revitalised'.

■ *Management.* All levels of management, but particularly departmental and supervisory management, have to be kept informed and be sufficiently briefed to be able to answer most of the initial questions raised by employees and correct any rumours or misunderstandings. It is of paramount importance that they should not feel that union representatives have been given more information than they have.

■ Summary propositions

■ The grievance/dispute process is an integral part of determining as well as interpreting and applying rules, and its effectiveness relies on employee and union acceptance of its integrity and usefulness in resolving their dissatisfaction.

■ While the formal disciplinary process is a management control process intended to 'penalise' employees whose performance or behaviour does not meet management's expectations, the disciplinary procedure within it requires management to be able to justify its actions to the employee and the outside world.

■ Management's objectives in any redundancy situation are to reduce its labour force and labour costs while maintaining the morale and goodwill of a future balanced workforce; the union's objectives are to resist, or minimise the extent of, the redundancy while securing the best possible financial compensation and assistance for those who are made redundant.

> **Activity** If you were able to obtain copies of grievance, discipline and/or redundancy procedures as part of the materials suggested in Chapter 7, you could examine them to compare and contrast them with the points made in this chapter.
>
> At the same time, you might like to consider going and sitting in on a Tribunal hearing to see not just how they are conducted but also the types of issues which arise in the workplace, how they are handled and what might lead people to seek a legal solution. Tribunal proceedings are open to the public; you will find them in the telephone book or contact your local ACAS office.

Further reading

- A. W. J. Thomson and V. V. Murray, *Grievance Procedures*, Saxon House, 1976. A very useful examination of both the theoretical and practical aspects of grievance procedures.
- P. K. Edwards, 'Discipline: towards trust and self-discipline', in S. Bach and K. Sission (eds), *Personnel Management* (3rd edn), Blackwell, 2000. This chapter discusses a variety of views relating to the disciplinary process.
- S. Wood and I. Dey, *Redundancy*, Gower, 1983. This book examines how people view and handle redundancy by examining a number of case studies.

References

1. A. W. J. Thomson and V. V. Murray, *Grievance Procedures*, Saxon House, 1976, p. 128.
2. ACAS, *Annual Report*, 1998, pp. 71–82 and table 7, pp. 132–3.
3. F. Lynch, 'You'll hear from my lawyer', *Guardian*, 10 January 2000.
4. *Grievance Arbitration: A practical guide*, ILO, 1977, p. 4.
5. Thomson and Murray, *op. cit.*, p. 18.
6. D. Torrington and J. Chapman, *Personnel Management* (2nd edn), Prentice Hall, 1983, p. 253.
7. D. Torrington and L. Hall, *Human Resource Management* (4th edn), Prentice Hall, 1998, pp. 550–1.
8. N. Singleton, 'Industrial relations procedures', *Department of Employment, Manpower Paper*, No. 14, HMSO, 1975, p. 16.
9. K. Hawkins, *A Handbook of Industrial Relations Practice*, Kogan Page, 1979, p. 141.
10. J. W. Kuhn, *Bargaining in Grievance Settlement*, Columbia University Press, 1961, p. 28.
11. Ibid., p. 81.
12. Thomson and Murray, *op. cit.*, pp. 76–83.
13. *Ibid.*, p. 79.
14. P. F. Salipante and R. Bouwen, 'Behavioural analysis of grievances: conflict sources, complexity and transformation', *Employee Relations*, vol. 12, no. 3, 1990, p. 20.
15. A. I. Marsh, 'Disputes procedures in British industry, Research Paper 2 (part 1), *Royal Commission on Trade Unions and Employers' Associations*, HMSO, 1966, p. 26.
16. *Ibid.*, p. 7.
17. Thomson and Murray, *op. cit.*, pp. 139–40.
18. Marsh, *op. cit.*, pp. 5–6.
19. Singleton, *op. cit.*, p. 20.
20. 'Represent and recruit!', *Labour Research*, September 1999, p. 16.
21. N. Millward, M. Stevens, D. Smart and W. R. Hawes, *Workplace Industrial Relations in Transition*, Gower, 1992, p. 200.
22. 'Discipline at work 1: the practice', *IRS Employment Trends*, no. 493, 1991, pp. 6–14.
23. P. K. Edwards, 'Discipline: towards trust and

self-discipline', in S. Bach and K. Sission (eds), *Personnel Management* (3rd edn), Blackwell, 2000, p. 325.

24. Torrington and Hall, *op. cit.*, p. 549.
25. Hoyt N. Wheeler, 'Punishment theory and industrial discipline', *Industrial Relations*, vol. 15, no. 2, 1976.
26. R. Smith, 'Work control and managerial prerogatives in industrial relations', Working Paper, Durham University Business School, May 1978.
27. M. Mellish and N. Collis-Squires, 'Legal and social norms in discipline and dismissal', *Industrial Law Journal*, vol. 5, no. 3, 1976 (referring to Ministry of Labour Report (1967), Donovan Commission Report (1968), 'In Working Order' (1975) and Industrial Relations Code of Practice (1972); this 'softer' approach can also be seen in the ACAS Code of Practice (1977)).
28. G. C. Walters and J. E. Grusec, *Punishment*, W. H. Freeman & Co., 1977, p. 31.
29. D. Rollinson, 'Individual issues in industrial relations: an examination of discipline, and an agenda for research', *Personnel Review*, vol. 21, no. 1, 1992, p. 53.
30. P. Edwards, 'Discipline and the creation of order', in K. Sisson (ed.), *Personnel Management* (2nd edn), Blackwell, 1994, p. 587.
31. Edwards (2000), *op. cit.*, p. 336.
32. Mellish and Collis-Squires, *op. cit.*
33. A. Fox, *A Sociology of Work in Industry*, Collier Macmillan, 1972.
34. S. Hill, 'Norms groups and power: the sociology of workplace industrial relations', *British Journal of Industrial Relations*, vol. 12, no. 2, 1974.
35. Edwards (2000), *op. cit.*, p. 329.
36. Mellish and Collis-Squires, *op. cit.*
37. G. Mars, 'Hotel pilferage: a case study in occupational theft', in M. Warner (ed.), *The Sociology of the Workplace*, Allen & Unwin, 1973.
38. R. T. Ashdown and K. H. Baker, *In Working Order: a study of industrial discipline*, Department of Employment, HMSO, 1973, p. 1.
39. W. B. Boise, 'Supervisors' attitudes towards disciplinary action', *Personnel Administration*, May/June 1965.
40. N. R. F. Maier, 'Discipline in the industrial setting', *Personnel Journal*, vol. 44, April 1965.
41. *R v Secretary of State for Employment ex parte Equal Opportunities Commission*, (1995).
42. *R v Secretary of State for Employment ex parte Seymour-Smith and Perez*, (1995).

43. *Western Excavating Ltd v Sharp*, (1978).
44. *Woods v W. M. Car Services*, (1981).
45. *Spencer v Paragon Wallpapers*, (1976).
46. *Wood v Heron Fabrics Branch of Courtaulds*, (1974).
47. *Laws v. London Chronicle*, (1959).
48. L. Dickens, 'Unfair dismissal law: a decade of disillusion', *Personnel Management*, February 1982, p. 25.
49. O. Aikin, 'Law at work: a need to reorganise', *Personnel Management*, February 1984, p. 37.
50. *Ibid.*
51. Dickens, *op. cit.*, p. 25.
52. P. Lewis, 'An analysis of why legislation has failed to provide employment protection for unfairly dismissed employees', *British Journal of Industrial Relations*, vol. 19, no. 3, 1981, p. 316.
53. *Ibid.*, p. 323.
54. ACAS (1998), p. 75.
55. 'Industrial and Employment Appeal Tribunal statistics: 1992–93 and 1993–94, *Employment Gazette*, October 1994, table 3, p. 369.
56. R. Snape, 'Legal regulation of employment', in G. Hollinshead, P. Nicholls and S. Tailby (eds), *Employee Relations*, FT Pitman, 1999, p. 292.
57. B. Capstick, 'Industrial tribunals: weeding out the "no-hope" cases', *Personnel Management*, August 1981, p. 44.
58. P. Wallace and R. F. Clifton, 'Pre-hearing assessments in unfair dismissal cases', *Employment Gazette*, February 1985, pp. 65–9.
59. ACAS (1998), table 7.
60. Dickens, *op. cit.*, pp. 26–7.
61. H. Concannon, 'Handling dismissal disputes by arbitration', *Industrial Relations Journal*, vol. 11, no. 2, 1980, p. 16.
62. Dickens, *op. cit.*, p. 27.
63. 'Disciplinary practice and procedure in employment' *ACAS Code of Practice 1*, HMSO, 1977.
64. P. J. White, 'The management of redundancy', *Industrial Relations Journal*, vol. 14, no. 1, 1983, p. 32.
65. R. J. Sutherland, 'Redundancy: perspectives and policies', *Industrial Relations Journal*, vol. 11, no. 4, 1980, p. 17.
66. B. Terryn, 'Redundancies in the UK', *Labour Market Trends*, May 1999, pp. 251–61.
67. Sutherland, *op. cit.*
68. P. Mumford, *Redundancy and Security of Employment*, Gower, 1975, p. 5.
69. Sutherland, *op. cit.*, p. 17.
70. *Ibid.*, p. 23
71. *Ibid.*
72. TUC *Annual Report*, 1983, p. 245.

73. 'Making way for the 35-hour working week', *European Industrial Relations Review*, no. 294, July 1998, pp. 19–25.

74. 'French cut hours to create jobs', *Labour Research*, March 1999, pp. 23–4.

75. O. Aikin and J. Reid, *Labour Law: Vol. 1 – Employment, Welfare and Safety at Work*, Penguin, 1971, p. 165. Reprinted by permission of Penguin Books Ltd. © Olga Aikin and Judith Reid, 1971.

76. *Ibid.*, p. 175.

77. A. Aikin, C. Mill, A. Burnage, J. Foulds, T. Lines, C. Pope, G. Thomason and E. Wooldridge, 'No escape from consultation', *Personnel Management*, October 1993, p. 56.

78. *Collective Redundancies and Transfer of Undertakings (Protection of Employment) (Amendment) Regulations (1995)*.

79. Aikin *et al.*, *op.cit.*, p. 55.

80. *Ibid.*

81. 'Commission issues national-level information and consultation proposal', *European Industrial Relations Review*, no. 299, 1998, p. 13.

82. 'Managing redundancy', *Incomes Data Services Study Plus*, Spring 1999, p. 2.

83. Mumford, *op. cit.*, pp. 42–3.

84. Incomes Data Services, *Guide to Redundancy*, 1980, p. 42.

85. Mumford, *op. cit.*, p. 47.

86. *Incomes Data Services Study Plus* (Spring 1999), *op. cit.*, p. 3.

87. Mumford, *op. cit.*, p. 50.

88. *Incomes Data Services Study Plus* (Spring 1999), *op. cit.*, p. 2.

89. *Ibid.*, p. 12.

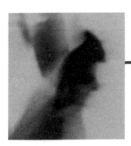

index

mediation, 265, 458–59, 474
 see also Advisory, Conciliation and Arbitration
  service; arbitration; conciliation
Mercury Communications, 438
mining, 65, 116, 175, 177, 291, 294, 300, 302, 428,
  432, 434, 436
Molestation of Workmen Act [1859], 101
Municipal Officers Association, 99

National Association of British Manufacturers, 276
National Association of Probation Officers, 145
National Association of Shopfitters, 272
National Association of Teachers in Further and
  Higher Education (NATFHE), 153, 154–56
National Association of Theatrical, Television and Kine
  Employees (NATTKE), 168
National Board for Prices and Incomes (NBPI), 295,
  517
National Coal Board (NCB), 65, 250, 291, 431, 445
National Communication Union (NCU), 168
National Economic Development Office (NEDO), 57,
  65, 121, 295, 313, 376, 524
National Farmers Union (NFU), 270
National Graphical Association (NGA), 168, 442, 451
National Industrial Relations Court, 478
National Joint Council or Committee (NJC), 350, 362
National Joint Industrial Council (NJIC), 350
National Joint Negotiating Committee (NJNC), 221,
  251
National and Local Government Officers Association
  (NALGO), 99, 123, 160, 169, 205, 217, 401
national minimum wage, 26, 47, 50, 68, 104, 292,
  296, 298–99, 305
National Minimum Wage Act (1998), 68, 104, 298
National & Provincial Building Society, 529–30
National Unilever Managers Association, 169
National Union of Agricultural and Allied Workers
  (NUAAW), 139, 168
National Union of Civil and Public Servants
  (NUCPS), 169
National Union of Dyers, Bleachers and Textile
  Workers (NUDBTW), 139
National Union of Elementary Teachers, 99
National Union of Knitwear Footwear and Apparel
  Trades (NUKFAT), 145
National Union of Mineworkers (NUM), 65, 68,
  103, 123, 142, 153, 160, 291, 426, 431, 445,
  451
National Union of Public Employees (NUPE), 169,
  205, 401
National Union of Rail, Maritime and Transport
  Workers (RMT), 112, 162, 413

National Union of Railwaymen (NUR), 160, 162,
  440, 446
National Union of Seamen (NUS), 162, 198
National Union of Sheet Metal Workers,
  Coppersmiths, Heating and Domestic
  Engineers (NUSMWCH&DE), 170
National Union of Teachers (NUT), 99, 160
nationalism, 32
Nationally Integrated Caring Employees, 147
negotiation, 66, 69, 207, 214, 219, 235, 244, 257,
  309, 331, 336, 338, 343–44, 379, 412, 414,
  416, 424, 457, 471, 491–511, 524, 554, 559,
  564, 565, 590
 bargaining limits, 340, 499, 501, 503, 506, 508,
  510
 and collective bargaining, 492
 and conciliation and arbitration, 459–60, 461–64,
  465–66, 471–72, 471–72, 473–74
 conventions, 510–11
 definition, 492
 encounter, 501–11
  adjournments, 499, 506, 508
  agenda, 502–3
  arguments, 495–96, 503–5
  concessions, 496, 503, 505, 506, 508, 509, 510
  dialogue, 497–98, 506–9
  informal meetings, 508
  mandate, 501, 508, 510
  opening, 505–6
  preparation, 501–5
  termination, 509–10
 failure to agree, 473, 510, 557, 562
 in 'good faith', 559
 and industrial action, 417, 421–22, 423–24, 443,
  494–95
 intra-organisational, 492, 499–501, 532
 power relationship, 78, 79, 492–93
 setting, 511
 team, 495, 498–99, 498, 508, 511
 trust relationship, 493–94, 507, 510
 see also bargaining; pay bargaining; productivity
  bargaining
negotiator, 492–501
 objective, 496, 506
 personal conduct, 511
 relationship between, 496, 499–500, 506–8, 509–10
 relationship with principals, 499–501, 508, 509,
  510–11, 531–32
 role, 492, 510
 skills, 493, 497–98
 stress, 496
 task, 496–99, 501, 505